HANDBOOK OF COUNSELING
TECHNIQUES

Handbook of
Counseling Techniques

EDITED BY

ERNEST HARMS

AND

PAUL SCHREIBER

PERGAMON PRESS

OXFORD · NEW YORK · LONDON · PARIS

1963

PERGAMON PRESS LTD.
Headington Hill Hall, Oxford
4 & 5 Fitzroy Square, London W.1

PERGAMON PRESS INC.
122 East 55th Street, New York 22, N.Y.

GAUTHIER-VILLARS ED.
55 Quai des Grands-Augustins, Paris 6

PERGAMON PRESS G.m.b.H.
Kaiserstrasse 75, Frankfurt am Main

Distributed in the Western Hemisphere by
THE MACMILLAN COMPANY · NEW YORK
pursuant to a special arrangement with
Pergamon Press Incorporated

Library of Congress Catalog Card Number 63–16089

*Set in Baskerville 11 on 12 pt by Santype Ltd., Salisbury
and printed in Great Britain by John Wright & Sons Ltd., Bristol*

Contents

Introduction

ERNEST HARMS and PAUL SCHREIBER

New School of
Social Research
New York City

Director
School of Social Work
Hunter College
New York City

ENCOURAGED by the reception of the *Handbook of Child Guidance* by the professional and academic communities and by the public at large, the Senior Editor conceived the plan to compile and publish a similar volume in the general field of Counseling. Recognizing the vast and relatively unchartered territory that counseling in its various branches represents, the need is evident for a publication which could serve as a map and a guide to the manifold varieties of the field. While obviously no single volume could attempt presentation of sufficient depth which could serve as a textbook for each and all of the specialities, it seemed important and timely to assemble a representative series of articles which could serve as descriptions and references for the student in any of the allied professions involved in counseling, for the worker engaged in a particular branch of counseling who wanted to inform himself of other areas of the field, and for the general reader who, either as a prospective consumer or as an intelligent layman in the community, wanted to gain some better understanding and knowledge of counseling in all its ramifications.

At this point, however, a word of caution seems in order. The editors have consciously and purposely limited the scope of this volume to counseling in the field of Human Relations. While recognizing fully the legitimate existence of programs identified as counseling, in other areas, such as, for instance, Investment Counseling, Consumer Counseling or Travel Counseling, it seemed appropriate in view of the origin and nature of counseling as a conscious process, to exclude from the purview of this volume all those programs and activities whose primary emphasis is not directed towards interpersonal relations.

Even within this limitation, the range of subjects is an extremely wide one as a glance at the table of contents will readily confirm. We have attempted to be as comprehensive as possible within the given limitation.

In line with the purpose of the Handbook we have tried and, we believe, have been successful in enlisting the cooperation of well recognized and competent experts in their own fields as contributors of the individual chapters. No attempt has been made to insure uniformity of presentation, style or arrangement. On the contrary, each author was given the fullest latitude in his approach to the coverage of his own field. This method presents, obviously, both advantages and disadvantages. While it produces more original and individualized writing, it results at times in duplication or in differential use of terms. While we have tried to eliminate some of the duplications, we have not changed any substantive parts of any contribution and have retained any contradictions and conflicts of opinions which might arise. We believe that the reader will be best in a position to form his own judgment and conclusions and to arrive at a proper formulation of essential concepts and terms.

In reviewing the 36 chapters which comprise the Handbook, we have been impressed by the fact that, in spite of the wide variations in presentation and the great range of content areas, there underlies this multiplicity of approaches a basic, uniform element. The essence of the counseling process as a problem-solving method emerges as a common thread, based on certain fundamental convictions about the individual, the growth and development of his personality, his rights and responsibilities, and on a shared understanding of the dynamics of human interactions, regardless of setting and content or discipline. We like to think that this aspect justifies our attempt to combine so many discrete activities in one volume.

We would like to express our thanks to the many colleagues who first helped with the planning of this book, and have since aided its execution with advice and corrections. And it goes without saying that we are also grateful to the contributors, who found, or made, time in their already full schedules to write these thoughtful, in the complete sense of the word, summaries of their experiences and ideas in counseling. Most of our gratitude, however, must go to Cora Kasius, editor of "Social Casework", who co-operated untiringly for uncountable hours in planning the format, suggesting the names of contributors, and adjusting details. At least half of the thought and work this book represents is hers.

Counseling: Some Historical Highlights

A. GORDON NELSON

Professor of Educational and
Vocational Guidance
Cornell University
Ithaca, New York

COUNSELING may be broadly and simply defined as the process of helping individuals cope with certain kinds of personal problems. The principles followed and the techniques employed in connection with a wide variety of such problems constitute the subject matter of subsequent parts of this book. The purpose of the present chapter is to sketch the development of certain aspects of the counseling movement in the United States, in order that students and practitioners may gain some degree of historical perspective, or avoid what someone has called "provincialism in regard to time."

To trace in detail the genesis of the many different sorts of counseling treated in this volume would require not only several chapters but also apperception beyond that of the writer. Hence the present account is limited to a survey of some of the outstanding trends and events that have been influential in the rise and development of a few major varieties of counseling selected from the many types provided today.

PRECURSORS OF COUNSELING

Counseling is, in an extended sense, one of the oldest of human relationships: from time immemorial individuals have "talked over" their personal concerns with acquaintances, friends and relatives. As a professional or semiprofessional service, however, counseling came into view during the first decade of the twentieth century. Why *then*?

First, the time was ripe, following the Industrial Revolution, for the emergence of services intended to promote human welfare. During the latter part of the nineteenth century, a philosophy of rugged individualism was beginning to give way to a sense of social responsibility, to the point of view that the well-being of individuals should be the concern of society as a whole. "Gradually . . . in the older and more densely populated countries of Europe, the economic and social problems created by the appearance of the isolated individual under the conditions of modern society proved so insistent and alarming that modifications of the policy of public non-interference were deemed increasingly necessary, until in the last quarter of the century rather comprehensive programs of social betterment, involving a new concept of society's duty to the individual, began to appear."[3] Anna Y. Reed summarizes the trend in these words: "During the closing years of the nineteenth century the civilized world replied affirmatively to the age-old question, Am I my brother's keeper? Society had accepted the theory of the unity of humanity and the brotherhood of man and was ready to begin translation of the theory into practice. . . . The years 1900 to 1910 were banner years for the expression of these newly accepted theories in terms of social and philanthropic efforts to serve humanity better . . ." (Reed, p. 2).[17]

A second factor that had a bearing on the rise of counseling services was the interest of psychologists in the nature and identification of individual differences. Although others had made a few fragmentary studies of such differences, Sir Francis Galton is often referred to as the founder of individual psychology and of mental measurement. Influenced by the work of Darwin, including his *Origin of Species*, Galton attempted to apply the principles of organic evolution to the study of human beings. In 1883, he published *Inquiries into Human Faculty and Its Development*, a book that many believe marks the beginning of individual psychology and of mental testing. But the psychologist who probably contributed more than anyone else to the early quantitative study of individual differences was James McKeen Cattell, who held the first professorship of psychology in the world, between 1888 and 1891 at the University of Pennsylvania. "In 1890 he published a notable paper on 'Mental Tests and Measurements' setting forth in detail his position on the measurement of individual differences, describing 10 tests which he was using, and recommending the use of 'mental tests' as apparatus in psychological experimentation" (Viteles, p. 31).[25] In 1896, with L. Farrand, he published in the *Psychological Review* a report of an investigation of the physical and mental status of Columbia University students, which was the first study of its kind. It is obvious that counseling today, which is so dependent on a knowledge of the nature, origins, and effects of individual differences, owes much to the pioneer work of Galton and Cattell, as well as to others who built on the foundations these men laid in the latter part of the nineteenth century.

Concurrent with the rise and growth of individual psychology, national, state and local surveys were being conducted which uncovered conditions that were indicative of a need for personal counseling services of one kind or another.[18] These surveys, which were undertaken by philanthropic, educational and industrial groups, thus played an important role in the rise of counseling during the early part of the twentieth century. Educational investigations revealed: that there was a lack of articulation between various school levels; that many pupils were retarded in achievement and grade-placement; that the drop-out rate was very high; that the schools were either unaware of or unconcerned about the educational implications of individual differences in children. Other surveys, philanthropic in origin and purpose, dealt with the types of employment into which young people went upon leaving school, the ways in which they obtained their first jobs, and the conditions under which they worked. Industrial surveys were conducted to investigate problems such as the inefficiency of workers, the causes of accidents, and the sources of labor disputes. Still other surveys made during this period dealt with social problems such as juvenile delinquency, mental deficiency, and mental and physical illness. The fact that all these inquiries were contemporaneously revealing different kinds of conditions and needs helps to explain why there appeared on the scene, at about the same time, a variety of personal-help services, such as vocational counseling, social work, educational guidance, the mental hygiene movement, juvenile courts, and personnel work in government and in industry. The following list of "firsts," although far from complete, gives an indication of the burgeoning of interest in the welfare of individuals having various kinds of personal problems:

1896—Founding of the first psychological clinic, at the University of Pennsylvania;

1898—Offering of first systematic training in social casework in the United States: a six-weeks summer course provided by the New York Charity Organization Society;

1899—Establishment, by Illinois, of the first juvenile court;

1903—First national convention of deans of women;

1904—One-year course in social casework offered by the New York School of Philanthropy;

1905—Beginning of medical social work, in the out-patient department of Massachusetts General Hospital;

1908—Establishment of the Vocation Bureau of Boston;

—Organization of the National Committee for Mental

Hygiene;
> 1909—Founding of the Juvenile Psychopathic Institute, Chicago;
> 1911—First state Workmen's Compensation Act passed;
> 1913—Organization of National Vocational Guidance Association;
> —Organization of American Association of Public Employment Offices.

CLINICAL PSYCHOLOGY

Many of the principles and procedures of counseling derive from clinical psychology, and some of the various types of counseling described in this book are properly the responsibility of clinical psychologists. The development of clinical psychology is therefore an integral part of the history of counseling. Watson,[27] in an article that is, so far as can be determined, the only general historical account of the subject, discusses seven "streams" that have contributed to "the torrent that is clinical psychology today." The four streams that the present writer considers most relevant to the history of counseling are referred to below, but the reader who is especially interested in clinical counseling is urged to read all of Watson's article.

Watson points out, first, that "the psychometric tradition in psycology," which originated with the work of Galton, Cattell, and Binet, is responsible for the clinical psychologist's interest in the quantitative measurement of individual differences. Among the many events that have contributed to this aspect of clinical psychology are the following: the publication of American revisions of the Binet Scale by Goddard in 1911, by Kuhlmann in 1911, and by Terman in 1916; the construction of performance tests, such as the Seguin and Healy Formboards; and the development of group tests to aid in the classification of military personnel in World War I.

Clinical psychology has also been influenced by what Watson calls "the dynamic tradition in psychology," which is quite different from the structural, sensationalistic approach of men such as Wundt and Titchener. One of the first psychologists to emphasize the importance of the clinical method for the study of behavior was William James, who was impressed by the work of two French psychiatrists, Janet and Charcot, and whose *Principles of Psychology* was published in 1890. James also supported the mental hygiene movement, particularly through his endorsement of Clifford Beers' book, *A Mind that Found Itself*, which was published in 1908. Another pioneer in the dynamic tradition was G. Stanley Hall, who is known chiefly, perhaps, for his studies of childhood and adolescence. He was one of a rather small group of psychologists of his time who showed an interest in psychoanalysis.

As president of Clark University, he invited Freud and Jung to lecture at his institution in 1909, when it celebrated its twentieth anniversary.

Theories and techniques developed in psychological and psycho-educational clinics, and the studies of individuals conducted in these clinics have, of course, contributed immeasurably to clinical counseling. It is generally agreed that the first psychological clinic was founded by Lightner Witmer at the University of Pennsylvania in 1896. In its early years Witmer's clinic dealt chiefly with mentally deficient and educationally retarded children, but later it began to serve other types of clients; thus, the diagnosis and remediation of speech defects was begun in 1914, and a vocational guidance unit was added in 1920. According to Wallin,[26] there were at least 20 psychological clinics in existence in the United States by 1914. In 1934, there were approximately 50 such clinics.[28] Today there are several hundred.

At about the same time that psychological clinics were being founded, a somewhat different type of service was also emerging, one that later became known as "the child guidance movement." Whereas the early psychological clinics were influenced greatly by the experimental and psychometric traditions and were concerned primarily with the intellectual aspects of personality, child guidance clinics grew out of the dynamic tradition and were therefore concerned chiefly with affective factors in behavior. The first clinic of this nature was the Juvenile Psychopathic Institute, founded in Chicago in 1909. Its director was William Healy, a psychiatrist. During the past fifty years child guidance clinics have been introduced into many communities. The period of their most rapid growth was in the 1920's, when the National Committee for Mental Hygiene established demonstration centers not only in cities but also in rural areas. These clinics usually have a minimum staff of a psychiatrist director, a clinical psychologist and a social worker, and deal primarily with the emotional problems of children who are maladjusted at home or at school.

THE VOCATIONAL GUIDANCE MOVEMENT

The opening of the Boston Vocation Bureau in 1908 is generally believed to mark the inauguration of formal vocational counseling services in the United States.[10] This Bureau was established, under philanthropic auspices, through the efforts of Frank Parsons, a public-spirited Bostonian who had for a number of years written and lectured on socio-economic problems, and had become especially interested in the education and work adjustment of youth. Parsons was the first director of the Bureau, the purpose of which was " . . . to aid young people in choosing an occupation, preparing themselves for it, finding an opening in it, and building up a career of efficiency and success."[4] Parsons was apparently the first person to employ the term "vocational guidance," and in his book, *Choosing A Vocation*, which was published posthumously in 1909, he set forth general principles with which there is little disagreement today. Moreover, he established courses for the preparation of counselors, employed the best tools and techniques then available, and was successful in promoting the idea that there was need for an expansion of vocational counseling services. It is not without reason, therefore, that he is often referred to as the "father" of the vocational guidance movement.

In this short survey it is not possible to refer to all the early workers in the vocational guidance vineyard, but one man, Eli W. Weaver, a teacher in the Boys' High School of Brooklyn, should surely be mentioned. As early as 1906, he was engaged in the placement of city boys on farms for employment during the summer vacation (Brewer, p. 89).[4] By 1908, under the sponsorship of the High School Teachers' Association, he had become the leader in the New York City schools of vocational guidance activities that were broader in scope than placement. In a number of schools, teachers served as counselors, without additional pay; pamphlets on occupational opportunities were made available to students; speakers on vocations appeared before high-school groups; and provision was made for follow-up supervision of those who had been placed in work situations (Reed, p. 8).[17]

As the work in New York and Boston began to attract national attention, other cities gradually began to introduce vocational guidance into the public schools. Among the first to initiate programs were Chicago, Philadelphia, Seattle, Grand Rapids, New Orleans, Minneapolis, and St. Louis.[17]

Reference has been made in a previous section of this chapter to the fact that studies in individual psychology were related to the rise of counseling services. It is appropriate at this point to mention three contributions that twentieth-century psychologists have made specifically to vocational counseling. In the first place, they have developed standardized tests, which facilitate the objective appraisal of personal traits that should be taken into consideration in the process of helping individuals to make vocational choices. Secondly, they have studied the psychological requirements of a number of occupations, and have thus provided data that enable counselors to compare persons with job requisites. Thirdly, they have demonstrated how the principles and procedures of clinical case-work may be applied in counseling with individuals who present vocational problems (Nelson, pp. 5–9).[16]

Many governmental, philanthropic, and private agencies in the United States currently offer vocational counseling services, of varying degrees of quality. A survey conducted in 1947 to determine the places of employment of members of the National Vocational Guidance Association revealed that 42 per cent were employed in elementary and secondary schools, and 16 per cent in colleges and universities. Fifteen per cent were working in government agencies, 6 per cent in business and industrial establishments, 5 per cent in social welfare and other community agencies, 3 per cent in rehabilitation centers, and 3 per cent in private counseling bureaus. The remaining 10 per cent were employed by a variety of organizations, such as churches, labor unions, service clubs, and libraries.[23] Since a very large proportion of NVGA members are known to be employed as counselors, this survey indicates the several types of places in which vocational counseling is offered.

COUNSELING IN COLLEGES AND UNIVERSITIES

From the year of the founding of Harvard, 1636, until the beginning of the last third of the nineteenth century, the counseling of college students was the responsibility of administrators and teachers; there was no formal or specialized service. The appointment of functionaries such as deans of men and deans of women came about as a result of a number of changes in higher education. The socio-economic developments contributing to these changes are succinctly described by Brubacher in the following passage:

" ... political and economic forces released by the American and French Revolutions, the Industrial Revolution and the American frontier began a radical alteration of the underlying sociological conditions that ... had given validity to the traditional ideal of liberal education. The growth of political democracy and the rise of the laboring classes seriously undermined the time-honored social system in which political power was restricted to a relatively small upper class and leisure was the privilege of the few. In a democratic society in which everyone enjoyed political freedom and in which this freedom gave new dignity to the labor of the common man, it became urgently necessary to reconstruct the traditional ideal of liberal education as the education appropriate to the political and economic interests of a small class of the population."[6]

Some of the ways in which colleges and universities began to change are as follows:

1. Total enrollments and the sizes of classes increased.
2. The student body became more "mixed" in respect to cultural background, intellectual potentiality, and motives for attending institutions of higher learning.

2

3. More students than had previously been the case entered college without having specific vocational objectives in mind.

4. There was a gradual expansion of the curriculum, especially in the sciences and the practical arts.

5. The elective system, which gave students a considerable amount of freedom (and responsibility) in the selection of subjects, came into being.

6. Women began to gain admission into colleges and universities, which gave rise to problems associated with coeducation.

6. As knowledge increased, faculty members became more specialized and began to assume greater responsibility for research in their respective disciplines.

One result of these changes was that there was a greater need for counseling but fewer administrators and professors had time for, or an interest in, talking with students regarding their personal concerns. This state of affairs led to the appointment of deans of men and deans of women. Initially, their chief function was that of dealing with disciplinary matters, but later they were expected to assume some responsibility for counseling.[15]

The array of student personnel workers available in present-day colleges is indicative of the extent to which counseling services in higher education have expanded over the years. Although administrators and professors have, in general, less personal contact with students than they had in early collegiate institutions, they still do a certain amount of "advisory work." Thus, it is common practice to assign a group of undergraduates to a faculty member, and give him responsibility for helping them plan their academic programs. Moreover, some college teachers enjoy, and seem to have a knack for, talking informally with students about their personal problems. Dormitory or residence-hall advisors are provided in many institutions; they are expected not only to supervise their charges and help them to profit from group living but also to advise with them or refer them to other sources of personal assistance. Deans of men and deans of women are counselors as well as administrators, particularly in smaller colleges where their administrative responsibilities do not preclude their spending the time required for effective work with students on an individual basis. In addition, there are, especially in the larger institutions, workers who specialize in vocational, disciplinary, health, financial, foreign-student, religious, and psychotherapeutic counseling. Thus we find that counseling in colleges today is performed by many different functionaries—a situation quite different from that of the colonial period, when " . . . the scholar served in a pastor-teacher-policeman relationship to the student, which demanded from the professor a combination of spiritual, instructional, and disciplinary counsel without modern counterpart ... " (Shank, p. 2).[21]

EMPLOYEE COUNSELING

Because employee counseling is a part of a total program of personnel services in industry, at least brief reference should be made, first, to the early history of what has come to be known as industrial psychology. It is interesting to note that the application of psychology to employee personnel problems began during the period when the other movements we have been discussing were initiated. Toward the end of the nineteenth century and in the first decade of the twentieth, a number of studies were conducted that helped to lay the groundwork for the use of psychology in the selection and training of employees. Among these were: the investigations of Marey, Mosso, and Imbert on bodily work and fatigue; Kraeplin's study of learning curves; the work of Bryan and Harter on the learning of telegraphy; and Lahy's investigation of psycho-physiological traits related to success in typewriting (Viteles, p. 40).[25] In 1911, Walter Dill Scott published *Influencing Men in Business*, a book that " ... represents the first studied analysis of workers' motives by one trained in the theories and procedures of psychology" (Viteles, p. 41).[25] But the psychologist who is usually regarded as the "father" of industrial psychology is Hugo Munsterberg, whose *Psychology and Industrial Efficiency* was published in 1913. Munsterberg presented the first formulation of the problems of industrial psychology. His investigations and publications were influential in stimulating others to conduct studies in this field of endeavour.

Although not necessarily labeled as such, "employee counseling" has, of course, existed for a long time in business and industrial establishments and in governmental agencies. The "open door" policy of many executives has enabled workers to talk over their problems with representatives of management and has also given the latter opportunity to become aware of employee attitudes. Moreover, many foremen and personnel workers have for years provided informal employee counseling.

The provision of *organized* counseling services for employees is a relatively recent development. One of the earliest formal programs was established at the Metropolitan Life Insurance Company in 1922, when it employed a full-time psychiatrist. In its early years the psychiatric program was concerned chiefly with the identification and treatment of mentally ill workers, but later it became a service designed to serve all supervisors and employees. "Its principal aim now is to prevent serious maladjustments by recognizing and helping to alleviate minor temporary abnormalities, and, by gaining acceptance of the service as one of value to 'normal people', to increase the understanding of human relations in the supervisory group and to improve the stability and efficiency of employees" (Baker, p. 12).[1]

It is sometimes stated that employee counseling "began" in 1927 at the Hawthorne Plant of the Western Electric Company. Referred to as "personnel counseling," it grew out of an investigation designed to determine the effects of physical working conditions on the morale and productivity of employees. One outcome of the research was the introduction in 1931 of a revised interviewing program, according to which Western Electric employees were not asked direct questions about specific working conditions, but were encouraged to give free expression to their feelings " ... in a friendly, confidential, and non-judgmental atmosphere" (Baker, p. 11).[1] This type of counseling has had a slow but fairly steady growth in industry since its inception at the Western Electric Company in 1931.

A different type of employee counseling came into prominence as a result of the expansion of industry during World War II. The influx of women workers led management to believe there was a need for a service that would deal specifically with the personal problems of women employees. Secondly, some companies set up advisory and informational programs to help both male and female employees cope with such problems as housing, gas rationing, and transportation to and from work.

The term "employee counseling" today connotes a variety of activities, including friendly listening, the giving of information about company policies and practices, the conducting of exit interviews, psychotherapy for the maladjusted, and the referral of workers to family welfare, medical and other community agencies that will help them with special types of difficulties. There is no set pattern of services characteristic of a majority of companies.

THE GROWTH OF COUNSELING

Having reviewed the early history of several kinds of counseling selected from the many types provided today, let us, in conclusion, turn our attention to some of the influences that have played a part in the growth of counseling in general during the past fifty years. It may be said at the outset that this growth represents a response to a need, and that the need for counseling has increased as a result of a variety of relatively rapid changes in our society.

In 1820, seven per cent of the population of the United States lived in urban areas, but by 1960 the proportion was above 60 per cent.

If it is granted that one of the chief functions of counseling is to help individuals make *choices*, and that there are more possible courses of action available to a person in a city environment than in a rural one, then it follows that as a nation becomes more urban, the need for counseling increases. In a city there is a greater number of occupational, educational, and recreational opportunities, and thus an increased possibility of an individual's making unwise decisions in respect to these opportunities. Moreover, as Tyler has pointed out, a city dweller is less likely than a villager to have available the kind of warm, informal counseling that an individual may need from " . . . an understanding old uncle, a family doctor or minister, or a teacher who has known him from boyhood."[24]

Changes in the world of work that have helped increase the need for counseling include: an expansion in the variety of occupations available; decreased opportunity for young people to explore their interests and abilities through home tasks and apprenticeships; shifts in demand for workers of various types, partly as a result of technological developments; fewer hours of work, which have brought increased leisure time and the problem of its use; rapid growth of the factory system and increased specialization of function in industry; and recurring periods of widespread unemployment. Problems of vocational choice and adjustment have been growing in number and complexity, with the result that individuals, unaided, tend to be less able to cope with these problems than they were at the turn of the century.

Schools have also changed, often in ways which make educational choices and adjustments more difficult. Curricular offerings have increased at both the secondary and post-secondary levels. The age of compulsory school attendance has gone up, and the high schools must deal with a much more heterogeneous pupil population. Our philosophy of formal schooling has changed from a "take-it-or-leave-it" attitude to a belief that educational institutions have a responsibility to help each individual develop to his optimum, in order that he may attain the greatest possible personal satisfaction and at the same time be of greatest value to his fellow men.

Judging from the reports of psychologists and sociologists, family life has been, and is, gradually changing. The home is losing some of its influence as "a haven of emotional support." The quantity and quality of guidance provided for youngsters today by many parents, leave much to be desired. A substantially greater proportion of mothers than in earlier decades hold jobs outside the home. One informed writer states: "It looks highly probable that the instability of family life will continue and probably get worse with more strains and stresses, both from the socio-economic insecurity and adverse conditions under which people are trying to live, and from the anxieties and conflicts inside the family due to the confusion of masculine and feminine roles, the inability to classify the patterns of relationships within the family. . . . As we already know, the children and youth will show the impact" (of this instability of family life) (Frank, p. 152).[7]

These are but a few of the socio-economic influences that have played a part in the growth of counseling services. Professional counseling has developed, also, as a response of society to the increasing prevalence of particular personal-social problems: juvenile delinquency, alcoholism, old age, crime, mental illness, divorce, *et cetera*—all of which require special types of assistance, as is made clear in subsequent sections of this volume.

BIBLIOGRAPHY

1. BAKER, HELEN: 1944. *Employee Counseling, a Survey of a New Development in Personnel Relations.* Princeton, New Jersey: Industrial Relations Section, Princeton University.
2. BORING, EDWIN G.: 1929. *A History of Experimental Psychology.* New York: The Century Company.
3. BOSSARD, JAMES H. S.: 1927. *Problems of Social Well-being*, pp. 600–1. New York: Harper.
4. BREWER, JOHN M.: 1942. *History of Vocational Guidance, Origins and Early Development.* New York: Harper.
5. BROTEMARKLE, ROBERT A. (Ed.): 1931. *Clinical Psychology.* Philadelphia: University of Pennsylvania Press.
6. BRUBACHER, JOHN S.: 1947. *A History of the Problems of Education*, p. 478. New York: McGraw–Hill Book Company.
7. FRANK, L. K.: 1947. *Some Postwar Social Trends which are of Special Interest to Orthopsychiatry.* American Journal of Orthopsychiatry, 16: 5–7.
8. HARMS, ERNEST (Ed.): 1947. *Handbook of Child Guidance.* New York: Child Care Publications.
9. HUTSON, PERCIVAL W.: 1958. *The Guidance Function in Education.* New York: Appleton–Century–Crofts, Inc.
10. JAGER, HARRY A.: 1948. *Vocational Guidance in the United States.* International Labour Review, LVII: 1–15.
11. KAPLAN, OSCAR J. (Ed.): 1948. *Encyclopedia of Vocational Guidance.* New York: Philosophical Library.
12. MARZOLF, STANLEY S.: 1956. *Psychological Diagnosis and Counseling in the Schools.* New York: Henry Holt and Company.
13. MATHEWSON, ROBERT HENDRY: 1962. *Guidance Policy and Practice.* New York: Harper.
14. MILLER, CARROLL H.: 1961. *Foundations of Guidance.* New York: Harper.
15. NELSON, A. GORDON: 1954. *The College Teacher is a Counselor.* The Educational Forum, XVIII: 349–357.
16. ——: 1954. "Vocational guidance," pp. 1–35. In *Areas of Psychology* (F. L. Marcuse, ed.). New York: Harper.
17. REED, ANNA Y.: 1944. *Guidance and Personnel Services in Education.* Ithaca, New York: Cornell University Press.

18. ——: 1927. *Human Waste in Education*. New York: The Century Company.
19. ——: 1946. *Occupational Placement*. Ithaca, New York: Cornell University Press.
20. Report of the President's Research Committee on Social Trends: 1933. Recent social trends in the United States. New York: McGraw–Hill Book Company.
21. SHANK, DONALD J.: 1948. *The Teacher as Counselor*. Washington, D.C.: American Council on Education.
22. SNYDER, WILLIAM U.: 1947. *The Present Status of Psychotherapeutic Counseling*. Psychological Bulletin, 44:297–386.
23. SPLAVER, SARAH: 1949. *Opportunities in Vocational Guidance*. New York: Vocational Guidance Manuals, Inc.
24. TYLER, LEONA E.: 1961. *The Work of the Counselor*, p. 9. New York: Appleton–Century–Crofts, Inc.
25. VITELES, MORRIS S.: 1932. *Industrial Psychology*. New York: W. W. Norton & Company.
26. WALLIN, J. E. W.: 1914. *The Mental Heath of the School Child*. New Haven, Connecticut: Yale University Press.
27. WATSON, ROBERT I.: 1953. *A Brief History of Clinical Psychology*. Psychological Bulletin, 50:321–346.
28. WITTY, P. S., and THEMAN, VIOLA: 1934. "The psycho-educational clinic." *Journal of Applied Psychology*, 18:369–392.

Principles of Counseling

CORA KASIUS

Editor of *Social Casework*
New York

COUNSELING as a professional helping service is a relatively new development in our society. In earlier days, when social relationships were less complex, troubled persons usually turned to relatives, friends, employers, lawyers, physicians, or the clergy for help and guidance. These sources of help are still used extensively and are unquestionably of value.

Relatives and friends can provide needed emotional support to a person under strain and they are often in a position to offer the kind of advice that will reinforce his strengths and capacities. The relative or friend selected as an adviser is likely to be a responsible person, who has status and prestige in the family or community. He is usually identified with the values and mores of the family or the community and therefore tends to emphasize the desirability of handling responsibilities in a socially acceptable way. Such lay guidance, however, contains many subjective elements and for this reason may fail to meet the real needs of the troubled person.

Members of the older professions—law, medicine, and the clergy—traditionally have given advice on personal and social problems as well as on matters related to their particular fields. Such advice, too, may have certain limitations since the consultant, by training, is oriented toward specific types of problems rather than toward the total needs of people. These professions, in recent years, have come to recognize that the responsibility for giving counsel on personal and social problems demands either additional training on the part of their own practitioners or the use of counselors specifically trained to give such help.

Counseling as a specialized service aims to provide guidance and support to persons who have encountered some problem in social functioning or who are facing new life situations that require a shift in their roles and responsibilities. Counseling services are available to persons who have such diverse problems as marital conflict, behavior difficulties of children, unemployment, delinquency, alcoholism, and so forth. They are also provided on a preventive basis to persons who are seeking guidance before critical problems arise. Both types of counseling are given by persons trained in any one of a number of professional fields.

At first glance, there appears to be no common denominator in these various counseling efforts, and one might, therefore, assume that the counselor's skill would derive from his knowledge about a specific area of social functioning. Although specialized knowledge is essential for counseling in a particular field, it constitutes only one part of the counselor's equipment. In addition, he must have sufficient psychological knowledge to be able to understand the emotional needs and reactions of the person seeking help or guidance. Both the social and psychological factors in the individual's adjustment problems must be understood and, in the counseling process, these two components must be appropriately related to each other.

In recent years psychology has provided new insights into human needs and strivings and new knowledge about the adaptive capacities of the individual. It has also thrown new light on the dynamic elements that are present in the helping relationship. Of special significance has been the illumination of the feelings and attitudes that are engendered, in both the counselor and the person seeking help, by the interaction between them. When positive feelings predominate, the relationship provides a medium through which the troubled person can gain emotional support and a new perspective on his problems. If strong negative feelings are present, the relationship loses its potential for effecting changes in the person's feelings and outlook.

RANGE OF COUNSELING SERVICES

The complexities of modern living place heavy social and emotional burdens on all individuals and, as a result, nearly everyone at some point in life feels the need to seek expert advice and opinion. Present-day counseling has emerged in response to this need. It has been made available by persons in various disciplines, including social work, psychology, education, medicine, nursing, and so forth. In the main, it is provided under the auspices of some organization or institution, such as welfare or health agencies, churches, schools, and colleges, labor groups, industry, courts, and military services. In recent years, various counseling services have also been provided by private practitioners who specialize in some aspect of social functioning.

In many instances, counseling is offered on an individual basis. The person seeking help or advice is offered private consultation about a personal problem. Under certain circumstances, such as instances of marital or parent–child conflict, the counselor usually draws other family members into the counseling process. The subsequent interviews may be conducted separately with each person; sometimes various family members are seen together, or are seen in a combination of individual and joint interviews. When various family members are involved in the process, the term "family counseling" is frequently used. If the central problem is the relationship between husband and wife, and they are both involved in interviews, the service is generally called "marriage counseling."

Providing guidance to the total family unit has become more widespread in recent years. The various helping professions have come to recognize the importance of family interaction in both the genesis and the solution of problems of social functioning. As a result, persons of all ages, both the young and the old, are observed or interviewed as part of the helping process. The base of counseling is therefore much broader today than it was a few decades ago. Many more men are drawn into active participation in child-rearing and child guidance programs. Sick and disabled persons are included in family discussions of plans for their medical treatment and physical care. In the same way, elderly people are involved in family planning that affects their living arrangements, finances, or physical care.

In recent years, many organizations and institutions have offered counseling services to a group of persons who have common concerns or common problems. This form of counseling has gained wide acceptance, largely because it seems to enhance the helping process. The group setting tends to reduce the sense of personal inadequacy since all members are struggling with the same concerns. Also, the exchange of experiences and opinions has the effect of reinforcing the ideas and principles that the leader is endeavoring to transmit. The aim of group counseling is the same as that of individual or family counseling, that is, to help the individual increase his capacity for social functioning.

Group counseling has proved to be particularly effective with persons who are assuming new roles that require new patterns of social adaptation. The following are familiar examples: adolescents who are passing through the phase of establishing independence; college students who are living away from home for the first time; the young person seeking employment; married couples expecting their first child; the parents of nursery school children, of teen-agers, of adolescents; and persons facing retirement. A number of agencies and organizations have also provided group counseling for parents of children who are physically or mentally handicapped.

Most counseling services are provided by organizations and are generally available to all persons. Many organizations, however, have adopted a fee plan which is usually administered on a sliding-scale basis. Private practitioners and a few agencies with limited clientele expect a fee payment.

PRINCIPLES AND PROCEDURES

Counseling, whether conducted with an individual, with one or more family members, or with a group, has certain common features. As has been indicated, the over-all aim of counseling is to help the individual enhance his capacity for social functioning. This goal is achieved primarily through bringing about changes in the individual's feelings and through increasing his self-awareness.

Changes in feeling take place largely through the medium of the relationship. The counselor endeavors to create an atmosphere that is conducive to frank discussion of the person's problems and concerns. He does so by maintaining an accepting attitude toward the person, and by encouraging him to express his fears, conflicts, and self-doubts. The experience of discussing his problems and his feelings about them gives the troubled person a sense of relief and hope that appropriate solutions can be found. He absorbs some of the counselor's calm, objectivity and confidence, and in this way gains emotional support.

Considerable attention has been given to ways of furthering the individual's trust in the counselor, and various techniques for establishing rapport have been developed. The troubled person should be encouraged to tell his story in his own way. The counselor should be alert to areas of tension and should respond sensitively to them. He should endeavor to secure relevant facts but should not push his inquiries to the point of making the person unduly anxious.

As the counseling process continues, the counselor undertakes to help the person gain a new perspective on his situation and some awareness of his attitudes and behavior that contribute to his difficulties. In order to engage the person in such an analysis, the counselor himself must have a clear understanding of the situation. The amount of information needed to understand a particular situation is determined by the nature and extent of the difficulty. The counselor must know which persons are involved in the problem, their respective reactions to it, and the character of their interpersonal relationships. His study and appraisal of the problem should encompass such factors as social strains and stresses, physical and mental health, and the capacity of the individuals to use counseling help.

Such appraisal is necessary whether the counseling is conducted through individual interviews or through group sessions. The facts on which the appraisal is made sometimes emerge slowly. Persons who seek help are likely to feel in a disadvantaged position, and they therefore tend to defend themselves against their feelings of inadequacy and inferiority in various ways—by underestimating or dramatizing their problems, by blaming themselves or others, or by searching for quick and magical solutions. Sometimes they endeavor to win the favor and approval of the counselor by withholding or distorting facts that put them in a bad light. Or they may feel too uncertain of the reactions of the counselor to present their difficulties fully and clearly. Soliciting information, therefore, requires special skill, both in selecting the areas to be covered and in timing the inquiries. The person in trouble or in conflict often cannot describe his problem adequately until he has gained confidence in the counselor.

As he makes an appraisal of the problem, the counselor must determine how the individual can be helped. The counselor may find that service for the particular person can be given more adequately by another resource, and if so, he makes plans with both the individual and the resource for the transfer. If continued counseling service by his agency is indicated, the counselor discusses the details of the plan.

Counseling involves much more than giving advice. It is true that the person seeking help often thinks he wants advice, but usually this is not true. What the person actually wants is an opportunity to discuss his confusions and conflicted feelings with someone who is not involved in his difficulties. Through these discussions he is usually able to arrive at a self-determined course of action.

The techniques of counseling, therefore, are geared to helping the individual engage in a process of examination. The counselor helps the person assess his practical difficulties and analyze his contradictory feelings about his situation. If counseling is successful, the individual is usually able to handle his personal relationships more satisfactorily and to take steps in the direction of improving his life situation. It should be stressed again that counseling is essentially a psychological service designed to strengthen the individual's capacity to handle his life's problems. Its aim is to relieve tension, to reduce self-depreciatory feelings, and to reinforce ego strengths. Such help, however, is conducted within the framework of the person's social needs and social responsibilities. The use of community resources—for education, recreation, employment, vocational training, and so forth—to aid the person in his problem-solving efforts is often suggested by the counselor. The counselor may make practical suggestions of various kinds and express his opinion about the advisability of a course of action. But he is trained to avoid the temptation of "taking over" the individual's problem and of imposing his own ideas on another person.

In the process of providing such help, the counselor uses many educational techniques. He provides the person with information about social resources, as mentioned above. He also exposes the person to psychological concepts by explaining them to him and by suggesting material for reading. The counselor offers the person an opportunity to discuss his newly acquired information, thus helping him assimilate it and relate it to his particular needs. Like all good teachers, the counselor recognizes that only a certain amount of information can be absorbed at one time, and that new ideas must be presented at an appropriate tempo.

CONCLUSION

Professional counseling is a relatively new development but it now has an established place among the helping services. Counselors are part of the structure of many community-sponsored social and educational services. In addition, counselors are engaged in private practice in increasing numbers.

Various counseling services are described in this volume. It therefore should have the value of orienting all persons in the counseling field to new developments and of providing them with an opportunity to study the common, as well as the specific, elements in these many professional undertakings. It is hoped that this short introduction will alert the reader to the common elements.

Child Care Counseling

RUTH STRANG

Professor of Education
University of Arizona
Tucson, Arizona

IN SCHOOLS and child guidance clinics workers constantly recognize that much of their guidance of serious cases is "too little and too late." So many of the existent problems of childhood and adolescence might have been prevented, or at least mitigated, by effective child care counseling.

Take the case of a delinquent Puerto Rican boy, for example. Child care counseling during preschool years might have started him off on the right track. Neither his mother nor his father was cruel or callous. They had their problems and they did not know how to cope with them. The father was indolent and easy going. He could have been helped to provide a home environment in which the child had some affection, more suitable activities, and a simple but adequate diet. The ambitious mother, whose role was that of a competent breadwinner, had never wanted the child and found little room for him in her life. She felt burdened by the care of the child and increasingly sorry for herself as his behavior became more outrageous. In the early years she might have been helped to accept herself, her ineffective husband, and her child. Counseling might have helped her learn some techniques of living in such a family constellation. If this help had been provided, the boy might never have started on the road to delinquency, and the efforts of the corrective institution to which he was sent later might not have been "too little and too late." Early child care counseling may not only prevent delinquency and serious emotional problems, but also help every child use his energy and ability more effectively.

Judges of juvenile courts, workers in mental hygiene clinics and others, while recognizing the multiple causes of disturbances of personal and social development, give a great deal of weight to parental guidance in the early years. They realize that it is worse than futile to blame the parents of maladjusted children. Instead, they see the need for concerted action to help parents provide the most favorable conditions for child growth. The late James S. Plant once said that he believed child guidance would eventually become largely parent guidance.

Skillful counseling can help parents change their day-by-day treatment of their children, even though it cannot change their basic personality structure or their deep-seated attitudes. Desirable changes in the parents' behavior toward the child evoke more acceptable responses on the part of the child, which in turn reinforce the parents' more positive behavior. Thus a beneficent cycle is set in motion.

BACKGROUND FOR CHILD CARE COUNSELING

To counsel parents effectively concerning child care practices, the worker must have a clear idea of which practices are psychologically sound. This is not so easy as it sounds. Over the years psychologists have changed their ideas on this subject. In fact, they have recommended quite opposite points of view at different times. A brief review of trends in child care practices is essential to a discussion of child care counseling.

Recommended Feeding Practices

Fifty years ago breast feeding was regarded as a moral obligation on the part of the mother. At that time unsanitary dairy practices and lack of scientific feeding formulas made breast feeding safer for the infant. By 1940 the point of view generally held was that breast feeding was preferred but not necessary. More recently the psychological value of close physical contact between mother and infant, and a calm, secure, and relaxed attitude on the part of the mother was emphasized. To feel secure and confident, the child needs to develop a sense of trust in the adult. The latest experiments with monkeys have shown that a warm, soft dummy mother may be comforting, but that is not enough. "Mothering" involves a more active response to the child's behavior.

Gradual weaning, with increasing bottle or cup feedings, has always been recommended. But the time recommended for beginning this process has varied. Earlier bulletins on child care suggested the sixth to eighth month as a good time for weaning, and even the fifth month was considered not too soon to begin. Later bulletins suggest an early but gradual introduction of strained and solid foods extending over a longer period of time.

There has been a shift from the rigid feeding schedule to one which accords with the baby's natural rhythm and the family's convenience. Around fifty years ago the mother was advised to feed the baby regularly on a three- or four-hour schedule until he was a year old. She was told to wake the baby at the end of the three-hour interval. If he cried before it was time for his next feeding, he must wait until the clock struck the hour. By mid-century the pendulum had swung to the other extreme—"self-regulated" or "self-demand" feeding. This was interpreted by some mothers as letting the baby eat what he wanted when he wanted it. Some modification of this extreme point of view was necessary. The sensible middle-of-the-road practice is for the mother to understand and to consider the individual infant's needs and to be guided by them, not by a rigid schedule nor by her convenience alone. She should try to judge when the baby is hungry by the way he cries, and act accordingly. Even though the baby's demands are at first erratic, he will gradually settle down to a fairly regular schedule which can be fitted into the family routine.

Solid foods are introduced earlier than they used to be. Less attention is now given to the order in which new foods such as fruit and cereal are introduced. More attention is given to the mother's attitude toward feeding, the mother-child relationship, and the conditions under which the baby is fed. The modern attitude is one of positive expectancy; the mother assumes that the child will eat small amounts of many wholesome foods. If he doesn't, there is no fuss about it. Later, when he is feeling well and happy, the food will be offered again. If he continues to refuse a certain food, some other food of comparable nutritive value can be substituted.

Toilet Training Suggestions

The trend in toilet training likewise has been toward more recognition of the child's bodily needs and rhythms; less insistence on early bowel and bladder control, and a more relaxed and accepting attitude on the part of the mother. Instead of starting toilet training at three months as was once advocated, mothers are advised not to begin toilet training until the baby can sit alone and has fairly regular movements. Bowel control takes about four to six weeks to learn and is usually established by the eighth or tenth month. Daytime bladder control may be expected between one and two years, and night control a little later.

By the time the child is four or five years old he may be expected to go to the toilet alone. However, lapses may occur when he is absorbed in new learnings or is emotionally disturbed. Anxiety on the part of the mother is to be avoided since it is often conveyed in subtle ways to the child.

These references to approximate times for acquiring different abilities do not imply that parents should be "time conscious" with respect to the child's development. Rather, parents should look for common sequences of behavior and be content if the child moves ahead at his own rate of development.

Research results on the effect of this child care practice on the child's personality are contradictory. A series of recent investigations has reported no relation between early and strict toilet training and personality development.

Right Attitudes toward Thumb Sucking

Earlier practices such as putting the baby's hand in a cotton mitten, sewing up the end of the sleeve, using a stiff cardboard cuff so he cannot get his hand to his mouth, putting a bitter substance on his fingers are now definitely condemned. Instead, the mother is urged to try to change conditions that are conducive to thumb sucking, such as lack of affection, few interesting things to do, and not enough opportunity to satisfy the natural desire to suck. Pacifiers are now permitted. If thumb sucking persists longer than usual, it only makes matters worse to scold the child or to make him over-conscious about it.

Changed Emphasis with Respect to Masturbation

Masturbation, once regarded as "an injurious practice which must be eradicated as soon as discovered," is no longer considered a cause for anxiety on the part of either the mother or the child. It is the feelings of guilt and fear often associated with the practice that are most detrimental. As in the case of thumb sucking, we should change the conditions that lead the child to seek this source of satisfaction rather than trying to change the child. Focusing his attention on the habit is one way of insuring its persistence.

Problems of Sleeping

General sleeping rules have not changed much during the past fifty years: 22–24 hours of sleep during the first two weeks of life; at six months about 12 hours during the night and 3–5 hours during the day; a regular routine; sleeping alone; and a quiet playtime before bedtime.

The modern emphasis is on recognition of individual differences and the child's need for the security that comes from knowing he is loved.

What to do about Crying

If a baby cries persistently there is a reason. Sometimes it is an obvious one; he is hungry, cold, wet, or otherwise physically uncomfortable. These conditions can be quickly corrected. However, crying may represent a demand for comfort of a less tangible kind. This, too, is a real need. If the former practice of letting him cry it out is followed in the first year, he may get a feeling about the world's indifference and his own helplessness that may persist for many years. If he is picked up only after he has cried for some time, he may learn to cry longer and harder each succeeding night.

The modern practice is to take plenty of time to make him comfortable and happy before putting him to sleep. If he whimpers a little, nothing need be done. Picking him up every time he cries a little may make him "more and more demanding and not a bit happier." But when he is really afraid and lonely and in need of comfort, it is better to meet this need than to let him exhaust himself crying it out.

Essentials of Discipline

Recommended practice in discipline has fluctuated between severe punishment and indulgence, between strictness and permissiveness. Some of the most important modern emphases are:

"Infancy is the time for the parents to be good and children to be bad"; the infant cannot understand why he should not do certain things; to punish him may only create anxiety.

Parents can "be good" by providing for the natural needs of the infant, creating conditions that will eliminate the need for imposing frequent restrictions on his behavior, seeing that he has few occasions to get into trouble rather than punishing him after he has got into trouble.

As the infant grows older he must learn to bring his pleasure seeking under control; he cannot always have what he wants when he wants it. He must learn to resist temptation and develop positive values. The development of conscience has its roots in various aspects of child rearing. Three kinds of maternal behavior have been found to be associated with strong conscience: (a) genuine affection toward and acceptance of the child; (b) "love-oriented" discipline—"what you have done makes me sad" and (c) the use of reasoning when the child has done something wrong.

Independence

There seems to have been a recent change in the attitude toward children's independence. Some persons now think we have gone too far in the direction of encouraging independence in children before they are capable of assuming responsibility for their actions. The little child needs the security of firm but reasonable limits maintained consistently by an understanding person. Within these limits he can develop an independence-dependency relation appropriate to his stage of development.

Current Emphases

The modern view was well summarized by Dorothy Barclay in a single sentence: "Live the good life and love that baby." Consideration for every member of the family, consistency in the parents' responses to the child, and constancy in their affection for him are the foundation of favorable child care practices. Parental motives and feelings are now recognized as equally or more important than their child care techniques and specific overt behavior. What a parent is and feels, speaks so loud that a child often cannot hear what he says. Both feelings and acts are important at certain stages and in different aspects of the child's development.[2] The young child may be more sensitive to his parents' behavior; the older child, to the parents' feelings.

A child's personality is not determined by a single event; repeated experiences of a similar kind are more likely to leave their mark. However, the child is flexible. He can unlearn and relearn. Even an intense experience may gradually fade away unless it is reinforced. Throughout life, important early personality trends are being modified by significant events in the individual's experience such as vocational success, marriage, and responsibility for bringing up a family of his own.

THE COUNSELOR'S ATTITUDE TOWARD PARENTS

In addition to the knowledge of child care practices already briefly reviewed, the counselor should have a positive attitude toward parents and their relations with children. The child care counselor should not blame the parents for the troubles of their children. Any censure that makes them still more uncertain, insecure, or fearful is likely to be unfavorably reflected in their children's behavior.

The counselor should recognize the complexity of parent-child relations. He should respect individual differences among parents as well as among children. Parents need help "in achieving their own unique kind of parenthood ... If we are to respect individual differences among people, then we must respect individually different patterns of parenthood."[1]

A mother who genuinely loves her child may make many mistakes in child care practice without causing serious harm to the child. On the other hand, a parent who knows all the answers and does most of the things advocated by child guidance specialists may fail to get the desired result because she has not learned to love. Her own emotional difficulties may prevent her from accepting her child wholeheartedly. To over-emqhasize the importance of a mother's love would only add to her feelings of guilt.

It is also important for the counselor to recognize the natural resistance of many parents to being helped. It is difficult for them to admit that they have problems in bringing up their children. Having problems seems to them an indication of inadequacy. Consequently the counselor should show appreciation of their efforts and praise their sound procedures. At the end of an interview one counselor said warmly, "You have helped me a great deal by coming here today and talking over Mary's problems."

When parents meet in small discussion groups, they are often reassured to find they are not alone in their difficulties. They learn that other parents have problems like their own. Sometimes they gain a great deal by hearing how other parents have handled situations similar to theirs.

WHO DOES CHILD CARE COUNSELING?

Many professional people work together on this problem of helping parents bring up children in the best way. The family physician, pediatrician, nurse, psychiatrist, psychologist, nursery school and other school teachers, the social worker in community service, family welfare agencies, and religious workers all share in this responsibility. Effective service requires broad preparation of personnel and close coordination among agencies.

To prepare workers for this responsibility, professional schools are broadening their curricula. Medical schools and schools of nursing recognize the interrelation between physical, psychological, and social factors in the lives of people. The training of psychiatrists and psychologists includes study of the physiological basis and causation of mental disturbances. Nursery school teachers are being prepared for work with parents as one of the most important parts of their job. More and more, elementary school teachers are being helped to conduct conferences with parents of their pupils during which they also discuss the preschool children in the family. All these professional people need a working knowledge of the many-sided development of children at different ages. This knowledge must be evaluated and organized for the preparation of workers in the broad field of child care.

Coordination among workers and agencies is equally important. This requires thinking together on cases and problems. Case conferences in which workers from different fields pool their information, understanding, and resources offer the most effective way of coordinating the efforts of all who are concerned with an individual case. It is also a slow but sure method for the in-service education of all the workers present. Seminars attended by representatives of various disciplines constitute the most effective means of thinking through basic problems of child care counseling. Panel discussions by doctors, psychologists, pastors, parents, and teachers held before an audience of teachers and administrators also represent an effective educational tool in this multiple approach to child care problems.

This pooling of resources does not mean that one professional person is to take over the responsibilities of another specialist. It means that each person is to be helped to work more wisely within the framework of his own situations. For example, nursery school teachers need psychiatric insights that can be applied within the framework of the nursery school. By working in the area of his special competence, with a recognition of related factors, each professional person can best help parent and child. Although he is not a therapist, he may have a therapeutic influence.

For example, the work of a child guidance or mental hygiene or psychiatric clinic would be related to all the forces affecting a particular child in the community. It would be concerned with the family, with neighborhood conditions related to the child's development, with economic conditions that determine whether parents can provide the essentials of food, shelter and clothing, and with the available health services and religious influences. The knowledge of mental hygiene possessed by the clinic workers should filter into everyday living and be used by parents in bringing up their children. It is important to find ways of coordinating all the forces that impinge upon a particular child.

There is another sense in which child care counseling requires a multiple approach. It should provide for simultaneous work with parents, with preschool children, with school children, with adolescents, with young married couples, with grandparents. All these persons contribute in some way to the care of young children. School children often have major responsibility for the care of their younger brothers and sisters. The development of these little children is greatly influenced by the older child's knowledge, skill, and attitude. A book by Florence

Nightingale published in 1861, *Notes on Nursing for the Laboring Classes*, includes a chapter for children who must take care of baby brothers or sisters.[9] Adolescents are beginning to look forward to homes of their own and would profit by effective education in marriage and family life. Young married couples meeting immediate problems of child care have a special readiness for counseling.

Though the role of grandparents in child care counseling has been given little consideration, the "numerous hazards of grandparent interference with parental control" have been pointed out. It has been observed that grandparents often have "unbending and didactic opinions concerning child care and an unwillingness to recognize the process of maturation" (Staples, *et al.*, p.91).[11] The differing views of grandparents and parents as to desirable child behavior frequently create conflicts for the children.

A comparative study of the "attitudes of grandmothers and mothers toward child rearing practices" confirmed the hypothesis that "the grandmothers as a group have the more strict, authoritative and punitive attitudes toward child rearing while the mothers are much more permissive in their ideas of adult control of children" (Staples, *et al.*, p.94).[11] This strict and authoritative attitude applied to all aspects of child rearing and not to specific aspects only. The permissiveness of both groups became more pronounced as their number of years of schooling increased. However, neither group was as permissive as were the specialists reported on in another study. It was also noted that grandmothers who live apart from their children and grandchildren have a more permissive attitude than those living in the home with their grandchildren. One explanation of this fact is that more tension-arousing situations arise when the three generations live together. The permissive attitude of parents a decade ago seems to have changed recently in the direction of greater firmness and the maintenance of standards.

In working with any individual or group it is important to understand their motivation; for example, why they don't do the things they ought to do, and what appeals are most likely to evoke their cooperation. Each should be approached in accord with his own point of view. A fundamental principle is to do things *with* people, not *to* them.

The Physician's Contribution

The family physician or pediatrician who has had training in psychology is in a strategic position to prevent or to ameliorate many emotional reverberations that may arise in connection with feeding, toilet training, and the daily schedule. The Physician's contribution is described in the chapter on Maternal Counseling.

The Role of the Nurse in Child Care Counseling

The nurses' responsibility for child care counseling has long been recognized. State laws require that nurses have some knowledge of pediatrics; the establishment of nursery schools in hospitals has enabled nurses in training to see how other professional workers handle problems of child care. Courses dealing with child care and parent education have been systematically introduced into the nursing curriculum.

Following are some of the questions which nurses are most frequently asked by new mothers:

Should every mother nurse her baby?

How are good eating habits developed?

How are good habits of elimination developed?

How much sleep is needed by normal children of different ages?

How are good sleeping habits developed?

At what ages can a child be expected to learn specific things such as walking, feeding self without spilling, dressing self, etc.?

What can be done about a child who is conditioned against some desirable action (i.e., drinking milk, going to sleep in the dark, etc.)? (Rood, *et al.*, p. 36).[9]

Though no nurse can escape such questions on child care, many are not prepared or do not take time to answer parents' questions adequately. Parent education is an inherent part of the work of all nurses. For this aspect of their work nurses feel the need of further preparation.

The Role of Psychiatrist and Psychologist

Many emotional disturbances in children stem from or are associated with faulty child care practices. By helping parents adjust their demands to the needs and temperament of the child, the psychiatrist and psychologist contribute to good child development. They recognize the emotional needs of both parents and child, and work toward helping the parents understand themselves as well as their child. Focusing on the security and personality development of the parent as a means of helping the child is an important modern emphasis. To this problem the psychiatrist and pyschologist bring their specialized skill in psychotherapy.

The Teacher as Parent Educator

All good nursery schools consider child care counseling as one of their most important functions. Taylor[15] lists a progression of five steps: acquiring knowledge of child development, discussing life experiences, engaging in guided observation and study of children at home and in nursery school, practicing child care under supervision, and taking full responsibility "for planning, carrying out, and evaluating experiences based on principles learned" (Taylor, p. 60).[15] Frequently the parent voluntarily initiates the discussion. Less often parent and teacher have observed the child at school and at home. Such observations enable both to see what forces are influencing the child. Most important is an understanding of the principles of human dynamics—why people behave as they do.

Parents may gain insight through skillfully conducted group meetings. In these meetings the skillful nursery school teacher shares leadership functions with the group of parents, recognizes the role each member plays and its contribution to the group goal, has an accepting attitude and a sense of humor, and helps each member make some contribution to the group.

In working with parents individually the teacher will meet similar problems. Also, sometimes he will encounter certain resistances on the part of parents. These should be recognized. Some stem from insecurity. The teacher, too, may feel insecure and uncertain. If he does, some of his anxiety may be transferred to the parent. Each may be afraid of the other for different reasons. The parent may feel inadequate in knowledge as compared with the teacher. The teacher may feel inferior to the parent in social prestige or in knowledge of the individual child. Actually, both have unique understandings to share with each other. Their conference should be a joint quest for the best possible conditions for the growing child.

The teacher should realize also that parents' attitudes change as the child grows up. A mother may feel much more loving toward the helpless infant than toward the two-year-old striving to leave the dependency of babyhood. A father may enjoy his active little boy more than the baby, with whom he does not know how to communicate. The teacher may help the parents to understand these changes in their attitudes toward their growing children.

It is difficult for teachers to feel sympathetic with some parents. If they see clearly that many of the child's difficulties stem from the parents' attitude and behavior, they tend to identify with the child and blame the parents. Their sympathy and understanding should embrace both parents and child.

The Social Worker's Conference with Parents

No other professional worker has so good an opportunity to understand the dynamic environment of the child as the social worker. As she observes parents and children together in a certain home, she gains an idea of the child care practices employed there and of their emotional concomitants. The social worker in a welfare agency also has the advantage of being able to give material assistance to the family; her efforts are not entirely blocked by economic need. She can draw on resources not available to the teacher and other professional workers. To the social worker, child guidance is family guidance and community guidance. Thus she is able to attack child care problems in a fundamental way.

The Church Worker

The pastor and his staff likewise have the advantage of working with a family group and having contact with the child from his earliest years. One church educational board has prepared a little book which will be sent to all parents as soon as the child is born. More and more, the importance of parents' values is being recognized, and the conflict between religion and the behavioral sciences is being reduced.

COUNSELING TECHNICS

It is difficult indeed to find any counseling technics that are used in child care counseling alone. The technics of counseling in general, and of counseling parents in particular, apply here. Consequently this section will consist of statements of a few basic, oft-reiterated principles followed by a specific application to child care practices.

Respect and Accept the Parent as a Person

The parents should be treated with courtesy, sincerity, and consideration. This is obvious. They should be regarded as capable persons with good ideas who have resources within themselves to solve many of their problems. Counselors should appeal to the parents' strengths rather than to their weaknesses. The counselor should not take responsibility away from the parents. The following case is a partial illustration of this principle.

A young father with active tuberculosis had just moved away from one community where the public health nurse had told him he must go to a sanatorium. In the new community another public health nurse visited the home. The father was taking care of the baby and two other small children while his wife was away at work. The nurse at first said nothing about the tuberculosis. She encouraged the father to talk about the children and about himself. He told about his anxiety for his family; if he went away for treatment, what would happen to them? His love for his family and his deep

concern for their welfare were uppermost in his mind. The nurse listened sympa-
thetically and showed, by an occasional reflection of his feeling, that she understood.
She suggested sources from which the family could obtain assistance while he was at
the sanatorium. She also showed him specific ways in which he could protect the small
children from infection. He began to look forward toward the future when he would
be cured and again able to play his role in supporting his family.

In this interview the nurse accepted and appreciated the father's
point of view and suggested resources in line with it. She listened. She
showed that she understood. And she helped him make plans that he
could not have carried out without her aid.

Control that Impulse to Give Advice

In general, advice is not welcomed by parents even though they ask
for it. The parent often will not follow the advice he or she requests.
Moreover, the counselor may be wrong; the advice may not work. It is
usually better to use and improve the approach the parents already
have in mind or to help them think through the problem in their own
way and arrive at their own decision. Success in doing this will help
the parent to feel more adequate as a person.

In one case the visiting nurse was called into a home to help the mother with a
feeding problem involving her three-year-old son. The mother, who called the agency,
said she had tried everything but still the boy would not eat. The nurse planned the
visit for 11.15 a.m., the time the youngster usually had lunch. Mrs. Jones had prepared a good, nutritious lunch for young Johnny, and the nurse proceeded to feed the
child without any difficulty. In the discussion between the mother and nurse that
followed it appeared that the mother's real problem was the conflicting point of view
between her husband and herself as to the feeding, schedule, and other aspects of
child care. In the course of the conversation, Mrs. Jones nervously said: "If I say
one thing, his father will tell Johnny just the opposite. I really don't know what to
do any more. And Johnny realizes it, too."
Nurse: "Why don't we have a talk with him together? Do you think that might
help?"
Mrs. Jones: "Oh, I don't think he'll like that. He doesn't like to be told what to
do, you know."
Nurse: "We won't tell him what to do. We'll just explain what seems to be best
for the child and for the happiness of both you and your husband."
It was arranged that the nurse would stop by when Mr. Jones would be at home,
not telling him that the mother had originally called her. After four visits Mr. Jones
began to understand the effect of his attitude on his wife and child. Both parents were
very appreciative of the nurse's interest and counseling.

The purpose of child care counseling, in a mother's advisory service,
has been to help the mother gain "an overall picture of the child's
situation and to discuss this with the mother, rather than to prescribe
a series of specific technics to deal with specific complaints."[3]

Making the Interview a Conference—a Sharing of Experience; an Interchange of Views, Information, and Attitudes.

One parent–teacher conference began in this way:

Teacher: How do you do, Mrs. Brown. It's so nice of you to come to the school. I hope you're feeling better.

Mrs. Brown: Oh, yes—a little. But it seems to be one thing after another. (Proceeds to tell about her illnesses.) And, of course, that made it necessary for my husband to spend so much time with me. I guess we've both been sort of neglecting Billy. We've been letting him do a lot of things on his own.

Teacher: I see. In my first grade class, too, Billy is a capable and independent child. When he finishes his work he finds something else to do.

Teacher and parent continued to work together on ways of helping Billy at home and at school.

Some parents are hostile and critical toward the world in general, or toward the school in particular; the counselor should realize that they are not hostile toward him as a person. Recognizing this, the worker will not feel apologetic or on the defensive. He may ask for their help or their suggestions.

Some parents are compulsive talkers; they go around in circles. It is difficult for the worker to keep the focus on the main purpose of the conference. Sometimes it is helpful to make a definite statement of the purpose of the conference. A question or comment often will bring the parent back to the major problems being discussed.

Many parents feel inadequate. So much is expected of them, according to radio, TV, magazine articles, and public opinion in general. Often the worker can praise some specific thing which the parent has done well and turn her thoughts toward some positive thing she can do.

Other parents are reticent; they resent anything that looks like an attempt to pry into their private affairs. The worker should be content with whatever specific information the parent chooses to give freely. No information is worth getting at the expense of a good relationship.

If a parent is non-communicative, the worker will try to find the reason: lack of language facility, unawareness of the child's needs, lack of trust in the worker, or some other reason. With this kind of parent, a concrete demonstration of some child care procedure sometimes helps to establish a more relaxed relationship. If the parent is relaxed and feels at ease, she is more likely to speak freely and frankly.

Many parents want the worker to take a frank approach so that they can get more help on their problems. They want to work together on conditions that need to be changed. They will accept constructive criticism that they can do something about.

If there are differences of opinion between parent and worker, each should state and interpret her observations of the child and explain why she thinks as she does. Sometimes they can recognize that their own deep-seated attitudes are responsible for their point of view about the child.

RESEARCH ON CHILD CARE COUNSELING

More research has been done on the effectiveness of group discussion and pamphlets than on the individual counseling of parents. Brim[2] (ch. 9) points out the deficiencies in research design in most of the studies of evaluation of parent education. Evidence is needed of the effectiveness of specific child care counseling practices. One of the most notable examples of this kind of research is the longitudinal study of the effects of parental guidance reported by Macfarlane.[7] In this research the effect of parental guidance on the behavior of children has been studied over a period of 35 years, beginning at birth. The 244 families were divided into an experimental group, in which the mothers were given guidance, and a control group given only mental tests and physical examinations. The home visits to the member of the guidance group were made by the psychiatric social worker who took a detailed habit and behavior history. The director of research followed up this initial interview by making a summary of the situation and discussing with the parents any questions which had arisen with regard to the bringing up of their children. Parents were also invited to describe the methods which they found to work best. From this continuing developmental study much will be learned about behavior problems at different ages, the relation between the child's typical behavior and his endowments and environment, and the relation between early emotional patterns and subsequent development.

One of the few experimental studies of the effectiveness of individual counseling was conducted by child health stations with mothers who reported feeding problems (Brim, pp. 294–295).[2] The mothers were interviewed and counseled individually, and permissiveness in handling the feeding problems was described and recommended. Only 8 of the 50 mothers adopted permissive practices. Those mothers who had had previous helpful suggestions, who cared more about the child's diet than his size, and who were open-minded were the ones who adopted or at least tried to adopt the methods recommended.

One other study of counseling programs reported improved behavior on the part of the children of the parents counseled. Another reported that the counseled group were initially more aware of family life problems than a group who were not counseled (Brim, pp. 301–303).[2]

Another kind of research in this field is the analysis of verbatim reports of interviews with parents of preschool children. Through such analysis one can note the insights gained by the parents during a series of interviews. Of course, the only insights which can be perceived by this method are those which the parents are able to verbalize. In some cases these insights may be merely intellectual, unsupported by the emotional drive that will make them functional. To measure the actual progress of the parent toward more constructive treatment of the child, it would be necessary to observe the parent–child relationship and have simultaneous interviews with the child.

Research and training may be combined through provisions for offering scholarships to promising young persons. These students may be expected to make creative, critical summaries of the literature on specific aspects of child care counseling, and to carry on research projects while they are being trained for key positions in the field. Such research requires a team approach with a competent director to set up the research design and evaluate the results. Problems would be attacked jointly by persons in different disciplines.

The so-called "action research" consists in applying the problem-solving method to practical unsolved problems recognized by practioners in the field. The results are applied to the local situation and immediately put to use there. Teachers and other professional workers are more likely to use the results of research which they themselves have initiated and carried out.

CONCLUDING STATEMENT

Child care counseling requires (a) a sound point of view toward parent–child relations, (b) knowledge of recommended child care practices, (c) knowledge of related disciplines, and (d) skill in counseling procedures. It is carried on by workers in many fields whose services should be coordinated with reference to the individual child in his family and community setting.

BIBLIOGRAPHY

1. BARCLAY, D.: 1955. "Tomorrow's Adults—the Readers Write." *New York Times Magazine*, January 9, p. 48.
2. BRIM, ORVILLE G.: 1955. *Education for Child Rearing*. New York: Russell Sage Foundation.
3. COOPER, M. M.: 1948. *Evaluation of the Mothers' Advisory Service*. Monographs of the Society for Research in Child Development, Vol. XII. Washington, D.C.: The Society.
4. KRAMER, D. and KARR, M.: 1953. *Teen-age Gangs*. New York: Henry Holt and Co.
5. LANGDON, G. and STOUT, I. W.: 1954. *Teacher–Parent Interviews*. New York: Prentice-Hall.

6. LEONARD, E. M., VAN DEMAN, D. D. and MILES, L. E.: 1954. *Counseling with Parents in Early Childhood Education.* New York: The Macmillan Company.

7. MACFARLANE, J. W.: 1952. "Research Findings from a Twenty-year Study of Growth from Birth to Maturity." Berkeley, Calif.: Institute of Child Welfare (mimeographed).

8. MACFARLANE, J. W. *et al.*: 1954. *A Developmental Study of the Behaviour Problems of Normal Children Between Twenty-one Months and Fourteen Years.* Berkeley, Calif.: University of California Press.

9. ROOD, D.: 1935. *The Nurse and Parent Education.* New York: Bureau of Publications, Teachers College, Columbia University.

10. SEARS, R. R., MACOB, E. E. and LEVIN, H.: 1957. *Patterns of Child Rearing.* Evanston, Ill.: Row, Peterson and Company.

11. STAPLES, R. and SMITH, J. W.: 1954. "Attitudes of Grandmothers and Mothers toward Child Rearing Practices." *Child Development,* 25:91–97.

12. STENDLER, C. B.: 1950. "Sixty Years of Child Training Practices." *Journal of Pediatrics,* 36:122–134.

13. STRANG, R. M.: 1959. *An Introduction to Child Study,* Parts II and III, 4th ed. New York: The Macmillan Company.

14. STRANG, R. M.: 1960. *Helping Your Gifted Child.* New York: E. P. Dutton.

15. TAYLOR, K. W.: 1954. *Parent Cooperative Nursery Schools.* New York: Bureau of Publications, Teachers College, Columbia University.

16. U.S. Children's Bureau: 1951. *Infant Care,* revised ed. Publication No. 8. Washington, D.C.: U.S. Govt. Printing Office.

Counseling Techniques in Child Guidance

—With an Appendix on Camp Counseling—

ERNEST HARMS

New School for Social Research
New York City

PRELIMINARY CONSIDERATIONS

SINCE the method chosen to execute a task depends to a considerable degree on one's interpretation of that task, what we may wish to call child guidance will be determined by our definition of child guidance. One widely accepted concept of child guidance is that of aid to the problem child and the mentally impaired child—a concept that excludes all but the abnormal child. Under this concept, child guidance is a practical method of remedial work with children. This writer believes that such a definition impermissibly narrows the area of child guidance, for there is an even greater need for guidance of the life and growth of the normal child than of the abnormal. This writer would like to see the common concept replaced by one that offers the widest possible latitude: the science of adjusting and guiding youth in its various stages of development to each phase of life and knowledge. This interpretation was the basis of his *Handbook of Child Guidance* (New York, 1947). As presented in that book, child guidance is the practical execution of all educational and social adjustment functions in the life of every child. In accordance with this idea, the author calls for the establishment of child guidance as a separate, autonomous field of science, superimposed on education as an enlarged field of practical education.

Counseling is the technique of child guidance in all of its phases. "Talking to" is not counseling, although some like to define it that way. There are certain ways of approaching and speaking to children at various age levels. Success in counseling depends on knowledge of these ways, which the counselor must learn. Knowledge of the social, ethnic, religious, and familial factors in the life of the child must be part of the counselor's professional tools. Careful discipline in acquiring knowledge of these many aspects is required of the competent counselor. Satisfactory child guidance requires detached insight into all child life and juvenile psychology. It requires also personal fitness for counseling, including all facets of personal health and ethical maturity.

Psychology itself must be a major contributor to all phases of counseling. Consulting psychology, which has become one of the largest fields of applied psychology, provides us with a major source of information on counseling techniques. Before the counselor can effectively use the methods of consulting psychology, however, he must have a solid basis of understanding of the child. This basis consists of information about the psychic constitution of the child, the characterological peculiarities of the child, the stages of development of the juvenile psyche, and, finally, knowledge of the effects of environment on the child.

Today, gaining such understanding seems to involve the administration of a battery of intelligence, personality, and projective tests, to which sometimes is added a check against an age-grade test, such as that of Gesell. These objective measures are preferred to what might be called subjective descriptive estimations. It is to be hoped that in the future it will be considered necessary to supplement these objective evaluations with more intimate, personal observations. Many diagnostic inaccuracies might be avoided if momentary indisposition, resistance to routine procedures, or social interference, as well as limitations in the reliability, validity, and applicability of tests were taken into account. Actually, no routine instrument can replace the personal psychological ability of a psychologist; successful evaluation of the psychological characteristics and qualities of a child depends on the flexibility of the observer. Accurate recognition of type variations and temperament predominance is as important as correct estimation of the specific tendencies of one of the major age groups. The factors which may distort test performance must also be taken into consideration in the guidance counselor's personal evaluation of the child. In addition, a case may be anomalous, or may present an unusual typological picture, and this should also be taken into account.

In sizing up the essential qualities of a young person, the developmental factor, that is, a combination of constitutional and environmental elements, must be given priority. Between infancy and post-adolescence, behavior patterns and dynamics change so rapidly that they ought to be measured by week-long periods in the early stage, and by no longer than five-year periods in post-adolescence. In contrast, changes in later life, when measured chronologically at all, usually are measured in ten-year periods. Advice given a young person as to conduct, for example, requires a realization of the differences that exist in these shorter periods between infancy and post-adolescence. Theoretical knowledge of these periods and the normal behavior patterns that occur in them, however, is not enough. There must be awareness of individual developmental tendencies, which can only be perceived phenomenologically and not as expressions of a denominator for a certain age group.

Developmental factors are especially important in pathological deviations; the rapidly changing background makes it difficult to fix the somatic picture of even the most common mental abnormality of childhood. When an older person, who may be considered more or less "completed," disintegrates into a pathological state, that state has a definite and identifiable appearance. In the case of pathological deviation in a growing child, one can count on healthy forces—on the innate developmental power and the desire to grow up and to learn. Here is a source of therapeutic power on which the adult can no longer rely. Of course, while in children there may occur pathological states so severe that even the basic forces are afflicted, these conditions are as rare as total idiocy or total imbecility.

This writer is convinced that in dealing with problems of children, constitutional and developmental aspects must be considered together, as influencing one another. This combined viewpoint must also be applied in evaluating intellectual capacity and ability. Although most educational psychologists firmly believe that present tests—or further modifications of them—are and will be sufficient and satisfactory for this purpose, one must come to the insight that the coordination of constitutional and developmental factors is necessary for a complete understanding of any child's intelligence. At present this insight is generally lacking. We do not take sufficiently into account that the slow learner progresses timidly because of an introverted type of constitution. We do not give the adolescent credit for capabilities which may be only temporarily obscured by the storms of maturation which flood his mind as well as his body. Furthermore, in complicated cases it is most important to identify the factor, constitutional or developmental, that is the major or primary cause of disability. Superficial examination will prove worthless. What may at first seem to be developmental conflict will often turn out to be based on constitutional disposition, or the reverse may be the case. Only careful investigation will bring the true cause to light, and this knowledge of the basic problem can be the only foundation for successful advice or therapy.

The multitude of environmental factors that shape a child, as well as his specific constitution and character traits and the course of his development, must be taken into consideration in proportion to their influence. Here again, concrete observations may show deviations from the observed "average" behavior or the most frequently applied theories. We may often observe how theories are not always backed up by concrete instances, as in the following examples: We know by now that the low-income groups are not the only sources of juvenile delinquents, that high-income groups are contributing to delinquency in an increasingly high percentage. We know that while the urbanite flicks switches or presses buttons to operate the complicated machinery that is a part of almost every city household, this does not mean that he understands technology. (Paradoxically, the average farm boy is more adept at operating and repairing complex mechanisms.) Finally, we have been forced, from observation of individuals, to give up evaluations based on stereotypes of group traits, which in turn are based on prejudice (e.g., that persons of African descent have less intellectual ability than those of European stock), and to recognize that environment plays a part in forming these characteristics.

In evaluating a child's condition for guidance purposes, the worker must be aware of his social class, the financial status of his family, whether he lives in the city or in a rural area; he should know his race and religion and the details of his schooling. He must be aware of the extent and the way in which each of these factors affects the individual with whom he is working, as well as how the individual feels about them. Environment means not only the physical and spatial outer world, but also the elements of time and change; even more important, it means the sociological, mental, and metaphysical factors which influence a child's life from the outside.

Even the physical outer world is more selective in its effects than is usually recognized. There are not only the obvious differences between rural and urban living. If one wanted to be more thorough, one could consider climatic differences, for example, which may play a part in an allergy as well as in emotional distress. The differences between maritime and mountain environment may play an important role in influencing the body as well as the mind of a child. We might add the semi-sociological conditions which make life on an Iowa farm different from that on a Texas range, or which make a coal-mining district different from a cottonmill village. We may go more deeply into different physical environments, in the manner of Clifford Shaw, who pointed out that certain city sections may be seedbeds of juvenile delinquency while other similar sections are not. We have begun to learn the extent to which environmental differences can be caused by local, political, and administrative variations, not to mention the far-reaching differences among classes, tribes, nations, and races. We have learned to our astonishment that even in the United States, where it is a part of the culture and of the Constitution of the nation not even to admit that physical differences can have any social counterpart, or that such a thing as "class" even exists, there is still, in twenty-four of the states, a legal prohibition against interracial marriage.

The last of the environmental factors to be considered —school and religion—are perhaps the most influential. Most children spend half of their waking hours, of at least their first eight to ten years of life, in a classroom. They are learning not only to read and write, but something about the world. They are part of a social group of children on whom teachers are a major influence. The school and the teacher are character-forming elements of the greatest importance; the school and the classroom, like the parental urban home or the farm, provide all kinds of different emotional and mental climates.

Finally, religion is not only the church or temple to which one goes on holidays; it is also a social community, which may sometimes also provide the schooling, and often represents the only people with whom one may socialize. One's religion usually limits the group from which a spouse is chosen, and may autocratically determine political choices. It is also the social agency to which one will apply when in need of social service or employment.

Of course, not all of these factors can be stressed in the actual process of guidance, but the guidance counselor must be aware of the part they played in shaping the child he is helping. He must realize how and where they aid or limit guidance.

Up to now we have discussed the three major factors of which the child guidance task is composed. The first, already considered, is thorough knowledge of the body and mind of the child, together with knowledge of the social conditions of juvenile life. The second set of factors consists of the qualities of personality and character which must be put into play if child guidance work is to be satisfactorily fulfilled. The third factor consists of the ways and means of the specific procedures and applications of guidance.

We come now to the second element of child guidance counseling, the specific professional features of the guidance counselor that make him a competent representative of his profession.

Let us first deal with the personality of the child guidance counselor. In recent decades it has been commonly acknowledged that merely routine information gained through reading and in college courses does not provide a person with the skills needed to do a satisfactory job. While child guidance is a professional discipline, it is above all a practical discipline and one in which innate abilities, like those of the artist, are a major prerequisite. Those who do not have this innate vocation for dealing with children, together with the infinite patience required in dealing with the problems and failures of children, should not become guidance counselors. I have often heard it said that a good child guidance worker must start out with a strong parental instinct, a strong desire, or pronounced ability, which he then transforms into a professional pattern. This, however, is far from enough. Child guidance demands great skill in observing and empathizing with the healthy and, even more important, the abnormal attitudes in children —a skill that one does not expect to find in the average parent. This is especially true for those abnormal behavior traits which are the special concern of guidance workers. It is necessary to train an innate ability by serious learning from books, but, still more, from observation and from experience in handling children. This learning, of course, should not stop with the end of formal training.

There are certain types of people who tend to seek personal compensation from being child guidance counselors; their strong desire to help children comes from a need to fill some lack in their own lives. For example, there are some unmarried women who, consciously or unconsciously, want to make up for their unfulfilled wish for motherhood by taking care of other women's offspring. Another type is the mother who has failed with her own family, or the wife whose marriage has ended in separation or divorce. By being good to the children or families of others, she finds justification of her worth. A third group are social workers or education workers who have failed in their work with adults, and who feel they might be more successful with children. Here one cannot emphasize strongly enough that while there may be more gratification, working with children is the more difficult task. Persons who have experienced failure in any sphere of life should be cautioned against entering the field of child guidance without first carefully examining their reasons for doing so. We are not condemning or excluding these groups as people; aside from the factors mentioned, they may be well or even extraordinarily qualified for child guidance.

All the factors mentioned up to now are only preliminary conditions to be required of the child guidance counselor. There are more intimate ones which should be stressed even more. The most important are, of course, a healthy personality and a healthy body, which are even more important for those counseling children than for those counseling adults. We have heard much about health requirements for teachers, who deal with presumably normal children; the guidance counselor, who deals mainly with abnormal behavior in a wider social setting, must be even healthier and more alert than the classroom teacher.

The counselor—and this is a most important point—must not only
be able to talk and to teach, but still more, to listen. He must be willing
and able, emotionally, to accept the most extreme behavioral deviations and must continuously make the effort to understand them. It is
necessary that he be able to live through the child's ordeals together
with him and to guide him through, and eventually out of, the under-
world of misbehavior and confusion.

Often the counselor's work is even more difficult than that of the
psychotherapist because he deals most frequently with the preventive
aspects and stages of deviation not fully developed, as well as with rarely
occurring pathological and infrequently observed somatic patterns.
He must cope with and handle with sureness the various stages of
deviations. He stands between sickness and health and has to deal
constructively with both. It happens frequently that parents bring
children with mild behavior deviations to the pediatrician, or even the
psychiatrist, and are sent away because the condition is not "severe"
enough to be considered pathological. Nevertheless, these children are
disturbed and are often more troublesome than really sick children.
It is precisely this rather frequent type which is the concern of the
guidance counselor. It was this situation that led the ingenious pediatrician and child psychiatrist Douglas Thom, author of *The Everyday
Problems of the Everyday Child*, to develop a type of behavior clinic that
dealt with this kind of pre-pathological child. In the struggle between
psychiatrists and psychologists over the right of treatment of any type
of behavior deviation, Dr. Thom's idea has been lost. The "psychiatric
clinic for children" and "child guidance clinic" concepts today lack
the depth and the wider-angled aspect towards which Dr. Thom was
striving.

More than in any other field of the scientific world, practical science
and personal maturity in the field of child guidance cannot be over-
estimated. While book study and administrative routine can help to
keep a counselor "in trim," only continuous practical work in the field,
even if only on a limited scale, can mature the worker. In addition to
physical and mental development, continuous practice is necessary for
professional growth, especially in a field as seriously involved with the
community and all social interrelationships as is child guidance.

There has been much argument among educators, psychologists, and
physicians as to whether married or unmarried status is preferable for
those working with children. I hesitate to make any definite statement,
preferring not to appear dogmatic. However, although one will find
unmarried workers whose counseling abilities are as good or even
better than some with parental experience, the feelings of parenthood
are of great value for counselors who may lack the ability to respond

intuitively to a child. Here like everywhere, intuitive response depends
primarily on innate abilities, and the less those abilities are intellectua-
lized, the better they are. The same may be said about all group relationships which are today considered so essential for counseling.

I do not adhere completely to the opinion that a counselor must
belong to the religion or race or class of his client. I have seen cases in
which Negro youths have been more attached to non-Negro than to
Negro workers. And I have found that a "neutral" religious attitude,
such as that of the Quakers, may prove most advantageous in a guidance relationship, since the pressures, often contained in a religious
dogma and which may cause problems and conflicts, are more likely to
be absent. In cases of adolescents and post-adolescents especially,
where elements of outside pressure frequently are the basis of conflicts,
religious neutrality is of considerable value, even if the religious factor
is not directly involved. The general feeling of neutrality and absence
of pressure will act as a denominator of confidence in the midst of
suspicion toward outside influence. Here, as much as anywhere else,
the guiding viewpoint should be the realization that each and every
case demands an individualized study that no dogmatic standardized
approach can fully illuminate.

In an era such as ours, when geriatric problems crowd our minds,
the employment of older workers in child guidance should not go un-
mentioned. Again, we feel that the particular quality of the individual
worker is the only sound measure. However, this problem ties in closely
with the one we have chosen to discuss last—that of whether, and when,
a male or a female worker is preferable. Our present social structure
does not provide as much opportunity for the grandmother in the raising
and educating of the next generation's offspring as was provided her
during the agricultural periods of Western civilization, when the mother
was tied down by housework or occupied with constantly arriving
infants. Then it was the grandmother who took over the educating
and guiding of the growing children. There was no doubt a great deal
of helpful influence on the child's development from this wisdom of
maturity; youth is often drawn to this maturity, especially when parental
authority or influence has failed.

Whether or not it is in general better, or in special cases advisable,
to use a male or female counselor is again primarily an individual
problem. However, we do know from general as well as developmental
typology that certain age levels have certain preferences, and these
should be considered. The "he-man" type of primary-school boy will
generally be drawn more to masculine guidance, while the same boy
after adolescence may be more open to maternal, female counseling.
Little girls on the primary-school level, on the other hand, will accept

female guidance far more easily; the "crush"-age post-adolescent "flapper" will in most cases have better transference with an older male counselor. In cases of broken families, the guidance counselor should realize that a part of the treatment may require that in some respects the counselor substitute for the missing parent, and in such cases the counselor should be of the same sex as the missing parent. Here again, however, sensitive empathy with the needs of the individual child, rather than a routinized approach, should determine the final decision.

Because of the importance that child guidance and childhood counseling have assumed in the educational world, academic schools have realized the need for adding to their training programs courses in guidance and guidance techniques. Most of the larger schools of education and schools of social work have begun to offer such courses. Full guidance counselor training programs, however, are, to my knowledge, available in only a very few schools.

Those who have worked extensively and done much thinking about educational and training needs in this field have realized that proper preparation requires considerable practical experience, and that we will not be able to speak of having satisfactory educational facilities for guidance counselors until adequate internship programs are developed.

We now arrive at the subject which some may consider to be the only appropriate one for this chapter—the counseling process in child guidance. We shall concentrate, in this section, on the counseling process itself, but without going into such corollary matters as testing or specific remedial techniques, although the latter are today considered more essential to the child guidance worker than the material to be presented below.

THE COUNSELING SETTING

The first question to be answered about the counseling process is that concerning its setting, that is, what environmental conditions are necessary for the successful execution of counseling and guidance. Conventional opinion today regards the guidance clinic as the only desirable setting, and guidance is the function of such an institution. A purely administrative and institutional approach to an essentially personal relationship between counselor and client would seem to have little value. In many cases the situation may be too complex to be handled by a routine procedure. The clinical setting may offer the advantage of the availability of both a psychiatrist and a social worker, but no matter what the amount of service available, the essential factor is still the personal relationship.

To be capable to develop this kind of a relationship with a counselor or other worker, a child must have some personal life of his own. In the case of an infant or nursery-age child, the advice or guidance must be given to the father or mother. In recent decades, techniques such as play therapy have been developed which are useful with very young children, but these special techniques are outside the scope of this general discussion. The age at which a constructive guidance relationship is possible is about the same as beginning school age.

Specific environments, which I have called settings, have either evolved or been developed to meet the needs of those who are interested in influencing others. These settings enhance the activity taking place in them. The best place for teaching is the classroom; for worship, a house of God; for festivity, the ballroom. Special problems arising in these groups, however, may require individualized settings. Children with certain deficiencies are better taught individually by means of private lessons than in a class. In the same way, some children needing guidance have special problems which make clinic treatment impossible or inefficient. Some authoritative workers are of the opinion that these children, since they cannot be treated in a clinic setting, should not be treated at all. We believe that since a considerable percentage of cases fall into this group, more tolerance and the invention of new and adjustable techniques are necessary. Cases of children who have a neurotic fear of contact with doctors and medical buildings, children who refuse to leave the house, or children whose resistance and bashfulness make it impossible for them to respond in the semi-public setting of a clinic, or in the presence of a third person in a doctor's office, are not uncommon. If we sincerely wish to help such children, the home is the only desirable setting, at least at the start, for counseling or therapy. In cases where the child is willing to leave the home, the intimate interview alone with a counselor is preferable.

Procedures in child guidance clinics vary. Generally, however, the preliminary interview procedure is similar to that currently followed in medical practice. A history is taken by a social worker; the child is then examined by a pediatrician; finally, a psychiatrist or psychologist administers psychological tests and examinations. Based on these investigatory and diagnostic preliminaries, therapy and counseling procedures are then initiated. Preliminary interviews may stretch over a period of weeks. Often actual counseling does not begin until three months after the first interview. In another type of child guidance procedure, child and counselor are brought together immediately, the history being taken by the counselor or an attending assistant. If physical and psychological examinations or tests prove necessary, these are carried out by special workers at the earliest possible date. The fastest method of preliminary interviewing, which was also the earliest, was initiated by Alfred Adler in Vienna at the beginning of this century. Under this procedure, a panel consisting of a medical or psychiatric worker, a counselor, and a social worker, study the child together and decide what help is to be given. This method is obviously not suited to those children who are disturbed or become withdrawn when they face a number of investigators.

The value of each of these three guidance procedures cannot be decided categorically; each has certain merits that the other two do not have. The procedure to be employed should be selected by the individual worker according to his own temperament and point of view, as well as on the basis of personality factors and availability of local facilities. Variants and new forms may be developed to meet the needs of the individual worker or clinic. This writer has always leaned toward what he calls the "short-term" guidance clinic, in which preliminary interviewing techniques are simplified so that the basically necessary techniques can be carried out within two hours, enabling therapist and counseling personnel to begin treatment at the first visit.

THE FIRST CONTACT

We have discussed the problems of choice of counselor from the point of view of sex, age, and marital status, and the settings under which child guidance procedures are conducted. The next problem is that of building a positive relationship between child and counselor, one in which the child accepts the advice and influence of the counselor. A good first contact is often of basic importance at this stage of therapeutic and guidance work. William Alanson White once said that establishing a good transference situation with a mental patient is as much as half the cure. This is equally true in guidance counseling.

A child will arrive in a counselor's office by one of three routes: the child himself feels he needs help and comes of his own accord; he comes willingly at the suggestion of parents or teacher; he is forced to come by parental, school, or legal authority.

If the child comes of his own accord, the problem of contact is minimal. If he comes simply for information or interpretation on some psychological or educational fact, the counselor does not have to build a personal "bridge." If the child is suffering from an inner conflict or insecurity, or if other social or educational conflicts must be overcome, the counselor's first task is to win the child's confidence. The child must trust the counselor socially and ethically as well as intellectually. He must feel that the counselor understands and accepts his faults and takes his problems seriously. Once the child is convinced that the counselor can help him, he is ready to accept the counselor's influence.

When a child comes to a counselor because he has been urged to do so by parent or teacher, the situation is more difficult. The parent or teacher will probably accompany the child. The counselor must get the child to realize that he needs help, and he must urge the need for this help even more impressively than the adult who brought the child. At the same time he must make the child feel that he, the counselor, can give this help, and that he can be trusted. Often this can be accomplished in one session, but the child must continue to feel, especially during the first contact period, when he may not be completely convinced of the counselor's ability to help him, that the counselor is a good, kind person with a warm personal interest in him.

In the third situation, in which the child is forced to come to the counselor, the counselor must overcome the resentment felt by a child who has been forced to do something against his own will. Here the process of establishing contact will be similar but much more difficult and complicated, since the child probably feels either that he does not need help of this sort, or that no authoritative adult can be friendly to children and trusted at the same time. Often simply the fact that the child is forced by the parent to face the counselor makes him unwilling to listen or even to look at the counselor. Often, too, children consider the forced visit to a counselor an act of parental punishment. It is an important first step for the child to like the counselor as a person. It may be wise not to discuss at first any serious personality problems or the events which brought the child to the counselor, but instead to learn the personal interests and likes of the child. In this way the child may come to feel that the counselor is really interested in him as a person rather than as a problem. If this approach is successful in establishing acceptance—and this may take several sessions—the child's problems may then be slowly brought out. In cases of severe resentment it is best not to discuss the child's particular problem at all, but rather in time to bring up general subjects related to the child's difficulty. This writer has found that this method is the only successful one in working with adolescent masturbators and sex deviates. Increase of tensions and conflicts must be avoided. It has happened that during a discussion of the reproductive processes of plants and animals with the friendly, accepting, and understanding counselor, and on the strength of the bridge that had been built during the contact period, the child will finally "have the heart" to speak up about his problems with confidence.

THE GUIDANCE PROCESS

First-contact procedure is necessary in all guidance; after the first contact, guidance may take various forms. It may be (1) simple advice;

(2) supervision; (3) psychological or educational therapy; or (4) actual guidance. Guidance may be given to an individual child or to a group. In recent years serious attempts have been made to develop the technique of group treatment. The validity and methods, and advantages and disadvantages, of group treatment will be discussed later.

Advisory and Supervisory Counseling

The simplest and shortest form of counseling is giving advice. A child may come to the counselor for advice via any of the channels discussed above. The relationship ends when the advice sought has been given; its application is the responsibility of the child or his guardian.

When advice is given repeatedly, in irregular sessions, it is referred to as supervisory counseling. The child may return to report on the success, failure, or other result of the earlier visit, but contact with the counselor is not a continuing relationship, nor does the counselor take any directing function over the total life of the child. Supervisory counseling is used by school psychologists to supplement classroom work and to eliminate or influence occasional behavior problems occurring in the life of the child.

Child Guidance Counseling

This term is usually used to describe over-all activities of a counselor. This writer prefers to limit its use to refer to a continuous process covering the total existence of the child. Guidance counseling involves a more intimate relationship than does supervisory counseling. It begins with a more refined form of contact, and it continues throughout the period during which the counselor "guides" the child. The period, sometimes lasting for years, is of necessity a longer one than in supervisory counseling. Whether the child needs guidance, and the kind of guidance he needs, is a matter to be decided by the counselor. If a child can help himself, he may benefit most from supervision. Guidance is called for when the child needs intellectual direction of his behavior. It is this function that distinguishes guidance from psychotherapy. The child in need of guidance usually suffers from indecision, which frequently is the cause of failure. His behavior may also deviate from that of his age group, or he may lag behind his age group. This may not necessarily indicate a neurotic pattern; erratic behavior is a common manifestation of modern juvenile life. The neurotic child needs more than intellectual direction.

Before any treatment is given, a careful diagnosis must be made. Examination should not be limited to behavior, but should include a medical review. In the recent psychologistic period in the social sciences we have experienced an overestimation of psychosomatic antecedents even in the area of physical disease and have seriously neglected those abnormal psychic conditions that are caused by physical pathology or to which physical pathology predisposes one. We have not, however, learned to be cautious of the superficial and routinized use of psychological and intelligence tests. If these tests are used, the tester must be fully informed as to their applicability and reliability. Special care is necessary in dealing with emotionally unbalanced children who may be hostile to the testing procedure or indisposed at the time of taking the test. In any case, when tests are given to such children, retesting should take place within a month or two. By that time the guidance counselor should be able to check the test results against his own evaluation of his client. It cannot be emphasized too strongly that personal evaluation should never be subordinated to scores on so-called objective tests. The former should always be the counselor's final guide. The counselor may of course feel surer in his judgment if that judgment is checked and supported by tests.

An atmosphere of confidence throughout the guidance relationship remains the basic denominator of all guidance work. The desire to help a young person cannot be fulfilled if confidence is not established and maintained.

A number of dogmatic descriptions of the guidance procedure have been attempted. One must read such descriptions with caution, since in most cases they are valid only for a specific type of child or for a specific social climate resulting from the special psychological or social concept on which they are based. Because there is the same variety of personality types among children as among adults, we cannot have one general and specific guidance procedure which will be valid for all children. In addition, some types of abnormality present further variation.

There are, of course, fundamental principles and functions of guidance procedure. In addition to the confidence relationship which we have stressed, it is necessary to have a total view of the life of the child —the elements of his environment, his physical health, the specific typological nature of his individuality, and his specific problem. While we know that "no one can know everything about anybody," in order to help the child to conduct his life meaningfully, we must know as much as possible about him.

A further basic function of guidance procedure is what this writer calls "aim-setting." There is an aim in every person's life. In most of those who need or seek guidance, this aim was never developed, or was lost through impairing circumstances, or was not the right one for the individual. Thinking in terms of "aim" is the central aim of guidance.

When advice or supervision is indicated, we assume that, with this help only, the individual can readily develop a satisfactory aim. The guidance counselor's job is to find the specific aim which is best for the child, and to help it develop properly. This is not an abstract task, nor is it limited to teaching specific skills. A counselor who recognizes that a youngster has musical ability and encourages him to become a musician will also see to it that he receives the training he needs, but this by no means exhausts the counselor's duty of "aim-setting." He must also deal with the youngster's intellectual development and emotional growth—in short, his total adjustment to life. Aim-setting difficulties may be the result of innumerable factors in a child's inner or outer life. The technique of guidance lies in the ability to find these inter-relationships and to untie the personal knots.

Another basic function of counseling is training the child to be self-sufficient. Guidance is more than the teaching of intellectual and manual skills and the supervising of a child's activities. The final aim of guidance is to enable the child being helped to live successfully without counseling. "Helping a person to help himself" is a trite phrase, but it expresses a basic truth.

Terminating a guidance relationship, especially a close one, should not be an abrupt procedure. It is often advisable to follow guidance counseling with a period of supervisory counseling which is allowed to taper off into occasional advisory meetings. The way in which a counseling relationship ends is as important as the initial contact. Frequently a child is reluctant to give it up. The secure child, however, will want to test his ability to get along by himself. The definite desire on the part of a young person for self-guidance is one of the surest signs of counseling success.

GUIDANCE THERAPY

The last guidance procedure we shall discuss is what this writer calls guidance therapy, which should not be confused with psychotherapy or social therapy of the non-medical kind. Since the borderline between medical and non-medical psychotherapy is today so much in dispute, it might be wise to refrain from making any definite separation; nevertheless we must create a "no-man's land" where psychotherapy is unavoidable in the field of child guidance. There can be no question but that all treatment which includes medical prescription, chemo- or physiotherapy, or physical examination belongs to the field of medical therapy, as does all treatment of psychotics and severe psychoneurotics. There is little chance that such cases will be brought to a guidance worker for assistance, but if this should occur, prompt referral to a psychiatrist is the only solution. In the same way, a guidance worker should not be expected to deal with physical symptoms which cannot be treated by first-aid, such as headache, dizziness, vomiting; or neurological and psychopathological symptoms, such as tics, headbanging, or drooling. Non-medical psychotherapy should be limited to mild neurotic conditions such as mild depressions, fears, insecurities, indecision, and unhealthy fantasizing. Guidance therapy may be prescribed for moral deviations such as pathological lying and stealing, and, finally, for special deviations such as speech pathologies, hysterical hearing failure, and learning difficulties. There is difficulty in being specific here, since, as we have already indicated, no precise borderline has been drawn. Anyone who is already working or receiving professional training in the guidance field will, from the above outline, be able easily to decide for himself which cases fall inside, and which outside, the domain of guidance therapy. Since in recent years more and better books on non-medical psychotherapy have been available, we need not go into more detail here.

Among certain circles in this country there has been a strict separation as between the tasks of guidance counselors working under the supervision of a psychiatrist and the tasks of those not under such supervision. The school guidance counselor, who in the last decade has become almost routine on the staff of the public school, deals mainly with diagnostic evaluation and handles therapeutically only children with mild deviational behavior problems. The guidance counselor who works in a child guidance clinic is permitted a considerable psychotherapeutic sphere of action which in one or another way is under the direction of a supervising psychiatrist. Since, as we have already pointed out, the question of the distinction between medical and non-medical psychotherapy has still not been determined, we believe it wise to refrain from making any definite statement on this point. In most cases collaboration between medical and non-medical workers in organizations where both are on the staff depends on personal and administrative policy and on personal tact, if not on governmental rulings which precisely define the tasks of each.

GROUP GUIDANCE*

Group therapy (to which group guidance is very similar) has been publicized to a degree that is out of proportion to its significance. A

* Some of the statements made in this section may be repetitious of statements made in a later general chapter on group therapy. The importance of group work in child guidance, however, would seem to necessitate discussion of specific aspects at this point.

decade ago this writer appealed for reason in the application of any technique which brought a number of patients together for collective treatment by one or several professional workers. The most frequently applied form of group therapy brings together a number of patients who are to receive the same treatment at the same time. Sociologically, such an assembly of individuals is not a group, but a mass. A group is a number of individuals united by nature or by society for a certain purpose. The most elementary group is the family. In the juvenile field it is easy to see the distinction between mass and group. When a number of children gather on the street or in the playground and simply stand around, each occupied only with himself, they form a mass; when they begin to organize themselves, whether in a folk dance or in a football or baseball game, they become a group. This clear distinction between mass and group should be made also between mass and group therapy. Mass therapy that gathers a number of patients together in one room, to be exposed to the same treatment by a therapist, has only an economic advantage. Its disadvantages lie in the lack of individual contact between patient and worker, and in the problems arising from the possible presence, in a collective assembly, of individuals in a disturbed state of mind. In group psychotherapy, members of the group influence one another's state of mental health. While there is no doubt that group influence may be of considerable value to patients with certain types of mental conditions, we are far from having established any really wider basic insight or methods in this area.

In child psychotherapy as well as in child guidance, mass handling does not promise success; children require more intensive individual attention than do adults. Nevertheless, group therapy and group guidance can be of considerable value. Handling a child in the framework of the family is in fact one form of group handling. Making professional workers as well as parents and teachers aware of this family group will help the family to act as a wholesome unit. Since one of the major elements in child development is learning to live in human society, group therapy and guidance can be of primary importance. This is especially the case in our modern cities with their small one- or two-child families. Nursery and kindergarten programs should be aware that one of their basic functions is group guidance for the child. It is in the nursery and kindergarten that infants learn to live with their own age group in the larger setting of communal living. This may be said also of the school class, which modern progressive education has tried to develop from a mass educational unit into a family unit with the advantage it has of being able to teach children to learn to live together. In individual therapy and guidance the group aspect has considerable merit also if there is awareness of the importance of adjusting the shy and, even more, the introverted or depressed child. Concrete help in this area can come only from some kind of group psychotherapy. From this point of view, group psychotherapy is a method of major importance. This aspect of group influence has up to now, however, not been satisfactorily developed.

TECHNICAL AIDS IN THE GUIDANCE PROCESS

Besides the more generally important elements of guidance, which have already been discussed, there are technical aspects which can help the guidance worker to achieve a definite "success."

Sizing up the Situation

By using routine procedures, guidance workers are often led into a scheme of handling their young clients which is not appropriate to the specific character of a child's condition—a situation that may lead to unsuccessful treatment. In gathering case information beyond what was obtained in the social work intake procedure, counselors must delve deeper than the requirements of any routine scheme, and must coordinate the information until a picture is formed in which all the specific problems of *this individual child* are spotlighted. No child should remain "a case of"; the child is "Jimmy, who had this or that experience, and who is now in this or that situation and condition. . . ." The individual personality factors, together with a sizing-up of the present situation, alone can enable the worker to act promptly and efficiently. This overall point of view will eliminate the dangers involved in applying routinized procedures to individual cases, and will give the security that comes from knowing that we have really touched reality in our work with human beings.

Multiplicity of Sources of Conflict

Some workers believe that they have established the sources of a child's conflict when they have identified an obvious social problem; the child has been unable to overcome his problems on his own because a one-sided typological constitution appears to be interfering internally. We often hear this diagnostic picture described. The attempt to work therapeutically with this diagnosis, however, fails. Careful observation will show that the diagnosis was superficial. For example, we may find in a child a strong emotional reaction to experience approaching him from the outside. We assume that he is an emotional youngster. But when we undertake to balance his emotionalism through therapy we are unsuccessful. The emotionalism is in itself the result of a conflict in which experiences in the rational or intellectual sphere of the child's inner life create a laming of all thinking, which in turn produces a strong unnatural emotional reaction. It is of course evident that the conflict in the rational life must be removed if we are to bring the child back to his normal abilities; this rational conflict proves to be the primary element in the entire pathogenic situation. Other similar conditions are frequently found. When we encounter approach difficulties in therapy, it may be well to reconsider our first diagnosis and attempt to arrive at a more sensitive understanding of the causes of the conflicts. Even if we do not subscribe to Freudian concepts which hold that the causes of obvious conflict are in most cases suppressed and can be uncovered only by the slow process of analysis, it would be well to consider whether our first diagnosis was not superficial. Causes of conflict must be uncovered over a period of observation of the child that may vary in length. If we observe sincerely and patiently we will only in rare cases fail to find the basic causes.

Continuity of Process

Any guidance or treatment experience, regardless of its length, must be considered as forming an episode in the life of the human being. It is not merely an "outside event," but a process which, if successful, will bring about more or less serious changes not only in personality habits but in the entire atmosphere and course of that life. Before, during, and after his contact with a counselor the individual is in a definite condition. If we are to achieve a sound change in his personality we must see the first period as the background behind the patient's changing condition. A measure of the changes and advances that occur during the counseling process, especially in cases where emotional strain makes progress not easily apparent, encourages both counselor and client. Every counselor must expect that his client will go through periods of setback. Such episodes should be seen, however, in the light of the total process of guidance and treatment; only in this way can we achieve clear insight into the condition and needs of the client. Since setbacks often considerably change the picture of development, we will need to see the various developmental patterns in order to guide the client to a final cure. It has often been demonstrated that the person receiving guidance is helped by sound self-evaluations, especially after setbacks, when such self-evaluations may lift the individual back to his former level.

5

RECORDS AND RECORDING

Records are taken more as a measure of self-insurance for doctors and counselors than for the benefit of the patient. But records which *are* taken for the patient's sake may be used in various ways and for a number of purposes. Records should serve the purpose of providing a quick survey and a clear picture of progress. Records should be short and to the point. Records may also be studies of a specific feature of the client's condition, and these should be more detailed. Often a combination of both types of record prove valuable. At Beth David Hospital's short-term treatment clinic the writer has developed a record form of the latter kind. The major facts and notes on progress are recorded in an easy-to-find way on the face sheet; in the follow-up sheets, details of significant individual factors are recorded so that the worker is not obliged to read numerous pages of reports to get a picture of the case.

COUNSELOR, PARENT, AND TEACHER

In the section on group counseling we commented on the family and its members as a group. Parents, however, are also involved in the counselor's task because of the part they play as a cause of the deviant behavior of the child. In both cases, part of the activity of the counselor may involve contact with parents. In many cases suggestions to parents may result in the correction of unfortunate conditions affecting the health of the child. Parents or other adults with whom the child spends the major part of his time must be solicited as part of the sphere of influence of the counselor. The counselor is in a position to exert influence on the child only during perhaps an hour every few days, or perhaps weekly or even less frequently; parents are continuously with the child so that it is important that they be instructed on how to make the influence of the counselor a continuous matter. The relationship between counselor and parents has been compared to that of the doctor and the nurse in the hospital situation. In the guidance situation the relationship is in many cases even more intensive.

In addition to the home, the school and its functionaries and teachers must be seriously considered as factors in the counselor's work. A child's unfortunate relationship to school should be taken seriously as a pathogenic factor. Insight into this factor, although frequently not too easily acquired, will help the counselor greatly in sizing up his work. The teacher may prove to be a primary helper in the readjustment of the child, often playing a more important role in the situation than the parents because of her professional insight into psychological conditions of the child.

Appendix

Special Aspects of Camp Counseling

SINCE the adult guardian in a summer camp is called a counselor, it might be thought that we plan to offer in this section a compendium for camp counselors. This, of course, is not the purpose of this short presentation. The counseling techniques discussed here relate to a particular aspect of counseling which is not the same as general counseling. The techniques of general counseling today come mainly out of the training of the kindergartner and the physical-education or leisure-time worker. The concept of counseling discussed here encompasses a different kind of task.

This author has in a number of publications advocated a specific concept of camping which he believes will especially benefit the majority of city children. This concept applies to an intensive guidance task. The writer calls this kind of camping "compensatory camping." At camp, away from school and city life, children should be compensated for the rigors of city and classroom. This calls for opportunities for healthy development not only on the physical level but on the mental and social levels as well. In addition, camp should build up children's resistance for the coming winter season. Seen in this way, camping assumes a special mental hygiene function which it does not usually possess. Camping can perform a special task in individualizing and socializing the child, features which cannot be properly developed in the city world of today and which are so important to a child's growing up.

More than these basic aspects, however, are appropriate subject matter for a discussion of guidance in camping. Let us briefly survey the most important additional points.

Detachment and Attachment

Family and home are the soil in which a child grows and to which he is attached by innumerable indissoluble bonds. When the child is transplanted out of this home soil for the first time, preliminary precautions must be taken. Detachment from his family makes an attachment to one or more camp staff members the most important initial step in a constructive camp experience. If at all possible, a child should be allowed to make friends with his camp counselor before the summer begins. This is important even though the child returns to the same camp from year to year.

Change in Environment

The change in climate and geography provided by camp will not of itself insure a successful camping experience. It is rather the change from the mechanized, routinized environment of the city and schoolroom to the freer life in nature that is the basis of successful camp living. The city child has been trained throughout his life to live with certain limitations that are unnecessary in natural surroundings. Even children who have been to camp before are restless and disturbed in their sleep during the first few days in camp before they have made the readjustment to their new life. Although they do not realize it themselves, many children are afraid when they are removed from their accustomed pattern of living even though these patterns may have caused them pain and suffering. The greater space, absence of noise, new sleeping and living arrangements, new people, and life among a group of children all of the same age are impressive experiences to a child accustomed to be alone with his parents.

Sometimes city experiences which have not been verbalized at home must be allowed expression at camp before adjustment to the new environment is possible, even if at times the form of such expression is violent. During the Second World War this writer found kindergarten children who had been completely immersed in the war atmosphere frequently did nothing during their first day at camp but play at "soldiers" and other war games. After a week or so, however, the same group of four-year-olds were seen in small groups, moving quietly on all fours. When asked what they were playing, they replied, "Cows and Bulls." Farm surroundings had changed their pattern of play.

Children are usually able to work out their first adjustments by themselves; the counselor does well to remain an observant bystander. He should step in to apply professional knowledge only when there are serious problems, such as emotional upsets, homesickness, withdrawal, sleeplessness, or nightmares. The counselor must realize that the child is going through a period of adjustment to his new environment. A child's misinformation about nature should be taken seriously. It is a tragedy of our times, and not to be laughed at, when a child asks if potatoes grow on trees, or if chocolate milk comes from brown cows, etc. The counselor must realize that city life has disoriented its children out of real nature and into a pattern of civilization that overemphasizes mechanical elements. The counselor himself must be able to represent the rural pattern of living if he is to help the child to get away from the influence of the city environment. He cannot be a city dweller who gathers together a few children and takes them to the country. He must be in command of the basic experiences of camp life before he can help children to gain the compensatory physical and emotional experiences of camp life.

The Individual Demands of the Camp Child

It is well to view the camp child as always not properly adjusted; this is the normal situation. Each child has his individual demands for compensation for the impairment he has suffered during the past school year in the city. Coping with these demands is not a job that anyone can handle. If one sees the camping experience as merely a stay in the country, or camp as a place to park a child for the hot months, nothing more than a little firm discipline is necessary to hold a flock of youngsters together. But if we see camp guidance as a function of social and mental health which offers compensation to each child individually, then we see also that a counselor must have specific abilities. He must possess a fair amount of general psychological knowledge of behavior, attitudes, and psychological types. He must possess the practical ability of the social worker to handle children. Finally, he should have a solid background of information in the clinical psychology of the everyday problems of the child, as well as of the most common forms of deviation in the neurotic city child. To all of this knowledge he must add knowledge of what we might call "camp neurosis"—deviations that may be caused by the camp environment itself.

From the above it will be clear that the camp counselor (who may be a school teacher or social worker during the winter) needs insight and training in specific camp tasks, otherwise he may be a failure in his summer job. This writer once emphasized in a paper (which received a poor reception from a large group of camp workers) that a good camp worker should be, above all, a social worker. I believe that the settlement house worker, in fact, has the best professional background for camp work.

There is at present a trend toward the specialized counselor (sports, handicrafts, arts) as distinguished from the general counselor. Only a large camp unit can successfully use specialist counselors. There should be no separation between counseling influence and activities. It is to be hoped that the pattern of specialization in camps will yield to the insight that the camp is an educational institution intended primarily to offer compensation for the factors inherent in city and school life which impair the healthy physical and mental development of the child, and not a teaching facility for things a child cannot learn during the winter.

Techniques of this kind of counseling are of course dissociated from any routine pattern of social and mass camp counseling. Camp counseling, as we see it, is an individualized job; techniques must always go beyond routine procedures. This of course does not mean that training in and keeping up with certain essential procedures should be neglected. There is a difference, however, between a militaristic Boy-Scout-like handling of bedmaking, bunk-cleaning, and canteen procedures, and individualized attention to help a child form acceptable habits in this less complicated, more primitive way of living. The same point of view must hold in helping the child to live in a group composed primarily of juveniles with a heightened desire for individualism and individualistic expression. Camp counselor instruction which sees the counselor's job as that of adjusting the individual camper so that he will be brought into line with the group is, according to our definition of camp experience, based on a false premise. The keep-them-quiet camp philosophy may make the job easier for the camp worker, but it does not help the individual child to find his compensating experience.

The best technical advice a camp counselor could be given is that he learn to observe his individual campers rather than overwhelm them with activities. If he wishes to help a child advance, the counselor must have good insight into the specific problems stemming from the child's disposition, from his home problems, or from his stay at camp itself. According to present clinical psychological concepts, it might seem that weeks of observation are necessary to obtain all this information. Intensive all-day living together, however, when supplemented by a good preparatory report from the home, may enable an observant counselor, after only two or three days, to know what kind of child he is dealing with and what the child's problems are.

A second piece of advice on good camp counseling techniques is that the counselor *live* with the child rather than lecture and correct him. The lecturing counselor arouses a serious resistance by stirring the child's bad memories of city, school, and home. Much of what could be achieved during the camping period may be lost if a new barrier is built up between the child and the adult at a time when help is needed. This does not mean, of course, that the endless questioning and the desire to know that characterize the child do not sometimes call for the lecturing method. The emphasis, however, must always be on decreasing tensions by any method available.

A third aspect of good camp counseling is the gearing of all action to developing self-confidence in the child. If this is the basic orientation in directing children at summer camp, most of the oppressive features of trying to teach a child to live in an unaccustomed environment will be avoided and many of the inner conflicts that the child has brought with him from the city will find release and solution. Following such a philosophy of course makes the counselor's work more difficult. Ordering children around is comparatively easy, but to encourage self-direction in a child calls for sensitive educational tact.

What we stress, then, is that only the person who can offer versatility in living with children should become a camp counselor. We reiterate that camp counseling is not an activity for everyone; it is a specialized educational task that requires specific training.

Specific Camp Problems of Children

Requests for advice on camp counseling in almost all cases center about specific camp problems of children. We must agree that there is no child who will not at some time during his growing years go through a period of troubles. The camp counselor should translate his realization of this truth into a basic attitude and should expect some kind of difficulty with every child. These troubles usually fall into the categories of episodes of severe misbehavior, enuresis, or homesickness. These problems should be dealt with by the trained therapeutic specialists. The camp counselor's role in relation to specific problems should be that of "trouble-shooter." The camp counselor should be ready at any time to assist in handling difficulties, but the camp is not a therapeutic institution, and the camp counselor is not a therapist. We do not expect that every child will have serious difficulties at camp, but they *could* have. The open-minded attitude of the therapist is the kind of outlook on the part of the camp counselor that this writer emphasizes as desirable.

Once, while the writer was presenting these thoughts on compensatory camping, he was opposed by a man who had been connected with a private educational institution which operated a dispensary. During one period this dispensary had a nurse who was eager to "doctor" the children, putting bandaids on the slightest scratch and handing out aspirin for any ailment. Of course, the entire population of the school was sick all the time. This nurse was replaced by one who had a more casual attitude toward her job, who did not feel it necessary to open her medicine cabinet for the slightest excuse. Under the new regime the sickness record remained minute for years. I cite this story in spite of the fact that it seems to go against my own point; in fact, however, it corroborates my thesis. When we look for troubles and woes we may actually be calling them forth. I do not believe that we should try to relieve *all* of a child's problems during his two months at camp, or that we should "soften" a child's personality by catering to his neuroticism or illness. We want a child to express his natural self and to be compensated for the defects of city life during the winter. In the case of real pathology, two months of camp cannot accomplish much, even if therapeutic assistance is available. There is no doubt, however, that a great deal of pathological development can be avoided if the camp counselor is trained to apply the techniques described here as the basis of compensatory camping experience.

BIBLIOGRAPHY

1. BENTLEY, JOHN E.: 1936. *Problem Children.* New York.
2. BLUM, MILTON L.: 1951. *Counseling and Psychology.* New York.
3. COX, DUFF, and McNAMARA: 1948. *Basic Principles of Guidance.* New York.
4. ERICKSON, CLIFFORD L.: 1947. *A Basic Text for Guidance Workers.* New York.
5. HAMRIN, SH. A.: 1950. *Counseling Adolescents.* Chicago.
6. HARMS, ERNEST: 1947. *Handbook of Child Guidance.* New York.
7. ——: 1948. "A Camp Counselor should be a Social Worker." *J. Social Case Work.* April.
8. ——: 1953. *The Intellectual and the Emotional Approach to Nature.* Progessive Education. April.
9. HURLOCK, ELIZABETH B.: 1949. *Adolescent Development.* New York.
10. JONES, ARTHUR J.: 1951. *Principles of Guidance.* New York.
11. REED, ANNA Y.: 1944. *Guidance and Personnel Services in Education.* Ithaca.
12. ROTHNEY, J. M. B. and ROENS, B. A.: 1952. *Guidance of American Youth.* Cambridge, Mass.
13. STOOPS, E. and WAHLQUIST, G. L.: 1958. *Principles and Practices in Guidance.* New York.
14. STRANG, RUTH: 1951. *An Introduction to Child Study.* New York.
15. THOM, DOUGLAS A.: 1934. *Everyday Problems of the Everyday Child.* New York.
16. THORNE, FRED. CH.: 1950. *Principles of Personality.* Brandon, Vt.
17. TRAXLER, ARTHUR: 1945. *Techniques of Guidance.* New York.
18. WATERS, JANE: 1956. *Techniques of Counseling.* New York.
19. ZACHERY, CAROLINE B.: 1940. *Emotions and Conduct in Adolescence.* New York.

Counseling in Child Welfare

LEONTINE R. YOUNG

Executive Director
Child Service Association
Newark, N.J.

CHILD welfare is one of those general terms that elicits a kaleidoscope of perspectives and attitudes. It has an emotional charge that can color realities to the point of unrecognizability and that can perpetuate particular assumptions and methods beyond the point of feasibility. In the popular conception it can mean hard-faced women who snatch children from the loving arms of helpless parents, or dreamy-eyed professionals following a will-o'-the-wisp. Even for the professionals it is not always easy to separate fact from fiction and perspective from mythology.

For the purposes of this chapter, child welfare will mean the protection of children by an authorized social agency when for whatever reason their natural parents are unable or fail to provide such protection. In our present society this can cover a bewildering variety of problems and situations, and can include children living in their own homes, as well as in such substitute care as foster homes and institutions. It can consist of many kinds of protection ranging from a need for food and shelter, to the expert counseling help that may unravel twisted emotions. However varying the needs, problems and services, they share one common determinant, the weakness and dependence of children; and one common objective, the protection of children until that dependence is past.

This may sound like one of those trite, taken-for-granted assumptions, but the reality tells a different story. Not even philosophically is it clearly accepted, and in application it encounters a whole thicket of obstacles. One has only to note the sharply contradictory attitudes of judges toward the question of parental rights vs the rights of children as noted in the Maas study, "Children in Need of Parents", to recognize the obscuring complexities. Nor are professional social workers themselves in agreement as to what specifically constitutes a need for protection, and what methods best afford that protection.

In any area effective counseling can proceed only from a clear philosophical base which determines the value criteria by which both objectives and means must be measured. The lack of such a generally accepted base renders any discussion of techniques a random procedure unless the assumptions underlying them are made explicit.

This discussion will be concerned with three basic assumptions of primary importance in determining the objectives and methods of child welfare counseling, and an evaluation of those assumptions in the perspective of current problems and needs.

One of the most important of these is the thorny question of parental rights, often seen as opposed to the rights of children. In the context of child welfare these rights are chiefly concerned with the extent of parental authority which may be exercised over children without intervention by any constituted agency of society. There are two sharply divergent points of view on this, and each has a profound influence on the objectives of counseling. One stresses the right of parents to almost unlimited authority over children, and the other stresses the responsibility of society to intervene on behalf of the children when parental authority threatens their well-being. The problem is confused by the fact that there is no precise clarification of the point at which society's responsibility should supersede parental authority. Even the legal definitions tend to be ambiguous here, and are subject to a considerable range of individual interpretation. Further, the whole situation is beclouded by the powerful emotional aura surrounding it.

The advocacy of parental authority as primary has, of course, strong historical roots. The Romans gave to the pater familias the power of life and death over his children so long as he lived, although that remarkable emperor Hadrian banished one man for exercising his prerogative in the murder of his son. The patriarchal family in general gave enormous power to the father over the lives of his children. But historically, the role and responsibility of the family was very different than it is now. Once it was the center of employment, education, religion, and the heart of life experience for its members. It provided the security, the life insurance, the roots.

In general, the family was based on a system of obligations and rights which were defined and enforced by the particular cultures. Obligations of parents and children were an integral part of rights of parents and children. This same concept is stated unequivocally in English common law—the rights of parents proceed directly from the obligations and responsibilities of parents. As the complexities of an increasingly impersonal society have infringed upon this traditional structure, a gap has been created between responsibilities and rights. The separation of the two is particularly noticeable in many of the families with whom child welfare is concerned. The present controversy which exists in both legal and counseling professions tends to overlook the structured relationship of responsibility and rights. Too often the gap is filled with an emotional bias, and a modern mythology substitutes for a clear, hard study of the facts. Thus, there grows up such an essentially modern assumption as all parents love their children or can with guidance come to do so. The parent who neglects his children even to the point of semi-starvation may be supported in a plan of keeping the children when he says he "loves them" or announces belligerently, "no one is going to take my children from me!" The contradiction between words and behavior can lead to the idea that this parent is expressing conflict in his feeling for the children, a conflict that may be resolved positively. When such an idea is translated into a plan of action without consideration of alternative explanations, the result can only reflect the accuracy or fallacy of the idea. The parental assertion of love may reflect community pressure rather than hidden feeling, possessiveness and power of ownership rather than devotion to the child.

Good counseling begins with the explicit assumption that contradictions require an explanation and that the explanation to be valid must be based on all the known facts and must be logically coherent. In the example cited it must answer such questions as—how consistent and continuous has the parental neglect been, what consistent and continuous responsibility has the parent carried in any area of his life; does he accept any responsibility for his behavior toward his children, or is that projected upon others? While the establishment of parental responsibility is a common objective of all counseling here, the crucial question arises around its feasibility. If it represents an unrealizable dream, counseling proceeds on a fallacious assumption. If it represents a practical reality within the short-time period set by children's chronological development, counseling proceeds on a clear and sound premise.

Unfortunately, such unexamined assumptions as "all parents love their children, or all parents have conflict and guilt when they neglect or abuse their children" tend to discourage an objective appraisal of all the relevant facts. On the other hand, a blanket assumption that the rights of children are primary can lead to chaos unless the specific nature of those rights is defined. It is ironical that at the same time one group of children may be deprived of even the most elementary rights such as food and physical protection, while another group is permitted to grow up with the emphasis so exclusively upon their rights that the concomitant concept of their responsibility becomes a shadow hovering in the background. There has been a tendency in one area of counseling to emphasize the responsibility of parents and the rights of children without sufficiently stressing the reciprocal nature of these two for both parents and children.

This has reflected the impact of modern economic and social change upon the role of the family in general, and upon parental authority specifically. It has given rise to that strange phenomenon, parents who doubt their right to set authoritative limits for their children, and who permit standards of behavior to be determined by the social milieu. The frequent accusatory nature of criticisms directed toward parents in general tends to undermine parental confidence and authority. At the same time, it fails to assess the tremendous demands now made upon the inner strengths of the family and the concomitant weakening of outer controls. The once powerful support and control of the extended family group, for example, has been reduced to an attenuated reflection of its former strength, and as demands upon parental strength and wisdom increase, the sources of personal support and guidance diminish. In this perspective, the whole question of rights, whether of parents or children, requires reassessment.

There are certain clear fallacies in some of the common assumptions surrounding this question. In the first place, parents are treated as an abstract group having social and psychological as well as biological factors in common. This rather naturally produces strong emotional responses to any blanket statement made about parents, and the nature of the response is rather naturally determined by what group of parents is considered as representative of all parents. Parents may be violently attacked or defended with little awareness on the part of the participants that they are talking about totally different sets of facts. In other words, parents are individuals, not an abstraction, and children given the common factor of dependence are individuals living in individual situations. This is not meant to imply that each family is unique in every respect, but there are decided and demonstrable differences in types of families which must be clearly taken into account in any assumption of rights.

Only in relation to some explicit and agreed upon standard of what constitutes adequate parenthood can the question of rights be resolved. The individual family could then be evaluated in the perspective of that standard. In a swiftly changing society it is obvious that the formulation of such a standard in any practical and total sense is probably impossible. Yet the objectives and methods of child welfare must make use of some standard however partialized if it is to maintain any consistent direction and serve the needs of today's children. One segment of the answer must lie in more precise and explicit diagnostic classifications which can be measured against at least such minimum agreed upon standards of parenthood, as adequate physical care of children, and which prevent making parents as such into a typology.

Another fallacy lies in the separation of rights from responsibilities. Such a separation must logically result in confusion since stability and order depend upon a balance of pressures. The rights of any individual or group are kept from extremes by the authority of structured responsibilities. The complexities and transition of modern society have tended to disturb or to weaken this structured relationship without delineating with clarity a new balance. This is most conspicuous with those families who depend more upon outer controls than inner strength to maintain stability. Thus the disorganized family with which child welfare is increasingly concerned is characterized to a considerable extent by a sharp disparity between what parents conceive to be their rights over their children, and what the community conceives to be their responsibility to their children.

Even in the fairly recent past, social controls tended to be personal, direct and persistent, enforced by the individual responsibility of community members. The small town knew its disorganized families personally, and enforced certain limits upon the behavior of those families. While this control could and did result in injustices, it also constituted a positive protection to children. Urbanization, population mobility, and a changing concept of personal responsibility have tended to make social (as differentiated from legal) controls more impersonal, sporadic and remote. As they tend to be enforced more and more by official agencies, there is a good probability that they become less effective in providing even minimum physical protection for many children. The impact of this upon the objectives and methods of child welfare counseling has yet to be thoroughly assessed.

It relates directly to another major assumption, that of self-determination. This concept has been widely interpreted as precluding the use of authority except when other methods of effecting necessary change have failed. Behind this interpretation are the tacit assumptions that authority is essentially unwelcome in any form to those upon whom it is imposed, and that it is in effect synonymous with a punitive and dogmatic approach. These assumptions are probably to some degree a reaction to a former period in child welfare when the major approach was punitive, and the standards imposed unquestioned. This reaction took little account of the fact that all social controls are essentially authoritative or of the consideration that the objectives of authority alter its nature and methods of enforcement. Further, punishment which is one means of enforcement was frequently confused with authority, a structure of control. As child welfare has been more and more faced with the problems of disorganized families, this confusion has had an increasingly deleterious effect upon the effectiveness of counseling.

It is interesting that therapeutic objectives and professional authority have frequently been regarded as opposed to each other. In a field such as physical medicine, no such question arises, and the average patient would be considerably confused by a doctor who prefaced his prescription with a qualification of his authority. Professional authority is, in fact, inherent in professional knowledge. Yet in counseling it has often been abdicated as a therapeutic device. Whatever the merits of such an abdication for counseling in general, its appropriateness to the present problems in child welfare seems clearly questionable. The weakening of social controls has created a structural vacuum for many families which is not likely to be filled by permissiveness or passivity.

In the first place, there needs to be a clear distinction between authority and punitiveness. Punishment uses fear as the motivating force for change, and its objective may be either a deterrent for future repetition of a behavior, or an expression of the feelings of the punitive agent. Authority defines certain arbitrary limits and channels for behavior. This may reflect no more than the power of the authoritative agent, but professional authority must seek to use its competence for a defined objective. In child welfare this objective is protection of children. This is very different than punishment of parents even when it involves legal action against parents. Protective authority is concerned with the direction and limits of behavior as these are determined by the needs of children, and part of the role of professional knowledge is the accurate perception of those needs.

Nor does this inevitably or even primarily, mean being "against parents." Disorganization implies clearly a lack of consistent direction, as well as a lack of consistent limits to behavior that is determined and maintained through individual responsibility. The assumption that this is a happy, carefree state for parents is a dubious one ill supported by experience with them. On the contrary, many of the parents with whom child welfare is now concerned reach out to a professional authority that offers them some of the structure they cannot achieve for themselves. The man who begged his caseworker to bring a non-support complaint against him in court so that he would be compelled to give part of his earnings to his family is not so atypical as has often been imagined.

This wish for an external authority which will require certain behavioral standards is probably to some degree true of most adults. If self determination is not to be construed as anarchy, it carries always a concomitant requirement of responsibility. For those people too dependent, too uncertain of their own standards and strength, too fearful of choices and decisions, responsibility for the consequences of behavior can be a heavy and frightening burden. With disorganized families such as those seen currently in child welfare, it is frequently an impossibility. Protective authority may be experienced by them as the first understanding they have known.

In the exercise of professional authority the weight of responsibility shifts to the counselor. The fact that many families may welcome such a shift does not diminish the weight of the responsibility. Not only perception of needs, but determination of standards, goals and channels of behavior becomes an obligation of professional knowledge. Consequences of behavior become a shared responsibility, with the counselor perhaps carrying the heavier share. The requirements on the counselor or caseworker for reality—focused judgment and the perspective of maturity increase with the responsibility. They are not easy requirements, and they are made more difficult by the current confusion in values and standards which are themselves authoritative structure imposed upon the individual by his particular culture.

Logically, this means that the counselor actively accepts the dependence of these families and precipitates such action as is necessary for the protection of the children. The inevitable question is, to what end? This encounters the third assumption, that the objective of the counseling is the independence of the parents, their ability to carry their own family responsibility directly. With the desirability of such an objective there can be no argument. The question concerns its feasibility. Any assumption that posits such an objective without the knowledge and guidance of specific diagnostic indices must risk confusion as the result, however meritorious the purpose. Further, where children are concerned, time is a great deal more than an academic question. Parental progress toward independence must occur within sharply defined time limits if children are to benefit materially from it.

The setting up of an ideal objective is important and necessary, but its confusion with the reality determined possibilities in any specific family can be and, in fact is destructive. It can lead to a counseling focus that ignores immediate problems and needs in its concentration upon an educational and therapeutic process that only the feasibility of the idealized objective could justify. It can lead also to the kind of what's-the-use hopelessness that has too often characterized work with disorganized families, and that is the obverse side of the idealized objective. This kind of all-or-nothing philosophy can deprive children of needed protection, and parents of the partial progress that might have been possible. It is also a potent barrier to the slow, laborious accumulation of the new knowledge that is so greatly needed and is so difficult to achieve.

Few assumptions have been so adverse and far reaching in their effects as this confusion of an ideal abstract objective with an immediate and specific goal. An under-estimation of pathology and an over-simplification of the process of change are only part of the not inconsiderable by-products. It has tended to support the popular misconception that with the magic of rehabilitation the problems will disappear, and it has contributed to the public disillusionment and punitiveness when they not only persist, but become more acute. It has forced social agencies into the untenable position of defending themselves against accusations of failure with problems they did not create and cannot solve. It has obscured the full extent of what the cost in human and financial terms must be if the problems are to find reality solution.

If parental dependence is to be accepted not simply as a prelude to independence, but as a potentially permanent status, much of the focus of counseling would be revised. The immediate question would be what degree of personal responsibility and maturity can specific parents be expected to achieve within a relatively brief time span that will have relevant and sufficient impact upon needed protection for the children. This would necessarily lead to the further question of what constitutes a minimum standard of protection for children and what indices provide reliable and valid diagnostic guides to prognoses of parental ability to achieve and maintain such a minimum standard. The ability to predict with at least a reasonable degree of accuracy becomes of major importance. Specific goals would then be measured against a minimum standard as well as in their relation to a maximum objective.

The number of cases closed would cease to be a criterion of success and to the factor of quantity would be added the no less important factor of quality. In a culture that increasingly confuses the packaging with the contents, the appearance with the substance, the words with the actions and efficiency with significance this would require the courage and the conviction that swim against the current and that prefer a difficult reality to the most entrancing and enticing fantasy. It could also mean new hope for many of our unprotected children and new horizons for a field that represents, as its name child welfare depicts, one of the finer flowerings of the modern day.

BIBLIOGRAPHY

1. ABBOTT, GRACE: *The Child and the State*. U. of Chicago Press.
2. GEISMAR, L. L. and AYRES, BEVERLEY: *Patterns of Change in Problem Families*.
3. ——: 1958. *Families in Trouble*.
4. ——: 1960. *Measuring Family Functioning*.
5. KLUCKHOHN, FLORENCE: 1958. February–March. *Variations in the Basic Values of Family Systems*, Social Casework.
6. MAAS, HENRY S. and ENGLER, RICHARD E.: 1959. *Children in Need of Parents*. Columbia University Press.
7. MURDOCK, GEORGE: 1949. *Social Structure*. New York: The Macmillan Co.
8. ST. PAUL: 1959. *Family Centered Project*.

Counseling in Schools

DOROTHY DAVIS SEBALD

Associate Professor of Education
Hunter College
New York

SCHOOL COUNSELING

SCHOOL counseling, traditionally a peripheral function of all members of the school staff, has become, in recent years a distinct, unique and highly specialized task of school personnel charged with responsibility for the academic, vocational, social and emotional guidance of school pupils. Within the larger framework of guidance, school counseling pervades every aspect of the school life of the pupil. Usually thought of as the heart or core of guidance services school counseling is an integral component of guidance. It is the place in guidance where pupils are met "face to face", either in individual counseling sessions or in multiple or group counseling activities.

Counseling in schools has developed from academic and vocational advisement to a highly complex system of leading children and youth to self-understanding, realistic self-appraisal, the establishment of value systems and awareness of their place and responsibility in the world of work and world society. School counseling is, as yet, a young and fluid function of guidance. Originally used by teachers and administrators, school counseling was considered to be an extension of the process of education or was patterned on legal counseling (advice giving) or on moral persuasion and exhortation.

When intensive study of the dynamics of behavior became an integral part of the training of school counselors, psychiatric counseling methods became, for the school counselor, a new, fascinating and absorbing technique with which to experiment in a new and growing field.

Counseling in schools is presently performed by administrators, deans, class-room teachers, teachers of special subjects, guidance workers, school nurses, attendance officers, social workers, psychologists, and in a few instances by psychiatrists. Each of these, by virtue of his training or by the authority and confidence placed in him by the school administration and the community, considers himself to be uniquely qualified to counsel school pupils. Because of the variations in the sophistication of school administrators concerning the purposes and importance of school counseling and the training necessary for personnel who perform it, school counseling procedures vary from simple advisement, orientation and information giving offered by the classroom teacher to the most sophisticated psychotherapy carried on by clinical psychologists, psychiatric social workers and psychiatrists.

Although large urban schools, because of the greater number of pupils, the extent, scope and complexity of problems, the availability of funds and trained personnel, often provide more extensive and highly specialized counseling services to pupils than do rural or small suburban schools there is a growing consciousness of the need for, and value of, counseling services for all children and youth.

Guidance services in schools have increased markedly in the past four decades and the training of personnel to meet the demands of the growing profession has broadened and intensified. As World War I brought to public attention the need for guidance services for school youth and World War II reemphasized its importance, the present cold war has directed the attention of the nation to the need for increased guidance of youth as an aid to national survival. The school counselor, therefore, has become a key figure, not only academically but politically and socially and his selection and training are of increasing importance.

The intelligence of the counselor, his basic knowledge of the dynamics of behavior, the extent and type of counselor training he has undergone, as well as his personality structure determine which pupils he counsels, the approaches to counseling he uses, the level, extent and duration of the counseling process, and the skill with which it is performed. Many states now require certification of school counselors and there are increasingly rigid requirements of academic training, internship and experience.

Therapeutic counseling, traditionally the prerogative and responsibility of the fields of psychiatry, social work and clinical psychology, and performed in hospital, clinic, private office or social agency has been modified and adapted by the school counselor to meet the restrictions imposed on counseling performed in an educational setting. Counseling in schools, because its clientele is captive, most often violates the assumptions that have been deemed basic to therapeutic counseling. In schools the counselee does not always come willingly to the counseling situation, he is often unaware that he has a problem to be solved, or after having been made aware of it has no desire to work toward its solution, and is hostilely resistant to any change in his behavior or attitudes whether it is the result of his own inner forces or outside pressures.

To the therapeutic counselor the individual being counseled is of the greatest importance and his needs transcend all others. To the school counselor the individual being counseled is of equal concern but the educational setting demands that the counselor be cognizant of the pupil not only as an individual whose needs are to be met but as a person functioning in an activity that has as its primary purpose the education and development of great numbers of pupils.

The form that the adaptation and modification of therapeutic counseling should assume for school counseling has been the subject of considerable controversy among those who practice counseling in schools and those who practice counseling in other settings.

The American Psychological Association, the American Guidance and Personnel Association, the American Psychiatric Association and the National Association of Social Workers at various times and with varying intensities, sought to define and delineate the counseling process in schools and to organize the functions and responsibilities of the school counselor. Great confusion still exists concerning therapy, psychotherapy and counseling in the minds of lay persons as well as in the minds of professionally oriented persons and grave concern is felt that psychotherapy will be undertaken by school personnel totally or inadequately prepared to render this service.

Most counseling in schools is done with pupils who do not deviate too markedly from "normal." Pupils with mental diseases, with serious personality disorders or with severe social or emotional problems are usually referred to hospital or clinic where they are counseled by psychologists or psychiatrists in a clinical setting.

The counseling systems used most often in schools are those which lend themselves most readily to work with normal children. Although Freud and his followers are recognized by school counselors as important contributors to psychological theories underlying school counseling there is comparatively little psychoanalytic therapy per se carried on in school settings.

Two systems which are widely used are the "directive" counseling of Williamson and Thorne and the "non-directive" or "client-centered" counseling of Rogers. These two systems are particularly appropriate for school counseling since they lend themselves either to individual or group counseling, both are suitable for work in an educational setting, and both, properly used by the school counselor, can be kept free from clinical or medical involvements. Rogerian counseling is based on the assumption that an individual, aware of a problem, under tension because of it, and seeking help in the resolution of it, can enter into a relationship with another individual that is sufficiently accepting and permissive to allow him to express freely his emotions and feelings and through this catharsis gain insights into the dynamics of his behavior and sufficient relaxation to allow the positive and integrative forces of his own personality to effect therapeutic change. There has been much controversy concerning non-directive counseling but there is little doubt that Rogers' philosophy and methods have permeated the thinking and the counseling activity of all school counselors, whether they attribute their methods to this counseling theory or some other.

Rogers gives six conditions which he believes to be necessary for personality change: "For constructive personality change to occur, it is necessary that these conditions exist and continue over a period of time:

1. Two persons are in psychological contact.

2. The first, whom we shall term the client, is in a state of incongruence, being vulnerable or anxious.

3. The second person, whom we shall term the therapist, is congruent or integrated in the relationship.

4. The therapist experiences unconditional positive regard for the client.

5. The therapist experiences an empathic understanding of the client's internal frame of reference and endeavors to communicate this experience to the client.

6. The communication to the client of the therapist's empathic understanding and unconditional positive regard is to a minimal degree achieved.

No other conditions are necessary. If these six conditions exist, and continue over a period of time, this is sufficient. The process of constructive personality change will follow."*

The simplicity of this position is more apparent than real. The therapist, to achieve these conditions, must possess sensitivity, self-discipline, deep understanding of human dynamics, unusual traits of empathy and communication, dedication to the worth of the individual and great skill in the recognition of the emergence of the client's constructive and integrative life forces. Because of its apparent simplicity and its non-threatening nature non-directive therapy has won

* ROGERS, CARL R.: 1957. "The Necessary and Sufficient Conditions of Therapeutic Personality Change." *Journal of Consulting Psychology*, 21, 95–103.

widespread acceptance among school counselors as a "safe" type of counseling.

In the extreme adherence to the non-directive approach the counselor is not so much concerned about the genesis of the client's problem or about a specific solution to the problem as he is about the changes that occur during the counseling process.

The second approach to counseling, the "directive" approach, is the oldest form of counseling in schools. It is based on the belief that in order to effect behavioral or attitudinal change learning of new adaptive patterns must take place in the individual and that these learnings can take place most readily under the leadership of a highly trained and experienced counselor who is competent to deal with all the factors involved in the client's problem. In the directive approach to counseling many of the techniques of psychotherapy and non-directive counseling are utilized to establish a comfortable working relationship, to allow free expression of anxieties, to trace the genesis of the problem, and to gain insights into behavior. In addition to these, however, directive counseling employs techniques of diagnosis, psychometry, information gathering and giving, and re-education with the aim of leading the client to objective self-realization and optimal development.

Thorne gives the following premises which underlie directive counseling:

"1. The therapist is essentially a master educator who takes over where society, family, education and the person himself have failed to condition healthy behavior.

2. The first stage of therapy consists in establishing suitable conditions for learning a new style of life. This includes establishing rapport, analyzing past conditions of a traumatic nature, releasing emotional repressions and blocks, and giving the client maximum opportunity to solve as much as he can by himself.

3. The concept of directiveness implies that someone must discover what is the matter and what is to be done, and then must see that it is done. This procedure involves diagnosis that cannot usually be accomplished by the client alone, and it also involves the issue of what is to be done therapeutically.

4. The issue is sharpened when facing the concrete decision of when, where, how, and why to interfere in another person's life. What is the authority for determining how another person shall be influenced therapeutically? In the past, such vested interests as religions, educational institutions, political parties and other pressure groups have regarded themselves as suitable authority. None of them is completely valid and satisfactory.

5. It is postulated that the scientific approach provides the most satisfactory authority for undertaking directive therapy. As here used, the scientific method is regarded as the ultimate method of establishing validity and must be given precedence. According to standards of time and place, the broad scientific training provides the highest standards of competence. Science is the common ground on which conflicting authorities must come to agree."*

The modifications and adaptations of various approaches to counseling have given rise to "eclecticism" in counseling. Fundamentally this is the selection by the counselor of an approach to counseling that meets the needs of the client, or is particularly adaptable to a problem or situation. Eclecticism assumes that the counselor is highly trained and experienced in a number of counseling approaches and, in the working situation, is equally at home in each. There is a further implication that a single counseling approach cannot be used in all situations and with all clients.

Because of the varying degrees of training and competence of school counselors it is reasonable to assume that in the past much of the counseling done in schools was on a "catch as catch can" or "trial and error" basis. With increasing research in the field of counseling and with more systematic and rigorous training of counselors, approaches to school counseling are receiving intensive study and analysis with common elements emerging which give direction and coherence to a complicated field.

Whatever system of counseling is used there are certain basic tenets recognized and accepted by all counselors. These are that a relationship established on mutual respect and trust must be developed before change can begin, that there must be readiness for counseling (and this despite sometimes seeming resistance), that the counselor must possess extensive knowledge of human dynamics, that the counselee has the capacity for growth and change, that communication between counselor and counselee must be present if change is to occur, and that broad training of the counselor in many areas is necessary if the pupil is to obtain the kind of help he needs.

GROUP COUNSELING

Counseling in groups was originally used in schools as a vocational guidance technique for the dissemination of information concerning the world of work and for orientation to occupations. Later its use for the appraisal of abilities, skills, interests and aptitudes necessary for

* THORNE, F. C.: "Directive and Eclectic Personality Counseling." *Six Approaches to Psychotherapy*. New York: Henry Holt, 1955.

various occupations and professions and for the re-evaluation of occupational choice in terms of self knowledge proved it to be an effective technique at all levels of guidance.

Concomitant with its success in vocational and educational guidance group counseling was proving effective in psychiatry, religion, social work and penology, and school counselors have seized upon it as a re-educative and therapeutic tool for pupils who are under-achievers, potential school drop-outs, chronic truants, school haters, as well as pupils who have situational problems or emotional difficulties engendered by home, school or cultural milieu. In group counseling pupils are brought together in either homogeneous or heterogeneous groups and given the opportunity to seek solutions to their problems through group discussion or group activity.

The form that group discussion or group activity will take depends upon the particular needs of the group or upon the philosophical and psychological orientation of the school counselor. Several methods of group discussion in school settings have been developed from existing group counseling methods and are being used effectively. The methods range from highly structured group situations led by psychiatrically or psychologically trained counselors to loosely formed groups without leaders.

The most highly structured group method is an outgrowth of psychiatry in which the individual is helped to develop new insights into his behavior through the interpretations of a trained leader and with the support of other members of the group who are working toward a common goal.

Next in structure is the method used most widely in group counseling in schools. This method, an outgrowth of individual non-directive counseling which was developed during World War II by Carl Rogers, assumes that the integrative forces of the individual will lead him to work through his problems in a permissive relationship within a therapeutic group. Less structured are an age-old method of allowing a group member to express his feelings and anxieties within a completely accepting group which at the same time sets an example by which he can pattern his behavior, and a method developed at Bethel which depends upon interaction among its members to effect attidudinal and behavioral change as a result of the individual seeing himself through the impersonal but sympathetic eyes of the group.

Group activity in school counseling may take as many forms as the needs of the group and the ingenuity of the counselor may allow. The best known of the group activities are psychodrama and role playing devised originally by Moreno for therapeutic group counseling of emotionally disturbed persons and adapted to school use. Basic to each is the assumption that the individual, freed from the responsibility of maintaining his ego-image, can bring to an imaginary situation his repressed needs and attitudes and through their expression can gain insights concerning them, can gain release of his tension, amelioration of his anxiety, and be given the opportunity for his positive life forces to emerge.

The success of group counseling in schools depends upon the skill and training of the school counselor and the appropriateness of the method employed.

Used widely at the secondary school level for many years, group counseling is becoming increasingly important for the elementary school pupil in the prevention of personality disorders, the amelioration of conflicts arising from present day culture and the establishment of positive social behavior. The successful leader of group counseling must have sound training in the dynamics of human behavior, be skilled and experienced in teaching and in group discussion, be comfortable in group situations, possess sensitivity to the unique flow of feelings and ideas inherent in group activity and be able to communicate effectively not only with members of the group but with their parents and teachers as well.

VOCATIONAL COUNSELING

Vocational counseling, historically the oldest of the guidance services in education, and which came under attack by psychologists impressed with the need to study the "whole" child, again stimulated by the recent interest in national manpower and survival needs, is regaining its status in the field of guidance. No longer practiced, or viewed, as an activity which considers one aspect of the pupil's life in isolation it is now recognized as a culturally oriented, developmental process, which, beginning in the earliest school years permeates the life of the school pupil and markedly influences his future as an individual and a citizen.

Vocational counseling is begun in the elementary school with generalized group orientation to occupations and to attitudes concerning them and shifts, at the Junior High School level, to occupational information, occupational exploration and in many instances to occupational choice. The curriculum selected for High School study is largely determined at the Junior High School level and often limits decisively the occupation or profession which the pupil can enter. Vocational counseling and academic counseling merging at the Junior High School level becomes of extreme importance to the pupil's future.

Vocational counseling at the High School level is accomplished both in multiple and in individual counseling sessions, usually under the leadership of counselors especially trained in this area. Attitudes, emotional factors, interests, aptitudes and abilities are all a part of the complicated process of vocational counseling and because the High School is often the termination of formal education for many pupils vocational counseling becomes an urgent need for the pupil and a grave responsibility for the counselor.

The United States Department of Labor, through publications of its Bureaus of Employment Security and Labor Statistics, offers considerable help to the vocational counselor and in many schools federal and state employment agencies offer counseling services by trained personnel. The National Vocational Guidance Association, the organization identified with the growth and establishment of vocational guidance also offers many services to vocational counselors.

The National Defense Education Act, as an expression of grave national concern about manpower shortages in science, engineering, teaching and medicine, has pointed up the need for mature and wise vocational counseling that will provide not only for the preservation of the nation and society but for the preservation of the pupil's right to follow his own aspirations.

ELEMENTARY SCHOOL COUNSELING

Elementary school counseling, a comparatively recent innovation, is probably the fastest growing branch of guidance. The downward extension of guidance services to the elementary school has been a natural outgrowth of the realization that guidance, to be effective, must begin as early as possible in the pupil's school life and that maladjustments often may be prevented by early identification of pupils with emotional and social, as well as learning problems.

Because of its recency elementary school counseling has not yet been shackled by traditional methods. Usually with the classroom teacher as the key guidance figure experimental methods are being tried and new approaches tested. Elementary school counselors systematically follow the progress of the individual pupil through the elementary school grades, constantly observing and evaluating his physical, social, mental and emotional development and by concerted action with teacher, nurse, social worker or psychologist strive to guide the pupil toward his highest achievement potential.

Concomitant with individual counseling the elementary school counselor recognizes and provides for the common needs of all pupils in the elementary school through group processes. Orientation to school, formation of social attitudes, provision of informational services, and interpretation of environment are among the functions of the elementary school counselor as well as record keeping, school placement, liaison between the home and school, and testing and evaluation.

In large city systems considerable experimentation with the team approach to school counseling has been initiated in elementary schools with teams usually consisting of school counselor, teacher, school social worker, psychologist and attendance officer. In addition the services of remedial specialists, visiting teacher and nurse are available for supplementary help.

The elementary school counselor uses the individual counseling interview either as an impromptu or a scheduled activity for those pupils for whom this type of communication is possible, or uses play techniques as a form of release and reeducation for pupils who are unable to communicate verbally.

Elementary school counselors are recruited principally from the ranks of elementary school teachers. Increasing numbers of them are trained guidance workers with particular emphasis in their training on child growth and development, dynamics of behavior, diagnostic and remedial techniques and parent-child relationships.

Referral of the elementary school pupil to outside agencies for specialized help is an important aspect of the work of the school counselor. Recognition of the need for referral, knowledge of services rendered by specific agencies, knowledge of community resources, appropriateness of referral, and methods of referral constitute a vital service to the elementary school child.

There are a number of counseling techniques that have been developed for use with elementary school pupils. Some of these have been adapted from techniques used in clinic and hospital, others are outgrowths of teaching methods. Among these are the case study, sociograms, language arts devices such as incomplete sentences, autobiography, word association and picture association, dramatic play, sociodrama, puppetry, and art.

Although there is a growing trend toward counseling with parents at all educational levels, from kindergarten through college, it is particularly important at the elementary school level. Since attitudes of the parent contribute heavily to the behavior of the child and in many instances are the cause of his problem it is almost impossible to counsel a child without the cooperation of the parent.

TRAINING OF SCHOOL COUNSELORS

Depending upon the level at which the school counselor functions his training varies from a few courses in essential skills and knowledge of counseling to the doctoral degree, with the standard preparation for most counselors at the master's degree level. Part time counselors in schools tend to have less training in guidance and counseling and more in subject matter fields, full time counselors, supervisors and directors of guidance and counseling services tend to have the higher levels of training.

One hundred and eighty-two degree granting institutions throughout the nation offer preparation in guidance and counseling to persons qualified to receive such instruction.

Many universities require teaching experience as a prerequisite to admission to such programs. Most universities offering training require one year of study for the master's degree but many require a two year program of study with increasing emphasis on counseling techniques, laboratory practice, and field experience or internship.

The National Defense Education Act of 1958, focusing the attention of the nation on the importance of guidance for national security, has given impetus to improved counselor training through the National Defense Education Act Counseling and Guidance Training Institute Program. The Institutes, under contract with universities throughout the country range from those offering the most basic preparation for counselors to those offering advanced training in counseling and guidance techniques for experienced and practising counselors. Regular session Institutes are held during the academic year and short term Institutes during summer sessions. In 1962 the congress of the United States voted a two year extension of the National Defense Act making possible Institutes for 1963 and 1964.

The training of school counselors has been studied extensively by the organizations most concerned with counselor competence, and selection criteria and formulations of training requirements leading to adequate preparation have been published over the years.

A policy statement issued by the American Personnel and Guidance Association in 1961 lists five basic qualities necessary to the effective school counselor: 1. belief in the worth of each individual, in his capacity to change, and in his ability to develop under conditions that are favorable for him; 2. commitment to human values; 3. alertness to the world; 4. openmindedness; 5. talent to communicate.

In the belief that the school counselor can emerge as a well qualified person following careful selection and sound preparation for counseling, the A.P.G.A. has proposed policies to guide the selection and preparation of school counselors. A minimum of two years of graduate education is recommended, with concentrations in (a) the behavioral sciences, the biological sciences, humanities; (b) processes of education; (c) professional studies in counseling; (d) supervised practice in counseling.

The policy recommends (1) flexibility of programming to meet individual differences; (2) a whole, integrated program with educational experiences spiral in nature, relating progressively more advanced work to earlier experiences and with a substantial portion of the two year period in full-time, continuous study; (3) a program emphasizing growth in self-understanding and professional attitudes as well as the development of cultural understandings, technical knowledge, and professional skills; (4) courses and other educational experiences conducted by faculty members well qualified through academic preparation and appropriate experience for counselor education or for the related discipline.

The policy statement further notes that counselor educators must be responsive to the standards set by professional organizations, to the needs of the counselors, and to the expectations of counselors held by the school, parents and the community.

Committees, representing Division 17, the Division of Counseling Psychology of the American Psychological Association have made recent recommendations for the preparation of school counselors in 1961 reports, "The Scope and Standards of Preparation in Psychology for School Counselors," and "The Current Status of Counseling Psychology."

The United States Office of Education invited representatives of counselor training institutions to take part in a conference to study counselor education and standards and in August 1960 issued a report emphasizing the responsibility of counselor educators in training counselors for work with elementary and secondary school pupils.

The Association for Counselor Education and Supervision (formerly the National Association of Guidance Supervisors and Counselor Trainers), a division of the American Personnel and Guidance Association, has an on-going project for the study of standards in counselor education. The study involves counselor educators and guidance workers working as local study groups on various aspects of standards for counselor education. The recommendations of these groups were presented in a series of "position papers" in 1962.

Ultimately, each state has the responsibility for certifying counselors for work in the schools but certification requirements differ widely and are often at variance with the requirements of training institutions and recommendations of professional organizations. Of the twenty-five states requiring thirty graduate credits for full certification many require only a small portion of the credits to be in guidance. The majority of the states permit courses to be taken "cafeteria style" with no unifying program of study and less than half of the states require a course in supervised practice in guidance and counseling. All the states require a teaching certificate as a prerequisite for certification.

The school counselor, more than any other member of the school staff, is responsible for the testing program of the school and for the tests used in counseling pupils. School tests are used for surveying class or school achievement, for school or grade placement, for admission to curricula or for college entrance. Tests in counseling differ from school tests in that they are used for obtaining information which the pupil himself can use or which can be used by the counselor for a better understanding of the pupil's abilities, potentialities, or personality structure.

Standardized psychological tests, used almost universally by school counselors, are classified in many ways, depending upon their structure and use. They are sometimes classified as tests of intelligence, of achievement, of aptitudes, of interests, and of personality. They may be structured or unstructured; may be administered in groups or individually; may be verbal or non-verbal; may be objective, projective, or subjective; may be used to survey the breadth and depth of subject matter fields or to diagnose subject matter weaknesses.

At the elementary school level tests are used by counselors chiefly to assess academic ability and achievement, explore interests, and to investigate personality. At the secondary school level the counselor uses tests chiefly for vocational planning, for academic advisement, and for college admission. National tests for college placement, while not the responsibility of the secondary school counselor, are of great importance to him, since in large measure they are setting the curricula of secondary schools throughout the nation. The question of whether this is a beneficial or detrimental outcome has been the subject of much controversy among counselors, administrators, college admission officers and test publishers.

Courses in tests and measurements are required in most training programs for counselors with emphasis on statistics, measurement principles, and the interpretation of tests. Knowledge of specific tests designed to assess intelligence, achievement, aptitude, interests, and personality traits and the levels at which particular tests are most appropriately used, as well as skill in the administration of tests, become a necessary part of the counselor's preparation.

The counseling of the academically talented or those who possess creative talents in art, music or other fields has become a specialized skill. Stimulated by the need to identify and educate all potential leaders as a source of national strength in a time of crisis, school counselors have been called upon to devise methods of identification of talented youth and through counseling and guidance to pilot them to the fullest use of their capabilities.

In large cities elaborate programs of identification, special education and intensive counseling have been developed. In smaller school systems or in individual schools each counselor is charged with this responsibility as well as with the responsibility for the counseling of all pupils within the school. The National Education Association in cooperation with related associations has sponsored a number of studies evaluating programs for the academically talented.

School counseling, still in a period of exploration in terms of status and function, is confronted with many problems which must be resolved before it can be accepted as a clearly seen body of persons engaged in a profession.

The whole question of professionalism is the most basic of these problems. Until there is agreement among related disciplines, as well as among school counselors themselves, concerning who shall counsel, what counseling is, the functions of the counselor, and the selection and preparation of counselors, school counseling cannot be regarded as a profession.

Closely related to this basic problem is the question of systematic research in the field of counseling. Although recent research in the field of counseling has become more rigorous and probing, there is great need to examine the degree to which the counselor is succeeding in his work and, indeed, the significance of what he is doing.

Another problem is the urgency with which the counselor is being exhorted by social and political pressure groups to discover and prepare scientists and leaders for specific purposes of national survival. Basic to the counselor's confidence in the value of his work has been a deep and persistent belief in the individual's right to make his own choices and to determine his own future. Now counselors are urged, by subtle implication, to direct and influence the pupil's choices toward certain professions or occupations as a patriotic issue. The conflicts aroused through the counselor's belief in individual freedom and his devotion to his country are very real and disturbing.

Vocational counseling, always a complicated process, presents many more problems for the present day school counselor. First among these is the vast knowledge necessary to keep abreast, not only of occupations of the near future, but those which will follow the swift and startling advances in science and in communication. Concomitant with this problem is that of automation, destroying whole areas of work and creating the need for the reevaluation of occupational opportunities.

The increase in college-bound youth creates many problems for the school counselor. Pressure from parents and the public, as well as the consciousness of status deriving from college training in the minds of young people, is placing the burden of responsibility for college advisement and placement on the counselor. Pressures from testing institutions, college admissions boards, expectations of parents, and hopes and aspirations of pupils add to the burden of an unanswerable and unsolvable problem.

More intelligent and adequate certification is another problem facing the school counselor. Certification requirements lag far behind recommendations of professional organizations and training requirements of universities and until these are brought into some semblance of agreement, school counseling will not be recognized and accorded professional status by related disciplines.

Unification of school counselors themselves is still another problem to be solved before professional status can be attained. Until school counselors labor together as a group to upgrade standards of preparation and of function and until there is common agreement concerning the aims and goals of school counseling the field will be too greatly influenced and molded by educational institutions and professional organizations.

School counseling is an important and significant part of the entire educational process. How it can reach its maximum effectiveness, what its content should be, which approaches should be utilized and who should be the persons to counsel are all questions to which answers are sought. That school counselors are searching for, and finding, the answers attests to the strength of an emerging profession.

The Faculty Advisor

JOHN W. M. ROTHNEY

Professor of Education
University of Wisconsin, Madison
Wisconsin

THE FACULTY advisor must often find himself in an anomalous position. Not usually a specialist in counseling, he is expected in the course of his advisory duties to do some of it, and he will often have doubts of his effectiveness. Under such circumstances there is a temptation for some advisors to simplify their tasks by giving a cursory glance at a student's study list in September, signing it, and telling him to come back to see him some time, "Say next May." Some will, of course, accept the challenge that advising offers and perform at a very high level despite their lack of specific training for it. Regardless of the degree to which they take their duties seriously however, many faculty members still maintain that advising is not one of their prime responsibilities and that it is a chore foisted upon them by the pressures of numbers of students who must be dealt with at such harassing times as marking and registration periods.

Educational institutions vary greatly in their provision of advisory services. In some colleges and universities all faculty members are given advisory responsibilities; in others combinations of trained and untrained advisors are used, and in still others there are counseling bureaus headed by highly trained specialists augmented by a few less highly trained faculty members whose teaching loads, salaries and promotions may be determined by the fact that they have special advisory duties. There seems to be, however, a general belief that the professor is inescapably a partner with the student in the quest of self-realization and achievement of common goals and that some association of students with mature adults is needed and can be

7

provided best when everyone has some hand in advising. In general there appears to be a trend toward the supplementing of casual student–faculty relationship by using a relatively small nucleus of faculty members who have been given some training, and topping the program with some highly trained persons who deal with special and difficult problems.

ADVISOR'S RESPONSIBILITIES

Although the duties of advisors vary with the policies of institutions they are generally guided by such instructions as the following.

"The advisor helps a student to select his subjects so that he will have a well-rounded education, interprets the requirements for the student, and helps him to meet all his requirements in their proper sequence. The responsibility for the selection of courses rests, in the final analysis upon the student and it is *not* within the province of the advisor to refuse approval of a course which the student is entitled to elect. At the opening of each semester the student is required to consult his advisor concerning his choice of studies and the advisor must approve the student's elections before he is permitted to enter classes."

The emphasis in most descriptions of advisor's duties is, as above, on assistance in the election of studies. Less specifically stated, but generally implied, is the hope that the advisor will pass on to the student particular kinds of information that he has learned as the result of his familiarity with procedures and circumstances not usually described in college catalogs. He is expected, for example, to pass on information about job opportunities in his own field. It is expected also that he will show interest in the student's problems and that he will refer him to such agencies as veteran's counselors, reading and study specialists, housing and employment bureaus, the football ticket office, and health or psychiatric services when he is unable to give the student particular help that is needed. In some respects the faculty advisor may be described as a combination listening post, information agency and switchboard.

MATERIALS FOR ADVISING

It has become fairly common practice to supply advisors with certain information about students that will presumably be of assistance in carrying out their responsibilities. Advisors generally receive photostatic copies of a student's record of grades in college (and, for freshmen, transcripts of high school marks), some group test scores, brief statements about the student's family situation, records of interests and activities, vocational experiences and a photograph. Some of these materials come directly from official records, some from questionnaire responses, others from freely-written statements of the students and still others from comments written by faculty members or ratings made by them. It is usually indicated that the advisor should study such data before the student is interviewed. The rest of this chapter is concerned with the values and limitations of such materials and methods by which they may be employed effectively in the advising relationships.

INTERPRETATION OF ACADEMIC RECORDS

One of the tasks most commonly allocated to the advisor is that of interpreting a student's record so that adequate consideration can be given to past performances in the selection of courses. If the student is an entering freshman the advisor will usually have a transcript of his grades and a number indicating his rank in class. Unless he is very familiar with the high school that the student attended the marks will be difficult to interpret. It is well known that marks vary greatly in validity and reliability and that they may have been subject to many influences. They *may* indicate excellent accomplishment and they *may* have high predictive value for college marks but they may only be indicators that the student has kept out of trouble, has performed well in certain extra-curricular activities and that he has created a good impression while he was in high school without high accomplishment or adequate preparation for the work of the college. Although marks in high school are generally the best single predictors of college performance they are not always good predictors of the success of particular individuals and the advisor must, therefore, view them with suspicion. He will find generally that the more the high school resembles the college (which usually means the larger the high school) the better predictors the marks will be. It has been demonstrated, however, that first semester marks in college are the best forecasters of what is likely to follow and, until these first marks are in, the advisor must realize that prediction is a hazardous process. He must do much investigation and ask many questions before he can get useful information from a transcript.

The rank-in-class figure that an advisor sees on a transcript may not have much meaning until he has examined the method of ranking used in the high school. If it is to be meaningful he must find out whether the rank was based on all the students in the graduating class and what proportion of them went on to college. He must determine whether the ranking was based on academic subjects only or whether it incorporated all subjects taken by all the students. He must realize that the averaging out of performances in many areas over the four

years of high school may have covered up more than it has revealed
about a student's strengths and weaknesses and he should know that
many secondary school personnel consider that the ranking of students
demanded by colleges is a highly unsatisfactory procedure. Some colleges
have evaluated high school ranking by observing, for a period of years,
the college performances of students who had earned certain ranks in
particular high schools. When such information is available to advisors
they can make increasingly valid judgments about such things as the
likelihood of a student's success in carrying specified subject loads, his
promise of achievement in certain areas of study, the desirability of
taking part-time jobs, participating in time-consuming extra-curricular
activities or the need for special help from specialists in reading and
study skills.

When the advisor is dealing with students beyond the entering
freshman level he will have at hand their records achieved during the
previous semesters. He will now have some (but not infallible, since
variations do occur) indication of a student's strengths and weaknesses
in getting marks within required areas of study and perhaps in electives
in which he has shown some interest. He will presumably have had
time to consider previous semester's records with his advisee and will
be in a position to give more adequate consideration to choices of
upperclassmen in the light of these data than he could give to the
entering freshman. As more records accumulate through the semesters
a longitudinal picture emerges so that when such decisions as the choice
of major fields or selection of an occupation are made the advising
should become increasingly more effective.

THE USE OF TESTS

In this section we shall be concerned only with devices that are commonly labeled as achievement, mental ability, intelligence and scholastic
aptitude tests. We are not concerned with the so-called personality
and interest tests since they cannot really be called *tests* in any common
use of that word and since their validity for advising purposes has never
been satisfactorily established. They will be used if at all, only by those
who have had long training and supervision in their development and
application.

On an advisee's record the advisor may find scores on some form of a
scholastic aptitude test. It will usually have been given by the college
during freshman week and the score will commonly be reported in
terms of quartiles, centiles or percentiles. If these have been computed
for local populations and some form of expectancy table has been
provided for the advisors, the figure given for a particular student may

prove to be very helpful in his advisement. The following expectancy chart, for example, indicates the chances that a student in a particular college has of making average grades of *C* or better (Grades below *C* carry no credit toward graduation) if he achieves scores on the test that lie within certain stated intervals. Thus if a student has scored above the 75th percentile there are only ten chances in a hundred that he will not get credit for his work (less than *C* grades) and the chances are even (50–50) that he will achieve a *B* average or better. If, however, he scores below the 25th percentile the odds are three to two (60 in 100) that he will not achieve the average of *C* that is necessary to get credit for his work and remain in college. Advisors who are thoroughly

EXPECTANCY TABLE

If Students score is	Chances in 100 of obtaining the following grades		
	Less than *C* average	*C* average or better	*B* average or better
Above 75%ile	10	90	50
Between 50th and 74th %ile	25	75	25
Between 25th and 49th %ile	40	60	15
Below 25th %ile	60	40	5

familiar with the way such tables are derived may point out such odds to their advisees after good rapport has been established and may consider with them what action seems advisable. They must indicate, however, that these are only odds in general and that they do not apply to particular individuals. They might for example discuss the desirability of carrying heavier or lighter course loads, the seeking of scholarship assistance, new ways of budgeting time, or improving study skills.

Advisors who have recourse only to results of tests administered to students while they were in high school must use extreme caution in the interpretation of the scores. Since less than a third of high school students go on for advanced training in colleges and universities some selection has taken place and a score that is high in a general secondary school population may be quite low when compared with the scores of college students. In Table I below, for example, we may see that a student who scored at the middle (50th percentile) of his high school class on this test would be only at the tenth percentile in the freshman class of the university at which this table was used. A student would have to score at the 86th percentile of his high school group to be at the average of the university freshman class. When such comparative figures are available for particular colleges the advisor may use the results of high school testing programs with some profit. In general, colleges are somewhat dubious about the use of results of high school testing programs and they prefer to administer tests after the student has enrolled in college.

The comments above concerning interpretation of scholastic aptitude test scores may be extended to include those devices that are commonly labeled achievement tests. The college or high school groups on which

TABLE I

NORMS FOR A MENTAL ABILITY TEST FOR HIGH SCHOOL JUNIORS CONVERTED TO NORMS FOR ENTERING FRESHMEN AT A UNIVERSITY

Percentiles for High School juniors	Converted percentiles for University freshmen
50	10
65	20
75	30
82	40
86	50
91	60
94	70
96	80
99	90

norms of the test were obtained must be examined for quantitative adequacy and qualitative representativeness. Determination must be made of the curricular coverage of the test items and consideration must be given to the instructional opportunities that the students have had. If examination of these factors gives the advisor reason to believe that the advisee has had adequate opportunity to show what he could do, the achievement test scores may be helpful in advising him concerning his choice of courses in college.

It is strongly urged that interpretation of test scores with or without the student present, should not be attempted unless the advisor has had considerable training in the development and use of tests. There are many pitfalls and numerous difficulties. These difficulties are becoming more clearly appreciated and it is to be expected that there will be significant improvements in the construction and use of tests in the future. Until such time certain cautions in their use should be noted. It is suggested, for example, that advisors avoid raising or discussing technical or statistical details with his students. In any event he should avoid defending the tests or trying to impress on advisees any results which are not acceptable to him. He should encourage the student to voice his own explanations, hunches, or feelings about the test scores and encourage him to relate his own experiences or other factors known to influence test results. He should not offer consolation except as it is incidental to supplying additional facts for interpretation although he should not, by silence or otherwise, seem to give approval to erroneous interpretations or to hasty interpretations that may lead to questionable conclusions. The advisor will always suggest that results must be interpreted in the light of other information and that, in the long run, the test scores are probably less important than many other data in influencing the advisee's course of action.

USE OF BACKGROUND DATA

From check lists, documents written by students, letters of recommendation, ratings or behavior descriptions of former teachers, statements on admission blanks, and many other sources the advisor may secure evidence concerning the advisee's usual behavior and significant variations from it as well as the hazards and opportunities the student has met in his environment up to the time the advisement begins. Since these devices may provide valuable information when they are used cautiously the advisor should be aware of their limitations and values.

Descriptions of a student's family tend to be concerned largely with its socio-economic level and the extent of the education of its members. Recently some investigations have revealed that data about families obtained from parents and students are not always dependable. Even if they are reliable, however, they seldom provide an adequate description of the psychological atmosphere of the home and if it seems that such information is needed it must be done by subtle questioning of the student. In the case of one student who was having trouble with grades, for example, the writer discovered that although the report about the advisee's home was very satisfactory from the point of view of socio-economic status, the home situation was the cause of his difficulties. He had come to a large university despite his parents' pleas that he attend a small sectarian college. When a first semester failure occurred the worry about it and the feelings of guilt about going against his parents' wishes combined to produce a condition of almost complete demoralization and failure. The advisor and the student drew up several optional courses of action and after weighing each of them, the advisee made a choice which resulted in a satisfactory solution to the problem. This was a fairly clear-cut case that could be diagnosed readily from scant data and careful questioning. Relatively few cases will be as easily recognized and treated. When the situation is more complicated the advisor will usually refer the advisee to special counselors who have the necessary training, experience and time to work with him. When situations at home are hazards to a student's successful performance it will usually require more competence and time than the advisor can bring to it.

Letters of recommendation from those who have known the student prior to his entrance to college, since their purpose is to recommend and commend, and since there is no control of the language that is used, are always suspect. If the writer is well known and there is evidence from follow-up data that his recommendations bear some relation to the performances of those about whom he writes, they can be used with confidence. Otherwise they should be left in the admissions office where they will not clutter the advisor's files.

PERSONAL DOCUMENTS

Papers written by advisees may be of considerable value in their advising if the adviser knows and heeds certain cautions about their use. It has been demonstrated that student autobiographies sensibly used can provide, at no additional cost to the college, the kind of advising material that no other instruments offer. They may give valuable indications of interests, clues about social attitudes, hints of a student's tendency to try to make a good impression when he is given the opportunity, and suggestions of his awareness of the feelings and attitudes of others. These clues, hints, and suggestions are obtained by analysis of what he has chosen to write about in the length and detail of his own choosing. There is, of course, the possibility of misinterpretation by both the writer and reader of the autobiography. There may be deliberate and unconscious omissions of important information and there may be bias in the selection of the experiences reported. For these reasons the autobiography cannot be used in isolation from other data. If, however, it is used cautiously in conjunction with other information that is available it can contribute valuable suggestions about that "inner half" of the advisee's life that is frequently hidden from those who seek only what they call objective data.

INTERPRETATION OF INFORMATION ABOUT HEALTH

The advisor must accept the fact that he is not a specialist in health and that he must depend upon experts in that field for his basic data and for their recommendations. He must consider the fact, however, that although information about the health of an advisee may be available in technical medical records the advisor faces the problem of considering with the student the effect that a health condition may have on his actions and choices. He must find the indications and contra-indications in terms of the course load to be carried by a student who has, for example, a particular kind of visual, heart or hearing difficulty. Until the advisor can secure fairly definite answers to his questions it is sometimes very difficult to keep an advisee from entering a program of study in which he is likely to fail or direct him toward one in which there is greatest chance of success. What the advisor needs here is not a formal diagnosis in technical terms but recommendations from medical personnel concerning what should be done on the basis of that diagnosis. The problems in this area will not be solved until the medical report that comes to the advisor contains specific answers to such questions as these: Is this particular student physically capable of carrying a full course load? Should there be restriction on the extra-curricular participation of this advisee? Is this particular student's visual condition such that he should or should not choose a course (such as medicine or law) that will require many years of intensive study? Unfortunately there are not enough research findings on the antecedent–consequent relationships in such matters so that advisors must often use their own often fallible generalist judgments on such matters even when there are excellent technical medical reports in their records.

In addition to the securing of good medical reports the advisor should concern himself with the student's attitude toward a health difficulty. It has been established that persons with almost identical medical diagnoses may respond to their handicaps in quite different fashion. One may use his handicap as a convenient alibi for every failure while another may accept it as a challenge and work very hard to compensate for it. The advisor who seeks to discover the student's attitude toward his difficulty and who discusses it with him may be helpful to him in overcoming an initial hazard to success in his academic work. Meanwhile he will make every effort to obtain medical reports that are meaningful to him and to his advisees and he will be ever alert to refer to specialists all cases in which he suspects that health is a limiting factor to accomplishment.

INTERVIEWING

The interview is, of course, the basic technique of the advisor. It is in this session alone with the student that the information obtained by use of the techniques described above is put to use in the student's service and it is in it that decisions are made or the bases for future choices are laid down.

The flexibility of the interview, the opportunity to personalize rather than generalize, and the very fact that it is centered upon just one person at a time makes it potentially the most effective of all advising procedures. Too often, however, the limitations of time and unsatisfactory other circumstances prevent the reaching of the potential. Registration periods, for example, usually require rather hasty interviews and even important changes of program may have to be made in too short sessions in order to meet certain arbitrary deadlines. Advisor and advisees alike feel the pressures of the academic calendar and the advantages of the leisurely prolonged and probing interview can seldom be realized at the times when they are often needed. There seems always to be another student waiting in the outer office.

Ideally, interviews in which important decisions about a student's choices are to be made should be preceded by introductory sessions designed only to develop rapport between advisor and student. After that first session the advisor should study the student's record and the answers to questions that remain unanswered after such study should be obtained at a fact-finding interview. After these two preliminary meetings advisor and advisee may then be ready to come to grips with some of the issues and make decisions that are based upon adequate information and careful consideration of alternatives. Rarely will these optimum conditions be met. Usually the student will meet his advisor for the first time to make his choices after he has had cursory orientation in group sessions that have only partially answered his questions, that have given him fragmentary bits of information and that may have, by the persuasiveness of some of the lecturers, left him with some strange notions about the opportunities in various areas and his own fitness for work in them. With several advisees waiting outside his door and with registration deadlines coming fast it is often impossible to answer the students' questions, provide the information they want, and give adequate consideration to the biased notions they may have obtained. This situation seems to account for the large number of students who get into courses for which they are neither prepared nor interested or who sign up for loads which they cannot possibly carry.

After the rush of registration period it is sometimes possible to get time and conditions for the kinds of interviews that were needed before that period. There may be time now for an advisor to see how the advisee perceives himself by letting him talk at length. There may also be time to be more concerned with the processes of making a decision than with the decision itself. There may be an opportunity to pass on to the student specific information about this particular college that an established faculty member has acquired but which may not appear in print. The time may be at hand when the student can develop that companionship with a mature adult which may be one of the best experiences in a college career. It is in these more leisurely sessions, too, that the student can feel free to raise questions about educational and vocational objectives, financial needs, homesickness, budgeting of time and even such matters as feelings of inadequacy in social situations. It is in such situations, too, that the ideal advisee-advisor relationship for which so many values are claimed may often be realized.

Although space does not permit thorough analysis of the strengths and weaknesses of the interview procedure in advising it may be well to note here certain precautions that advisors must take if the interview is to be effective. Faculty members who were themselves successful in college must not let emphasis upon marks become too great. They must not mistake the classroom for the world or the honor student for the best person. They should not let one outstanding characteristic of the advisee, desirable or not, blind them to the possibility that the student may have other traits which need further development or re-training. They must not retain too great confidence in their own judgment about the diagnostic efficacy of certain clues such as particular gestures or "looking one in the eye" when their effectiveness has not been established, or may even be rejected by, research findings. They should not use themselves as examples of what every advisee should be, and they must ever be alert to the difficulties involved in the use of words that have meaning to them but that are not clear to the student. In advising, one of the major difficulties pointed out by one writer is that, "We confuse fact and feeling, project old memories and pre-judices into new pictures and report the mixture in words colored by our own personal semantics." The advisor who has recognized these difficulties and has attempted to avoid them in his interviews is likely to be vastly more effective than those who have not analyzed their own procedures. Those who wish to analyze their performances with the objective of improving them may do so by making some tape recordings of their interviews, by reading of discussion and research reports on counseling methods, and by informal follow-up of a sample of their advisees to discover whether or not their advising has been effective.

RECORD-KEEPING

Since advisors usually have many advisees and since they have contacts with many other persons it is often difficult to remember what has happened in the case of a particular counselee. Since, too, they are often required to report about a student on short notice it is essential that they keep careful records of what has transpired in their interviews and the action that has resulted. The making of notes after each interview and meticulous filing of records can become an onerous chore unless a carefully considered plan has been developed. Advisors simply cannot remember all that takes place during interviews and some provision must be made for the writing of notes that will serve as reminders of past actions and suggestions for the future. In doing so they must choose one from among three methods. They may summarize the action in a few carefully chosen phrases, they may attempt to reproduce almost photographically the proceedings, or they may select a few key points for statement, elaboration and interpretation. The first of these methods may seem most expedient but notes which seemed adequate at the end of the interview may be so unclear at the next meeting that valuable time may be lost in going over again what had been covered previously. Reproduction of all the proceedings, besides being too time-consuming must result in the retention of much unnecessary material. Careful selection of a few key-points with a sentence or two of elaboration and interpretation may best present a cumulative and meaningful picture of the advisee's chief problems and accomplishments, developments with respect to them, and the next steps that must be undertaken. Such records will be helpful in a review of the case before the advisee is seen the next time, will be useful if it is necessary or advisable to transfer the student to a new advisor, and may be useful to the advisor himself when called upon to describe his duties or even to justify his position. If such records are made immediately after interviews with the advisee, if, in them, interpretations are separated from facts, and if no incident is reported unless it clearly serves a purpose they are likely to be most useful. It is particularly important that unless observations or incidents or interpretations seem likely to serve in the understanding of the individual or as a stimulus to further discussion or action they should not be recorded.

SUMMARY

In this chapter the chief duties and responsibilities of faculty advisors have been sketched, the materials for advising usually available to them have been scanned, and some techniques for using the materials have been described. It has been suggested that the trend in advising of students is toward the provision of personnel in counseling bureaus who assist a relatively few troubled students with severe problems, to train selected faculty members as advisors and to give them special opportunities to take care of the general advising problems, and to try to develop a personnel point of view throughout the whole faculty. An attempt has been made to show how advisors may secure information about their advisees and how they may be used in routine advisement. Controversial issues concerning the highly technical types of counseling required when deep emotional problems appear have not been covered here since, presumably, advisees with such problems will be referred to highly trained personnel in special counseling agencies. Detailed discussion of the contributions to student welfare made by faculty members who profess no skill in counseling but who do yeoman service by excellent teaching in, before, and after classes has not been presented in this chapter but the absence of such discussion must not be construed as failure to appreciate their contributions. Advising services are commonly provided by all faculty members even though everyone is not qualified to perform all advising services.

Advising is part of the tradition of American education. Changes in populations, purposes and forms of educational institutions, and advancement in knowledge about behavior of students, has resulted in the moving away from the pastor–policeman–teacher relationship of tutor and student that was common in colonial days, and the moving toward use of professionally trained advisors. It has been well said, however, that no corps of professional advisors, essential as they now appear to be, can replace the variety of personal approaches and the normal student classroom contacts that members of the faculty can offer.

BIBLIOGRAPHY

1. ARBUCKLE, D.: 1959. *Student Personnel Services in Higher Education.* New York: McGraw-Hill Book Company.
2. AIKEN, D. W.: Autumn, 1949. "Securing Faculty Cooperation in the Student Personnel Program." *Educational and Psychological Measurement.*
3. BROUWER, P. J.: 1949. *Student Personnel Work in General Education.* Washington, D.C.: American Council on Education.
4. CARMICHAEL, L.: 1950. "A College President Looks at Vocational Guidance." *Occupations,* Vol. 28.
5. CARPENTER, M., HOPKINS, E. and HILTON, M.: May, 1953. "College Guidance. Whose Job Is It?" *NEA Journal.*
6. COTTINGHAM, H. F.: May, 1955. "Roles, Functions, and Training Levels for College Personnel Workers." *Personnel and Guidance Journal.*
7. DARLEY, J. G.: December, 1956. "The Faculty Is Human, Too." *Personnel and Guidance Journal.*
8. EDDY, E. D.: 1959. *The College Influence on Student Character.* Washington, D.C.: American Council on Education.
9. GORDON, I. J.: January, 1953. "Guidance Training for College Faculty." *Journal of National Association of Deans of Women.*
10. HARDEE, M. D.: July 7, 1951. "General Education and General Education Counseling." *School and Society.*
11. HAVIGHURST, R. L.: 1960. *American Higher Education in the 1960's.* Columbus, Ohio: The Ohio State University Press.
12. JACOB, P. E.: 1957. *Changing Values in College.* New York: Harper.

13. KIMPTON, L. A.: 1950. "Student Personnel: Sense and Nonsense." *College and University*, Vol. 25.
14. KOILE, E. A.: 1955. "Characteristics of College Teachers Interested in Faculty Counseling." *Journal of Counseling Psychology*. Vol. 2.
15. KOILE, E. A.: April, 1954. "Faculty Counseling in Colleges and Universities." *Teachers College Record*.
16. LLOYD-JONES, E. and SMITH, M. R.: 1954. *Student Personnel Work as Deeper Teaching*. New York: Harper.
17. ROTHNEY, J. W. M.: 1958. *Guidance Practices and Results*. New York: Harper.
18. SHANK, D. J.: 1948. *The Teacher as Counselor*. Washington, D.C.: American Council on Education, 1948.
19. TEAD, O.: May, 1953. "Integrating Personnel and Teaching Functions in College." *Educational Forum*.
20. THORNTON, J. W.: 1960. *The Community Junior College*. New York: John Wiley and Sons.
21. TINSLEY, M. A.: December, 1955: "The Faculty Advisor in the Liberal Arts College." *Personnel and Guidance Journal*.
22. TRAXLER, A. E. and TOWNSEND, A.: 1953. *Improving Transition from School to College*. New York: Harper.
23. TYLER, L. E.: Revised 1961. *The Work of the Counselor*. New York: Appleton–Century–Crofts.
24. WILLIAMSON, E. G.: 1960. *Student Personnel Services in Colleges and Universities*. New York: McGraw-Hill Book Company.

Child Protection

ROBERT M. MULFORD

General Secretary
Massachusetts Society for Prevention of Cruelty to Children
Boston, Mass.

BEGINNING OF PROTECTIVE SERVICES

IN ORDER to approach a discussion of counseling techniques in the field of child protection, a brief description of the so-called child protective agency program is in order.

The organization of child protective agencies dates back to 1875 when the New York Society for Prevention of Cruelty to Children was founded as a result of a case involving cruelty to a young girl which was referred to the New York Society for Protection of Cruelty to Animals because of the lack of any child protective service. Since that time, SPCC's and child protective agencies have developed in many parts of the country and, although there has been some difference in the way in which these organizations have functioned, their basic purpose has included the investigation of cases involving neglect, abuse and cruelty to children. Most protective agencies, in addition to their concern for individual cases reported to them, also carry on a program for the improvement of community conditions affecting children and participate in efforts to improve legislation affecting children. These agencies originally were founded at a time when there were no well organized public welfare departments and when no one had a particular responsibility for the protection of children either from neglecting parents or others who were exploiting them. The early efforts of these agencies were largely devoted to investigation of complaints and prosecution of offenders. Casework or counseling techniques as we know them today were unknown. The field of psychiatry had not yet developed and private social work was limited to programs of friendly visitation with limited financial assistance, and the care of children in orphan asylums, institutions and, in a few instances, foster homes. From their experience in dealing with neglectful parents, some of the pioneers in the field of child protection began to see that their work should not be limited to investigation and prosecution and that some parents could use and needed advice and help in correcting conditions which caused neglect. This was the beginning of the casework method which today is the basic program of progressive child protective agencies.

PRESENT PHILOSOPHY

The present casework approach to parents who are neglecting their children is based upon the insights into human behavior which have been contributed by the fields of medicine, psychology and psychiatry. As a result of the contributions from these fields, it is clear to social workers in child protection that the great majority of parents want to be good parents and do not intentionally neglect their children. By the same token it is widely accepted that the best place for any child is in his own home with parents who love him, if that home can be preserved and can offer at least minimum standards of child care. These concepts repudiated some of the earlier assumptions in the field of child protection, chief among which were: (1) that parents neglected their children because of their innate cruelty or because of wilful intent, and (2) that the best treatment was to rescue the child from the neglectful parents and place him in a substitute environment. It should be pointed out that child protective workers were not the only ones who held these now outmoded assumptions, for in truth thousands of children have been placed away from parents who should have been helped to express their natural love and concern for their children through adequate care. Today, the basic goal of child protective agencies is that of strengthening family life, of helping parents to solve their own problems so that they can be adequate parents, and of helping children to stay in their own homes with parents who want them and who are being helped to provide at least minimum standards of child care.

FUNCTION OF CHILD PROTECTIVE PROGRAMS

A description of counseling techniques in the field of child protection needs to commence with the recognition that this service is materially different from other casework services. In the first place, however, we should perhaps recognize the fact that for the purpose of this discussion the word "counseling" is taken to mean the casework process through which the caseworker in a child protective agency carries out the agency's function. Counseling in the field of child protection, then, is a process which is different from counseling in other fields because of the essential differences in the problems and needs of parents and children who are referred to those agencies offering protective services to children. Most casework or counseling services exist for persons who recognize that they have problems with which they need help and who are able to move to get that help from an agency set up to serve them. The child protective agency exists to serve children whose parents for the most part do not recognize their need for help and who have not been able to move to get help from other casework resources in the community. It is here essential to point out that the term "protective service" is not used in the sense of a wide variety of general casework services, but rather as a limited function carried on by child protective agencies which are set up to serve only children whose parents cannot or will not take steps themselves to get needed assistance in solving their problems involving child-parent relationships and personality difficulties which cause child neglect.

One such agency has defined its function as that of "protecting children from abuse, neglect or other types of substandard care when parents are unwilling or unable to recognize the need for help and to do something about it." This definition of function makes it clear that the protective agency focuses its primary attention on the needs of children, although in its casework efforts, direct help to parents may be its primary method of achieving this purpose.

PROTECTIVE CASE WORK DIFFERENCES

There are at least four specific characteristics which differentiate the child protective service from other casework or counseling programs. First, the service to the client is initiated by the agency on the complaint of neglect or abuse of someone other than the parent. Second, the parent to whom help is being offered is not free to decide that he does not want the services of the agency. Third, the agency is not free to terminate the service only because the parent has refused or is unable to use help. Fourth, if the parent is unable or unwilling to improve conditions which are endangering children, the agency must bring the situation to the proper court with recommendations for the care of the children. It should be pointed out that all of these responsibilities must be carried out by the agency if it is to call itself a child protective agency.

THE INTAKE PROCESS

There are two ways in which the process of counseling in a child protective agency is materially different from that of other agencies.

8

The first has to do with the way in which the protective agency receives referrals or requests for help. The second has to do with the way in which the caseworker in the protective agency approaches the family. The first of these, or the intake process, starts with some one other than the parent. Some person in the community takes note of the fact that a child is being neglected and feels concerned enough to make a report of this fact to the child protective agency. The agency is called upon since it represents the community's concern for neglected children. Just as we have police departments which are skilled in crime detection and prosecution, so do we have child protective agencies whose staff are skilled in the investigation and treatment of situations involving neglect of children and, where necessary, the prosecution of offenders under the community's laws. The beginning of an effective counseling program in these situations depends upon the way in which cases are processed by the agency at the point of complaint. In the first place, not all cases referred to the agency represent valid complaints of neglect. Some situations are referred purely on the basis of spite by people who have "an axe to grind" against parents or children. Some cases are referred to the agency by persons who have heard a story about a situation from someone else and by the time the matter is reported to the agency, it is a question as to how much of the complaint is true and how much is fiction. The protective agency therefore has a responsibility to examine very carefully the requests for service which come to it in order to determine which ones represent valid complaints for which the agency has a responsibility. In evaluating the validity of a complaint, the agency's casework staff must take into consideration first of all the source of the complaint. Does the complaint come from a reliable person whose integrity assures the authenticity of the facts presented? Is the complaint made because of the complainant's concern about children, or is there some ulterior motive which prompts the complaint, such as the desire to have the family move by a landlord who has a grievance? Secondly, the agency must inquire into the content of the complaint. Are there facts which substantiate neglect of children? Does the complainant have specific information which tells the agency that this is a situation meriting its interference in family life? Is there sufficient specific information concerning the neglect of children so that the agency's caseworker can go into the situation with conviction? This is important, since social workers today recognize the right of the family to pursue its own ways without interference as long as the rights of others are not violated. Parents have certain rights which agencies must respect, and interference is justified only when the rights of children are not being protected by parents. Because the agency wishes to work in efficient co-operation with other agencies, it will inquire as to whether any other agency is presently helping the family, usually through the Social Service Index, and if so, will clear with that agency and then decide whether or not it needs to go into the family situation. When these questions have been thoroughly answered, and the agency has accepted the case for service, the caseworker can approach the family with conviction and with a reasonable hope of carrying on a counseling service which will be helpful to both children and parents.

APPROACH TO THE PARENT

The problem which has to be treated has a good deal to do with the techniques used in carrying out counseling. Certain skills need to be developed in relation to the type of the agency's counseling program. In the field of child protection, counseling to the parent of a neglected child begins with the agency's entrance into the situation unasked and, in most instances, unwanted. The caseworker, therefore, becomes the symbol of unwanted intrusion and is an outside threat to the family from the standpoint of the parent. In many cases the parent has a feeling of guilt about his inadequacy which is brought to the surface on the entrance of the caseworker into the situation. A defensive mechanism is immediately set up which frequently leads the parent to become hostile, resistant and denying. His hostility is directed toward the person who made the complaint, who is unidentified by the agency according to policy, and toward the caseworker who confronts him or her with the complaint of neglect or abuse. This hostility may take a violent form in angry denunciation of the complainant and the worker and usually is accompanied with a denial of the accusation.

What is involved in approaching the parent in a neglect situation? Many protective agencies make their approach to the parents by letter. Unless the complaint is such as to indicate the desirability of immediate investigation and/or action to protect the child, it is felt that writing a letter is preferable to a home visit. This gives the client time to consider the matter and organize his defenses before confronting him personally. It also starts the relationship on a more professional basis in that an office appointment is usually made.

Whether the approach is made by letter or in person, the following responsibilities must be carried out by the worker. First of all, the worker has the responsibility to identify himself and the agency which he represents. Involved in this is a description of the agency's function and its responsibility as a representative of the community's concern about children. Secondly, the caseworker must inform the parent as to the content of the complaint which has specifically brought him into

the situation. Thirdly, the caseworker indicates to the parent his desire
to be of help in the situation, his need to know more about it, and his
readiness to help the parent. The way in which this is done gives the
parent his first impression of what protective service may be. The
importance of conveying to the parent the worker's real, genuine desire
to be of help cannot be over-emphasized. The worker who has a need
to punish parents and who approaches them in an authoritative, condemning manner cannot be an effective protective caseworker. In
order to be successful in the child protective agency, a caseworker must
have a strong and genuine conviction that most parents want to be good
parents to their children. He therefore approaches the parent without
violating his dignity, self-respect and without implying unnecessary
threat or blame. As the parent responds to the caseworker's presentation
of the complaint, the counseling process begins with the handling of
the client's hostility, resistance and denial. The way in which this is
handled by the worker determines in part whether or not there can be
a casework relationship and thus whether counseling can be effective.
If the caseworker retaliates, on the basis of his own need to defend himself against the client's aggression, and adopts a punitive or prosecutory
attitude, there will be little opportunity for counseling. There will be
no casework relationship and perhaps the caseworker's activities will
be limited to that of making an investigation rather than involving the
client in a relationship in which study, diagnosis, and treatment become
integrated in a helping service. Whether or not the parent responds to
this offer of help which comes with an implied threat depends not only
on the caseworker's approach to him but also on the parent's ability to
use help. Some parents are so disturbed emotionally that they cannot
use help and cannot see the need for it. Others have subconsciously
wanted help and will respond readily to the opportunity to get it, even
though it comes to them unasked. Furthermore, in some instances, the
parent's insecurity and fear of the implied threat of possible removal of
his children may be so strong that he will immediately grasp any
opportunity to prevent it.

AUTHORITY

Much has been written concerning the relationship between authority
and case work. For many parents who are neglecting their children,
the authority of the protective agency to be in the situation and to
insist upon adequate care for children is an emotional prop which has
far more positive than negative connotations. The particular characteristic of counseling in the child protective field is that this authority
is given to the agency by the community and is administered by the

caseworker in such a way that it does not constitute a personal authority through which the worker meets his own emotional needs. In other words, where authority becomes a negative instrument, it is usually because of the way in which the caseworker approaches the client and carries out his authority. For years, caseworkers have feared to use authority because of its negative connotation. Today we see authority as a part of reality. None of us lives without limitation of our activities in terms of laws, mores and customs. These, in a way, serve as a protective framework within which we can move with confidence and security. This concept applies very directly to the authoritative role of the child protective agency. In the relationship with the protective caseworker the client learns what society expects of him as a parent— the boundaries within which child–parent responsibilities must operate —and receives help in carrying out those responsibilities. He thus has an opportunity to become secure in his role as a parent.

Thus, if the approach to the parent is made with genuine regard for the parent and in a skillful manner without violating basic casework principles, the agency authority produces the framework for constructive counseling in which both the parent and the child can have their needs met. The counseling process here is carried on with the parent in terms of his responsibilities to his child. Thus, the counseling is continuously related to the reason for which the agency came into the picture, namely, the neglect of the child.

DIFFERENCES IN PROTECTIVE COUNSELING

A description of the approach to the client has already pointed out a basic difference as between counseling in the child protective field and counseling done by family agencies. The agency has gone to the client. The caseworker has been faced with the necessity of handling extreme hostility and establishing a basis for continued relationship with the client.

TIME LIMITATIONS

In this setting it is the caseworker rather than the client who sets the pace at which some change must take place. Where a child is severely neglected, the focus must be on the needs of the child, and movement in treatment must be related to relief of the child's suffering. The caseworker may not be able to take the time to work through all of the problems which beset the parent and cause him to be unhappy and maladjusted. It may well be, then, that change must occur fairly quickly if the child is to remain with the parent. The responsibility then rests with the caseworker to decide how quickly and how much change. This of course presupposes the caseworker's evaluation and diagnosis of the way in which the situation is affecting the child. It is this determination which forms the basis of the caseworker's treatment schedule. In some instances the conditions affecting the child are so damaging and the opportunity for immediate change of these conditions so unlikely that the caseworker must move toward the removal of the child. From this, it can be readily seen that there are two types of evaluations which must be quickly made: first, an evaluation of the effect of these conditions on the child, and second, an evaluation of the parent's capacity to change the situation quickly enough to meet the child's present needs. These determinations are necessary and present in every case the child protective agency receives. In most instances, the effect of conditions on a child are not so deleterious that hasty decisions need to be made. The worker, however must be prepared to move according to the needs of the child in every situation. In most cases this means that a casework relationship is established within which counseling can proceed on the basis of helping the parent to meet both his own and the child's needs within the home. Where the prospect of care outside the home enters the situation, the caseworker is confronted with a new set of problems.

QUESTIONS CONCERNING PLACEMENT

When the worker reaches the point where he must consider the possibility of placement of a child outside his own home, a number of questions will be raised. Has the parent failed to respond to the caseworkers' efforts to help him become an adequate parent? Is the child so seriously affected by the home situation that the trauma of separation is less than that of continued substandard care? Can this child learn to accept substitute parental care? Are there relatives who might assist? Can the parent be helped to release the child for placement voluntarily, or will it be necessary to invoke court action to secure the removal of the child? How can the worker prepare both the child and the parent for placement? If court action is contemplated, is there sufficient legal evidence available to bring such action? Can the parent be helped to participate in the court action so as to reduce the amount of trauma for the child? If relatives are not available, what are the possibilities for placement of the child? Does this child need a placement with foster parents, or would a group setting better meet his needs? These questions must be carefully considered and, in the final analysis, one additional question—does the community possess the type of placement resources which will meet this child's needs? In no other casework program does the worker have to consider so many factors as in the field of child protection. It can be seen that the counseling process must be developed in terms of the specific responsibilities which the child protective agency has assumed. The four characteristics of this type of service impose responsibilities which necessitate an adaptation of counseling techniques and processes usually employed in other casework programs.

USE OF THE COURT

When working with the parents toward a successful adjustment of problems has failed to produce the necessary change, the caseworker in a child protective agency must consider the question of taking court action to protect the children. It should be noted that court action has different purposes according to the needs of the individual situation. In some situations the use of the court may be based upon the hope that, with the realization by the parents that this is something serious which may result in the loss of their children, they may decide to attempt to correct conditions which heretofore they have been unwilling to change. In this situation, there is no intent that the children shall be removed as a result of the action, but rather that the parents may be motivated to improve conditions which the caseworker feels they are capable of improving. On the other hand, in many situations the court is used as a tool in achieving the protection of children where parents have failed, and where in the opinion of the caseworker they are unable to change conditions. In using the court for either purpose, the child protective worker has a responsibility to prepare both the parents and the children for the action and for possible results. The worker here has to have a knowledge of the law governing neglect cases, a knowledge of the rights of the parents, and a knowledge of court procedure. He must be able to point out to the parents how they can participate constructively and how they can help the child even at this point. Where the evidence is strong both from a social and legal standpoint for the removal of children, the parents still may be able to help the child accept placement and adjust in it. Even in gross neglect situations, there are few children who really wish to be placed away from their parents, and in most instances parents can be of help in preparing children for placement, even though it is on the basis of a neglect complaint. Strange as it may seem to those who have had no experience in this field, in many cases the casework relationship does not end at the point the caseworker brings the neglect case into court. Where there has been a real casework relationship with parents and where parents have come to trust the caseworker, they can accept the fact that it is necessary for the worker to carry out his responsibility to bring the case into court and to prosecute it. This is one of the aspects of counseling within the protective setting which is not to be found in other casework settings. Not all caseworkers can adapt themselves so as to carry this important responsibility. To do this requires tremendous conviction on the part of the worker as to the necessity for this function and his desire as a professional person to serve children through an agency which must carry out this function. The way in which a worker carries it tests his integrity and ability as a professional person.

CLOSING THE CASE

Another point at which the counseling process differs from that of other fields is at the point of closing the case. In other casework settings, the client decides when he has received the service he has wanted from the agency and therefore terminates the relationship. In the protective setting both the worker and the client decide whether he can now withdraw from the situation. When the counseling process has proceeded to the point where the parents have been able to take over their full responsibility for the care of their children, and the children are now receiving adequate parental care and supervision, the agency's responsibility ceases. It is the caseworker who must determine at what point the parents have reached the goal of responsible parenthood. In some situations, however, the unfortunate fact is that parents have not been able to use the agency's service and court action has been initiated and carried through. When the matter has been referred to the court, and the agency has participated in court action with recommendations, the matter then becomes the responsibility of the court, not the agency, and the agency may then withdraw from the situation. In some cases where parents have not been able to respond, the agency may withdraw because it feels that its presence in the situation is no longer constructive and there is no legal evidence to support a charge of neglect in court. At this point, if it does withdraw, the agency has a responsibility to inform the parents that if additional complaints are received, the agency may reactivate its interest in the situation. Some cases may be closed as a result of the parents' willingness, through the intervention of the protective agency, to accept help on a voluntary basis from another casework agency which is willing to accept the parents' request for service and proceed to help them. In each instance, noted above, it is the caseworker rather than the parents who has the final responsibility for terminating the agency's interest.

SUMMARY

Counseling techniques are materially affected by the particular responsibility which the child protective agency is charged with by the community. The four fundamental differences between child protective agencies and other casework agencies call for an adaptation of counseling techniques to meet the needs of practitioners who carry out this important agency function. The specific points at which these techniques are modified are: (1) in the intake process, in which the agency seeks to determine whether or not it has a responsibility to enter a particular family situation referred to it by complaint or some one other than the parents; (2) in the agency's approach to parents which involves the identification of the agency and its purpose, explanation of the complaint, the handling of the client's hostility, and the movement into a treatment relationship which attempts to remove the causes of child neglect; (3) in the process of evaluating the need for placement of the child and preparing the child and parent for placement where that is deemed necessary; (4) in preparing parents and children for court action and carrying the case to a successful conclusion in terms of that action; and (5) in closing cases, after the agency's evaluation of the situation indicates there is no further need for that service.

BIBLIOGRAPHY

1. Standards for Child Protective Services—Child Welfare League of America, New York, 1959.
2. DeFrancis, Vincent: 1955. *The Fundamentals of Child Protection: A Statement of Basic Concepts and Principles.* American Humane Association, Children's Division, Denver, Colorado.
3. Mulford, Robert M.: October 1958. "Emotional Neglect of Children: A Challenge to Protective Services." *Child Welfare.* Also available from American Humane Association, Denver, Colorado.
4. Gordon, Henrietta L.: 1956. *Casework Services for Children.* Houghton, Mifflin Co., Boston, Chapters 15, 16.
5. Mulford, Robert M., Wylegala, Victor, B., and Melson, Elwood F.: 1956. *Caseworker and Judge in Neglect Cases.* Child Welfare League of America.
6. Sandusky, Annie Lee: 1957. *Child Welfare Services.* U.S. Children's Bureau Publication No. 359.
7. Kaufman, Irving, M.D.: February 1957. "The Contribution of Protective Services." *Child Welfare.*
8. DeFrancis, Vincent: 1958. *Let's Get Technical: The Way and What of Child Protective Services.* American Humane Association, Children's Division, Denver, Colorado.
9. Beck, Bertram M.: "Protective Casework Revitalized." *Child Welfare*, Part I —November 1955, Part II—December 1956.

The Counseling of Delinquents

RICHARD R. KORN

Lecturer in Criminology and Penology
City College, New York City
Formerly Director of Counseling
New Jersey State Prison

INTRODUCTORY

THERE has always been a large and respectable body of opinion to the effect that, for the more important problems of human life, teaching, training or the giving of advice of any kind—are fruitless. The argument, briefly put, runs as follows: "For those who can profit from it, the advice is unnecessary. For those who need it, the advice is futile." It has been pointed out that those who insist on the futility of advice are violating their own principle in the very act of uttering it—for, if it is fruitless to give advice then it is equally fruitless to advise against advising. In any event, those who assert the futility of education in general can take comfort from the admonitory literature dealing with the treatment of delinquents in particular.* Rarely in the history of social endeavor has so little been accomplished by so many on behalf of so few.

The present writer must reluctantly concur with this disheartening observation—though with reservations strong enough to mention. If teaching in this area is a poor substitute or preparation for experience, then experience alone is frequently a very poor, and certainly a most inarticulate, teacher. Furthermore, if those who instruct or advise about the treatment of delinquents have had little success, it is also true that those who rely exclusively on practical experience have hardly done better. The uncritical repetition of poor practices is probably

* They will undoubtedly draw comfort from this chapter.

more harmful than the reiteration of impractical doctrines. One possible insight into the dilemma may derive from the frequently cited (but nonetheless estimable) observation that the teachers rarely practice —and the practitioners rarely teach. *One reason why experience alone may be a poor teacher is that the practitioner does not usually become aware of what he himself is doing except in the attempt to communicate it to others.* It is in this sense, perhaps, that to teach is also to learn.

As a reading of the preceding pages of this volume might suggest, both theory and practice in the field of counseling are highly controversial. An equally thick cloud of controversy and ambiguity obscures the fruitful discussion of the causes and remedies of crime and delinquency. As in similarly uncertain fields, the relative lack of reliable knowledge has had its usual consequences in the proliferation of countless nostrums by innumerable medicine men; the vacuum has been filled, and the inverse relationship between demonstrated truth and insistent dogma has held with a vengeance.* It is to be expected, then, that a combining of efforts in the fields of counseling and delinquency will lead to a compounding of uncertainties. It is for this reason that the student and practitioner about to begin the application of his craft with delinquents would do well to spend considerable time in the largely intellectual, self-critical task of questioning his own preconceptions concerning both.

Since most unresolved problems in each of these areas are related to most others, the process of self-questioning, once begun, may appropriately begin at any point. The counselor might start by asking: How may the potential client population of delinquents be differentiated from other client populations—and to what extent do these differences pose problems requiring modification of standard counseling techniques? Equally important, to what extent do delinquents differ significantly from each other—what are the sources and ranges of variation within the client population itself? Under what circumstances will the counselor and the delinquent encounter each other—and under what circumstances will counseling be carried on? How will the counseling process and its consequences be affected by these situational factors? What are the relations between various forms of delinquency

* The absence of reliable knowledge typically has direr consequences in the applied social sciences than in the physical sciences, partly because of the unremitting social pressure for remedial action. Like disease, crime and delinquency pose continuous crises, in response to which the specialist is continually required to operate in spite of his uncertainty: even if he does not know what he is about, he is expected to act as if he does. The demand for concerted, consistent, and defensible action tends to harden tentative expedients into fixed social institutions whose very existence limits the range of further experimentation. The prison system itself represents the literal concretization of an historically convenient expedient into a social institution remarkably resistant even to repeated demonstrations of its inadequacies.

and various categories of psychological maladjustment? Are these relationships relatively constant—or highly variable? Specifically, under what circumstances is psychological maladjustment a cause, a result of, or irrelevant to the outbreak of delinquent behavior? In each of these contingencies, what is the appropriate counseling strategy—and the appropriate goal?

How shall the counselor evaluate the effects of his procedures? More fundamentally, how may he become critically aware of what he is doing in the first place? All may agree that the objective of correctional counseling is *rehabilitation*—but the assertion of the objective offers little guidance toward its attainment. Rehabilitation involves at least four different things: it is, firstly, an intention or aspiration of the therapist, secondly it is *something he does* in order to carry this intention out, thirdly it is something that happens to the client, and finally it is something that the client does or refrains from doing presumably as a consequence of what happened to him. Unless the counselor is able to conceptualize the relatedness, the distinctiveness, and the conditionality of each of these aspects, he has no basis for evaluating whether he is actually doing what he intends to do, whether what he believes is happening to the client is actually happening to him, and whether any of these events are consequential for his client's subsequent behavior.

If the counselor cannot hope to find answers to these questions, he must nevertheless be continually aware of them, if for no other reason than that, in the absence of a constant self-questioning attitude, he may continually be answering them—unknowingly and incorrectly.

1. CHARACTERIZING THE CLIENT POPULATION:

What is Delinquency? Who are the Delinquents? How do they differ from Non-delinquents?

Discussions of the extent and treatment of delinquency are limited by conceptions of what delinquency is. As the following analysis will indicate, the question, What is delinquency? may itself be highly misleading because it seems to suggest that a single answer is possible. In view of the variety of legal, administrative, clinical and behavioral definitions available, the assumption that any directly factual, mutually consistent answers are possible may itself be one of the principal sources of confusion. Consequently, one of the first requirements of discussion is a rejection of the simple question, What is delinquency? and the substitution of the question, What is meant when the term *delinquency* is used?

(a) The Legal Definition

As a legal concept, delinquency is considerably broader and vaguer than the legal concept of crime—for two reasons: (1) it includes many behaviors which would not be considered illegal if committed by adults and (2) the description of these behaviors is frequently much more ambiguous than would be constitutionally acceptable in criminal statutes, which generally require precise specifications of the activities labelled as illegal. The New Jersey Juvenile Delinquency Statute provides a representative modern example:

NEW JERSEY STATUTE 2A: 4–14

Juvenile delinquency is hereby defined as the commission by a child under 18 years of age of (1) any act which when committed by a person of the age of 18 or over would constitute:

    a. A felony, high misdemeanor, misdemeanor or other offense, or
    b. The violation of any penal law or municipal ordinance, or
    c. Any act or offense for which he could be prosecuted in the method partaking of the nature of a criminal action or proceeding, or
    d. Being a disorderly person,

or (2) the following acts:

    e. Habitual vagrancy, or
    f. Incorrigibility, or
    g. Immorality, or
    h. Knowingly associating with thieves or vicious or immoral persons, or
    i. Growing up in idleness or delinquency, or
    j. Knowingly visiting gambling places, or patronizing other places or establishments, his (or her) admission to which constitutes a violation of law, or
    k. Idly roaming the streets at night, or
    l. Habitual truancy from school, or
    m. Deportment endangering the morals, health or general welfare of said child.[8]

The most cursory reading of this typical inventory of delinquent behavior should make two conclusions abundantly clear: (1) many of the activities specified as delinquent are no different from those engaged in, at one time or another, by all children: (2) since either all or the vast majority of children at one time or another engage in these activities, and since only a small proportion of these children are either socially labeled or officially processed as delinquents, *something more than the mere engaging in these activities is required for the social identification of a child as delinquent.* This "something more" is formal, administrative action on the part of the law-enforcement agents of society.

(b) Administrative Definitions of Delinquency

Formal administrative action by law-enforcement agents may take several forms, and estimates of the extent of delinquency will vary according to the index used. If *police complaints* are used, one figure will result; if *court appearance* is used, the figure will be different; if *commitment to an institution* is used, a third figure will result. In a study investigating the estimates of delinquency made on the basis of these different indices of delinquency, Kobrin found the following:

> During the seven year period 1927–1933 the rate of (institutional) commitment per 100 boys of juvenile court age residing in Chicago in the ten square mile area with the highest rates was 6.1. . . . During the same period the rate of official court delinquents . . . was 14.6. . . . In contrast to both commitment and juvenile court appearances . . . the average rate of delinquents based on police complaints . . . was 20.6.[6]

Thus, when *police complaints* were used as the index of delinquency (in contrast to court appearance or commitments to institutions), the rate of delinquency in the area "rose" to more than one out of 5 children in the neighborhood studied. Then Kobrin looked further. The rates just cited were based only on *one year* of the seven year period under study; as such they did not provide an estimate of the incidence of delinquency during the entire age range of eligibility for these children (age ten to seventeen). On the basis of a survey of police complaints throughout the entire seven year period, Kobrin was able to estimate that 65.9 per cent of the children in the area had engaged in behavior "serious enough to warrant recorded police attention" between the ages of ten and seventeen.

What is essential to note here is that the formal law-enforcement action often went beyond "recorded police complaints". These children were *not* taken to court, they were not formally adjudicated delinquent —and they were not institutionalized—though there is no reason to believe that their misbehavior was significantly less serious than the behavior of the adjudicated and institutionalized children. Thus, what differentiated these non-adjudicated, non-institutionalized delinquents from the others was not what they did but what was done to them by agents of the society.

Commenting on the problems of definition raised by Kobrin's figures, George Vold has raised these questions:

> How delinquent does a boy have to be before he is found delinquent? Is a boy delinquent whenever a social worker, or a neighbor, or some other citizen so reports him? If that criterion is accepted, it seems clear that the proportion of the total number of delinquents in any area called delinquent would be greatly increased. It might even be true that the majority of all juveniles in all areas would be found to be delinquent—in which case one would be confronted with the awkward conclusion that all areas are delinquency areas![12]

The suspicion voiced by Vold to the effect that most children in all areas might be found delinquent, on the basis of a purely behavioral criterion, has been strongly supported. In a study comparing rates of delinquency based on institutionalization with rates based on reported behavior, Short and Nye found evidence which strikingly refutes the common and still current assumption that delinquent behavior is disproportionately higher in the lower socioeconomic status levels.* The class-distribution of delinquents in the institution studied by these authors confirmed the conventional expectation, revealing 50.0% of the inmates in the lowest socioeconomic stratum, 32.9% in the next higher, 13.0% in the second upper stratum and only 4.1% in the highest stratum. However, when they turned their attention to offenses of equal seriousness admitted by juveniles in the open community, the authors found that only 16.0% of the juveniles reporting similar behavior belong to the lowest stratum, 38.4% in the next higher stratum, 34.6 in the next and 11.0 in the highest.[10]

Commenting on their data, the authors criticize the "usual procedure of assuming that a group of institutionalized children are 'delinquent', [in contrast to] a group of non-institutionalized children who are defined as non-delinquent." Contrasting these more conventional procedures with the data revealed by their own, they add, significantly:

> For purposes of etiological inquiry, such data have the advantage that they can recognize the existence of institutionalization and in fact study its influence as an etiological process.[11]

We are now in a position to summarize our conclusions regarding the question *how does the delinquent client population differ from other (nondelinquent) client populations?* (1) There is no valid basis for assuming that the behavior of officially adjudicated delinquents differs significantly from the illegal behavior of a vastly larger population of children, committing similar acts, who are not formally processed as deliquents. (2) What strikingly differentiates the officially processed delinquents from those whose behavior is either not detected, or not officially acted upon, is a chain of socio-legal processes ranging from (a) arrest, (b) formal adjudication as delinquent, (c) official supervision and restriction within the open community to (d) brief or prolonged incarceration in the enforced company of similarly processed children in correctional institutions.

* See also PORTERFIELD, AUSTIN L.: 1946. *Youth in Trouble*. Fort Worth, Texas: The Leo Potishman Foundation. In this early study of reported delinquency Porterfield found that the violations admitted by college students of Texas Christian University exceeded, both in number and seriousness, the charges brought against a comparable sample of delinquents brought before a nearby juvenile court.

II. HOW DO DELINQUENTS DIFFER FROM EACH OTHER?

In the foregoing discussion we have already suggested a partial and tentative answer to the question *what differentiates delinquents (as delinquents)* from each other?* Our conclusion was that the most visible and demonstrable difference derives not from the nature of the delinquent behavior itself, but rather from the nature and extent of the community reactions to this behavior—reactions ranging from tolerance or indifference to prolonged correctional incarceration. We have, in effect, implied that it makes a difference whether or not juvenile misbehavior is tolerated and ignored ("Don't worry, he'll grow out of it"), informally dealt with in the family setting ("He'll get what's coming to him when Dad comes home") or formally punished by the impersonal law-enforcement agents of society ("We hereby commit you, during the period of your minority, to the New York State Training School at Otisville").

We will now examine the hypothesis that the nature of the societal reaction is not only the most visible and demonstrable source of differentiation, but the most crucial and consequential as well—not merely for the child and the society at large, but for the character and course of his relationship with the therapeutic resources made available to him, among which is counseling. For it must also be pointed out that, just as the vast number of children committing delinquent acts never come to the attention of the community as *delinquents,* so also do they rarely, if ever, come to the attention of counselors as delinquents. With distressingly few exceptions (some of which we will discuss) the overwhelming number of delinquents seen by counselors are seen after they have been formally processed, and most frequently as a result of or in connection with this processing. It follows, then, that a chain of events so consequential to the child must be of similar consequence to the counselor.

The most consequential experience in this chain of events, and the most extreme and prototypical expression of the formalized societal response to the delinquent is correctional incarceration. Partly because of its eventfulness and the fact that, in itself, it initiates a train of experiences and consequences entirely novel to the delinquent himself and to other misbehaving children, and partly because it focuses the problems of the delinquent–counselor encounter in their most glaring form

* Our focus of concern here is, of course, one of gross, global differentiation. Nothing in this discussion implies a denial of the existence or significance of individual differences of all kinds—though it should be pointed out that efforts to establish systematic or significant individual differences between delinquents and non-delinquents have so far proven unvalidatable.

and clearest light, we shall concentrate our discussion upon the counseling situation in the institutional setting.

Before turning to this, however, it might be useful to consider a number of objections and alternatives to the conclusions we have advanced.

(1)

We have suggested that the most significant basis for distinguishing delinquents from non-delinquents—and delinquents from each other—is not their behavior, but rather the extent and severity of their treatment, the most consequential and severe form of which is incarceration. *Is it not more plausible to assume that the degree of severity or extremity of this treatment is, itself, an expression of and reaction to the seriousness of their original delinquency in the first place?*

A number of considerations militate against agreement with this more comfortable explanation. (a) An increasing number of studies, such as that by Short and Nye (cited above) indicate that delinquent behavior is more or less normally distributed among all socioeconomic status levels, while rates of incarceration are disproportionately concentrated at the lower end of the socioeconomic continuum. (b) The credibility of the explanation that less privileged children tend, on the whole, to commit more serious delinquencies is lessened by the findings of several careful studies which indicated that the delinquencies reported by middle and upper class children at least equal and may even exceed, in extent and seriousness, those charged against adjudicated and institutionalized delinquents. (c) The well-known and frequently demonstrated fact that the greater financial and social resources of more privileged families provide them with many more non-public remedial resources than are available to the less privileged in the event of all types of family crises (including physical and mental disease, as well as delinquency) *together with the fact that differential risk of exposure to law-enforcement processes is demonstrably a function of socioeconomic status* suggests that the basis of the differential is not the more serious delinquency of the poorer delinquent but rather the inferiority of his social alternatives. The parents of the well-to-do child apprehended for a serious delinquency have a number of alternatives. They can hire private professional help. They can send the child to a private boarding school or psychiatric facility. As a last resort, they can move out of the neighborhood and the jurisdiction. Since most conscientious juvenile court judges seek to avoid institutionalizing a child and actively reach out toward any plausible alternative compatible with community protection and the welfare of the child, one or a combination of these dispositions is likely to forstall incarceration.

9

(2)

There is a second category of objection to the line of reasoning we have advanced. *If, as is alleged, the institutionalized delinquents were originally, on the whole, not essentially different and not more seriously "delinquent" than other delinquents, then how and why does mere institutionalization make them so different after? What is so consequential, so serious and so differentiating about institutionalization? If they were not, somehow, different before, they would not be different later.*

Dealing first with the question of the "seriousness" or "consequentiality" of institutionalization: (a) statistical studies of criminal careers indicate that the large majority of persistent adult offenders have prior records of juvenile adjudication, including institutional dispositions; (b) comparative studies of those juvenile offenders discharged without adjudication, those adjudicated but granted probation, and those sent to institutions indicate the factor of previous institutionalization greatly increases the statistical risk of later recidivism. It is, in fact, the single best predictor of subsequent delinquency and crime.

Dealing with the question *why institutionalization introduces such drastic, consequential, and differentiating changes in delinquents who originally may have been no different from other juveniles who misbehave* leads us into the heart of our discussion and provides the framework for our analysis of the prototypical situation in which the delinquent and the counselor encounter each other.

By way of preface, it should be noted that the general conception of *drastic situational factors inducing drastic personal changes in individuals and groups* is novel neither to behavioral theory nor to human experience. There are many situations and experiences which drastically reduce the range of variation among those exposed to them. The population of today's *young married fathers* is drastically different from the identical population of yesterday's *gay young bachelors*—though exactly the same individuals are involved. They are not only different from what they once were, but less different now from each other than they used to be. And they are very different, as a group, from that other population of gay young bachelors, their old companions, who are still gay young bachelors: an almost unbridgeable chasm separates them, though only a few years have passed. Again, contrast the rough and ready population of ten-year-olds who "don't care at all about girls" with the identical population six years later—who care about little else.

Consider, as more appropriate to our own problem, the vast contrasts between the collection of raw recruits entering the Marine "Boot Camp" and the same individuals emerging a few months later. Each is still the "same" person but the attitudes and behavior of each is significantly more similar, in part at least, because their experiences and present situations have induced and require a rigid conformity to identical norms. *If they did not conform they could not survive as Marines.* Consider, finally, the case of a twelve-year-old, removed from his family, his home, and his neighborhood and required to live in a society of older, more powerful juveniles from whose 24-hour association there is no escape, from whose punishments there is no redress, to whose leadership there is no alternative, from whose code there is no appeal, and in whose way of life there are only two alternatives: emulation and conformity or resistance and humiliation. In the chronicles written by the survivors of concentration camps there are isolated instances of heroes and martyrs who risked their lives in order to preserve their human dignity. In the case-histories of training schools there are doubtless instances of twelve-year-olds who found it possible to survive without becoming liars, thieves, connivers and bullies—and who somehow managed to emerge, years later, with an unshattered integrity. Whenever they can be found their names deserve to be enrolled on the same roster of heroes and martyrs.

Though it is difficult to be dispassionate with this issue, it is essential that it be stated clearly and without risk of unintentional misunderstanding. We are not asserting that the greater liability of institutionalized delinquents to future criminality "proves" that correctional institutions "cause" delinquency. To say this would be tantamount to asserting that mental hospitals cause mental disease—simply because rates of mental illness always rise when new mental hospitals begin functioning. What we are suggesting is that confinement to a correctional institution exposes the delinquent to the identical social pressures and influences which were largely responsible for his original delinquencies—with the important difference that these factors are severely intensified and there is no escape from them. One need do little more than go down the list of delinquent activities cited in the New Jersey Juvenile Statute quoted above—and match these activities with the characteristics of what Goffman has knowingly called the "underlife of a total institution."[2]

"Incorrigibility." An indispensable requirement for social prestige in the inmate social system is effective resistance to the staff's attempts to make one a "good boy". (Effective simulation is tolerated—but only if it is really simulated.)

"Immorality." The incidence of homosexuality in juvenile institutions, though difficult to calculate with ideal accuracy, is considered by experts and most candid inmates to be extremely high. In some institutions it is endemic.[*]

* See Kinsey: "We have never secured histories from any long-term institution in which fewer than sixty per cent of the men were engaged in such activity, and in one institution we had over ninety per cent of the inmates admit such experience within the institution." Private communication cited by Barnes & Teeters in *New Horizons in Criminology*, 3rd Ed. New Jersey: Prentice–Hall, 1959, p. 373.

"Knowingly associating with thieves or vicious or immoral persons." As commanded by the Juvenile Court, which, ironically, may send the child back to the institution if he is later found to be associating with the same "thieves or vicious persons" on the street.

The list of delinquent activities to which the child is exposed and with which he is required, under terrific social pressure, to conform in the juvenile institution, would greatly exceed the list compiled by the less vivid criminological imagination of the adults who write the delinquency statutes. What is more home to our purpose is the awareness that the pressures which maximate antisocial attitudes and behavior in the institution are precisely those which confront the counselor in his attempt to change them.

One further set of citations before we turn to consider the situation confronting the correctional counselor, the first from that astute prison-visitor George Bernard Shaw, the second from a more recent observer. Though Shaw rigorously repudiated the Lombrosian notion of a "criminal-type," he could not deny that a "prison-type" existed. With characteristic acuteness, however, Shaw pointed to the prison environment as the source of the stereotype, and his comment, foreshadowing Clemmer's brilliant later studies of "prisonization" describes the de-differentiating effects of institutional life:

> ... The criminal type is an artificial type, manufactured in prison by the prison system .... The type is not one of the accidents of the system but must be produced by imprisonment no matter how normal the victim is at the beginning, or how anxious the authorities are to keep him so. The simple truth is that the typical prisoner is a normal man when he enters the prison and develops the type during his imprisonment.[9]

In his study of total institutions of all kinds, Goffman writes of the "moral career of the mental patient" in terms directly applicable to the confined offender. As we have suggested of the delinquent institution, Goffman suggests that the mental hospital, though not responsible for the patient's original disease, envelops him in an environment in many ways conducive to its perpetuation:

> Persons who become mental patients vary widely in the kind and degree of illness that a psychiatrist would impute to them, and in the attributes by which a layman would describe them. But once started on the way, they are confronted by some importantly similar circumstances and respond to these in importantly similar ways. Since these similarities do not come from mental illness, they would seem to occur in spite of it. It is thus a tribute to the power of social forces that the uniform status of the mental patient cannot only assure an aggregate of persons a common fate and eventually, because of this, a common character, but that this social reworking can be done on what is perhaps the most obstinate diversity of human materials that can be brought together by society.[2]

Though a number of the foregoing observations were drawn from adult institutional life, they do not importantly deviate from conditions known to workers in juvenile institutions.* They may, in fact, be even more exacerbated—for one important reason. Though isolated from the world and life of adults on the outside, the inmates of adult institutions are cared for, controlled, and treated by fellow adults. The juvenile offender suffers from a double isolation, the first common to children and adolescents, the second unique to young persons who are institutionalized. The counselor confronting the juvenile in an institution must struggle to reach him over this double gap, a distance of age widened by institutional alienation. Thus, to the difficulty of meeting an individual enmeshed in an environment largely incomprehensible even to those who work but do not live in it is added the difficulty of dealing with a person in another world of life—a world in which the adult once lived but from which, except for the uniquely gifted, his maturity has permanently exiled him. Intimate communication over this chasm is rendered even more difficult by the fact that the juvenile endures his double exile in a crowd of other exiles for whom the gap is a heavily protected barrier against a hostile adult world—a barrier the counselee may cross only at great personal risk.

III. THE COUNSELING SITUATION:
Under what circumstances will the counselor and the delinquent encounter each other? Under what circumstances will the counseling be carried out?

Irrespective of whether the counselor meets the delinquent in an institution, in a probation setting, or in a private agency, the circumstances in which typically they encounter each other differ in many ways from those obtaining in the usual counselor–client interaction. In order to explore the novel problems presented by these circumstances, and to relate them to the goals of counseling itself, it is first necessary to establish some basis of agreement about what those goals are. We have chosen to stress goals rather than techniques, at this point in the discussion, for two reasons: (1) while there is considerable variation and

* In a recent review of Gordon Trasler's book, *A Study of Foster Care*, Professor Harris Chaiklin takes note of the author's observation that the highest rate of failures on foster care—and the sickest children—spent their early life in institutions. Commenting on this observation, Professor Chaiklin writes: "This agrees with repeated studies about the effects of institutional life. ... The evidence indicates that when children are placed in large, congregate institutions ... society is initiating a long drawn out process of ritual murder. We need fewer studies of adjustment to institutional life and more on how to get rid of institutions." *Journal of Health and Human Behavior, 1962: **3**, p. 62.*

some disagreement about appropriate techniques—not only in the field of counseling, but in any psychotherapeutic field—there is much greater agreement concerning the desirable objectives of any method; (2) since the techniques themselves are designed as means to achieve certain ends, the evaluation of the efficacy of those techniques is to be made with reference to those ends.

Some years ago, the writer attempted a survey of contemporary treatment theories for the purpose of extracting a core of shared principles. The following represents his understanding of the aims common to all techniques, from short-term counseling to extended depth analysis;

1. The client must somehow be helped toward an awareness that his difficulties are, at least in part, related to motives and patterns of perception within himself. His attempts to account for all or most of his difficulties by blaming a hostile or indifferent human environment must be understood by him to derive, at least in part, from a natural human tendency to avoid feelings of guilt, inadequacy, or self-rejection. He must be assisted toward the gaining of an awareness of the necessity of taking a present initiative toward change within himself, and he must be helped to see the fruitlessness of evading his responsibility toward himself by futile attempts to change merely his environment, or other people.

2. This assistance toward understanding comes about in the course of the relationship with the therapist or the therapeutic situation in which the individual invariably first attempts to make his faulty modes of perception and behavior work. Repeated demonstrations of his failure may be necessary before he is able to abandon them. It is important, however, that these failures be used as a basis for further exploration rather than interpreted by him as merely confirming his feelings of helplessness or worthlessness. He must be helped toward understanding that even these feelings are, in a certain sense, excuses for evading his primary responsibility of self-help.

3. Finally, the client must be shown (or provided with opportunities for) the learning, testing, and fixating of newer, more effective modes of perception and response. As these new learning patterns emerge and are found rewarding in terms of increased success with the self and others, they tend to become more and more established in the individual's total pattern of adjustment.*

It is widely agreed that the therapeutic changes based on these processes are critically dependent on the person's taking the essential first step of acknowledging that he is in difficulty—that "something is wrong". The nature and extent of this acknowledgement—which can vary from "something is wrong with *me*" to "something is wrong with everybody *but* me" may be said to define the client's *accessibility* to counseling in the first place; it is usually implied when the individual decides to seek help.

It is now possible to make some general observations with respect to how the typical circumstances of the delinquent's encounter with the counselor reflect upon the delinquent's accessibility for counseling.

* Adapted from the chapter, "Problems, Issues and Alternatives in Correctional Treatment" in the author's text, *Criminology and Penology*. New York: Henry Holt, 1959, p. 533.

(1) *The decision to seek help in the first place is rarely, if ever, made by the delinquent himself.* Though counseling is occasionally sought by persons with antisocial feelings, self-referral by delinquents as such is virtually non-existent. Almost invariably, the delinquent is sent for counseling by someone else who has defined him, in one way or another, as a "boy in trouble"—frequently the first words the counselor hears are some variant of the comment, "*They* sent me because *they say* I need help." In many cases, "they"—the source of the referral—represent, in the delinquent's mind, the source of the trouble as well, as in the case of the persistent school problem referred to the guidance counselor by the principal, or the probationer referred to court clinic and required to attend as a condition of his probation. (2) *The counselor dealing with delinquents is usually connected with an agency or institution having either direct or implied commitments and responsibilities to community policy concerning delinquency.* As a paid employee or a salaried consultant, the counselor has considerably less flexibility than his colleague in private practice—and both he and his delinquent client know this. Moreover, if there is not a close harmony between the counselor's own therapeutic orientation and agency policy, the delinquent is bound to know this too—and likely, as well, to exploit it since, as frequently happens, the delinquent's own "program" for himself may be in conflict with agency policy. This situation is extremely vulnerable to the unwitting transformation of the counseling relationship into a kind of tacit anti-agency alliance between the counselor and his client—and a consequent reinforcement of the delinquent's already intense attitudes against authority. (3) *Most clients receiving professional help are expected or required to pay for it as part of their own contribution to self-help or recovery; as agency clients or institutional inmates, delinquents lack or are denied this opportunity.* Though there is considerable room for debate over the question of whether and how much underprivileged clients, including delinquents, should be required to contribute, there is general agreement that effective treatment requires strong involvement and "self-investment" by the client. Indifferent or grudging participation can be as harmful as excessive dependency. However, in a context in which participation by the delinquent is frequently obligatory rather than voluntary, it is hard to see, at this point, how the motive to contribute can arise. (4) *As a client group, delinquents tend to be excessively committed to the kinds of associations and relationships which have contributed to their difficulties—and isolated from the kinds of associations which could support and reward non-delinquent behavior.* With the possible exception of the deteriorated drug addict and alcoholic, the seriously delinquent child is uniquely isolated within, and dependent upon, a social context which is supportive of his problems, and hostile to their solution. This isolation is directly fostered by the administrative

processes which formally and publicly differentiate him from "non-delinquent" children, processes which attain their maximum efficiency and ultimate effect when the child is forcibly incarcerated with other delinquents. The counselor is thus required to deal with a client whose social world is not only empty of significant positive figures, but dominated or powerfully influenced by negative figures. These associates of the client—often defined as "all the friends I've got"—are, moreover, typically hostile to counseling and to the counselor. Since they are also, simultaneously, large contributors to the client's continuing delinquent activities,* a counseling situation which fails in one way or another to deal with their "hold" on the client is constantly in danger of losing the client himself. One of the advantages of group counseling, as a technique, is the possibility it offers of dealing with the client in his own social world, reaching him in and through the group that reached him first—and which still holds him. *Conversely, one of the disadvantages of individual counseling with delinquents is the counselor's lack of contact and influence with the delinquent's group—a group to which he may return immediately after each counseling session.*

All of the forementioned factors reflect negatively in the deliquent's *accessibility to counseling.* Because these factors operate with maximal intensity and effect in the juvenile institution, it is profitable to examine them in that setting. Before turning to this examination, however, it would be useful to discuss one further basic question which bears directly on the problems presented by delinquents and the alternatives and resources available to the counselor.

IV. THE RELATION OF PSYCHOLOGICAL MALADJUSTMENT TO DELINQUENT BEHAVIOR

In considering his strategy, the counselor must make some assessment of the psychological resources and liabilities his client brings into the counseling situation. This assessment in the case of each individual client will be influenced by the counselor's general orientation to the client population as a whole. Professional opinion concerning the incidence and relation of psychological maladjustment to delinquency and crime is very sharply divided, the viewpoints ranging, at one extreme, from the conviction that delinquency is invariably an effect of

* In a study comparing 500 delinquents with 500 non-delinquents in the same area, the Gluecks found that 98.4 per cent of the delinquents associated with other delinquents, while only 7.4 per cent of the non-delinquents had delinquent associates. (Sheldon & Eleanor Glueck, *Delinquents in the Making.* New York: Harper. 1952, p. 89.)

mental disturbance, to another extreme, which asserts that delinquency is most often an *alternative* to mental disturbance.

The discussion is as heated as it is divided. Thus, for example, writes the noted forensic psychiatrist Dr. David Abrahamsen:

> In all my experience I have never been able to find one single offender who did not show some mental pathology, in his emotions or in his character or in his intelligence. The "normal" offender is a myth. . . . There is little doubt that if we had sufficiently refined methods of examining delinquent persons, we would find that all of them suffer from some form of mental disorder.[1]

Commenting on this statement, the sociologist George Vold writes:

> If this is to be accepted at face value, one can only marvel at the ability of this psychiatrist to maintain contact for many years with groups of prisoners and not to have encountered the business in crime, the "operator" who functions in crime in a manner similar to that of his counterpart in legitimate business activity. The author seems unaware of the well-established fact that about 90 per cent of the offenses known to the police are not those directed against persons but against property, in the understandable quest of getting a maximum return for a minimum of effort.
>
> If the phenomenon of crooked and dishonest dealing, of which crimes against property represent a small fraction, is interpreted as mental abnormality, this is in effect saying that the entire population is sick and abnormal, except, perhaps, for the few misunderstood psychiatrists so vainly struggling to stem the tide of all-pervasive misconduct.[12]

Despite its persistence in many schools of current psychiatric thinking, the identification of delinquency and mental disorder no longer goes unchallenged by individual psychiatrists. The sharpest skepticism is expressed by those who have worked in close contact with offenders. Thus, Dr. Richard Jenkins:

> . . . The assertion that all or a major fraction of delinquency can be accounted for as neurotic behavior neither rings true nor makes sense.
>
> Inner conflict and neuroticism are typically associated with a high level of inhibition, sense of duty, introjected standards and super-ego controls. The typical delinquent, on the other hand, is characterized by a personality and way of life relatively free from the dominance, let alone the tyranny, of such inner tendencies. In this regard, he is quite likely to be freer than the rest of us. Usually he has a certain earthy realism *and is less, rather than more, inclined to be neurotic than is the non-delinquent.*[46] [italics supplied]

Sociologists have long held the view that many forms of crime and delinquency may be well within the range of normal behavior. Merton, for one, has pointed out that certain types of illegality "constitute a 'normal' response to a situation where the cultural emphasis upon . . . success has been absorbed, but where there is little access to conventional and legitimate means for becoming successful."[7] Dr. Jenkins concurs in this view and describes a major proportion of delinquency as the product of "the same motivation our culture sanctions as the force which keeps our competitive economy ticking . . . "⁵ Jenkins has called this type of delinquency "adaptive". Adaptive delinquents are distinguished from those whose clearly disturbed adjustment and poorly integrated behavior indicates an etiology based on compulsive response to frustration rather than on discriminative and adaptive goal-seeking.

A close reading of the opposing positions of Abrahamsen and Jenkins reveals a certain similarity in conceptualization, despite the fact that each arrives at a different conclusion. Each assumes a fairly direct, implicitly uncomplicated relationship between the offender's mental condition and his illegal behavior. Having invariably found some form of mental disturbance in the offenders he studied, Abrahamsen concludes implicitly that their illegal activities *were caused* by their pathology and must, ipso facto, be pathological activities. Where Abrahamsen conceptualized in a one-way direction from mental condition to activity, Jenkins, starting at the activity end, worked in a one-way direction back to the mental condition. Having ascertained that certain types of crime and delinquency were highly rational, goal-directed, and rewarding, he concluded that the offenders engaging in these activities were, ipso facto, rational. What both conceptualizations ignore is the possibility (1) that persons who are disturbed may engage in certain rational and rewarding activities and (2) that essentially healthy persons can behave in ways which are maladaptive, illogical, and unrewarding. In effect, each assumed that the relationship between psychological condition and type of activity is invariate and unmediated.

The inappropriateness of this limited frame of reference becomes apparent when one attempts to apply it to other activity or career patterns. There are healthy bankers and unhealthy bankers, disturbed shoemakers and non-disturbed shoemakers. Moreover, certain disturbed bankers and shoemakers are quite efficient and successful as bankers and shoemakers—while certain healthy members of these professions are professional failures. Presumably, there may also be healthy and disturbed, successful and unsuccessful professional thieves, bankrobbers, and confidence men as well. These examples suggest another line of possibility.

Unquestionably, a very severe degree of maladjustment will ultimately interfere with functioning. The disturbed banker may become so disturbed that he can no longer function effectively as a banker. *So, too, may the disturbed bank robber, the disturbed shoplifter, the disturbed juvenile thief.* If it is plausible to believe that effectiveness in carrying out skilled non-criminal tasks requires a certain minimal degree of adjustment, there seems no reason to exclude the skilled activities of many delinquents and criminals from this general rule. Seen in this light, the relationship between good psychological adjustment, *as such* and criminal behavior *may frequently be mutually supporting rather than mutually exclusive.**

Pursuit of this line of reasoning raises an equally plausible but much more frightening possibility. When the banker and the shoemaker become so disturbed that they can no longer function, they may turn to psychotherapy in the hope that effective treatment may, among other things, help them to function better. Presumably, effective treatment for their psychological problems will do just that: they will emerge from their treatment to function effectively again as bankers and shoemakers. What, then, of the juvenile gang leader who suffers from a psychic trauma which reduces his *élan* and *éclat* but which leaves his antisocial values and aggressive interpersonal orientations intact? Presumably, a course of therapy which *effectively restores his feelings of adequacy but fails to change his values and attitudes will enable him to be a more effective gang leader.*

These considerations suggest that a full grasp of the whole range of possible relations between psychological adjustment and delinquency is an absolute prerequisite for determining the appropriate strategy and the appropriate target of counseling in the individual case. For purposes of clarity we will now attempt to summarize and schematize this range of possible relations.

A. From a purely mental health standpoint, a given delinquent may be:
    1. Relatively disturbed or
    2. Relatively symptom free
B. If he is relatively disturbed, his delinquent activities may be:
    1. Largely irrelevant to his disturbance
    2. Largely caused by his disturbance
    3. Largely the cause of his disturbance
C. Whether he is disturbed or symptom free (i.e., in either case), the personal consequences of his delinquent activities may be:
    1. Relatively rewarding, materially or socially
    2. Relatively unrewarding, materially or socially

Implicit in this outline of the possible relations between personal adjustment and personal activities are two assumptions: (1) the individual's total personal adjustment influences not merely *what* he chooses to do and *why* (his motivation) but also *how* he succeeds in doing it (Thus an individual can, for the most neurotic reasons, decide on a

---

* The relationship is frequently seen in precisely this light by law-enforcement authorities—and by offenders themselves. The police tend to regard the clever and calculating professional with considerably more apprehension than the terrified and bungling amateur. The discriminating bank robber will have nothing to do with a get-away man upset by neurotic feelings about bank-theft.

line of activity and have sufficient resources to carry it out efficiently);
(2) a line of activity, or a way of life (adopted because of any combination of psychological and situational determinants) involves the individual in *consequences* which are more or less rewarding or unrewarding
in a social context and network of close relationships which are relatively
supportive and approving or relatively non-supportive and disapproving.
Sufficient reward and social support gives rise to *attitudes and values* in
favor of the activity and powerfully reinforcing it. When these attitudes
and values become firmly and harmoniously established in the self-
concept (i.e., become "egosyntonic") the individual's continuing commitment to the activities become less and less dependent on his original
motivation, *and hence, less relevant* to it and more and more dependent
on the context of reward and social approval supporting those values and
attitudes. At this point *his purely psychological condition* tends less and less
to influence *what* he does and tends primarily to affect *how he does it.*
What we are thus, in effect, saying is that the complex of determinants
which were originally etiologic to the behavior may not be the same
which determine its continuity and persistence.

At some point a decision, a commitment is made: the bank clerk has
decided to become a banker, the apprentice has decided to become a
shoemaker, the juvenile delinquent has decided to become a professional
thief. Sick or well, they will attempt to continue to function in these
activities and they will function, efficiently or inefficiently until such
time as they are either too disturbed to go on, have ceased to like or
enjoy what they are doing, or have found something better.

We will now suggest a working typology of delinquents based on the
variable relationships of these factors or dimensions, using the terms
"disturbed and symptom-free" to refer to the continuum of mental
health, the terms "adaptive and non-adaptive" to refer to the continuum
of rewarding or non-rewarding consequences, and the term "pro-
delinquent attitudes, values and associations" to refer to the presence
or absence of personal commitment to delinquent roles.

Analysis of Table I suggests a basis of expectation for the kinds of
problems to be presented by each psychosocial type of misbehaving
child, a basis of predicting the social impact of their institutional experiences and a basis of speculation concerning their accessibility and
the probable consequences of effective counseling directed at one or
more aspects of their total psychosocial situations.

In general, Types I through IV will be minimally accessible to
counseling, being committed to a system of values and variously enmeshed in a social system which is hostile and punitive to the acknowledgement of personal difficulties. Moreover, while Types I and II are
in actual need of psychotherapeutic help, successful counseling aimed

exclusively at their disturbances is likely to improve the effectiveness of their delinquent behavior in two ways: (1) increasing their ability to relate to other members of their delinquent reference groups; and (2) improving their general competence and, consequently, the probability of reward. Type III will, in most cases, enjoy high status among other delinquents, both in and out of the correctional institution, will

TABLE 1

PSYCHOSOCIAL TYPOLOGY OF DELINQUENTS

Psychosocial type	Presence of psychic disturbance	Commitment to pro-delinquent values, attitudes, and associates	Rewarding consequences
I Disturbed, adaptive socialized delinquent	YES	YES	YES
II Disturbed, non-adaptive socialized delinquent	YES	YES	NO
III Symptom-free, adaptive socialized delinquent	NO	YES	YES
IV Symptom-free, non-adaptive socialized delinquent	NO	YES	NO
V Disturbed, non-socialized non-adaptive delinquent	YES	NO	NO
VI Disturbed, non-socialized adaptive delinquent	YES	NO	YES
VII Symptom-free, non-socialized non-adaptive delinquent	NO	NO	NO
VIII Symptom-free, non-socialized adaptive delinquent	NO	NO	YES

frequently occupy a position of leadership because of his higher efficiency and superior interpersonal competence—and will be maximally resistant to counseling. Type IV, though less efficient in delinquent skills, will also enjoy a relatively high status among other delinquents; for him the institution will provide a social reinforcement of delinquent attitudes and the opportunity of improved training in delinquent activities.

In general, Types V through VIII will experience moderate to very severe interpersonal difficulties with other delinquents, especially in an institutional setting. Type V, the classic prototype of the neurotic delinquent, will be severely traumatized and victimized. Types VII and VIII, prototypes of the occasional delinquent, will be able to cope somewhat more effectively with other inmates, but their superior inter-personal competence will expose them to pressures of inducement to join with the healthier socialized delinquents in their anti-institutional activities. *Nevertheless, a group counseling situation capable of enlisting their support will provide a powerful wedge into the inmate social system, particularly if they have been able to form personal friendships with the healthier, socialized delinquents.*

Counseling experiences with each of these types in an institutional setting leads to some pessimistic conclusions. (1) A case-load based on self-referral (or, in most instances, even on staff referral) will tend to become saturated with the disturbed, least effective delinquents, many of whose problems are exacerbated by traumatic experiences with other inmates. Such a caseload will rarely include the less disturbed, more effective delinquents whose activities are being socially and materially rewarded and who, for this reason, are more likely to persist in delin-quency. (2) Even in the cases of the most disturbed and most accessible delinquents, individual counseling effectively directed at their psycho-logical difficulties is likely, with the possible exception of Type V (the disturbed, non-socialized, non-adaptive delinquent) to *improve* the effectiveness of their delinquent activities.

V. EVALUATING THE RESULTS OF COUNSELING

Carefully gathered, objectively evaluated research evidence con-cerning the presumed effects of counseling is rare and hard to come by. Nevertheless, the two most impressive and thorough studies available lend support to the pessimistic conclusions cited above.

The Cambridge–Somerville Youth Study

In one of the most ambitious and carefully organized attempts to determine whether early and prolonged counseling can prevent de-linquency among vulnerable children in the city of Cambridge, 325 boys between the ages of 9 and 11 were given counseling for a median period of five years. The boys receiving treatment (hereafter referred to as the T-boys) were selected on the basis of nominations as "pre-delinquents" by teachers and a committee of experts. The treatment group was carefully matched with an equal number of predelinquent boys, nominated by the same technique, who did not receive treatment and who thus represented the experimental controls. (They are here-after referred to as the C-boys.)

The results of the experiment were evaluated by means of a comparison of the behavior of both treated and non-treated boys following the termination of counseling and after the elapse of a period of exposure time in the community. Rates of court appearances and rates of institutional commitments, together with estimates of the seriousness of the delinquencies were used as indices. The following summary of findings is derived from the analysis made by Powers and Witmer; and is, except where indicated, cited verbatim:

COMPARISON OF THE T- AND C-BOYS IN RESPECT TO FREQUENCY OF COURT APPEARANCES

1. We first compare the frequency of offenses and of court appearances of the 325 T-boys and the 325 C-boys as of July 1, 1948 regardless of age at that time or the length of time the T-boys had remained in the treatment group.

Court Appearances	T	C
Number of boys	96	92
Number of offenses	264	218

2. We now compare the T-boys who had reached the age of 17 before July 1, 1948 with the C-boys matched with them in respect to the frequency of court appearances.

Court Appearances	T	C
Number of boys	68	63
Number of offenses	141	132

3. Compared to C-boys, how many T-boys committed offenses for which they were brought into court *after* their 17th birthday? (Comment: an extremely important measure of *later* post-treatment recidivism)

NUMBER OF BOYS IN COURT AND NUMBER OF OFFENSES CHARGED AGAINST THEM BETWEEN THE 17TH AND 22ND BIRTHDAYS

	Number in Court	Number of offenses
T-boys: 17th year	21	30
C-boys: 17th year	27	40
T-boys: 18th year	20	36
C-boys: 18th year	14	19
T-boys: 19th year	23	37
C-boys: 19th year	13	19
T-boys: 20th year	12	13
C-boys: 20th year	6	8
T-boys: 21st year	3	7
C-boys: 21st year	—	—

Total number of Offenders	T	123
	C	86

(*Comment:* What is particularly noteworthy here is that, with the exception of the 17th year, the number of T-boys charged with offenses progressively exceeded the number of C-boys charged with offenses during each succeeding year. By the 20th birthday, *the ratio was two to one in favor of the untreated boys.* By the 21st birthday there are no reports of C-boys appearing in court.)

(In an attempt to compare the *seriousness* of the offenses committed by the two groups, Powers and Witmer devised a "scale of seriousness" in consultation with the law-enforcement authorities of Cambridge and Somerville. All offenses were assigned a seriousness index and the number of offenses by each group was tabulated against the appropriate index.) The following data summarizes the totals in each category:

	T	C
A. Least serious	76	57
B. Fairly serious	52	31
C. Serious	88	72
D. Most serious	48	58

(Powers and Witmer note that the number of C-boys committing the most serious offenses exceeds that of the T-boys. Nevertheless, when one compares the comparative incidence of different types of offenses within this "most serious" category an interesting finding emerges. *The overall advantage of the treated boys was precisely in those types of offenses associated with severe emotional disturbance, typical of the disturbed, non-socialized non-adaptive delinquent.* The following extracts, drawn from Powers and Witmer's tables, compares the incidence of maladaptive and adaptive offense types for the two groups:

"Maladaptive" Offenses

Offense Type	T	C
Lewdness	2	2
Indecent assault and battery	0	4
Unnatural and lascivious acts	1	2
Abusing female child	1	1
Carnal abuse	0	1
Sodomy	0	1
Assault with intent to rape	1	0
	—	—
	5	11

Criminally "Adaptive" Offenses*

Offense Type	T	C
Carrying dangerous weapon	4	0
Breaking and entering	32	40
Assault and battery with dangerous weapon	2	0
Possession of burglary tools	1	0
Arson	2	1
Robbery, unarmed	2	2
Robbery, armed	0	2
Robbery by force and violence	0	1
	—	—
	43	46

What these figures suggest is that the principal advantage of counseling for the treated boys was that treatment tended to reduce the

---

* Because of its ambiguity, we have left out *manslaughter* in which the distribution was: T: 0, C: 1.

incidence of offenses more or less directly associated with psycho-pathology. The matched control group, lacking this treatment, may have been more vulnerable to the onset of the kinds of pathological adjustment associated with these acts. Nevertheless, the counseling received by the T-boys was much less effective with respect to the more adaptive offenses typically associated with gainful, goal-directed criminality. Only in the *most serious* category of this type or offense did the C-boys exceed the T-boys (46–43). In all other categories of seriousness, the T-boys committed more offenses than the C-boys (216–160) and in the total number of offenses of all types and serious, still exceeded the untreated boys (264–218).

Commenting on the failure of the experiment, Powers and Witmer state, in a footnote: "Just why the T-boys showed a slightly excessive (*sic*) number of appearances over the C-boys we cannot say. The counselors did not believe, naturally, that their influence was adverse...."*

The PICO Project

Though the counselors in the Cambridge–Somerville study shrank from the possibility that "their influence was adverse," the evaluators of another experiment in the counseling of delinquents did not. In an exceptionally careful study of counseling with institutionalized older delinquents at the Duel Vocational Institution in California, the staff of the project divided 1600 inmates into two categories: *amenable* and *nonamenable* for treatment—categories roughly equivalent to our own categories of accessibility and adjustment.† They then further divided both groups equally into treated and non-treated controls, thus obtaining four groups:

Treated Amenables
Control Amenables
Treated Nonamenables
Control Nonamenables

After the termination of treatment an evaluation was made of post-treatment behavior on the basis of a number of criteria, including *failure on parole*, length of time spent in the return to custody *after*

* All data and citations quoted from Edwin Powers and Helen Witmer, *An Experiment in the Prevention of Delinquency*, New York: Columbia University Press, 1951, pp. 320–338.

† The most salient ingredient of amenability appeared to be the quality of anxiety. ... In addition, the judgment of amenability was also influenced by evidence of "awareness of problems," "insight," "desire to change," and "acceptance of treatment." Stuart Adams, "Interaction between individual Interview Therapy and Treatment Amenability". Sacrimento: California Board of Corrections, 1961, p. 28.

failure on parole, time spent in lock-up and other measures of institutional and post-institutional adjustment.

One finding was startling. As expected, the treated amenables fared significantly better than did all other groups, while the untreated amenables and the untreated nonamenables fared about the same. However, the *treated nonamenables fared worse than the untreated nonamenables*. Facing the possibility that counseling might have been related to these results, Adams writes:

> The possibility that the treated nonamenables received the "wrong kind" of treatment is one that needs serious consideration. Jenkins has given this possibility some credence in his discussion of treatments for antisocial personalities: "If one attempts to treat the unsocialized aggressive child by the methods suitable for the overinhibited, neurotic, withdrawn child, his behavior will typically get worse." ... It is possible, therefor, that much more radical procedures are needed for (delinquents) of the kinds defined here as nonamenables.[20]

One of the contributions of the PICO study is the decisive manner in which it related treatment accessibility to treatment outcome.* It follows that a clear understanding of this relationship is a prerequisite of effective correctional counseling.

VI. THE CRITICAL PROBLEM OF ACCESSIBILITY IN CORRECTIONAL COUNSELING

It seems axiomatic that any treatment based on the variables of an interpersonal relationship requires some nexus of need or mutual interest between the participants. In the case of the neurotic, the motive force for treatment is the client's anxiety and his awareness of his failure to cope with his problems. In contrast to the neurotic whose experiences have confirmed his inadequacies, the typical delinquent has had many experiences which have confirmed the effectiveness of his adjustment. He has learned that others can be intimidated or manipulated. He has learned a contempt for authority as ineffectual or dishonest—or both. In effect, he has succeeded in establishing a

---

* Accessibility to treatment requires an acknowledgement of personal difficulties. But it is against this first and all-important acknowledgement that the delinquent peer-group and the inmate social system mobilizes all its forces and values. This mobilization typically takes the form of defining all problems in terms of grievances and demands justified by these grievances. On the basis of this orientation, the delinquent value-system divides the world of other people in terms of a simple dichotomy: there are people who exploit one, and people one exploits. This value-orientation may be an aspect of a more general response to social rejection. In many ways, the delinquent's outlook enables him to minimize the otherwise devastating effects of converting social rejection into self-rejection. In effect, it permits him *to reject his rejectors rather than rejecting himself*.

picture of himself and others which is based on a feeling of his own superiority and greater strength.

Thus, while the neurotic comes to the therapy as a consequence of his failure and with a desire to have his adjustment *changed*, the adaptive delinquent comes with a relatively undiminished confidence in his success and with the intention to continue his adjustment, in spite of environmental obstacles. This crucial distinction in the motivation for therapy determines the manner in which the therapist is defined. Where the neurotic seeks to find a person who will assist him in the modification of uncontrollable feelings and reactions, the adaptive delinquent seeks, in the therapist, a person whom he can maneuver and exploit for the purpose of attaining situational objectives with greater efficiency. Thus, in striking contrast to the neurotic whose desire for treatment is an outcome of his sense of failure, the adaptive delinquent's request for "psychological help" is frequently the outcome of the reverse motivation: an expression of confidence in his ability to manipulate human relations.*

This divergence in treatment objectives lies at the heart of the accessibility problem. The delinquent comes to the treatment situation with his true purpose of manipulation disguised in the form of a request for help. Unlike the neurotic, however, who is to some extent ready for treatment at the point he seeks it, the adaptive delinquent must be *readied* for treatment. In order to create this readiness for therapy, the therapist must somehow assist in the creation of a need for it within the delinquent. In the face of the adaptive delinquent's typical confidence in his ability to exploit human relations, this objective requires that the delinquent be provided with an experience where his manipulative skills are thwarted and revealed to be inadequate.

The therapist's first opportunity to expose the inadequacy of the delinquent's manipulative techniques comes in the earliest stage of treatment; it is an opportunity which must be grasped. It occurs when the delinquent attempts to maneuver the therapist into accepting the

---

* In common with practically everyone nowadays, the well-informed adaptive delinquent is aware of the universal preoccupation with matters psychological. In those institutions where treatment is emphasized, the inmates are well aware of the practical importance of "getting in good" with the psychologists and of showing the "right" psychological attitudes. In one juvenile institution known to the author a delinquent, in a moment of candor, revealed the "formula" he found most effective: "The best way to get out of here real fast is to get in trouble right off the bat. You act real bad and bitter. Then you get some counselor to pay attention to you. He talks to you a coupla times. You still act bitter. Maybe you even get worse. He gets more and more interested in your problems. Then, one day, you suddenly see the light. Presto—chango, you're a real good boy. Everybody gets excited because you're rehabilitated. It works every time."

delinquent's definition of him as a sympathetic supporter in his struggle against an unjust world. Though the delinquent appears to be asking for help, he is actually asking the unverbalized question: "*How can I control this relationship?*" Accordingly, the first task of the therapist is to smoke this motive out and to point out that the delinquent's request for help is really an attempt at using the therapist to manipulate others.

In dealing with this attempt, the therapist will begin to employ the strategy he will use throughout the treatment: an insistence on answering the real but unverbalized question and unmasking the pseudo-questions as red-herrings. Perhaps the most vivid way to describe the progressive stages of accessibility is in terms of these unverbalized questions and communications which form a continuous counterpoint to whatever is said in the interviews.

VII. APPLICATION TO A SPECIFIC COUNSELING SITUATION

The problems and methods discussed in the previous pages may be concretely illustrated by the record of a fairly typical first counseling session with a non-neurotic, averagely intelligent delinquent transferred, as a disciplinary case, to an adult institution.

The counselor opened the session by asking why the inmate had come to see him.

Delinquent: Well, I've been talking to a few of the guys. . . . They said it might be a good idea.

Counselor: Why?

Delinquent (in a fairly convincing attempt to appear reticent): Well . . . they said it did them good. . . . They said a guy needs somebody he can talk to around here. . . . Somebody he can trust. A . . . a friend.

Counselor: And the reason you asked to see me was that you felt I might help you— that I might be a friend? Why did you feel this?

Delinquent (a little defensively): Because they told me, I guess. Aren't you supposed to be a friend to the guys?

Counselor: Well, let's see now. What is a friend supposed to do? (Delinquent looks puzzled.) Let's take your best buddy, for example. Why do you consider *him* a friend?

Delinquent (puzzled and a little more aggressive): I dunno. . . . We help each other, I guess. We do things for each other.

Counselor: And friends are people who do things for each other?

Delinquent: Yes.

Counselor: Fine. Now, as my friend, what is it you feel you'd like to do for me?

Delinquent (visibly upset): I don't get it. Aren't you supposed to help people? Isn't that your job?

Counselor: Wait a minute—I'm getting lost. A little while ago you were talking about friends and you said that friends help each other. Now you're talking about my job.

Delinquent (increasingly annoyed): Maybe I'm crazy, but I thought you people are supposed to help us. . . .

Counselor: I think I get it now. When you said "friends" you weren't talking about the kind of friendship that works both ways. The kind you meant was where I help you, not where *you* do anything for *me*.

Delinquent: Well . . . I guess so. If you put it that way.

Counselor: Okay (relaxing noticeably from his previous tone of persistence). Now how do you feel I can help you?

Delinquent: Well, you're supposed to help people get rehabilitated, aren't you?

Counselor: Wait. I'm lost again. You say I'm supposed to do something for *people*. I thought you wanted me to do something for *you*. Do *you* want me to help *you* get rehabilitated?

Delinquent: Sure.

Counselor: Fine. Rehabilitated from what?

Delinquent: Well, so I won't get in trouble any more.

Counselor: What trouble?

At this point the delinquent launched into a vehement recital of the abuses to which he had been subjected, starting from his first contact with the juvenile authorities to his most recent difficulties with his probation officer immediately prior to the offense (stealing a car) leading to his present sentence. During the entire recital he never referred to any offense he had committed but, instead, laid exclusive emphasis on his mistreatment.

The counselor heard this account out with an expression of growing puzzlement which was not lost on the counselee, who continued with increasing vehemence as his listener appeared increasingly puzzled. At length the counselor, with a final gesture of bewilderment, broke in:

Counselor: Wait . . . I don't understand. When you said you wanted me to help you stop getting into trouble I thought you meant the kind of trouble that got you in *here*. Your difficulties with the law, for example. You've talked about your troubles with different people and how they get you angry but you haven't talked about what got you into jail.

Delinquent (visibly trying to control himself): But I am talking about that! I'm talking about those bastards responsible for me being here!

Counselor: How do you mean?

The delinquent again repeated the tirade, interspersing it with frequent remarks addressed to the counselor. ("What about this? Do you think *that* was right? Is that the way to treat a young guy?" etc.) The counselor once more seemed just as puzzled, and broke in again.

Counselor: I still don't see it. We'd better get more specific. Now take your last trouble—the one that got you into the reformatory. This car you stole . . .

Delinquent (excitedly): It was that f—— "P. O." (probation officer). I asked him if I could get a job in New York. He said no.

Counselor: What job? (The counselee allowed that it wasn't a specific job—just "any job in New York.")

Counselor: But I still don't follow. The probation officer wouldn't let you work in New York. By the way—don't the regulations forbid probationers from leaving the state?

Delinquent: Well, he could've given me a break.

Counselor: That may be—but I still don't follow you. He wouldn't let you work in New York, so you and a few other guys stole a car and went to Pennsylvania. How does that figure? Did you have a job there?

At this point, the counselee "blew up" and started to denounce "bug doctors who don't help a guy but only cross-examine him."

Counselor: Wait a bit, now. You said before that you wanted me to help you. We've been trying to find out *how.* But so far you haven't been talking about anything the matter with you at all. All you've talked about are these other people and things wrong about them. Now are we supposed to rehabilitate *you* or rehabilitate *them*?

Delinquent: I don't give a f—— who you rehabilitate. I've had about enough of this. If you don't mind, let's call the whole thing off.

Counselor: But I do mind. Here you've been telling me that my job is to rehabilitate you and we haven't talked five minutes and now you want to call the whole thing off. Don't you want to be rehabilitated? (Delinquent is silent.)

Counselor: Let's see if we can review this thing and put in in the right perspective. You said you wanted to be rehabilitated. I asked you from *what* and you said, from getting into trouble. Then I asked you to talk about your troubles and you told me about this probation officer. He didn't give you what you wanted so you stole a car. Now as near as I can understand it, the way to keep you out of trouble is to get people to give you what you want.

Delinquent: That's not true, dammit!

Counselor: Well, let's see, now. Have I given you what you wanted?

Delinquent: Hell, no!

Counselor: You're pretty mad at me right now, aren't you. (smiles).

(Delinquent is silent, looks away.)

Counselor (in a half-chiding, half-kidding tone) : Here, not five minutes ago you were talking about what good friends we could be and now you're acting like I'm your worst enemy.

Delinquent (very half-heartedly, trying not to look at the counselor's face): It's true, isn't it?

Counselor: C'mon now. Now you're just *trying* to get mad. You won't even look at me because you're afraid you'll smile.

(Delinquent cannot repress a smile. Counselor drops his kidding tone and gets business-like again.)

Counselor: Okay. Now that we've agreed to stop kidding, let's get down to cases. Why did you come to see me today?

(Delinquent, very half-heartedly starts to talk about rehabilitation again but the counselor cuts in.)

Counselor: Come on, now. I thought we agreed to stop "conning". Why did you come?

Delinquent: Well . . . I heard you sometimes see guys . . . and . . .

Counselor: And what?

Delinquent: Help them.

Counselor: How?

Delinquent: Well, I tell you my story . . . and . . .

Counselor: And then? What happens then?

(Delinquent is silent).

Delinquent: You tell *them* about it.

Counselor: Who do I tell?

Delinquent: You know—people who read them.

Counselor: Should I write a report on this session?

Delinquent: Hell, no!

Counselor: What do you think we should do?

Delinquent (looking away): Maybe I could . . . (falls silent).

Counselor (quietly): Maybe you could come and talk to me when we really have something to talk about?

Delinquent: Yeah. . . . Aw, hell . . . (laughs).

DISCUSSION: This interview illustrates the problems and possibilities presented in the crucial first counseling session with an adaptive delinquent of average intelligence who attempted to conceal his true feelings and his motive to manipulate under the disguise of a request for friendly help.

Any hope of therapeutic contact with this individual was dependent on the counselor's ability to unmask his actual attitudes and motives in a manner enabling the delinquent to continue and develop the counseling relationship with dignity and candor. Failure to pierce the disguise—which characteristically, was designed to tempt the counselor by flattering him—would have foredoomed the counselor to a relationship with a mask. Behind this mask the delinquent, entirely untouched and unreached, would merely be congratulating himself on his success in deceiving and manipulating the naive adult world. Needless to say, the anti-therapeutic consequences of this relationship —involving, as it did, a high-statused expert in "rehabilitation"— would have been severe.

The special character of the adaptive delinquent's motivations around treatment requires a special counseling technique. The usual methods of permissiveness, non-directiveness and acceptance require modification. To have permitted the counselee to "define the relationship" would have been disastrous, since that definition would have left the counselor no alternatives to the roles of dupe or oppressor ("sucker or s-o-b"). Similarly to have encouraged this adaptive delinquent to "solve his problems in his own way" would have been merely to collaborate with him in the continuation of his anti-social pattern: the manipulation of personal relationships for the purposes of self-aggrandizement and non-mutualized exploitation.

The first job of the counselor was to convey the fact that he was aware of the delinquent's underlying motive and his attempt to control the counseling situation. This accomplished two objectives: (1) it unmasked the attempt to manipulate; and (2) it uncovered the delinquent's true feelings of hostility. These jobs had to be done with an easy casualness and an absence of moralistic condemnation, with the counselor conveying the impression that the delinquent's behavior was entirely "natural" and to be expected. The absence of a condemning attitude is essential for, while the delinquent's hostility must be laid bare he must not be given any realistic basis for it. In effect the therapist says: "You are angry at me not because I have hurt you but because you weren't able to 'con' me. You're also angry because I haven't given you a real reason to be angry."

The subsequent course of a therapeutic relationship initiated in the manner described above will depend on many factors, not all of which

are under the direct control of the therapist. In many instances—
perhaps in the majority of cases—the experience of failure in manipulating the counselor will be insufficient to modify the pattern, and the
therapeutic situation will require broader support from the total
institutional environment. The mere failure to manipulate the therapist
will be of little value if, after leaving the therapist's office, the delinquent
is able successfully to deceive his work supervisors, his house-parents
or the custodial personnel. In order to reinforce the insights achieved
in the counseling sessions the delinquent's continued attempts to engage
in devious environmental manipulation must be frustrated.

VIII. THE CONSEQUENCES OF FAILING TO COPE WITH THE ACCESSIBILITY PROBLEM

In a paper of this scope it would be impractical to attempt a more
detailed exposition of the critical concept of accessibility and its special
implications in the case of adaptive offenders. In concluding this paper
it would be appropriate to discuss certain of the pitfalls which beset
a treatment relationship that fails to take the accessibility problem into
account.

It cannot be overemphasized that the delinquent's accessibility determines not merely the character, evolution and progress of the relationship but, at all times, the level at which the therapist can work. It is
of little use for the therapist to *inform* the delinquent about what
his difficulties "basically" are or to tell him how he "really" feels
about himself. From a diagnostic point of view the therapist may
well be correct, but unless the problem is one about which the delinquent is concerning himself, the information is useless. It may do no
more, in fact, than to make the delinquent aware that the therapist
is disturbed about something concerning which the delinquent is not
troubled at all.

The failure to recognize the true stage of accessibility leads to a
standard approach which frequently involves the therapist in answering
the right questions at the wrong time. Thus—for example—it is fruitless
for the therapist to offer warmth and affection to a delinquent engaged,
at that moment in deceiving or defying him. The delinquent may well
be in need of affection, but he is clearly not accessible to it. The question
he is consciously asking is not, "Do you love me?" but "can you stop
me?" Should the therapist ignore this conscious question and attempt,
prematurely, to answer the unconscious one, he probably will not
succeed in reaching the delinquent on any level.

This error is directly related to another which arises, similarly, out of a standard approach employed with little relevance to the realities of the initial treatment relationship. This error arises out of the therapist's naive and premature acceptance of the adaptive delinquent's definition of him as a friend. Unaware that this definition is merely a way of neutralizing him, the inexperienced therapist—who may be as eager to be liked as the delinquent is eager to exploit him—frequently falls into the trap. Once the delinquent feels he has succeeded in getting the therapist to accept this definition, the second phase of the strategy is quickly commenced. In this—which might be called the "pay-off "phase—a demand is made that the therapist assist the delinquent in some particular aspect of his struggle against the unjust world. In effect, the delinquent is saying: "Since you are now my close friend, I have every right to expect that you will at all times be my ally and supporter and that you will not question my version of things."

Little time is wasted in testing this alliance. In a typical testing maneuver the therapist is asked to extricate the delinquent from some disciplinary action or to "go to bat" for him for some special—and usually unwarranted—privilege. Any balking by the therapist at this point—especially after he has committed himself as the delinquent's "friend" will be viewed as a betrayal, enabling the delinquent to say, in effect: "I knew it all along. You were only pretending to be my friend. Now you too have let me down, just as all the others have done."

This denouement is inevitable; actually it is what the delinquent wanted in the first place. Having shown that he can manipulate the therapist (thus re-inforcing his ideas of power and his contempt for the "sucker") he can now celebrate his victory in a dramatic denunciation scene, pointing out (1) that the counselor was not only insincere but weak and foolish to think that he could "bribe" the delinquent into reforming by doing him favors, and (2) that he, the delinquent, now has a renewed license to misbehave since he has been "betrayed" once again. Needless to say, when matters have reached this pass, the therapeutic objective has long since been lost.

CONCLUSION

The attention of professional personnel engaged in the counseling of juvenile offenders needs to be directed to the special problems presented by the adaptive delinquent. This increasingly recognized type of offender presents distinctive counseling difficulties centering around the motivation for and the accessibility to treatment. As a widely distributed but theoretically novel type of client, he presents a special challenge to both theory and practice. The evolution of an adequate theoretical foundation for sound treatment techniques with this widespread category of delinquent is urgently needed in the field of correction. Unless the implications of this problem are frankly faced it is doubtful that an improvement in the statistics of recidivism will parallel any further refinement in the current apologetics of rehabilitation.

BIBLIOGRAPHY

1. ABRAHAMSEN, DAVID: 1952. *Who Are the Guilty*, p. 125. New York: Rinehart & Company.
2. GOFFMAN, ERVING: 1961. *Asylums*. New York: Anchor Books (Doubleday Inc.).
3. ——: *op. cit.*, p. 129.
4. JENKINS, RICHARD L.: October, 1955. "Adaptive and Maladaptive Delinquency." *The Nervous Child*, **2**, pp. 9–11.
5. ——: *op. cit.*, p. 11.
6. KOBRIN, SOLOMON: October, 1951. "The Conflict of Values in Delinquency Areas." *American Sociological Review*, **16**, p. 654.
7. MERTON, ROBERT K.: 1949. *Social Theory and Social Structure*, p. 136. Glencoe, Ill.: The Free Press.
8. Report and Recommendations of the State of New Jersey Youth Study Commission: 1957. *Helping Youth in Trouble*, p. 131.
9. SHAW, GEORGE BERNARD: 1946. *The Crime of Imprisonment*, p. 105. New York: Philosophical Library.
10. SHORT, JAMES F., Jr. and NYE, IVAN F.: Winter, 1957. "Reported Behavior as a Criterion of Deviant Behavior." *Social Problems*, **5**, pp. 207-213.
11. *Ibid.*
12. VOLD, GEORGE: "Discussion of Kobrin's Findings" (Appended to Kobrin's article, *op. cit.*).

Marriage Counseling

ALBERT ELLIS

New York City

HISTORY

IN ITS non-professional phases, marriage counseling is as old as the institution of marriage itself: since, from the earliest days, there have always been relatives, friends, officials, and religious leaders who have helped people with their marital difficulties. As a recognized profession, marriage counseling is of more recent origins, and may be said to have begun with the investigations and teachings of Professor Ernest R. Groves in the 1920's. Not long after, Paul Popenoe founded the American Institute of Family Relations in Los Angeles; and by the early 1940's the profession of marriage counseling had gained enough reputable adherents to make it feasible to form the American Association of Marriage Counselors, Inc., whose early members included individuals of such stature as Robert L. Dickinson, Lester Dearborn, S. Bernard Wortis, Robert W. Laidlaw, Abraham Stone, Emily H. Mudd, and Gladys Groves.

During the last decade, marriage counseling has continued to grow as a profession, with graduate programs in marriage and family living being given at several leading American universities and with full-fledged clinical training programs being pursued at various institutions, including the American Institute of Family Relations, the Marriage Council of Philadelphia, the Menninger Foundation, and the Merrill–Palmer Institute. In other countries, as David Mace has recently shown,[30] marriage counseling also has been making considerable progress, particularly in England, where the National Marriage Guidance Council was set up in 1938 and has grown to a large organization having eighty highly active centers.

WHO DOES MARRIAGE COUNSELING?

Marriage counseling is done today by a large number of professional workers trained in different disciplines. Most reputable counselors have their basic training in one of the clinical or social sciences, such as medicine, clinical psychology, social work, sociology, law, or religion. Increasingly, however, a group of individuals is coming into existence whose members have been specifically trained in marriage counseling rather than in some other basic discipline. Some of the older members in the field question this new trend, on the grounds that marriage counseling is basically a clinical or psychotherapeutic procedure, and that therefore its practitioners should be recruited from one of the clinical disciplines. But other authorities feel that marriage counselors may be trained in their own right, provided that they recognize their limitations.

TRAINING OF MARRIAGE COUNSELORS

Marriage counseling is too new a profession to have very definite training standards. A joint subcommittee on standards of the National Council on Family Relations and the American Association of Marriage Counselors has given much serious consideration to the problem of standards and has made some interesting recommendations. In regard to academic training, the committee feels that counselors should have a graduate or professional degree from an approved educational institution in one of the following fields: education, home economics, law, medicine, nursing, psychology, religion, social anthropology, social work, or sociology. In whatever field the counselor selects for emphasis, he should have specific accredited training in the psychology of personality development and interpersonal relations; elements of psychiatry; human biology, including the fundamentals of sex anatomy, physiology, and genetics; sociology of marriage and the family; legal aspects of marriage and the family; and counseling techniques. To be recognized as a reputable marriage counselor, the candidate should additionally have at least three years of professional experience subsequent to obtaining his degree, including actual experience as a clinical assistant in marriage counseling under approved supervision.

A marriage counselor's qualifications should also include, says the report of the Committee on Standards for Training of the American Association of Marriage Counselors (1958), "a knowledge of human growth and development, and of the dynamics of human behavior and human motivations; a capacity to differentiate between normal and abnormal behavior mechanisms; and some understanding of the everyday give-and-take problems of family living and relationships within the family group. In addition, the marriage counselor needs to be skilled in the use of basic counseling techniques, and to have developed an awareness and disciplined control of his own biases, prejudices, attitudes and needs as these may affect his work with clients."

TECHNIQUES OF MARRIAGE COUNSELING

In one respect, marriage counseling is similar to other forms of psychological counseling, since it usually is concerned with individuals who are in trouble and who frequently have severe psychological difficulties. The one outstanding difference, however, between the two types of counseling is that marriage counseling is concerned with at least two (and often more) individuals, while general counseling or psychotherapy may only be concerned with one client. Most marriage counseling clients come for help because they are having trouble relating their present or future mates. To some extent, therefore, a marriage counselor diagnoses and treats an interpersonal *relationship* rather than only an individual.[6] He must continually orient his efforts so that they benefit two or more individuals rather than merely one.

In consequence, it is most common for a marriage counselor to see both marital (or premarital) partners. On occasion, he may see only one mate, while some other counselor or psychotherapist sees the other. Or he may first see both partners and later refer one of them for treatment elsewhere. But more often than not he will see both partners himself and often continue to see them for a series of sessions.

Perhaps the most common procedure is for the counselor first to see one of the mates or would-be mates and then separately to see the other. At the initial contacts with the counselees, this is a preferred procedure, since one partner may be reluctant to reveal certain material while the other mate is in the same room. At times, however, both individuals may be seen together, either initially or regularly.[25,32,34,38]

In the individual or joint marriage counseling sessions, which usually are from 45 minutes to an hour in length, each spouse is encouraged freely to ventilate his or her feelings and attitudes toward himself and his mate. In this manner, the counselor ultimately—and sometimes fairly quickly—determines what the basic marital differences are, and what the partners may do to try to resolve these differences. Some counselors favor non-directive techniques of counseling; but the majority seem to favor a democratic but still fairly directive approach.

MARRIAGE COUNSELING AND PSYCHOTHERAPY

In theory, marriage counseling is different from general psycho-therapy, since it is done mainly on a conscious or ego level, and does not attempt to get at underlying or unconscious personality factors in emotional disturbance. Moreover, marriage counseling often includes a considerable amount of information or education, particularly in the area of sexual problems, while psychotherapy tends to include less factual information.

There are, however, many authorities in the field who contend that marriage counseling is not essentially different from psychotherapy, but is a form of therapy.[1,7,9,12,17,18,21,22,24,28,29] These writers feel that marriage counseling clients are often just as severely disturbed as are psychotherapy patients; that the main sources of premarital and marital difficulties are the personality disturbances of the individuals having such difficulties; and that many counseling cases will never be resolved unless the counselor gets at underlying and even unconscious thought and emotions which are troubling the clients. Whether competent marriage counselors realize it or not, these authorities contend, they are frequently doing psychotherapy and should consequently receive training in therapeutic techniques if they are to function properly.

GOALS AND OUTCOME OF MARRIAGE COUNSELING

As defined by Godwin and Mudd,[20] marriage counseling is "the process by which a professionally trained counselor assists a person or persons to resolve the problems that trouble them in their interpersonal relationships, as they move into marriage, live within it, or make a decision to terminate it. The focus is on the relationship between the two persons moving into marriage, or already in a marriage, rather than, as in psychiatric therapy, on the reorganization of the personality structure of the individual."

Some authorities feel that a marriage itself can be sick, and that there-fore the marriage, or the relationship between husband and wife, is the thing to be treated. Other authorities emphasize that marriages con-sist only of individuals, and that it is the individuals who are to be treated rather than their marriage. Most counselors take a rather middle-of-the-road stand and treat the individuals *in* a marriage rather than the individuals by themselves.

It is generally agreed, however, that it is not the function of a coun-selor to try to hold a marriage together at all costs, even though it is his function to try to help in every possible way to remove the emotional blocks that may be impairing the relationship. Counselors usually take the stand that since the marriage exists at the time the partners come for counseling, and since marriage is a serious business and often involves other family members, sincere efforts should be made by the clients and the counselor to work out a good relationship. If, however, this is impossible, then the counselor should try to be of aid in the fairest and least upsetting separation or divorce that can be worked out.

Although facts about marriage counseling outcome are almost non-existent, it is generally felt that most couples who come for counseling are helped to some extent by the counseling process, and that many marriages which were dreadful before the mates came for counseling are helped to become tolerable and even happy. Only in a minority of cases, apparently, does separation or divorce ensue.

In a review of one hundred marriage counseling cases seen by the writer, most of which were treated by the recently developed method of rational-emotive psychotherapy,[10,11,13,14,15,17,18] it was found that 42 per cent of the couples seen effected a considerable improvement in their marital relationships, 40 per cent effected a moderate improvement, and 18 per cent showed little or no improvement. This, considering that these couples came for counseling because their relationships were exceptionally poor, would appear to be a fairly good showing.

THE FUTURE OF MARRIAGE COUNSELING

Marriage counseling may well be said to be in its infancy today and to be slowly approaching its adolescence. It requires much experimentation and research before it comes of age. New tendencies in the field include approaches to group counseling techniques; cooperative consultations between different counselors; experiments with one counselor seeing both partners during the same session; and counseling which includes the entire family rather than only the husband and wife. A notable recent development in the field has been the organization (especially in the State of Ohio) of marriage conciliation services in the domestic courts.[2,4] It is difficult to predict exactly what the future of marriage counseling will be, but it is safe to say that a decade or two from now will show further progress in the field and a degree of increased maturity among marriage counselors and their methods that is perhaps barely imaginable today.

FURTHER SOURCES OF INFORMATION

Professional articles on marriage and family counseling continue to appear in *Marriage and Family Living*, *Family Life*, *Marriage Guidance*,

Social Casework, Social Work, and the *Advances in Sex.* The main professional organizations specifically for marriage counselors are the American Association of Marriage Counselors, the Academy of Psychologists in Marital Counseling, the Marriage Counseling Section of the National Council on Family Relations, and the Society for the Scientific Study of Sex.

BIBLIOGRAPHY

1. ACKERMAN, NATHAN W.: 1958. *The Psychodynamics of Family Life.* New York: Basic Books, Inc.
2. ALEXANDER, P. W.: 1954. "Legal Science and the Social Sciences." *Missouri Law Rev.*, **21**, p. 111.
3. American Association of Marriage Counselors, Committee on Standards for Training: 1958. Report on Standards for Training. New York: American Association of Marriage Counselors, Inc.
4. BRIDGMAN, RALPH: 1961. *Marriage Conciliation.* In Albert Ellis and Albert Abarbanel, *The Encyclopedia of Sexual Behavior.* New York: Hawthorn Books.
5. CUBER, J. F.: 1948. *Marriage Counseling Practice.* New York: Appleton–Century–Crofts, Inc.
6. EISENSTEIN, V. W. (Ed).: 1956. *Neurotic Interaction in Marriage.* New York: Basic Books, Inc.
7. ELLIS, ALBERT: 1953. "Marriage Counseling with Couples Indicating Sexual Incompatibility." *Marr. Fam. Living,* **15**, pp. 53–59.
8. ——: 1954. "Psychosexual and marital problems." In L. A. Pennington and I. A. Berg, *An Introduction to Clinical Psychology.* New York: Ronald Press.
9. ——: 1956. "A Critical Evaluation of Marriage Counseling." *Marr. Fam. Living,* **18**, pp. 65–71.
10. ——: 1957. *How to live with a Neurotic.* New York: Crown Publishers.
11. ——: 1958a. "Rational psychotherapy." *J. General Psychol.,* **59**, pp. 35–49.
12. ——: 1958b. "Neurotic interaction between marital partners." *J. Counseling Psychol.,* **5**, pp. 24–28.
13. ——: 1959. "Rationalism and its therapeutic applications." In Albert Ellis, *The Place of Value in the Practice of Psychotherapy.* New York: American Academy of Psychotherapists.
14. ——: 1960. "Marriage counseling with demasculinizing wives and demasculinized husbands." *Marr. Fam. Living,* **22**, pp. 13–21.
15. ——: 1961. "A rational approach to premarital counseling." *Psychol. Reports,* **8**, pp. 333–338.
16. —— and ABARBANEL, ALBERT: 1961. *The Encyclopedia of Sexual Behavior.* New York: Hawthorn Books.
17. —— and HARPER, ROBERT A.: 1961a. *Creative Marriage.* New York: Lyle Stuart.
18. —— ——: 1961b. *A Guide to Rational Living.* Englewood Cliffs, N.J.: Prentice–Hall.
19. FITZSIMMONS, M.: 1951. "Collaborative Treatment in a Marriage Problem." *Marr. Fam. Living,* **13**, pp. 52–55.
20. GOODWIN, HILDA M., and MUDD, EMILY H.: 1961. "Marriage counseling." In Albert Ellis and Albert Abarbanel, *The Encyclopedia of Sexual Behavior.* New York: Hawthorn Books.

21. HARPER, ROBERT A.: 1951. "Marriage counseling: art or science?" *Marr. Fam. Living*, **13**, pp. 164–166.
22. ——: 1953. "Should marriage counseling become a full-fledged specialty?" *Marr. Fam. Living*, **15**, pp. 338–340.
23. ——: 1958. "Communication Problems in Marriage and Marriage Counseling." *Marr. Fam. Living*, **20**, pp. 107–112.
24. ——: 1960. "A Rational Process-centered Approach to Marriage Counseling." *J. Individ. Psychol.*, **16**, pp. 197–208.
25. HERBERT, W. L., and JERVIS, F. V.: 1959. *A Modern Approach to Marriage Counseling*. London: Methuen.
26. KARPF, M. J.: 1951. "Marriage Counseling and Psychotherapy." *Marr. Fam. Living*, **13**, pp. 169–178.
27. ——: 1952. "Premarital Counseling and Psychotherapy: Two Cases." *Marr. Fam. Living*, **14**, pp. 56–73.
28. LAIDLAW, ROBERT W.: 1957. "Marriage counseling." In Samuel Liebman, *Understanding your patient*. Philadelphia: J. B. Lippincott Co.
29. LAWTON, GEORGE: 1958. "Neurotic Interaction Between Counselor and Counselee." *J. Counseling Psychol.*, **5**, pp. 28–33.
30. MACE, DAVID R.: 1957. *What is Marriage Counseling?* New York: Public Affairs Committee, Inc.
31. MUDD, E. H.: 1952. *The Practice of Marriage Counseling*. New York: Association Press.
32. MUDD, EMILY H., STONE, ABRAHAM, KARPF, MAURICE, and NELSON, JANET (Eds.): 1958. *Marriage Counseling: a Casebook*. New York: Association Press.
33. ROGERS, CARL R.: 1951. *Client-centered Therapy*. Boston: Houghton Mifflin.
34. SKIDMORE, REX A., GARRET, HULDA VAN STREETER, and SKIDMORE, C. JAY: 1956. *Marriage Consulting*. New York: Harper.
35. STOKES, W. R.: 1951. "A Marriage Counseling Case: the Married Virgin." *Marr. Fam. Living*, **13**, pp. 29–34.
36. STONE, ABRAHAM and LEVINE, LENA: 1956. *The Premarital Consultation*. New York: Grune & Stratton.
37. VINCENT, CLARK E.: 1957. *Readings in Marriage Counseling*. New York: Thomas Y. Crowell Co.
38. WALLIS, H. J. and BOOKER, H. S.: 1958. *Marriage Counseling*. London: Routledge, Kegan Paul.

The Pre-natal Pediatric Interview

MILTON I. LEVINE

Associate Professor of Clinical Pediatrics
Cornell Medical Center
New York Hospital
New York City

WITHIN recent years an increasing number of prospective parents have been requesting an interview with the pediatrician prior to the birth of an infant.

This interview, if given sufficient time, usually proves of great value to both the parents of the baby-to-be as well as the pediatrician and serves many purposes. It should provide far more than the mere opportunity for the prospective parents to appraise the pediatrician. Rather, its primary object should be to establish a mutual relationship, and to give the parents a valuable opportunity to clarify their own ideas and prepare for changes in home and family relationships which of necessity occur when a new infant arrives.

To the physician it offers an opportunity to develop an understanding of the parents' needs and how they will best be handled. All parents differ, and some people with deeper anxieties will need greater help and support through the years of child development. This interview also offers the physician the occasion to demonstrate to the father and mother his personal interest in their problems, his attitudes and opinions on the subject of child care, and his willingness to spend the necessary time if it should be needed in the future.

With few exceptions, all parents desire and need re-assurance and need to be relieved of any misunderstandings, misgivings and feelings of guilt. There are a great many people who still feel that they are incapable of being good parents; some who are worried lest they will be unable to change a mode of life; others who fear that the birth of a new child might deeply hurt a very much loved first child. Then there are mothers greatly concerned because they do not feel maternal and are worried lest this will bring abnormal and incomplete relationships. There are parents completing unwanted pregnancies and parents who have their hearts set on a particular sex of the child.

It is obvious that many of the questions asked and the answers given will depend largely upon the family structure, the home environment, and the personalities of the prospective parents. No two family situations are entirely alike, no two sets of parents have the same temperaments, the same emotional make-up, and the same upbringing. Some parents have a great deal more knowledge than others. Some are relaxed and assured, others tense and anxious.

Although it is preferable that parents start the conversation and proceed to present the problems foremost in their minds, it is also important that the physician, through his own questioning, gain a fairly clear picture of the family and the home environment.

The answers and suggestions given by the physician to the parents will depend largely on whether or not there are other children in the home and, if so, the age levels of these children. The ages of the parents, their professions or businesses, the number of rooms in the home, the number of people outside of the immediate family in the home—all of these are among the many important facts to be considered by the physician in his parental counseling.

What about the fact that I don't feel maternal? Just how important is breast feeding? What about a self-demand feeding schedule? If rooming-in is available at the hospital, is it advisable? If the infant is a boy, is there a real need for circumcision? Is it preferable to have a baby-nurse at home? Are pacifiers advisable? Should a crying baby be picked up? Should the baby sleep in the parents' room? If there is an older child, how should he be handled? Such are a few of the numerous questions usually asked by expectant parents.

In relation to a new mother, it should be the effort of the pediatrician to reassure her in her ability to be a good mother and to rear her child successfully.

The mere fact that a woman in her late pregnancy does not as yet feel maternal is not of extreme significance—for numerous mothers have this same reaction and only develop maternal interests after the birth of the baby.

It should be emphasized that "there are no perfect parents." It is natural for all parents to make mistakes and even the so-called authorities make mistakes in the upbringing of their own children. It is one thing to read articles and attend lectures on child care; it is another matter, and not always so easy, to put into practice the principles so advised. The most one can ask is that the parent do the best he can.

BREAST FEEDING OR FORMULA

Probably the most frequent questions asked by prospective parents are those relative to breast feeding. A modern trend of idealizing and exalting breast feeding has caused a great deal of confusion among parents. Many mothers have gained the impression that the desired warm relationship between mother and child can be fully attained only through breast-feeding.

The answer to the question "Should I nurse my baby?" is not always easily answered. Is the mother desirous of nursing or will she nurse the baby because she has been told it is best for the baby? Does she have no opinion one way or the other? Would she prefer to nurse and if so—why? And if she plans to nurse—how many months should she continue?

It should be emphasized that most mothers are physically capable of nursing their infants if given the opportunity and adequate encouragement. However, even with this realization, the advisability of recommending breast feeding is still often open to discussion.

There are working mothers who must place their infants on formula feeding immediately after birth. There are mothers who have no desire to nurse, who do not enjoy or may even abhor the idea of breast feeding. There are mothers who do not want to be tied down by breast feeding, others who would avoid any possibility of obesity during the nursing period and still others whose husbands object to the idea.

For these mothers the whole problem will be simplified if they are brought to the realization that there is no sole answer to the problem of optimum feeding procedure. The factor of primary importance is that the feeding should be of mutual satisfaction and pleasure to both mother and child.

With this in mind one might roughly divide all new mothers into the following categories:

A. *Mothers who are Anxious to Nurse*

These should receive every encouragement not only during the interview, but later, in the hospital, by the obstetrician and the nurses as well. Practically 100 per cent of this group are capable of nursing their infants if given the opportunity and the proper emotional support.

B. *Those Mothers Who Have No Feeling Pro or Con but Will Nurse if it is Considered Best for the Baby*

Experience has proven that if these mothers are given every encouragement the great majority will find enjoyment in the experience of breast feeding.

C. *Mothers Who Would Rather Not Nurse but Will Do So if it is Considered Best for the Baby*

In such cases the physician should discuss the mother's feelings with her and attempt to determine the factors which produced her attitude. At times such a discussion will relieve anxieties and misconceptions, but the final decision should be made by the mother herself. If a mother chooses to try nursing she should be given the understanding that breast feeding may be discontinued if the experience is not a happy and satisfying one. But whatever method is chosen she should be given every reassurance and encouragement.

D. *Mothers Who Prefer Not to Nurse for Fears of Obesity, Breast Abscesses, and the Fear of being Tied Down*

Generally speaking this group should not be pressured to nurse, for these mothers would breast feed their infants under feeling of anxiety or frustration. It is much more desirable that an infant should be bottle fed by a relaxed mother, rather than breast fed by one who is tense and anxious about her well-being.

E. *Mothers Who Dislike and Those Who Loathe the Thought of Nursing*

Such mothers should not be encouraged or directed to breast-feed. This could only prove harmful to the mother–child relationship. These mothers always have some deep seated reason for their aversion —and this feeling cannot be removed by logic or a single discussion.

F. *Mothers Who Cannot Nurse Because, Due to Economic Conditions, They are Forced to Work*

These mothers often develop feelings of guilt or inadequacy and suffer remorse over conditions they cannot control. They should be reassured that their babies will thrive very well on the formula and that given close attention by them in the mornings, evenings, at night, and over the week-ends their children will not suffer emotionally.

One further problem, also often arises and that is the advisability of breast feeding an infant when there is an older child at home. Or, if the decision has been made to nurse, should this always be performed in private away from the observation of the older child? This should be no reason to deprive the baby of breast feeding nor is there any gain in excluding an older child during the nursing. The older child can simply be told that this is the way little babies are fed before they have teeth, and the mother should add (if true) "you were fed this way when you were a little baby." The older child should also be reassured that the baby is not hurting the mother or eating the mother—a common misconception of little children.

FEEDING SCHEDULES

Once the subject of breast feeding has been discussed and some fairly definite decision reached, the way is open for a discussion of general feeding attitudes. This not only involves feeding schedules, but the attitude of the parent toward feeding. Most informed mothers today have some knowledge of the meaning of self-demand feedings—but all of them ask about its use. Again, the advice of the physician should depend upon the temperament of the mother, the size of the family and whether or not there is assistance in the necessary household routines.

Obviously, if there are other small children, a complete self-demand feeding schedule would not only be extremely difficult, but would in all likelihood increase feelings of sibling jealousy. In such instances it is preferable to advise some modified self-demand schedule, with certain approximate hours for feeding, but with a leeway of one hour before and after the specified time. This usually permits the mother sufficient time and flexibility to give adequate attention to the other children. Usually the infant himself forms a feeding cycle in approximately four weeks.

But when discussing feeding practices with prospective mothers, they should be strongly warned against two common errors. The first is forcing an infant to eat and the second, permitting an infant to cry from hunger for long periods of time.

Bottle-fed infants are particularly prone to the feeding pressures of over-zealous mothers. The physician has given the directions for formula preparation and, unfortunately, the average mother feels that the infant should receive the whole amount in each bottle at every feeding. She does not realize that the milk intake of a baby fed on the breast varies greatly at the individual feedings. A six week old baby may nurse 4 ounces at one feeding and 7 ounces at the next.

The harmful effects of these feeding pressures may be of long duration. Not only do they break down the desired relationship of a mother with her child, but by making the feeding an unhappy experience, may tend toward the development of a chronically poor appetite.

One other point of information should be directed to all mothers, especially those who plan to use the self-demand or modified self-demand schedule. Every whimper or cry of an infant does not necessarily mean that the child is hungry.

THE QUESTION OF TRAINED INFANT NURSES

A problem not infrequently presented to the physician is whether or not an experienced infant nurse is a necessity after the baby is brought from the hospital. Does she interfere with the optimal mother–child relationship? Will she be an intruder into a family unit? Would not the infant's maternal grandmother serve better in the same capacity?

Experience has demonstrated that although not by any means a necessity, an experienced infant nurse may be of the greatest assistance to the mother of a newborn, whether or not there are siblings in the family. Such a nurse not only can relieve and dispel many of the unnecessary anxieties of the new mother, but also show her how to organize her day. She also relieves the mother of many of the necessary routines, permitting her time for relaxation and time to devote to other children who may have been waiting at home during her hospital stay.

This does not imply that the care of a newborn infant should be given over entirely to the nurse. The prospective mother should be warned against accepting a secondary place in the life of the child. She should take over as many of the feedings as possible, she should bathe the baby and cuddle him as much as she desires. The physician cannot over-emphasize the concept that "this is your child."

The selection of a suitable nurse requires great care. She should be calm and relaxed, not possessive or imperious, and certainly not one that tends to make it appear that infant care is extremely difficult or a great hardship. The new mother must be reassured that millions and millions of newborns have been handled successfully without the aid of nurses—but if one can have the aid of an experienced nurse during the first few weeks at least, there are certain definite advantages.

One further important consideration in the selection of a nurse is that she should not only qualify for the care of the infant, but that she should fit into the family picture without too much difficulty. It is not easy to have a third adult enter closely into the family relationship; and this should be borne in mind when interviewing nurses.

The length of time advisable for the assistance of an infant nurse varies with the individual family. Some mothers, through experience or personality, are more assured than others, some need more rest before assuming complete care, some need more aid in organizing their work and in carrying out the necessary routines. There are certain mothers who must work and will need a good mother substitute for the hours when they are away, and then, there are a certain few women who would never be happy assuming the full care of their children.

If it is at all possible, the physician should have a list of capable nurses whom he can refer and personally recommend, or he should refer the mother to a good agency for baby nurses to whom he has already designated the type of nurse he desires for infants under his care. Unless the physician or the prospective mother have personal knowledge of the personality and background of a baby nurse, it is always advisable for the mother to investigate carefully all letters of recommendation. A great deal of unwritten and important information may be obtained by telephone conversations with previous employers—for a good infant nurse must be far more than one whose quality lies in her ability to care for the child.

CIRCUMCISION

Discussing the possible birth of a male infant often brings up the question of the pros and cons regarding circumcision. Omitting religious considerations, the question usually pertains to its necessity as a health measure. If circumcision is advisable, how soon should it be performed?

There is, of course, a great deal of dispute on the necessity or advantages of circumcision. Those who advise it maintain that the foreskin may collect irritating smegma beneath it, that it may predispose to masturbation, and that in adult life, a certain percentage of men develop cancer of the foreskin.

These arguments may be countered by the facts that if the foreskin is free and can be easily retracted, there should be no fear of the collection of irritating substances. Furthermore, there is no evidence to show that the foreskin, unless very elongated, encourages masturbation—but, disregarding this, there is no evidence either that masturbation is in any way physically harmful. Finally, the percentage of men who develop cancer of the foreskin is so small that it may be considered as negligible.

On the other hand, there are those who argue that the act of intercourse is more satisfying when the foreskin is present—an argument which so far has received no scientific or statistical support to confirm or disprove it.

We have learned, however, from a great deal of psychological data, that circumcision may be a great harm psychologically if performed during later childhood or adult life. There is even some question as to the trauma caused when the operation is performed on an infant of more than a few weeks of age, when his nerves are already organized and when pain following an operation is acute and sustained.

Apparently during the first week or ten days of life, the nervous system of a newborn is so poorly organized that in the vast majority of cases, a circumcised infant will resume the quiet sucking of a nipple immediately following the circumcision.

The prospective parents should be told that circumcision is advisable in every instance where marked phimosis prevents retraction of the foreskin or prevents normal urination.

It should be remembered however, that the foreskin is normally adherent to the head of the penis for several months after which it separates spontaneously. From this period on, it can usually be retracted with comparative ease. But if circumcision is to be performed, it is best done during the first two weeks of life.

PREPARING A SIBLING CHILD FOR THE ARRIVAL OF THE NEW BABY

A good many parents already have one or more children in the family when expecting the birth of a new baby. To the physician are brought the sibling problems which usually accompany this event.

The parents should be given the realization at the outset of such a discussion that sibling rivalry always exists and that sibling jealousy is almost as frequent. Their effort should be to minimize these as much as possible. This is a most important concept for parents to accept, since many who have sincerely attempted to ward off such rivalries and jealousies feel that they have failed if these responses become evident.

The questions relating to the sibling adjustment are numerous. How do you prepare a child for the new baby? When is it best to tell him about the expected infant? Who should care for the older child or children when the mother is in the hospital, and where should the child stay? When the mother returns from the hospital, should the older child remain with a relative until the home environment is settled? If the older child remains home, should he meet his mother at the door when she returns, or should he go to the hospital and ride home with his mother and the new baby? What room is best for the infant? Should the older child see the baby being nursed? These are among the most frequent questions asked by expectant mothers who have one or more children already at home.

Of course, the manner in which the questions are answered and even the content of the answer depends largely upon the age of the siblings. It is obvious that the small child, especially one between eighteen months and five years of age, who depends almost entirely on his mother, will suffer much more than an older child, not only because of his great sense of loss during the period of separation, but also because he is not as a rule prepared to share the affection of his mother.

The parents of small children are therefore advised to withhold the announcement of the expected birth from a child under the approximate age of six years until the last month of pregancy or until the child himself asks a leading question, possibly brought on by conversations he may have overheard or by observation of his mother's changing contour. From that time on, the child can enter actively in the preparations—even to the extent of aiding in the selection of clothes and equipment for the newborn, and to packing the mother's valise with hospital necessities.

The arrangements for the care of this child during the mother's stay in the hospital will depend on adequate mother substitutes. Usually a grandmother, for whom the child has great affection and confidence is the best substitute for this period. If at all possible, the child should remain at home with pictures of the mother in evidence, and even with some of her clothing, such as shoes, coats, and hats where they can easily be observed. If no grandmother is available, then some other person in whom the child has confidence should be found. If a temporary nurse must be obtained, then she should live with the family and have close contact with the child for a week or more before the mother enters the hospital, in order that the child may know her well and learn confidence in her. It should be arranged also that the father be home much more and spend extra time with the child during the period of separation from his mother.

In furtherance of the plan to include the older child in the family arrangements for the entrance of the newborn into the home, it is important that he be taken to the hospital to greet his mother and aid her in bringing the infant home.

The real impact of the new arrival on the life of an older child rarely begins until the baby arrives at home. So much depends upon what parents and relatives say, how much time they spend with the infant, what comparisons are made and what room the newborn occupies.

Whatever other arrangements are made, it is rarely advisable to place the crib or bassinette in the parents' bedroom while the older child remains in his own room. Only too often an older child feels that this indicates a greater love for the baby than he himself receives. It is also inadvisable for parents to remove the older child from his accustomed room and turn the room over to the infant. Again, the older child will usually gain the impression that he is being displaced.

Most parents with other children have given some thought to the problem of sibling rivalry before the birth of the baby. Often in their attempts to eliminate potentially difficult situations, they lean too far in the opposite direction. An example of this is in the effort of mothers to prevent the older child from observing the breast-feeding of the infant. Often doors are shut to the consternation of the older child while the mother secretes herself with the newborn. There is no need for nursing to be withheld from the view of the older brothers or sisters.

The siblings should be told that this is the way babies are fed and, if true, "You also were fed this way before you had teeth."

Most of the other problems relative to sibling rivalries and jealousies may be discussed with the physician after the birth of the baby. These pertain to infantile regressions and efforts in making the older child feel his advantages in being older, as well as means of demonstrating to him that although a new child has arrived, he is still loved as much as before the arrival of the infant.

DISCIPLINE

Parents will often bring up the subject of "spoiling the baby." How much can one indulge an infant? Must one pick him up the minute he cries? Should you feed him at the hours he selects? Should you rock a baby in the carriage so that he will go to sleep quickly?

Fathers and mothers should realize that an infant, during most of the first year of life is helpless and completely dependent on his parents or parent substitutes to satisfy his needs. He is unable to reason but quickly expresses his hunger, discomfort or other needs by crying. And every parent responds to the infant's crying by the desire to satisfy these needs. This is instinctual and during almost the whole of the first year these instincts may be followed without fear of spoiling the child. For with the satisfaction of his needs the infant learns trust in his parents, an important factor in the normal emotional development of every child. When we realize that the parent is the representative of all people to the infant and young child we can understand the importance of establishing this confidence and this warmth of relationship.

This does not mean, however, that an infant should be picked up every time he whimpers. At times babies will cry for a few moments and return to sleep. If a parent is busy she can wait a few minutes before picking the baby up without fear of upsetting the infant too greatly.

When children approach one year of age and develop a degree of understanding then some form of discipline may be exercised. Then a baby can start to learn that he can't have everything he desires, that his wishes cannot always be satisfied immediately and that there are other people in the world also who must be considered.

Parents and potential parents must be warned against being over permissive and over indulgent. These can be just as destructive to a child as over restriction. A growing child needs guidance and authority almost as much as he needs love. But authority must be reasonable and just, permitting the child a good deal of independence and the opportunity for exploration, discovery and experimentation.

Numerous other questions are also brought to the physician, although less frequently. These include the subjects of rooming-in where it is possible in maternity services, questions on pacifiers and thumbsucking, grandparents, and even how to aid the new father to accept gracefully the inevitabilities of his wife's divided attention.

Before the pre-natal interview is completed, the physician should attempt to impress the prospective parents with three points to remember:

1. Enjoy your infant.

2. Don't try too intensely or too strenuously to be the perfect parent.

3. Don't hesitate to call your physician if problems arise that cause you anxiety, either psychological or physical.

Counseling Methods of the Family Service Agency

RALPH ORMSBY

Executive Director
Family Service of Philadelphia
Philadelphia
Pennsylvania

THE CENTRAL purpose of the family service agency, according to a report of a Committee of the Family Service Association of America, is "to contribute to harmonious family interrelationships, to strengthen the positive values in family life, and to promote healthy personality development and satisfactory social functioning of various family members."[1] The report of this Committee on the scope and methods of the family service agency is a principal source of the concepts expressed in this article.

The major function by which the purpose of the family agency is carried out is family casework service. Family casework is derived from, and in fact is practically synonymous with, the professional method of helping known as social casework.[2,3] While some persons in the field differentiate "counseling" as a method within social casework, and some use the term interchangeably with "casework," the point of view expressed here is that the helping method of the family service agency is best termed "social casework."

CLIENTELE

The clientele of the family service agency is an extremely varied one. In terms of problems of life adjustment, the family agency clientele includes persons with marriage difficulties, parent–child relationship problems, maladjustments in social relationships, trouble in facing crises and limitations caused by environmental pressures, tensions on the job, and internal family frictions. Applicants for the service come from all walks of life, have varied educational backgrounds and are from different economic levels. Business and industry recognize the value of family counseling for their employees.[4] A growing percentage of clients of the family agency pay fees for the service rendered. Whereas in the past an applicant usually expected a social agency to give him something material or to take some specific action on his behalf, it is recognized today that the family agency provides expert, professional help to aid the client in solving his family relationship and social adjustment problems.

The family caseworker therefore must have a wide range of skills, applicable to varied problems and to clients of different age levels. Thus the caseworker may work directly with one or both marriage partners, with an aged family member, with an adolescent, a young adult or with a young child.[5] Often, when more than one family member needs casework service, the agency must plan to have more than one caseworker available for service to the family unit.

Today there are family service agencies in most cities in the United States of 50,000 or more population. In 1961 there were 302 agencies in the membership of the Family Service Association of America, including five in Canada.[6]

RELATIONSHIP

The principal medium of casework service is the personal communication or *relationship* established between the client and the caseworker. An atmosphere is created in the interview by the quality of the worker's attitudes and feelings that enables the client to define his problem, to explore its ramifications and the impact on his life adjustment, and to use professional help in working out a solution.

The caseworker consistently brings attitudes to the relationship which are supporting and enabling. For the client whose personality difficulties stem from inconsistent, dominating, unresponsive, repressive and hostile relationship experiences, the casework relationship is itself a new and corrective experience providing encouragement and increasing the client's self-respect. This is a first condition toward helping the client to mobilize his inner capacities and environmental resources on his own behalf.

On the other hand, the caseworker must be in control of attitudes on his part which may be overstimulating or guilt-producing for the client. For example, indiscriminate kindness by the caseworker may add to the burden of an already guilt-laden client and cause him to react aggressively or with depression. While the caseworker strives to keep the relationship on a predominantly positive level, he must be able to accept negative feelings expressed by the client without retaliation, whether or not the feelings are realistic and appropriate to the situation. The relationship offered by the caseworker is a warm and human one but it is controlled professionally with understanding of its effect on the client. The professional casework relationship is reliable, supporting and thoughtful rather than impulsive.

The caseworker must also be sensitive to the development of too intense an attachment by the client to him. Some of the techniques usefully employed in keeping the relationship on a realistic level are: regulation of the frequency of interviews, encouraging healthy outside interests and activities, and deflecting the client's positive feelings to appropriate members of his family and other persons in his environment. It is also important to prepare the client for separations from the worker at times of vacation, transfer to another worker, and termination of the treatment.

The pervasive importance of the client–caseworker relationship in the helping process may tempt the social caseworker to base his help solely on the development of skill in the management of attitudes and feelings. Relationship must be correctly handled for the particular client; it must be syntonic with sound psychosocial diagnosis, selection of treatment method and use of techniques appropriate to the treatment method selected.

PSYCHOSOCIAL DIAGNOSIS

From the moment a client comes to the family agency for help, the caseworker observes the client, studies him, obtains information about his current functioning, is interested in his past history as it relates to current behavior and, in short, attempts to understand the client and his problem. Because the caseworker seeks to know the psychological and social factors that are operating in the client's life and how inner and outer pressures are interrelated and together affect his social functioning, such diagnosis is termed "psychosocial."[7]

The caseworker estimates the reality pressures on the client, how he deviates from others in his handling of them, and whether or not his anxiety is "normal" for the circumstances, realistically overwhelming or out of proportion to the actual situation. All of this means that facts must be learned about the client, his problem and his behavior which add up to knowledge usable in planning treatment with him.

In the main, psychosocial diagnostic material is obtained in the casework interview. It may be confirmed or enlarged by a plan of analyzing data with a psychiatric consultant and by arranging for psychological testing. Collateral information obtained with the client's permission from schools, employers and others is an essential part of fact-finding.

Since social casework is concerned with everyday life adjustment, data which helps to determine the degree of the client's ego strength are important. Technically, such data are needed because, as will be described later, the predominant treatment aim of family casework is supportive, but supportive of strengths rather than a buttressing of personality weaknesses. If strengths are to be supported, they must be identified and understood. A practical guide to the most important ego functions and how they can be distinguished, although it is recognized that they overlap in the healthy well-integrated personality, is set forth in an article by Dr. Sidney L. Green.[8] The ego functions described are: object relationships, reality testing, judgment, motility patterns, tolerance for frustration, affectivity, defense mechanisms and basic intellective capacities.

A large part of the casework activities of the family agency may be classified as short-term service[9] involving only a few interviews with each client, although collateral work may be considerable. In this grouping, sufficient knowledge of each case is needed to help the client consider immediate alternative choices and decisions in handling a problem, to plan with him for referral to another agency or resource or to consider with him further use of the agency on a continued and sustained basis. Understanding of the client and his problem may be limited at this point but some diagnostic appraisal of available data is required in responding to his problems. Continued service, often involving complex family relationship problems such as marital discord, requires completion of a study process which will produce enough data to make an initial formulation on which to base a treatment plan.

The initial diagnosis may, of course, be revised as further knowledge of the client is obtained. Since treatment must be based on psychosocial diagnosis, evaluation and prognosis, the earlier an initial diagnosis is achieved, the earlier treatment techniques can be selectively employed. It is usually possible to complete a study process and arrive at the first diagnosis in five interviews with the client plus necessary collateral interviewing.

EVALUATION

Diagnosis, as described above, seeks to define the client's problem. In making use of the diagnosis in treatment, the client must be evaluated by the caseworker in terms of his treatability, how he can be helped and how he may be expected to respond to treatment. Before treatment is undertaken, therefore, some estimate or prognosis must be made. Just as the professional use of the relationship continues throughout the period of activity with a case, so diagnosis and evaluation continue and treatment is modified in the light of further knowledge and understanding of the client.

FOCUS AND GOAL

The counseling methods of family casework are focused on improving the social functioning and social relationships of the client and his family. While social adjustment and psychological balance are inseparable, the focus of the social agency is on how the client gets along in his daily living. The *focus* of treatment is therefore on the client's social adjustment problems, including his ability to get along with his family members. When the client's problem is predominantly intrapsychic, the casework task may be to help the client to use psychiatric help rather than to treat the emotional difficulty.

Family casework is not concerned with the individual client alone.[10] Throughout treatment, the family caseworker is concerned with how other members of the family are functioning, how the client's behavior and social adjustment affect other family members, and what casework treatment of the client will mean for other family members. As has been stated, more than one family member may be included in the treatment plan, as both husband and wife in a marriage conflict problem, or parent and child where there are relationship difficulties.

The ultimate goal of family casework is to help the client to achieve reasonably successful daily living in his environment and with his family rather than to effect complete personality re-organization. Family casework therefore may be classified as a brief treatment method. The goal is to provide maximum help in as brief a period of time as possible. When it is realized that appointments with the client are seldom held oftener than once a week, the goal of family casework treatment is seen as limited rather than extensive.

Treatment, in terms of the specific goal with a particular client, may be subdivided into: A. Treatment aimed at maintaining adaptive patterns, and B. Treatment aimed at modification of adaptive patterns. Both types of treatment require an equal degree of skill and competence; diagnosis and evaluation indicate which type of treatment is appropriate for the particular client.

Treatment aimed at helping the client to *maintain* his adaptive patterns is directed toward supporting his existing strengths within the framework of his maximum usual pattern of functioning. It attempts to alleviate undue pressures in the client's social reality, and to strengthen the client in his emotional reactions to psychological pressures. As the client, with the support of the caseworker, experiences success in making better use of his capacities to deal with everyday living problems, the integrative capacity of his ego is increased, tensions are reduced and he is then able to continue on his own with restored functioning.

This type of treatment is appropriate when diagnosis and evaluation reveal that:

1. the client usually functions adequately and needs help only in social planning to overcome a temporary crisis.

2. the client has a weak ego structure which would be threatened and debilitated by directing him to further self-examination of his attitudes and emotional involvement in his problem. It should be pointed out that the ego may be weak because of overwhelming reality pressures as well as because of faulty personality development. Also the developmental stage of the client, for example in adolescence and old age, may place him in this category.

3. a preliminary period of ego-supportive help is indicated to prepare the client for some other form of treatment, often requiring preparation of the client to accept referral to psychiatric or other forms of help.

The techniques suitable to this type of treatment include: manipulation of the environment, direct advice and guidance, logical discussion, the exercise of professional authority, reassurance, and encouragement to take steps toward desirable objectives.

In employing this type of treatment, it is important that the caseworker estimate the dependency needs of the client. In providing needed gratification of dependency needs, which has immediate therapeutic value, the caseworker must avoid establishing a neurotic dependency relationship. The supportive work must be strengthening of healthy personality trends and directed towards socially desirable objectives. If diagnosis is inadequate, the caseworker may fall into the trap of supporting weakness indefinitely without benefit to the client.

In helping the client to maintain his adaptive patterns or restore him to his usual adequacy in coping with everyday problems of adjustment, the client may gain some self-awareness although this is not the aim of this type of treatment.

Treatment aimed at helping the client to *modify* his adaptive patterns is directed toward increasing the client's understanding of his behavior and attitudes, of his habitual patterns of behavior, of his relationships to other persons and his reactions to specific life situations. By helping the client to increase his ability to distinguish between his own part in his problem and the effect on him of reality factors, the client is gradually able to exercise more control over his behavior and develop better ways of handling himself and his situation.

Treatment of this type is appropriate when the diagnosis and evaluation show that the client has sufficient ego strength and flexibility to make constructive use of a process of self-examination.

The technique of this type of treatment is *clarification*. The emphasis of clarification on helping the client to understand himself may lead some practitioners to encompass the whole counseling process within this technique. The point of view of this article is that increasing the client's self-understanding is only a part of the total counseling method.

Clarification may range from a simple intellectual process of helping the client to think through matters that are relatively uncomplicated by strong emotion, to achieving a deeper comprehension of attitudes and feelings of considerable emotional content.[11]

Clarification is accomplished by helping the client to express himself and what is troubling him, and then, by questions and comments regarding inappropriate and inconsistent material, helping the client to think more clearly without distortion and confusion. The verbal activity of the caseworker is usually kept at the minimum necessary to keep the client on the track of increasing his self-understanding. When the worker, zealous to increase the client's self-knowledge, is too active and is not tuned to the client's emotional capacity to assimilate understanding, the client achieves only an intellectual grasp of his difficulties and modification of his behavior does not occur. However, it may be important to go over the same material repeatedly with the client until he has gained sureness in his self-knowledge and is able to see its application to different aspects of his behavior and feelings.

Clarification, as thus described, is not to be confused or equated with the technique of helping the client to achieve *insight* into his emotions, attitudes and behavior. Insight therapy involves techniques of uncovering repressed psychic material and unconscious conflicts and utilization of the client's transference reactions with a goal of bringing about basic changes in the client's personality structure. It is the point of view of the author that treatment of the insight type, while occasionally practised by caseworkers, is not sufficiently developed as a standard method, to be presently included in the range of social casework expected of caseworkers in the family agency. It is obvious that a client, through clarification, may achieve a degree of self-understanding approaching insight which helps him to change his behavior, but use of the techniques of insight therapy in a technical sense is not included in our definition of clarification.

TERMINATION

It has been stated that the family caseworker's goal is to provide maximal help with daily living problems in as short a period as possible. While treatment may extend over a period of months, the caseworker is alert to the client's progress in learning to handle his problem. In supportive treatment, just as the caseworker guards against undue dependency, he prepares the client in advance for termination of help by gradually withdrawing his technical support. Where the treatment aim is to help the client to modify his behavior in some particular aspects of his social adjustment, the caseworker in the later period of treatment helps the client to integrate understanding rather than to open up new areas of exploration. It can be observed in family agency practice that, where thoughtful termination of a helping process has occurred, the client may not need to return, and if he does at a later time, there is a new problem focus and new readiness to assume responsibility in working on the problem himself.

MEASUREMENT AND FOLLOW-UP

The evaluation of results of family casework help involves, of course, difficult measurements. A method of measuring movement or change occurring in an individual client or his environmental circumstances during the period he receives casework help was reported in 1950 by J. McVicker Hunt and Leonard S. Kogan.[12] This method involves the standardizing of judgments by caseworkers on the following:

1. Adaptive efficiency
2. Disabling habits and conditions
3. Verbalized attitudes or understanding
4. Environmental circumstances.

Follow-up studies of clients who have received casework help also have been undertaken with considerable care for accuracy and scientific evaluation. While much needs to be done in this area of evaluative research, the findings to date give precise indications that casework help is effective and produces positive results.

THE FUTURE OF FAMILY CASEWORK

Family casework has developed a method particularly suitable in helping many troubled people with problems of family relationships and social adjustment. While use of the professional staff of a social agency for such help was relatively unknown before the thirties, it has become an accepted source of personal counseling in the last two decades. This cultural change in the attitude of the average citizen has been accelerated by the fact that family casework agencies have uniformly set a high standard of qualifications for their professional staff members. A basic requirement for employment on the professional staff of a family casework agency is achievement of a Master's degree from an accredited graduate school of social work with a two-year curriculum encompassing both academic work and supervised field placement experience. Thus family casework can look forward to an increasing demand for its counseling services.

BIBLIOGRAPHY

1. "Scope and Methods of the Family Service Agency," 1953. *Family Service Association of America*, New York.
2. HAMILTON, GORDON: 1951. "Theory and Practice of Social Casework" *Columbia University Press*, New York.
3. "Principles and Techniques in Social Casework," 1950. *Family Service Association of America*, New York.
4. "The Family Agency: Its Value to Business and Industry," September, 1960. *Family Service Highlights*.
5. "Family Casework in the Interest of Children," February–March, 1958. *Social Casework*.
6. "Directory of Member Agencies," 1961. *Family Service Association of America*, New York.
7. HOLLIS, FLORENCE: June, 1951. "The Relationship Between Psychosocial Diagnosis and Treatment." *Social Casework*.
8. GREEN, SIDNEY L., M.D.: December, 1954. "Psychoanalytic Contributions to Casework Treatment." *Social Casework*.
9. KOGAN, LEONARD S.: May and June, 1957. "The Short-Term Case in a Family Agency." *Social Casework*.
10. BEATMAN, FRANCES L.: March, 1957. "Family Interaction: Its Significance for Diagnosis and Treatment." *Social Casework*
11. HOLLIS, FLORENCE: June, 1949. "The Techniques of Casework." *Journal of Social Casework*.
12. HUNT, J. McVICKER and KOGAN, LEONARD S.: 1950. "Measuring Results in Social Casework." *Family Service Association of America*, New York.

Group Counseling Methods

HYMAN SPOTNITZ

Formerly Jewish Board of Guardians
New York City

GROUP counseling is a systematic mode of giving advice, opinion or instruction in the presence of two or more persons for the purpose of influencing their judgment, their conduct, or both. The practice awaits empirical definition and distinction from related activities, especially from group psychotherapy; but, on a broad continuum of these services, group counseling is rather commonly accepted as the most ego-centered and closely geared to immediate realities. Within its own sphere, various methods are employed. These too form a continuum, based on the relative directiveness of the counselor's approach to the needs and difficulties presented by those requesting his services.

With more or less clinically normal persons who seek clarification of their sense of personal identity or help with some adjustment problem of which they are fully conscious, he appropriately carries on an ego-oriented process. With personalities whose predispositions hamper effective responses to advice, the counselor may find it necessary to address himself to uncovering conflicts and stimulating verbal release. With due recognition of the fact that my formulation of the indirect method may be regarded as crossing the almost imperceptible boundary into psychotherapy, I shall encompass within this chapter the principles and procedures implicit in the broader concepts of group counseling.

Demonstrations that the group setting has certain intrinsic values that do not exist in the bipersonal setting have added stature to group counseling during the past decade. Nevertheless, it has its limitations as well as its positive aspects. Both have to be evaluated in relation to an individual's specific need for counsel before it can be determined how beneficial a counseling experience in a group would be for him.

Advantages of the Group Setting

The most obvious advantage of group counseling is that it enables several persons to be helped at the same time. Obviously, this is an important consideration, in view of the great demand for assistance in dealing with personal problems. For those seeking such aid who are willing to secure it in the company of individuals with similar motives and needs, group counseling is a boon.

But exigency is not the only advantage. For a considerable number of persons who wish to obtain the type of counseling most appropriate to their needs regardless of its cost and other practical aspects, group counseling may well recommend itself as the method of choice.

Many people feel more secure as members of a group seeking counsel than if they were soliciting it individually. Uneasiness or fear of the counselor as an awe-inspiring or threatening figure seems to be diluted by the insulating effect of the group setting. The attitude of the counselee is therefore more relaxed, as a rule, in a group than if he were closeted privately with the same counselor. Besides, once the group member discovers that both his problems and his response to counseling are not very different from those of his co-members, it usually becomes easier for him to talk about his problems, to request the information or advice he needs, and to assimilate it.

With the growing realization that his basic urges and reactions to his urges are similar to those of others in the group, the counselee's previous sense of isolation about his own personality problems tends to evaporate. Mounting feelings of kinship and intimacy ultimately stimulate latent abilities to maintain socially constructive relationships.

Individuals who seek help primarily for dealing with problems of social adjustment have most to gain from group counseling. States of anxiety and psychoneurotic or psychosomatic symptoms that are significantly exacerbated in the presence of two or more persons are types of distress which usually respond well to this procedure. Questions about interpersonal functioning—how to make friends at college, for example, or how to be a good member of a team or avoid various sorts of conflicts—are much easier to handle after they have been ventilated in a group session, with appropriate discussion and study.

That is why someone requesting help with some problem arising out of his relations with several persons may be invited to discuss the situation in a group. It may be explained that the presence of other counselees often makes it easier for people to absorb information and utilize it constructively.

In the dynamics of the group setting, moreover, the beneficial results of counseling are more quickly to be discerned. The interaction of the participants facilitates the digestion of the psychological nourishment offered.

Disadvantages of the Group Setting

Since the counselor's time and attention have to be shared with others in a group, each member naturally receives less than he would command if he were alone with the counselor during the same period. Besides, one member may have problems that are decidedly different from those of the other counselees and make inordinate demands upon the group leader.

To his co-members, the person with special problems may become a source of irritation. Conversely, the resentment building up against him may expose him at any moment to their combined hostility. Supplementary counseling on an individual basis may enable him to function more cooperatively in the sessions; otherwise, his removal from the group becomes necessary.

The group setting tends to inhibit the communication and handling of bi-personal problems. The one-to-one relationship is preferred for the resolution of personality difficulties rooted in experiences during the first two years of life, the pre-verbal period when an individual is primarily involved with one person at a time, usually his mother. If the group is structured to deal with one person at a time, or if the counselee concerned relates to it as to a single transference object, such intimate problems may be effectively dealt with through group counseling. However, successful results in cases of this nature are exceptional and hard to predict. Even in individual counseling or analytic psychotherapy, years of treatment may be required to alter personality elements patterned during early childhood. It has yet to be determined whether a proportionately long exposure to the group climate will also counteract deviant tendencies which originated in the pre-verbal period and stimulate personality maturation in those areas.

DIRECT GROUP COUNSELING

The counselor's goals will naturally dictate his methods of working with a group. If his chief aim is to instruct, he may deliver inspirational talks or lectures and provide opportunity for planned discussions.

Such procedures, which are primarily authority-directed, were originally described by Pratt in 1905 for the "class" treatment of somatically ill patients.

Since then, many other methods of working didactically with groups have been developed. A counselor may, for example, give informal talks on subjects in which group members express some interest, and encourage them to verbalize their reactions to the instructions or explanations he provides. He may arrange a wide variety of group activities. His counselees may go on trips with him, visit one another, exchange gifts. They may produce plays or arrange screenings of films bearing on significant ideas related to the educational process going on within the group milieu. A statement and discussion of these themes under the counselor's direction often follow the presentation. Environmental manipulation may be utilized.

Through methods such as these, a counselor conveys information, introduces stimulating ideas, or teaches important lessons. Activities of this nature do provide new experiences, but they do not produce intrapsychic change.

Counseling becomes more complex when a group focuses on the personality problems of its members. If the individuality of only one of them is under consideration during a session, the rest of the group may helpfully center on him in any one of a number of ways.

His problems may be dramatized in an impromptu or prepared psychodrama, the form popularized by J. L. Moreno. Discussion and interaction designed to assist the member in resolving his difficulties supplement the role-playing elements of such a presentation.

If Klapman's system of "affective re-education" is followed, the counselor assumes a more authoritative role. Programs are planned and reading assignments are handed out to the counselees. They may be called on to report on their reading, to submit questions for the group leader to answer or for the whole group to discuss.

In groups organized to help persons with similar problems, the counselor may carefully study their behavior and make pertinent comments about it. Inspirational talks stimulate the confession or admission of problems. Authoritative advice, guidance or direction may be supplied. Some group programs provide the members with opportunities to live or work together.

In anonymous organizations, such as Alcoholics Anonymous, the counselor devotes himself principally to the suppression of a specific pattern of behavior. Loyalty to the group, mutual support and the unqualified acceptance of cultural, religious or moral values may be required of the members. Solemn appeals to reason and ambition may be made.

The more experience one acquires in instructing and advising a group, the more one comes to realize that deficiencies in judgment and conduct must often be attributed to something other than ignorance about the nature of the demands which external reality makes upon the individual, generally or in a specific situation. Inappropriate or inadequate functioning can often be traced back to shortcomings in the biologically, culturally and psychologically determined elements of the personality.

Some people with such shortcomings have sustained serious psychological scars that make them emotionally incapable of solving their own problems. They approach a counselor with the notion that his advice will make it possible for them to solve the problems. Whether it will or not depends on their ability to accept and utilize the advice for the exercise of good judgment and the improvement of their conduct. If they can not absorb and act on the advice, it may serve to point up their inadequacies, intensify their feelings of helplessness and paralyze whatever capacity for functioning they do possess. To those who are so incapable of perceiving the motivations determining their behavior that they are unable to accommodate themselves easily to the demands of reality as they perceive it, the responsible counselor may have to explain that advice as such would have little if any value at the time. In these cases, some procedure other than direct counseling is indicated.

INDIRECT GROUP COUNSELING

What some people require is a form of counseling that is directed toward an improvement in their current psychological functioning more basic and general than the immediate solution of the particular problem they present would produce. To bring about such improvement, so that they may convert advice and information to their own needs and to socially constructive ends, is the purpose of indirect counseling.

If a person's current functioning is inadequate because his early training in the family group and his psychological development were inadequate, indirect group counseling is designed to help him become psychologically adequate to solve his present problems. Actually, that is the realistic goal of the individual who seeks counsel.

Indirect group counseling becomes highly complex and makes stiff demands on the group as a whole when the counselor sets out to acquire thorough understanding of its members and to help them effect substantial personality changes. To liberate them from outmoded patterns of behavior, he must recognize, on the one hand, whatever immaturity, deviation, disorganization or disintegration of personality they manifest and, on the other hand, their potentialities for regrowth. Obstacles causing arrests in their development may thus be removed, deviations may be corrected, and each counselee may be helped to achieve the maturation of his personality.

The more extensively and intensively indirect group counseling addresses itself to these tasks, the closer it gets to the realm of analytic group psychotherapy. Indeed, the goals and methods of the highly skilled and understanding counselor may eventually become indistinguishable from those of the analytic psychotherapist.

Nevertheless, the counselor and the psychotherapist operate within different frames of reference, and the initial orientation of each to his group members differs accordingly. The therapist takes it for granted that help in changing attitudes and improving behavior is required of him because his group members are in treatment for some condition recognized to be more or less pathological. Some of these people may respond more quickly than was anticipated, either because the diagnosis of emotional illness was incorrect or because they required little assistance to achieve the limited goals they set for themselves in psychotherapy.

On the other hand, the counselor assumes that advice and information—what people come to him for, often voluntarily—are the only services that they will require from him. But he has to exceed the scope of his initial assumptions in working with counselees who are unable to respond to an exclusively ego-oriented process. Their abilities to handle the problem they present not infrequently have to be released as well as directed, or they turn out to have another problem that is more acute and basic. The counselor has to be sufficiently trained to recognize what goes on in such cases and to refer appropriately those he can not handle himself. For some who consult him, indirect counseling is the alternative to psychiatric study or intensive psychotherapy.

Various personality theories, approaches and techniques are encompassed in indirect group counseling. Within the conceptual framework of one system, the counselor may employ numerous techniques as suitable in each situation, or he may be rather strictly limited by the system itself to a characteristic attitude. Those who adhere to the so-called client-centered system developed by Carl R. Rogers focus on clarifying the feelings of their counselees. The reflection of feelings may be flexibly interspersed with other techniques by the counselor who operates eclectically, drawing on whatever procedures are available to him to secure his immediate objectives. The inspirational, didactic, authoritarian or psychodramatic approaches employed in direct counseling to work on a specific problem are also employed in indirect counseling to secure the more general objectives associated with personality change and maturation.

What follows is a presentation of the general principles, conceptual tools and dynamic phenomena that characterize indirect group counseling that is oriented to these broader objectives.

Selection of the Group

When individuals assemble and talk about themselves spontaneously, they tend to be dominated by emotional currents that move them in opposite directions. These currents, one of libidinal and the other of aggressive impulses, find expression eventually in feelings, thoughts and modes of behavior. Both currents must be controlled and utilized; if kept in proper balance, they promote a healthful group process.

The libidinal current then operates to facilitate the development of feelings of intimacy and understanding. The aggressive current also serves as a constructive force when it is controlled; if not, it can operate to violate the rights of counselees and even destroy their group as a functioning unit. Well regulated, the aggressive current helps to maintain individuality, to set limits to personality encroachment and to push aside obstacles to psychological growth. This will go on steadily, if imperceptibly at times, if the emotional climate of the group is thus controlled.

On the other hand, excessive domination of the group by one current or the other may lead to undesirable behavior and other untoward developments. The counselor has to give much thought to the effect which each candidate for a group might have on the others. Some types of personalities would facilitate the development of one of these emotional forces, or the other. Their selection is made with a view to promoting a conglomerate of group activity that would help to equilibrate the libidinal and aggressive currents.

A group is ideally constituted for indirect counseling if some of its members have the ability to instigate verbalization, others can help to maintain a stable climate, and still others are able to act as pacifiers and prevent the group from becoming overexcited. Rather than marked diversity or similarity, the membership should also be well balanced with respect to personality formation. A withdrawn person and one who is emotionally outgoing in nature function well together; an inhibited individual counterbalances one who is impulsive. A blending of schizoid and manic, and of obsessional and hysterical types helps to create an effective synthesis of personalities.

Age, sex, intelligence, socio-economic backgrounds, sexual attitudes and situational concerns are other factors to be weighed in terms of the aims of the counseling experience. The rule of thumb is that heterosexual groups of diverse types generate emotional interaction and highly charged relationships, whereas groups of relatively similar people tend to engage in quiet discussion and develop mild interest in one another.

Full particulars on each candidate for a group should therefore be at the disposal of the counselor. He may procure the information needed through a series of individual or group interviews. So-called group screening is now employed in many agencies. From an interview group of about forty candidates, it is usually possible to select from five to ten who could form an effective unit. An even larger number of candidates may be assembled for screening if several counseling groups are to be formed.

Group Procedures

Once the composition of a group has been determined, questions of procedure should be settled. Many arise when the group begins to function. In harmony with its objectives, decisions are usually in order on such points as the following:

Is the group to meet at regular intervals or just occasionally? Shall members be required to attend every meeting? How long are the meetings to last? Who is to talk first? How much time may each counselee have for direct verbal communication? Are interruptions to be permitted? May all subjects be discussed? How much of what goes on in the group sessions may be disclosed and discussed outside? What in general is the counselor's role to be? When shall he intervene? Shall decisions be arrived at unanimously, or by majority vote? Or shall they be handed down instead by the counselor in an authoritarian manner, or adopted by a different method during each stage of the group's development?

Decisions of this nature often have more than a *pro forma* importance. If, for example, one of the group objectives is to stimulate the emotional development of its members, that would be furthered whenever a unanimous decision was demanded. The process of achieving unanimity in a counseling group, as in a jury, often stirs up very lively, even explosive forces.

If maximum self-revelation and self-understanding are goals of the counselees, the group is encouraged to remain as unstructured as possible as it begins to function. After routine arrangements have been agreed upon, the members may do as they please about talking or remaining silent. If one of them seeks direction, he is informed that it is his duty to talk freely about himself and to help his co-members understand themselves better. The counselor participates chiefly as an observer, saying little unless paralyzing anxiety has to be allayed or one group member needs to be protected from the effects of an overly destructive attack by another.

Dealing with Resistances

If this general plan of operation is followed, sooner or later the counselees will show obvious interest in doing something besides relating personal problems and helping one another achieve self-understanding. Their new interests take many different forms, but all of them obstruct their emotional development.

One counselee may try to use the group setting for the solution of some urgent personal problem. Another may object that the time is not ripe for the discussion of a particular subject, or that the subject itself is unsuitable for group discussion. Someone else may want to use the meeting time for something more enjoyable than talking and listening to problems. It may be asked whether one member has the right to monopolize the group's attention for several consecutive sessions. Finally, the group may become preoccupied with the personality of the counselor himself and question him about his private life and activities.

Such obstacles to group progress, typical methods of resisting meaningful communication, are consistently studied and worked on by the goal-oriented counselor. When the resistances begin to operate within the group, they assume different forms and appear at different times; the type of resistance patterned by each member is apt to be highly expressive of his personality. When these so-called *individual resistances* are in the process of being resolved, the counselees will begin to manifest *common resistances*—jointly activated methods of obstructing the ultimate goals of the counseling experience.

Crucial for its success is the correct handling of the resistance patterns. Their resolution is both an art and a science.

Before anything can be done with or about a resistance pattern, it must be recognized for what it is. The counselor must be able to detect the various methods employed by the group members, individually or collectively, to resist self-revelation and self-development.

Recognition of a resistance is usually followed by a strong impulse to overcome or demolish it. But this is not the approach that I recommend to a counselor who functions characteristically as a participant-observer. Quite the contrary. A resistance pattern helps to *maintain the equilibrium* of the person who is resorting to it. Instead of trying to help him give it up, the others in the group should attempt to persuade him that such behavior is unnecessary—assuming, of course, that it serves no useful end in that situation.

The resolution of a resistance pattern usually begins with a careful investigation of its current and historical meaning for the counselee. His own interest in its past and present significance for his psychic economy is usually heightened by this approach.

Sooner or later, the resistance patterns are *conceptualized and verbalized* —that is, interpreted—in the group setting. One member frequently does this for another in a well-functioning group, while the counselor assists without taking too active a part in the process. Ultimately, the behavior of all of the members should be fully interpreted.

It is desirable that the counselees do this themselves, as much as possible, but the counselor should have various techniques at his disposal to help them. For example, he may ask questions that may evoke detailed information about the resistance patterns manifested in the group. The artful use of "why" requires that he follows the *stream* of the group's communications and intervenes briefly at well-spaced intervals, so that his counselees will gradually acquire the ability to investigate, to explore and to understand each other without developing undesirable states of irritation and tension.

After the resistance patterns have been resolved, the group as a whole tends to be more respectful of the rights and privileges of each member. Whatever is said in the sessions is treated as a privileged communication. The counselees display more confidence and reliance in one another. As mutual respect is established, they work toward unanimity of opinion in some areas, while manifesting a tolerant awareness of the reasons why their opinions diverge in other areas.

Thereafter, there is little if any need for the group to operate with fixed rules of procedure. Democratic principles of human relationships are usually taken for granted, because the group experience itself has demonstrated that these principles are the key to desirable social functioning.

Other Aspects of Indirect Counseling

Pressures inherent in the group counseling situation cause feelings to build up, and these lead to the development of latent psychological tensions. In a series of stages the concealed tensions mount, are recognized, understood historically and mastered. Inhibitory patterns holding the energy in check have to be understood. Verbal release patterns are formed and utilized to permit the discharge of the energy. This patterning and the resolution of the obstacles or resistances to communication occur in a wide variety of combinations, some of which overlap.

The art of indirect counseling involves the ability to recognize the presence of states of aggressive or libidinal tension and to secure their discharge in language—not in behavior—in the group setting. The counselor has to be able to distinguish between the two emotional currents and find out how and why they are concealed. His attitudes and interventions are designed to aid the counselees in overcoming obstacles to the verbal release of their impulses. While he remains on the alert for aggressive tensions that would interfere with smooth group functioning, he must bear in mind that their presence may be exaggerated to mask libidinal impulses.

He conveys the idea that the counselees should allow themselves to become aware of all their impulses, feelings and thoughts, so that the connections, associations, and origins of their verbal productions may be understood. After the counselees get to understand their own feelings, thoughts and limitations, the group works to achieve a synthesis of healthy impulses, feelings and thoughts.

In this process of emotional education, the group itself is employed as a force with which to influence and correct. The counselor's attitudes and verbal communications create a climate in which the group members may experience types of emotions that are conducive to their progress in one sphere or another.

One of the counselor's tasks is to facilitate the development of situations which will expose the participants, whether actively or passively, to more stimulation or frustration than their respective ego structures can endure. In such situations, the latent inflexible attitudes which have made it impossible for them to cope with their immediate problems are manifested in the sessions. The counselees then tend to behave in ways that make it possible to recognize developmental arrests and deviations which disrupted the mind's hierarchical continuity and allowed rigidity to set in. Although he does not focus on unconscious behavior as intensively and extensively as the analytic group psychotherapist, the counselor employs methods of counteracting the effects of untoward experiences of the past that interfere with appropriate functioning in the present, so that the group members will become capable of solving the particular difficulties about which they have consulted him.

Because he maintains the attitude of a sympathetic and interested observer, the counselor attracts special attention in the group. Eventually, as its members tend to reactivate their previous attitudes toward persons in authority, their feelings about him resemble those they had for their parents. Though transference is not stimulated and employed as significantly as in analytic psychotherapy, its development in the indirect counseling group enhances the influence of the leader as a sort of psychological parent. He exploits transference phenomena to confront the members with their troublesome attitudes and to contrast these with other points of view that would favor more constructive solutions to their problems. The transference reactions that the counselees develop for one another are also utilized to make them aware of alternative forms of behavior.

The study of an emotion in its successive phases helps the counselees recognize how it can lead to self-defeating forms of behavior. Their verbalization of the various emotional configurations that develop in their interaction with each other and with the counselor promotes the mastery of impulse patterns. The group situation provides many opportunities to practice new forms of behavior that emerge in the course of the counseling experience. Ultimately, the group members acquire the freedom of choice to behave in consonance with their own objectives.

PREREQUISITES OF THE COUNSELOR

Ample knowledge of the subject on which he tenders advice, a positive and perceptive approach to troubled human beings and the ability to handle them well together are essential qualifications for direct group counseling. Obviously, the indirect counseling of groups imposes more exacting professional and personal requirements.

The capacity to develop emotionally understanding relationships is the most essential prerequisite. Latent abilities for leadership emerge swiftly as one gains experience in handling groups.

In indirect counseling, the practitioner has to draw upon a series of related disciplines—general medicine, psychiatry, psychoanalysis, group psychotherapy, clinical psychology and social casework. Besides being well trained in his own particular field, the counselor should have a reasonably good working knowledge of the others. Skill in handling intergroup relations is also valuable equipment.

It is desirable that indirect counseling by non-medical professionals should be carried out in cooperation with psychiatrists trained in group dynamics as well as in medical diagnosis and psychotherapy. The group leader is exposed to the significant data and emotional impact of several persons at the same time. Regular psychiatric consultations serve as a check on diagnosis and the therapeutic approach to their problems, and also help the counselor to maintain balanced judgment in coping with the emotional impact of the group. The stiff demands made on his skill, judgment and personality also make it desirable that he should have undergone psychoanalysis and taken part in a group training program.

13

CONCLUDING OBSERVATIONS

Group counseling is intended primarily for people who seek help in handling problems involving their relations with several persons. In terms of their own understanding of these multipersonal problems, information and advice will clear the way to desirable solutions. Whether this does or does not prove to be the case depends on how accurately they have evaluated their problems.

Direct counsel will be of benefit to those whose appraisal of their own difficulties is sound. Placed in a group with people with similar problems, they will respond in a few sessions. They will find it possible to act as they have been advised and to function effectively in accordance with their objectives.

Others who solicit counsel in connection with an immediate problem have incorrectly evaluated it; more often than not, they are handicapped by some more basic emotional problem of which they are not aware. Indirect group counseling is designed to prepare them to utilize the information and advice they seek, so that it will actually benefit them.

The more emotionally disturbed these people are, the more intensive the psychological assistance they need. Some will require individual counseling, or a combination of individual and group counseling. No matter how intensively the counselor works with them on their problems, he may find it necessary to refer a few of these people for psychiatric treatment. He is faced with the responsibility of assisting them in getting whatever kind of help they need to solve their particular problems.

With those who are responsive to indirect counseling, he functions in the group setting like a psychological parent as well as a dispenser of information and advice. Through this activity, he helps them acquire the freedom of choice to function in accordance with their own potentialities and goals in life.

The presence of other counselees similarly engaged in self-understanding and self-mastery appeases the group member's social hunger in a constructive and gratifying way. The experience of learning how to deal with one another's inappropriate attitudes in the group setting, and of observing how deviations in personality structure may be corrected, often proves to be of great value in dealing with siblings, parents, classmates, business associates and others with whom the counselee is in daily contact.

In the setting of a group receiving indirect counseling, one observes under controlled conditions how society may contribute to personality disorders, and how pathological patterns of behavior may lead individuals to social deterioration. The counselor provides a milieu for emotional interaction in which these object-lessons may be learned in a vividly convincing and gratifying manner, with a minimum sacrifice of time and other potentialities for development. As he helps individuals to evolve psychologically in the group setting, the counselor also illuminates many desirable pathways for the evolution of society.

BIBLIOGRAPHY

1. ACKERMAN, N. W.: 1961. "Symptom, Defense and Growth in Group Process." *Int. J. group Psychother.* **11**, pp. 131–142.
2. AMSTER, F.: 1954. "Application of Group Psychotherapy Principles to Non-structured Groups." *Int. J. group Psychother.* **4**, pp. 285–292.
3. ANONYMOUS: 1959. "Group Counseling in Wakefield Prison." *Lancet* **2**, p. 1022.
4. APPEL, E. and MARTIN, C.: 1957. "Group Counseling for Social Adjustment." *Amer. J. ment. Def.* **62**, pp. 517–520.
5. BROEDEL, J. W.: 1959. "A Study of the Effects of Group Counseling on the Academic Performance and Mental Health of Underachieving Adolescents." *Disserta. Abstr.* **19**, p. 3019.
6. CRAIG, V. W. and BROWN, W. H.: 1956. "Group Counseling for Administrative Personnel." *Nursing Outlook* **4**, pp. 378–380.
7. CORSINI, R. J.: 1957. *Methods of Group Psychotherapy*, McGraw-Hill (Blakiston), New York.
8. DREIKURS, R., CORSINI, R., LOWE, R. and SONSTEGARD, M. (Editors): 1959. *Adlerian Family Counseling; Manual for Counseling Centers.* Oregon: Univ. of Oregon Press, Eugene.
9. DRIVER, H. I.: 1958. *Counseling and Learning through Small-Group Discussion.* Madison, Wisconsin: Monona Publications.
10. FAMILY SERVICE ASSOCIATION OF AMERICA: 1959. *Use of Group Techniques in the Family Agency* (Pamphlet) FSA, New York.
11. GASKILL, E. R. and MUDD, E. H.: 1950. "A decade of group counseling." *Social Casework* **31**, pp. 194–201.
12. GINOTT, H. G.: 1957. "Differential Treatment Groups in Guidance, Counseling, Psychotherapy and Psychoanalysis." *Int. J. soc. Psychiat.* **3**, pp. 231–235.
13. ——: 1956. "Group Screening of Parents in a Child Guidance Center." *Int. J. group Psychother.* **6**, pp. 405–409.
14. GOLUB, F. R., McBRIDE, J. F., and STILLWELL, HAMILTON: 1956. "Retirement: An Experiment in Group Counseling." *Personnel*, **32**, pp. 544–547.
15. GRUNWALD, H.: 1957. "Group Counseling in a Family and Children's Agency." *Int. J. group Psychother.* **7**, pp. 318–326.
16. HARROWER, M.: 1956. "Projective Counseling, a Psychotherapeutic Technique." *Am. J. Psychother.* **10**, pp. 74–86.
17. HOBBS, N.: 1951. "Group-centered Psychotherapy." In Rogers, C. R. (Ed.), *Client-Centered Therapy.* Boston: Houghton–Mifflin.
18. KADIS, A. L.: 1960. "Analytic Group Work with Teachers." *J. National Ass. Women Deans and Counselors* **33**, p. 78.
19. —— and LAZARSFELD, S.: 1945. "The Group as a Psychotherapeutic Factor in Counseling Work." *Nervous Child* **4**, pp. 228–238.
20. KELSEY, C. E., Jr.: 1960. "An Annotated Bibliography of Group Counseling." *J. Psychol. Studies*, **11**, pp. 84–92.

21. LEICHTER, E.: 1956. "Family Casework Through the Group Method." *J. Jew. commun. Serv.* **33**, p. 376.
22. LERNER, A.: 1955. "Self-evaluation in Group Counseling with Male Alcoholic Inmates." *Int. J. group Psychother.* **5**, pp. 286–298.
23. LEVINE, L., "Sex and Marriage Problems." In Slavson, S. R. (Ed.): 1956. *The Fields of Group Psychotherapy*, Ch. 14. New York: Int. Univ. Press.
24. —— and BRODSKY, I.: 1956. "Taking Stock of Marriage: an Illustration in Group Counseling." *Marriage & Fam. Living*, **18**, pp. 162–167.
25. LIFTON, W. M.: 1961. *Working with Groups: Group Process and Individual Growth.* New York: John Wiley.
26. LUBIN, B. and SLONIMSKI, A.: 1960. "A Counseling Program with Adult, Male, Palsied Patients." *Cerebral Palsy Review* **21**, p. 3.
27. MENSH, I. N.: "Research in Counseling and Psychotherapeutic Process." In Brower, D. and Abt, L. W. (editors): 1956. *Progress in Clinical Psychology.* New York: Grune & Stratton.
28. MUDD, E. H.: 1957. "Knowns and Unknowns in Marriage Counseling Research." *Marriage & Fam. Living* **19**, pp. 75–81.
29. NOYES, A. P. and KOLB, L. C.: 1958. *Modern Clinical Psychiatry.* Philadelphia: W. B. Saunders.
30. REDWIN, E.: 1955. "The Behind-your-back Technique in Marriage Counseling." *Group Psychother.* **8**, pp. 40–47.
31. ROTHMAN, R.: 1956. "Group Counseling with Parents of Visually Handicapped Children." *Int. J. group Psychother.* **6**, pp. 317–323.
32. SHERMAN, S. N., "Group Counseling." In Eisenstein, V. W. (Ed.): 1956. *Neurotic Interaction in Marriage*, Ch. 16. New York: Basic Books.
33. SLAVSON, S. R.: 1950. *Analytic Group Psychotherapy.* New York: Columbia University Press.
34. ——: 1961. "When is a Therapy Group Not a Therapy Group?" *Int. J. group Psychother.* **10**, pp. 3–21.
35. SLAVSON, S. R. and MACLENNAN, B., "Unmarried mothers." In Slavson, S. R. (Ed.): 1956. *The Fields of Group Psychotherapy*, pp. 187–194. New York: Int. Univ. Press.
36. SPOTNITZ, H.: 1952. "A Psychoanalytic View of Resistance in Groups." *Int. J. Group Psychother.* **2**, pp. 3–9.
37. ——: 1961. *The Couch and the Circle*, Ch. 10. New York: Alfred Knopf.
38. VINCENT, C. E.: 1957. *Readings in Marriage Counseling.* New York: Crowell.
39. WOLFF, W. M.: 1956. "Group Counseling in a Neuropsychiatric Hospital." *Personnel Guidance J.*, **34**, pp. 504–507.

Counseling in Public Assistance

KERMIT T. WILTSE

Associate Professor of Social Work
University of California
Berkeley, Calif.

WHAT IS PUBLIC ASSISTANCE?

PUBLIC assistance is the provision by government of a minimum subsistence to people without income. In an industrial economy people cannot obtain the essentials of living without money. When income ceases due to death of breadwinner, disability, old age, loss of job or some other reason, sooner or later some people will exhaust all their resources and need financial aid. In the United States public assistance is provided as a joint undertaking of the state, local and federal governments.* There are currently five main types, called categories, of public assistance in use in the United States, although not all five are utilized in every state and territory. The names of the categories—Old Age Assistance, Aid to the Blind, Aid to Dependent Children, Aid to the Permanently and Totally Disabled and General Assistance†—indicate both their purpose and the historical fact that

* The Social Security Act of 1935 encompassed two basic approaches to the problem of financial dependency in our modern industrial economy, namely insurance and assistance. The insurance provisions were expressed through setting up the program of pre-paid benefits through employer–employee contributions that is now termed Old Age and Survivors Insurance; the federal grants-in-aid for assistance to those individuals and families whose financial dependency fell outside the insurance provisions or for whom the insurance payment was insufficient to meet their needs. For a thorough exposition of the subject of social security in the United States, see Vasey, Wayne, *Government and Social Welfare: Roles of Federal, State, and Local Governments in Administering Welfare Services*, New York: Henry Holt and Co., 1958. 506 pp.

† Although these are the names given to the categories in most states, there are a few variations. For example, in California it is Old Age Security rather than Old Age Assistance and Aid to Needy Children rather than Aid to Dependent Children, but the purpose is substantially the same.

the first four were developed to separate out of the undifferentiated mass of financially dependent individuals and families certain types of need for special attention.

It is not necessary to the purposes of this article to explore the detailed features of each category or the intricacies of eligibility for each. But it is necessary to keep clearly in mind that eligibility to any type of public assistance is based upon proven financial need. The applicant for public assistance must assert his financial dependency and cooperate with the public assistance worker in proving it. In our society financial dependency tends to be equated with total dependency. This fact creates the implications of inadequacy and failure that cluster around receipt of financial assistance both in the feelings of recipients and in the attitude of society toward them. The helping process in public assistance hinges upon the meaning which the application for or receipt of public assistance holds for each individual person who experiences it.

This process can be expressed as the process of eligibility determination but the phrase "eligibility determination" must be conceived in a very broad sense. The process of eligibility determination ranges from a relatively simple kind of help in making their application and proving their need for assistance required by some of the clients of the public assistance agency to a quality and degree of help required by others that demands of the public assistance worker the highest degree of ability to initiate and sustain change in these clients' relationship to employment, to spouse or children, or to other realistic factors in their lives. It is this very range of expectation placed upon it that renders the effort to describe the total function of the public assistance agency as a single entity which we term "eligibility determination" of limited usefulness. We must examine in some detail the clientele of a public assistance agency and the problems they present in order better to understand the essential nature of the public assistance worker's job.

WHO COMES TO THE PUBLIC ASSISTANCE AGENCY AND FOR HELP WITH WHAT PROBLEMS?

The only common denominator of the people who come to a public assistance agency is that each is unable or believes he is unable to manage without financial aid. The extremity of need to which he has subjected himself before taking this step, his feelings about having to apply for aid, and the emotional and material resources he may have for self-support in the future are as various as are the age and family characteristics of any cross section of the American population. Many—in fact the largest single group—are persons past 65 years of age who tend to see old age assistance as a "pension" to which they are entitled by right of their years. They are often understandably very resistant to accepting the idea of their right to it being contingent upon clear proof that they have no other resources with which to manage. The public assistance worker must help them to face this fact in order that they can engage themselves positively in the process of establishing their eligibility if they are really in need, or in discovering and using alternative resources where any exist. The larger proportion of recipients of this type of assistance can manage their own affairs beyond this point with the interest and concern of the worker available to give further help in times of acute emergency or emergence of new problems. Some—a smaller but uncertain proportion—may need and want more frequent or a more profound quality of help because of conditions or emotional problems peculiar to them and to their situation. An example of this is the elderly woman who is in conflict with her daughter with whom she is living, yet no other plan is feasible or acceptable to all the persons involved.

The attitude of our American culture toward its aged members might be described as one of kindly considerateness, and the laws governing assistance to the aged in the various states express a social policy of humane and considerate treatment of the dependent aged. The original Social Security Act did not specifically express an additional mandate to state and local administrations. Not until the 1956 Amendments was a new legislative policy asserted by additions to the "purpose" clauses leading into the provisions for each category that expressed a new emphasis on services. With reference to the aged these clauses stated that self-care and self-dependence of the aged was to be promoted by local administration.* The implications of this renewed emphasis on services to the aged are many and far-reaching. Simply stated they mean that the federal government will encourage with leadership and share in the costs of administering programs to assist aged recipients with all kinds of individualized services that will contribute toward maintaining or restoring their capacity for physical and psychological self-care and self-dependence. This is not to imply that services to the aged by local welfare departments were discouraged prior to 1956, or that departments did not have such programs. Rather it means that there is a positive policy of encouraging the efforts of local departments toward all kinds of counseling and group activities with aged, a fact which has great implications to the thesis of this chapter.

The same attitude of tolerant concern is likely to adhere to all

---

* For a full discussion of the exact wording and the implications see Schottland, Charles I., "Social Security Amendments of 1956: A Summary and Legislative History," *Social Security Bulletin*, Vol. 19, September 1956, pp. 3–15.

individuals regardless of age who are dependent upon public assistance because of specific and clear-cut physical disability, such as blindness, tuberculosis, heart disease, or due to the state of being a child. We commonly speak of the socially acceptable reasons for financial dependency, meaning those reasons which in our society have the least connotation of individual fault or failure. Age and physical disability are generally the most socially acceptable. Financial dependency due to inability to find a job even in times of economic prosperity, dependency due to personality problems of the individual, or dependency of one's children due to loss of breadwinner if that loss were caused by desertion or divorce tend to carry an implication of personal fault or failure. This fact is of significance to the worker who seeks to help his clients, regardless of the reason for their financial need, to come to terms with their feelings about their situation and to put their energy into making constructive use of public assistance while they must have it, and into finding ways and means of restoring themselves to self-support when it becomes feasible.

The importance of individualized counseling and other services to assist individuals and families maintain or restore their social functioning has long been recognized as a most important aspect of the public assistance agency's function. In other words the money grant was an essential aspect but not the total of the public assistance worker's task. Service, a single word embracing a multitude of distinguishable activities, has been seen since the inception of the public assistance programs as a necessary adjunct to the granting of financial aid. Service must be individualized to the specific problem or problems of each recipient. For one family, it might be helping a father maintain his psychological health while he is helped also to work towards restoring his physical capacity or acquire a new trade. A new concept of rehabilitation has emerged during the last generation, a concept that embraces the social, the psychological, and the physical. The availability of a comprehensive program of vocational rehabilitation services with offices covering every local community bears an important relationship to any consideration of counseling with reference to public assistance.* For another it may be helping a young mother, a recipient of Aid to Dependent Children, find a way to manage her life without a husband and be an adequate mother to her children. Each of the verbs in the preceding sentence suggests the careful counseling that the public assistance worker is called upon to do.

* For a full discussion of the development of vocational rehabilitation services in the United States see Black, Bertram J., writing on the topic "Vocational Rehabilitation," *Social Work Year Book 1960*, National Association of Social Workers, Inc., 2 Park Avenue, New York 16, New York, pp. 600–607.

The 1956 amendments to the Social Security Act previously referred to included a new phrase with reference to the Aid to Dependent Children program, namely that administration of the program should include services to preserve and strengthen family life.* The addition of these words means that the federal government will give positive encouragement and leadership to the states and localities toward the development of such services; it does not in any sense imply that nowhere did such services exist prior to 1956. The fact that in nearly 90 per cent of the families receiving aid under this category the dependency is due to either divorce or desertion of the father or illegitimacy of the children suggests the problems related to preserving and strengthening family life. "Preserving" and "strengthening" are action words that imply not only that the public assistance worker has the responsibility to do something, but also that he must have the capacity. What is involved in helping people preserve or strengthen so complicated a social and psychological condition as "family life"? What is implied in terms of knowledge and skill?

Another significant point to emphasize is that the public assistance worker is expected to motivate toward self-support any individual client for whom employment or self-maintenance is a reasonable possibility. The aged and those with certain kinds and degrees of disability are more or less exempt from this expectation. Any adult less than 65 years of age without a specific disabling condition is expected to strive toward eventual self-support, and the public assistance worker is clearly charged with the responsibility of motivating him in this direction wherever it is a feasible objective. It is not a feasible objective usually where there are young children and no father in the home. Inherent in this pervasive and far-reaching mandate is the core of that which makes the function of the public assistance worker a professional service. A person who seeks to motivate another person toward any particular goal is thereby taking a conscious responsibility for helping that person to change his current orientation of himself to reality. The public assistance worker is directed by law and policy to help some of his clients to change. He cannot implement this mandate unless he knows how—in other words, unless he possesses the profound knowledge and skill that is involved in helping people find within themselves the motivation and the strength to change.

In our knowledge of human behavior we are long since past the stage when we believed a person really changed because some other person—a social worker perhaps—told him what he should do and exhorted him to do it. We know that the confused and emotionally

* *Op. cit.*, Schottland.

conflicted person, deeply involved in his own inner struggle between
his impulses toward growth and mature responsibility and the opposite
pull towards dependency and evasion of responsibility, will not immediately resolve this conflict because a public assistance worker tells him
to get a job. Or to use a different kind of example, a mother whose
conflicted and ambivalent feelings toward her children are expressed
through neglectful and indifferent care of them does not resolve her
feelings because a social worker tells her to clean up her house and be a
better mother.

The point of this discussion is to emphasize that public assistance is
not a single function requiring a single type or quality of help from the
public assistance worker. Space does not permit even an enumeration
of the variety of types and shadings of people's problems which come
to the public assistance agency. Many of them can be categorized as
simple problems of financial need fully resolved by a monthly check
granted in a courteous and considerate manner. Many others cannot
be so easily resolved. Only the diagnostic skill of the worker plus his
readiness to offer help can make the necessary distinctions. He does
not have clear guidelines either by category or by type of situation. The
mandate to preserve and strengthen family life, or to promote self-care
and self-dependence, must be operationalized into actual behavior
expressed within the context of a psychological relationship generally
characterized as rapport. The mandate to motivate clients toward
self-support where this can be seen as a feasible objective contains no
definite lines as to which of his clients are to be so motivated or which
are to be exempt from such effort. Public assistance in this country is a
mixture of a need-meeting institution—that is, financial aid in and of
itself meets basic human needs—and of a social welfare service—that
is, a service which helps people resolve problems that interfere with
normal social adjustment. It is neither wholly one nor the other.
The worker who is sensitive to people and their problems sees many
opportunities to help the people who come to him for financial aid—
problems in parent–child relationships, marital relationships, relationships to other people in the home or in the community. Realistically
these problems are always directly related either to the client's need
for financial aid or to the use he is able to make of it. If the worker has
the requisite knowledge and skill and is given the time and administrative support from his agency, he can do an extremely important
preventative, ameliorative and rehabilitative job. Without these elements, public assistance becomes a routine service with little that
speaks of professional service to people in helping them achieve more
personally and socially satisfactory life adjustments.

In the discussion of the "what" and the "why" of public assistance thus far in this article, neither the terms "counseling" nor "social casework" have been used. Counseling is a more general term that might be applied to any situation in which one person takes responsibility for advising or giving help or guidance to another. It may or may not be under agency auspices and may have more or less the qualities of a professional relationship—one characterized by the fact that the counselor takes conscious responsibility for bringing special knowledge and skill to help the other person to solve his problems. In line with this general definition of counseling, all social casework could be called counseling but not all counseling could be called social casework. By definition social casework is the implementation of a social purpose through a social welfare agency that has been created either by public law or by community sanction usually expressed through a formal charter or some form of community mandate.

The help given to people with problems in their social living through the public assistance agency is more appropriately referred to as social casework rather than counseling although the terms overlap. This is true because it is always implemented through a social agency purpose which in itself gives direction as to who is to be helped and with what problems. The social worker must be as clear as possible about the social purpose of his agency and have achieved a quality of emotional identification with that purpose if he is to implement it into a real helping process. The attention given to the "why" and the "what" of public assistance in this section was necessary to an understanding of the "how" it is to be done.

HOW DO WE HELP PEOPLE IN A PUBLIC ASSISTANCE AGENCY?

In the public assistance agency the worker uses the same principles that are applicable to helping people with their problems through a social casework or counseling relationship in any other setting. In its simplest terms a helping process is one in which the relationship to the helping person is used as the medium in which the client can examine the problem with which he is confronted and gain increased capacity to resolve his problem or to reduce or control it. This over-simplification of an extremely subtle and complex process adds little to our understanding of how it is done.

Ability to help others is grounded upon a total attitude toward people which we characterize by such phrases as respect for the individual and for his uniqueness, belief in his fundamental worth, and a conviction about the desire and capacity of people to change, to adjust, to be in some kind of harmony with his culture that will give him satisfaction and give satisfaction to others. Behind the attitude which these phrases express is a philosophy of life from which stems an approach, a way of looking at and relating to one's fellow man. Human beings do not acquire this attitude solely through the normal process of growing up. Neither can it be developed solely by a formal educational process, such as professional education for social work. Anyone who would seek to help people with their problems must possess certain basic personality traits, which might be characterized in a shorthand way as an ability to feel concern for the other person, to identify with him, to project oneself into his needs—in other words, a warm, sensitive, outgoing, yet emotionally mature personality. Then, as one acquires technical knowledge of how human nature is shaped by individual life experiences and understanding of the social forces of the cultural milieu, he gradually gains the ability to put purpose and direction into his efforts to help people. Professional education for any of the fields of activity loosely termed counseling—including social work—utilizes a combination of classroom and field practice instruction in the training of practitioners. Academic knowledge means little unless it has been tested and integrated into practice. Likewise, natural warmth and sensitivity, though absolutely essential, unless combined with real knowledge of the human material to which it is directed will always be limited and often purposeless.

Acquiring an ability to help people with their problems is a lifelong process involving in a very true sense the development of the total personality of the person. Formal academic education gives one the tools of understanding, but only by trying to be of help to troubled people, examining and re-examining one's use of himself in the helping relationship, can one gain the degree of understanding that one must have if he would seek to help people with their more profound problems of social adjustment.

In the following brief example drawn from a typical experience of a worker in a public assistance agency, we see the elements common to all helping illustrated in a seemingly simple yet basically very profound manner.

Mrs. B., a 34-year old woman with two children ages 11 and 13, had been receiving the Aid to Dependent Children category of public assistance since her divorce from her husband three years ago. The alimony which her husband was able to pay met part of the family's needs and the agency made up the difference. Mrs. B. had worked as a cook and caterer in various restaurants before her marriage to Mr. B. and it seemed to the worker now that since Mrs. B.'s children were getting older and less dependent upon her and she did have a skill that is in demand, it would be possible for her to seek employment. When the worker raised the question of employment with Mrs. B. during a home call, Mrs. B. was very resistant to the idea, emphasizing how much the children needed her at home, the danger of their getting into difficulties if she were not at home at all times to supervise them, was pessimistic about employment prospects, and was altogether very negative about the whole suggestion. This worker tended to handle her objections "head on" attempting to convince her she was exaggerating the dangers and difficulties, and finally insisting that Mrs. B. seek employment and that she come to the office each week and make a report on her efforts to find work. The next three weeks Mrs. B. came in each week promptly at the appointed time. Scarcely sitting down, she recounted in rapid fashion the places she had been to ask about a job and the reason none were available or at least none were offered her that were feasible for her to accept. During the fourth week a new worker took over in the district in which Mrs. B. resided and the following is this worker's description of what occurred in the interview when Mrs. B. came in during that week to report.

"Mrs. B. entered the interviewing room with a quick 'let's get this over with' air, and sitting on the edge of her chair began a rapid recounting of her efforts to find work during the past week and why nothing was materializing. I immediately sensed that she was on the defensive and was trying to prove something to me, namely that feasible employment was not available. As soon as I could interrupt the flow of words I asked Mrs. B. for whose sake was she trying to find this job, for herself or for me because I represented this agency. She was a little flustered by this question but quickly went on to say the previous worker had told her she must seek reasonable employment and she was just reporting her efforts. Very gently and carefully I said to Mrs. B., 'Mrs. B., if you feel from us that the agency is trying to make you do something of which you do not really want to be a part, it is all wrong, and we should stop right here. If this is the way it is I'm sure you have strength enough to manage not to find a job, or if you should happen to be cornered into accepting one, it will be my job, not yours, and you will probably make it fail.'

"I had to say several times in different ways that I had no desire or intention to push her into doing something she felt she did not want before Mrs. B. could feel I really meant what I said. Gradually she relaxed and was able to respond positively to my invitation to examine together her total situation, what was good and bad about it as she saw it, and what I might be able to help her to change. Before the hour was over Mrs. B. was talking realistically about the pros and cons of employment, could see both the positive and negative values, and was exploring the different alternatives that were open to her to improve her situation."

This brief case story illustrates all the essential elements of social casework and of the broader concept of counseling. It is particularly typical of public assistance. Society's expectation that each of its members carry his own weight if possible is expressed in law and policy in the requirement that the public assistance worker motivate recipients toward self-support wherever it is feasible in view of their age, family responsibilities, and conditions of the labor market. The task of implementing this mandate effectively is a most subtle and complicated one.

The public assistance worker must have acquired by study, by self-examination, and by testing it out in numerous individual situations a profound understanding of and conviction about the basic need inherent in every individual to be in some degree of harmony with his culture. Often, of course, this basic drive is obfuscated by emotional conflicts, by age or illness, but it is always there in some degree no matter how attenuated. In the case of Mrs. B. the worker as a representative of society and Mrs. B. had become protagonists. Mrs. B.'s real strength, her drive toward adequacy and independence, was mobilized by the worker's pressure against the agency's (and therefore society's) demands. When this occurs, as it so often does, the agency is doomed to almost certain defeat. This statement is both a recognition of and a tribute to the inherent strength of human beings.

If we are to help people, to motivate them toward change, toward carrying their responsibilities more adequately, we must be able to identify with and support their fundamental ego strength. Too often, particularly in public assistance, the worker attempts to make the choices, in effect to substitute his ego for that of the client. By saying that he did not intend to try to push Mrs. B. into doing anything she did not want to do (and meaning it!) the second worker gave direction of her own life back to Mrs. B. Behind this seemingly simple act is a whole social philosophy of respect for the individual that is not just an esoteric ideal, but an attitude and an approach developed by real knowledge of and understanding of human behavior. When Mrs. B. felt the worker's identification with her and with her needs and desires, a new kind of mutuality developed. Then she could use the worker's understanding of her and of the demands of society and the worker's emotional support that flows through that subtle thing we call relationship to move toward a real change in her orientation to the realities of her life.

Although much more could be said about the points illustrated by the case of Mrs. B., a different type of case situation is introduced because it emphasizes some of the same basic points through quite a different problem.

Mrs. P., age 76, has been a recipient of Aid to Needy Blind category of public assistance for the past two years. She lives in a tiny shack situated at the top of a steep hill overlooking a deep canyon. She lives alone and depends upon neighbors and friends to bring her groceries and mail to her. She seems extremely set in her ways and refuses to consider moving. Various friends and neighbors report that she is very fault finding and they are tired of helping her, as she shows little appreciation. The shack can accommodate only one person, and that plus Mrs. P.'s refusal to have a stranger come in to help her makes it very difficult to supply her with paid help. There are no relatives who can assist her. The problem is how to handle the living situation so that Mrs. P. will be safe as well as content in her little home. Because of her blindness and general frailty she is in danger from the possibility of an accidental fall and from being burned in her efforts to keep herself warm and do her cooking.

The kind of problem which the case of Mrs. P. presents to the public assistance agency is a common one. It poses the fundamental question of how and by what behavior does a member of a democracy forfeit his right to self-determination when his behavior is neither criminal nor within the definition of legal insanity. In a culture which emphasizes an individual's right to take his own risks and encourages independence and self-responsibility is not Mrs. P.'s behavior really within the socially sanctioned range? Yet attempted suicide is a punishable offense in the laws of all the states, and Mrs. P. is in real danger of self-destruction.

A sampling of the reactions of the general public to the situation of Mrs. P. would no doubt bring forth reactions ranging from a vehement "leave-her-alone—it's her own business if she kills herself!" on one hand to an equally vehement "she must be protected from herself by legal action!" on the other. The public assistance worker is likely to get caught in conflicting demands from neighbors, police, and from his own conscience when he is faced with a situation like that of Mrs. P.

There are no easy answers to the problem which Mrs. P. presents to the worker and to the whole of a local public assistance agency. The community is likely to hold the agency responsible if something serious happens to a person known to be one of its clients. For this reason the worker's immediate supervisor, and in many instances the agency executive, should know of the situation and share in the responsibility for the decisions that are made.

First of all, of course, the worker should endeavor with all the skill at his command to help Mrs. P. to see the risks she is taking plus the demands she must make on her friends and to accept a different living arrangement, such as a boarding home. Any chance of success will depend upon the worker's ability to truly identify with Mrs. P., to let himself feel what it is like to be old, alone, nearly blind and financially dependent and that clinging to a small piece of independence which the little shack of her own represents is a very human reaction—in fact an indication of real strength. It is possible that Mrs. P. could trust the worker enough to accept a new arrangement. It is possible the worker might have to use someone whom Mrs. P. does trust as an intermediary. When the neighbors and others are demanding of the worker that he "do something" because they want to be relieved of the burden of responsibility and perhaps guilt, it is essential that the worker hold each of them to the fact they too bear part of the responsibility for Mrs. P. Specifically, the worker might suggest that the group of neighbors and others who are concerned about Mrs. P. get together and agree on exactly what they will do and what they cannot do for her and then fulfill their agreement. In other words, the worker can take leadership in stopping the "buck-passing" process that is going on and always goes on when individual problems become a community concern.

These two brief case examples, seemingly very different, yet the same in the essential humanness of the respective responses of these people to the life problems confronting them, have been used to illustrate the basic principles of helping people in a public assistance agency. Space permits no more than brief reference to some of the over-all principles; the finer points of helping public assistance clients with appropriate illustrations would go far beyond the limits and perhaps the purpose of this chapter. Inherent in all that has been said about how to help people who come to the public assistance agency are the three elements in the helping process, which can be reviewed again in summary: (1) Understanding of human behavior, which means real knowledge of the whole process of growth and development from infancy to old age in all the sociological, psychological and cultural implications of this statement, for it is only upon knowledge that a sensitive awareness of the meaning of behavior can be built. Self-awareness is an essential part of this. We cannot really understand the behavior of other people except as we understand and have come to terms with our own. Clarity and soundness in the diagnostic interpretations which must be made are absolutely essential. Diagnostic ability stems from knowledge tested by actual experience. (2) Identification with the social purpose of the agency service we represent. In relation to public assistance there must be clear understanding of the social purpose and objectives of public assistance in America, with appreciation of the implications of each category of assistance. This requires knowledge of the program in its historical development, its current status, and the direction of its future development. A quality of emotional identification with the fundamental purpose is necessary if one is to psychologically cut through the morass of procedural detail and hold steadfastly to the basic objectives. (3) Elements (1) and (2) are blended into skill in the process of actually helping real people who come to the agency for help. No other social welfare service in America presents those who implement it a greater range of different types of life problems than does the public assistance agency. Knowledge is never enough; knowledge must be translated into skill. Conversely, there is no such thing as skill without knowledge. There is an element of art in any professional skill. The surgeon translates knowledge of anatomy and physiology into skill in knowing when and how to perform an operation; the teacher translates knowledge of subject matter and of child development into skill in helping children to learn; the social worker translates knowledge of human behavior, of agency purpose and function and of community resources into skill in the process of helping people toward more satisfactory social adjustments. Describing the determination of eligibility for public assistance as skill in involving people through the medium of the relationship with the worker in a process of examining and coming to some resolution of the problems related to their need for financial aid expresses its bare bones. Acquiring this skill is a lifelong process in which formal education plays an essential part but is not the whole of it. Helping others is in last analysis a way of behaving. He who seeks to know this "way" must engage himself in a process of real personality growth.

BIBLIOGRAPHY

1. BALL, ROBERT M.: September 1947. "Social Insurance and the Right to Assistance," *Social Service Review*, pp. 331–344.
2. DE SCHWEINITZ, KARL and ELIZABETH: July 1948 and October 1948. "The Contribution of Social Work to the Administration of Public Assistance," *Social Work Journal*, pp. 153–177.
3. HOEY, JANE M.: January 1947. "The Content of Living as a Basis for a Standard of Assistance," *Journal of Social Casework*, pp. 3–9.
4. WILTSE, KERMIT T.: March 1958. "Social Casework and Public Assistance," *The Social Service Review*, XXXII, pp. 41–50.
5. ——: October 1958. "The 'Hopeless' Family," *Social Work*, pp. 12–22.
6. ——: 1959. "New Approaches to the Administration of ADC Programs," *Casework Papers, 1959*, pp. 20–30. Family Service Association of America, 215 Park Avenue South, New York City.

PAMPHLETS

7. AMERICAN PUBLIC WELFARE ASSOCIATION, *ADC: Problem and Promise*, American Public Welfare Association, 1313 East 60th Street, Chicago, Illinois, 1960.
8. GREENLEIGH ASSOCIATES, INC., *Facts, Fallacies and Future: A Study of the Aid to Dependent Children Program of Cook County, Illinois*, Greenleigh Associates, Inc., 437 Fifth Avenue, New York City, 1960.
9. MARCUS, GRACE, "The Nature of Services in Public Assistance Administration," Public Assistance Report No. 10, Federal Security Agency, Social Security Board, Washington, D.C.: Government Printing Office, 1946.
10. TOWLE, CHARLOTTE, *Common Human Needs*. An Interpretation for Staff in Public Assistant Agencies, University of Chicago Press, 1952.
11. WILTSE, KERMIT T., *Public Assistance Personnel: Educational Requirements and Training Facilities*, Bureau of Public Administration, University of California, Berkeley, 1959.
12. ——: "Social Case Work in Public Assistance," Testing Method and Skill in a Selected Case Load, California State Department of Social Welfare, 1952.
13. PERLMAN, HELEN HARRIS: 1957. *Social Casework: A Problem Solving Process*, Chicago: University of Chicago Press.

Counseling Adults
in Leisure and Recreational Activities

E. DeALTON PARTRIDGE

President Montclair State College
Upper Montclair
New Jersey

LEISURE A RECENT HERITAGE

ONE of the really significant developments in America during the twentieth century is the increase in leisure time available to young and old of both sexes. A variety of social and cultural changes have contributed to this increase in leisure hours.

Working hours have decreased. With more efficient methods of production, increased use of automation, better communication, and improved transportation it has become possible to increase production tremendously and at the same time decrease the number of hours of work per day and the number of days worked per week.

Not only have the weekly work period and the work-day been shortened, but the length of productive life has decreased continually in relation to the total life span of the individual. Compulsory education and child labor laws have delayed the time of steady gainful employment. The prolonged life span of the individual combined with more universal and earlier retirement have created a growing "leisure class" in the upper age brackets.

Communications have greatly improved. Shopping can now be done over the telephone or if necessary by automobile. Visits with friends or relatives can be more frequent and involve less time. Travel for business purposes can be fast and efficient.

Work in the home has been simplified. Labor-saving devices have made the life of the housekeeper less taxing. The vacuum cleaner, the deep-freeze, the automatic dishwasher and clothes-washer, frozen and canned foods . . . all of these and many other new devices or techniques have helped to bring a dividend of leisure to the housewife.

As serious students of society would expect, there has been a considerable cultural lag between the frontier of increased leisure and a development of constructive means for evaluating or utilizing it. On the time span of social change the increased leisure has come about so rapidly that there has been insufficient opportunity to develop a set of folkways or mores to deal with it.

Furthermore, the distribution of this new leisure has not been universal. Certain occupations enjoy the dividend of leisure hours much more than others. For example, the reduction in the work week has been much more marked for the trades than for the white-collar worker. The classifications of professional occupations enjoy less of an increase in leisure hours than the non-professionals. This is due in part to the fact that in our expanding economy the number of highly trained professionals has not kept pace with the demand for their services. This has meant in turn that the work week for these professions has not been reduced commensurate with other occupations.

This disparity in the distribution of leisure time has had an interesting effect upon the patterns of leisure time use in the American Society.

Historically, leisure has been the privilege of a wealthy minority. This minority was usually the best educated segment of society and hence in a position to set a culturally high tone on the use of leisure. In American society this is no longer true.

Today the exploitation of leisure is a source of livelihood for a sizeable and growing portion of the population. Since a large proportion of the family budget is spent in the pursuit of leisure activities, there is keen competition in the market-place, on the air, on the highway for the "leisure dollar." Those who spend these dollars are the ones who have leisure. Since this represents to a large extent the working population, it is this group that sets the cultural tone of many organized leisure pursuits. It is evident under these conditions that a wide distribution of leisure time may not necessarily be a social blessing.

Many of the current attitudes toward leisure time are a direct carry-over from an earlier period of our history when play and recreation were frowned upon. There was a day not many generations ago when adults who played or sought activities for the sheer joy of doing them were considered anti-social. Indeed, in those days such persons were not contributing their share to the production of useful goods or services. Leisure was a luxury that few people could afford.

With the increased tempo of life growing out of a rather completely mechanized society, periods of relaxation have come to be a necessity for many people. The art of using leisure time advantageously is one that doctors now encourage. Play and recreation are just as important today to the success and stability of our society as production and distribution. In fact, there is reason to believe that in terms of the needs of the human personality the proper and constructive use of leisure time is a vital necessity.

Along with the increase in leisure time there has come a corresponding growth in enterprises designed to gain profit from this leisure. The movies, radio, TV, comic books, automobiles, hobby clubs, high fidelity recordings, camera shops and a myriad of other schemes have sprung up to capitalize on this important dividend of the machine age. Leisure which has been created by the machine age has in turn created a whole galaxy of business activities to exploit it.

Students of leisure time and its use have long been concerned with the growing popularity of spectator amusement. While there is a definite place in society and in the personal life of the individual for wholesome amusements where he reacts only as a spectator, it is also true that the great value of leisure is lost if there is complete lack of creative activity during leisure hours. Creative activity such as constructing, painting, collecting or playing a musical instrument provide for the individual a real integrating experience . . . an opportunity to express himself as an individual, to develop skills that gain response from other human beings and often a basis for companionship where no other basis may exist.

PATTERNS OF LEISURE ACTIVITIES

As important as leisure is in modern society there is no organized program today to prepare individuals with regard to the proper and constructive use of leisure time. Most hobbies are acquired more or less accidentally and depend upon the home environment and the neighborhood in which one happens to grow. From what we know of the development of leisure interests and activities, it is quite evident that they are learned just as one learns to speak or walk. It is quite obvious, too, that many human beings grow into old age without ever having sampled a wide range of leisure activities. One who works in the field of adult education is impressed with the sense of discovery that older people have when they develop a new skill or interest. In some communities the adult schools are full to over-flowing with talented persons who have never before had an opportunity to paint, sculpture, make a leather purse or turn a wooden dish on a lathe.

PREPARING FOR RETIREMENT

The transition from full employment to partial or complete retirement can be a difficult one for a person who is not prepared for a sudden on-rush of leisure time. This preparation should start many months before actual retirement if the individual is really to be ready. Those who counsel older adults should stress this point strongly.

While generally it is easier, and possibly better, to build leisure patterns in retirement upon earlier interests, this is not actually necessary. The old adage about teaching old dogs new tricks has been thoroughly discredited. Older persons *can* learn new things if they *will*. It is a matter of motivation and it should be the responsibility of the counselor to furnish some of this motivation.

The recommended leisure pattern for the adult will depend considerably upon the type of gainful employment he pursues. For those who earn a living in a swivel chair active leisure pursuits should be considered. For those who are indoors continually there is great advantage in a leisure activity that combines sunshine and fresh air. The postman will probably find stamp collecting more in keeping with his needs than a hiking club. The teacher who spends hours a day with children might well consider activity with adults in the leisure hours, or indeed, some hobby that takes her away from people entirely for a few hours a week.

Ideally the mature adult will have not one interest, but several that will each meet a different need. The well rounded adult should have an active and wholesome interest in each of the following areas:

Something to do alone. There is need in these times to have a hobby where one can bury himself and do just as he wishes for a while, dig in as deep and stay as long as pleases him. The types of activities that fit into this category are: Reading, music listening, fishing, whittling, painting, carpentry, photography, collecting, and cooking.

Something to do with others. Human companionship is satisfying and stimulating. The rounded personality will find some activities that involve other people so that the give and take of human companionship continues through life. Here are some of the possibilities: Folk dancing, hiking, poetry, bridge, forums, literary clubs, making music, volunteer leadership, and drama.

Something active. The human body needs movement. There is good mental and physical health to be found in hobbies that provide physical exercise within the limits of age and ability. Suggestions? Here are a few: Dancing, swimming, bowling, golf, hiking, tennis, archery, skating, and gardening.

LEISURE AND FAMILY LIFE

The increased leisure now available in America can be either a boon or a liability to family life depending upon how it is utilized. If the increased leisure means to the head of the house more time to be away from home . . . more time with the "boys" . . . more opportunity to pursue individual whims and interests then leisure will not add to the richness of family life. If to the mother it means only more cocktail parties, more hands of bridge, more fashion shows, more gossip, then society would be better off with less leisure.

To parents who seriously wish to enrich the lives of their children increased leisure will provide an opportunity to create a constructive atmosphere in which family relationships can develop. There are few better ways for a father and mother to become acquainted with their children and to be in a position to influence the development of their character than to share leisure-time activities with them.

Fortunately, along with the increased slice of leisure time, modern civilization has also provided the average American family with the means to use that leisure in a vast variety of constructive ways. The modern family can, if they have the imagination and interest, transform their humble abode into an interesting and living center of activities that will widen the eyes of youngsters of both sexes and of any age. Parents can now bring into their home at little expense the best of entertainment, music of the masters, reading material of great variety, tools for creative projects.

While a generation ago the automobile was drawing youngsters away from the home and entertainment and self-occupation was less and less on the family hearth, today there are other equally powerful influences that are magnetizing the home for the youngster and making it a place of culture and participation. Even the automobile, which has made it possible for the family to spend much time away from home can be used to enrich family life and solidify the family unit. Picnics and family tours to near and distant places are now possible for the great bulk of Americans.

THE ARMY OF VOLUNTEERS

Visitors from other countries never cease to marvel at the number of organizations and activities in America that are carried on by volunteer help. Many important facets of community life depend upon the steady and skillful energy of the unpaid worker who gains satisfaction from participation. The army of volunteers is a direct outgrowth of the leisure-time individual. It represents one of the constructive results of the new leisure.

There is for the individual, a real mental health value in this volunteer work. For the personality that is naturally egocentric the volunteer activities nearly always furnish an opportunity to serve others, to become concerned about the health or welfare of less fortunate persons. This process naturally draws the egocentric person away from his own troubles and projects his interests outward. The energy that normally would go into brooding is sublimated into activities with a purposeful end.

Opportunities for this type of service are available for persons of both sexes and a wide range of abilities. Such organizations as the Boy Scouts, the Camp Fire Girls, the Girl Scouts, the Y.M.C.A., Boys Clubs, to name but a few, are dependent almost entirely upon volunteer leaders. In the Boy Scouts alone there are no less than 375,000 men and women giving their time to help bring the program to American youth.

The youth serving agencies have carefully developed personnel procedures which are designed to recruit and select competent volunteers. In most cities of any size in the country these organizations maintain an office with a small professional staff. The main responsibility of the professional staff is to recruit volunteers and assist them in gaining the necessary skills to lead their groups.

The main requisites for leadership of youth groups are good moral character plus intelligence and a desire to learn. The youth agencies usually provide regular training courses and well written literature to help those who are willing to serve. Usually, too, there are periods of apprenticeship during which the novice can gain the skills and knowledge needed to succeed.

Most of the leadership recruiting in the so-called "group work" agencies is done through the local group. Fathers, mothers, older brothers and those who have established roots in the neighborhood make the best leaders of groups. One need not have extensive experience to get started but can learn as he goes with the help of more experienced leaders.

In addition to the extensive field of opportunity to serve in leadership capacities for youth groups there are scores of openings for both round and square pegs to serve in community enterprises during the leisure hours. A complete list of such opportunities would take too much space, but here are a few of the better known ones: Community Chest, Red Cross, church groups, March of Dimes, Civilian Defense, P.T.A., League of Women Voters, American Legion, political organizations, dramatic groups, musical organizations, garden clubs, ethnic groups, neighborhood associations.

BACKGROUNDS FOR COUNSELING

In order to counsel adults with regard to their leisure pursuits one needs to assemble a considerable amount of data about the individual and the community in which he lives. Leisure pursuits depend upon the individual, his pattern of capacities, his training, his interests and his life history. These individual characteristics in turn must find expression in a particular type of environment. The pattern of leisure pursuits will depend upon the possibilities that the environment provides. To use an extreme example, there is little point in advising a person to take up skiing if he lives below the Mason–Dixon line unless he has resources and time to travel.

Individual Background

Below are the types of information that one must assemble in order to understand the individual potential for leisure pursuits.

age
family relationships
vocation or profession
economic status
schooling
existing interest patterns
physical abilities or disabilities
perceptive abilities
   blindness
   color blindness
   tone deafness
personal history of leisure pursuits
attitude toward others . . . sociable or withdrawing

The Environment

In order to advise individuals intelligently about leisure and recreation one must know what the possibilities and limitations are within the environment in which the individual moves. A competent counselor in this field would have access to information about existing interest groups or physical facilities that might be used. The following list is suggestive.

Community Facilities
Indoor
   swimming pools
   bowling alleys
   libraries
   art galleries
   gymnasiums
Outdoor
   hiking trails

camping spots
swimming pools
boating facilities
skating rinks
tennis courts
play fields
gardening areas
Clubs and Organizations
   hiking clubs

folk dancing groups

music groups

bowling leagues

sand lot leagues

youth groups

   Boy Scouts

   Girl Scouts

   Camp Fire Girls

   Y.M.C.A.

   Y.W.C.A.

   Y.M.H.A.

adult education schools

hobby groups

models

   aircraft

   railroad

   boat

craft

collections

   stamp

   antiques

   insect

gardening

painting

photography

carpentry

In connection with all of these specific data one must be aware also of the costs that are apt to be associated with the various leisure pursuits. There are recreational activities ranging in cost from a few cents a year up to hundreds of dollars. One must be realistic about these costs and not advise activities beyond the reach of the person seeking help.

Just how one would go about assembling this type of information would depend upon the community. In many communities the local library would be of help. The newspaper will nearly always carry news items about the activities of groups. Some newspapers in the larger cities have regular sections devoted to leisure activities.

The names and addresses of such organizations as the Boy Scouts and the Camp Fire Girls can be found in the phone book. If there is a Council of Social Agencies in the community a complete listing of volunteer agencies can be had readily. Indeed, it would be a fine service to the adults of a community to assemble and publish information of this kind. A guidebook to local leisure-time activities should find extensive use.

Another resource that will be helpful in counseling with regard to leisure activities is a list of persons who have skill and interests in various lines. It is not probable that any one person who is advising others about leisure pursuits would have all of the interests and skills that represent possibilities for leisure activities. He may, however, have the assistance of many others who are willing to teach others their own hobby. One of the usual characteristics of a hobby fan is that he likes to spread participation in his particular interest. Today it is largely through such person to person influence that hobbies spread in a community.

Guidance in the development of leisure and recreational activities is important. It is important to the individual and to society. Sociologists have long been convinced that much of the social breakdown in our society stems from the improper use of leisure time. If the increased leisure that modern technology has brought results in growing crime rates, increased gambling, higher accident rates, more frequent alcoholism, more family breakdown, then the Puritans will have been right after all when they contended that the Devil will find work for idle hands. Proper planning and education can avoid this and turn leisure into the great boon that it should be.

BIBLIOGRAPHY

1. CLOSE, KATHRYN. *Getting Ready to Retire.* Public Affairs Pamphlets, 22 East 38 St., New York 16. $.25
2. DONAHUE, WILMA (Editor). *Free Time: Challenge to Later Maturity.* University of Michigan Press, Ann Arbor. $4.50
3. GLEASON, GEORGE. *Horizons for Older People.* Macmillan Co., 60 Fifth Av., New York 11. $2.95
4. HART, GIFFORD R. *Retirement: A New Outlook for the Individual.* Harcourt, Brace, 383 Madison Av., New York 17. $3.95
5. LAWTON, GEORGE (Editor). *New Goals for Old Age.* Columbia University Press, New York. $3.00
6. NATIONAL RECREATION ASSOCIATION. *Recreation Activities for Adults.* Association Press, New York. $3.00

The Counseling Process
in Community Planning

LESTER B. GRANGER

President International Conference of Social Work
New York

To THE average observer of the American social scene and indeed to many practitioners in the field of social work itself, the process of counseling is *ipso facto* a one-to-one relationship. These observers see counseling in the traditional framework where the counselor deals with an individual or with a family group in an effort to help the client solve personal or family problems which baffle and handicap him. It is out of this counselor-client relationship that the modern practice of casework has evolved.

Within the last several decades, however, the concept of counseling has been enlarged to include not merely the individual or his family as client, but a larger social group—on occasion the entire community. The process of community counseling has come to be known in some of its aspects as community organization. When applied by competent practitioners the community counseling process can be used for the purposes of community education and development, intergroup relations, social action and a variety of other objectives which too often in the past have been sought by the hit-or-miss, trial-and-error method.

A principal characteristic of community organization which distinguishes it from the practice of case work is that whereas casework seeks to use the group to affect the individual and prepares the individual for more effective management of his affairs within the group, community organization seeks to recruit and weld together the strengths of many individuals and their organizations into a group force conscious

211

of its objectives and disciplined to achieve them. In this way organized action can be applied to improving the conditions of the entire community; thereby living opportunities and personal expression for the individual members of the group are enhanced. Community organization (or community counseling) can of course be viewed, not merely from the standpoint of the social work profession but also from the standpoint of the civic-minded community at large. In either case, however, the process is aimed at the same objective—to improve through organized effort the conditions under which people live. This presupposes not only the interposition of knowledgeable leadership but also the involvement of the people who are affected by and will directly benefit from the changes that are being sought.

COUNSELING IS A PART OF PLANNING

The very concept of a planned community is comparatively recent in American experience and even yet is not accepted with equal readiness and understanding by all elements in our population. There are enough remnants of laissez-faireism in American thought for the more resistant-minded to look upon community planning as a vague threat to free enterprise and therefore something to be considered with suspicion and accepted with reservations.

Yet the need for such planning has become ever clearer as the American community has taken its modern shape. It was revealed in the mid-nineteenth century, as our society shifted from an agrarian to an industrial pattern of living. The larger cities grew still larger in answer to the demands of expanding business and industry. They became prototypes of urban community growth in general, not only in governmental forms, residential patterns and essential community services, but also in the types and seriousness of problems that arose from the very fact of community growth. The community-wide ramifications of expanding finance and industry have continued to produce extremely complex economic–social–political relationships. Their complexity is natural, since *the modern community is only a vast collection of conflicting individual and group interests linked together by a common need.* People come together for community living because in this modern age it is impossible for them to survive alone or in mere family groups. Once together, however, they find themselves constantly in competition or conflict as their personal and group interests collide. In order for them to continue to live together, and thereby survive, they must work out a design for community existence, one that will maximize their realization and development of common interests and minimize the impact of colliding interests.

It was Edward C. Lindeman who pioneered in expressing this concept in his still-pertinent "The Community," published as long ago as 1921. The very word, "community," connotes a common sharing—a sharing of material possessions and their use, of essential services and of specialized skills and intelligence. It connotes, also, however, *a sharing of the inescapable problems that emerge when large numbers of people live closely together.* The larger the community and the more intense its vitality, the greater its common needs and problems—and the greater its need for constant planning to solve those problems. It is upon such planning that the two great pillars of modern society are established, these being law-and-order (courts, police and attendant regulations) and common services (such as streets, sanitation, hospitals and schools).

The community counselor is a naturally-evolved product of such planning, as well as its initiator. At the bottom of all community planning is the personal relationship, whether developed between individual and individual or individual and group, or indirectly—between group and group. This relationship can be extended through a natural or chosen leader, or through the efforts of the community counselor. The difference between these two approaches marks the difference in methods between direct and indirect leadership.

COUNSELING IS INDIRECT LEADERSHIP

In the political and frequently in the economic field planning is generally, of necessity, carried on by direct leadership. In the field of social needs and problems, community planning depends for solid and continuing development upon the indirect leadership provided by the community counselor. Each type of leadership has its strengths and weaknesses. For instance, *direct leadership* makes greatest use of the skill, dynamism and prestige of the strong leader. The very force of his personality impressed upon a planning group can frequently carry through to a successful conclusion plans that would have been unlikely without his exerted influence. On the other hand, direct leadership is apt to be so much an extension of the leader's own personality that when he steps out of the picture all planning stops, until another "strong man" comes along to pick up along the lines of his own personal ideas.

The *indirect leadership* exerted by the community counselor (i.e., a specialist in the process of community organization) is by its very nature less dynamic. It gets under way more slowly in most instances. Frequently, the finished plans are quite different from those hoped for in the beginning. Yet if the counselor's work is competently performed, those plans that are adopted have a far better chance of maturing than if one dynamic leader had assumed prime responsibility for them and forced them upon an unconvinced or reluctant group. The indirect leadership method employs not personal, but group dynamics. It actively involves more people. Their interest grows as their participation increases. The community is apt to respond with stronger support because of the cross-sectional representativeness of the leadership endorsing the plan.

In the first instance, the plan may die if the direct leader moves out of the picture. In the second instance, long before the plan has been put into operation the community counselor, as the indirect leader, may have moved on to other projects without his absence being noted.

This is one reason why the community organization specialist, as community counselor, has made his most significant contribution in the area of social needs and services, rather than in such economic affairs as business or industry planning. One cannot conceive that a Henry Ford or a Charles Schwab could have built an auto or steel empire by employing the committee approach and waiting for "the educational process" to develop a consensus among their associates. But it is even more inconceivable that such men, of whatever intelligence and driving energy, could use their empire-building methods to establish a public school system for Detroit, a hospital system for Pittsburgh, or a department of parks and playgrounds for New York City. Satisfying the social needs of a community is a far more complex undertaking than manufacturing or trading for a profit. A social program that is most efficiently constructed in terms of dollars-and-cents operational standards can utterly fail of its purpose by failing to adjust to the emotional and physical needs of the people—and only the people through their authorized and trusted representatives can make this determination.

A KEY ROLE

The community counselor, therefore, becomes the key person who is able, by training, inclination and natural gifts, to initiate, encourage and "direct through indirection" efforts in the community to improve living standards and relationships of the people. He may be trained as a social scientist or a social work practitioner. He may have moved into the community counseling field from some related area of experience, developing his skills in the process. But whatever his background of training, the counselor must be expert in two important areas of his responsibility. He must understand people in their emotional make-up and their social reaction and inter-action; he must know the history and salient characteristics of the community with which he is dealing, whether it be homogeneous neighborhood or heterogeneous metropolitan area.

In other words, whether the counselor be professionally classed as a sociologist, economist or social worker, his responsibility requires that he be versed in the fundamentals of groups dynamics and social research. The reason for this is clear. Some of the toughest community problems are those arising out of inter-group relationships in which social inter-actions are as illogical as they are important. Their treatment calls for the specialists' knowledge of "why we behave like human beings." Inversely, other problems which seem to be hopelessly entangled in a web of group suspicions and hatreds may, upon examination and analysis, turn out to be caused principally by lack of fully understood and shared information. In such cases, the community counselor may be rendering the crucial service through the mere act of clarifying the issues and authenticating the facts underlying them.

TAPPING COMMUNITY RESOURCES

Already the list of specifications for the successful community counselor builds up into a formidable assortment—group dynamist, social researcher or fact-finder, social analyst and interpreter. Fortunately, however, the job does not require perfect mastery of all these professional assignments. In fact, though the community counselor is usually called a specialist in community organization, actually he is apt to be more of a generalist than a specialist. He has a *general* knowledge of each of these speciality fields, but he has *special* knowledge as to the appropriate field to be tapped in case of need and the agency resources that can be depended upon.

Not all resources that will be needed are of the agency variety. Far more important are those of key voluntary leadership. Audrey and Harley Trecker, in their provocative little volume on the common-sense of committee work,* remind that tens of thousands of organiza-tions with millions of committees and possibly tens of millions of members are in existence throughout this country. Even making allowances for those that are "paper" committees only, and for those that bloom like flowers in May and expire in June, there are still millions of committee members busily at work in big city, small town and countryside. Any community larger than a cross-roads settlement is certain to have its quota of committee leadership, with new recruits ready to step in as old veterans fall out. Forming a committee is a favorite year-round American sport; nowhere in the world will a community worker find a greater wealth of earnest volunteers panting to do good works at the drop of a handkerchief.

* TRECKER, A. R. & H. B.: 1954. *Committee Common Sense*. Whiteside and Morrow.

But in this very wealth there can be poverty. *Readiness to do good works is no guarantee of readiness or ability to do a good job.* The very intensity of community interest may be a handicap in getting a job done; over-zealous leadership has been known to confuse action with activity. Whether activity can be harnessed as constructive action depends largely upon the kind of planning and coordination that are achieved. And this will depend upon the experience of the community counselor involved, the resources provided by his agency, his knowledge of the leadership personalities in the communities and the records they have established—and the prior steps taken in preparation for lining up members of his community team.

Consider the counselor, then, as a *conscious catalyst of community development.* Catalyst, because without his presence many of the things that happen would never come to pass, and most would be delayed. Conscious, because the counselor is never satisfied merely to cause events to "happen." They are planned in advance and, as far as possible, guaranteed on the basis of the counselor's sure knowledge of the personalities he is dealing with, their special interests and prejudices, the history of social developments and economic–social forces in the community—and on the basis of plans made for taking full advantage of all these factors.

BASIC PROCESSES THAT MAKE FOR SUCCESS

As a recognized professional specialty, community counseling is a fairly new arrival. This is not to say, however, that the counseling process has not been going on for generations under the direction of devoted or shrewd individuals who would have been amazed to learn that they were "counseling" their communities. In their own opinions, they had been only trying to "get things done"; their natural gift for "indirect leadership" had led them to take those steps and adopt those approaches best calculated to encourage others to invest time and effort in community development. In this modern age, with the constantly increasing pressure of community development problems, we cannot wait for natural leadership to assert its influence in solving mammoth and growing problems. Counselors must be trained and assigned to the tasks needing their services. Certain techniques instituted by the pioneers have been refined and improved through professional application and testing. They can be safely used almost anywhere in the American community.

Wayne McMillen, one of the authorities in the field of community organization, years ago indicated some of the basic processes involved in successful community counseling. He stressed *getting acquainted with* *the community* as the counselor's first task.* Here is where the fact-finding technique becomes important, as the worker analyzes his community's social needs, its strength and its weaknesses. As an action program is contemplated, priorities of interest must be set up, with first attention being paid to those which are not only most important but also reasonably feasible. Interesting effective leadership, tentatively formulizing program, organizing task forces in the shape of committees, setting up interpretive programs designed to win public support for the project—all these become second nature to the experienced community counselor, who may never have read a book on "how to make friends and influence people."

INDOCTRINATION THROUGH ANALYSIS

Arthur Dunham, from his vantage point at Michigan University, has constantly stressed the importance of thorough advance-analysis of the problem as the foundation of successful community development programs.† Most projects that are worthwhile are going to require real time and effort on the part of those interested. It is the counselor's task to get this across to the project's sponsors, tactfully enough not to frighten off needed support but strongly enough to make certain that those who stay will work. And the best guarantee of obtaining and retaining such seasoned leadership is to include it in the analysis process.

The average volunteer leader is convinced that he knows his community thoroughly. He may be sure, for instance, that juvenile delinquency is merely a matter of careless parents, slack courts and lazy police. "Do some jacking up," he advises, "and the problem will cure itself. But let him sit down for a series of interesting meetings concerned with disturbing aspects of juvenile delinquency; plan those meetings so as to reveal more and more of the grim facts under the surface of youthful misbehavior. The committee member is at first irritated, then puzzled and finally challenged. He is then ready for the "what, who, where, when, why and how" of the Dunham analysis process.

ANALYZING A COMMUNITY PROBLEM

1. *What* is the problem? . . . How long has it existed? What is the setting and background?

2. *Who* are the persons or groups involved? . . . What personality factors . . . are significant . . . ?

3. *Where* is the problem? What relationships . . . with other units or levels are involved?

* McMILLEN, W.: 1945. *Community Organization for Social Welfare.* University of Chicago Press.

† DUNHAM, A.: 1954. Colorado Social Welfare Journal, Annual Conference Proceedings.

4. *When* is the problem? Is it immediate ... short-time or long-range? Is there a time limit ... ?

5. *Why* is this situation a problem? What would happen if nothing were done ... ?

6. *How* may the problem be best approached? What are some of the chief alternatives?

As questions such as these are pursued with increasing interest on the part of committee members, answers to other questions naturally evolve. The objectives of proposed action are considered more seriously than in the light-hearted way so characteristic of the average "civic affairs" group. Those most capable of assuming initiative are spotted for future assignments. Organizations, agencies and individuals in the community whose help may be valuable are listed for later calls. Practical attention is given to the question of who is going to do the job—and with what? If employed staff will be needed, budget discussions are opened, together with the question of how the money is to be raised. Principal community blocks are identified well in advance of opening operations, and strategies for getting around these blocks are discussed. By the time that the problem analysis has been completed, the committee has become a team. It knows its job and, what is more important, the members know each other and their possibilities.

Nelson Jackson, assistant executive director of the National Urban League's staff, an able practitioner of community organization on the national scene, is another who stresses the fact-finding-analysis approach to the community counseling job.* He points out that research inquiries, to meet the needs of a given social action project, need not satisfy all the stern tests of the research scientist. What is required is that all necessary facts be assembled into a coherent picture of the social problem to be attacked, that they be thoroughly tested for accuracy *and that their authenticity be accepted by those who will be forced to depend upon them in the future.* Much of this kind of fact-finding can be done by committee members with no previous research experience, but to make certain that it is soundly done it needs the planning and checking which the community counselor can supply—or can persuade other, qualified experts to supply.

THE PLACE OF SOCIAL RESEARCH

There are times, however, when the "generalist" approach of the community counselor is not sufficient for the job ahead—when fact-

---

* JACKSON, N. C.: 1953. "Methods of Social Action," Proceedings of Institute on Social Action, Louisiana Conference of Social Welfare.

finding must be done so carefully and expertly as to meet the searching criticism of other research specialists as well as the more inarticulate opposition of the general public or vested interests. Here is emphasized the need for a community counseling "team"—for having available other specialty resources, either on the counselor's staff or on the staffs of cooperating agencies. And of prime importance among those specialists is the social researcher.

Ten years ago, thoughtful leaders in Miami, Florida, took to the Welfare Planning Council their growing concern about health and welfare conditions in the Negro neighborhoods of that resort city. Racial conditions in general were so bad as to have earned for Miami a reputation for being one of the country's very worst communities in this respect. Behind the high rates of disease, delinquency, dependency and crime that disturbed welfare leaders were shocking conditions of housing, police brutality, denial of common services, poor schools and the rest of the calendar of racial discrimination.

Not one white Miamian in ten would have admitted the high incidence of racial discrimination. Probably even fewer would have agreed that the welfare problems were as serious as reported or susceptible to radical improvement. The response of the Miami public to these racial challenges was strikingly similar to that of the Chicago public to its slum problem, or of New Yorkers to the question of Puerto Rican assimilation—of any typical big city public to a serious problem which has been "lived with" over a long period of years.

ABSORPTION BY EASY STAGES

Miami Council leaders discussed the problem brought to them, not as one of race, but as one of welfare needs. Warren M. Banner, of the National Urban League, was asked to come in as a community consultant. An experienced social researcher, he went to work with a committee of citizens appointed by the Council. It was interracial in its composition, but it was also broadly representative of the community's various influence groups, including the Chamber of Commerce, Junior League, the city government and county officials, and board members of various social agencies. The study director took responsibility for digging out the actual facts of Negro life and Negro–white relationships in Miami. Members of his committee took the responsibility for studying the facts, sifting them for possible error, absorbing their import and assisting with their interpretation.

There was not one member of that committee, including even the most experienced social agency representatives, who did not gain in factual knowledge and social insight regarding a problem with which they had lived for so long that some considered it impervious to attack. The Banner reports brought them to see it as not one big problem but as an accumulation of larger and smaller problems, strung together by a prevailing racial attitude among the white majority of the city's population. The presentation of each problem was accompanied by a proposal for its amelioration or solution. These were discussed by the committee with an eye to their timeliness and practicability in light of prevailing racial attitudes. When the time came for action on the report as a whole, the committee astonished many of its observers—and probably some of its own membership—by a unanimous acceptance of the facts presented, the conclusions drawn and the recommendations for attack on the problems.

The full report was adopted by the Welfare Planning Council as an action-guide for improving health and welfare conditions in the Negro neighborhoods, which were the special responsibility of the Council. But the most important effect of the report was not confined to the Council; it reached out into areas not usually concerned with welfare services as such. The prestige of the Council's advisory committee was such that its endorsement of the report could not be shrugged away. It gave courage to lesser leadership in speaking out against other forms of racial iniquities. There was more than a little justification for popular reference to the report as "the Banner bible of race relations."

ELEMENTS OF COMMUNITY ACTION

None of this "just happened." It was the perfect demonstration of the role of the "conscious catalyst of community development." It had all the necessary elements of successful community action. There were, first of all, the interested citizens who realized that they were dealing with a problem too complicated for easy handling. They took it to the organization geared for handling such problems, the Welfare Planning Council. Here was a community planning agency which recognized the need for action, but which also recognized the situation as one outside of its usual area of competence, deeply impregnated as it was with racial questions in a highly race-conscious community. The Council, being well aware of the agency resources available, called in the research specialist of a community counseling organization, the National Urban League.

The study director could have made his investigations, buttressed his facts with proof, presented his findings in a neatly-drafted report to the Welfare Planning Council, and then left town. If he had done so, he would have been the social researcher, but not the community counselor.

What put him in the counselor's role was his relationship to his committee. His first action was to satisfy himself, through Council assurances, of the committee's representative nature. He sought a prestige based not upon social or financial position, but upon proven integrity and intelligence in dealing with the community's interests. He did not demand a "liberal" attitude on the part of the white or colored members so much as openmindedness and willingness to take a position and defend it.

The study director's second action was to insure regular attendance of committee members by warning them in advance that many of his findings would deal with "tough" questions and would be regarded by some as controversial. This warning stimulated both the conservative and the liberal members of the committee, the latter hoping to attack the status quo and the former determined to defend it. Committee meetings never lacked a quorum.

The study director, who had now become the community counselor, then began to feed into the committee meetings preliminary reports that outlined the areas of interest in which information would be sought —and samples of the kinds of facts that cursory investigation yielded. When he had brought his committee to the point where facts were challenged and proof was asked for, he then had a community planning group in operation.

DEVELOPING MUTUAL CONFIDENCE

By the time that the full report was ready for discussion by the committee, its members and their counselor had developed mutual respect and confidence. They knew that when he made a statement of fact, he could back it up with proof. He knew that when they challenged an opinion or method of approach, they were expressing their honest convictions, and, therefore, the convictions of a large number of citizens whom they represented. There was, for instance, a considerable minority with grave reservations about the "timeliness and practicability" of the recommendations. They wondered if the time was ripe for an out-and-out attack on the racial inequities in the Miami community. They questioned the strategy of "covering the waterfront" of more than a score of separate problems and thereby risking a massive opposition opinion. All of these reservations were frankly discussed in committee meetings. First one and then another of the doubters was satisfied. When the report was voted on every one of its twenty-three recommendations were approved, and by a unanimous vote.

AVOIDING SWITCH-OFFS

During the progress of this project there were a number of possible switch-off points at which action could have been side-tracked. If the original interested group had merely met to view-with-alarm and point-with-distress, it would have become nothing more than another *ad hoc* protest group. Justified protest always has its educational effect, if skillfully expressed, but *unimplemented protest is little more than vocal exercise*. Implementation of the original interest was made possible by referring it to a stable agency with resources of staff and board experience.

The second possible switch-off was avoided when the Welfare Planning Council escaped the trap of *volunteer* fact-finding and turned to the experienced professional for a solid research job. The reference to the "trap of volunteer fact-finding" is not in derision of the method but with emphasis on certain dangers implicit in its use. Such dangers were evident in observing the rash of community self-studies that broke out around the country during the post-World War II period, largely inspired by the highly-advertised "Monclair (N. J.) plan." The studies were initiated by individuals and groups disturbed by economic and social inequities experienced by some population elements. "Inventory" was taken of racial, religious and other social attitudes revealed in the survey. The final accounting ranked the community as "good," "fair" or "poor," and generally suggested steps for improvement.

But in both the fact-finding and the evaluatory phases of such a study, professional consultation is imperative. For without it, questionnaires may prove to be "loaded," however innocently, findings can be in-conclusive or premature, prejudgements by "researchers" may be translated into survey conclusions and public confidence or attention may be irretrievably lost even before it is won. Properly protected against such dangers, the volunteer study can be an effective community organization tool but, as is indicated, such protection almost always demands professionally-experienced consultative service.

In the case of Miami it would have been expecting too much of volunteer leaders to have given them the job of challenging established racial attitudes and practices surrounded with so much emotionalism. The average committee member, if asked to accept such an assignment, would either have shirked off from the whole job or would have avoided its tougher commitments. It was easier for the public to accept such a job being done by a professional brought in for the purpose; it was easier for the committee to endorse his proven findings than to have dug them out themselves.

When the community counselor arrived on the job, he had no prestige in the Miami community, except among his professional colleagues and those few citizens who were acquainted with the work of his agency. He wisely declined to assume any spokesmanship role, for spokesman-ship without prestige is like an orange without juice—completely unsatisfying. The counselor, therefore, devoted himself to assurance of prestige on the part of his committee. His indirect leadership asserted itself as he provided his committee members with facts and reinforced *their* prestige with authority and conviction. The Junior League member who went back to her volunteer activities in child welfare could never again be unconcerned over the welfare of Miami's Negro children —or uninformed, for her quickened interest would spur her to keep abreast of developments within the Negro community. And so with the Chamber of Commerce leader, and the member of the Board of Education.

Indirect leadership paid its dividends, not only in the immediate public response to the recommendations of the Miami study, but also in improvement activities carried on over a long period of years. Ten years after the "Banner bible" was put in circulation, the counselor was asked to return for an evaluatory check-up on what had happened as a result of the study. Using several of the original members of the advisory committee as the core of a re-activated group, the Council sought to answer the questions "Where do we stand today?" and "Where do we go from here?" Dr. Banner found that of twenty-three major action recommendations, nineteen had been largely complied with, and there had been some tentative progress on the remaining four. The new committee followed the guide lines of the old one; in its report on progress made during a ten-year span, it included recommendations for the next ten years of progress.

WORKING WITH COMMITTEES

By no means is every community action program so successful in its attainment of objectives, nor is every community counselor as fortunate in his relations with his planning committee. Yet, in the Miami experience there are illustrations and precedents that can be taken to heart by any counselor working anywhere in the country,—provided, that is, that certain guide lines are always kept clearly in view. Much stress has been placed upon the counselor's use of committees—the exertion of indirect leadership in guiding and supporting direct leaders. It has been pointed out that the committees are most effective when they are most representative of the general community. Yet it must be remembered that it is easier to organize a "representative" committee than it is to keep working smoothly and effectively. The representative committee must first of all acquire a shared conviction that the job accepted is of real importance. There will be varying opinions on that point at the outset, depending upon the interest-base of the representatives involved. Constant indoctrination, through individual and group approaches, must be carried on by the counselor or the committee leader until such a conviction is fully shared.

This means that committee members should be chosen with an eye to their adjustability of viewpoint. They should have strong convictions, but these should be susceptible to readjustment in the face of compelling arguments. The charge to the committee must be clearly expressed and understood in the same way by all members of the committee. This may require frequent counselor's reference to the committee's purpose and its specific commitments. Finally—or not finally at all—there should be a clear understanding not only of what the committee will seek to do but also of what it will not attempt to do. Leadership, once installed, must be respected; the more "representative" the committee is, the more important is this stipulation, for when such a committee acquires several spokesmen it ends up with no effective spokesman.

STEPS IN THE COUNSELOR'S JOB

Here, then, are the various steps included in the community counselor's job, any one of which may be required in any one planning operation and all of which may be needed in some projects:

1. *Identifying the problem.* The problem must be identified so clearly that the counselor has no difficulty in interpreting it to others. He should be able to refer to the community complaints regarding the conditions that produced the problem, sample opinions as to the need for action, and have recourse to official records showing the actual state of affairs and indications of the reaction of leadership when and if social action is initiated.

2. *Enlisting Community Cooperation.* In smaller communities the enlistment of leadership support will probably begin with civic groups. As the community becomes larger, other leadership forces will be available for recruitment. Public officials should be brought into the picture early in the process. In social work practice, as was noted in a Brandeis University International Workshop report on "Community Development and Community Organization,"* there is too often noted a tendency to foster avoidance of political activity as decisions are made affecting the community. This is not only illogical but also fatal to success in many instances. The American community is a political entity quite as much as economic and social. The increasing complexity of social problems and the growing involvement of government in the affairs of citizens make imperative the participation of government

* Brandeis University International Workshop: Community Development and Community Organization, 1961; National Association of Social Workers.

officials in interest areas where they carry responsibility, even when the community organization project is initiated by citizen leadership. And nothing is more apt to stimulate such participation than the creation of political support for their constructive involvement.

Interested social agencies should be canvassed for possible support from their staff or members of their boards. The press, radio and television should be used to the full limits of their availability. However, until the problem has been clearly defined and there is some assurance of some action, it is probably not well to publicize plans too widely.

3. *Studying the Community.* The counselor should make use of every possible source of information regarding not merely the problem itself, but also that part of the community's history which bears upon the problem. Every community has special alliances and factions. It suffers from certain fears and enjoys certain emotional prides which may be the result of historical developments or the reflection of current forces exerted by vested interests. All of these help to create the framework for community planning and the counselor cannot afford to have others better informed on such subjects than himself. And if he should not have mastery of such information, he should have ready access to those who have.

4. *Enrolling Leadership.* Potential leaders in a community development project do not line up waiting for enrollment. They have to be found—sometimes with infinite pains and great care. The community counselor should keep a file of lists of organizations and their key leaders, with notes indicating the major interests and effectiveness of each. In this way the rifle is substituted for the shotgun as a method of selection and the chances of choosing unsound leaders are greatly reduced. The counselor's involvement with leadership, however, does not end with the selection of members of his "team". He must spend a great deal of time, broadening their knowledge of the problem faced, and increasing their confidence in his own expert's status.

5. *Analyzing Community Opinion.* Three general types of opinion may be expected on the subject of any important community development project. One opinion group, which is generally fairly small, is composed of the project's supporters. The second group consists of the active opposition—and in most cases it is even smaller than the first. The great majority of the general public, however, can be expected to be either uninformed, indifferent or half-interested. It is this uninformed and indifferent majority that should be a principal concern of the counselor, for the project's success is apt to depend upon the effectiveness of interpretation among the public majority.

6. *Interpreting the Project.* With this uninformed and indifferent neutralist majority, the support of newspapers, radio and television can

be of great importance. Few who are not originally interested in a project's aims will catch fire from a single interpretive contact. The message must be dinned against the public's attention again and again until it begins to make an impression. There is no communication medium that offers so much opportunity for repetitive interpretation as television, radio and the press, in that order. It is obvious, therefore, that the community counselor must, as a part of his job, maintain continual and closely-amicable relationships with those who direct the major communication media.

7. *Guiding the Committee.* The best committee can get off the path of its original objective if its guide-posts are not constantly pointed out. Committee members are, ideally, busy people with other concerns that have high priority. They are apt to come to meetings only partly prepared for discussions; or in the interim since the last meeting, other problems and programs will have absorbed their attention. The counselor, therefore, must be ready with tactful suggestions and reminders to keep committee members abreast of discussion and moving toward the agreed-upon goal. Similarly, a prod may be needed when committee interest threatens to flag. A few visits to key members, the introduction of new subject material for considerations, a pat on the back at the right time—these are ages-old devices for inspiring and maintaining group action which the counselor must be ready to employ.

9. *Inventory and Recapitulation.* Not only the action group, but the counselor as well is helped by the inventory of community assets and recapitulation of committee progress that should be reported now and then. Especially is the inventory-and-recapitulation important in the case of long-term projects, when committee spirits are most apt to flag because the world refuses to be turned over in a hurry. The committee should be persuaded itself to make such a retrospective analysis, so that it can thereby convince itself as to the worthwhileness of its job. If this is not possible, the counselor should do the job himself, making sure that the members check and double-check his findings. Nothing encourages continued effort like assurance that past efforts have paid dividends.

CONCLUSION

The counseling process in community planning can be one of the most frustrating or rewarding of all professional experiences. And it is not necessarily the counselor himself who is responsible for the outcome. It is as apt as to be the community as the counselor. Some communities are at the stage where planning is resisted and the counselor's proffer of services scorned. Others may have the will-to-do but lack the leadership with know-how plus influence. And still other communities, on the right track and making progress that gladdens the counselor's heart, may overnight be swept by some new wave of interest or reaction that cancels out plans and gains—and postpones a fresh start until some indefinite future.

But, regardless of inconclusive result or heartbreaking failure, the community counselor still has one of the most enrichening assignments in the American community. More than most, he is so close to the heart of the community that he can feel its pulse and diagnose its social, its *spiritual* health. He works with the community's "best" people and finds himself opposed by the worst. He comes to know intimately, from behind the scenes, the personalities who "count" in the community. And in all of this, the counselor has the joy of seeing individuals and leadership groups grow in wisdom and influence, and witnessing community situations improve as a result of that growth. The counselor is seldom a hero and never gets rich, but his work is one of helping his America to become better and stronger—and realization of this can be the richest reward of all.

And as for the community itself, the process of community organization is one which, once learned and applied by one leadership team, can be adapted and readapted to varied purposes by as many teams as find challenging social ends to pursue. It is used profitably in stimulating neighborhood rehabilitation or in supporting or watch-dogging urban redevelopment programs. Increased voter registration, creation of new or enlarged social services in suburban areas, developing youth-aid programs for combating delinquency, organizing consumer education programs—these are only a few of the civic improvement efforts once carried on by the trial-and-error method which are now employing the experience and training of the community counselor.

But it is important to keep in mind, as India's Prime Minister Nehru has pointed out respecting that country's community development program, that the greatest benefits to come from the process of community counseling need not be readily identifiable. They may well be the intangibles of social result which appear belatedly—when recognized at all—in more cooperative attitudes between leadership personalities and groups. Or the benefits may come in the form of a more critical citizen attitude toward the coverage and quality of public service—an attitude growing out of deeper awareness of the public's needs and rights.

Community organization, as the vehicle for the community counseling process, is an essential part of healthy community life in today's America. It is to be hoped that the social work profession, which is best geared to use this vehicle in a fashion consonant with the greatest social health of a modern community-in-change, will be alert to shape the counselor's role toward maximum use of the vehicle.

BIBLIOGRAPHY

1. BUELL, BRADLEY: 1952. *Community Planning for Human Services*, New York: Columbia University Press.
2. COLCORD, JOANNA: 1947. *Your Community*, New York: Russell Sage Foundation.
3. DUNHAM, ARTHUR: 1958. Community Welfare Organization, "Principles and Practice," New York: Thomas Y. Crowell.
4. FRENCH, DAVID G.: 1952. *An Approach to Measuring Results in Social Work*, University of Columbia Press.
5. GRANGER, LESTER B.: 1954. "Changing Functions of Voluntary Agencies," New Directions in Social Work (Ed.) Cora Kasius, Harper.
6. ——: 1961. "Community Organization." *Values and Ideals of American Youth*; Eli Ginzberg (Ed.). New York: Columbia University Press.
7. ——: 1947. "Educational and Promotional Process in Community Organization." Proceedings, National Conference on Social Welfare.
8. HUNTER, FLOYD: 1953. "Community Power Structure—A Study of Decision Makers." Chapel Hill: University of North Carolina Press.
9. JOHNS, RAY and DEMARCHE, DAVID: 1951. "Community Organization and Agency Responsibility." New York: Association Press.
10. KING, CLARENCE: 1948. *Organizing for Social Action*, Harper.
11. KVARACEUS, WILLIAM C.: 1954. *The Community and the Delinquent*, World Book Company.
12. LINDEMAN, EDUARD C.: 1929. *The Community*. Association Press.
13. McMILLEN, WAYNE: 1945. *Community Organization for Social Work*, University of Chicago Press.
14. MURPHY, CAMPBELL: 1954. *Community Organization Practice*, Boston: Houghton Mifflin.
15. OGDEN, JEAN and OGDEN, JESS: 1946. *Small Community in Action*, Harper.
16. ROSS, MURRAY G.: 1955. "Community Organization, Theory and Principles." New York: Harper.
17. TRECKER, AUDREY R. and HARLEY, B.: 1954. *Committee Common Sense*. Whitside Morrow.
18. WEISMAN, IRVING: 1959. "Social Welfare Policies and Services," Social Welfare Education XII, New York.
19. WILENSKY, HAROLD and LEBAUX, CHARLES: 1955. *Industrial Society and Social Welfare*. New York: Russel Sage Foundation.
20. BRANDEIS UNIVERSITY: 1961. *Community Development and Community Organization*; Report on International Workshop; New York: National Association of Social Workers.
21. NATIONAL CONFERENCE ON SOCIAL WELFARE: 1957. *Planning Social Services for Urban Needs*, Papers on Community Organization, Columbia University Press.
22. —— The Social Welfare Forum, Official Proceedings (Annual); Columbia University Press.
23. INTERNATIONAL CONFERENCE OF SOCIAL WORK: 1958. *Mobilizing Resources for Social Needs*, Proceedings of the Ninth Biennial Meeting, Tokyo, New York and Bombay.
24. SOCIAL WORK YEAR BOOK: Annual.

Vocational Counseling

JANE F. CULBERT *

Supervisor of Counseling Services
Vocational Advisory Service
New York

VOCATIONAL counseling began about the turn of the century, its birth-date usually given as 1908, the year in which Frank Parsons opened a boys' work bureau in a settlement house in Boston. Himself an engineer, and later a lawyer, who had worked in a rolling mill as well as taught in high school and college, Mr. Parsons had seen that the young people who came to the settlement house were eager for "advice" as to their choice of work, how to prepare for it, how to find an opening in it, and how to advance beyond that beginning job. On his executive committee were men from industry and business, labor and education. His staff combined experience in industry, employment, vocational training and adult education with thorough knowledge of the community and its resources. Their concern was with the vocations of young people, and they called their service "Vocational Guidance." Its originators recognized that in an industrial world in which even then all processes were becoming more and more complicated, the traditional advisors of youth —parents, teachers, friends—were no longer adequately equipped to give vocational advice.

Vocational counseling, meeting a social need and involving techniques used by social workers such as interviewing, evaluation and follow up, had its beginning in a social agency. Once initiated, its contribution was speedily recognized, and similar services were established in a number of cities, in different settings, and with varying emphases, but all concerned with helping young people work out vocational plans.

(* deceased September 29, 1962)

IN THE SCHOOLS

In Boston, as in other cities, it was a social work agency which pioneered in introducing vocational guidance into the public schools. In New York City, it was a demonstration counseling project of the Vocational Service for Juniors that led to the appointment of licensed counselors in the public schools. Most large and many small school systems now provide this service.

In the early days, emphasis was primarily on the relation of the individual to the working world, and his finding a suitable place in it. After the service was extended to the schools, its focus was considerably changed from vocational to educational counseling. Though in some school systems there were full-time vocational counselors, in many certain teachers were relieved of teaching duties for a limited number of hours daily, to take over this new service. Often these teachers had little knowledge of the world of work, but were aware of the need for educational guidance and for help with personal problems. In time, as a result, more emphasis was put on requirements for college entrance, and less on knowledge of employment possibilities, the requirements of employers, and opportunities for beginning workers. Duties assigned to the vocational or guidance counselor, besides conferring with individual students on their future "careers," may include providing vocational materials for a course on Occupational Information, in form of lectures, films or discussions. In some schools placement is a function of the guidance counselor. Students may be referred to the guidance counselor because of "failures," discipline problems, or any deviating behavior. In schools employing a psychologist, sometimes besides carrying responsibility for the testing he also counsels individual students. In most school systems today, these functions fall to people from the academic world, so that with increasing emphasis on college preparation, the vocational aspects are apt to be obscured, and more value attached to knowledge of the educational field than to practical and specific knowledge of the working world.

CHANGING EMPHASIS IN GUIDANCE

Gradually the emphasis on the relation of the young person to the world of work has given way to the inclusion of educational, personal, psychological and other sorts of guidance, to the extent that in 1929 there was a move to have "Vocational" dropped from the name of the professional organization of vocational counselors, founded in 1912: The National Vocational Guidance Association. This effort failed at the time, but in 1952, when the NVGA merged with four other national groups, the name of the resulting organization became the American Personnel and Guidance Association. Local branches have also become Personnel and Guidance Associations, with the preponderance of their membership coming from school personnel.

As the guidance movement has thus become more and more identified with education and psychology, the training in guidance, especially for school counselors, has been taken over by the schools of education and by psychology departments. The M.A. in Guidance now generally required of a counselor, given in graduate schools of education, usually includes some courses required in case work training, such as community resources, and interviewing, but with much less provision for field work under close supervision than is required in a school of social work. Some courses in vocational guidance are given in departments of psychology. In either case, despite courses in occupations, there is not much stress on knowledge of the facts of working life—the technological changes and trends, the evolving requirements—nor on the relationship of the individual to the opportunities and exactions of the working world.

It would be desirable, in addition to theory courses in guidance, if all vocational counselors would serve an apprenticeship, or a period of field work training in a vocational counseling agency. The experience of helping young people seeking to enter the working world, or trying to come to grips with problems in their first employment, or looking toward ways of advancing in that employment or toward a longer-term objective in another job or another field of work adds immeasurably to the counselor's equipment.

OUT OF SCHOOL COUNSELING

Vocational counseling is carried on in various community agencies.* Whether in an agency offering vocational counseling only, or providing vocational counseling as one of its services, in most sizeable communities today there is at least one source of vocational counseling for out of school youth and adults. Many of these agencies also do job placement; and in some communities, organizations formerly offering placement only, including the state employment services, now offer counseling as well.

Vocational counseling is concerned with helping young people select a field of work suitable to their aptitudes and interests. To do this effectively, the counselor needs not only the personal qualities, the training and experience which make him skillful in dealing with young

* The American Board on Professional Standards in Vocational Counseling, Inc., publishes a directory of approved vocational counseling services in each state.

people and their problems; he must also know his community—not only its socio-ethnic composition and income level; he must know it vocationally. This involves knowing what business and industries exist, especially those which offer jobs to beginning workers; it involves being in touch with local employer groups, fraternal organizations, labor unions. It involves full knowledge of training resources, opportunities for apprenticeship, and trade schools.

The vocational counselor is work oriented, seeing the vocational problem as basic, with its solution contributing to the solution of other problems. Once a work adjustment has been made, the young person is better able to cope with other problems. A satisfactory work experience has a stabilizing effect on emotional adjustment. It has been said that work itself is therapy.

Vocational problems are, of course, closely associated with other problems and therefore counseling on personal and social development and adjustment is included in the functions of the vocational counselor. He is aware of these; he is also aware that he is trained especially to deal with the vocational aspect of the young person's need. If the problem is one related closely to the client's work—his difficulties in the training process, lack of understanding of what he might gain from a seemingly dead-end job, his relation to supervisor or fellow workers—the counselor would probably deal with it himself. Where problems other than vocational are the overriding need, he would arrange for help from those whose function it is to deal with these problems.

Vocational counseling, in common with other forms of counseling, deals with the individual. It recognizes that the client must be seen, listened to, and understood as an individual—one whose present is the result of a past that forms the basis, but not the measure, of his future. He must always be thought of, too, as a growing and developing individual, even where at first he might seem to have reached the limit of his development. The vocational counselor, while considering immediate work possibilities, must always think in terms of the potentialities of the individual, and his capacities for realizing them, in terms of training and other developing experiences.

REQUIREMENTS

Formal requirements for guidance workers vary from state to state.* New York was first to require certification for school counselors, in

* *Guidance Workers Certification Requirements*, OE-25005, Bulletin 1960, No. 14 by Royce E. Brewster, Specialist for Guidance Practices, U.S. Department of Health, Education, and Welfare, Office of Education, lists the certification requirements for guidance workers by states.

1926. Thirty-four states now have mandatory certification for this position, four have optional certification and twelve have none. Several states are in process of setting up requirements for certification or have already done so, effective at a future date. As an example, in New York State at the present time, in addition to completion of an approved curriculum leading to the baccalaureate degree (or approved equivalent preparation), a candidate must complete thirty hours in approved graduate courses, including: Understanding the individual (dynamics of behavior, etc.); Principles and Practices of Guidance; Techniques of Counseling; Measurement and appraisal for the use of counselors (including statistics); and Survey (organization and use of educational and occupational information). There is provision for substitution of equivalents. Candidates shall also have completed two years of teaching in an approved school, and one year of work experience other than teaching. (This latter may be another year of teaching combined with field work courses providing observation, study and discussion of occupational and training opportunities and community resources.)

Requirements for vocational counselors outside the school setting also vary from agency to agency. In one, acceptable graduate study is described as "in the field of economics, sociology, psychology, social work or allied subjects," and there is an additional requirement of several years' "experience in business and/or industry" for which also there are equivalent positions.

The requirement "personal equipment adequate to insure constructive work with individuals in a counseling situation" is harder to define. Like any person who deals with individuals having problems, the vocational counselor must understand the dynamics of human behavior. Because in working with young people one of his aims will be to help them understand themselves, he must have a basic understanding of the development of personality, the stresses of adolescence, the impulsiveness and other traits of youth. He must also be able to recognize serious deviations that may indicate the need of therapy, though usually he does not consider this therapy as his responsibility. Counselors who are clinical psychologists sometimes include therapy in their services. The counselor must be able to distinguish unrealistic vocational interests that stem from parental pressure or sibling rivalry, and perhaps the equally unrealistic goal which represents a genuine interest but too little understanding of the intellectual requirements and the preparation involved. He must be able to measure interest against the ability to complete successfully the training required to meet employment demands as to skills. He must know how to assess the young person's ability to cope with pressures and other stresses. He must be able to help him explore his interests, and understand the reasons for them.

He must know how to observe the individual with perception and to define his problem, how to interview the client so as to gain his confidence and at the same time secure the information necessary for good vocational planning; how to help the young person think for himself, how to prepare him for making his own decisions.

The client must also know what, in his interviews with the client, is pertinent for the case record; and how to write records clearly, as if for someone else to read, rather than as notes to himself.

In addition to all of this—all of the qualities and equipment which he shares with other kinds of counselors—the vocational counselor must have a fund of information about vocations, a clear and constantly refreshed and replenished knowledge and understanding of the working world.

KNOWING THE COMMUNITY

Anyone serving young people must have a good grasp of the sociological and cultural background of the community—the values held; the standards and customs to which the young are expected to conform; economic levels and housing problems; and resources for recreation, community association, and education. In addition the vocational counselor must acquire a vocational knowledge of the community.

One excellent source of information and assistance is the public employment service. Direct contact should be made with their offices, and this should be maintained and furthered, in order to keep in touch with changes in requirements and in opportunities for employment. Other local sources of information and assistance are the business bureaus, local chambers of commerce, business men's and women's associations or professional groups, and the civic-minded fraternal organizations such as the Rotary Club. The members of such groups not only can provide information on the shops, businesses and industries of the community, but often can arrange for the counselor to visit local firms and plants to learn first hand of the manufacturing or other processes involved. Where the community is primarily a one-industry town—as where a steel mill or a paper mill dominates the employment scene— the vocational counselor will want to make contact with the personnel department or plant manager and if possible arrange for a visit to the plant, to learn directly the types of work, entry jobs, unskilled and skilled requirements, training provided on the job, and opportunities for advancement. Whatever his other qualifications, without accurate and up-to-the-minute information no one is fully equipped to give vocational counseling to those who seek help in finding their way in the working world.

"WHO NEEDS IT?"

It is to be noted that to most young people vocational counseling seems a normal need, as natural a step toward employment as going to a placement service. They do not feel they are "letting the family down" in seeking it, nor that it marks them as "odd," inadequate, coming from a "poor family" or in some kind of trouble. They seek it because they are uncertain as to choice of work, or their ability to succeed in what they think they would like to do or in the training that must precede employment in it. They need evaluation of their interests, as well as their capacities. They want to confer with someone who is objective as well as knowledgeable about their vocational aims, or their confusion of purpose; someone who knows the working world and its requirements as well as the available educational or training resources and requirements for admission to them.

The ability to support oneself being the customary measure in our society of the individual, a feeling of success in work is of signal importance to youth—"the mark of a man." Therefore, because of the connection of vocational counseling with the world of work, with the adult business of earning a living, young people are not ashamed of having to ask for it, and it can sometimes reach out to the hardest to reach.

Often young people undervalue their abilities. A poor record in school courses for which he was inadequately motivated may have given an intelligent boy a faulty measure of his endowment, so that without enlightened encouragement he would put aside all thought of any occupation requiring further education. Young people not only need help in assessing their capabilities, but clear information as to the time, effort and money needed in order to reach a certain goal. In many cases they also need to learn of short-term alternatives that will help them earn, or learn, or in some way advance toward that goal. Ways and means of financing training, granted abilities to justify this effort, may be part of the planning between client and counselor. Where no strong vocational preference exists, the young person needs help in selecting a field or a course of training broad enough to serve as a foundation for further development and growth.

Urban living in some ways tends to decrease rather than enhance youth's knowledge of occupations. The number of men and boys watching an excavation or a construction through openings in the side-walk wall attests that there is very great interest in building processes and technology. But the passive observers are far removed from sharing in these processes, or being able to discuss them with those who do them, or trying themselves out in this occupation. And while part-time or summer employment may provide the basic values of any work experience, it often gives little opportunity to observe or learn about the processes and products that engage permanent workers, and even less opportunity for try-out employment in actual production. Modern industry to a great extent is carried on in large plants behind closed doors, and the work involved is quite unknown to the young people of the immediate neighborhood. Although the public invests enormous funds in educating our youth, they do not yet get enough guidance in how to relate this education to their work lives. All of these factors make the choice of a vocation difficult for most. They need vocational guidance.

Although both boys and girls need vocational counseling, a larger proportion of boys and men seek it, obviously because most of them feel that their work life will continue at least to retirement age, whereas—though this concept is changing—many girls still think of a work life lasting only to marriage.

Nor is vocational counseling a need only of the young. This is not a service which once given is never needed again. Greater maturity may change basic interests, and drastic changes within an industry are the order of today. Thus even mature young men and women, with successful employment experience, may want to discuss with a vocational counselor which of several new roads to follow. In an era of continuous industrial and technological change, with old jobs vanishing and new skills required, there is continuing need of vocational counseling.

THE COUNSELING PROCESS

Counseling procedures include interviews and testing.

As in the first interview in any counseling, the vocational counselor must be able to establish a good relationship with the client; must know how to secure the needed basic information and at the same time convey to the client an understanding of how this information relates to his current problem. Though it is not unlike an interview conducted in a case work or related agency, there is in the vocational counseling interview a difference in emphasis. It is likely to center around a young person's work interests and plans, even vague ones. More attention is given to his employment history, however brief,—things he liked or disliked about his jobs, his own ideas about his success or failure in them, and what he learned from them as a basis for practical thinking about a field of work and his future in it. Careful attention is given to his school experience, the subjects he liked, and those he disliked or found most difficult. If he has an unsatisfactory school record, there may be some discussion of his study habits, or of situations which make study difficult; what he feels are the reasons for his school failures. Where the client can be helped to see that it is pertinent to his vocational problem, no question will be regarded as impertinent.

Discussion usually begins at whatever point seems most natural, most interesting to the client (as revealed by statements in the application form he has filled out), and most likely to draw him out. If he seems confused about the function of the counseling service, or if he has come with the expectation of being given a "test" which will give a definitive answer to his problem and provide the key which will open the door to success, a brief, clear and simple explanation may be first in order.

Although the first interview must deal with a series of questions which will provide information for the counselor's use, these questions and the answering of them should also be revealing to the client. They may show him how little he knows about the field in which he has expressed interest, or that the reasons for his interest were not well founded. Discussion may also bring to light an interest in something related to his social or recreational activities. The counselor's role must also be that of the listener. He will want to know the client's reasons for coming for consultation, the problem as the client sees it, the depth of the vocational interests, the degree of knowledge he has about the occupation of his choice, his family's agreement or disagreement, and the degree of their willingness to help him follow his vocational interests.

Usually covered in a first vocational counseling interview—their order depending on circumstances or the client's sense of priority or urgency—are: his plans if any, with the reasons for his choice, and examination of earlier vocational interests that he may have discarded; his educational foundations and employment experience; his recreational activities and hobbies which throw light on the validity and quality of his interests; and the family situation in relation to his own plans, whether it is comfortable and happy or full of stress and opposition.

While discussing all of these matters, in his first impressions of the client's manner, appearance, perception and sensitivity, the vocational counselor will be seeing these personality traits as factors that would strike an employer either favorably or unfavorably.

Beyond the establishing of a good relationship, and securing basic information, an important objective of the first interview is to stimulate the client to think for and about himself, and about the world of work. Too many early school leavers, and even high school graduates of today, have slid along painlessly from elementary to junior high to high school with little thinking or conscious decision. These sometimes have the idea that they will slide into the working world somehow, without making any decisions or acquiring the competence that any employer would demand of them. One of the first things a counselor tries to do is to start a youth thinking seriously about his various interests—which may range from vague dreams to hope, from purpose to determination. He must be helped to think of fitness for various fields in light of the requirements—in education, skills and personality traits that his fields of interest will demand. The more serious, the more gifted person also often finds it difficult to make a vocational choice for the very reason that he usually has many interests as well as the ability to succeed in a number of occupations.

Often a new concept of work has to be developed. Basically, a vocational counselor must have an interest in and a real respect for the non-professional, mechanical, service or craft occupations. Nothing is worse for a young person than the feeling that the thing he can do and wants to do is regarded as beneath the family standing, or will be looked down upon by his fellows. Only if he himself respects all kinds of work will the counselor be able to combat the misconception that "you can never get anywhere without a college education"—an idea which is a source of destructive frustration to many young people with good capacities, but neither good prospects for getting into college, nor any interest in doing so.

Other misconceptions that the client should be helped to think through are first that vocational counseling must lead to a final and irrevocable choice of the vocation in which he will work for the rest of his life. The rapid and profound changes in all the processes of business and industry today make this concept invalid. Changes in family circumstances, increased self understanding through the work experience, further education or growth in maturity may permit his viewing as possibilities the training, or type of work, that once seemed beyond him. Also, a client's vocational thinking should not be restricted by the notion that there is just one right job for everyone. He should know that most people have the capacity to do, or to learn to do, many things.

It may help to carry forward the client's thinking about his plans if he is asked to secure some specific information, or take responsibility for some agreed-upon action, before he is seen again by the counselor. Before the interview ends, the matter of tests will be explained, and ordinarily an appointment for testing will be made. By the time it ends, too, the client should feel that the counselor has a genuine respect for him and for his vocational problem; and that, working together, they will arrive at plans practical enough to take care of his immediate need yet flexible enough to allow for change and development, in himself and in his vocational goal.

TESTING

Almost as soon as tests were developed, vocational counseling services began to use them as an aid in evaluating a young person's capabilities. Sometimes tests had not been sufficiently validated; often too much emphasis was put on particular scores. In the earlier days, and in some places today, testing is done by counselors who have had courses in the theory of tests, but not sufficient practice under supervision to insure the validity of the tests or their interpretation. As John M. Brewer, a major historian of the vocational guidance movement, has said: "Testing is a sharp tool that in careless hands can do much harm."

Today most vocational counseling services include a testing program designed to supplement the school record and the counselor's impression of the client's intelligence and ability to plan. The variety of tests give more exact information about his intellectual functioning, his strengths and limitations, and how he compares with others in his age group. In addition to gauging his performance at clerical work, or with numbers, or in tasks requiring manual dexterity, tests are given which afford some indication of the client's feelings about himself, his accomplishments, his relations with other people and his outlook on life.

The psychological examiners also report their observations of the client's reaction to various tests, their behavior during periods of difficulty; the anxiety, irritation, discouragement or frustration which may be shown; differences in approach to varying materials; meticulous work habits or carelessness in performance; and their relation to others during the tests. These observations are of great value to the counselor in estimating his client's ability to meet employment demands or to withstand competitive pressures and other stress.

Psychological tests are a valuable instrument in aid of the vocational counselor, but cannot in themselves determine a vocational plan. They deepen the counselor's understanding of his client, and often are helpful not only in measuring present levels of development, but also in uncovering the client's latent possibilities for growth and achievement.

EVALUATION AND PLANNING

Before he sees the client again, the counselor will carefully review and evaluate all the information he has gained through his first interview, through the school and social agency reports, and through the results of the psychological tests and the observations of the psychologist who administered them.

Sometimes this evaluation takes place at a conference attended by the employment worker, teacher or social worker who referred the client; sometimes a more experienced staff member is present; sometimes the psychologist also attends. But whether it is done by the counselor himself, or in a conference, this evaluation is a most necessary step in counseling. Many factors must be considered and weighed. Not school achievement alone, not test results, not the client's present state of self esteem, neither the "impressive personality" nor the current poor prospects for sympathetic backing or financial aid should determine the long-range vocational plan. All of them, and the relation of each of them to the others, have a place in the evaluation which is to form the basis for a vocational plan. Together, they may add up to an indication that the client's vocational goal or tentative plans are not feasible. In that case they serve as the framework within which to work out alternate plans, related to the client's interests but within his capacities. These plans will be discussed with him at the next, or planning interview.

THE PLANNING INTERVIEW

The planning interview is somewhat unpredictable because in the time since the first interview the client may have changed some of his ideas—under stimulus of the first discussion and his beginning to think for himself, or through new information he has secured about his earlier interest.

Though the evaluation and pre-planning may have produced very definite recommendations, the counselor will not merely enumerate and discuss these recommendations, for his function is to help the client think for himself, and to express himself as to any change in his plans or his thinking. Time must be given for consideration and decision, and there must be attention to what is most immediate, such as the possible necessity of securing some kind of work without delay. Alternative goals should be considered with the client, even where he comes with a fixed idea and a fairly practical plan. Time may be needed to help him see the relationship of his chosen occupation to other lines of work in which, with some further training or a broader experience, he might advance himself.

Most clients will want to know the results of the tests. This information should be given with discretion and judgment as to how it can be helpful. Positives should be emphasized; indeed, great care should be taken to present this information in a way which will not be a source of discouragement. Single test scores are to be avoided but the total test pattern, showing relative strengths, may be very helpful. Tests should not be regarded or presented as a single determining factor, but in their relation to the client's vocational interests and to sound planning.

If evaluation has invalidated the client's first objective, he must be helped to think this through, perhaps to a modification which is more feasible. If a young person with a poor school record shows genuine interest—based realistically on a work experience, or success in a hobby, for example—in some vocation which would require more academic work, it might be wise to plan further schooling in a different environment for an exploratory period. With strong motivation toward a definite goal and a clear understanding of the need for doing well in a formerly disliked subject if he is ever to reach that goal, a young person often surprises himself by his improved academic achievement.

For the young person whose social life is very limited, especially where the choice of vocation would require a degree of social development, the counselor might explore with his client the possible development of avocational interests through a general education course of evening study, or joining in youth groups, or participating in neighborhood cultural or recreational activities.

Since one of the chief purposes of counseling is to get the client's plan under way, in most cases a definite course of action will be discussed before the end of the planning interview. Through the broader understanding of his client which the preceding evaluation has given him, the counselor is better prepared to answer questions and meet resistances. If, however, the client is not yet ready to give up an unrealistic objective, a second planning interview may be scheduled, giving him a little more time to think about the plan, and to secure further information about the field of his choice.

To be effective any planned course of action should be arrived at with the client's participation, or at least his genuine acceptance of it. A plan reluctantly accepted and undertaken half-heartedly, is not likely to be effective, however practical and wise.

HELP WITH PARENTS

A vocational plan often will have more chance of effectiveness, if it is also accepted by the parents; in any case the cooperation of parents is usually essential to sound and comfortable vocational planning. If the client is still in school, the school counselor may wish to talk with the parents, in order to see the problem from the family standpoint, and to help them understand the situation as the child and the counselor see it, so as to enlist their constructive cooperation in the plan, even if they are disappointed.

With young people who come through referral by other than family, or "on their own", it may be wiser for the counselor not to see the parents but to treat the client as an adult, and help him see how he might go about securing his parents' cooperation. This might prove a learning experience in growing up, freeing himself from over-protection, or domination, and dealing with a difficult situation in which two points of view must be considered.

Sometimes a young person needs help in changing his parents' point of view about a field of work, and the loss of status they may see as inherent in such work. Or a youth may be having to cope with the paralyzing effect of parental pressure to enter a profession for which he has little aptitude and less liking.

If the client asks for and needs help with his parents, in vocational planning, the counselor will suggest an interview. Only in extreme cases, where there is obvious need of psychiatric or medical care, should a parent be seen contrary to a client's wishes.

FOLLOW-UP INTERVIEWS

Vocational counseling seldom ends with the planning interview. Sometimes the counselor knows the client's response and through evaluation of his ability to plan and to follow through, that he will need help and encouragement in carrying out the decisions that have been made, especially where his situation is involved and difficult. In these cases he will arrange to keep in active touch with the client.

Though in every case the counselor tries to help the client become able to handle his own problems, he will also want to show an interest in the outcome of the plans, and to assure the client that he may return if difficulties arise in carrying out these plans. For experienced and mature young people it is often enough to point them in the right direction, for immediate work, or for the preparation which has been decided upon. Most young people, however, do need a follow-up service to be sure that their progress is not interrupted, or thwarted by disappointment in the nature of their job, or lack of understanding of what it might teach them; or supervision that is misunderstood and resented; or by failure or other difficulty which they, because of their inexperience, may have magnified out of proportion or seen out of perspective.

Many young people need help in beginning jobs because of old ideas of work that have given them unfortunate attitudes. The necessity for skills and competence in some line, sufficient to warrant a pay check, is a new idea to some inexperienced, unsuccessful young workers. There are boys who regard work as an inevitable necessity to be avoided if possible. A job adapted to the interests and abilities of a youth may in itself develop a more constructive attitude. In follow-up, the counselor must often deal with problems of adjustment to work, and he will help the young person toward greater understanding of his relation to regulations, to a foreman or supervisor, and to the requirements and conditions of industry or business, as compared with school. The vocational counselor will need to distinguish between a problem of vocational adjustment, and failure to adjust because of emotional difficulties.

THE UNADJUSTED

The question is often asked: how much personal counseling is done by a vocational counselor? In general, vocational counseling agencies do not accept a young person because he is unadjusted; neither do they refuse to accept him because he is. A decision must be made whether an applicant's degree of unadjustment is so severe, or its nature such as to prevent his being able to profit by vocational counseling. Many unadjusted young people become good and satisfactory workers in the right field or niche. They are often referred to vocational counseling agencies by psychiatrists, for help in selecting the most suitable job within the limits of their tolerance and their capacities. Others with poor emotional adjustment come to vocational counseling through social workers or employment counselors. There are agencies which not only accept the unadjusted for vocational or placement counseling, but also supplement their service with work tryout programs in a sheltered workshop, where work limitations can be taken into account, and help given in overcoming them.

There are instances, of course, where the counselor, through obvious indications, realizes that before a client can make any headway toward securing training, or planning for employment, he will have to work out his emotional or personality problems. In such event, steps will be taken to put the client in touch with such help as is needed, giving care to handling the referral in the way that will be least destructive to the client. Similarly, the counselor may see that a plan cannot be carried through until there are decided changes in the family situation, changes which the young person cannot bring about unaided. Here too referral will be made to an agency which can give the particular kind of help that is needed.

Primarily, the province of the vocational counselor is vocational. He deals with vocational choice and preparation, and generally with concrete and practical aspects of work adjustment and fulfillment. He gives consideration to the other problems faced by his clients primarily in terms of their bearing on the vocational problem. Yet he does not regard his field as a narrow one. Work is certainly one of the most important and enduring adjustments each individual must make. Therefore the vocational counselor feels that, in helping young people find that work which will be most conducive to the fullest use of their present and potential abilities, he is giving them a long start toward stable and good lives.

Counseling in an Employment Agency

MARGUERITE H. COLEMAN

Supervisor of Special Placement Services
New York State Division of Employment
New York

CHARACTERISTICS OF EMPLOYMENT AGENCY APPLICANTS

PERSONS seeking service through an employment agency have one characteristic in common—they are all looking for a job, most of them need and want an immediate job and most of them feel very keenly the financial and social pressure of unemployment. Few such applicants come to an employment agency requesting counseling service and many who have the greatest need for employment counseling service are least receptive to it—and least able to participate intelligently in it—at that particular moment in their lives. They want a job and they want it immediately. True, they all want a "good job" and some recognize that they know too little about their own capabilities and interests and labor market possibilities and requirements. Nevertheless, in many instances the pressure for immediate employment makes applicants reluctant to postpone actual referral to a specific job for even one day. Hence employment agency interviewers find themselves in a very difficult situation. They are dealing with applicants at a time when the applicant's need for employment counseling may be most acute if he is to achieve satisfactory job adjustment and yet because of the pressure of unemployment, he is frequently literally unable psychologically to participate in the very process which should be of assistance to him in getting and holding the good job he so desperately wishes.

Fortunately, for the sanity of employment agency interviewers, the majority of persons who seek employment help through an agency have already made a choice of an occupation. They have had work experience or specific training in that occupation, they are at least reasonably satisfied with the occupation they have chosen and they have engaged in it successfully. They wish that kind of employment again, they are familiar with and ready to accept the wages, hours and conditions of employment prevalent in the occupation in the locality in which they are seeking employment. Such jobs do exist and employers do have vacancies. Therefore, the major task of the employment agency interviewer is one of matching, as well as he can, the qualifications and desires of the applicant against the employer demands and requirements in respect to orders the agency already has on file or orders which the interviewer can secure by contacting employers with whom previous contact had already been established.

Stating the major function of an employment agency this briefly and bluntly is not intended to minimize the skill necessary to do a good placement matching job. Only a thoroughly experienced placement interviewer who has considerable knowledge of industries, occupations and people can be a successful placement interviewer. However, this matching of occupationally set job applicants with employer orders already on file or reasonably easily obtainable, is a placement job and not a counseling job.

While, as has been stated, a sizeable percentage of applicants coming to an employment agency need and wish good placement matching assistance, another sizeable percentage (variously estimated at 20–40 per cent of all agency job seekers) do need some kind of counseling or special placement assistance before they can be referred to a position or before they will achieve satisfactory job adjustment. The kind and extent of assistance needed by these applicants varies greatly and the technical demarcation between "good placement assistance", "employment counseling" and "vocational guidance" is a fine hair-line that will probably never be settled to the satisfaction of the semanticists. Whatever the process is called, however, all employment agency interviewers recognize the fact that a significant number of job seekers do need some kind of special placement or counseling service.

KINDS OF COUNSELING PROBLEMS

Among the most frequent employment counseling problems presented by applicants in an employment agency are:

1. Inability to decide on a field of work or an occupation because the applicant has had no previous work experience or specialized training. Such an applicant may have outstanding abilities in a single field of work or in several unrelated fields. He may or may not

recognize his own abilities, potentialities and interests but he usually has insufficient labor market information to relate his abilities to occupations or fields of work. Such applicants are frequently found among recent high school graduates or school drop-outs, some recent college graduates, some veterans, and many women in their 30's or 40's entering the labor market for the first time. These are the applicants, who when asked what kind of work they want, frequently answer earnestly, and they believe honestly, that they will take "anything".

2. Lack of apparent relationship between the kind of job the applicant says he wants and his apparent qualifications. These applicants have usually had little, if any, previous work experience. They may have had some specific training in an occupation different from the one in which they are now expressing interest. They may express interest in two or more unrelated occupations, each of which requires different preparation. It is important to recognize that such applicants may be expressing interest in an occupation that seems to be below their education, training and potential abilities as well as above their education, training and potential abilities. Many inexperienced or relatively inexperienced applicants applying at employment agencies ask for kinds of work in which they could probably perform successfully and for which they would meet employer and job requirements but which would be at a level considerably below their potentialities.

3. Desire or interest for changing occupations. Such applicants have usually had specific work experience or specific training in a particular occupation but they may be dissatisfied with or unsuccessful in their present employment, or they may have been displaced for technological or sociological reasons, or age or disability may be forcing a change in occupation, or the acquisition of additional training or skill may motivate an applicant to seek other or "better" employment. Some applicants in this group may have to seek employment in a field other than that in which they have had recent training simply because insufficient work opportunities exist at a particular time in the labor market to absorb all of the people who have been trained in and desire work in a particular occupation. Applicants in this group include some veterans who are no longer interested in the kind of work they had previous to entering military service, older workers, some applicants who are re-entering the labor market after a serious accident or other physical or medical disability, and workers left stranded because entire factories have closed down or moved out of town.

4. Expressed desire for training or request for information about specific training facilities or expressed interest in apprenticeship

opportunities. Frequently applicants asking for information about training resources or apprenticeship need assistance in making a sound vocational choice before they embark on training or apprenticeship. Such applicants may be considering a type of training that seems unsuitable in terms of the applicant's potentialities and abilities. It is not infrequent too, to find that the applicant has only a vague and nebulous notion of the relationship between the kind of training in which he has expressed interest and the kind of requirements, demands and possibilities for which the training will prepare him. Employment agencies deal every day in the week with sizeable numbers of people who inquire about some specific kind of training, with little if any notion about either the content, cost or length of the training, or their own potentialities to profit by the training, or the marketability of the training after it has been completed. There is no question whatsoever that additional training may be helpful and in many cases necessary to successful job adjustment and promotion, but only if the training is being undertaken to further a basically sound and thought-through job plan.

5. Unsuccessful search for work. Many applicants who seem to have the qualifications for the kind of job they are seeking and who may have had previous successful experience in the occupation, encounter unusual difficulty in a particular labor market in finding employment. Such applicants may be looking for work in their own occupational field at a higher level than that for which they are qualified, or they may be seeking work at a level that is attained only as a result of promotion from within, or the opportunities in their occupation may be shrinking, or they may be demanding higher wages than employers are paying, or they may be too restrictive in regard to hours, location, travel, etc., or they may need help in preparing résumés or in participating effectively in the employer interview.

6. Inability to hold a job. There are some applicants who seem to have little trouble getting jobs but considerable trouble holding jobs. Such applicants may become dissatisfied too quickly and not try jobs long enough, or they may expect promotion too quickly, or they may be unable to work harmoniously with supervisors or fellow workers, or they may have poor work habits or personality difficulties that interfere with successful job adjustment. Some of these are helped by employment counselors but many of them need medical, psychiatric or psychological help and the sooner the employment counselor can recognize the need for referral to another agency, the better it will be both for the applicant and the agency.

While the material listed above is suggestive of the more frequent types of counseling problems presented by applicants in an employment agency, each applicant is different and his counseling problem must be specific to him, directing attention to the major obstacles or difficulties which must be faced in his particular situation or the issues with respect to which decisions must be made for satisfactory solution of his particular problem. One of the fascinating aspects of employment agency counseling by all experienced counselors, is that if the counselor lives to be 100 he will never encounter exactly the same problem twice.

THE COUNSELING PROCESS

The process of counseling in an employment agency situation does not differ basically from counseling in any other similar situation. The same general method applies, that is:

1. Assisting the applicant to recognize and to agree on the problem.
2. Ascertaining and agreeing on the facts that are related to the problem.
3. Supplying and discussing pertinent labor market and similar information.
4. Discussing and agreeing on possible and practical solutions to the problem.
5. Agreeing on at least a tentative plan.
6. Assisting the applicant in taking action on the plan.
7. Following up with the applicant to determine progress or difficulties he may be having.
8. Assisting the applicant to progress in or to modify the plan where necessary.

ASCERTAINING THE PROBLEM

If applicants at an employment agency were asked what their problem was they would undoubtedly answer "Unemployment." To them their problem is their need for a job. The experienced employment counselor sees the problem somewhat differently. He recognizes completely that unemployment is a serious problem and that the only satisfactory answer is suitable employment but the employment counselor realizes that the need for a job is not the real problem; the problem is rather why the applicant is having trouble either in deciding on the kind of job he wants, or in getting the job, or in keeping the job after he gets it. Until the applicant and the counselor can discover why the applicant continues to be unemployed or unsuccessful in his employment, and can remove or modify the reasons for the continued lack of success, no satisfactory solution to the problem can ever be found.

In attempting to formulate and to understand the specific problem, the counselor would do well to keep the following questions in mind:

1. What does the applicant say his problem is, or, from what he says, what does it seem to be?

2. What specific factors in the applicant's situation point up the difficulty or obstacle?

3. Why do these factors prevent or hinder immediate referral to a suitable job or why is the applicant having trouble getting or keeping a job?

4. What assistance does the applicant need before suitable placement can be effected?

GETTING PERTINENT INFORMATION

In most employment agencies, the usual tool or method for securing and giving pertinent information is the individual interview supplemented, where necessary, and when available, by standardized and validated aptitude and proficiency tests. The areas which the employment counselor is interested in exploring are the applicant's skills, knowledge, abilities, physical characteristics, aptitudes, personal traits and interests. No hard and fast rules can be established concerning the relative significance, in an individual case, of these various items of information but no valid counseling plan can be made until information is secured and considered on all seven of these factors. Nor is there one best order of eliciting this information. Since, however, the applicant has come to the employment agency for a job it usually seems more logical to him to start discussing jobs—the kind of job he would like and the kind he has had in the past.

SKILLS, KNOWLEDGE, ABILITIES, APTITUDES AND INTERESTS

For applicants who have had previous work experience, this experience is the most important and most significant information to be obtained, analyzed, and discussed. Although the applicant may wish to or have to change his occupation, the knowledge he has obtained, the skills he has developed, and the work habits and relationships he has formed on his previous jobs are usually his most important vocational assets. Very few such experiences contribute nothing to his chances for successful employment in his next job and the negative as well as the positive aspects are important. It is important to know the jobs the applicant did not like or in which he was not successful and why—which components of each job he liked best and least and

17

why. While it is not always possible or desirable to attempt to place a worker in precisely the same occupational category in which he was previously employed, it is frequently very possible to utilize parts, at least, of the knowledge and skills he has acquired to make an occupational transfer to a related occupation. Many older workers and physically handicapped workers are placed most successfully through the use of this careful analysis and re-synthesis of previous work experience.

What the counselor wishes to know and to evaluate in respect to each job the applicant has had is what tasks the worker performed, why they were performed, what was involved in performing them, and what was the worker's reaction in terms of liking or not liking them and in terms of his estimate of success or lack of success. After all of this information has been obtained for each job the applicant has had, some of it may well turn out to be relatively unimportant or insignificant in the total situation, but the counselor cannot possibly know what will be important or significant until he has secured it and has evaluated it in terms of all other information.

The significance of specific training usually varies directly with the recency of the training. If the training was very recent, and especially if the applicant is inexperienced or relatively inexperienced, complete and accurate information on training is extremely important. As in the analysis of work experience, the employment counselor should know precisely what was included in the training, what skill or skills were acquired and what level of skill achieved, the length of the training, why the applicant took training, his reaction to it and to the various parts of it, his degree of success in it and what further training, if any, he is now taking or plans to take. Popular opinion to the contrary, many employers realize that all applicants cannot have previous work experience and many employers, for many jobs, are willing to consider and sometimes prefer inexperienced applicants who have successfully completed training in recognized training facilities. Proficiency tests if well standardized and validated are helpful in determining the level of skill the applicant has achieved or the extent of specific knowledge he has acquired in the occupations in which he is claiming experience or specific training.

For younger relatively inexperienced applicants, general school achievement is also important—level of schooling reached and at what age, kind of course taken, specific subjects liked or disliked, relative success in general education and in specific subjects, why the applicant left school and plans, if any, for further education. School reports giving not only information on courses and grades but also evaluative comments by teachers and counselors are frequently extremely helpful in employment counseling. Aptitude tests when standardized and when used and interpreted wisely are helpful in the counseling of inexperienced applicants. They can never be the sole determining factor nor can they ever be regarded as a short cut to arriving at a sound employment plan but when used as they were intended to be used they provide an excellent source of objective information of an applicant's probable job potentialities.

Interests check lists too, when used as they were intended to be used, are frequently helpful in aiding the applicant to articulate his vocational interest and in aiding the counselor to relate expressed interest to fields of work. Interest in a particular field of work or occupation is extremely important if it is a real or marked interest, and if it is real or marked either for or against, its evidence will usually appear and reappear throughout the total interviewing situation. This evidence may appear directly or indirectly in the discussion of jobs liked or disliked, of school subjects liked or disliked. This evidence may appear in avocational hobbies or activities engaged in, and as was stated earlier, this evidence may appear in interest tests or interest check lists. Every so often a counselor will encounter an applicant who has an unusually strong interest in or preference for a particular occupation or field of work, an interest that is completely supported not only by what the applicant says but by almost everything he has ever done—his education, hobbies, leisure time activities, reading preferences, etc. Such persons are rare, however. Most applicants have a greater variety of less intensive interests some of which can be more successfully satisfied by avocational than by vocational activities. It is probably reasonably safe to assume that if an applicant has a really marked interest for or against a particular field of work, the counselor will scarcely be able to miss it if the counselor really listens to the applicant while the applicant talks.

PHYSICAL CHARACTERISTICS AND PERSONAL TRAITS

The sole concern of an employment counselor in an applicant's physical characteristics and physical capacities is their relationship to job performance and job adjustment. His primary interests are in evaluating whether or not an applicant can perform a job successfully in terms of his physical capacities, whether or not a particular kind of work would aggravate a disability, and whether or not a disability would jeopardize the life and health of other people. He approaches the employment counseling problem of a physically disabled applicant precisely as he approaches the employment counseling problem of any other applicant. He realizes that first, all jobs do not require the same physical capacities or physical characteristics; second, all applicants and all human beings are "physically handicapped" in one way or other and to some extent; third, careful matching of physical capacities with physical demands is important in the vocational plan of all individuals including the so-called physically handicapped; and fourth, physically handicapped applicants are "people" with the same individual skills, interests, and abilities as all other people. The presence of a physical disability is simply one more factor that must be considered but it should be considered in its proper perspective and not as the over-riding all important aspect of the total problem.

The relationship between personal traits and personal characteristics to job interest and successful job performance and adjustment is probably the area about which we know least. That there are relationships between personality traits and job interests and satisfactory or less satisfactory performance in a particular field of work seems fairly evident, but exactly what the relationship is and how you ascertain the kind and degree of relationship in any objective or practical manner is an unsolved problem at the present time. There are, however, some generalizations and cautions which may be helpful to the employment counselor:

1. Personality traits are desirable or undesirable in relation to a specific job in a specific establishment and they may be important or unimportant because of popular or specific prejudice, or whim rather than inherent in actual job demands or requirements.

2. Personality traits which happen to be distasteful to the employment counselor are not necessarily undesirable.

3. In determining the possible effects of personality traits and attitudes on job adjustment, the counselor must be careful to consider these in relation to other assets and liabilities of the applicant. Studies of factors which contribute to success in a given occupation have shown that adjustment in any field usually depends not upon any one factor but upon various possible combinations of factors.

4. Discussion of personality factors about which the applicant can do nothing should be avoided if possible and certainly never unduly emphasized.

5. Some applicants applying for job help have such involved personality or emotional problems that psychiatric help should, if possible, be sought.

GIVING PERTINENT INFORMATION

The employment counselor limits the information he gives to that which is pertinent to the particular applicant situation, that is, the information the applicant needs or wishes to enable the applicant to arrive at a sound and practical solution to his particular problem. Since this is an employment counseling situation, the kind of information needed usually includes occupational and labor market information specific to the particular problem; for example, the relationship between demand for and supply of workers in a particular occupation or occupations, specific job requirements and conditions of work including wage information, opportunities for promotion and additional training or education necessary for promotion, and perhaps some information on employment trends by occupation, industry or geographic area. The necessary information may also include information on training facilities, requirements, cost, length of training, etc., information on services available through other agencies, information on how to conduct a job search, and for young applicants, information on labor laws and working papers. In some instances the counselor may find it necessary or desirable to refer the applicant to other or additional sources of information, for example, selected books or pamphlets, employer or labor organizations, college or other educational counseling facilities.

ASSISTING THE APPLICANT TO DEVELOP A PLAN AND TO ACT UPON IT

The counseling process to this point has consisted of identifying and agreeing on the problem and ascertaining and discussing pertinent facts both about the applicant and about the labor market. In developing the plan, which of course should be the possible solution or solutions to the problem, the counselor and applicant will be reviewing and weighing all of the facts within the framework of the problem. Since this is an employment counseling situation the plan will be in terms of the fields of work and specific occupation which, considering all of the applicant's qualifications, potentialities and interests governed by the facts of the labor market possibilities, both immediate and long range, seem to offer the best possibilities of successful employment and successful job adjustment. In most instances the possible plan will not be limited to one occupation and frequently not even to one field of work. Since this is true the counselor will help the applicant think through all of the possibilities and their relative advantages and disadvantages. In most instances it will be necessary to discuss both the immediate job plan and the long range goal since, while the two are related they are not necessarily the same. As was stressed in the beginning of this chapter, most employment agency applicants need and want an immediate job and no long range plan, however appropriate, will solve one of the primary facets of the applicant's immediate problem unless the plan embodies both the immediate and the long range. Sometimes the immediate and the long range can be very closely related, that is, the immediate job the applicant can obtain is a first direct step toward achieving the long range plan. In other cases, the immediate job may not be so directly related to the long range plan and in these cases it is important that the applicant understand the total as well as the immediate possibilities. In all of these decisions, the role of the counselor is that of supplying information and assisting the applicant to focus all of the information and all of the facts toward the possible decision and solution. All of the decisions and all of the solutions are, however, in the last analysis, the applicant's and not the counselor's. As the discussion proceeds, the applicant himself usually starts narrowing down the various possible solutions to the one he prefers until finally the applicant and the counselor agree to proceed on a plan. When this step has been achieved, the next step is to start action on the plan. Here it is extremely important to decide and to state clearly who, that is, the counselor or the applicant, is to do what, when and how. Many completely sound and practical employment counseling plans fail of achievement because the counselor did not tie the final knot on the package by insuring that the applicant knew and agreed with the precise clear-cut actions that should immediately follow.

FOLLOW-UP

The final and important step in employment counseling is the follow-up. The applicant should feel that the counselor has a continuing interest in him until he seems to be firmly set on the path to good job adjustment. The counselor will also have the very human desire of wishing to know how good his counseling was, wherein it might have been better, and if it apparently was not successful, why it was not. The applicant, as he progresses in his job plan and job adjustment, may need additional information. In some instances, circumstances make modification of the plan or modification of the action steps toward the ultimate plan necessary.

And finally, no employment counselor will ever be successful all of the time. Since, however, in our civilization, work and work adjustment are so important, both to individuals and to society, good employment counselors wish to learn through their errors. There are few achievements in life so satisfying as the knowledge that you have helped a person solve his job problem successfully.

BIBLIOGRAPHY

1. Employment Counseling in the Public Employment Service, United States Employment Service 1949.
2. Handbook on Placement Counseling, New York State Employment Service 1954.

3. BREWER, JOHN M.: 1941. *History of Vocational Guidance.* Harper.
4. BLUM, MILTON L. and BALINSKY, BENJAMIN: 1957. *Counseling and Psychology.* Prentice–Hall.
5. CULBERT, JANE F. and SMITH, HELEN R.: 1939. *Counseling Young Workers.* Vocational Service for Juniors.
6. FITCH, JOHN A.: 1935. *Vocational Guidance in Action.* Columbia University Press.
7. GALLAGHER, JAMES ROSWELL, and HARRIS, H. J.: 1958. *Emotional Problems of Adolescents.* Oxford University Press.
8. MILLER, CARROLL H.: 1961. *Foundations of Guidance.* Harper.

Counseling in Business and Industry

LEROY N. VERNON

Staff Director
The Vernon Psychological Laboratory
Chicago, Illinois

THE CONTEMPORARY concept of counseling is, in some ways, a new thing on the face of the earth. While it has origins in the thinking and practice of great teachers and spiritual leaders of all generations, counseling as it is professed and practised today differs in some fundamental aspects from inherited traditions. Teachers and religious leaders have generally assumed that in giving counsel they speak from some wisdom, knowledge or spiritual authority, but the counselor of today makes no such assumption. He has no "message". He does have a technique born of an attitude, and while there is no conflict between this attitude and those of religious and educational authorities, the counsclor's attitude keeps him from doing certain things normally expected of them. He does not preach, and he does not teach. His conversation is conducted with the expectation that there will be change of attitude, new insight, or new convictions which will grow in the mind of the counselee out of his own critical evaluation of whatever they talk about.

Counseling, as a technique, grew out of the experience of clinical psychologists who were dealing with maladjusted and neurotic individuals. If the same process is to be applied to employees in business and industry, it will be because there are needs to be served in these situations which can be met by the counseling process. It is being done to a limited extent, and is frequently mentioned by writers on personnel and industrial relations as one of the activities necessary to a well rounded personnel program. Nevertheless, acceptance of the idea of counseling as a legitimate and desirable personnel function in a business organization is by no means universal or even wide spread.

The interest is undoubtedly wider than the practice. There have been significant and well publicized experiments in the field, some of which have produced permanent programs. There are also strong educational forces at work in the business world which may be expected to produce wider acceptance and application in the future. The extent to which counseling becomes established business practice will depend on the acceptance and support it is able to win from business management and on the resources of trained men which can be made practically available at the point where the work is to be done.

While it would be beyond the scope of this discussion to trace the history of industrial counseling in any detail, it may be worthwhile to refer the interested reader to some of the more significant experiments which have stimulated public thinking along this line, and also to allude to some of the forces and agencies which hold promise of expanding this work in the immediate future.

In about 1929, R. H. Macy & Company, Incorporated hired V. V. Anderson, a psychiatrist, for work of this nature. He was primarily concerned with the selection and evaluation of store personnel with the objective of reducing costs and increasing sales, but he did have opportunity to apply therapy in cases where it would eliminate problems or contribute to the effectiveness of the employee. He found that about 20 per cent of the store personnel were classifiable as "problem individuals" and a large proportion of these conditions represented personality disturbances.[1] At that time, this program in which a psychiatrist was employed by a business concern, was ahead of its time. However, attention still was centered upon dealing with the problem employee as an efficiency problem. There was little expectation of applying any kind of psychotherapy to any sizeable proportion of the working force, and little expectation that management would support anything which did not result in tangible improvements.

At about the same time, W. J. Dickson of the Western Electric Company, was conducting interviews with over 20,000 employees. He says, "Our work at that time was primarily intended to determine the aspects of the worker's environment that were regarded favorably or unfavorably. Having made this analysis, our purpose was to take corrective action where needed in an effort to remedy deficiencies in policies, practices, and working conditions. As this work progressed, we became more and more aware of two things. First, frequently the complaint as stated was not the real source of the individual's trouble . . . secondly, our attention was arrested by the observation that when employees were given an opportunity to express themselves freely, many complaints were restated, or disappeared entirely. We also observed that this talking out process had a beneficial effect upon the individual. It seemed to provide him with a release from tension and a new zest for work. We had all this as background when we decided to inaugurate our present plan of counseling."[2]

Since the counseling program at Western Electric has been widely reported, there is no need to describe it in detail here, except to note that it is a large scale counseling program for rank and file employees which has now persisted for about twenty years. In this situation, management has supported work which is believed to improve the mental health and morale of employees, and the nature of the program is such that its continuance shows an interest on the part of management in the problem of mental health in addition to the efficiency objective.

In spite of the wide publicity attending some of these projects, there are still surprisingly few programs like that at Western Electric. However, there are agencies at work which may be expected to promote acceptance of the idea, to find better ways of doing it, and ultimately to promote a wider use of counseling in industry. A number of universities now maintain bureaus which conduct psychological experimentation in industry; for instance, Harvard School of Business, University of Wisconsin, Purdue University, Wayne University, Michigan State College, and the Massachusetts Institute of Technology. As university departments, their primary function is research and not a service functioning on a continuing basis. Unless they produce facilities and operating plans which can be incorporated into the business world, they do not constitute an answer to the need for services of this nature.

Probably the strongest force for extending the practice of counseling in industry on a continuing basis is the growing group of industrial psychological consultants. There are now in this country about 177 members of the American Psychological Association who are full time psychological consultants to industry. The industrial division of the American Psychological Association (one of seventeen divisions) lists 518 members and most of them devote some time to consulting or research in industry. Some of these men are spending most of their time as counselors, usually with executives or supervisors, but sometimes with workers at all levels.

Among the activities of consulting psychologists in industry, two types of program deserve consideration in a discussion of counseling. One of them is closely related to the work of management engineers, and the other is the application of psychological testing to industrial employees. Both types of program are usually addressed to supervisory and executive personnel, and only occasionally do they reach to the lower echelons.

Management engineering, which began as consulting service to management concerned with methods, systems and policies, has turned sharply in the direction of the personnel aspects of management. While management engineers still offer specialized services in such areas as methods analysis, market analysis, cost and compensation systems, etc., a frequent attitude of the consultant now is "We cannot supply answers to your problems, but we can help you select as members of your organization men who will". The response of businessmen to this approach has been good, and some of the strongest management engineering organizations in the country have been built almost entirely on the basis of this approach.

Man evaluation, the selection of candidates for responsible positions, is at times a ruthless and presumptuous undertaking, and management engineers, remembering the hostility generated by "efficiency experts", have become sensitive to the public relations aspect of their jobs. Single minded absorption with their task of evaluating men can be destructive of the morale of companies and the realization of this danger has turned both executives and consultants toward a counseling approach in which the consultant is as much concerned with the development of executives as with their selection.

Counseling with executives is a logical and necessary part of such a program. A leading organization in this field composed entirely of professional psychologists (currently employing seventy psychologists with Ph.D. degrees) regards their function as twofold: One—counseling with executives for the sake of clarifying ideas of themselves, defining personal objectives and reducing interpersonal tensions, and two—promoting changes in organizational structure so that confusions will be reduced and areas of responsibility will be reasonably within the power of available men.

Psychologists in this situation have used a clinical approach in which case studies of individuals are carefully prepared. Some have relied on interviewing as a technique; others have used psychological tests in addition to interviewing.

In work of this nature, the benefits of counseling are a kind of by-product of the process of man evaluation. There may be some loss in the efficacy of counseling when the counselor has some other objective, and one of the problems of the counselor–consultant is to achieve the status of counselor to employees and still function as a consultant to management.

When tests are used, they frequently are the principal basis for the evaluative judgment. The resulting interviews can then more clearly be "counseling" interviews, with the primary purposes stated earlier in this discussion as objectives of counseling. It is estimated that 80 per cent of our larger companies are now using psychological tests as a part of their basis for selecting men, and increasing numbers of these companies provide counseling service following testing.

A typical program of this nature in a middle-sized steel company was introduced by the following letter:

Subject: Executive Management Survey
To: Management Personnel
From: The President

All of us who carry executive responsibility have, for some time, been conscious of the problem of providing for future company leadership.

Because the present average age of men in responsible positions in our company is surprisingly high, we want to consider the probable changes which will take place during the next ten years and to be sure that we are doing everything possible to provide continuity of policy and a high quality of future leadership.

To provide continuity of policy, it is necessary that men who are to determine policy in the future have some part in establishing policy at present so that we never come to the time when one "regime" retires and another "regime" takes over.

We feel that we can be helped in this process by an outside specialist and we are fortunate in having a man who has worked closely with us for the past ten years. He will bring to us the advantage of an outside perspective, and he makes available to us the methods and viewpoints of management planning which have been perfected during the period encompassed by two World Wars. We regard him as an analyst and adviser who can help provide the basis for the planning which we must do.

The man we refer to is Dr. ——. He has already started the accumulation of data about the company and will be in touch with you during coming weeks to ask for some of your time and your earnest cooperation.

We believe that the work he will undertake can be interesting and valuable to all of us as individuals, as well as to the company.

Each man, from President down through foreman, was visited by a psychologist who undertook to have him:

1. Tell the story of his life in order to provide his counselor (and also himself) with a perspective on his present situation and prospects.

2. Accept this program as a worthy company effort which he can sincerely cooperate with and support.

3. Learn that the purposes of the psychologist are constructive for him as well as the company, so that he need not be anxious.

4. Understand something of the idea of psychological testing as a basis for guidance for both him and management, and so be prepared for a subsequent counseling interview.

A second interview is devoted to gathering information about job content that will lead to a job description and a manual of organization.

The third interview is purely counseling in nature. It begins with a review of the test findings and later leads to a free discussion of any aspect of his job or life situation he wants to discuss. It has been estimated that 50 per cent of these interviews produce discussion of problems which could not be discussed in this way in any other relationship.

Counseling with men at executive levels is an important function and a rewarding experience. The man who heads a business enterprise carries a heavy load of responsibility (witness the frequency of ulcers!) and the chance to talk freely, privately and personally with a scientifically trained counselor is needed and usually welcomed by these men. Furthermore, if, as psychologists believe, the essence of executive ability is the integration of personality which comes with social and emotional maturity, these interviews make an important contribution to the building of executives, for counseling is a maturing experience. Thus, it serves both a need felt by individuals and an important objective of the corporate enterprise.

While these programs are going forward and there is a gradually increasing acceptance of the value of counseling in industry, the total number of employees who are reached by any such program must be very small in proportion to the working force. The progress of the movement is slowed by the fact that business executives fear what they call an "academic" approach, and organized labor fears what they regard as a possible encroachment on the relationship between worker and labor leader. If labor leaders could see the constructive possibilities of employee counseling, they could be a major force in accelerating its use. Business executives have come a long way toward a professional attitude, and as they adopt broader objectives for themselves, they see more reason to use counseling for its social value as well as its practical utility. However, there is need for more clear statement of the objectives of counseling in terms of which to justify its broader acceptance. Does counseling serve purposes which are consonant with the objectives of business?

The objectives of an industrial organization are not always the subject of clear thought or clear statement. To say that a business exists purely to make a profit is not telling the whole story, though many business executives would still accept such a statement. If profits were the sole purpose of business, counseling, like a number of other personnel functions, might still be defensible—but the defense would be more difficult. Counseling probably can increase the efficiency of workers and reduce the danger of industrial strife, but evidence that it has done these things in specific situations would be hard to produce.

For a more adequate statement of the objectives of business, we may refer to the organizational manual of a company manufacturing earth moving equipment—The Koehring Company of Milwaukee. It says, "The primary purpose of this company is to serve the needs of three groups of people: customers, employees and stockholders. From the viewpoint of those who need shovels, cranes, pavers, etc., the primary reason for the existence of this company is to produce these products. From the viewpoint of those who work here, the primary purpose is to create jobs where people can work, produce useful goods, and receive security and the means of livelihood as well as the satisfactions of being part of a fine company. From the viewpoint of the stockholders, the primary purpose of the company is to pay a good return on their investment, and to lay the foundation for a better return in the future. Products, people and profits are the problems of business, and the success of business management can be measured in terms of how well they serve in these three areas."

From this viewpoint, management is in the position of integrating and reconciling the pressures of these three diverse interests, and the well managed company will operate in terms of all three kinds of objectives. It should be recognized that the objectives of service to the public, profits and good industrial relations are not the same; and while they can be reconciled or their differences kept in balance, it is also possible for them to be in direct conflict. For instance, a company might make more money by producing a poorer product, or it might produce a superior product at the cost of poor industrial relations.

A program for counseling with employees serves the industrial relations objective directly, and the other two objectives indirectly. The type of justification which will be presented by industrial psychologists and accepted by business management will depend on the type of management with which they are dealing and on the security of the organisation being served. The large scale and more permanent programs in the past have been in companies which were financially secure and which had a professional type of management. The smaller companies which are reached more largely by the consultant organizations operate under different pressures and may need to be approached with different appeals.

All of this assumes that counseling is effective in producing a healthy psychological climate in which workers can live and work. It is not a foregone conclusion that this is true, and the basis for such an assumption needs to be carefully examined.

It is a safe assumption that any sizeable working force includes individuals who are frustrated, confused, bitter, and antagonistic and uncooperative—in a word—neurotic. Failing to find the satisfactions they need, these individuals live in a state of chronic tension, unhappy about themselves and ready to find faults in their environment which will relieve them of their self-condemnation. They are the focal infection centers from which tension continually spreads to those around them. If counseling can change the attitudes of these people toward themselves and thus reduce their tensions, it can have a salutary effect on the whole organizational body.

Counseling has been shown to be effective in changing the attitudes of individuals toward themselves and toward other people. Under the direction of Dr. Carl E. Rogers, research has shown that the amount of self-criticism of a counselee showed a marked decline as he progressed through the known stages of the counseling process. At the same time, his criticisms of others and expressions of antagonisms and hostility showed a parallel diminution. Attitudes toward self parallel attitudes toward others, and when the attitude is one of critical hostility, the individual is in a state of tension, unhappiness and confusion.[3]

In a work situation, the cumulative effect of tensions of this kind can effect the morale of the whole organization because of the "feed-back" effect. Worker "A" is disturbed and hostile, perhaps because he is not happy about himself and not sure that he can cope with the problems he faces. His hostility is directed toward worker "B" who is driven to the defensive and also becomes hostile, aggressive, critical and unco-operative. In this state of mind "B" constitutes a new threat to the security and poise of "A". Thus tension mounts by self-excitation like "feed-back" in a radio circuit, and the result is a raucous growl where there could have been music. If counseling can reduce the tensions of an individual, it can forstall this undesirable situation.

The evidence accumulated through research directed by Dr. Rogers has been mentioned. There is an interesting sidelight illustrative of the same process from quite a different source. It appears that a similar reduction of tension and the freeing of individuals for constructive activity takes place when workers are asked to express themselves in attitude questionnaires, as well as in counseling. For a number of years one of the leading department stores of the country conducted an annual morale survey. An anonymous questionnaire was prepared by a con-sulting psychologist, asking employees to express what they think and how they feel about all the known issues with which employees are concerned. The store workers were gathered together by groups to fill out the questionnaires so that a return was received from all employees in one day's time. For the first three or four years this was done, there was measurable increase in the total volume of store sales for a number of days immediately following completion of the questionnaires. It was concluded that the opportunity to express themselves had a measurable beneficial effect before anybody had time to even read what had been said.

The same kind of effect was much in evidence in the Hawthorne experiment at Western Electric. George C. Homans says in describing this experience:

"The results of the interviewing program were interesting from the first. The program was received with enthusiasm by both supervisors and operators. 'This is the best thing the company ever did' and 'The company ought to have done this long ago' were the sort of comments commonly encountered. The employees seemed to enjoy the opportunity of expressing their thoughts. They felt some kind of relief, as if feelings that had long been pent up within them had found an outlet. Requests for interviews were received, some from the supervisors themselves.

"Evidence soon accumulated that the interviews not only gave expression to attitudes hitherto pent up, but also, in giving them expression, changed them. The report of 1931 explained this rather unexpected result by an analogy: It has long been known that one who writes a memorandum greatly clarifies his thought upon the material to be presented. Exaggerations, distortions, emotional reactions, defenses, etc., are largely dissolved when thus viewed objectively. In a similar way, employees who express their thoughts and feelings to a critical listener discharge emotional and irrational elements from their minds. Many personal and individual problems and attitudes have been improved by the verbal expression which the interview affords. Taking account of the employees' expressions recorded in 20,000 interviews, we feel that this value in interviewing cannot lightly be overlooked."[4]

It may very well be that the progress of counseling in industry is retarded as much by the lack of trained men who are able to function in the business situation as it is by lack of acceptance on the part of management. As noted earlier, there are about 177 psychologists engaged full time as consultants, in business, and to this must be added the part time activities of many college and university professors. Altogether, this is a small supply of trained men to serve a working force of some 62,000,000 people in office and factory.

In the November, 1946, issue of *The American Psychologist* Ross Stagner reports a study carried out under his direction at Dartmouth College. Questionnaires regarding the application of psychology to personnel work were sent to the presidents of seventy large corporations. Of the thirty-six that responded, 42 per cent reported the existence of an employee counseling system and 53 per cent considered such a program desirable. However, the nature of these counseling programs is not specified.

This particular study sampled primarily the policies of large corporations which can stand the overhead cost of a substantial personnel department, and the results from smaller enterprises might not be so encouraging. Nevertheless, Dr. Stagner concludes that it does suggest the presence of a substantial opportunity for qualified people.[5]

Opinions about the qualifications of counselors differ between wide extremes. In 1947 the American Psychological Association set up the board of examiners in professional psychology to grant diplomas to men qualified in specialized fields, and counseling and guidance was one of those fields. The standards set up by this examining board required the guidance counselor to have a Ph.D. degree.

Psychiatrists as a professional group have set even higher standards, and have questioned the capability of psychologists for doing anything which would classify as psychotherapy.

At the other extreme, we find personnel men, foremen, and supervisors and managers encouraged to learn counseling techniques, to use them in their daily contacts with workers, and as far as possible to gain the advantages of a counseling relationship. In this connection, Norman R. F. Maier says, "Because training in counseling develops skills which are useful to a discussion leader and is an aid in dealing with all inter-personal relations on the job, any time spent on the subject would be useful, even if it did not develop all the essential counseling skills. However, the prospects that even limited training in counseling will be of some value in performing the counseling function are assured by the fact that training in leading group discussions facilitates training in counseling. Thus the mere fact that counseling skills and leadership skills require similar attitudes and similar methods makes the training in both an efficient procedure." He goes on to say that if the counseling done by these people is of the "non-directive" or "client-centered" type, it can have no harmful effects, even though it does not accomplish all that might be desired.[6]

It is true in some sense that there is an element of what we are calling "counseling" in all inter-personal relations. Every exchange between people involves attitudes implemented through techniques, and it is both possible and desirable that these attitudes and these techniques can and should be taught wherever possible. However, it would be a mistake to suppose that the average foreman or the average personnel man exposed to these ideas could accomplish the same kind of results which are accomplished by professionally trained counselors. One of the legitimate objectives of the psychologist in industry may be to disseminate the attitudes and techniques of counseling among personnel and supervisory people and executives, but what the latter do should not be confused with the work of a trained man who makes counseling his profession.

The significance of a counseling approach to the industrial relations problem is that it implements an important social philosophy. If it is true that the interests of workers, owners and customers make different and, at times, conflicting demands on management, management may meet its problems in a variety of ways. One approach is to keep each group from knowing what is done for the others. Secrecy and absolute control have frequently been the operating policy of ownership, but it is increasingly untenable as workers become better educated and better organized. Another approach is to "sell" or propagandize so that repeated presentations of a viewpoint overpower opposing interests with persuasion.

Counseling is a third kind of approach, based on the belief that all human beings are capable of understanding the interests of others, even when those interests are opposed; and of tempering the pursuit of their more selfish objectives with an appreciation of mutual interdependence. A good counseling program with employees is quite free from any hidden objectives. It does not propagandize, but has as its first purpose to listen and understand, and as its second objective to build in every person the belief that he can be understood.

BIBLIOGRAPHY

1. ANDERSON, V. V.: 1929. *Psychiatry in Industry.* New York: Harper.
2. HOSLETT, S. D.: 1946. *Human Factors in Management,* p. 230. New York: Harper.
3. ROGERS, C. R. and DYMAN, R. F.: 1954. *Psychotherapy and Personality Change,* pp. 167–195. The University of Chicago Press.
4. STAGNER, R.: 1946. Attitudes Regarding Psychological Methods In Personnel Work. The American Psychologist, 1: 540–541.
5. MAIER, N. R. F.: 1952. Principles of Human Relations. New York: John Wiley and Sons, Inc. 413–414.
6. LEVINSON, HARRY: "The Psychologist in Industry." *Harvard Business Review,* September–October, 1959.
7. PERRY, JOHN: "When The Boss Interviews." *Personnel,* July–August, 1960.
8. AMERICAN PSYCHOLOGICAL ASSOCIATION, "Division of Business & Industry." *The Psychologist in Industry,* 1959.

The Mediation of Labor Disputes

JULIUS J. MANSON

District Supervisor
New York State Board of Mediation
New York City

IN THE belief that a mediation conference is an extraordinary example of how parties under stress attempt to resolve their difficulties, the writer invited two trained psychologists to act as observers at the New York State Board of Mediation. The hope was that after they were immersed in this untapped reservoir of experience, they would be able to salvage some points from which mediators could profit. After several months of observation, they came as guests to a luncheon-discussion attended by the staff mediators and some Board members. The mediators pressed the psychologists for specific answers, and the psychologists reacted by pointing to the signs of anxiety, obsession, regression, projection and rigidity among mediators. This evidently revealed that each group was human, albeit professional.

The mediation process may not easily respond to convincing analysis, or precise formulation. But mediators and social scientists could agree that generally labor relations are a specific aspect of human relations; a labor dispute is a human dispute. The economic issues are far too often the external garb for psychological friction. Irritation and resentment, frustration and fear are chronic elements in the work-place. Each of these emotional ingredients plays a varying role in the final precipitation of a labor dispute.

There are, of course, valid economic controversies which will separate management and union. The conference table, however, around which negotiators proceed to resolve the issues, becomes an arena for emotional salvos. Instead of an atmosphere of sweet reason, in which logic and facts prevail, the air is charged with tension, as each side tries to maim the other's stability and move in for the kill.

This freedom of the parties ultimately to engage in trial by battle is remarkable in the American economy which is a delicately balanced mechanism with many exposed nerve endings.

The pinch of a strike may disrupt a basic function or make the entire organ quiver. Naturally, then, the government directs its attention to the maintenance of peaceful labor relations in order to protect the health, welfare, comfort and safety of the people. Bearing in mind constantly, however, that our way of life rests upon democratic foundations, we must use only those techniques and methods for the adjustment of labor controversies which, while easing strife, preserve liberty. Mediation is such a technique, bridging differences within the framework of democracy—emphatically bringing to focus the basic elements of our democratic system of government.

In theory, the process of mediation encourages the union and the employer to use reason instead of force. Thus the conference table replaces the picket line. Men of good will can talk themselves into an agreement, particularly where the commonwealth is endangered; given the place and opportunity, they will employ intelligence rather than belligerence. The mediator, therefore, proceeds to arrange a conference. As an impartial third party, he invites or persuades—but never orders—the principals to meet in his presence to iron out their differences. The meeting ground is preferably on neutral territory, usually the office of the mediator. If the dispute is imminent or threatened and not yet in the open warfare phase, then that first conference is likely to be well-behaved. If a strike or lockout has already begun, evidence of frayed tempers appears at the first session. There is no set pattern and the mediator accordingly must be sufficiently flexible to expect anything.

In fact, rarely do the disputants reveal at the outset exactly what each wants. An accumulation of grievances, major, minor, real and imagined, plus petty peevishness and clashes of personalities, all take turns bobbing up to the surface of the discussion for an airing. In such sessions, the mediator mainly listens. And he may be the only one doing so. Sifting fact from figment, he distinguishes the chief areas of disagreement. Acquiring that knowledge demands extraordinary patience. Indeed, "Sitzfleisch"—the capacity to outsit the parties—often solves the problem. If the mediator sits long enough, both sides may sufficiently exhaust each other and be willing to accept what the mediator suggests.

After temperatures have subsided and every man has spoken his piece, rightly or wrongly, the mediator consults with each group separately. Thus he can ascertain, in confidence, precisely how far each will travel, what each will take, and what each will give. More often than not, the real positions and the apparent ones of the bargaining agents differ greatly. At this stage of the mediation process, the actual boulders of disagreement emerge. From now on to the finish, the mediator chips away the differences, suggesting to each side in turn a formula to fit the facts. Long experience in such matters establishes the importance of appreciating the psychological elements which play upon and intermingle with the industrial, economic, social and political factors in a complicated case.

On occasion, the mediator may stand by, leaving the parties to themselves, ready to intervene if needed. And the case is settled not because of the air-conditioning system, but essentially because the principals have met in an atmosphere of free discussion. The mediator's chief contribution lies in providing the opportunity to settle disputes in a democratic way.

The entire mediation process is the very essence of a free people. The union and employer appear voluntarily; there is no element of compulsion. At any point in the proceedings, anyone can pick up his hat and go home. The parties can ignore the advice of the mediator. Sometimes they do! In that event, a costly operational stoppage may follow, probably to end with the ultimate acceptance of the mediator's original proposal. At least, there is no restraint upon the rights of conferees to disagree.

In direct negotiations, the participants may conduct their conferences as they choose, say what they please, and conclude a contract or not. The principle of voluntary action is preserved intact in the mediation process. During the course of the talks, the mediator may find that after securing agreement on various points, one or two valid issues block complete adjustment. He would then propose arbitration of these differences. With the consent of the disputants, an arbitrator enters the situation, listens to their testimony, and then hands down an award which is binding on both sides. The mandatory character of the arbitrator's award distinguishes arbitration from mediation. Since the parties, however, in an effort to arrive at an amicable solution, agree in advance to submit their differences for a final decision by an impartial person, they voluntarily obligate themselves to comply with the arbitrator's award. The union and the company thus in reality continue their freedom of action from the very outset to the very end.

The mediator imposes no penalties for he has no law to enforce, no oaths to administer, and no subpoenas to issue. Mediation deliberately replaces compulsion by volition, preserving the will of the parties and not the order of the court. The backbone of our national character is independence, vividly demonstrated in the arena of industrial controversy; and when the disputants are mindful of their responsibilities to the community, mediation, safeguarding their independence, becomes an indispensable highway toward enduring cooperation.

The realities of mediation experience, however, are somewhat more complicated than the foregoing description.

In the papers which have been written about mediation, the "great questions" still remain open:

1. What are the mediator's goals: To settle the symptoms or the causes; the immediate or the long-term issues? To settle practically or ethically; in the parties' interest or the national interest?

2. When should the mediator intervene?

3. Is mediation art or science?

For example, running through the discussions of the past are references to the elusive attitude of the community toward collective bargaining. Collective bargaining appears to be socially acceptable. Men are free to strike but the right to strike remains acceptable so long as it is not used. Thus an unhappy and hazy society establishes devices for dispute settlement but no clear goal exists for the basis of settlement, so settlements, because of this lack of clarity, are on a case by case basis and the mediators must improvise.

The ambiguous attitude toward collective bargaining, strikes and settlement, and specifically the role of the mediator, was sharply brought to focus in an editorial which appeared in the *New York Times* on July 4, 1961. The advent of a Presidential Fact-Finding Board had led to a settlement for one segment of the maritime strike. The Editor after referring to the "senseless" labor dispute and the cynicism of some of the participants, raised two questions among others in the following language: "What behind-the-scenes role, if any, was played by high level Federal authority in forcing such a costly settlement as has been agreed on in a large segment of the industry? . . . Was the emergency so great as to warrant tremendous pressures on the President's Board to get the strike settled at all costs?" The inference is that mediators have another standard by which to be judged: How an Editor may feel about a particular settlement. Who is to judge whether a "senseless" labor dispute has been settled "at all costs"?

Mediators are aware that some of the settlements are as sturdy as rice cakes. Many are wrapped in cellophane, giving a smooth exterior through which are still visible the underlying troubles. As already noted, the familiar symptoms of labor disputes are distillations of chronic conflict within the shop and that long term solutions would require far more comprehensive training and techniques than mediation alone can provide. Effective mediation in the sense of enduring solutions is an ideal aim. It would require thorough familiarity with the idiosyncrasies of the parties in their daily interaction and this would require a massive staff of more than mediators. A more limited and attainable goal for mediation would be the application of those civilized procedures which have enabled men to deal with each other.

When should the agency intervene? Should the agency beat the bushes for business or await a wail for help from the weaker side? The issue here is Cool Indifference versus Hot Pursuit. A parlor game may be set up of the possibilities ranging from a "hands-off" to "feet-in" policy. For example, would the agency intervene where:

1. Both sides call
2. One side calls
3. No side calls
4. One side rejects
5. Both sides reject.

We take for granted that the first possibility clearly requires the agency to intervene. Consider, however, the abuse of mediation in the instances of an industry where both sides cynically invite every mediation agency in sight to soothe the consumer and other publics. While the mediators have a hotel corridor to themselves, the parties are working out their own destinies in some mediator-proof shelter. In these hardened situations, the mediators are "props", and professionally superfluous. Veteran mediators could give ample evidence for moving North, South, East and West of a dispute instead of entering storm center for any of the foregoing possibilities. The Federal and State statutes searching for objective standards have directed the mediation agency to intervene under various conditions which sometimes do, and sometimes do not, consider the parties, as, national safety, community health and welfare, interstate commerce, business volume, size of staff. There are clearly other elements to consider. The question of when to intervene, stated simply, is complex.

Another open question is whether mediation is art or science. It is unlikely that mediation will become more scientific or less artistic. Among professionals, the mediator is distinguished by having neither tools nor rules. He uses no stethoscope, calipers, Bible or couch. There is adequate reason for loose procedure. Conflict in collective bargaining has infinite variety. The mediation process must be liquid enough to fit the shape of the vessel.

An underlying philosophical framework, however, need not create rigidity in treatment. In the ordinary case, there are different concepts by which a mediator can approach his task. None of them is a complicated theoretical framework. Each may have an appropriate role, singularly fitting the occasion. If the parties are frayed by each other, the mediator may inject humor; if they are not talking, he can restore communication; if they misunderstood one another, he can introduce clarity; if they fail to see a solution, he can uncover it.

Obviously, experience should test the most workable concepts. Mediation is essentially a clinical operation. The word "clinical" comes from a Greek root meaning "bed," and now relates to the investigation of disease in the living subject by observation as distinguished from controlled experiment. Sometimes all a mediator needs is a bedside manner. And occasionally none of these techniques works, especially where institutions are adversaries. It should be clear that groups, as well as individuals, are in conflict when the union bargains for employees. Although the union often assumes the role of a "manager of discontent," in major labor disputes, particularly, the institutional roots of industrial conflict embrace more than individual malaise. Then the factor of economic and ideological cleavage transcends the frictions arising from the limits of individual perception and the imperfections of emotional unbalance.

The task of the mediator is burdened by still another force. For example, the general impression flowing from the writer's mediation experience is that there are two kinds of logic in collective bargaining: (1) The common sense which flourishes when both sides enjoy equivalent power; (2) The common sense which is extracted from the fellow who is over a barrel. The first point is obvious. The second may be illustrated by Thucydides who gives an account in the Sicilian Expedition of the way in which the Athenians negotiated with the inhabitants of the small Island of Melos. Thucydides, a general who saw needs realistically and noted them carefully, recounts that Melos had observed strict neutrality during 15 years of war. Athens wanted to use Melos as a Naval Base and sent envoys to invite the Melians to become an Athenian satellite. The Melians realized that the choice was between death by battle, or slavery by submission. The logic was precisely stated by the Athenians:

... We Athenians will use no fine words. ... We both alike know that into the discussion of human affairs the question of justice only enters where the pressure of necessity is equal and that the powerful exact what they can and the weak grant what they must.

Mediators are not divinities. A mediator cannot grant the weaker party the power it lacks. Where strength is uneven, a union representative whom the employer regards as an insulting psychopath may be replaced by an impeccable finishing school type who will make and ultimately get the same demands. The mediator in such unbalanced situations would have to produce a face-saving formula to make a harsh settlement seem palatable. Lay psychotherapy in these circumstances would merely be a fringe benefit of mediation.

At present, there is less government control of labor relations in the United States than in virtually any of the Western industrial nations. To an observer, even from shores regarded as democratic, it is baffling to find that the government cannot force a settlement when the disputants disagree. Other modern nations have a wide range of tools often used as weapons in the national interest to impose a settlement on unwilling parties. Our democratic tradition limits the number of devices in this field. Dictatorial instruments are automatically barred. Our stated public policy commits us to foster free collective bargaining. Within that framework, labor and management may shape their own relationships, wage their own economic wars, and reach their own agreements with a minimum of government entanglement. The accompanying emotional wear and tear should be an expected feature of "antagonistic cooperation". Mediation seeks to reduce that antagonism, and would welcome the insight of trained psychologists to enhance the mediators' skills.

Rehabilitation Counseling

WILLIAM M. USDANE

Professor of Education
Co-ordinator, Rehabilitation Counseling
San Francisco State College
San Francisco, California

THERE are approximately 2,230,000 physically handicapped adults in the United States who are feasible of rehabilitation to the point of re- munerative employment. Nearly half of this group, however, will find employment after rehabilitation only in sheltered workshops. Each year an additional 250,000 disabled persons come to need vocational rehabilitation. An estimated 16,000,000 people in the United States are suffering from some form of mental illness. This means that one in every 10 persons is now suffering from some type of emotional dis- turbance. There are estimated to be 3,800,000 problem drinkers in the United States, 950,000 of whom are people with severe chronic alco- holism. About 3 per cent of our entire population, 5,400,000 children and adults are mentally retarded. Three children out of every 100 born are destined to be mentally retarded.[27]

Of all the patients who go to general hospitals for treatment for physical ailments annually, it is estimated that six millions are suffering from serious mental and emotional illnesses which are partly responsible for their physical complaints. According to a survey completed in 1954 by the Menninger Foundation, emotional ills in industry cost the nation billions of dollars in productivity each year. Absenteeism costs more than nine billion a year, while accidents, at least 70 to 90 per cent of them, are due to psychological causes. Alcoholism represents a loss to industry in excess of a billion dollars. One out of every 50 workers is a problem drinker and 89 per cent of these are in the 35–55 year range.[28]

There is extensive statistical documentation for the conclusion that increased state legislative appropriations to provide intensive treatment with new tranquillizing drugs, and increased professional staff have finally achieved the cumulative force needed to reverse the seemingly inevitable annual rise in mental hospital populations. Day and night hospitals, half-way houses and newly sponsored government support of voluntary agency rehabilitation facilities with funds for demonstration and research projects are also responsible for the increased return of the mentally ill to community and work.[29]

Richard M. Titmuss states that all collectively provided services are deliberately designed to meet certain socially recognized "needs"; they are manifestations, first, of society's will to survive as an organized whole and, secondly, of the expressed wish of all the people to assist the survival of some people.[21] He states further that "needs" could be thought of as "social" and "individual", and mutually related, as inter-dependent essentials for the continued existence of the parts and the whole.

The public program of vocational rehabilitation "needs" started in 1920 with its beginnings in World War I, since it grew out of rehabilitation services established for disabled World War I veterans. From 1920 until 1945, 250,000 disabled persons were rehabilitated by the Federal government. A Federal-State program, vocational rehabilitation was greatly expanded with the passage of Public Law 565 in 1954 which provided for training grants to encourage formal professional training of Rehabilitation Counselors. In 1961, a record number of disabled persons rehabilitated into employment was set under the public program. The figure of over 92,500 provides a basis for predicting that 200,000 persons a year may be rehabilitated by 1970.

During the last ten years, 351 new rehabilitation facilities and 153 new sheltered workshops have been established throughout the nation. Emphasis has been placed on occupational centers for the mentally retarded, work evaluation for the cerebral palsied, work adjustment for disabled persons with emotional problems, occupational services for epileptics and services for the homebound. Current estimates indicate that there are over 800 sheltered workshops providing services of varying nature for the disabled in the United States.

Since the passage of Public Law 565 in August of 1954, and with basic support from the Vocational Rehabilitation Administration in the Department of Health, Education, and Welfare to start graduate training programs in Rehabilitation Counseling, approximately thirty universities and colleges have begun graduate two year programs. These programs have attempted to supply what is needed in professional education for practice in rehabilitation counseling.

The rapid, evolutionary progress exhibited in the development of graduate curricula in the training of Rehabilitation Counselors has resulted in an emerging profession with growth problems. Contingencies of professional differentiation are the initial difficulties to be faced by a profession which subscribes to a basic tenet of rehabilitation as comprising a team of professions.

The answers will undoubtedly continue to emerge along with the profession, based primarily, it is hoped, upon an acceptance of change and modification within the scope of the rehabilitation process itself. While all professional fields within the inter-disciplinary complex serving the handicapped individual have common problems of integration of theory and practices, there are many implications for graduate training in Rehabilitation Counseling. Basic curriculum content denoting the specialization itself must be combined with a frame of reference about personality and human pathology and its treatment basic for all the helping professions.

THE REHABILITATION COUNSELOR

Rehabilitation Counseling subscribes to the hard core counseling requirement of all the counseling professions: a face to face relationship enabling the individual to internalize an awareness of his problems and his potentialities toward a program of adjustment and self-improvement.[24] But there is a cluster of skills which provides the Rehabilitation Counselor with a distinctive focus. He works with the physically or emotionally disturbed, including the mentally retarded. There is primary emphasis upon the vocational aspects of the total rehabilitation process which includes medical, personal and social adjustment. Vocational planning as well as implementation of the individual's occupational goals are indigenous to the counseling interaction. Vocational counseling as it is professionally practised by trained Rehabilitation Counselors with the handicapped becomes the distinct focus, and as a member of the professional team, the counselor also recognizes his several quasi- and non-counseling roles. With this recognition, furthermore, he is able to differentiate administrative from professional duties, quasi- or non-counseling from counseling interaction, and the major contribution of this distinct professional role from that of other members of the rehabilitation team.

This chapter will not be concerned with those elements necessary for inclusion within the graduate training curriculum for Rehabilitation Counseling, but with those distinct techniques which are the perquisite of his counseling relationship. Material is already available from yearly curriculum seminars concerned with curriculum development for Rehabilitation Counseling Training programs[30,31] and previous publications in this regard.[12,19]

One of Greenwood's[11] attributes of a profession to distinguish it from a non-profession is that the skills that characterize the profession flow from and are supported by a fund of knowledge that has been organized into an internally consistent system called a body of theory. As a starting point for the continuing examination of its systematic body of theory, the following might serve as an initial group of undergirding concepts:

(a) Recognition of the Rehabilitation Counselor's final aim as the appropriate level of *vocational* rehabilitation of the handicapped individual.

(b) Recognition of the conscious furtherance of a relationship between the Rehabilitation Counselor and the handicapped individual to help him understand both his problems and his potentialities to carry through a program of adjustment and self-improvement so that his optimum personal and social adjustment will be concomitant with his vocational adjustment.

(c) Recognition and acceptance of the other professional and non-professional roles of those working with the handicapped individual as an application of the philosophy of rehabilitation as a composite science.

(d) Recognition of the initial starting point of the handicapped individual as he sees it, keeping the perceptions and needs of the Rehabilitation Counselor relevant to the reality needs of the individual.

(e) Recognition of the medical, psychological and social aspects of the handicapped individual's problems as they interpose, supersede, or coincide with vocational adjustment.

(f) Recognition of the agency strengths and limitations in achieving the requests or needs of the handicapped individual.

(g) Recognition of the interaction between internal strains and external pressures relevant in the socio-economic scene which are present in the vocational adjustment of the handicapped individual.

(h) Recognition of the community's felt needs for services and facilities affording appropriate vocational adjustment of the handicapped individual.

(i) Recognition of the handicapped individual's strength to develop increasing initiative and capacity for self-help through initial vocational satisfying experiences in order to tolerate future frustrations or failures normal to family and community relationships.

(j) Recognition of the Rehabilitation Counselor's depth knowledge of the world of work as his contribution to the handicapped individual, the other team members, and the community through an understanding of the sociology of occupations, labor market and occupational information, and the employment levels for the handicapped within the larger community.

(k) Recognition of the need for flexibility in adapting to new and different vocational problems precipitated by the uniqueness of the multiple medical, psychological and social problems of the handicapped.

Vocational rehabilitation is considered one of the stages of the fuller process of complete rehabilitation of the adult disabled, including the habilitation of the congenitally or early disabled young person. At one time rehabilitation was defined as the restoration of the handicapped to the fullest physical, mental, social, vocational, and economic usefulness of which they are capable.[25] More recently, Whitehouse defined the term from the standpoint of a community interpretation to include the young, the adult and the aged in all their capacities and possibilities: "the cultivation, restoration and conservation of human resources."[23] The latter comprehensive definition clearly implies prevention and a life-process view of a whole person as a reference point for community planning. Vocational rehabilitation is defined as the stage in the total rehabilitation process concerned with the individual's optimum vocational and economic capacity through the maximum use of necessary facilities providing vocational counseling, assessment and evaluation, vocational training, specialized placement or full employment.

A philosophy of rehabilitation itself is suggested in the following four concepts: (1) the worth and dignity of the disabled individual and his basic entitlement to becoming an economically and socially useful member of his community; (2) rehabilitation is a composite science bringing into focus all of the various professional services required by a severely handicapped individual to achieve normal living to the best of his ability and capacity; (3) rehabilitation is a continuous process, linking all services for the severely handicapped through the teamwork approach from the initial referral or case finding to the eventual goal commensurate with the optimum achievement possible; (4) rehabilitation is a community responsibility and must be supported both nationally and locally for the total rehabilitation of the severely handicapped.[22]

THE COUNSELING ROLE OF THE
REHABILITATION COUNSELOR

The Rehabilitation Counselor is faced with little written information in the field concerning the actual techniques of counseling with the disabled. Plentiful are generic counseling texts, and within the past few years, there has been increasing literature on theory and practice, specialized demonstration projects, and the role and function of the

Rehabilitation Counselor. But little has been concerned with some of the specialized counseling techniques themselves.

One of the more comprehensive texts is a book of readings in rehabilitation counseling[18] but the editor expressly states in the preface that "although counseling is broadly conceived, the book does not attempt to cover the basic substantive or technical aspects of rehabilitation counseling." Apparently then, there are such techniques distinct to the Rehabilitation Counselor.

The graduate of a professional curriculum in Rehabilitation Counseling may find his quest for answers concerning specialized techniques in counseling the handicapped through (a) his supervised field experiences accompanying his academic university coursework, (b) a practicum involving supervised counseling interaction at the university counseling center or at a local rehabilitation facility in the community, (c) any combination of coursework and fieldwork, or (d) through practical experiences on the job which latter approach may necessitate his understanding of counseling at the level of his client's willingness to be thus served.

What then are the specialized counseling techniques which might differ from the counseling core of techniques discussed pertinently in the other chapters of this Handbook? Is there one approach to any of the disabling conditions? Are techniques in the counseling process with the cerebral palsied transferable to the counseling process with the epileptic? Are the emotionally handicapped a group which necessitate still more specialized techniques than the physically disabled? Does the stress upon the vocational aspects in counseling the handicapped stated previously suggest any more specialized approach than a normal face to face relationship?

1. It might be helpful to conceive of two assumptions that appear to be more evident in counseling the handicapped than the non-handicapped; (a) the inevitability of human progress, and (b) the uniqueness of the individual. Counseling the cerebral palsied youngster of sixteen whose life has been spent as much in hospitals and rehabilitation centers as in schools must be predicated on the rapid progress, for him, that will be made once he is exposed to the world of work through the vocational rehabilitation assessment and evaluation process of reality reinforcement. Today, as he sits before you, his vocational fantasies show little rein, and his inappropriate job identifications are difficult to accept. Face to face counseling could do little more than assure him that in non-authoritarian fashion, he will be helped to gain confidence through the counselor's support and acceptance of necessary dependency. The primary purpose at this initial stage would be to promote or increase initiative and capacity for self-help. Without the

assumption of the individual's inevitable progress, despite apparent overwhelming limitations medically, psychologically and socially, the counselor could easily find himself avoiding an initial step of acceptance as necessary in this case as in counseling with a gifted, non-handicapped high school valedictorian. While the cerebral palsied individual and the valedictorian are each unique in individual presentation, the Rehabilitation Counselor must be aware of the several other team members who currently are involved with the cerebral palsied person who must be made aware, as a result, that *this* counseling session has vocational planning as the primary orientation of the interpersonal relationship.

2. The nature of the agency of facility in which the Rehabilitation Counselor will be working provides him with a somewhat different *milieu* than is afforded other Counselors. The rehabilitation center, sheltered workshop, hospital, State Vocational Rehabilitation Agency and other facilities add another dimension to the problem of the initial counseling session. Medically, the overt physically handicapped announces this problem as he enters the counseling room. There is little opportunity for the Counselor here to sustain the type of objectivity possible by eschewing a look at the case folder prior to the first interview as to what are some of the problems. Studies have indicated the possibility of a bias of some professional workers with certain disabilities. The roots of prejudice may lie within the professional worker as Gellman points out,[9] and social distance between the Rehabilitation Counselor and the handicapped person may be increased by prevailing counselor middle-class stereotypes as goals for patients. The majority of rehabilitation clients come from lower-level socio-economic groups, and the Rehabilitation Counselors must be insightful of his own preconceived perceptions which may provide a negative psychological climate for a positive relationship with the handicapped.

3. Specific knowledge about the medical problems of various diagnostic categories will be of help to the Rehabilitation Counselor. Certain basic understanding is implicit: the deaf individual should not face any position which would make it difficult for him to read the Counselor's lips; the blind person should be allowed to take the Counselor's arm when both are walking together toward the counseling room, or any other new location within the agency; stabilizing the chair as the orthopedically handicapped attempts to sit before you for the first time is a normal procedure if done with understanding rather than fright or uneasiness. Several of the national organizations for specific disabilities distribute "do's and don'ts" in this respect. But there is a need to know more than these apparent amenities. The epileptic with *petit mal* seizures has often found it difficult to overcome initial writeups

about his minor attack that colored the report far out of proportion to its significance. The individual with multiple sclerosis must be understood with reference to the current nature of the disease; neither his medical prognosis nor his psychological overlay can be neglected. The use of medical consultation and the capacity to request meaningful medical reports for vocational planning are a part of the professionalism of the Rehabilitation Counselor's counseling techniques.

4. Curriculum developers in Rehabilitation Counseling agree generally that the most essential characteristic of counseling is the interpersonal relationship between the client and counselor.[32] This relationship was stated as possessing "a unity which was violated by attempts to describe it in terms of technical competencies."[33] Here is a dilemma for the writer of a chapter on Rehabilitation Counseling Techniques! And yet the understanding of the utilization of specialized techniques is a part of the Counselor's professional ability to deal in depth with the client's motivational system. The counselor must be aware of the dynamic aspects of personality through the use of personality theory in helping the client extend his area of self awareness. But more than an awareness of personality theory is necessary. The Rehabilitation Counselor must add to his familiarity with general principles in the psychology of motivation, learning, personality development and organization, perception, and social behavior. He must go beyond a general understanding and further explore the sociological principles of group relations, cultural dynamics and the relation of culture and society to personality.

There are two related but distinguishable types of problems of which he must be aware: (1) adjustment of the individual to disability, including acceptance of loss, modification of the self-concept, role of the body image, personality factors, situational factors; (2) disability as a social-psychological problem, including the social-psychological significance in western culture, group status of the disabled, and social barriers to improved rehabilitation procedures.[34] The need for the Rehabilitation Counselor's critical self-examination of his personal attitudes toward the disabled has already been underscored.

In addition to the field-theoretical formulations of R. G. Barker, et al.,[1] and the "adjustment to misfortune" hypotheses of T. Dembo, et al.,[3] Janis utilized Freudian concepts with hospitalized patients admitted for surgery.[15] Grayson also discusses the psychological problems of the disabled within a rehabilitation center in psychoanalytic constructs.[10] Lee Meyerson has critically reviewed theory and research in rehabilitation psychology with especial reference to some experimental application based on the behavior and learning theories of B. F. Skinner, Spence, Hull and others.[16] The Vocational Rehabilitation Administration has supported special seminars, conferences, study groups, and curriculum studies with special reference to the counseling role of the Rehabilitation Counselor. Copies of published reports are available either from their Central Office in Washington D.C. in the Department of Health, Education, and Welfare, or from the host university or association that sponsored the conference or institute. There are a number of national organizations who have also thus participated. While no list should be considered complete, the following are somewhat representative: National Rehabilitation Association, National Society for Crippled Children and Adults, American Psychological Association, American Personnel and Guidance Association, Council on Social Work Education, International Society for the Rehabilitation of the Disabled, National Association of Sheltered Workshops and Homebound Programs and the Association of Rehabilitation Centers. Two of the major rehabilitation centers in the United States have also published extensively in this field: Institute of Physical Medicine and Rehabilitation and the Institute for the Crippled and Disabled, both in New York City. Other facilities especially engaged in publication of their demonstration and research efforts in the rehabilitation counseling area are the Jewish Vocational Service of Chicago, The Association for the Help of Retarded Children and the Altro Workshop and Federation of the Handicapped in New York City, the Woods Schools in Langhorne Pennsylvania, Highland Hospital and the Cleveland Rehabilitation Center in Cleveland, the Massachusetts Association for Mental Health and the World Federation for Mental Health in New York. A total list of those engaged in or allied to vocational rehabilitation areas has been published in an annotated listing entitled, "Research and Demonstration Projects," Office of Vocational Rehabilitation, U.S. Department of Health, Education and Welfare, Washington 25, D.C. (1961).

Several of the national disability group organizations have also distributed literature relating to the counseling process of a particular category: American Foundation for the Blind, United Cerebral Palsy, National Association for Retarded Children, National Association for the Deaf, National Association for Mental Health, National Epilepsy League, National Tuberculosis Association, American Heart Association, National Foundation (polio and birth defects).

5. *Personal Adjustment Counseling.* The Rehabilitation Counselor is often faced with the types of maturation problems which are frequently found in the young adult handicapped due to delayed adolescence. At the Institute for the Crippled and Disabled, the author found during his five years of vocational counseling that the young adult handicapped between the ages of sixteen and twenty appeared approximately five years younger in adjustment maturity and three to five years younger

in school progress. The Institute for the Crippled and Disabled includes full time teachers from the New York Board of Education. In one of these classes, considerable remedial work was handled by a teacher whose primary focus was on the fundamentals that had been perceptibly missed through sieges of hospitalization, intervening physical therapy, intermittent home instruction, and confounded by parental dependency relationships. The inevitability of human progress is perhaps one of the few clues to the continuing counseling relationship toward long range vocational goals.[36]

As a result, Personal Adjustment Training has become one of the early stages in the counseling process of the handicapped. Agencies dealing with the blind, the mentally retarded, the multiply handicapped cerebral palsied have developed specialized units within rehabilitation facilities where, in group interaction through both vocational and recreational tasks, the following items are covered:

> Personal health and appearance
> Manners
> Means of getting employment
> Means of adjusting to accidents and unemployment
> Ways to get along with the "boss"
> Ways to get along with fellow workers
> Budgets and banking
> Ways to travel
> Suggestions for living at home
> Suggestions for living away from home
> Recreation
> Personal relationships
> Group relationships
> Citizenship

These items appear as much geared to some of the activities of daily living as to vocational adjustment, and impinge upon some of the specialized techniques in assesssment and evaluation which will be covered later. Emphasis in personal adjustment training has been found helpful as prerequisites to successful employment with the mentally retarded, while travel training is essential to the total adjustment of the blind. The above list of 15 items contains, undoubtedly, a considerable amount of reinforcement of content hopefully covered in special education classwork. But again the vocational focus of such training expands the adjustment horizon of the handicapped especially as rehabilitation counseling is concurrent with the personal adjustment training.

Counseling sessions include the reactions of the disabled to his personal adjustment training, and inappropriate behavior can be brought to his attention through empirical evidence within the group task setting. As Lofquist states, "While the counselee has need for anxiety reduction concerning his vocational problem or set of problems, psychopathology is not involved and the counselee is capable of learning new attitudes and appraising vocational realities with reference to his unique assets and liabilities without first requiring a major restructuring of his personality."[17] This is not to state that psychotherapy may not be occurring, but more to underline the utilization of the rational powers of the client, with focus on the reality aspects of the individual's situational encounters. To engage in depth counseling alone presupposes a unilateral team approach by the Rehabilitation Counselor. The importance of vocational rehabilitation counseling is best conceived through the understanding of the disabled individual as a total personality. One of the most difficult constructs in the philosophy of rehabilitation to be understood by the Rehabilitation Counselor is his need to know, understand and be guided by a theory of personality without identifying or portraying himself as a psychotherapist. The client's problems are dealt with as they are relevant to vocational planning.

The essential focus in Personal Adjustment Training should be upon the development within the handicapped individual of what might be termed an acceptable "work personality." In the achievement of this goal, and during the rehabilitation process, there will undoubtedly be the need of several of the team members to assist the individual. Unless the Rehabilitation Counselor, however, recognizes his role as the vocational adjustment contributor within the understanding spectrum of health, physical, personal and social problems, the client may continue to have problems of motivation for self-support, training, evaluation, or any level of employment.

6. *The work sample within the situational technique.* In recent years a new method of vocational evaluation and assessment has appeared. It has been known variously as work exploration, pre-vocational evaluation, guidance testing, job test evaluation, work adjustment and other titles indigenous to individuals or facilities throughout the United States. In no way does this approach rule out the use of the standardized, psychological tests for the disabled. The evaluation of the disabled in these tests must be based on the non-handicapped or normal population. Outside of contributions for the use of psychological tests with the handicapped in the area of the blind[2] and projective personality tests for the emotionally disturbed, there has been virtually very little published for handicapped groups.[4]

Situational techniques have in common the fact that actual work tasks are used for evaluation purposes. The work sample or job task is a sample of an actual type of work. If challenged by a test which resembles an everyday activity, or which offers purpose and realistic achievement, the handicapped individual can be motivated along with an appraisal of his aptitudes. Assessment and evaluation of the handicapped with their multiple medical, psychological, social and vocational problems can best be accomplished through developmental tasks as defined by Havighurst.[13] It is the seriously disabled individual's gradual successful achievement in vocational developmental tasks that affords him the opportunity to learn. Success with sub-units of the final task reinforces the strength to sustain the final result. A similar approach is expressed in Dollard and Miller in what they term graded situations where the patient can learn during therapy. They point out that "the goal is a bit-by-bit revelation, since the bits are all the patient can stand at any one time," but that "in order to grade the units of a task, the whole task must be conceived."[5]

This technique provides the Rehabilitation Counselor, as well as the rest of the team, an opportunity to observe and evaluate the integration of the individual's physical, mental and emotional make-up within a work environment. A habilitant might be chronologically 18 years old, but because of restricting and over-protective family attitudes, he may not have the emotional experiences necessary to cope with the demands of work and relationships with other workers. Poor performance during a situational evaluation can easily be misinterpreted as caused by motor involvement and/or mental retardation. The habilitant may first have to be taught the proper use of basic tools, measuring instruments and machines.

It is not necessary to provide monolithic monuments containing huge pre-vocational shops or units with expensive machinery. Unfortunately the work sample approach appears destined to eliminate basic theory and behavioristic fundamentals in favor of bigger and better plants.

Two basic features are perhaps the more important texture of the situational technique, and each is founded on two theoretical constructs.

(a) *Operant conditioning.* This is a term devised by B. F. Skinner[14] consisting of reinforcing spontaneous activities of the subject. In operant conditioning, the experimenter waits for the subject to do something spontaneously, and then rewards it. If, however, this theory is applied to the mentally retarded or the emotionally disturbed in a sheltered workshop evaluation unit consisting of graded tasks, the reinforcement or reward constantly appearing after every completed sub-task will increase output significantly and distractability decreases. It is suggested that the reward not be in the form of material substance, but to be found in (b) which follows.

(b) *The counselor in the role of workshop floor supervisor.* The therapeutic milieu afforded through the relationship of the workshop floor supervisor and the handicapped individual offers professional support and understanding for total growth. Within the relationship comes the praise for work well done as well as support during failure, which support in itself is rewarding to the handicapped. His failures must be minimized before successes can build toward his feeling of self reliance and achievement vocationally. While some experiments have utilized pennies for reinforcement or other non-relationship awards, it is the rewarding experience of the counseling relationship that will eventually prepare the handicapped to sustain his relationships during employment with other workers, the boss, or the foreman of the plant. Mention was made of the mentally retarded and the emotionally disturbed specifically. The point to be emphasized is that with the physically handicapped, the counselor works with their fears and problems, not with their physically incapacitating phenomenon. The latter adjusts itself through the support offered in the relationship and through the reinforcement of successes in the use of equipment, jigs, tools and directions.

To recapitulate, it is hoped that the theories of operant conditioning and interpersonal relationship will form the basis for the use of the situational technique in the assessment and evaluation of the skills as well as the work personality of the handicapped individual. The author suggests here primarily the work of Skinner and associates as well as the work of Harry Stack Sullivan to provide a framework for an approach to the use of the work sample within the situational technique. The role of the Rehabilitation Counselor, trained in psycho-dynamics of interpersonal relationships, becomes that of the Workshop Floor Supervisor. The situational technique may fail with the referral "off the floor" of the handicapped individual for "counseling."

Experiences by those utilizing the relationship between the individual and the Rehabilitation Counselor on the workshop floor or in the work adjustment setting have shown that the serious barriers to employability are anxiety, hostility, fear of authority figures, lack of confidence, lack of understanding of appropriate work behavior, awkwardness in relationships with co-workers, and similar interpersonal variables.[8] The industrial insurance compensation case responds to the technique wherein he cannot hide behind a barrage of physical complaints. Once engaged in work with others, he begins to recognize his remaining or newly found skills in the company of others who may appear more physically handicapped than he.

The specialized technique of the situational setting utilized by the Rehabilitation Counselor as the counselor *within the setting* should afford a contribution to the total picture of the client within five areas: (1) what is his concept of self as a worker, (2) what is his use of his abilities in a work situation and his aptitudes for further training, (3) what are his interpersonal relations with supervisors and co-workers and his amenability to the counseling process on the floor, (4) what are his interests and work satisfactions, and (5) what is his adjustment to work pressures and his level of employability currently and diagnostically for further vocational planning?

The past ten years have found more and more Rehabilitation Counselors in workshop floor settings. The initial difficulty of accepting a position which appears less than professionally "white collar" has been resolved by several elements, among which have been possibility of research, employment success of the "unemployable" mentally retarded and emotionally disturbed clients, and of course, higher salaries.

The specific approaches of types of equipment, job areas for work samples, workshop procedures, space, number of clients to each workshop supervisor and other mechanical problems can be found in the literature of the Office of Vocational Rehabilitation as well as in the library maintained by the National Society for Crippled Children and Adults in Chicago. The National Association of Sheltered Workshops and Homebound Programs in Washington, D.C. and the Association of Rehabilitation Centers also maintain information and suggestions in this regard.

7. *Occupational Information and Employment.* Occupational information includes theories of vocational choice, labor market analysis, job analysis and the psychology of careers as well as the gathering, filing and dissemination of information regarding the world of work. This is a broad definition of the area, but the content coverage in the professional training of many counselors tends to be involved with an overwhelming catalogue of pamphlets, books, Department of Labor publications, Chamber of Commerce information and the development of a library in "the outer office."

The technical matching process of job information and client traits has lately added a current emphasis on emotional and sociological factors.

The writer is indebted to Sidney Fine for the following approach.[6] In his recent analysis of the use of occupational information for employment in the Rehabilitation Counseling process, he has differentiated between "discovery" and "invention." Starting first with a definition of a job as a job-worker situation, he further elaborates a job-worker situation as a behavior situation involving an interaction among three parameters: what a worker does, what he knows, and what needs to get done. Fine structures each parameter as having Things, Data, and People characteristics, and charts how work meets the needs of worker as reflected in the personnel function. He poses the question for the

Rehabilitation Counselor thusly: Can a rehabilitation counselor really "discover" the job that suits the total dynamics of his client, his need structure, his aptitudes, temperament, physical capacities, etc.? Obviously not. No job is a static fixed thing represented by the typical job specification developed through current job analysis techniques. Any job-worker situation occurs in a dynamic context. The same job-worker situation can have significant variations depending on the over-all employment situation. The Rehabilitation Counselor must essentially complete a "job of engineering," both from the physical and social aspects. Rather than "discovering" through more intensive job analysis the appropriate job, the Counselor's problem is one of "invention." The job need can best be understood as a given placement for a unique individual. If the use of occupational information and job search is approached through Discovery, the counselor's attitude may tend to be one of sympathy rather than empathy. The handicapped individual becomes less than "normal"; how can he be fitted to the less than "normal" job?

If one's approach is that of Invention, the challenge is as much to the Counselor as it is to the client, and within an emphatic framework. Effective placement is a mutually creative act, and the less the capacity for Invention on the part of the Rehabilitation Counselor, the less vocational counseling is meaningful—even necessary. And eventually, as a result, the less suited the job is for the handicapped.

Invention focuses on the handicapped individual and his problem, especially in his involvement of his own vocational plan. It is important that the Rehabilitation Counselor recognize the continuity of work behavior with behavior in school, leisure, social and other situations. Viewing the world of work as another point on the life span continuum, the Counselor's understanding of personality theory helps understand the psycho-dynamic use of occupational information toward the placement process. Occupational information must be an essential aspect of the interacting counseling process before it can become effective information of any kind. If Invention rather than Discovery is utilized with occupational information toward the counseling placement process, such information then becomes as integrated within the counseling relationship as personality theory.

Additional techniques involve the understanding and usage of Interviewing Guides, Worker Trait Materials, and the Occupational Outlook Handbook. Since small business enterprises are often entered into by many handicapped who obtain compensation settlements, "Small Business Enterprises for the Severely Handicapped,"[38] "The Placement Process in Vocational Rehabilitation Counseling"[20] and issues of the "Employment Security Review"[26] will prove helpful. In addition, the Twelfth Annual Workshop on Guidance, Training, and Placement, Report of Proceedings, Part II"[39] includes information regarding special techniques in this area supported through Public Law 565, Section II, (2) (5) of the Vocational Rehabilitation Act of 1954. An excellent small business bibliography is listed in Appendix III.

At the Alabama School of Trades in Gadsden, Alabama, the Office of Vocational Rehabilitation has established a project entitled, "Techniques and Procedures for Rehabilitating Severely Handicapped People in Small Business Enterprise." Information and copies of reports can be obtained through OVR or from the Project Personnel or through any State Division or Bureau of Vocational Rehabilitation. This material is helpful in working with industrial compensation cases who are contemplating a small business enterprise. Additional pamphlets underscoring special techniques in the placement counseling process for the mentally retarded and others are "Preparation of Mentally Retarded Youth for Gainful Employment,"[35] "Selective Placement,"[37] and "The Mentally Retarded and Their Vocational Rehabilitation."[7]

SUMMARY

Rehabilitation Counseling is an emerging profession currently passing through rapid, evolutionary changes in its graduate training programs at approximately thirty universities and colleges. Some of its systematic body of theory has been mentioned in this chapter as represented by an overview of certain counseling techniques. These techniques are currently in process of being organized into an internally consistent system, or a body of theory. Graduate training in the profession of Rehabilitation Counseling imparts to the Rehabilitation Counselor extensive education in the theory of his discipline. As Greenwood points out, this specialized type of knowledge is the basis for the professional's authority within the client–counselor relationship.[11] Sanction of the community is clearly in the creation of thirty government supported curricula throughout the United States due to an overwhelming need in rehabilitation agencies of various types. The profession itself has recognized the need for professional associations, and two groups are currently engaged in the development of standards, code of ethics, encouragement of research and the further development of graduate training. These are the American Rehabilitation Counseling Association (Division VI of the American Personnel and Guidance Association), and the Rehabilitation Counseling Division of the National Rehabilitation Association. The former publishes its own journal, "Rehabilitation Counseling Bulletin" which is in its fifth year. The latter publishes a "Professional Bulletin," "The RCD News," and has completed a study of hiring standards and practices for Vocational Rehabilitation Counselors in private and public agencies.

The title, Rehabilitation Counselor, has been established and appears in the Department of Labor's publication, "The Dictionary of Occupational Titles" with a professional code number. University trainers and State and Federal personnel meet annually both together and separately to encourage the further development of selection and recruitment standards, field supervision standards and other curricula aspects.

As part of the profession of counseling, the Rehabilitation Counselor is emerging as both part of the psychological counseling movement and containing unique, specialized techniques which appear to afford it distinct professionalism.

BIBLIOGRAPHY

1. BARKER, R. G., WRIGHT, BEATRICE A., MEYERSON, L., and GONICK, MOLLIE R.: 1953. *Adjustment to Physical Handicap and Illness.* New York: Social Science Research Council.
2. BAUMAN, MARY K.: 1958. *A Manual of Norms for Tests Used in Counseling Blind Persons, American Foundation for the Blind,* 15 West 16th Street.
3. DEMBO, TAMARA, LEVITON, GLORIA, and WRIGHT, BEATRICE A.: "Adjustment to Misfortune," *Artificial Limbs,* pp. 4–62.
4. DiMICHAEL, SALVATORE G.: "Applicability of Standard Psychological Tests to the Disabled," in *Clinical Aspects of Counseling with the Disabled,* Office of Vocational Rehabilitation, Washington 25, D.C., Rehabilitation Service Series No. 343, 1954.
5. DOLLARD, JOHN, and MILLER, N. E.: 1950. *Personality and Psychotherapy,* p. 350. New York: McGraw-Hill.
6. FINE, SIDNEY A.: 1960. "Comments on Dr. Roe's Paper" in *Occupational Information in Counseling,* pp. 44–47. Boulder, Colorado: University of Colorado.
7. FRAENKEL, W. A.: 1961. *The Mentally Retarded and Their Vocational Rehabilitation— A Resource Handbook,* National Association for Retarded Children, Inc., New York: 386 Park Avenue South.
8. FRIEDMAN, S. B., and NEFF, WALTER S.: September, 1957. "Use of a Simulated Work Environment in Vocational Rehabilitation," *Employment Security Review,* U.S. Department of Labor, 24, pp. 8–11.
9. GELLMAN, WILLIAM: 1959. "Roots of Prejudice Against the Handicapped," *Journal of Rehabilitation,* pp. 4–6, 25.
10. GRAYSON, M., POWERS, A., and LEVI, J.: 1952. *Psychiatric Aspects of Rehabilitation.* New York: Institute of Physical Medicine and Rehabilitation Monograph II.
11. GREENWOOD, ERNEST: "Attributes of a Profession," in *Man, Work & Society,* edited by Sigmund Nosow & William H. Form, Basic Books, 1962, pp. 206–218.
12. HALL, J. H., and WARREN, SOL L. (Eds.): 1956. "Rehabilitation Counselor Preparation," National Rehabilitation Association and National Vocational Guidance Association, Washington, D.C.
13. HAVIGHURST, R. J.: 1953. *Human Development and Education,* p. 2. New York: Longmans, Green.

14. HEBB, D. O.: 1958. "The Motivating Effects of Exteroceptive Stimulation," *American Psychologist*, **13**.

15. JANIS, I. L.: 1958. *Psychological Stress—Psychoanalytic and Behavioral Studies of Surgical Patients*. New York, N.Y.: Wiley.

16. LEVITON, GLORIA (Ed.) : *The Relationship Between Rehabilitation and Psychology*, Clark University, Worcester, Massachusetts, 1959, Lee Meyerson, "Theory and Research in Rehabilitation Psychology," pp. 7–26.

17. LOFQUIST, LLOYD H.: 1959. "An Operational Definition of Rehabilitation Counseling," *Journal of Rehabilitation*, XXV, No. 4.

18. PATTERSON, C. H.: 1960. *Readings in Rehabilitation Counseling*, Preface, ix. Champaign, Illinois: Stipes Publishing Co.

19. SEIDENFELD, MORTON A.: July–August 1962. "The Need-Oriented Profession of Rehabilitation Counseling: Implications for Selection, Training, and Services," *Journal of Rehabilitation*, pp. 11–14.

20. THOMASON, BRUCE, and BARRETT, ALBERT M. (Eds.) : September, 1960. *The Placement Process in Vocational Rehabilitation Counseling*, Office of Vocational Rehabilitation, Department of Health, Education, and Welfare, Washington 25, D.C.

21. TITMUSS, R. M.: 1960. *The Social Division of Welfare*, pp. 10–11. Liverpool University Press.

22. USDANE, W. M.: 1955. "A Comparative Analysis of Legislation for the Severely Handicapped Civilian Orthopedic in Great Britain and the United States," unpublished doctoral dissertation, New York University.

23. WHITEHOUSE, FREDERICK A.: June 6–8, 1956. "Rehabilitation as a Concept in the Utilization of Human Resources," pp. 20–43. Institute on Rehabilitation, Bryn Mawr College.

24. "An Introduction to the Vocational Rehabilitation Process," GTP Bulletin No. 3, Rehabilitation Service Series No. 555, 1960, U.S. Government Printing Office, Washington 25, D.C.

25. Definition adopted by the National Council on Rehabilitation (now defunct) in August, 1943.

26. *Employment Security Review*, U.S. Department of Labor, Bureau of Employment Security, U.S. Employment Service, Washington 25, D.C.

27. "Facts on the Major Killing and Crippling Diseases in the United States Today," The National Health Education Committee, Inc., 135 East 42nd Street, New York, N.Y., 1957.

28. *Ibid.*

29. *Ibid.*

30. "Occupational Information in Counseling," A Report on the Harvest House Conference. Boulder, Colorado: University of Colorado, 1960.

31. "Preliminary Seminars on Curriculum Development for Rehabilitation Counselor Training Programs." San Francisco: San Francisco State College, 1960.

32. *Loc. cit.*, pp. 21–27.

33. *Loc. cit.*, p. 24.

34. *Loc. cit.*, p. 28.

35. *Preparation of Mentally Retarded Youth for Gainful Employment*, Bulletin 1959, No. 28 Office of Education Rehabilitation Service Series No. 507, Office of Vocational Rehabilitation, Department of Health, Education, and Welfare, Washington 25, D.C.

36. *Rehabilitation Trends—Midcentury to 1956*, Institute for the Crippled and Disabled, New York 10, N.Y. 400 1st Avenue.

37. *Selective Placement*, Personal Methods, Series, No. 9, U.S. Civil Service Commission, Washington 25, D.C., October, 1958.
38. *Small Business Enterprises for the Severely Handicapped*, Rehabilitation Service Series No. 320, Office of Vocational Rehabilitation, Department of Health, Education, and Welfare, Washington 25, D.C., 1955.
39. Twelfth Annual Workshop on Guidance, Training, and Placement, *Report of Proceedings, Part II*, Office of Vocational Rehabilitation Department of Health, Education, and Welfare, Washington 25, D.C., 1960.

Counseling in The United States Army

FERNANDO G. TORGERSON

Formerly
Lt. Col., United States Army
Washington, D.C.

INTRODUCTION

THERE are few social institutions in America in which counseling is
more pervasive than in the United States Army. The responsibility of
officers and non-commissioned officers for the welfare of the personnel
in their unit or organization is a military value enforced and reinforced
by custom, tradition, practice and regulation. This fact, alone, would
appear to establish the importance of counseling, but this compounded
with our national value system of concern for the individual and his
welfare, makes it doubly significant.

In tracing the development of individualized services for the common
soldier in our own Army, which has been traditionally a citizen Army,
there is no indication, earlier than the Civil War, that concern for the
individual was reflected in programs of institutionalized services in
which counseling was a core activity. While it is not supported by clear
evidence, it is reasonable to assume that the personal and sentimental
needs of individual soldiers were met by the soldier's immediate family,
his buddies, or his Commanding Officer in the period prior to the
Civil War.

The first organized program of individualized relief services for the
common soldier was that of the U.S. Sanitary Commission, a volunteer
organization which developed very early in the Civil War, and after
some struggle, gained a quasi-official status. It became apparent, early
in the Civil War, that in the large-scale mobilization of a volunteer

Army there were bound to be individuals with unique problems which the traditional military bureaucracy was not designed to meet. At first, it was thought that these were, perhaps, of a temporary nature and would soon be provided for through the Army as it became more capable of meeting problems, following the initial inundation of volunteers occasioned by Lincoln's call for volunteers. However, it became apparent, even as it is today, that no matter how perfect the system, no matter how carefully planned, there will always be the situation which falls outside general policies and provisions, and must be decided upon and provided for individually. To provide against breakdown in the system, or the unfavorable incidents accruing to the large bureaucratic structure of the Army suddenly being required to meet enormous demands, the United States Sanitary Commission made provisions, through its Special Relief Department. As the War progressed, the Special Relief Department expanded so as to provide individualized attention and care through services which involved interviewing on a one-to-one basis.

The methodology employed by special relief agents was predicated on the existence of unique problems of individuals which required handling on an individual one-to-one basis. The service provided was characteristically in the form of a tangible or practical service, consisting of advice, money, information, comfort items, lodgings and meals, clothing, referral to another agency, or help in military administrative problems. Less commonly, the help was in the nature of sympathetic listening, emotional support, or help through relationship. The special relief agencies did not have a scientific understanding of relationship, or discipline in its use, but a few were aware of some significant aspects of using relationship in helping others. In some instances, the agents employed principles of helping people which are similar to those used by social caseworkers today (the closest modern day counterpart), but it would be inaccurate to assert that the special relief agents employed these principles for the same reasons, or with the same underlying rationale as modern social caseworkers. The agents differed from modern social caseworkers in their lack of self-awareness, and in their lack of a scientifically based understanding of human behavior.

The program of individualized social services was recognized and supported by the general public, and by a majority of military and Government leaders. Not all of these, however, recognized the relationship between the provision of special relief services and maintaining maximum fighting strength.

In historical retrospect, this program must be considered a most significant event in the development of military bureaucracies, since it recognized the need for the employment of the concept of individualization. It established, in as alien a setting as one could imagine, a program predicated on the unique needs of individuals. Armies historically had been oriented toward the rational military purpose of success in combat. Army commanders were not concerned with the concept of individual differences or unique needs of individuals. But the Sanitary Commission bridged this apparent dilemma and introduced the principle of individualization on these grounds, "Its work is, in the highest degree, humane and charitable, for it visits and relieves the sick, the destitute and miserable, but its ultimate end is neither humanity nor charity. It is to economize for the National Service the life and strength of the National Soldier."* For the first time in the history of the Army of the United States, it was recognized that the concept of individualization is not incompatible with the impersonal goal of success in combat. In fact, they are mutually supporting.

This manifestation of regard for the individual, in the Army, is of course, more understandable if viewed in relation to evolving social thought just prior to the Civil War. The tiny, dispersed Regular Army of 16,000 found itself, at the beginning of the Civil War, suddenly engulfed by a huge volunteer Army that brought with it concepts of social welfare evolving at that time. It was the spirit of social reform so evident in the nation as a whole, which imposed itself on an, at first, reluctant Medical Bureau of the Army and manifested itself in the form of the Sanitary Commission. It was not a development from within the Army, but an almost literally forced imposition from the outside.

Just as in the Nation as a whole, which was rapidly becoming an industrialized society at that time, the Army primary groups' compassionate functions in regard to the individual needs of its members became grossly inadequate to the task at hand. When the tiny Army was dispersed on the frontier in groups of 20 to 40, there was no need for institutionalized services to meet individual needs through professionally administered counseling processes. The Civil War, then, marked the turning point and the advent of counseling on a large scale.

In today's Army, however, an entire array of uniformed professionals provide for the individual needs of soldiers through various levels of counseling activities. Counseling services are provided for the soldier from induction into the Army to separation from the Army. It is

* Lt. Col. Fernando G. Torgerson, MSC, Social Service Consultant, Office of The Surgeon General, Headquarters Department of the Army, Washington, 25, D.C. "A Historical Study of the Beginnings of Individualized Social Services in The United States Army." Unpublished Doctoral Dissertation, University of Minnesota, 1956, p. 269.

practiced by enlisted men and officers, professional as well as line officers. It is taught as a method in service schools, and acquired through on-the-job training. It ranges from simple, direct advice to the employment of more complex techniques involving attitude change. Counseling is done individually and in groups. It is a technique used in disciplinary facilities, induction centers, separation points, hospitals, and even in Combat Units engaged with the enemy. Counseling services are provided for cadets at the United States Military Academy, and it is also taught the cadets as an essential element of the knowledges and skills required of a commissioned officer.

THE SOCIAL WORK OFFICER AS COUNSELOR

Clinical social casework in the Army is defined as a process of helping an individual come to a decision with reference to a social or personal problem so that he is enabled to move toward a solution of the problem with conviction and with the strength to live with the consequences of that decision. This treatment process may involve the use of any number of resources, collaboration with other disciplines, as well as contact with key persons in the individual's life.

The treatment goal of clinical military social casework is to help the individual whose ability to function adequately is impaired by reality problems to regain maximum effectiveness as a soldier. The treatment goal is achieved through a selective use of casework treatment techniques and social resources.

As a specialist in the treatment of problems of social reality, the clinical social work officer must identify himself with the Army structures and mission and adapt his casework goals, procedures, and techniques accordingly. He must develop an understanding of the Army environment, which represents the reality to which the patient must adjust, and a sensitivity to those factors in a soldier's situation which can be changed so that he can become a more effective soldier. In each specific setting there are well-defined limits arising out of the Army's mission and structure which will affect the focus of the casework process and require further adaptation of procedures and techniques.

The social work officer observes the principles of professional ethics, including the ethical obligation of confidentiality in respect to information about patients. (This term is used in the sense of client.) The confidential material gained by the social worker comes to him by virtue of his official position, and can be used only for professional purposes. It is discussed only with persons who are authorized access to such information. Within the Army, certain administrative channels have been established for the transmission of clinical information to non-military agencies and individuals. These channels must be observed. If progress or final reports are submitted to the source of referral, they must be so organized as to portray objectively the patient's situation as seen by the professional team without giving details which might unnecessarily jeopardize the patient's military relationships upon return to duty.

The information obtained by the social work officer is not privileged information in the legal sense. Because the social work officer is in an official position, information he obtains about the patient is available for use by courts-martial and civilian courts if properly called for.

Under the stress of illness or injury, few individuals are able to remain objective or realistic in their reactions to situations. This is accentuated when the individual is exposed to the stress of rigorous training, combat, or other conditions of severe deprivation or special demands. Under these conditions, which are to be expected in the Army, some soldiers are consciously or unconsciously inclined to exaggerate their illness or injury or develop psychosomatic complaints for the purpose of avoiding the stress situation. The secondary gains realized by the soldier when he is able to escape the tension producing situation through medical treatment operate to reduce his motivation toward return to duty. When this is found to be true during the course of treatment, it is most profitable to avoid discussing with the patient his symptoms or illness. The chances of returning the soldier to a duty status are much greater if the social worker encourages him to talk about his feelings concerning the training or combat situation and conveys to him an implacable conviction that he can and will return to duty. It is also important that the social worker recognize the opposite tendency in soldiers, that of denying illness or injury to avoid separation from their organizations. Because of strong unit identification, they are reluctant to risk hospitalization for fear of not being able to rejoin their organization. The social work officer must be aware of the possible range of reactions from minimizing of illness and injury to exaggeration of illness or injury, if casework treatment is to be of maximum effectiveness in maintaining the soldier's effectiveness.

A number of circumstances not always within the control of the clinical social worker influence treatment, but the goal of treatment always remains the same—restoration of the effectiveness of the patient. To achieve this goal, the social worker helps the patient maintain constructive relationship to reality, solve problems related to social reality, and achieve adequate and satisfying independent social functioning within the existing personality structure. This is accomplished through a relationship with the patient developed through regulated face-to-face interviews which convey acceptance and understanding of the patient and focus on social realities. The social worker handles resistance and anxieties through skilled use of psychological support, explanation, clarification, and practical assistance. At the same time, the patient is encouraged to use current strengths to act and decide on his reality problem, with the social worker helping through intelligent use of authority and other techniques mentioned above. Thus, treatment includes all the services and activities which the social work officer directs toward the relief of personal and social problems of ordinary living, as well as the modification of attitude and behavior. The degree of emotional health or illness within the individual or the nature of the illness is not itself the determining factor in judging the suitability of social casework as a treatment method. Patients in reasonably good mental health may have social and interpersonal problems that require the services of a social work officer. At the other end of the scale are patients with diagnosed mental illness who are able to make use of casework help in limited areas of their difficulties, usually focused upon specific problems of social adjustment. Between these two extremes is the large number of patients with neurotic traits, symptom neurosis, or character disturbances whose emotional disorders or deviations in behavior are expressed through interpersonal and social problems.

The techniques of clinical military social work are based on understanding of human behavior and skill in relationship (interviewing). Techniques are selectively employed according to the needs of the individual and in relation to the demands of the Army situation. The major techniques can be grouped in several ways. As one major group, they can be considered as those employed to alter or modify the patient's outer situation through the use of reassurance, direct advice and guidance, suggestions, logical discussion, or exercise of professional authority through active intervention in the patient's behalf. A second group would be those techniques which are used to modify the patient's attitude and pattern of behavior by increasing his understanding of himself, his problem, and his part in creating them. The predominant technique here is clarification. Reassurance and educational techniques similar to those used in the first method are also utilized when appropriate. All of the techniques of social work are closely interrelated and cannot be considered as distinct techniques used independently of each other. In practice, they are used as needed, in a mutually related and supporting manner, and the typical purposes of one may be achieved indirectly or secondarily by the employment of the other. For example, real insight may be derived from simple clarification, although insight was not the central casework goal. Likewise, a patient may gain considerable clarification of his situation through the caseworker's use of such elements of support as acceptance, interest, encouragement, and ventilation. The utilization of these techniques is influenced by the military situation. For the purpose of pointing out how specific techniques are applied in the military-medical setting, they will be grouped under the headings of environmental modification, psychological support, clarification, insight development, and psychotherapy, although psychotherapy is not a technique of social work, but rather a unique method of treatment employed by specially equipped and trained social work officers.

Environmental modification is used when patients are unable to move toward relief of incapacitating environmental pressures. It may also be used in the treatment of patients who, because of illness, are unable to help themselves or, by reason of their illness or overwhelming stress, have regressed to an immature adaptive state. Environmental modification should be used only after careful evaluation indicates that the patient cannot accomplish the necessary changes himself, or that time factors require the worker to act to prevent serious deterioration in the situation. In the Army setting, where patients may be referred on a basis other than voluntary, Army necessity may require the use of this technique with or without the patient's consent. The applicable principle here is that treatment starts where the patient is and this dictates that, in the case of the grossly immature patient, the social worker assumes the responsibilities of the good parent. This role often requires courses of action which the immature patient is not capable of understanding or to which he will not give assent. In view of the authoritarian structure of the Army, environmental modification is often a sharp and readily available instrument in the armamentarium of the Army caseworker, however, it should not be used when it is reasonable to expect that the patient is able to make necessary changes himself within the Army structure. The social work officer contributes most to the effectiveness of the soldier when the individual is helped to adapt himself to the Army rather than when attempts are made to adapt the Army to an individual's immature reaction pattern.

The social work officer, by his position and uniform, is easily identified as related to the command structure of the Army and thus representing that with which the soldier may be in conflict. Initially, this can operate as either a negative or a positive force in developing a relationship. In either case, it is through his skill in the development and use of relationship that the social work officer must establish himself as an understanding person who is interested in the soldier and his problems. The Army social worker who identifies himself with the Army and its mission provides the patient with direct evidence of encouragement and understanding in an environment which he may have otherwise concluded was indifferent to his feelings and problems. It is the combination of acceptance and understanding, firm conviction in the importance and necessity to adapt, and belief that the individual can adjust that results in the most effective support. For this reason, the social work officer must be fully aware of his own feelings with reference to the Army and the installation to which assigned. The use of psychological support is particularly helpful with young trainees away from home for the first time and initially unable to adjust to change of environment. Because of the time limits in the Army situation, this technique must be used with caution and only to a degree that enables the soldier to regain or maintain effectiveness.

Clarification is accomplished by psychological support and involves establishment of the right perspective—the separation of the objective and the subjective. The dominant note is the patient's understanding of himself, his environment, and the significant people with whom he is associated. This is of importance in Army social work because the soldier is frequently prone to project his problem upon such factors as the Army structure, his senior commissioned and non-commissioned officers, the locale of his assignment, and the nature of his duties.

Insight development goes beyond clarification in that it includes a reliving within the treatment situation of feelings from both past and current life situations. It is accompanied by some degree of clarification and psychological support. It involves carrying understanding to a deeper level than in clarification. The purpose of this method is to increase the patient's understanding of himself and his situation so that he can manage his life more realistically. Insight development is an advanced casework technique to be employed by experienced caseworkers. Because of the length of time required, the spatial mobility of military personnel and the necessity of expenditure of professional efforts where the largest number can be served, this method is used only infrequently in most military situations.

THE COMPANY COMMANDER AS A COUNSELOR

As indicated in the Introduction, concern for the welfare of men has been an important value among Army officers from the beginning, although the primary sources which have been searched reflect little in the way of techniques that were employed in helping soldiers. Van Steuben, the Prussian Advisor to the Continental Army, advised Lieutenants:

"He should endeavor to gain the love of his men by his attention to everything which may contribute to their health and convenience . . . He should pay attention to their complaints and when well founded, endeavor to get them redress, but discourage them from complaining on every frivolous occasion." *

In today's Army, the Company Commander's or Unit Commander's counseling responsibilities are so extensive as to be difficult to discretely describe. The range of counseling problems which may arise for the Company Commander or his subordinate officers and non-commissioned officers include: military discipline, appearance, effectiveness, personnel management, health of the individual soldier, legal problems, and even the athletic and recreational activities of the soldier. Such personal problems as the following are also in the province of the Company Commander: requests for special privileges, sickness or death in the soldier's family, indebtedness, affairs of the heart, and homesickness.

Fortunately, the Company Commander in today's Army has a number of resources to assist him in the discharge of his tremendous responsibilities. The personnel officer in higher headquarters can assist him in counseling on personal affairs. The Chaplain is available for problems relating to the soldier's spiritual and personal life. The Legal Assistance Officer is available to help the soldier as well as the Company Commander on legal problems. If the soldier has a specific complaint which he would rather not discuss with his Commanding Officer, he has the privilege of talking to the Inspector General. The American Red Cross can help the soldier with family problems through the provision of funds or loans, as well as in getting health and welfare reports concerning the soldier's family, which may be helpful in maintaining his morale. The troop Information and Education Officer can assist the Company Commander in providing for off-duty education, in addition to providing services aimed at keeping the soldier informed.

The most skilled counselors for psycho-social problems available to the Company Commander are the professional officers assigned to the Mental Hygiene Consultation Services located on most military posts. The mental hygiene team consists of psychiatrists, psychologists and social work officers. All of them are professionally trained and experienced in providing both direct counseling services to the individual, as well as consulting with Company Commanders on individual and group problems.

Patricia E. Grant, an officer in the Women's Army Corps, prepared a thesis in connection with her work for a Master's Degree at the University of Pennsylvania in 1956, on the subject of, *Counseling in the Women's Army Corps*. An interesting aspect of her study involved asking some 43 officers and enlisted women what they considered important

* William A. Ganoe, *The History of the United States Army* (New York). (D. Appleton–Century Company, 1942, p. 59.)

characteristics and traits for an effective counselor. The most frequently cited characteristics were these:

a. likes people	i. good listener
b. unselfish	j. humility
c. sincerity	k. confidence in ability to help others
d. understanding of people	l. good health
e. approachability	m. good sense of humor
f. consistency	n. enthusiasm
g. fairness	o. patience
h. sets a good example	p. sympathy

That the Army recognizes the importance of the Company Commander as a counselor is evident in many ways. The basic Field Manual on military leadership, FM 22-100, makes clear a Company Commander's responsibility in this area. Department of the Army Field Manual No. 21-13, *The Soldier's Guide*, informs the soldier that his first resource in the solution of personal problems is his Company Commander. The "Officer's Guide," which is described as a "Ready Reference on Customs and Correct Procedures Which Pertain to Commissioned Officers of the United States Army," makes a special point of the commissioned officer's responsibility in counseling his men. A 1961 Department of the Army Pamphlet No. 355-26, entitled, *Your Soldiers*, forcefully reminds commissioned officers of their responsibilities to the soldier. The memoirs and autobiographies of successful officers are replete with injunctions to the aspiring military leader on the importance of counseling.

CHAPLAINS AS COUNSELORS

Department of the Army Pamphlet No. 16-60, entitled, *The Chaplain As Counselor*, is a 68-page document, intended to serve as a guide for Chaplains in their role of counselor to military personnel and their families. The following is extracted from the Manual, under the heading, "Purpose":

"It outlines the different theories, techniques and circumstances which Chaplains may use advantageously for the improvement of themselves in the interpersonal relationship of counseling. . . . It embodies modern studies, research, and practices of counseling which have made significant contribution in understanding, evaluating and applying principles of psychology for the relief and treatment of personality problems."

But the pamphlet makes clear, under "Purpose," that the Chaplain is not attempting to invade the fields of other disciplines, such as psychiatry, psychology, and social work. The intent is to make intelligent applications of some of the principles and techniques employed by these disciplines in their own work as Chaplains. The pamphlet urges Chaplains to work cooperatively with other professional disciplines engaged in counseling. It states that counseling for Chaplains consists mainly in dealing with military personnel and their families, "In the interpersonal relationship of interviews." It cautions the Chaplain that he is limited in the methods, the intensity, and the results of counseling. It is considered proper for the Chaplain to deal with conscious material, but he ought not to handle unconscious material which he may, by his experience or training, learn to recognize. He must learn when and how to make an appropriate referral to other disciplines better qualified to handle the soldier's problem.

The pamphlet points out that Chaplains can become efficient counselors if they have: "1. A love for people; 2. A desire to help them; 3. A knowledge of their own capabilities and liabilities; and 4. A technical awareness of the dynamics and treatment needed in the counseling relationship."

If the reader is interested in further details, he is encouraged to consult this official pamphlet which, in considerable detail, discusses concepts of counseling, techniques of various types of counseling, qualities and skills of a good counselor, and general problems in counseling.

THE PERSONNEL MANAGEMENT OFFICER AS COUNSELOR

Perhaps no other military occupational specialty is engaged in more day-to-day counseling activities than the personnel officer and his enlisted assistants. From the moment the soldier is inducted into the military service until the time he is separated from active service, he has frequent occasion to be counseled by representatives from his personnel division. Army Regulation 601-270 outlines the personnel officer's responsibility in the area of counseling the new inductee into the military service.

Army Regulation 635-15 outlines responsibility for readjustment and orientation activities at transfer and separation points. Department of the Army Pamphlet 608-2, *The Army Personnel Affairs Handbook*, provides general information of special importance to the soldier. It includes rights, benefits and privileges available to the soldier while on duty in the active Army, as well as the rights, benefits and privileges available to survivors should the Service member die while on active duty. It includes detailed suggestions and advice for arranging and keeping personal affairs in order. Finally, it lists the persons the soldier should contact when counseling and assistance is needed with personal affairs.

In addition to informing the individual Service member and his dependants, *The Personal Affairs Handbook* is also intended as a source book for Commanders, Personnel Officers, Personal Affairs Officers, Survival Assistance Officers, Legal Assistance Officers, and others in discharging the duties of their office.

Another pamphlet, published by the Department of Defense, entitled, *Your Personal Affairs*, describes to the individual Service member the counseling services that are available to him during active service as well as in retirement. These documents are cited only to indicate the importance that the Army attaches to guiding and counseling all members on personnel matters.

The Department of the Army encourages personnel officers and non-commissioned officers to acquire and develop skill in the area of counseling as it relates to the discharge of their responsibilities through attendance at short courses, reading, and consultation with professional counselors.

THE LEGAL ASSISTANCE OFFICER AS COUNSELOR

The Legal Assistance Program was originally adopted on 16 March 1943, with the joint sponsorship of the American Bar Association and the War Department. Because personal legal difficulties may contribute to a state of low morale and inefficiency and result in problems requiring disciplinary action, the Army considered it in the best interests of the Service to provide legal assistance in resolving these difficulties as an effective preventive measure. Army Regulation 608-50 currently prescribes the procedures by which legal assistance is provided.

The Legal Assistance Officer interviews, advises, and assists military personnel and their dependants or, when appropriate, refers such persons to civilian counsel of their choice for needed legal advice and assistance concerning personal-legal problems.

The skill and competence of the Legal Assistance Officer as a counselor is related to his personal aptitude, experience and training, since the Army provides no specific course of instruction in counseling for the Legal Assistance Officer. However, the Judge Advocate General does circulate materials, and encourages Legal Assistance Officers to develop skill in interviewing and other counseling techniques.

COUNSELING IN PERSONNEL MANAGEMENT

Department of the Army Pamphlet No. 600-3, *Career Planning for Army Officers*, states: "The importance of, and requirement for, periodic counseling of officers cannot be overemphasized. Counseling must be initiated early in the officer's career, and conducted periodically, particularly during the junior officer development phases." The pamphlet goes on to say that it is the duty of all officers who have responsibility for an officer's career development to point out, in the initial counseling session, the scope of his work, objectives to be attained, job expectations, standards of performance, and conduct expected. Subsequent counseling sessions should be scheduled in order that necessary guidance can be accomplished prior to the date that an efficiency report must be rendered on the officer. The pamphlet advises the counselor to be informal, personal, and purposeful in manner. The counseling sessions are to be used to inform the officer of his weaknesses and deficiencies, together with positive suggestions for improvement. Only in situations when distances or other geographic and situational exigencies preclude personal interviews, should written communications be used.

Army Regulation 623-105, "Personnel Efficiency Ratings," provides guidelines for formal counseling in connection with officer efficiency reports (The Efficiency Report provides an evaluation of the individual in the form of a standard record designed to meet the requirements of a centralized personnel management system), including the purposes of counseling, how to prepare for a counseling session, techniques useful in the counseling session itself, possible reactions of the counselee, and how to close a counseling session.

The December 1961 issue of *Army Information Digest* (an Army magazine with articles of interest to military personnel) included an article on performance counseling by Major General R. A. Hewitt, in which he expands on the provisions of Army Regulation 623-105. He reminds the reader that Army Regulation 623-105 requires that the Rating Officer counsel the rated officer several months prior to the rendering of an efficiency report. In addition to its use in connection with efficiency reporting, he makes clear counseling is also a means of developing the individual's self-confidence in his ability to accomplish assigned tasks, and to meet new situations and problems. General Hewitt specifically points out that the counseling session should not be a recounting of a list of plus's and minus's on a ledger. It should furnish concrete assistance and provide a basis for increased responsibility. He sees counseling as a tool of leadership.

The Army considers that counseling, as a demanding aspect of leadership, is an exercise in human relations. Both counselor and counseled must be regarded as people, both of whom are more important than any set of techniques. Inexperienced counselors can and should improve their counseling skills by study, in practice, and by discussing counseling problems with more experienced officers. Because techniques of one counselor are not necessarily the best for another, the best guide is—be yourself.*

SUMMARY

Counseling, in an unsophisticated form, has likely been practiced in the United States Army from the beginning, but an organized program of counseling-type services was not instituted until the Civil War, when the United States Sanitary Commission established the Special Relief Department to provide for the individual needs of soldiers not met by the military establishment, itself. The American Red Cross, through its service program for the Armed Forces, is the modern day counterpart of the Special Relief Department.

The emerging and progressive development of counseling services in the Army has been a concomitant of the growth and complexity of the Army as a military bureaucracy. Just as in the Nation as a whole, there developed a need to provide individualized services through institutionalized programs which could no longer be met by the primary group.

The present day Army provides an entire array of counseling services for the soldier from the time he is inducted to the time he is separated, which cover almost every contingency, circumstance, or forseeable need. Most of these counseling services are provided by officers and non-commissioned officers as a part of their primary duty, but other officers, such as the social work officer, provide counseling-type services as their primary duty.

Although the Army provides counseling services for personal, legal, spiritual, emotional, and social problems, effective counseling is considered one of the more demanding responsibilities of troop leaders. This latter should be regarded as the most important area of counseling in the United States Army.

BIBLIOGRAPHY

Army Information Digest. December 1961. pp. 20–25.
Department of the Army Pamphlet 16–60. *The Chaplain as Counselor.* (Washington: U.S. Government Printing Office, 1958.)
Department of the Army Pamphlet 600–3. *Career Planning for Army Officers.* (Washington: U.S. Government Printing Office, 1961.)
Department of the Army Technical Manual 8–241. *Army Social Work.* (Washington: U.S. Government Printing Office, 1958.)
Department of the Army Technical Manual 8–242. *Military Clinical Psychology.* (Washington: U.S. Government Printing Office, 1950.)

* Department of the Army Pamphlet 355–25, *Officer's Call.* 1961. p. 14.

Department of the Army Technical Manual 8–246. *Army Social Work Handbook.* (Washington: U.S. Government Printing Office, 1962.)

The Officer's Guide. The Stackpole Company, Harrisburg, Pa., 1961.

GRANT, PATRICIA E.: "Counseling in the Women's Army Corps." (Unpublished Master's Thesis, University of Pennsylvania, 1956.)

HUGG, WILLIAM STIMMIE: "Counseling Responsibilities of a Company Commander in an Army Training Division." (Unpublished Master's Thesis, Ohio State University, 1950.)

MORGAN, RALPH W.: "Clinical Social Work in the U.S. Army 1947–1959." (Unpublished Doctoral Dissertation, The Catholic University of America, 1960.)

ROONEY, WILLIAM S.: "Army Emergency Relief as a Social Welfare Program." (Unpublished Doctoral Dissertation, Western Reserve University, 1956.)

TORGERSON, FERNANDO G.: "A Historical Study of the Beginning of Individualized Social Services in the United States Army." (Unpublished Doctoral Dissertation, University of Minnesota, 1956.)

Counseling Techniques from the Catholic Point of View

ROBERT P. ODENWALD

Formerly
Professor, Catholic University of America
Washington, D.C.

THERE seems to be a commonly accepted notion that there is "a" Catholic point of view on most public questions, running the gamut from national to international politics, from cold war to hot war, from the matter of over-population in some world areas to the problem of displaced persons in others. However, if one took the trouble to read extensively in Catholic publications that deal with such issues, one would find as wide a difference of opinion among Catholics on questions of this type as there are among any other segment of our country's population.

Here is the essence of the matter: Catholics, by reason and by faith, believe in certain fundamental laws that govern the whole of creation. These laws are of divine origin and are unalterable. One of them is that God holds certain rights over men. Another is that man has certain rights and certain obligations. Once these fundamental concepts are accepted and respected, one is free to discuss any subject and to hold views on any subject, as for example, means of alleviating population problems. (Since contraception is opposed to the fundamental laws, it is not open to question or to argument.) No Catholic has to be a Democrat or a Republican, an isolationist or an interventionist, on religious principles. He is, of course, not allowed to engage in or to foster political dishonesty, or to neglect his duties to the State.

When we consider counseling, a similar situation exists. The Catholic viewpoint limits the therapist and the techniques to be employed only insofar as these may tend to transgress the law of God.

NO CATHOLIC SYSTEM OF COUNSELING

It thus becomes apparent that a single approved system of Catholic counseling is out of the question. Good Catholics, of course, are faithful to their Church dogma, but on subjects beyond its boundaries they form a group of varied thinkers, for the most part independent, and occasionally even radical. It is true that there is a large majority of Catholic opinion that is in agreement concerning many aspects of the counseling relationship, of the techniques to be employed, of the goals to be achieved. However, we should bear in mind that there is no one system of counseling that Catholics as a whole would unanimously endorse. Let us cite as an example the variant opinions held by different Catholic priests, each of whom is prominent in the field of psycho-therapy. The Rev. Charles A. Curran is a strong proponent of non-directive counseling. On the other hand, the Rev. Dom Thomas Verner Moore could probably be classed as a psychobiologist; he strongly favors the psychoanalytic viewpoint. There are a number of attitudes on counseling techniques on which men as far from each other in certain respects would be in agreement because of their religious back-ground. Some of these points—in fact, most of them—will not be limited to Catholics. Non-Catholics who follow the moral law will find themselves in considerable, if not in complete, agreement with this point of view. Although Pope Pius XII frequently spoke or wrote on problems in this field, what he did was simply to restate the divine moral law, or to apply it more specifically. Accordingly, non-Catholics should not be surprised to find themselves in agreement with the Pope's state-ments on psychotherapy, just as any number of non-Catholics found truth and leadership in the statements of Leo XIII, Pius I, Pius XII and others, on such socio-economic problems as the living wage or labor-management relations.

INDIVIDUAL INTEGRITY

Official Catholic dogma has always maintained that Christ died for every individual and that each human is, in a very real sense, a child of God and brother of Christ. Each individual has an inviolable right to be the master of the citadel of his own mind. Even God Himself does not normally usurp this right of man to think his own thoughts and decide on his own actions. Therefore, the counselor must take great care not to apply undue pressure—whether of a psychological or physiological nature—in probing the secrets of a man's mind, without that man's implicit permission and without sufficiently grave cause. From this it follows that anything which is revealed to the counselor during treatment must be kept sacred and inviolate, not only to preserve the good rapport of the counselor-client relationship, but even more importantly, to protect the individual's right to his own integrity. The Code of Canon Law puts the habitually insane on the level of children who have not reached the age of reason. In this connection it should be borne in mind that children have rights as do the insane and the neurotic. Usually the rights of children are respected by professional people. Unfortunately, the same is not always true of the chronically insane or even of neurotics, although it is generally agreed that they are entitled to good care, to protection from those who might take advantage of them, and to the respect of their fellowmen. They, too, are the creatures and the adopted sons of God. This principle of preserving man's integrity forbids any indiscriminate use of the individual for scientific research. Such research may, of course, be conducted, but its goal must be the advancement of therapy. Hazards must be kept to a minimum.

PERSONAL RESPONSIBILITY

Any system of counseling which would deny the responsibility of the individual would soon find itself aiding and abetting personal immorality, social dissolution, and world anarchy. In spite of weaknesses incurred through the sin of our first parents and in spite of the strength of Satan in tempting man to evil, the Church steadfastly maintains that in general man is responsible for his actions and must answer both to the State and to his Creator for his evil deeds. However, in this dogma, the Church is neither rigid nor radical. She is aware of and recognizes many factors which can influence man's choice and thus lessen his responsibility. Psychotherapy also takes into consideration these factors in dealing with disturbed individuals. Emotions, such as fear or envy or lust, and ignorance for which one is not to blame, are such factors, and they lessen man's moral guilt. In its desire to give man "insight" and "control," counseling seeks to remedy the effect of these factors. According to Dom Thomas Verner Moore, "Not only ignorance but also emotional conditions affect human responsibility. Whenever one is in such a violent state that he does not see clearly what he is doing or is driven to act impulsively and without reflection, responsibility is diminished and perhaps to such an extent that it is taken away entirely and the individual is not guilty of doing what is itself a wrong and criminal act."[9]

INDIVIDUAL POTENTIALITY

From what has just been said about the individual and his responsibility it is easy to understand that the Catholic point of view favors the concept that every normal individual possesses tremendous powers of self-direction and of self-improvement. Eugene Cardinal Tisserant in his preface to Father Curran's *Counseling in Catholic Life and Education* writes: "But, among the many things the Catholic Church through her great scholars has given mankind, is an abiding confidence and assurance that man can, with God's help, overcome the disorder of his wounded nature in the saving Grace of Christ."[2] This general theme is the central tenet of the nondirective school of counseling. According to Frederick H. Allen, "At a time when the world needs new orientation to the essential place of the individual, we need to emphasize the strengths of human nature and its capacity for self-responsibility."[1] This concept, however, is not uniquely nondirective, nor is it uniquely Catholic. The Church has always maintained its truth; the nondirective school of counseling has emphasized its importance. Their common interest in the inner strengths of the individual does not necessarily make nondirective counseling the most acceptable form from a Catholic point of view. To make it seem so is a totally unwarranted assumption.

THE COUNSELOR

Because of the attributes of the individual mentioned above, there are certain characteristics a counselor should have, to be properly equipped for his role. The chief of these is altruism. Curran says that "... the counselor must spend himself for others."[4] The substance of the concept is well expressed in the following remarks of Garrigou-Legrange with respect to the spiritual counselor: "His charity ought to be disinterested and to incline him, not to draw hearts to himself but to lead them to God. On this point, Tauler is exacting and says that certain directors who draw souls to themselves are like hunting dogs that eat the hare instead of bringing it back to their master."[5] The counselor's first responsibility is to keep the good of his patient ever foremost in his mind. He must not use his client to satisfy his own needs. He must have, at one and the same time, both disinterestedness and interestedness; the disinterestedness that protects him from the pitfalls of counter-transference, that is, of the transference by the counselor of his suppressed desires upon the client as object, and the interestedness that enables good rapport between himself and the client to be maintained.

THE COUNSELOR NOT A MORALIST

That the counselor should not dominate his patient is a general principle of great significance. This is true even when moral issues are involved. A physician must treat endometritis, even though it may be the direct result of a criminal abortion. As a doctor, it is not his role to pass upon the moral, or for that matter, upon the legal aspects of such an abortion. On the other hand, he cannot morally advise such an abortion or condone it, explicitly or implicitly. These same general principles apply in the field of psychotherapy.

What leads individuals to counseling are, essentially, psychological problems. Moral issues may be involved, but it is not the counselor's function to attack them on moral grounds. He must, it goes without saying, not advocate or condone immorality. This is not always an easy middle course to steer. It is in such situations that a nondirective technique is often the more helpful, for it places responsibility on the client, where it belongs. There remains the possibility that the counselor's silence will be construed by the client as meaning approbation. In such a situation the counselor seems morally bound to express himself in some such manner as the following: "I feel it is my duty to tell you that my own moral principles forbid the course of action that you are proposing. In such matters you are free to follow and, in fact, you must follow your own conscience. I merely want to say that I cannot give you support in this matter." Fortunately, the need for such remarks is rare, but at times they may be necessary.

THE WHOLE MAN

The present-day psychosomatic approach in medicine and in psychology has popularized an ancient concept that was first clearly outlined by Aristotle, and, centuries later, masterfully developed by St. Thomas Aquinas. The Baltimore catechism in 1884 presented the basic idea in these words: "Man is a creature composed of body and soul . . . ." The insoluble riddle resulting from Cartesian dualism is incompatible with the attitude of the Church. So is the mechanistic outlook that flows from modern behavioristic monism. If man is a composite instead of a unit, then his body demands physical treatment and his soul demands psychological treatment; then there is not relationship between body and soul, or between psychotherapy and physical medicine. However, in their work, nearly all medical men and most psychological counselors do not accept such a notion, if not explicitly, or least by implication. A materialistic monism actually would leave no need for counseling as such; it could merely manipulate the environment in some form of situational therapy. Even environmental manipulation would be almost impossible since it implies some choice. There would be nothing left to do but to follow fate. Spiritual monism is not today a popular philosophy. Yet, it would leave a broader field for counseling than, by implication, materialism does. Catholic counseling techniques should concern itself with the whole man and with all the factors that affect him, whether they be psychological or physical. As Curran puts it: "Man is not only motivated by ideas but by what he feels in the dark and deep recesses of his emotional and instinctive being. . . . In the Christian Apostolate we must meet the needs of the whole man."[4]

A HIERARCHY

Since man has many powers or faculties which frequently are in disharmony, it is a quite natural consequence that some type of ordering be initiated, so that the personality may be saved from internal chaos. Perhaps the principal function of counseling is to assist the individual to arrive at a satisfactory state of inner equilibrium. It is generally conceded that, theoretically speaking, reason or intellect must rule over the emotions, and that within the realms of reason and of emotion there are greater goals and lesser goals. Agreement would be less unanimous as to the further application of a hierarchical system as proposed by Garrigou-Legrange: "We ought to live as reasonable beings and also children of God redeemed by His only Son. We must not only submit our passions to reason but subordinate reason itself to faith, to the spirit of faith, and subject all our natural activity to the life of grace and charity, in fidelity to the Holy Ghost."[6] Counseling, whether of a devout Catholic, or of other pious theists, must take into consideration and respect this natural hierarchy in their lives.

A PHILOSOPHY OF LIFE

As a corollary to helping in the development of an inner hierarchy, the counselor assumes some responsibility for establishing a philosophy of life in his client. It is only by such a course of action that psychological gains made in the counseling situation become permanently valuable to the individual. One is reminded of Gordon Allport's remarks in this connection: ". . . a third, integrative factor is required in the mature personality, namely a unifying philosophy of life." And later he writes: "Religion is the search for a value underlying all things, and as such is the most comprehensive of all the possible philosophies of life."[2] Here is another reason why a counselor should not impose his own philosophy of life on a client. The counselor can and should encourage the client to formulate and adopt a sound philosophy of life, but it would be beyond his function and undesirable, for him to decide what that philosophy of life should be. Furthermore, the counselor must be attuned to the possibility that his client's philosophy of life may be more noble than is his own. He must guard against evaluating such concepts as out of touch with reality.

GOAL OF SECURITY

Everyone, consciously or unconsciously, seeks security. From the security of the womb until life ends in the surety of the grave, man strives to secure some guarantee of stability. Insecurity is the principal factor that brings people to psychological counselors. The client has, previous to the initial interview, set up in his own mind certain expectations as to counseling. He hopes and expects that counseling will bring him security. He may be ready and willing to go through the stress of greater insecurity necessitated by the counseling techniques; but the goal is always the same. When all is over, he must be able to feel secure. There are situations, however, where it seems impossible to bring a person to the peace of security. What does one tell the incurable cancer patient? What does one say to the parents whose only son has just been killed in an accident? What philosophy can a mother adopt whose husband is an habitual drunkard? How does one help a marriage relationship when the children are hungry and inadequately clothed? For economic as well as for other reasons, situational therapy is not always feasible. Frequently the only real security that individuals can be offered is the spiritual security of resignation to the will of God and trust in His loving care. Only in terms of such spiritual values can some people be given inner peace, for the problems of life for some persons are impossible of happy solution. Listen to Bishop Fulton J. Sheen: "The modern soul is not going to God through order in nature, as he did a generation ago, but through his disordered self; he is looking for God not through a search for a cause of the cosmos, but through a yearning for redemption from his own frustration."[11]

SOURCE OF MORALITY

This seems an appropriate place to say something about the Catholic opinion regarding the origin of moral law. Many counselors maintain their adherence to what they refer to as "moral standards." But these may be different from the moral standards of the Church. The reason for the difference arises principally from the fact that the Church recognizes that morality is based on the immutable natural law given by God to man, while others hold that morality is based upon and essentially equivalent to social norms. Duncan Whitehead, in an interesting discussion of changes in morality, as an editorial comment in the *Psychiatric Quarterly*, defines the attitude of "social moralists." "By 'morality' is meant the principles generally accepted at any time or place to govern right conduct; by 'immorality,' the disregard of moral principle and the practice of conduct held to be wrong." Later, Whitehead remarks, "It is primarily as a moral creature that psychiatry deals with man. The well-adjusted man, who is psychiatry's goal, is the man who lives at peace with his morals. The man whose life and morals clash is the sick man we, as psychiatrists, treat."[12] This is further evidence for the opinion that the counselor should not become a moralist, since the norms of morality are not the same for all. As Allport mentions, in *Personality, a Psychological Interpretation*, quoted above, it is dealing in ethics to say how one ought to behave; it is both legitimate, however, and essential for the psychologist to point out the probable consequences of certain behavior.

CONSCIENCE

A Catholic point of view on counseling techniques would hardly be complete without some mention of conscience. Conscience has been equated by some with the superego. However, the superego has the same source and the same criterion of excellence as has "morality," based, as they both are, on social standards. True conscience has its source from God through society, and it has the criterion of its validity in the moral law of God. Conscience is something more than the superego; it demands settlement with God while the superego demands only that one's peace be made with society. Psychotherapy may relieve man of the *guilt feelings* resulting from his depravities, but it cannot relieve him of his *guilt*. The superego may be satisfied, but conscience will not be quieted until God is asked for forgiveness. Thus, counseling can never, for Catholics, substitute for the Sacrament of Penance, nor in the case of others can it substitute for repentance. Paul J. Glenn's description of conscience is a good one: "Conscience is the intellectual consciousness or reasoned awareness of right or wrong in a situation here and now to be judged. ... It is the same cold reason with which we work out a problem in mathematics—only, to be entitled to the name of conscience, it must be engaged upon issues of right and wrong, good and bad, and not upon mathematical quantities."[7] Counseling cannot remove guilt for the simple reason that it cannot undo the offense to God. As Thomas Aquinas states: "Now the past has become a kind of necessity, since what has been done cannot be undone."[3]

SEX COUNSELING

Sex counseling or sex education, for individuals when they are ready for it, falls within the scope of Catholic counseling. Such sex counseling should not be given in groups of mixed sexes, nor should the more intimate details be given before large groups. Sex instruction should be individualized and is best given by the parents, but it may be given by any conscientious person with a mature outlook on sex, one who will treat the subject with the reverence and delicacy to which this divine institution is entitled. Such a counselor must have a mature attitude toward sex. He or she will show respect for the subject and for those who have problems or questions with regard to it. The keenest skills of the counseling profession should turn their attention to the problem of imparting sex knowledge and counsel to the young people of our land. Well might the words of Pope Pius XII be applied to sex counseling: "Give them also a knowledge of their own personality and thus of the greater treasures of freedom; train their minds to sound criticism, but at the same time imbue them with a sense of Christian humility, of just submission to the laws and the duty of mutual dependence among men."[10]

VOCATIONAL COUNSELING

"Vocation" is here used in the sense of a state in life rather than as a profession. This is the special aspect of counseling of particular significance from the Catholic point of view. The basic principles of counseling as well as most of the techniques are applicable in this specialized field. Particular attention must be given to allow full freedom of choice as to vocation. Because of docility in the personality, many who come for vocational counseling are influenced by the counselor to enter the religious life, or in some cases, not to enter it, and this may be to the detriment of the individual, and of society. In dealing with the problem of choosing a state in life it is important to discuss with the individual the pros and cons of the various possibilities. It is quite wrong to emphasize God's will as the course to be followed. This leaves the individual more emotionally disturbed and less capable than before of deciding the issue on the basis of reason. If he feels that he is the master of his own fate, that he can freely choose between one or another state of life, then he has a better perspective for considering and evaluating the factors in his own personality and the conditions of a particular life's role. Then and only then can he decide the degree of compatibility or incompatibility between the two.

There is a special personality problem involved in religious counseling. This is well expressed by Father George A. Kelly: "It is not inconceivable that young men and women might enter religion without having accomplished any real separation from the parental apron strings. . . . In fact, even for those who are not unduly dependent, the religious life of its very nature contains certain dangers to proper growth in maturity. This type of life calls for much more dependence than is normally had in adult life; if this is pressed too far it can readily change childlikeness into childishness."[8] The wise counselor will weigh the maturity of the individual against his dependency. If necessary, the client may be helped to greater maturity before or even after joining the religious life. If the dependency needs seem to be the primary motive for entering the religious life, then, of course, the client should be given this insight.

CONCLUSION

St. Thomas Aquinas, the Catholic Church's greatest philosopher, learned much from his pagan predecessor, Aristotle. Thomas kept within the bounds of his own faith. Guided by his own reason, he developed to full flower what is now called the *"philosophia perennis."* In other words, St. Thomas kept an open mind with respect to the thoughts and experimental data of those who went before him. Much the same holds true for the Catholic viewpoint on counseling techniques. Valuable data are being arrived at experimentally; various counseling techniques are constantly being tested and developed. Any number of new and stimulating theories of the personality are being discussed. As we have observed, the Catholic viewpoint demands only that the bounds of morality be respected. Experimental data are welcomed and encouraged. Theories are discussed as freely and as wholeheartedly among Catholics as they are among other groups. With regard to techniques of counseling, there is no specific Catholic approbation or disapproval. Here, as in the medical specialities, the wisest rule is for the counselor to be governed in his choice of techniques by two considerations: his patient's needs, and his own intelligent use of whatever techniques appear best suited to these very needs.

BIBLIOGRAPHY

1. ALLEN, FREDERICK H.: 1942. *Psychotherapy with Children*, p. 306. New York: W. W. Norton.
2. ALLPORT, GORDON W.: 1948. *Personality, A Psychological Interpretation*, pp. 214, 225. New York: Henry Holt and Co.
3. AQUINAS, THOMAS: *Summas Theologica* II Q 49, A7, 8.
4. CURRAN, CHARLES A.: 1952. *Counseling in Catholic Life and Education*. New York: Macmillan.
5. GARRIGOU-LEGRANGE, R.: 1947. *The Three Ages of the Interior Life*, Vol. I, p. 262. St. Louis: B. Herder Book Co.
6. ——: 1947. *The Love of God*, pp. 299–300. St. Louis: B. Herder Book Co.
7. GLENN, PAUL J.: 1936. *Psychology*. St. Louis: B. Herder Book Co.

8. KELLY, GERALD S. J.: 1947. "Emotional Maturity." *Review for Religious*, 7, 1.
9. MOORE, DOM VERNER: 1937. Principles of Ethics, Philadelphia: I.P. Lippincott, p. 34.
10. PIUS XII: 1949. "Papal Guidance for Teachers." *Catholic Action* **31**, p. 18.
11. SHEEN, FULTON J.: 1949. *Techniques for the Convert Makers*. New York: The Paulist Press.
12. WHITEHEAD, DUNCAN: 1954. Editorial Comment. *The Psychiatric Quarterly*, **28**, 323–328.
13. Academy of Religion and Mental Health: Religion, Culture and Mental Health: Symposium 1959. Academy of Religion and Mental Health, NYU Press, 1961.
14. Academy of Religion and Mental Health: Religion in the Developing Personality: Proceedings of 2nd Academy Symposium, 1958. Academy of Religion and Mental Health, NYU Press, 1960.
15. BIDDLE, W. EARL: 1955. *Integration of Religion and Psychiatry*. New York: Macmillan.
16. BRACELAND, FRANCIS J.: 1955. *Faith, Reason and Modern Psychiatry: Sources for a Synthesis*. New York: J. P. Kenedy and Sons.
17. CAVANAUGH, JOHN R. (Ed.): 1957. *Fundamental Marriage Counseling: A Catholic Viewpoint*. Milwaukee: Bruce Publ. Co.
18. CURRAN, CHARLES A.: 1952. *Counseling in Catholic Life and Education*. New York: Macmillan.
19. DAMAL, WILLIBALD: 1955. *Pastoral Psychology in Practice*, trans. by Conway, Joachin, W. New York: J. P. Kenedy and Sons.
20. EWALT, JACK R., STRECKER, EDWARD A., and EBAUGH, FRANKLIN: 1957. *Practical Clinical Psychiatry* 8th ed. New York: Blakiston Div., McGraw–Hill.
21. GEMELLI, AGOSTINO: 1955. *Psychoanalysis Today*. New York: P. J. Kenedy and Sons.
22. HAHN, MILTON E. and MACLEAN, MALCOLM S.: 1955. *Counseling Psychology*, 2nd ed. New York: McGraw–Hill.
23. KELLY, Rev. GEORGE A.: 1959. The Catholic Family Handbook, Random House.
24. ———: 1958. The Catholic Marriage Manual, Random House.
25. ODENWALD, ROBERT P.: 1958. *Your Child's World*, Random House, 1958.
26. ———: 1955. "Medical Guide to Vocations" by Biot and Galimard, translated from the French and adapted into English by Robert P. Odenwald, M.D., F.A.P.A., the Newman Press, Westminster, Md.
27. ———: 1958. "Psychiatric Factors in Marriage Counselling and Counselling Problem Parents with Problem Children" as part of a book *Marriage Education and Counselling* edited by Alphonse H. Clemens. The Catholic University of America Press.
28. ———: 1961. "How to Maintain a Cheerful Attitude," as part of the book, *The Catholic Guide to Expectant Motherhood*, Random House.
29. ODENWALD, ROBERT P.: Mental Hygiene and the Priest, *The Homiletic and Pastoral Review*, December 1950.
30. ———: Psychiatric and Religious Aspects of Marriage Problems, *Marriage and Family Living*, February 1952.
31. ———: Counseling the Homosexual, *The Priest*, December 1953.
32. ———: Mental Health and the Schoolroom, *Education*, Sept. 1954, Vol. 75, pp.18–23.
33. ———: The Priest as Counselor: The Normal Personality, *Conference Bulletin of the Archdiocese of New York*, Feb. 1956, Vol. 33, No. 1.

34. ——: The Priest as Counselor: Family Counseling, *Conference Bulletin of the Archdiocese of New York*, Sept. 1956, Vol. 33, No. 2.

35. ——: Punishment From the Viewpoint of Psychiatry, *The Catholic Lawyer*, Spring 1960, Vol. 6, No. 2.

36. RINGEL, ERWIN and VAN LUN, WENZEL, trans. by Mayrick Booth: 1954. *The Priest and the Unconscious*. Westminster, Md.: Newman Press.

37. ROYCE, JAMES E. S. J.: 1955. *Personality and Mental Health*. Milwaukee: The Bruce Publishing Co.

38. STERN, KARL: 1954. *The Third Revolt: A Study of Psychiatry and Religion*. New York: Harcourt Brace.

39. TERRUWE, A. A. A.: 1959. *The Priest and the Sick in Mind*. Transl. by Baars, C. W. and Aumann, J. London, Burns & Oates. New York: J. P. Kenedy and Sons.

40. WATKINS, JOHN G.: 1960. *General Psychotherapy*. Springfield, Ill.: C. C. Thomas.

41. WHITE, ERNEST: 1955. *Christian Life and the Unconscious*. New York: Harper.

42. YOUNG, RICHARD K. and MEIBURG, A. L.: 1960. *Spiritual Therapy, How the Physician, Psychiatrist and Minister Collaborate in Healing*. New York: Harper.

43. VANDERVELDT, JAMES H. and ODENWALD, ROBERT P.: 1957. *Psychiatry and Catholicism*. New York, Toronto, and London: Blakiston Div. McGraw-Hill.

The Protestant Point of View in Counseling Techniques

WALTER HOUSTON CLARK

Professor
Andover Newton Theological School
Newton Center, Mass.

PSYCHOLOGICAL research in recent years has made much of three separate approaches to human relations: the *authoritarian*, the *laissez-faire*, and the *democratic*. These terms may be said to outline roughly three different emphases in Protestant counseling, and since they have evolved successively one out of the other, we may start with a brief historical introduction to the subject.

The traditional role of the Protestant pastor, and often of the elders in a Christian community, has been that of a mentor and a custodian of the morals of the parish. This concept has by no means been completely outgrown, and there are many churches and denominations where the Christian duty of the counselor is to point out to others the way they should go. The purpose of the old-time, and some new-time, evangelists has been to soften the hardness of sinners to the end that a conviction of the enormity of their transgressions will prepare the way for more individual approaches, which might be thought of as counseling in nature.

But even though, psychologically considered, the results of much of this type of personal evangelism have been superficial in nature it must not be thought that such techniques have been completely devoid of constructive effects. The Oxford Group, now known as Moral Re-Armament, a movement rooted in the Protestant evangelistic tradition, may be used as an example both of the strength and weakness of this approach to counseling. The Group features four Moral Absolutes as a rule of life together with the Guidance of God as the effective means of achieving goodness. Particularly in the past it has emphasized an experience of conviction of sin in the individual not only through a program of public witness but very largely through personal contact by members, which might be considered an informal mixture of counseling and group therapy. There have been cases where the experience of sin has been very directively manipulated in private interview. The author has demonstrated that this has sometimes resulted in a very disillusioning reaction to religious experiences, but probably more often in profound personality change rivaling and perhaps surpassing in depth occasionally the results of the most skilled efforts of modern psychotherapy.*

This movement has now a world-wide following, while its techniques have been adopted, though in less provocative form, by Alcoholics Anonymous, religiously oriented therapy for alcoholics, of whose value there is little serious doubt. Here the authoritarian nature of the counseling therapy has been considerably softened, though it is still directive in the sense that certain procedures are set up and prescribed for every alcoholic who sincerely wishes cure.

These two movements, stemming from the Protestant tradition, though not confined to it, will also serve to illustrate early attempts to make religious counseling self-conscious about methods to be used. Alcoholics Anonymous will also illustrate another trend in counseling: cooperation between psychological science and religion, for Alcoholics Anonymous has received much commendation and study from psychologists. In another form, one of the chief milestones in this cooperation was the collaboration of the physician, Richard Cabot, and the clergyman, Russell Dicks, in the writing of *The Art of Ministering to the Sick* in 1936.

Here can be seen an important effect of scientific thinking on Protestant views of counseling, the lessening of authoritarian emphasis. This has led in some cases to the other extreme, a recommendation of *laissez-faire*, where the counselor is supposed to develop an almost compulsive horror of imposing his views on the counselee in any way.

The psychologist who has most strongly influenced this stream of Protestant counseling theory in recent years has been Carl Rogers with his leadership of the non-directive movement. The most articulate spokesman for the Protestant counseling theory in this tradition has been Seward Hiltner of Princeton Theological Seminary.

But even as Rogers himself has begun to realize that complete non-direction is an impossibility, so that he now refers to his school as

* See *The Oxford Group*, Chapters 2 and part of 3.

"client-centered" rather than "non-directive," so there has been a parallel development in Protestant counseling theory. An illustration of this would be the emphasis developed at Boston University School of Theology's Counseling Center, whose Director, Dr. Paul E. Johnson, has described what he calls the method of "Responsive Counseling" in his book, *Psychology of Pastoral Care*.* While the method is hardly distinguishable from Hiltner's in practice, it differs in theory in that it acknowledges more explicitly that insights developed in the counseling situation are the joint products of both counselor and counselee working together. This justifies the identification of Johnson's method as *democratic*, rather than *authoritarian* or *laissez-faire*.

While the *authoritarian* or highly directive method of counseling among Protestants is by no means dead, the *laissez-faire* and *democratic* approaches are much more self-conscious and currently influential, so that our exposition will apply more particularly to them. Since the distinction between them is so slight in practice, we will not use our limited space to underscore their differences.

The essentials of these Protestant techniques are identical with those advocated by the non-directive or client-centered school of Rogers. These involve: (1) the assumption that the aim of the counseling interview is that of personality change; (2) the fact that the interview is initiated by, or at least involves, a felt need on the part of the counselee, who comes to the counselor with a view to expressing this need; (3) the receiving of confidences by the counselor in an atmosphere of acceptance involving neither censure nor approval; (4) understanding by the counselor not simply of the words of the counselee but more especially of the feelings behind the words; (5) an accurate reflection by the counselor of these ideas and feelings so that the counselee may objectify them and clarify the issues of his problems in his own mind; and (6) a belief underlying this process of the capacity of the counselee to resolve the issues for himself and so to grow in self-knowledge and maturity.

The question next arises: How do Protestant religious concepts modify these techniques and distinguish their religiously oriented function from their secular use? Here are four points of fundamental significance. It should be noted in passing that these techniques commend themselves to Protestants in the more liberal traditions.

(1) Behind the counseling process stand certain theological preconceptions. In simplest and most essential form these are the acknowledgement of the fatherhood of God and the brotherhood of man. This is not a mere form of words, as secularists might tend to believe, but a

* See Chapter 3.

COUNSELING TECHNIQUES FROM PROTESTANT VIEWPOINT   323

conviction which, when sincerely held, affects the relationship between counselor and counselee. It supports and strengthens the special concern that the counselor feels for the counselee. The counselee is similarly supported in his expectations of this concern on the part of the counselor, which means that he will more readily respond with confidence to the warmth and acceptance that is offered. Thus the relationship between the two is enriched by the theological dimension when "two face a Third," as Cabot and Dicks have put it.

(2) The relationship is of course importantly affected by the fact that the counselor is usually a clergyman. Not only is the counselee more apt to accept implicitly a commonly held theological position but he expects certain ethical attitudes. Though these are not injected into the interviewing process by the counselor, they frequently are by the counselee, who, through sermons and other methods, has been instructed in Christian teachings and is acutely aware of them. While these may have sharpened his guilt feelings often to a neurotic degree, and so make the initial contact more painful, nevertheless it may be the confidence of the counselee in the moral and religious integrity of his counselor that brings him to this particular source of help. It is this source of anxiety in guilt feelings that makes it important for a clergyman to avoid censure about ethical and moral matters. Once the counselee discovers that his disclosures are accepted with understanding but without censure, he feels freer to explore the implications of ethical behavior before someone he knows to have certain pretty well-defined standards of right and wrong. Hence in many cases this unspoken factor eventually makes for a greater feeling of support and consequent lowering of anxiety.

(3) Particularly when the counselor is a clergyman, the Protestant emphasis is on what he *is* as a person. This is not emphasized as so necessary when the religious tradition is sacramental and the clergyman is thought of merely as the instrument of divine authority or the ordained agent of God, as in the sacrament of Confession and accompanying Absolution. The therapeutic effects of the Sacraments operate in another way. The Protestant has always expected something additional of his ministers in the way of righteous living, and insists on looking on his Pastor as to some degree the prototype of God or Christ. Even though the counselor may deprecate this flattering estimate of his virtues he cannot escape the implications for the success of his counseling; for it is not only what he says in his sermons but how he lives his life that will determine how many seek his help in private. Consequently, more than the secular counselor, he is ready to sacrifice his time and convenience; while the counselee, on his part, is ready to interpret the acceptance that he discovers as an expression of that forgiveness he has

associated with God. Indeed, when authoritarian pastors have been involved, it is the very lack of an assurance of the "forgiving" attitude that has led the Protestant often to prefer a psychiatrist, particularly when concerned about matters of morality. This has been one of the reasons for the decline of authoritarianism in Protestant counseling.

Yet even when this forgiveness is suggested by the manner of the counselor it has not assured the client; for it is not merely that client-centered theory holds that the counselee is ultimately responsible for his own decisions, but Protestant tradition itself has always held that the individual is held to account for his own transactions with God. The attitude of the counselor merely reminds the religious counselee of the forgiveness of God and so makes easier the reconciliation that is part of the process of growth.

(4) Not so much in the actual counseling interview as in what may be called the "pre-counseling" situation, the prospective counselee is made aware of the value of the *ideal*. Though in the very process of aspiration there lurks the danger of an anxiety-producing situation, religious tradition has always insisted on the paramount demands of Truth and the importance of certain Absolutes. The very concept of God involves erecting ideals of perfection that no man can achieve, and much of that measure of moral virtue achieved by mankind owes itself to a certain level of tension involving some anxiety. Though the average secularist counselor will not be unmindful of the importance of religious values in the personality structure of his client, he may feel that these should be sacrificed if they interfere with adjustment. The religious counselor, on the other hand, though he acknowledges the importance of adjustment, is likely to discover certain religious values that in comparison make personal adjustment pale into insignificance. The Protestant duty of discovering God for oneself, for example, has led in the past to much personal conflict and tribulation. Yet taking things on the whole Protestantism would not exchange this emphasis for even a considerable measure of the mental health that may have gone by the board in the search for God.

The Protestant searcher in his quest for the ideal may have lost his way, and in his sense of estrangement may long for reconciliation with what he identifies as God. This quest assumes a certain loneliness as an essential part of the process. The Protestant counselor consequently, no matter how consecrated and pure an individual he himself may be, recognizes the arena in which the counselee is struggling as holy ground. Aside from according the support of his acceptance and understanding from the sidelines, he keeps hands off, knowing that in the last analysis the final decisions, for good or evil, must be those of the individual. In this process previously accepted teachings about the Ideal will play their parts, along with the somewhat paradoxical abdication of authority by the very individual who may originally have been responsible for the implanting in the mind of the counselee the teachings that are now causing so much anxiety and confusion.

It is obvious that the problem of the exact role of the Ideal in counseling is a very complex one, and we cannot do justice to it here. It is subject to distortion and may appear in very unwholesome forms. But on the other hand it may be the issue whose confrontation may spell the attainment of wholeness on a much deeper level than if mere "adjustment" were the goal of the philosophy of both counselor and counselee. It will suffice here to point out that this is an aspect of the counseling process that will have a place in situations under Protestant influences.

It remains to make a few brief comments on religious resources that are not part of the counseling process proper but which may be used by the Protestant counselor, particularly when he is a clergyman.

The Bible. As the traditional source of authority and instruction the Bible will in some way influence counseling process under Protestant auspices. Usually this will be an important implicit element in the pre-counseling *Gestalt*, though often the teaching of the Bible may be an explicit point at issue. Its wisdom may illuminate, or be illuminated by the experience of the counselee. On the other hand, confusion may arise through a too narrow interpretation of its words, and the counselor may have to explain the difference between literal and spiritual truth. The insight into God's nature revealed by the Parable of the Prodigal Son, for example, is of considerably more importance than whether the story had a literal foundation or not.

Doctrine. Much the same comments might be made as to the place of church doctrine, which may often give rise to conflicts and confusions to be resolved in the counseling session. Again the counselor may be called upon to clarify and explain doctrine, but if he is well advised he will not attempt to force articles of faith on the counselee. Authoritative utterances on doctrine may be appropriate in the pulpit, but not in the counseling chamber if the counselee is to benefit from the growth consequent to his working out a faith of his own.

Sacraments, rites, and liturgy. When he senses that it would be appropriate, the counselor may make it clear to the counselee that he is welcome to partake of the sacraments and participate in services of the Church. These may have the effect of consolidating gains made during counseling. The counselor here may find it wise to warn against the essentially magical use of the sacraments, where they are assumed to be merely a kind of automatic means of appropriating the Grace of God or influencing Him rather than a means of strength as a road to greater insight into His will for man.

The Church as a Community. More obvious from the psychological point of view is the tremendous asset available to the pastoral counselor in the church community as a resource for group therapy. Often the counseling problem will involve a sense of estrangement or rejection on the part of the counselee. Through participation in church activities the individual may find acceptance that will consolidate inner psychological growth. Furthermore, there are some forward-looking churches which not only have sponsored counseling programs, but have organized group therapy as well; as in the case of the Marble Collegiate Church in New York City.

Prayer and meditation. Many of those who come to their pastors for counseling are people of piety for whom prayer may be a comforting or strengthening experience. Consequently all theorists in the field of pastoral counseling devote some attention to the use of this resource. While its most appropriate use may be with the sick and bereaved, there is always the danger that it may be overdone. The judicious counselor will sense when and with whom it will be effective. Here again the counselor must be careful that prayer is not conceived as a piece of magic, and so constitute merely an escape mechanism. One of its leading functions is to quicken a sense of relatedness between counselor and counselee as well as to make more real to both of them their relation to the Divine. Meditation as well is often encouraged as a means of psychological appraisal and spiritual direction.

This short sketch of the Protestant point of view in counseling has attempted to highlight some of the chief emphases distinguishing it from other points of view. In these emphases there has been some inevitable distortion, since for the most part the total counseling process does not differ so very markedly from other types in various psychological traditions. It has been remarked that nearly all approaches to counseling may show their achievements, and it has been suggested that the essential element common to all of them is the presence of an accepting counselor willing to devote his entire attention to the counselee in identifying understandingly his problems and feelings. It may well be that this fundamental attitude rather than a particular technique is the key to therapeutic result. But if so the Protestant sees in this merely the expected outcome and confirmation of the value of Christian concern for the welfare of the individual.

BIBLIOGRAPHY

ANONYMOUS: 1942. *Alcoholics Anonymous.* New York: Works Publishing Co.

BOISEN, ANTON T.: 1936. *The Exploration of the Inner World: a Study of Mental Disorder and Religious Experience.* New York: Harper.

CABOT, R. C. and DICKS, R. L.: 1936. *The Art of Ministering to the Sick.* New York: Macmillan.

CLARK, W. H.: 1951. *The Oxford Group: its History and Significance.* New York: Bookman Association.

HILTNER, S.: 1949. *Pastoral Counseling.* New York: Abingdon-Cokesbury Press.

HILTNER, SEWARD: 1958. *A Preface to Pastoral Theology.* New York: Abingdon.

JOHNSON, PAUL E.: 1953. *Psychology of Pastoral Care.* New York: Abingdon-Cokesbury Press.

KEMP, CHAS. F.: 1961. *The Pastor and Vocational Counseling.* Chicago: Bethany Press.

KEW, C. E. and KEW, C. J.: 1953. *You Can be Healed.* New York: Prentice Hall.

MAY, ROLLO, *et al.*: 1956. *Existence: a New Dimension in Psychiatry and Psychology.* New York: Basic Books.

MORRIS, C. E.: 1954. *Counseling with Young People.* New York: Association Press.

MOSER, L. E.: 1962. *Counseling: a Modern Emphasis in Religion.* Englewood Cliffs, N. J.: Prentice Hall.

OATES, WAYNE E. (Ed.): 1959. *An Introduction to Pastoral Counseling.* Nashville: Broadman Press.

OUTLER, ALBERT C.: 1954. *Psychotherapy and the Christian Message.* New York: Harper.

Pastoral Psychology. *A Monthly containing Many Articles dealing with the Protestant Approach to Counseling.*

ROGERS, C. R., *et al.*: 1951. *Client-centered Therapy.* Boston: Houghton Mifflin Co.

TILLICH, P.; 1952. *The Courage to Be.* New Haven: Yale Univ. Press.

WISE, C. A.: 1951. *Pastoral Counseling: its Theory and Practice.* New York: Harper.

The Rabbi as Counselor

HENRY ENOCH KAGAN

Rabbi, Sinai Temple
Mount Vernon, N.Y.

THIS essay on the Rabbi as Counselor will include first, a theoretical rationale to justify the Rabbinic counseling role and second, some observations on how a modern Rabbi with a contemporary psychiatric orientation can function in this role. In the theoretical part we shall deal with the impact of psychiatry on religion with special reference to Judaism and in the functional part we shall deal with the pastoral counseling techniques especially applicable to the Rabbi.

There is confusion about the relation between religion and psychiatry in general because, too often, the experts do not know what their opponents mean either by religion or psychiatry. Partly because they do not speak the same language and are confounded by semantic differences, religionists and psychiatrists appear to be in an irreconcilable conflict over the nature of man. It will be helpful if we begin with at least some simple definition of religion and of psychiatry. Because man has been engaged in defining religion for five thousand years and has produced a tremendous sacred literature in half a dozen major faiths a simple definition of religion is obviously not easy. The same may be said about psychiatry. Even though by comparison with religion it is less than one hundred years old psychiatry now also boasts of a voluminous literature in half a dozen different schools of thought. Indeed, some psychiatric denominations are as dogmatic as some theological ones. Nonetheless, at the risk of oversimplification we shall advance two definitions based upon the semantic meaning of the words religion and psychiatry.

The word religion could be derived from the latin "religere" meaning to bind together or also from "religo" which means to feel cared for in opposition to "negligo" meaning to be neglected. Using both origins, religion becomes a faith which helps man to relate himself to himself, to others and to the world by believing there is a divine power in the cosmos which cares for him. Psychiatry, derived from the Greek "psyche" meaning soul and "iatria" meaning healing, is a method for healing sick souls. Religion is a self-confidence producing belief; psychiatry is a scientific therapy to cure the loss of self-confidence.

The specific sphere of religion is the knowledge of God or theology. The specific sphere of dynamic psychology is the knowledge of the nervous and mental functions of man. However, both ask questions about the general nature of man and how he lives as well as ought to live, and the area wherein they overlap may be defined as the psycho-religious experience. When, through prayer or ritual, man has a religious experience, it is of course irreverent as well as futile to inquire about the effect of this experience on God; but it should not be irreverent to study the effect of this experience on man. To my knowledge, scientific research on the psychological effect of prayer upon man has never been attempted, but such a study could fittingly challenge the combined talents of the theologian and the psychologist. All great advances in knowledge in our day have resulted from combinations of learning and new hyphenated terms have been created. Today we speak of bio-chemistry, geo-politics, socio-economics, psychosomatic medicine and cybernetics. Discoveries have been made because separate disciplines have joined together in their pursuit. Indeed, the anticipated voyage of manned spaceships to the planets millions of miles away will be the direct result of such a development; the intellectual revolution which turned physics away from a rigid deterministic view of the nature of the universe to an uncertain, inexact, probable and contingent view. The great mathematician, Norbert Wiener, who has traced this evolution in physics not to Einstein but to Gibbs has written: "one interesting change that has taken place is that in a probabilistic world we no longer deal with quantities and statements which concern a specific real universe as a whole, but ask instead questions which may find their answers in a large number of similar universes." In other words, one set of knowledge which excludes all others cannot survive in the Space Age.

In any team approach, each member must surrender the idea that he possesses a monopoly on truth. This is especially difficult for the religionist for he is committed to a dogma and vested ecclesiastic authority. When Copernican astronomy in the sixteenth century disproved the centrality of the earth, it took the Catholic church more than a century to accept the place of our small earth in the cosmic planetary system. When Darwinian biology in the nineteenth century

22

denied man's self-glorifying claim of miraculous separateness from the animal kingdom in the evolutionary scale, fundamentalist Protestantism reacted violently and in many places still refuses to assimilate the new knowledge. The intellectual challenge to religion in the twentieth century is Freudian psychology which took from man divine will and made him subject to primordial instinct. Of these scientific challenges to religion it would seem psychiatry would be the least difficult to assimilate into religious thinking. Psychiatry deals with a subject which is not only religion's primary interest but also with a subject which is invisible. Psychiatry may call this subject the psyche and religion the soul, but both are not available for exact scientific terms of measurement. The second half of this century finds the conflict between religion and psychiatry in a new phase in which, in all probability, religion will make adjustments to Freud as it did to Darwin and Copernicus.

The effect of Sigmund Freud on the religious thinking of our times is as revolutionary as the effect of the new atomic science on physics. As the new physics has made it possible to explore formerly inaccessible regions of space, so Freudian psychoanalysis has made it possible to explore previously inaccessible regions of the mind. The depth psychology of the unconscious has laid the foundation of a new science of human relations which, although it is still in its early stages of development, has already vitally affected religion.

At first, religion was antagonistic to depth psychology, not because of its methods, but because of its theory. Freud's emphasis on sexuality and its sublimation as the primary civilizing motive, as well as his contention that man created God instead of vice versa, blinded religion to the significance of his therapeutic method. When Freud's theories were radically modified by the rebellion of his former students, Alfred Adler and Carl Jung, who pointed out, respectively, the importance of the inferiority complex and of the collective unconscious, religion passed from the phase of belligerency to peaceful co-existence and is now in active cooperation. Such influential theologians as the Christian Paul Tillich, who encourages the use of psychiatry when it differentiates between pathological and existential anxiety, and the Jewish Martin Buber, who advocates a psycho-synthetic method in which the private man to man counseling situation becomes in itself the best way to an awareness of God, have both become rallying points for the alliance between religion and psychiatry. Dr. R. Finley Gayle in his inaugural address as the President of the American Psychiatric Association took note of this common interest religion and psychiatry have in guiding the unconscious motives of man when he said "for the clergyman as well as for the psychiatrist the question is not so much *whether* he will deal with some of the unconscious material, as it is *how* will he deal with it." It is much more important for the welfare of man that religion arrive at a working alliance with psychiatry than with astronomy or biology. The revolution of the earth about the sun and the evolution of the human species deal with external material aspects of life, but psychiatry deals with the functioning of man's inner life, with his very being. The problem of the twentieth century is less a matter of science than a matter of the science of human relationships. As Charles de Gaulle aptly remarked "We may well go to the moon, but that's not very far. The greatest distance we have to cover still lies within us." We know very much about the atomic structure of nature and more and more about interplanetary communication. We know very much less about the structure of personality and how humans may control their inner selves to achieve a happy life in a more harmonious society.

Judaism has survived many cultural changes over the centuries as a continuing living religion because it had the genius to harmonize itself with new knowledge. Up to the twentieth century the challenge of new knowledge to it came primarily from non-Jewish sources. In the first century, Philo successfully defended Judaism in his Hellenistic world by his attempt to incorporate Platonic and Stoic philosophy; in the twelfth century Maimonides explored Judaism to harmonize it with Aristotle and Moslem metaphysics; in the eighteenth century Moses Mendelssohn applied the rationalism of Leibniz and the German enlightenment to the problem of revelation in the Bible. In our twentieth century the challenge to Judaism as to so many other contemporary religious and cultural expressions has come not from a non-Jewish source but from a Jewish source—from Freudian psychoanalysis. The intellectual fermentation now going on between Judaism and psychoanalytical theory is still too young to have as yet produced a fine mellow synthesis such as Philo's *Legum Allegoria*, or a Maimonides' *Guide to the Perplexed* or a Mendelssohn's *Jerusalem*. No Jewish thinker has yet essayed a comprehensive harmonization of Judaism with modern dynamic psychology.

Because Freud was not only born a Jew but was also proud of his Jewishness, it is ironic to find that his influence thus far has been taken more seriously by Catholicism and by Protestantism than by Judaism. In 1956, when the world was celebrating the centennial of Freud, no Jewish organization but at least one important American Christian church formally commemorated the birth of this "infidel Jew," as Freud defined himself. Certain reasons may be advanced to explain why Judaism has been slower than Christianity in dealing with its relationship with psychiatry, despite the fact that at first psychoanalysis appeared to be almost a Jewish monopoly in practice. Protestant theologians find in Freud's concept of the instinctual id a confirmation of their doctrine of the inborn sinfulness of man, a doctrine so foreign to Judaism. Catholic thinkers concern themselves with the differences between the confessional booth and the analyst's couch. Judaism is primarily a way of life which includes a healthy sense of reality including the wholesome reality of sex, while Christianity is a system of theological salvation rooted in the denial of this world. Therefore, Judaism was not so disturbed by Freud and aroused to make a defense against it as was Christianity. Finally, there were extenuating circumstances which explained the hesitancy of Judaism to make adjustments to the psycho-analysis of the individual. While Christianity continuously emphasized the salvation of the individual soul which brought its interest into psychiatry, the virulence of anti-Semitism which was concurrent with the rise of Freudianism made it necessary for Judaism to be so pre-occupied with the sheer group survival of the Jew that it had little time to devote to the emotional needs of the Jew as an individual.

Nonetheless, modern psychiatry has awakened Judaism at last to a re-examination of those elements in it which are contributive to mental health. That the modern investigation of the subconscious motives in mental healing is having a great impact on contemporary Judaism is best evidenced by the concurrent revival of interest in an earlier Jewish movement called Hassidism. It was a religious movement of joyful pietism which arose among East European Jews in the eighteenth century after a period of dark despair which followed a decimating persecution. The Hassidic Rabbis were concerned about the abnormal sense of guilt which profoundly depressed the Jew, derived as it was from his belief at that time that his suffering was a punishment by God. Rebelling against the purely legalistic interpretation of Judaism, these Rabbinic pietists tried to help their followers recapture a confidence in the joy of living by emphasizing joyful prayer and even introducing in the Synagogue the group therapy of communal dance and communal singing. Hassidism even devised a technique a century before Freud for a talking method to aid a person achieve renewed confidence in himself and in life. To quote one Hassidic teacher, Rabbi Simcha Bunam of Parshisha, who lived one hundred and fifty years ago, "It is highly necessary for every human being to have at least one sincere friend. One true companion. This friend must be so close to us that we are able to tell him even that of which we are ashamed." Another Hassidic Rabbi observed, "Supposing someone comes to you and asks your help. You shall not turn him off with pious words, saying 'Have faith and take your troubles to God.' You shall act as though there were no God, as though there were only one person in all the world who could help this man—only yourself." In part, Hassidism was a tremendous effort to rescue guilt from the abnormal and neurotic. It was profoundly opposed to an intensification of guilt because it reduced a sense of selfhood. A piquant example of their effort to normalize guilt is the Hassidic explanation of why the liturgical listing of sins recited on the Jewish Day of Atonement is arranged in a prayer in an alphabetical order. "If it was not otherwise," these Rabbis said, "we should not know when to stop beating our breasts for there is no end to sin and no end to being aware of sin but there *is* an end to the alphabet."

It is probably through a modern reinterpretation of Hassidism that the eventual confrontation of Judaism with Freudianism will be made. Seventeenth-century Jewish mysticism did deteriorate into a neurotic, abnormal, abortive messianic movement. However, a late nineteenth-century revival of Jewish mysticism has proven to be along the more normative forms of Judaism and is known as Habad Hassidism. Its leader was Rabbi Schneur Zalman. His work *Tanya* attempted to invigorate the power of conscious free-will over subconscious instinct and shows insight into Ego psychology. His grandson, the psychiatrist Dr. Joshua Fishel Schneierson, who founded the Mental Hygiene Institute for Children in Tel Aviv, has incorporated Jewish religious insights in his Hebrew works such as *The Psychology of a Child's Intimate Life, The Turning Point in Modern Psychology, The Road to Manhood* which await an English translator. Martin Buber's philosophy about "the Thou-and-I" which is making such a profound influence on certain psychotherapeutic circles is derived from his studies in Hassidism. A preliminary study of the relation between Freudianism and Hassidism has been made by Professor David Bakan in his fascinating study, *Sigmund Freud and the Jewish Mystical Tradition.* With some very convincing arguments Bakan supports the thesis that psychoanalysis is no less than "a scientific secularization of the religious Kabbalah." Kabbalah was the mystical philosophic basis of Hassidism. The Jewish mystical definitions of the soul are to be found in the outstanding collection of Kabbalistic ideas developed throughout the Middle Ages and which are contained in a book called the Zohar. The Zohar was almost as popular among Jewish mystics as the Bible itself. In the metapsychology of the Zohar we find startling parallels with Freudian psychology. The Zohar's definition of the soul as containing three parts in conflict with each other anticipated Freud's tripartite psyche. Freud's emphasis on sexuality as the motivation for civilization is reflected in the Zohar's definition of the creativity of the Divine as being erotic in character as well as the Zohar's view that salvation may be achieved through sexual experience. Indeed, there are more than mere intimations of an Oedipus incest in the Zohar with its yearning on the part of man to be related to the Shekinah, God's female partner in mystic Kabbalah. Freud's fascination with demonology, his frequent metaphorical use of the devil image as his ally in his effort to expose areas considered inviolate, Freud's awareness of the diabolical Faustian aspect of transference by which the patient must fall in love with the analyst—all reflect the pact with Satanic powers in the Kabbalistic mystical system. The Kabbalistic technique of "temurah" by which the order of a word's letters are changed recalls Freud's antithetical reversal of words in dream work. Freud's *Interpretation of Dreams* is closely related to Solomon Almoli's *Pitron Cholomot* to which Freud referred in his own book on dreams which he considered his greatest effort. In *Pitron Cholomot*, the fifteenth century Jewish physician Almoli, drawing on the psychological insights in the dream found in the Talmud tractate Berokoth, described the sex symbolism, wish fulfillment and word play as elements of the dream which are strikingly parallel to psychoanalytic theory. Freud's use of free association in analysis recalls the striking similarities in the thirteenth century Kabbalist, Samuel Abulafia, who employed "Kefitsa," a skipping from one concept to another in order as Abulafia said, "to unseal the soul, to untie the knots which bind it."

Through his Jewish family background which had been associated with Hassidism Freud was familiar with Kabbalistic metapsychology. It may well have been to this Jewish mysticism as the origin of some of his novel ideas that he was referring when on his seventieth birthday Freud spoke in veiled terms to the B'nai Brith of Vienna about his Jewishness as coming from "many dark emotional forces" as the "clear consciousness of an inner identity," and an "intimacy that comes from the same psychic structure." It was because of its Kabbalistic birthplace that Freud could come to make the startling statement that psychoanalysis could have been discovered only by a Jew! Of course, Freud separated and abandoned the supernatural elements in the Jewish mystical tradition and used its insights for his own psychological purposes.

That the healing of sick souls involved not only medicine and psychology but also religion Dr. Freud eventually understood well. His first publication was *Studies in Hysteria* but his last was *Moses and Monotheism*. Freud started as a medical man and ended as a theorizer about religion. It is true that Freud called the religion of a father God the "illusion" of infantile minds and said that religion had no "future." In his earlier period he believed that religion was on the wane and probably hoped that psychoanalysis might replace religion to keep men from falling back into primitive savage instinct. Theodore Reik insists that Freud was anti-religious; whereas Ernest Jones holds Freud was only non-religious. Probably Freud who understood ambivalence so well became ambivalent himself on the subject of religion. Unsound as his Biblical exegesis is in his last work, *Moses and Monotheism*, this Jewish genius nevertheless wrote in that book, "Judaism is a triumph of spirituality over the senses and a self-confidence that accompanies progress in spirituality."

The authority of Freud cannot be quoted to disprove the real existence of God, but only to expose the basis of man's need for the existence of God. In this regard it would be helpful to the religious critics of Freud to read his correspondence to his student, the Swiss Christian clergyman, Oscar Pfister, whom in good humor Freud called "a true servant of God, the very idea of whose existence seems to me highly unlikely." Pfister was much interested in the psychoanalytical principle of the transference of love by the patient to the analyst. In his correspondence with Pfister on this subject Freud came to recognize how a religion that emphasized the ethics of a loving God could be valuable in sublimating the primitive libido in man. I choose three of the many letters which Freud wrote to Pfister over a ten year period. In 1909 Freud answered, "in itself psychoanalysis is neither religious nor the opposite but an impartial instrument which can serve the clergy as well as the laity when it is used only to free suffering people. I have been very struck at realizing how I had never thought of the extraordinary help the psychoanalytic method can be in pastoral work, probably because wicked heretics like myself are far away from that circle." In that same letter this strictly moralistic heretic suggests that it is because most people are no longer really religious that those who cannot endure their suffering must needs turn to psychoanalysis to master "obdurate instinct." Freud even admired proper religious sublimation but he added, and this is important, that such religious success would depend on the maturity of the person to person relationship between pastor and parishioner. Freud wrote to Pfister, "you are in the fortunate position of leading them to God and reconstructing conditions of earlier times, fortunately in the one respect that religious piety stifles neuroses." In discussing transference which he considered to be a "curse," Freud wrote to Pfister, "psychoanalysis perhaps achieves a cure but not the necessary degree of independence or a guarantee against relapse," and to this clergy therapist trained by him Freud continued, "it is easier for you in this respect than for us physicians because you sublimate the transference on to religion and ethics and that is not easy with seriously ill people. From the therapeutic point of view I can only envy your opportunity in bringing about sublimation into religion. But the 'beauty of religion' assuredly has no place in psychoanalysis."

Since Freud made this statement forty or more years ago, has the development of dynamic psychology reached the point, unrelated to the present popular and suspect religious revival, where the "beauty of religion" can take place in the psychotherapeutic process? In the long run, Freud's critique of religion may prove to be more constructive than Jung's so called affirmations of religion which are so frequently referred to in order to bring the "beauty of religion" into therapy. It should not be forgotten that Jung made the following statement, "any statement about the transcendent" is "always only a ridiculous presumption of the human mind which is unconscious of its boundaries" and Jung also said, "God for our psychology is only a function of the unconscious." In Jung we are dealing with a religious illusion but it is not religion. Religion does glorify man for being able to communicate with God but it is also humble enough not to make God's existence depend upon man. The religious philosopher, Martin Buber, properly criticizes Jung for failing to make this distinction between the religious and the pseudo-religious in which every "alleged colloquy with the Divine is only a soliloquy."

In dealing with religious factors in counseling, a sensitive distinction must be made between the religious and the pseudo-religious if any positive values are to be derived in religious counseling. The religious connotations and even stubborn religious convictions that do underline many factors in the therapeutic relationship cannot be categorically denied by the rigid formulas of frigid counselors, nor be cavalierly circumlocuted by a confidant because of that counselor's own religious uncertainty. For example in dealing with one of the most anxiety producing emotions, namely, that of guilt, how can this feeling in our culture be completely separated from the religious concepts of sin? The anxiety of guilt is one of the most painful of psychic illnesses just because its roots are deep in the religious origin which intensify guilt.

Today, it is popular to accuse the psychotherapist of *relieving* the person of all sense of guilt for the sake of his physical health and to charge the clergyman with *inducing* a sense of guilt for the sake of the person's spiritual improvement. Such can only be the case when either party is insensitive to the distinction which must be made between normal guilt and neurotic guilt. Failure to make this distinction can be as harmful as being unable to distinguish between existential anxiety and pathological anxiety. Into this area of guilt there can impinge the theological concept of Original sin which does compound anxiety because it bears with it not only the sinfulness of sex but also the forfeiture of free will. Judaism does not ascribe man's conscious awakening to sexuality as punishment for Adam's fall from grace. Therefore, Judaism does not believe men are predetermined by the act of birth to be evil. However, regarding religious concepts which *do* abnormalize the natural, the observation of the Christian theologian, Paul Tillich, is relevant. "If religion," he says, "does not lead to or does not directly support pathological self-reduction, it can reduce the openness of man to reality, above all the reality which is himself. In this way religion can protect and feed a potentially neurotic state."

Returning to Freud's observation to the clergy therapist, Pfister, about the clergyman being in "the fortunate position of leading them to God and reconstructing conditions of earlier times, fortunate at least in the one respect that religious piety stifles neuroses," we may ask wherein does Judaism specifically make such a contribution to mental health and wherein, to paraphrase Tillich, does Judaism not reduce but rather increase "the openness of man to reality, above all the reality which is himself?" As we examine Biblical, Talmudic and especially Hassidic sources from a modern psychological orientation we are impressed with the remarkable sensitivity and insight Jewish religious thinkers had on the nature of man as well as on the guidance of human behavior. A comprehensive study of the psychodynamics of Judaism has yet to be made but a preliminary exploration confirms the observation of Ernest Jones, the biographer of Freud, namely, that Freud did not discover much that was brand new. He did rediscover with greater clarity many ideas which were always intuitively inherent particularly in classic Biblical Judaism. Modern Judaism, with its preoccupation with the ecclesiastical, the legalistic and the organizational, has tended to neglect these psychological insights. However, by reason of the impact of modern psychiatry, Judaism is now reawakening and bringing to attention the special psychological values in it.

First, Judaism has always had a profound insight about the therapeutic importance of talking out emotions which trouble the soul. In fact, it had an intuitive knowledge about the psychosomatic illnesses caused by guilt if the acknowledgment of guilt is repressed resulting in the weakening of bodily strength. Just because classic Judaism did not, as do other religions, make a radical separation between the body and the soul, it arrived in ancient days at an understanding of man's illnesses that is surprisingly modern. Many are the passages like "Better is a dry morsel and quietness therewith than a house full of meat with strife" and "A merry heart doeth good like medicine but a depressed spirit drieth up the bones" in the Book of Proverbs which make it read like a text in modern psychosomatic medicine. The concept of catharsis and transference are directly referred to in such passages in Proverbs and Psalms as "If there is worry in the heart, let one talk it out," and "When I kept silent my bones wore away through my groaning all the day long, then I said I will make confession and Thou didst forgive." While psychiatrists seem to have supplanted clergymen who once were called "the physicians of the soul" and the role of the clergy today has become primarily that of a preacher or of an ecclesiastical functionary, it should be recalled that in Biblical days there were not only the religious specialists as preacher or prophet and as priests but also what the Bible calls the Wise Men or Hacham. Their writings in the Wisdom books of the Bible show what insightful counselors they must have been to the individual Jew. The Prophet, Jeremiah, recognized their worth when in one sentence he equated their value to be on a par with that of the Priest and the Prophet saying: "The Torah shall not perish from the Priest, nor the word depart from the Prophet, nor counseling from the Hacham, the Wise."

In classic Judaism God's work was being done when any man was kept from becoming sick. Created in the "image of God" man received his body in trust from God and therefore should take care of it. The ancient Jewish attitude toward medicine was based on this Jewish theology. Judaism was the first religion to reject, therefore, the ancient medical theologies which ascribe diseases to the bewitchment of evil gods. As the first monotheism, Judaism held that only one God alone cared for the health of His people. "I kill and I make alive; I wound and I heal." Therefore, Judaism rejected all magic medical practices and denounced witchcraft, magicians and astrologers. "Regard not them that have familiar spirits, neither seek after wizards to be defiled by them." "There shall not be found among you one that uses divination." "Be not dismayed by the signs of Heaven." Health was a blessing divinely conferred on those Jews who lived righteously. "If thou wilt diligently harken to the voice of the Lord thy God and wilt do that which is right in his eyes and will give care to his Commandments I will put none of the diseases upon thee, for I am the Lord that healeth thee." On the other hand, if the Jews transgressed the Law of God "The Lord shall smite thee with the boils of Egypt, with emerods and with scurvy and with the itch, whereof thou canst not be healed. . . . The Lord shall even smite thee with madness and with blindness and with astonishment of the heart."

The Jewish Priests in Bible times were not only in charge of sanitation but also were medical healers. And in later Talmudic times the only profession regarded in Jewish Law as compatible with the divine mission of the former priest was medicine. The physician in the Talmud was also a Rabbi and was not regarded as a secular practitioner, but as a legate of the Divine, the earthly helper of God. In the Book of Ecclesiasticus written by Ben Sirach in the second century, we read, "My Son, in sickness be not negligent; pray unto God for He will heal; and to the physician also give a place for there is need for him likewise. For there is a time when in his hand is good success for he too will supplicate unto God that He will prosper to him the treatment."

Probably the most renowned physician of the Middle Ages was the Rabbi Moses Maimonides of Cairo, court physician to the mighty Sultan Saladin. "Among a thousand people only one dies a natural death," observed Maimonides, "the rest succumb to irrational modes of living." Reference has already been made to the role of the Hassidic Rabbi in the eighteenth century as an intuitive psychological counselor. Today with the rise of specialization and the training and certification in pastoral psychology, the time may be ripe for making available in the American Synagogue the pastoral Rabbi just as clergymen specializing in psychology have already appeared in certain Christian churches. The Rabbi as listening pastor will supplement the Rabbi as talking preacher. Psychologically trained and certified he may cooperate with the other "scientific" members in the team of modern therapists.

Second, in addition to providing a method of talking out for the healing of souls, Judaism has always concerned itself with strengthening character to resist breakdowns. It has been aware of how the personalities of parents unconsciously effect the development of their children's character structures. Judaism has emphasized the important function of the home as a "mikdash me'at", a "little sanctuary", because it has always been sensitive to the proper role the father and the mother should play at home because their children identify with them. The Biblical account of the sibling rivalry, for example, between Jacob and Esau, is as modern as any case history in dynamic child psychology. The Bible says the father Isaac loved Esau; the mother, Rebecca, loved Jacob. This division in family love resulted from the personalities not of the children but of the parents. Isaac was dominated in his own childhood by his strong father, Abraham. Abraham rebelled against his own father and left home. But he dominated his own son, Isaac, even to the point of sacrificing him if this had been necessary. At the same time, Isaac was over-protected by his elderly mother, Sarah, and chided by his half-brother as a momma's boy for his delayed weaning. Isaac accepted the wife chosen for him by his father. When Isaac first met his wife, Rebecca, he considered her, the Bible says, to be a comfort for his recently deceased mother. In other words, Isaac was an over-maternalized, submissive person, who was looking not for a wife, but for a mother. In contrast, his wife, Rebecca, was an active shepherdess, aggressive in welcoming strangers at the well. Despite oriental society with the inferior status of woman, her father had to seek her consent to the marriage. She ran the family afterwards and planned the advantage of her own favorite, Jacob, which involved deceiving her husband. The boys might have been equally loved by both parents had the parents considered the needs of their sons. Instead, the parents projected into their sons compensations for their own frustrations. The submissive father, Isaac, liked in Esau what he was not allowed to have in his own childhood, namely, the freedom of the hunter. The aggressive mother, Rebecca, liked Jacob more because she could not dominate the freer Esau who selected a wife whom she did not approve. Each of the twins was only half-loved. Insufficiently loved by his feminine father, Jacob was filled with fear. Insufficiently loved by his masculine mother, Esau was filled with hate. It took these twins many years to mature and reorient their feelings toward each other before they could eventually embrace each other again as brothers. The Bible clearly shows that Isaac's home life was unhappy because the father and the mother were in conflict over what should be their proper roles in the family. Judaism has always had something to say about the role which is appropriate to the father and appropriate to the mother and appropriate to the child so that "the hearts of the parents will be turned toward the hearts of the children and the hearts of the children to the parents, strengthening the bonds of devotion and love in the home and making it a sanctuary worthy of God's presence."

Third, modern psychiatry has been working its way back to what Judaism long ago declared to be the only road to personal stability, namely, the capacity to hope in order to enjoy the capacity to love. The need for psychic healing methods, secular or sacred, might be reduced and healthier parent-child relations might become almost automatic if we understood how to achieve this capacity in the human for an affectual relation with another person. Probably the most profound psychological truth ever uttered was the Bible's command "Thou shall love the neighbor as thyself." Hate stems from self hate which in turn stems from the incapacity to love another, which in turn is the result of having been inadequately loved.

The Judaic tradition has always recognized sex as an important, indeed, a divine element in this drive to achieve love. However, Judaism has long had the psychological wisdom of recognizing that the separation of sex from love is not the sign of happiness, but a symptom of emotional sickness. The Biblical book, the Song of Songs, makes a healthier effort to lift sex from mere animalism or body chemistry when it sanctifies sex as the glorification of God. In my premarital counseling, I always recommend to the couple that they read this Bible book alongside the modern books on mating. It balances these books' overemphasis on the techniques of sexual mating, an overemphasis that stems from the typical American pragmatic idea that all problems can be solved if you simply have the technical know-how. It is fortunate that Western society has finally made public recognition of the physical reality of sex, but it is a tragedy that at the same time it has lost the significance of the psychological reality of love. Modern man has lost the meaning of love because he has lost the meaning of life. It is only when we have confidence that life itself has meaning, that love can be affirmed as being more than sex.

The Bible believes that life is good because God made it good and, therefore, you find in the Bible men who had a very high opinion of the capacity of a man and a woman to love each other. Believing that life has purpose, they use human love as a metaphor to describe God's providential love for his people. A prophet of Israel thus declared, "for thy Maker is thy Husband for the Lord has called thee to Himself as a wife of love in his youth." If one believes that life has meaning and purpose sufficient to make one hopeful despite the mysterious unknowns of life, then one can love another person also with hope. Those who think with Macbeth that life is "but a tale told by an idiot, full of sound and fury, signifying nothing" do become as emotionally distraught and hopelessly depressed as Macbeth. The recent psychiatric studies of Harold Wolff lead to the conclusion that where there is hope that one is loved there is greater success in enduring pain, in healing and prolonging life. Men today are victimizing themselves by what Ian Suttie has called their "flight from tenderness and compassion," the most healing of all agents. The restoration of a capacity to love which many psychotherapists hold to be the major goal in psychotherapy is handicapped without a capacity to believe in life.

Fourth, Judaism has held that it is not only healthier for the person to trust in another person by believing in life but even healthier to belong to a group which believes that life is trustworthy and holy. "Thou shalt be a kingdom of priests and a holy nation" from the Bible has more than mere theological connotations. The problem of aloneness, alienation, rootlessness, or "anomie" as Durkheim called it, is pandemic in our world today. This not belonging anywhere is not overcome by industry's artificial creation of "the organizational man." The paradox of the present day disassociation and disorientation is that it also diminishes a sense of individuality. Not belonging with anyone else makes us feel not merely alone but alien to ourselves. Only a people with a very strong feeling of cohesion by reason of a sense of high purpose and spiritual destiny can produce fearless individuals with a sense of themselves as persons of independence and worth. Judaism has attempted to give this sense of mission to its adherents. A man can do almost anything and even bravely face the challenge of standing alone so long as he believes he is wanted by someone. And if he feels he is wanted by God, he can even challenge God as did Abraham, Moses and Job and insist as the Jew has always insisted that everything is in the hands of God except man's own right to choose, except man's will which is, according to Judaism, free. Therefore, nothing could be more mistaken than the attitude of certain sophisticated parents who think that for the sake of their child's individuality formal religious affiliation with Judaism should be deferred until a child is old enough to make decisions. Piaget's significant studies in child development show that little children graduate out of their infantile and frightened sense of the magical omnipotence of everything about them and first begin to develop a healthier, realistic idea of causality by the answers which are given to their insistent questions about who made me and this world. Failure to make this step to reality can have damaging psychological effect in meeting later life's crises which do call for independent decisions. Children intuitively have expressed this basic need for a belief in causality, for as the Gesell statistical studies indicate interest in religion does reach a peak around the age of six. To know that life is not a meaningless, fatalistic accident but is purposely caused gives man the feeling that he has a right to decide in order that he can participate in its purpose.

Hope which has such therapeutic value vanishes when the need to belong, the need to be loved and the need to believe are unmet. These three needs appear to be so closely interrelated that it ought to be investigated how the absence of belief will warp the capacity for human love, physical and psychic, and will abuse companionship to conquer loneliness. As the case histories of Mortimer Ostow in his book *The Need to Believe* show, the disavowal of religion does not cancel out this need to believe. The so called non-believer may place his faith in scientific method or economic Utopia to protect himself against the feeling that the world in which he lives is hostile. The object images he creates are quasi-religious. Their self-made fantasies compare to religious superstitions in that both are used by the self to protect it against what it considers a hostile world. They are intra-psychic. In contrast, Judaism is inter-psychic in that it would have its followers believe that the world is not hostile but hospitable and, therefore, a place in which the self can relate itself to other selves in trust and confidence.

These are four factors in Judaism which have a direct bearing on present day treatment of mental and emotional problems: namely, the talking out method inherent in ancient Judaism; the parent–child relationship in the proper family roles; and the need to be loved and the need to belong which cannot be fulfilled without the additional ingredient of satisfying the need to believe.

Because our society is no longer made up of integrated communities with religious orientation, there is a crisis in meeting the need to believe. A recent study of the changing role of the clergyman shows that his role of ritual symbolizer or congregational leader has declined.

His role as pastoral counselor has grown because there are isolated, mobile individuals in our extensive, secularized and atomized society in search of roots they hope to find through a personal, spiritual relationship which they can no longer find in traditional, theological symbols. This will not sound sacrilegious to those who remember that the founders of all religions clearly differentiated between the outward symbolic and the inward spiritual. To them the beginning of the latter was a unique relationship of man to man, each concerned for the other's mutual sanctity. Thus conceived, therapeutic counseling, whether done by a secular therapist or by an equally trained clergy therapist (whose role must become a new religious specialization relieving him of the more obvious judgemental, ecclesiastical functions), may well be in itself a religious value. This relationship deals with value judgments intrinsic to the counselor as well as to the counselee no matter how objective and non-directive the technique. When a congregant comes to a Rabbi for counseling it is a mistake on the part of the secular therapist to consider the situation in competition with medical or psychological psychiatry. The religious counselor, even one with psychological training, does not divest himself of his religious role in his counseling function. Linn and Schwarz correctly point out that it is a mistake to eliminate religious vocabulary in religious counseling and substitute symptom for sin, psyche for soul, super-ego for conscience and cure for salvation. There is a significant degree to which theological language expresses psychological truths and traditional religious practices fulfill special psychological needs. This is especially true in the area of bereavement in which the religious counselor can help re-establish a recathexis of love during the healing time of grief. Victor Frankl has demonstrated this in his logotherapy.

Because of the modern specialization in pastoral psychology the modern Rabbi who counsels should distinguish between pastoral care and pastoral counseling. A consultation, limited to a single or several visits to encourage the sick, to console the bereaved, to instruct pre-marital couples, to advise on family relations, is pastoral care. Such supportive aid is helpful to individuals in situations in which they may feel that their own adequacy is challenged. A Rabbi's success in this service will depend on the extent of his formal knowledge of the dynamics of the psyche, especially its ambivalent nature. In these varied pastoral situations, the Rabbi must be aware not only of conscious pain but also of unconscious fear in sickness; not only of the loss but also of the guilt in grief; not only of the fulfillment but also of the frustrations in sex and love; not only of the joys but also of the resentments of parenthood.

In addition to psychological understanding of these situations, the

Rabbi must know something about the techniques for establishing rapport with another individual. This means creating a confidential atmosphere which stimulates verbal response from the congregant. While preaching is a one-way communication, pastoral care is a two-way communication. It requires the preacher to assume the unaccustomed role of listening more than he talks. This major emphasis on listening is advisable even though at the conclusion of such single or brief consultations, the pastor is expected to and should direct the attention of the counselee to the more wholesome goals of living.

The Rabbi's success in pastoral situations will be conditioned by his own personality. His success is related in some degree to whether he is an extraversial or an intraversial type. But this is less important than the Rabbi's ability to subordinate his own need to express himself and even his natural need for friendship to the same need in the parishioner he wishes to help. In the pastoral relationship, the congregant literally uses the Rabbi.

Thus the Rabbi's knowledge of dynamic psychology, his technique for interpersonal communication and the degree of his own personal needs will determine the fruitfulness of his efforts in the more or less routine and limited relationships of visiting the sick, comforting the bereaved, and giving marital and family advice. This is pastoral care.

Pastoral counseling is a term I use to define a much more extended and intimate relationship. In the observations which follow, I am referring to cases which covered one hour a week for ten weeks, to three hours a week for four months. The Rabbi here assumes the role of a therapist in a psychotherapeutic situation in which the congregant is conscious of the fact that he is coming to the Rabbi for "soul healing." Perhaps that phrase will sound less remote and unrealistic if we use the exact Greek words, "psyche iatreia." Medicine preempted the Greek and narrowed its meaning to the specialization of psychiatry. Until the more recent rediscoveries of psychosomatic medicine, psychiatry not only limited its services to mental diseases but confined its healing to pathological conditions, resisting all references to unconscious psychological processes. Today, because of the influence of psycho-analysis as well as psychosomatic medicine, psychiatry has been adopting more and more of the techniques of therapy through verbalization. Psychological religious counseling is also therapy through the talking out of emotions that trouble the soul.

The first problem, therefore, which faces a Rabbi who acts as such a psychologically trained counselor is to differentiate between himself and a psychiatrist. As a clergyman, the Rabbi does have historical, religious, and moral grounds for justifying and renewing his classic role as physician of the soul, but the average clergyman is not yet trained to know whether medical treatment is indicated or not. It is now common knowledge that the diseases which extend from headache to high blood pressure, from indigestion to ulcers, from asthma to arthritis, may originate in and become aggravated by such emotions as anger, anxiety, loneliness, and unloveableness. But counseling is no substitute for medical treatment of specific bodily ailments. We are reminded of Judaism's ancient warning to anyone who does not receive medical attention when needed. Counseling is valuable when undertaken concurrently with medical treatment when necessary. It should be axiomatic, therefore, that whenever a Rabbi functions as a counselor, he should always have with the congregant's consent a reliable medical report about the congregant's physical condition. Unless the Rabbi himself qualifies also as a clinical psychologist, he should have this diagnostic service available to check on the depth of the emotional disturbance to be able to determine whether the congregant should be referred for psychiatric or psychoanalytic treatment. The Rabbi need have no fear that such referrals will injure the religiosity of his congregant, first because no competent psychiatrist teaches irreligion, and secondly because no sick soul can have a healthy religion unless emotionally secure.

Only after all these medical and psychiatric precautions are eliminated, should the Rabbi enter into the role of counselor. When a shy, cultured, unmarried man in his early thirties came to me for such counseling, among his complaints was an irritating skin eruption on his right hand, the hand he used as a consultant chemist in his father's factory. He was referred to a dermatologist for examination. The dermatitis did not respond to treatment until after 25 hours of counseling during which he revealed his extreme anxiety under the severe domination of his less educated, unsympathetic father. Seen one hour a week for three more months, he was able to re-orient his attitude toward and accept his father and gain adequate self-confidence to establish himself in different employment. His dermatitis was a psychosomatic conversion of his anxiety which, when released, facilitated therapy. However, his timidity was made more painful because of his sibling rivalry with a younger, successfully married, more energetic, outgoing brother. He found it difficult to establish an affectional relation with a woman, with the exception of one successful though casual sexual encounter under circumstances away from paternal influence. Further insight into his emotional problem was gained from the fact that his mother had come a year before for a short period of counseling, during which she spoke of her frigidity which, she said, was induced by sexual incompatibility with the father. These conditions affected the son's capacity for love as well as his self-confidence, which were worked through in counseling while receiving medical attention.

23

A Rabbi psychologically trained to function as a counselor should be able to confirm such diagnoses of the emotional problem as expressed by this counselee, either by administering tests to him, as Rorschach and Murray TAT, if the Rabbi is competent to do so, and, if not, by the services of a clinical psychologist, and also by competence in interpreting dream material which the counselee may bring up. The counselor may arrive early in the relationship at a reliable diagnosis of the emotional difficulty. He must not force this diagnosis on the counselee, not only because the diagnosis can not be exact in all details, but also because part of the therapy is to allow the counselee to work through his own diagnosis and arrive through his own efforts at an understanding of his problem. Furthermore, inner conflicts can not be typed into set categories. Rather should the progress of the healing fit each individual. This is why patient listening and taking the time not to go faster than the counselee is so important in psychotherapy. In this process, the Rabbi trained as psychological counselor must be aware of the appearance, the tone of voice, and the gestures of the counselee. He must be alert not only to trivial statements, but also to pauses, which are often more significant than words. He must be able to discern how seemingly unrelated items repeat themselves to form a pattern. And at all times, the Rabbi must detect his own limitation which manifests itself in his lack of empathy with the congregant. The latter is the real test of whether a Rabbi can counsel or not, for he must not feel antagonized if the person he helps may express immoral, irreligious, or anti-Semitic views and even hostility against the Rabbi.

The primary attitude of the Rabbi in the counseling situation is full acceptance of the person who has come for help. No matter what be the state of his morals, or the attitude of others toward him, or the attitude he has toward himself, the person must feel that in the presence of the Rabbi, he is an individual of worth. This alone has healing qualities. For, of course, most individuals who come to a Rabbi for counseling, will not come because of physical ailments but because of emotional insecurities.

Anxiety caused by the unrelieved tensions which unresolved fear, hate or guilt produces, is the major reason why a person will seek religious guidance. Indeed, the most astute students of psychotherapy today find anxiety to be the most pervasive mood of our times. The outstanding symptom of this anxiety is the loss of a sense of personal significance, the feeling of not belonging anywhere, not even to ourselves. The existentialists have made quite a case out of this phenomenon, which Kafka symbolized in his novel *The Castle*, and which is so aptly described by W. H. Auden in his classic poem entitled *The*

Age of Anxiety. Rollo May, a former clergyman and now a practicing psychotherapist, has brilliantly analyzed the centrality of anxiety which he illustrated with case studies in his book *The Meaning of Anxiety*. And anxiety is the major assumption upon which one of the great theologians of our times, Paul Tillich, has developed the thesis of his book *The Courage To Be*, the very title of which is significant. By joining depth psychology with religion, Tillich has given us a profound insight into the ontology of anxiety, differentiating between existential anxiety which can only be assimilated and pathological anxiety which can be eliminated. "Pathological anxiety," he writes, "once established, is an object of medical healing. Existential anxiety is an object of priestly help. Neither the medical nor the priestly function is bound to its vocational representatives; the minister may be a healer and the psychotherapist a priest, and each human being may be both in relation to the 'neighbor.' But the functions should not be confused and the representatives should not try to replace each other. The goal of both of them is helping men to reach full self-affirmation, to attain the courage to be."

As I study the histories of eight consecutive cases recently counseled, I find the "courage to be" fundamental to each one. They include a shy adolescent who, though attractive, is an isolate, because she was made to feel inferior by a dominating over-extraversial father, who at the same time challenged her because she had no dates with boys; a woman tied to a deceased mother who reared her in Christian Science which almost proved fatal to herself when her own child was born, and who now sought the courage to be independent that she might establish rapport with her own Jewish-minded husband; a girl in the twenties with a repressed hatred for a strong, non-demonstrative father, desirous of acquiring a sense of her own worth to free herself from numerous temporary liaisons with inferior, weakling boy friends; a father of 50 feeling defeated in his domestic life though successful in business, trying to understand his only daughter, herself undergoing psychoanalysis; a married woman in menopause, troubled by self-hate as a Jew, and an incapacity to demonstrate love for husband or son because of the depersonalizing coldness of her beautiful, vain, selfish mother toward her; a nervous boy of 17, highly talented, ignored by a father who was neurotically preoccupied with hiding his own Jewishness from his business colleagues; a young woman attached to an attractive father whose infidelity to her mother she had discovered and because of which she felt threatened by a deterioration in her own relations with her own husband; a man in his climacteric, tolerating a less intelligent wife and losing a sense of meaning to his life.

Now the dilemma of the Rabbi-counselor in helping these persons find the "courage to be" comes from the peculiar dual role he occupies. As a religionist, he is expected to represent and demand fixed standards of moral conduct. This is the major reason why a congregant emotionally troubled hesitates to consult the Rabbi. He may not be embarrassed by telling the Rabbi he has lost faith in God, but he does fear he will be chastised if he expresses, for example, hate instead of love for a parent. The Rabbi does represent moral value judgments, and yet he can not be condemnatory if he is to succeed as a counselor; the counselor can not change the counselee. The counselee must change himself. Furthermore, successful counseling does not mean changing a specific conflict, but developing such insight in the person that he is able to cope in a more mature manner with his style of life and its problems, as they will continue to confront him day to day. To be able to do this, the counselee must first be able to see himself as he really is. This requires a permissive situation in which he may express himself without fear of punishment or reprisal. This in itself has cathartic value, because it allows for an airing of repressed emotions which helps to release tension.

The Rabbi's uncritical acceptance of a person's uncensored revelation of unhealthy negative actions or feelings does not mean approval of them, for in good counseling the counselee soon becomes aware that the counselor also does not proffer special approval for his expression of healthy positive attitudes. Blame or praise may be the methods of authoritative preaching, but they are not the instruments of counseling. The individual must not be deceived by ideal pictures of himself so that he does not recognize his own need, or distort reality to conform to his imaginary needs. Freed from being on the defensive through the counselor's accepting attitude, which is reassuring, the counselee more frankly faces himself and accepts himself. Acceptance of self is the beginning of a reorientation of attitudes which will lead to an acceptance of value judgments which the counselee himself will eventually make. Only when for example he tells himself that promiscuity is a neurotic sickness, will he seek a moral way of living. Only when he realizes that sadistic pleasures or masochistic ones are infantile attention-getting devices based on the feeling of unwantedness, will he cease to abuse love.

The counselor will see these patterns of behavior long before the counselee, but he must resist the temptation to interpret too quickly. Insight is an experience which is achieved, not an experience which can be imposed. Interpretative suggestions and help in recognizing choices may therefore be made by the Rabbi only on the insight already achieved by the counselee. Certainly, to argue interpretation is a waste, especially with the intellectual type who comes for help, but prefers these exercises in abstract religious thinking to divert his attention from his feelings which he does not want to recognize. To interpret unexpressed attitudes is definitely dangerous. Even after the counselee has gained insight into his own feelings, he may retreat from it because it is a painful revelation. The Rabbi must be prepared for this resistance which may even result in the breaking off of the relationship. As Karen Horney has pointed out, a high percentage of those who begin analysis sincerely want to have all the inconveniences of their neurosis removed without relinquishing the neurosis itself. But the fact that most people with emotional problems desperately need a confidant will usually sustain the relationship over this critical moment.

The Rabbi-counselor, therefore, should be patient and expect this irregular progress to maturity without falling into the mistake of encouraging exhortations or premature ready-made answers and solutions. It is just at this point of greatest struggle to gain insight, that the troubled person needs someone who believes in him. The fact is that the Rabbi-counselor as confidant and therapist can be the decisive difference as to whether the counselee will retreat behind old defenses or move forward to confront a positive choice of more satisfying goals.

"In such moments," David E. Roberts writes, "the therapists are mediators of a kind of faith in the ultimate meaningfulness of life which is at the core of religion. . . . The danger of 'playing God' in the lives of people, which certainly must not be minimized, should not blind us to the fact that men can be instruments in the service of healing power. The endowments and skills of the religious therapist as an individual are immeasurably enhanced by the fact that he is the symbol of something much greater than himself—namely, the drive towards fellowship, wholeness and honesty which is deeply rooted in human life." The fact is that some transfer takes place between the congregant and the Rabbi in this extended counseling relationship, and when the congregant arrives at sufficient insight in himself to adopt a course of action more rewarding than his neurotic temporary satisfactions, his evaluation of this choice will conform more to the value judgments associated with that Rabbi who has functioned as his counselor.

The proof of a moral decision is action and only the counselee can carry out the action indicated. This he will do only if the decision is his. This is why the Rabbi must be sure that the decision is not dependent upon the Rabbi, for this means that the counselee has not matured to accept responsibility for himself. So long as self responsibility is not achieved, so long will the congregant use the counseling experience as a crutch and even make demands on the Rabbi-counselor beyond his capacity. While self-acceptance is a turning point in counseling, independence and responsibility is its termination. It is not expected that all problems will be solved through counseling, nor is this assumed to be a desirable goal. As Carl Rogers indicates in his classic book, *Counseling and Psychotherapy*, satisfying living consists not in a life without problems but in life with a unified purpose, and a basic self-confidence which gives satisfaction in the continual attack upon problems.

In all that has been said here, we have underlined the limitation of the role of the Rabbi as counselor. To recapitulate, the Rabbi with only a superficial psychological training should be careful not to go beyond the area of pastoral care. One minister, nationally famous in the field of pastoral counseling, says he has a rule of thumb. Whenever he has more than seven interviews with a person, he knows he is getting into depth therapy. That is not the field for the average Rabbi who, unless he has the training and skill, should set even a lower limit and early refer persons in deep emotional problems to other competent authorities. To prepare himself adequately even for this limited counseling, he should acquaint himself with dynamic psychology, the techniques for personal communication, and have as clear an awareness of himself as is possible. To function in the role of pastoral counselor on the other hand, as herein defined, we must require of the Rabbi an extensive psychological training. To the writer, it appears that if we are serious about our present interest to ally religion with psychiatry, we should begin to develop Rabbinic specialists in counseling, just as we have been developing specialists in the Rabbinate in education. A healthy motivation toward this desirable goal would be staffing our larger synagogues with one psychologically trained Rabbi to act solely as a counselor in individual and in group therapy.

While serious mental illnesses are the province of medical psychiatry, most persons only need short term counseling to understand their emotions. As a measure of preventive psychiatry against emotional strain in this age of increasing anxiety, our congregants could use a Rabbi to whom they could turn and receive complete confidence and sympathetic counseling. We do not mean someone who will take their responsibilities away from them and tell them what to do, nor one who will sit in critical judgment upon their actions, but one who helps them gain insight into themselves so they can resolve their own emotional problems.

The matter of relationship between religious counselor and scientific therapist may well depend upon how both look upon themselves as persons as well as upon the other they help as a person. This applies to the therapist and the clergy alike. Whether the one or the other conceives of himself as acting in the role of intermediary or in the role of relationship will not depend upon whether he feels he is especially ordained by God or ordained by his scientific degrees. All of us are persons of doubt as well as faith. Some of us consciously devout are unconsciously skeptical; and some consciously skeptical are unconsciously devout. Therefore, as persons we must not assume an omnipotence which is not ours. The expectancy of such omnipotence in us by our respective clients or parishioners is indeed a measurement of their neuroticism. Furthermore, we cannot look upon ourselves solely as the experts who have the exclusive skill to help others. Sometimes total preoccupation with techniques, theological or psychological, may conceal one's own uncertainty in one's own art of living. Rather we should say to ourselves, "I am a person who is myself helped when I help others." This requires the intimate converse of two in a dialogical interchange whose essential element is experiencing the other side. In the first attitude the relationship is that of subject to an object, an I to It; in the second attitude the relationship is one of person to person, an I to a Thou relationship, which in Martin Buber's definition is itself a religious experience. Such an interhuman relationship is of the rarest sanctity beyond the most knowledgeable psychology and theology which one Hassidic Rabbi said he learned indeed from an untutored peasant.

Said Rabbi Moshe Leib of Sasov, "How to love man is something I learned from a peasant. I was at an Inn where peasants were drinking. For a long time all were silent until one peasant, moved by the wine, asked one of the men sitting beside him, 'Tell me, do you love me or don't you?' The other replied, 'I love you very much.' The intoxicated peasant spoke again, 'You say that you love me but you do not know what I need; if you really loved me, you would know.' The other had not a word to say to this and the peasant who put the question fell silent again. But I understood the peasant; for to know the needs of men and to help them bear the burden of their sorrow, that is the true love of men."

Quaker Counseling

CLARENCE E. PICKETT

Philadelphia, Pennsylvania

IF THERE is anything different or distinctive about Quaker counseling, it can be explained against a background of Quaker history. Consider how Quakerism began and how much counseling and pastoral care have become an integral part of it.

Three hundred years ago in England amid great religious unrest and activity there separated from the mass of "seekers" somewhat like-minded groups of people soon called Friends or Quakers. One belief which helped mark them off as different from others was their doctrine of the "inner light." They held that one needed no professional priest or pastor to interpret the Bible or preach. Each for himself might read and be led or guided to understand or interpret, or to preach, by the divine spirit within him, that same spirit which inspired the Bible. So, as to religious activity, personal conduct, and all affairs of life, any person, man or woman, was to follow what guidance or "opening" he could experience by attention to his own "inner light," "that of God" in himself, subject always in major concerns to the corporate "light" of his group or congregation.

As neighborhood Meetings for Worship were organized, they soon needed business meetings. Since there was no paid person to do "pastoral work," it was done by committees or volunteer individuals. They gave relief in poverty or suffering, counseling in religious matters, or on problems of personal conduct. Some Friends became especially "gifted" in close attention to inner "leadings" which enabled them in Meetings or in family gatherings for worship to "speak to the condition" of someone whose need was thus met, though at the time of the "ministry" the speaker did not understand the need.

In the early decades of Quakerism activities of Meeting committees were directed largely to relief on account of imprisonment or other conflicts with the law "for conscience' sake." But distress of mind needed relief too, and often found it with the help of a friendly visitor. Courage, patience, tolerance, loving forgiveness, were strengthened by wise counseling and the assurance of the Meeting's interest. "When differences" . . . meaning interpersonal tensions . . . "arose and became known," efforts were made by an "overseer" or other Friend, on behalf of the Meeting, with "a gracious tact" to reconcile them. The Puritan doctrine of total depravity assumed an authoritarian approach by the counselor. In contrast, the *Quaker* counselor appeals to the "light" in the conscience of the counselee and asks, "does thy decision make thee feel comfortable?" "Can we find and discuss the cause of thy inward lack of peace?"

The Quaker plan for pastoral care of a congregation includes positive religious teaching and preventive effort designed to bring about a condition where personal difficulties would be self-resolving and remedial counseling less needed. "Guarded education" with emphasis on cultivation of the religious life for children is a part of this process. In the 18th and early 19th centuries Friends private schools were started in England and America long antedating public education. Most of them are still maintained.

Over the centuries a practice has developed of reading in public Meetings a series of queries raising questions of religious thought, life, and conduct. These are intended to provoke among all Friends a self-examination which is a part of the process of counseling. These queries, 12 in number, cover the corporate life of the Meeting but are especially directed to matters of personal conduct such as: "Do you manifest a forgiving spirit and a care for the reputation of others?" "Do you endeavor to express in your daily lives the love and brotherhood, the sincerity and simplicity which Jesus Christ lived and taught?" These and other queries are periodically read, to be answered individually, and as a Meeting.

References in this article to present-day Friends apply mostly to the "Yearly Meetings" of Philadelphia and nearby parts of Pennsylvania, New Jersey and Delaware. Their total membership is near 17,000. In the United Kingdom Friends number about 20,000. Their organization and practice are comparable, as indeed they were once the parent body. Elsewhere in the United States, in Europe, the Near East, Africa and Asia are more Friends totalling over the world approximately 180,000. Among many of these, and among two-thirds of Friends in the United States, the "pastoral system" prevails. Paid pastors, often having special training, are expected to do pastoral counseling in addition to conducting worship services.

Present-day Quakers are part of the modern world with its rapid social and political changes, its continuing tensions. In the old days there came strength and support to many through the sense of belonging to a coherent family and to a group of families which was the Meeting, or Quaker community. Now with urbanization and rapid travel there may be less sense of community. But the tradition of volunteer service goes on.

In the first and second World Wars Friends were faced anew with decision about their traditional peace testimony, their conscientious objection to war. Though they were brought up to be well aware of the Quaker pacifist position, and often in peace time supposing they would be conscientious objectors, the actual coming of war demanded difficult prompt decisions. Closely knit Quaker communities had gone, and their "moral support" to young people was less evident. Young men were away at college and subject to the currents of thought and influence that prevailed everywhere. In varying numbers they chose (1) to accept military service, (2) to accept non-combatant military service, (3) to refuse any service in the military organizations (these were assigned to "civilian public service" groups), or (4) to refuse even to register for any service (these as a rule were brought to trial and sent for a term to federal penitentiaries). Much time and effort was and is now spent in counseling with these young men, "conscientious objectors," not so much to persuade or advise toward this or that choice, as to help each one reach his own clear decision with the knowledge that his family and his Meeting stood ready to back his decision with warm interest and friendship.

A helpful service has been given by concerned and eager volunteer Friends who visited "conscientious objectors" in prison, and visited wardens and prison officials with friendly explanations. Older Friends attending trials were often helpful in court, testifying as to character and explaining religious attitudes and beliefs.

The recent wars resulted also in the development of Quaker relief organizations, partly as an alternative service to war. The Friends Service Council in England and the American Friends Service Committee in the States were motivated by the common desire to provide relief and rehabilitation. But with and beyond physical relief they sought to bring reconciliation and a healing of the spirit, to distribute the material aid as far as they could with personal warmth and friendship, and to build a reservoir of hope and good will in areas of conflict. Because Friends did not proselytize and became trusted as free from political motive, their relief units were allowed or invited into many of the world's most troubled places.

The same interest in reconciliation has led to efforts by Quakers to increase international understanding through the United Nations, through informal gatherings of diplomats from various countries, and through organized study in seminars.

In a large Friends Meeting in the present century the overseers are an active group, meeting frequently. They take some thought for absent members by letters at times, or news sheets. They scan the list of resident members, hoping to keep alive relationships which will be a ready channel for practical help, advice about education, vocation, marriage, or counseling on personal problems. They try to have knowledge of the available sources of help, family societies or other social agencies. Quaker biographies and history attest to much success in the type of interpersonal relationship which could be considered counseling.

Marriage is considered by Friends a religious sacrament and not merely a civil contract. It is, therefore, a solemn undertaking, and special provision is made for counseling persons anticipating marriage and for assisting them in preparing for the ceremony but also discussing the problems of married life.

Recently more and more concerned Friends are realizing that some troubled members want to consult with a counselor not so close to the group, to get a still more objective hearing. Also at times the involvement of specially-trained counselors is desirable. The Philadelphia Yearly Meetings of 1954 approved the setting up for a trial period of a professional counseling service for Friends. After only a few months of operation, demand for the service seemed to justify its continuance. This is thought of not as a substitute for, but a supplement to, the traditional and continuing work of "overseers." The variety of problems matches that of any counseling agency. A number of clients say they come not only because of the professional training of the counselors, but because they feel unwilling to take this particular problem to anyone who knows them at home and in their own Meeting, and because they particularly want a counselor who will understand, appreciate, respect and help strengthen religious motivation in human behavior.

Counseling With Older Adults

JOSEPH H. BRITTON*

Professor of Child Development and Family Relationships
Pennsylvania State University
University Park, Pennsylvania

RECENT population changes throughout the world have brought to scientific circles the gerontologist—the scientist who through his field of specialty is particularly interested in problems of aging. Gerontologists are providing some fundamental knowledge of the aging process and to some extent they are solving problems of application of existing knowledge about older people.

Persons with knowledge and understanding of aging men and women increasingly will be required to fill many kinds of positions, and personnel workers in business and industry, case workers in many public and private agencies, rehabilitation specialists, recreation leaders, clinicians, ministers, and educators will have to become sensitive to the needs of older people and the opportunities to work with them. The greater the number of persons who live to old age and the more power they wield, the more essential it is that they be effective personalities.

Counseling with older adults is an area in which there is a dearth of knowledge of both the fundamental nature of aging personalities and of how counseling may influence them. Much of what is presented here, then, must be considered as tentative working hypotheses in need of refinement and testing. First to be presented will be some indications of need for and potential value of counseling of older adults, followed by a discussion of some special problems of counseling older persons as

* The author is greatly indebted to Dr. Jean O. Britton, Associate Professor of Psychology, for her assistance and suggestions. This paper is submitted as Publication 172 of the College of Home Economics, The Pennsylvania State University, University Park, Pennsylvania.

distinguished from this activity with younger people. Some necessary qualifications or attributes of counselors of older persons will be discussed, and some of the techniques they may employ will be examined. Finally, some problems which need study will be listed.

The term *counseling* refers to "a relationship in which one person endeavors to help another to understand and to solve his adjustment problems" (English & English, 1958, p. 127). As used here, however, counseling should be distinguished from psychotherapy. In counseling, attempts are made to rehabilitate the individual in reference to his personal problems, but those in which profound personality reorganization is not required. In psychotherapy, attempts are made to provide rehabilitative treatment of a relatively deep-seated personality disturbance. Counseling does involve personality reorganization to some degree, but here the discussion does not concern the process of administering psychological treatment to the severely emotionally disturbed individual of advanced age.

In his bibliography of gerontology and geriatrics, Shock (1951, 1957) included relatively few titles in the area of counseling. For the most part the publications cited have dealt with the social and psychological problems of aging and to a lesser extent with counseling as such. Within the area of counseling most attention has been given to vocational and employment counseling (for example, the research reported in *Counseling and Placement Services for Older Workers*, 1956), and some attention has been given to psychotherapy and to guidance of older persons. Some aspects of counseling older adults with personal and social problems have been described by de Gruchy (1947), Garrett (1951), Kent (1956), Klein and Moffitt (1946), Lawton (1942, 1948), Lockwood (1954), Martin (1944), Scott (1949), Stern (1948, 1950), and Vickery (1955). These authors report use of several approaches to counseling and underscore the need and potential benefits to be gained from counseling older persons. The publications of Birren (1959), Burgess (1960), and Tibbitts (1960) have summarized what is known about human aging and provide some scientific and conceptual bases for practical programs of service to the aged.

It can be said that our society is one which traditionally has either ignored or looked unfavorably on old age (Havighurst, 1949). As a people Americans have put emphasis and value on persons and things youthful. Doubtless this has been a deterrent to professional individuals who might otherwise concern themselves with older persons. In a practical way, the emphasis upon serving the young has been demonstrated in the ways in which limited professional services are used. When a choice must be made, many counselors and agencies have felt that most of their energies and skills must be directed toward adolescents and young adults. This attitude is expressed by Posner as a basic issue in casework: "We still hold little belief in the creative potentialities of the older person. . . . We have not yet related our theories of growth and change to those in the ending phase of life" (1961, p. 235). Some psychotherapists also feel the pressure to concentrate on the young and indicate that they must limit therapy to those persons under the age of fifty (Snyder, 1961).

THE NEED

The National Conference on Aging in 1950 brought attention to the need for counseling services for the aged in several fields, among them vocational, health, and family relations (*Man and His Years*, 1951). This need was underscored by the White House Conference on Aging in 1961 (*The Nation and Its Older People*, 1961), when it was pointed out that the majority of older persons are capable of managing their own affairs, given the essential resources with which to meet their needs. Personal counseling is often indicated when they are faced with difficult decisions: how to adjust to a necessary change in living arrangements, how to meet a health problem, how to manage on lowered income, and how to prepare for retirement. These decisions are difficult not only as practical problems to be solved but also because they involve the person's evaluation of himself and his world. It was emphasized that early attention to small symptoms of social and personal maladjustment may help to delay or to avoid more crippling conditions later (Anderson, 1960).

There is indication that professional services for the aged are often available but that they are not in great demand by older adults themselves (Britton & Britton, 1962; Kutner, 1956). However, whenever programs are especially organized for the elderly or where an agency staff has given special attention to their needs, counseling has been in heavy demand. For example, in one study of 18 private family agencies, most of which offered a general counseling service only, it was reported that 2,432 persons used their services on a sample day but that only 5.8 per cent of them were over the age of 65. On the other hand, in another group of family agencies which have concentrated on service to those aged 65 and over, 25 per cent were in this age group. It is estimated that about one-third of all the agencies associated with the Family Service Association of America now have some special programs for the aged, and plans are underway for the enlargement of these programs (Anderson, 1960, p. 19). It appears that with the development of services will have to come the education of the older population to the potentiality and availability of services.

Another factor affecting the need for counseling and other services for the aged is that the proportion of the aged in the population varies geographically (Anderson, 1960, p. 60). For example, small towns have a disproportionately high ratio of older persons. Nearly 12.2 per cent of the population in places of 1,000 to 2,500 population are aged 65 and over as compared with the national percentage of 9.2 per cent (*New Population Facts on Older Americans, 1960*, 1961). However, the numbers of the aged in absolute terms in these areas are often too few to support the services which are needed.

SPECIAL PROBLEMS IN COUNSELING OLDER ADULTS

In order to be effective personalities older people must satisfy essentially the same needs as other persons do. Like others, each older individual must feel that he is, and is recognized as being, a worthwhile and useful person in his own right, that he is approved of and reasonably successful in his endeavors. In other words, the relationships among an older person's perception of how he is (his "real" self) and how he wants to be (his "ideal" self) and how other people think he is (his "social" self) must be reasonably close. It might be expected that abilities and opportunities to meet one's needs and to realize one's goals and aspirations vary with age. It should be helpful, then, to examine briefly the period of later maturity and old age as a stage in the life cycle.

Probably in the later periods of life especially, problems seldom occur alone. In one study of counseling of older persons (Vickery, 1955), 84 per cent of the cases were individuals who were involved with a constellation of problems. Apparently a number of stress situations often arise within a short period of time. For example, a man may retire, making necessary major economic and activity rearrangements; his spouse may die, requiring profound emotional readjustments and radical changes in living pattern. Each of these events by itself ordinarily would be filled with anxiety, but having them occur together may be almost catastrophic.

Lack of consistent expectations for older people on the part of society as a whole may complicate these "tasks of living." The expectation for each person to be independent and self-sufficient (Britton, Mather, & Lansing, 1961) and to withdraw from the labor force on inadequate funds, for instance, is one potential conflict. One observer has said that our society tends to regard old age as "a kind of anti-climactic superfluousness which may be thought of as the outliving of usefulness" (Linden, 1959, pp. 482–483).

Great stress is placed on individual responsibility and independence in American society. In fact, one social psychologist has said that in America "to be a person is to be independent, responsible, and self-respecting, and thereby to be worthy of concern and respect in one's own right. To be a person, in this sense, is to be an autonomous and responsible agent" (Williams, 1959, p. 435). And in counseling, generally one goal is to help the individual to function more independently. As an individual advances in age, however, he sooner or later arrives at a point when he becomes partially or totally dependent upon others. Eventually it may be necessary for him to have assistance from others on the most intimate levels for extended periods of time, but at first it is often necessary that he accept some assistance as essential to his continued independent functioning in other areas of behavior. The counseling experience may provide an opportunity for an older person to function somewhat dependently and to recognize that he can still be a person deserving his own respect and the respect of others and that he is not totally incompetent nor immoral for accepting such a role.

In discussing results of a community survey on aging, Kutner, *et al.* (1956), stated that "consideration should be given to sustaining long-range supportive professional contacts with older people whose dependency needs may be so great that attempts to give strength to the ego through a therapeutic relationship prove fruitless. Such supportive relationships encourage dependency but, considering the relatively hopeless dependent needs suffered by some isolated and friendless old people, a portion of professional time might usefully be spent in indulging of them" (p. 262).

Related to the problem of dependency is the idea that aging itself may be considered "an inevitable mutual withdrawal or disengagement, resulting in decreased interaction between the aging person and others in the social systems he belongs to" (Cumming & Henry, 1961, p. 14). This theory is in contrast to the often implicit theme "that the life span must, in order to be successful, undergo steady expansion" (p. 18)— that "the middle-aged state (of persistent extroversion) is much preferable to the aged state, and that to remain in it indefinitely is to succeed, while to leave it and shift openly to a different stage of the life cycle is to fail" (p. 22). According to the theory of disengagement, a long life necessitates an older person's release from it. Counseling may well provide opportunity for personal exploration of this possibility.

It is well to recognize, then, that coming to a professional person for help may well signify different things to an older client than to a younger one. To a younger or middle-aged person who has grown up in a period of preventive medicine and mental hygiene, seeking professional help or counsel for assistance with difficult problems is a practical thing to do. To an older person the act of seeking help is often perceived as an admission of incompetence or failure (Britton & Britton, 1962).

A further consideration concerning older adults and their problems is not usually true of younger persons: The realities for older people themselves and their life situations often have an unfavorable prognosis. Ordinarily opportunities for new jobs, even for those in middle age, are not great; with individuals for whom paid work denotes social worth and self-respect, retirement from the life-long occupation may come as a real crisis. The health problems during the later periods of life are usually those which appear gradually and then become chronic; medical science has yet to conquer these diseases, and often the most that can be done is to offer temporary relief.

Concurrent with solving problems of retirement and health, the older person often must make financial readjustments. At a time when some expenses go down, medical costs, for example, frequently go up markedly. Satisfactory living arrangements within the budget may be difficult to secure and to maintain. Difficulties in establishing and maintaining relationships with one's friends and in meeting one's civic obligations may be partly financial. To the extent that status in one's community depends upon finances, such prestige is also in jeopardy. Moreover, an inflationary economy presents an unfavorable outlook for the unprotected person on a fixed income.

Separation from family or isolation from friends or other social contacts may bring untold hours of loneliness to the old person. After many years of marriage, the loss of one's spouse can be profound; the usual situation, of course, is for the wife to out-live her husband. For persons without families close friendships may take the place of intimate contacts with one's family, but to form new friendships as old friends leave may present great difficulties.

For the older person who has children and grandchildren there can be many positive aspects in his relationships with his family. Many older persons seem to feel their children and grandchildren provide them with perhaps the greatest sense of joy and fulfillment. They remark also that they can enjoy their grandchildren without assuming much responsibility for them. This relationship, however, may be interpreted by some as one of decreased authority and status, with a loss in feelings of usefulness for the older person.

There are other aspects of old age to be considered. Not infrequently older persons express real pleasure with their later years when the pressure "to be somebody" is reduced; at last, they say, they can relax and be themselves. They express joy in a sense of fulfillment, of having accomplished their life tasks, and of having now the deserved time to gain personal satisfactions. To be able to look forward to an afterlife with faith and assurance is another pleasure some achieve in the later years.

The orientation to time is a problem which seems unique to counseling with older adults. In counseling young persons, the focus is on the future; the early years of adulthood are times of preparation and expansion, of hope and optimism. There is plenty of time. In 1959 an American white man of 20 had an expectation of life of 50.1 years, a white woman of 20 an expectation of 56.0 more years. Compare them with the man of 65, whose life expectancy was 12.7 years, or the woman of 65 who could expect to live about 15.6 additional years (*Longevity At All-Time High*, 1961). What is the older individual's orientation to time? Knowledge of the basic orientation to time would seem of importance for counseling anyone in later maturity, but especially crucial for counseling the person who feels his life has not been successful. If his past and present do not provide him the feelings of personal worth necessary for maintaining his morale, how does he then perceive the future? What does the future hold for him? Counseling may entail significant change and change might be perceived as a real threat for which there is hardly time to work out. The feeling for time which the counselor himself has for older clients is undoubtedly relevant also, and is related, probably, to the effectiveness of the counseling experience.

A further question concerns the criteria for evaluating the mental health of an aging person. To what extent is the concept of good mental health dependent upon a youthful ability to change, to be flexible and resilient? To what extent does it require a long-range orientation to the future, in contrast to such a view toward the past? And how do the counselor's attitudes about success in aging affect his relationship with the older client?

There may be other special problems of the relationship between an older client and the counselor (Stern, Smith, & Frank, 1953). In the counseling relationship the older client may assign to the counselor the role (and, indeed, the counselor may assume it) of the knowing, authoritative parent, while the client necessarily assumes a child-like position of dependency. To what extent is an older person able to return to such a position? If he has been a proficient member of society throughout his life, what does it mean for him to admit that he does not now have the answers? To himself, the very act of seeking aid from another person may be seen as failure. How well can an individual grow up from childhood and adolescence, to achieve independence through his early and middle adulthood, then to become dependent often on the very people he himself had advanced into independent positions? To what extent does he associate the young counselor with his own children? What are the effects of this association?

QUALIFICATIONS OF COUNSELORS FOR OLDER ADULTS

In addition to the usual qualifications of counselors of younger persons, what kind of person should a counselor of older adults be? Probably he should be an individual who is maturely motivated to help older persons achieve a deep satisfaction in their later years. Certainly he must know and appreciate the problems older people face; he must also know and appreciate the problems families and associates of older persons encounter. This is particularly true of counseling within the framework of a social agency. At a time of crisis when some plan must be made for the older person it is usually necessary for his children to be involved. For example, most states require that an application for financial assistance be accompanied by an investigation of the ability of the older person's children to assist him. The children may be required by legal means to contribute financially, but unless the children are also encouraged to help voluntarily in the planning and provision for the parent's care, the result may be increased estrangement and hostility (Lazarus, 1961, p. 231). The counselor of older people, then, must be one who can communicate effectively and interpret and clarify to significant persons in the client's life his understanding and appreciation of the older person. The counselor should also be able to assess the client's own resources and those of his family, and to know the resources in himself and in the larger community upon which he can draw to assist the client at this time of life.

The importance of the counselor's awareness of the various social and cultural factors which have shaped the older client's life, his living patterns, his values and attitudes has been emphasized by Posner (1958). The counselor should have some knowledge of the dynamic technological and social changes which have taken place over the past several decades in society at large and typically within the family. Older Americans today have lived through two world wars and a third major conflict, they have experienced a great economic depression, and they have seen amazing changes in the physical and economic and social aspects of day-to-day living. Surely these kinds of changes in the culture influence personality development. The counselor's concern for the individual should not permit him to undervalue the importance of such socio-cultural factors as he works with older adults.

The counselor needs to analyze some of his own feelings about aging as they may influence his perception of the older client's problems. What are the counselor's feelings about his own aging, his concern for the future, his anxiety for and guilt surrounding his responsibility to his own aging parents, his own fear of death?

Theoretically the counselor of older persons should be able to distinguish between individuals who, on the one hand, have inner resources and potential for personal growth, and on the other hand, those whose inner resources and growth potential are quite clearly limited. This is not so much a technique as it is an ability to see and to discover within the human person these capacities. This also requires that the counselor be able to differentiate between the problems expressed by the client and the "real" problems underlying them.

The process of counseling older adults entails serious responsibility. On the practical level it requires the ability to decide when it is worthwhile for the client to understand the total picture, when, for example, the realities of the situation indicate that little can be done about them anyway. What has been gained if the client comes to the realization that his life has been a failure and that there is no opportunity to make up for that misfortune? What are the ethical considerations involved?

TECHNIQUES OF COUNSELING WITH OLDER ADULTS

Some of the techniques used in the eclectic approach to counseling presented here need special consideration for work with older people. Counseling is as much an art as it is a science, and "techniques" cannot be interpreted as mechanical methods of counseling. Discussions of techniques of counseling with younger persons are relevant here, but what should a counselor of older adults do?

First, a counselor of older adults must listen. Too often counselors are led to accept an older client's request or statement of his problem at face value rather than looking at it in depth and making every effort to utilize his capacities to the full. Through his being silent, through reflecting and clarifying the client's feelings, he should be able to communicate his acceptance of those feelings in much the same way as does the client-centered therapist (Rogers, 1951).

There is some indication that it may take a longer period of time for a counselor to build a relationship with an older client because the older person tends to move more slowly into a new relationship. The counselor must be prepared to offer support during this process.

The counselor may need also to give information to the client— information about the aging process and of possible ways of solving problems and accomplishing goals. In the course of this procedure he may need to ask questions and bring pertinent issues to the client's attention. Knowledge of how people grow old, the social milieu in which they age, and the problems they face during this time will be needed. Results from appropriate psychological tests, properly inter-preted, may provide useful data about the individual himself.

One function of the counselor may be assist to the older person in perceiving his situation in several ways. This role is suggested by a study by Thaler (1957), who found that older people "may try to adjust by sheer attempts to recognize aspects of their environment and be unable to form inferences and conceptually interpret what is going on around them. . . . These aged persons may feel there is only one meaning to a situation, may fail to see other meanings, and hence have the 'rigidity' so often attributed to the elderly" (p. 408). The counselor's suggesting additional facts and ideas may help to compensate for this tendency.

Much of what is done in information-giving involves interpretation by the counselor of what appears significant to provide. He may also interpret directly to the client what seem to be the physical, social and psychological realities the individual faces in himself and in his life situation. He will need to be able to communicate effectively to the client his knowledge of the dynamics of the situation, selecting and interpreting what he deems desirable to have the client consider.

An important function of the counselor for the older client may be to sum up for him and to integrate into meaningful relationships the events of the client's lifetime all in perspective to the present. The pur-pose of this phase of counseling is to assist the client in gaining perspec-tive and in analyzing for himself the positive and negative elements of his situation so he can take constructive action toward solutions of his problem. This action may be the developing of legitimate defense mechanisms which will make life meaningful and worthwhile.

To accomplish this latter purpose the counselor may suggest possible avenues of action; in the interests of rehabilitating the client the counselor may recommend participation in certain activities, such as jobs and avocations, social, educational, or religious activities. He may refer him to other persons or agencies which could be of aid to him— to physicians, ministers, employment agencies, and homemaker services, for example. He may refer the client to reading materials which might be helpful. These suggestions may be for diagnosis and remedial action and for the development of the client's personal resources. They might also serve to divert the client's interests toward new experiences which could function as compensatory activities.

During counseling, older adults may need to be reassured that they are themselves worthwhile in their own right; the counselor may need to provide such reassurance and to encourage them in setting realistic goals and in reaching for them. Reassurance may play an important part in their facing the realities of life and in maintaining their sense of personal dignity and worth. Reassurance may be important, too, in helping older persons to be patient with themselves and to expect and to hope for what is still possible.

With older persons the counselor should also be ready to help manipulate the environment so as to enable him and his family and associates to work out and maintain satisfactory relationships. Often on a very practical level, small changes in the living arrangements and management within the home can assist the older person to feel he is still a part of things and worthy of consideration. Suggestions of ways for family members and others to meet older persons' needs to feel wanted and useful can assist materially the ease with which they can live and work together. The interpretation of the client's situation to others and aid in changing that environment so that it is friendly to the aging person may be as important as any phase in the process of personal rehabilitation.

RESEARCH NEEDS

Much of what has been said here may be considered as working hypotheses which need refinement and testing. Adequate theory as a basis for research in pursuit of knowledge of personality development during later maturity and old age is lacking. Given such knowledge, valid criteria of mental health in this period of life might be developed and means for evaluating these refined. Hence, basic research on personality and aging and on the counseling process as such should be conducted.

To be able to predict man's life patterns with accuracy is a goal of the gerontological sciences. What are the "normal" patterns of aging? What are the effects on old age of preventive and meliorative programs of mental health through the adult years? What is the effect on personality functioning of social environments which place high value on being old?

To what extent and with what kinds of older individuals are various techniques and approaches of counseling effective? What types of persons are good risks for the expenditure of counseling efforts? In what areas of life can change be made? What types of environmental manipulation are possible without undue sacrifice to others? What are the effects of different approaches to counseling?

Each counselor brings to the counseling situation himself, with his own personality characteristics. What is the relation of these characteristics of the counselor to the effectiveness of the counselor-client relationship? (See Snyder & Snyder, 1961.) What effect does the counselor's age and maturity have upon success in counseling? What is success in counseling older persons? What success can be had with group counseling? What do older people want in a counselor? What characteristics of older clients and their difficulties are related to the success of the counseling?

SUMMARY

In this paper, discussion has been limited to counseling with the presumably "normal" old person who is not severely emotionally disturbed. Older people are motivated by essentially the same needs as other persons, yet live in a society which traditionally has placed greater value upon the young than upon the aged.

A number of problems related to counseling older adults have been enumerated. Older people's problems are often complicated by occurring together almost simultaneously, and often none of them can have a very happy outcome. How both the client and the counselor view these facts in reference to the future is important. The counselor must understand and appreciate the problems older people and their associates face, and he must be able to evaluate the resources for growth within the individual and within the environment.

The counselor must be a good listener, acceptant of feelings, able to give needed information on the processes of aging and to draw on resources in the community. He must be able to interpret the problems to the individual old person himself and to his family and associates. It may be necessary for the counselor to help manipulate the environment to effect the most satisfactory relationship for all persons concerned.

If counseling is to become a truly useful tool for man in the latter span of life, it must be based on knowledge of personality development throughout all the adult years. Research must be conducted in this area as well as in work on the effectiveness of various counselors and of counseling techniques with older adults.

BIBLIOGRAPHY

1. ANDERSON, J. P. (Chrmn.): March 1960. *Background Paper on Social Services for the Aging.* Washington: White House Conference on Aging.
2. BIRREN, J. E. (Ed.): 1959. *Handbook of Aging and the Individual: Psychological and Biological Aspects.* Chicago: University of Chicago Press.
3. BRITTON, J. H., and BRITTON, JEAN O.: 1962. "Expectations for Older Persons in a Rural Community: Solving of Personal Problems." *Geriatrics,* **17**, 602–608.
4. —— MATHER, W. G., and LANSING, ALICE K.: 1961. "Expectations for Older Persons in a Rural Community: Living Arrangements and Family Relationships." *J. Gerontology,* **16**, pp. 156–162.
5. BURGESS, E. W. (Ed.): 1960. *Aging in Western Societies.* Chicago: University of Chicago Press.

6. *Counseling and Placement Services for Older Workers* (BES No. E-152). Washington: U.S. Dept. of Labor, Bureau of Employment Security, February, 1960.
7. CUMMING, ELAINE, and HENRY, W. E.: 1961. *Growing Old.* New York: Basic Books.
8. DE GRUCHY, C.: 1947. "Counselling the Aged." *Geriatrics,* **2**, pp. 183–187, 189.
9. ENGLISH, H. B., and ENGLISH, AVA C.: 1958. *A Comprehensive Dictionary of Psychological and Psychoanalytical Terms: a Guide to Usage.* New York: Longmans, Green.
10. GARRETT, J. F.: "Counselling and Rehabilitation of Older Persons." In *No Time to Grow Old,* New York State Joint Legislative Committee on Problems of the Aging, Legislative Document No. 12, 1951, pp. 176–179.
11. HAVIGHURST, R. J.: 1949. "Old Age—an American Problem." *J. Gerontology,* **4**, pp. 298–304.
12. KENT, A. P.: 1956. "An Experiment in the Counseling of Older People." *Geriatrics,* **11**, pp. 44–48.
13. KLEIN, P. E., and MOFFITT, R. E.: 1946. *Counseling Techniques in Adult Education.* New York: McGraw-Hill.
14. KUTNER, B., FANSHEL, D., TOGO, ALICE M., and LANGNER, T. S.: 1956. *Five Hundred Over Sixty: a Community Survey on Aging.* New York: Russell Sage.
15. LAWTON, G.: 1942. "Psychological Guidance for Older Persons." In E. V. Cowdry (Ed.), *Problems of Ageing.* (2nd ed.) Baltimore: Williams & Wilkins, pp. 785–809.
16. ——: 1948. "Counselling the Older Person." *J. Gerontology,* **3** (Suppl. to No. 4), p. 8.
17. LAZARUS, ESTHER: 1961. "The Influence of the Social Structure on Casework Practice with the Aging." *Social Casework,* **42**, pp. 227–233.
18. LINDEN, M. E.: 1959. "Cultural and Socio-Psychological Considerations in Work with the Aged." *Social Casework,* **40**, pp. 482–483.
19. LOCKWOOD, W. V.: 1954. "Adult Counseling for Better Adjustment to Problems of Aging." *Teachers College Record,* **55**, pp. 183–189.
20. Longevity at All-time High. *Statistical Bulletin of Metropolitan Life Insurance Company,* 1961, **42** (August), pp. 6–8.
21. *Man and His Years: an Account of the First National Conference on Aging.* Raleigh, North Carolina: Health Publications, Institute, 1951.
22. MARTIN, LILLIEN J.: 1944. *A Handbook for Old Age Counselors.* San Francisco: Geertz Printing Co.
23. *The Nation and its Older People: Report of the White House Conference on Aging, January 9–12, 1961.* Washington: U.S. Department of Health, Education, and Welfare, 1961.
24. *New Population Facts on Older Americans, 1960:* staff report to the Special Committee on Aging, United States Senate. Washington: U.S. Government Printing Office, 1961.
25. POSNER, W.: 1958. "Socio-cultural Factors in Casework with Adult Children and Aged Parents." *J. of Jewish Communal Service,* **35**, pp. 193–201.
26. ROGERS, C. R.: 1951. *Client-centered Therapy: its Current Practice, Implications, and Theory.* Boston: Houghton Mifflin.
27. SCOTT, W. G.: "Counselling Older Workers can Succeed." In *Never Too Old,* New York State Joint Legislative Committee on Problems of the Aging, Legislative Document No. 32, 1949, pp. 116–120.
28. SHOCK, N. W.: 1951. *A Classified Bibliography of Gerontology and Geriatrics.* Stanford: Stanford University Press.
29. ——: 1957. *A Classified Bibliography of Gerontology and Geriatrics. Supplement One 1949–1955.* Stanford: Stanford University Press.

30. SNYDER, W. U.: Personal communication. November 12, 1961.
31. —— W. V. and SNYDER, B. June: 1961. *The Psychotherapy Relationship.* New York: Macmillan.
32. STERN, K.: 1948. "Observations in an Old Age Counseling Center: Preliminary Report on the First 100 Clients." *J. Gerontology*, **3**, pp. 48–60.
33. —— "Problems Encountered in an Old Age Counseling Center." In N. W. Shock (Ed.), *Conference on Problems of Aging.* New York: Josiah Macy, Jr., Foundation, 1950, pp. 30–32.
34. —— SMITH, J. M., and FRANK, M.: 1953. "Mechanisms of Transference and Counter-transference in Psychotherapeutic and Social Work with the Aged." *J. Gerontology*, **8**, pp. 328–332.
35. THALER, MARGARET: 1957. "Relationships among Wechsler, Weigl, Rorschach, EEG Findings, and Abstract–Concrete Behavior in a Group of Normal Aged Subjects." *J. Gerontology*, **11**, pp. 404–409.
36. TIBBITTS, C. (Ed.): 1960. *Handbook of Social Gerontology: Societal Aspects of Aging.* Chicago: University of Chicago Press.
37. VICKERY, FLORENCE E. "A Study of Personal Counseling Needs of Senior Citizens." In *Old Age in the Modern World,* report of the 3rd Congress of the International Association of Gerontology, London, 1954. London: E. & S. Livingston, 1955, pp. 603–605.
38. WILLIAMS, R. M., Jr.: 1959. *American Society: a Sociological Interpretation.* New York: Alfred A. Knopf.

Counseling in a Hospital

MINNA FIELD

Formerly Director
Social Service Department
Montefiore Hospital
New York City

COUNSELING in a hospital, as in any other setting, is a service intended to help the troubled person deal effectively with the problems which confront him. In a hospital, counseling is designed to help the sick person and members of his family with the problems created by the illness and its aftereffects. This requires an evaluation of the strengths and weaknesses of the persons concerned, the mobilization of existing resources which can be utilized for the achievement of maximal benefits from medical treatment, and helping the people involved accept the limitations of the illness, develop the ability to cope with its frustrations, and function with some satisfaction despite the limitations imposed.

The professional relationship on which the counselor relies in carrying out his duties derives its strength from the basic concepts generic to all counseling. These concepts emphasize the importance of a permissive relationship, an understanding of the individual involved, an appreciation of his values and goals, and a respect for his worth and dignity as a human being as well as his right to self-determination. Thus, counseling in a hospital shares with other counseling fields a common philosophy, common goals, responsibilities and problems, as well as common knowledge, skills and techniques in meeting the problems presented and attaining the goals outlined. The nature of the setting, however, and the specific problems encountered require the development and utilization of additional specialized techniques.

The problems which call for special counseling techniques can be divided roughly into two categories, namely: those created by the nature of the setting and those inherent in the fact that the counselor is dealing with people who are sick. In actuality, however, no clear-cut division is possible, since the very nature of the setting accentuates the problems inherent in being sick.

PROBLEMS INHERENT IN THE NATURE OF THE SETTING

We have been witnessing within recent years an increased acceptance of the concept of total medical care. This concept implies the recognition of the interrelation and interaction between social, emotional and physical factors and the way in which this interrelation influences the treatment of the patient's physical condition. The clearer this recognition on the part of the medical personnel, the greater the demand for the provision of adequate quantitative and qualitative social counseling as an essential component of comprehensive medical care.

This broadened concept of the importance of the social and emotional factors imposes upon the counselor the obligation to develop a special body of knowledge and specialized techniques. In addition to the knowledge of man and his needs, a requirement basic to all fields of counseling, the counselor in a hospital must have an understanding of the particular disease entity, of the interaction between the demands of the illness and the patient's emotional needs as well as the ravages— physiological, social, economic, familial and emotional—the medical condition may bring in its wake, affecting both the patient and the family group.

Patient is Unaware of the Need for Counseling

While modern medicine operates on the premise that treatment of the medical condition must take into consideration the interrelation between emotional strain and somatic disturbance, the patient is for the most part unaware of this philosophy and its implications, or of the need for counseling. His purpose in coming to the hospital is, as he sees it, the treatment of his physical condition. Though illness may, and often does, cause social, economic and emotional upheavals, their importance may be temporarily obscured by the overwhelming threat of the illness to life and limb. Even when these problems press heavily upon him, the patient may lack an appreciation of their effect on his response to treatment, and may be unaware of the facilities available within the hospital for help with such problems as confront him.

The counselor in the hospital is thus faced with the need to render service when such service is not requested and may not even be considered relevant. This attitude on the part of the patient demands a change in the usual counseling techniques. The counselor must take the initiative in helping the patient understand the effect of his social problems on medical treatment and the importance of help in those other areas if the medical condition is to be treated adequately and successfully. To offer service in the absence of a specific request for such service and without threatening the patient's feelings of independence and self sufficiency, requires of the counselor a high degree of skill in the interpretation of his function as well as an increased sensitivity to the feelings underlying the patient's attitudes.

Need for Teamwork

The recognition that the physical, emotional and social components of illness must be considered together and not as separate entities has given rise to an entirely new approach to the treatment of the patient. It is recognized that no single profession can be knowledgeable in the treatment of all the problems facing the patient and that the rendering of comprehensive medical care demands the skills of various professional groups. While the counselor may be specifically charged with the responsibility for helping the patient and members of his family with such social and emotional problems as interfere with the rendering of adequate medical care, it must be kept in mind that the patient will turn to and receive counseling from other hospital personnel. This is particularly true of the two professional groups most intimately concerned with the patient's treatment: the physician and the nurse, who frequently become involved in counseling, whether planned or unplanned, formal or informal.

It is important to remember that the patient comes to the hospital primarily, or even exclusively for the relief of his ailment. It is therefore natural that he should turn to the physician for advice and guidance in many areas which he recognizes as impinging upon his medical condition and having a direct bearing upon it. Furthermore, the physician, if he is to discharge his responsibility, must counsel the patient on the necessary changes in his way of life, affecting his future living arrangements, his work, his diet, etc. The authority vested in the medical practitioner gives his counseling added weight.

Similarly, the nurse, rendering the necessary physical care and ministering to the patient's personal needs, establishes a relationship with the patient which encourages confidences and advice-seeking on his part. Also there are times when the nurse is the only person available with whom the patient may share such fears and anxieties as are particularly pressing at the time. It is therefore understandable that the nurse may become involved in a discussion of problems not directly related to her professional role.

Other professional personnel may also be drawn into a discussion of the patient's problems, which on the face of it fall within the area of the counselor's role. How deeply any of these members of the hospital staff will become involved in active counseling, and how helpful such counseling will be, will depend to a considerable degree upon the particular person's background, his knowledge and attitudes as well as upon his concept of his professional responsibility. While we may feel that it would be preferable and in the best interests of the patient, if each professional discipline assumed only those responsibilities which his profession assigns to him, we must recognize that it is the patient himself who often decides upon the person with whom he will discuss his problem. Frequently, he discusses his problems with more than one person and may receive contradictory advice.

If the patient is not to become confused as a result of such contradictory advice as he might receive, it is important that all those who are intimately concerned with his care learn to work as a team, with the patient's welfare as the primary focus of their activity.

The dictionary defines teamwork as "work done by a number of associates, usually each doing a clearly defined portion, but all subordinating personal prominence to the efficiency of the whole." Underlying teamwork activity there must be a common recognition of the need to work together and a willingness and flexibility in adjusting one's part in the process of achieving a common aim.

This concept of teamwork has several implications as far as counseling is concerned. It means that the counselor must learn to define his function and be able to interpret it to the other members of the team. At the same time he must be willing to learn to understand the function of the other members, to respect the contribution they are able to make, and integrate such understanding into his own thinking. Teamwork, based on such mutual understanding and a willingness to share and integrate all available knowledge not only does not detract from the value of each individual's contribution, but actually increases its value. To insure maximal benefits of such sharing and integration, various channels of communication must be developed.

Although the goal of the team's activity is always the same, namely the patient's maximal adjustment, the focus shifts in line with the needs of the individual patient at a particular time, demanding of the counselor a considerable degree of flexibility, if his activity is to remain in line with the total treatment goal.

Timing and Tempo

An area where counseling in the hospital presents a special problem is the one which relates to timing and tempo. One of the fundamental concepts of counseling is the need to proceed at the client's pace. As a result, counseling is usually a slow process, progress being determined by the client's emotional readiness to move forward. In a medical setting, however, where the final responsibility rests with the medical authority, the tempo of counseling must at all times be strictly related not only to the patient's emotional, but his medical readiness as well. The exigencies of the medical situation, or the physician's decision that counseling service at any point is medically counterindicated, may influence and alter both the timing and tempo of counseling, accelerating or retarding it, in line with the medical needs of the moment. Furthermore, in a hospital, crisis situations occur frequently, and their intensity, which is seldom duplicated in other settings, may confront the counselor with problems which involve matters of life and death. Such problems demand of the counselor an ability to change his slow evaluative approach and proceed at a quickened pace both in arriving at an evaluation of the problem and in taking the necessary steps towards its solution.

PROBLEMS INHERENT IN DEALING WITH SICK PEOPLE

Illness is not merely a set of symptoms. It is an intensely personal, subjective experience. What it may mean to the patient and the kind of counseling he may need, or be willing to accept, depends on a variety of factors.

The problems which illness creates will vary not only with each individual patient, but with the different stages of the illness and at different points of the patient's hospital experience. When the patient first realizes that he is ill and needs hospitalization, he is confronted with problems which in nature and intensity differ from those with which he has to deal once he is in the hospital. The problems of the patient who is getting better differ from those of the patient who feels himself going downhill. The incapacitated person in the hospital contends with difficulties which in degree and in kind cannot be compared to those he encounters as a handicapped person in the community.

Individual Reactions to Illness

Different as these problems may be, the common factor in assuring the provision of adequate counseling lies in the understanding of the meaning of illness to people in general, and the meaning of the specific illness or disfunction to the individual patient needing help. Consequently, a careful appraisal of the effect of the illness, and its possible residual disability, on everyday living is of primary importance. Even more important, however, is the patient's reaction to his illness, a reaction which is determined to a great extent by his entire life experience, his personality before he became ill, his pattern of meeting and dealing with life's exigencies, strains, stresses and frustrations, his strengths and his weaknesses. Therefore, if we are to understand what problems confront the patient, how he reacts to them, and what help he will require to achieve maximal adjustment, we must learn to deal not with a diseased organ, but with feeling, thinking people whose entire emotional well-being is endangered by the disease process, and whose emotions in turn affect the disease and its progress.

In dealing with sick people, the counselor must keep in mind that they are particularly susceptible to strains, stresses and conflicts; they are often complaining, demanding and fault finding; they may be inclined to misrepresent and not hear what is said to them. The problems, frustrations and annoyances of everyday living frequently become accentuated and aggravated by the very helplessness which illness and hospitalization impose. Some of these problems can be ameliorated if the counselor is able to maintain at all times an appreciation of the dignity of the individual, and a respect for his rights as a functioning human being, regardless of the stage of his illness, or the incapacity it produces. Since the counselor in a hospital functions as a member of a team, this understanding of the patient's reactions and their bearing on the problems he faces must be shared with other team members, if it is to be used constructively in the treatment.

What are some of the problems with which sick people require counseling? What help can counseling provide?

Fear, Anxiety and Frustration

Hospitalization brings the patient face to face with the need to acknowledge the apparent seriousness of his condition. The uncertainty as to the meaning of the diagnosis and its implications, the strain and tension of facing an unknown future often give rise to feelings of helplessness, bewilderment and insecurity. Loss of security as to what will happen to him is likely to create for the patient the same emotional problems as accompany loss of security in any other area, namely fear, anxiety and frustration.

In counseling the patient, emphasis must be put on devising ways to reinforce his feelings of worth and importance, which would help to counteract existing anxiety. The threat of the illness, however, is real and acute. The anxiety the patient feels cannot be alleviated by superficial or false reassurance. It can only be helped through the provision of reliable and authoritative answers to the questions which trouble him. While the counselor is not in a position to supply such answers, he has the responsibility for creating an atmosphere in which the patient is free to raise whatever questions he has with the assurance that his anxiety will be treated with understanding.

A thorough knowledge of the patient and an understanding of the implications of the illness will help the counselor determine when normal anxiety is intensified by long established patterns of reaction to tension and strain. Such understanding, shared with the physician, will help the latter gear his answers to the patient's questions so as to meet not only such concern as is openly expressed, but his more deeply rooted needs as well.

The patient must be helped at all times to accept the reality of the situation in which he finds himself so that he neither exaggerates the seriousness of his illness, nor minimizes its impact on the adjustments he will be compelled to make.

Loss of Self-Sufficiency

Besides the normal anxiety about his physical welfare, the patient is also concerned with the sudden change in his usual way of functioning, with separation from his accustomed surroundings and everyday associations, with a need to accept a milieu which is strange and therefore frightening, and to submit himself to procedures which are alien, often uncomfortable, sometimes painful. All these threaten and disturb the patient, for he cannot help but feel that this new force which came into his life interferes, at least for the time being, with his customary role of an independent, self-sufficient and self-directing member of the community.

This feeling of dependence and loss of self-sufficiency is reinforced by the reality of the patient's situation. The standards of self-sufficiency set by our society and by the patient himself are, as a rule, in direct opposition to the type of adjustment demanded by the usual routine of a hospital and the requirements of his medical condition. The very fact that the patient is in bed and requires help with the performance of everyday functions, encourages dependency. Some patients may welcome this enforced dependence, for it may satisfy a profound, long suppressed need. Others may remain in constant conflict between their need to be dependent, which circumstances encourage and their desire for independence which society demands. Still others, deprived of the ability to be self-sufficient, may come to view even a temporary dependence as a complete obliteration of themselves as individuals.

The value of independence to different individuals, the degree of mature, independent adjustment the patient achieved in the past, his concept as to what constitutes an adequately functioning individual, as well as his reaction to his inability to live up to that concept, all must be taken into consideration in setting counseling goals. One patient may need to be helped to accept and submit to the enforced dependence without surrendering his individuality or engendering a feeling of uselessness. Another may need help in seeing temporary dependence as a means of returning to an independent existence. Still another may require assistance in giving up some of the satisfactions illness holds for him, if he is to readjust to normal community living following his hospitalization.

Reaction to Authority

The patient's feeling of insecurity engendered by illness and helplessness is further aggravated by the need to submit his daily activities to outside control and accept another's decision as to what is best for him.

Traditionally medicine has been associated with an authoritative approach. Since the primary obligation of the physician is to alleviate suffering and save life, he has learned to exercise authority as an effective way of accomplishing this end. Through the years, the authoritative attitude of the physician has been adopted by other hospital personnel. The patient is constantly advised and urged to comply unquestioningly not only with the doctor's advice, but with the hospital routine as well. This, coupled as it often is in a busy hospital, with minimal sharing as to what is actually being done or planned, has the effect of depriving the patient of any right to self-determination.

The aim of counseling, however, is to restore to the patient his sense of self-responsibility. If the counselor is to succeed in this, he must divorce himself from the authoritative aspects of the setting of which he is an integral part, while at the same time helping the patient to accept and follow the prescribed regimen. The counselor must be able to accept the patient's reaction to authority, and allow him free expression of hostility to all those who exercise such authority—physicians, nurses and the hospital routines in general. In addition, the counselor must impart to the physician his conviction of the patient's right to participate actively in arriving at decisions which vitally affect his future. Free expression of his feelings, by relieving tension, and active participation in planning give the patient visible assurance of his importance as a self-directing person whose right to free choice is recognized by the people in the hospital environment and particularly by the doctor to whom he looks for help. He is then able to accept the necessary course of treatment to which he might have been resistant.

Loss of Status

The feeling of loss of independence and self-sufficiency induced by illness affects not only the patient's estimate of himself, but his relationship to his family and the members of the community as well. In our culture, the ability to perform the traditional functions which society assigns to us is often the accepted measure of the individual's worth. The incapacitated person is particularly vulnerable in this respect. The very separation from family and friends necessitated by hospitalization, lack of participation in normal family living, and the inability to discharge his customary obligations and duties, affect the patient's feelings of security and usefulness. He thus fears to lose his accustomed place in the scheme of things and his sense of importance in the family constellation is threatened.

If the illness interferes but temporarily with the patient's usual pursuits, he may respond to a sustaining, reassuring relationship over the period of his incapacity, provided the reassurance is based on reality. If, however, the disability is likely to be protracted or even become permanent, the counselor will need to help the patient develop a new set of values. This can best be accomplished through a sustained emphasis of the positive aspects of the patient's personality, uninjured by the disease process. The patient must be drawn into participation in family living which would help him see that his dignity and worth as a human being, and his value to the family depend less on what he is able to do physically and more on what he is, what he thinks, what contribution he can make despite the disability.

Counseling of Families

It is evident that in order to carry out a program designed to enhance the patient's sense of continued participation in family living, counseling cannot be confined to the patient, but must be extended to family members as well. The role of the counselor in his work with families of patients lies in several areas.

By virtue of the strong ties which bind members of the family group, the social, economic and emotional problems which illness creates for the patient, have repercussions on family members as well. They respond to and are influenced by changes in the patient's condition, his inability to perform as usual, his fears, anxieties, misgivings and apprehensions. The family's concern about these matters coupled with their need to contend with frustration, suppress irritation and exercise patience and forbearance, in turn react upon the patient affecting his feelings about himself, his readiness to abide by the necessary medical recommendations, and may seriously interfere with the program of necessary medical care. If the patient is to profit by counseling, and thus help toward his own medical improvement, it is important that an attempt be made to relieve family members from some of the tensions which illness creates for them.

At the same time the counselor must utilize the positive values inherent in family living and sharing, by conveying to them his own belief in the intrinsic worth of the patient as a person, regardless of the degree of the incapacity. He can also help families gear their demands in accordance with the limitations imposed by the illness, and assist them in utilizing imaginatively whatever potentialities the patient possesses for active participation in family living. Armed with such an understanding of the patient's needs and reliable information about his medical condition, as given by the physician, family members can be helped to develop an appreciation of the values the patient has for them and become an important part of the patient's total treatment plan. Such participation of families in treatment is particularly helpful if we are to secure for the patient as full and meaningful a life as his condition permits, for it is the attitude of family members which determines the patient's feelings about his own importance.

Problems at Discharge

Difficult as the adjustment to the hospital may be, the prospect of returning to the community often confronts the patient with different but equally difficult problems. This is particularly true when the patient faces discharge while carrying within him an incapacitating residue of the illness which is likely to interfere either temporarily or even permanently with normal functioning. The patient, aware of his inadequacy, cognizant of the difficult adjustment which lies ahead, may view discharge with misgiving and lack of faith in his ability to resume an independent existence.

If the patient is not to be overwhelmed by the reality which awaits him, counseling with the problems to be faced upon discharge must begin while the patient is still in the hospital. Encouraging the patient to participate actively in planning for his return to normal living is a helpful device in preparing him to assume a greater degree of self-direction.

Such help as the counselor may give in assisting with living arrangements, work adjustment, or the securing of medical follow-up is of value not only because these are concrete services, essential for the patient's well being, but because it is a means of enhancing the patient's feeling of importance. Given this visible proof of interest in his welfare, the patient begins to see himself as a person of worth who possesses positives despite whatever disabilities may still remain.

SUMMARY AND CONCLUSIONS

The aim of counseling in a hospital is to help patients and members of their families with problems which illness and disability pose for them.

The direction of counseling activities and the extent to which they can be helpful are influenced by limitations inherent in the individual patient, the requirements of the setting, as well as the counselor's own attitudes.

The problems with which the patient requires help, such as fears, anxiety, guilt, the struggle between dependence and independence, are generic to all counseling. The counselor in the hospital must evaluate these reactions not only in relation to the patient's usual response to stress situations, but to the reality which illness creates as well. To do this effectively, the counselor must have a thorough understanding of the patient's personality make-up as well as a knowledge of the patient's medical condition and its social implications, the limitations it imposes, the readjustments it requires and the way in which the individual's residual potentialities can best be utilized.

If the counselor is to help patients achieve a satisfactory adjustment, his activities must be based on the conviction that patients have rights and responsibilities, hopes and desires, ambitions and goals. The extent to which illness interferes with their attainment and the patient's reaction to the frustration thus caused, will determine the severity of the problem. In other words, the counselor must learn to deal not with disease, but with feeling, thinking people whose entire emotional well-being is endangered by the disease process, and whose emotions in turn affect the course of the illness.

The hospital setting itself creates and accentuates problems. The unpleasant aspects of life in a hospital, the impersonal routines, the unfamiliarity of the complicated procedures, the fact that he is but one among many sick people—all tend to rob the patient of his individuality and demand a special effort if the patient's feelings of worth and status are to be preserved.

The counselor is not the only one involved in a counseling relationship with the patient. This requires an ability to function as a member of a team, free sharing of information about and responsibility for the patient. The need to identify both with the hospital and the patient, and to adjust the tempo of one's counseling to the exigencies of the medical condition require the acquisition of specialized techniques.

Certain limitations are imposed by the attitudes of the counselor himself. Dealing with people in trouble always carries with it certain threatening aspects. In dealing with sickness, these threatening aspects are aggravated because of the recognition that illness is no respecter of age, social standing, or intellectual endowment. The fear that the problems created by illness may become part of the counselor's own experience for himself or a member of his family group, may affect his response to illness and disability, which in turn may influence his approach to the patient's problem, and consequently his ability to offer the help required.

All these limitations, within the setting, within the patient and within the counselor must be taken into consideration, if the counselor is to make a contribution to the maximal adjustment of the sick people needing help.

SUGGESTED READINGS

APTEKAR, HERBERT H.: 1955. *The Dynamics of Casework and Counseling.* Boston: Houghton Mifflin Co.

BARTLETT, HARRIET M.: 1940. "Emotional Elements in Illness: Responsibilities of the Medical Social Worker." *The Family.*

——: 1940. "Influence of the Medical Setting on Social Case Work Services." *Proceedings of the National Conference of Social Work.* New York: Columbia University Press.

COCKERILL, ELEANOR: September 1951. "The Contribution of Medical Social Work to the Team of the Health Professions." *Medical Social Work.*

FIELD, MINNA: June 1955. "The Nurse and the Social Worker on the Hospital Team." *The American Journal of Nursing.*

——: 1958. *Patients Are People* (2nd Edition). Columbia University Press.

FRIEDMAN, SIGMUND L., M.D.: May 1947. "The Medical Social Worker Sees the Human Being First." *Modern Hospital.*

HAMILTON, KENNETH W.: 1950. *Counseling the Handicapped in the Rehabilitation Process.* New York: The Ronald Press Co.

HEMMY, MARY L.: 1951. "Case Work Services Today in a Hospital Setting." *Selected Papers in Case Work.* National Conference of Social Work.

RANDALL, OLLIE A.: January–February 1950. "The Essential Partnership of Medicine and Social Work." *Geriatrics.*

RICE, ELIZABETH P.: April 1949. "Generic and Specific in Medical Social Work." *Journal of Social Casework.*

ROGERS, CARL R.: 1942. *Counseling & Psychotherapy.* Boston: Houghton Mifflin Co.

Teamwork: Philosophy and Practice. Practice in Medical Care and Rehabilitation Settings. Monograph II. The American Association of Medical Social Workers. July 1955.

WHITE, GRACE: 1951. "The Distinguishing Characteristics of Social Work." *Medical Social Work.*

Counseling in Nursing Practice

HILDEGARD E. PEPLAU

Professor of Nursing
Rutgers University
New Brunswick, N.J.

COUNSELING is one of the many sets of role-actions which make up the workrole of generalized nurse practitioner. Staff nurses and private practitioners who work in homes, hospitals, public health agencies, schools, camps, industrial plants, and the like, have many professional contacts with individuals in regard to health problems. In the ordinary course of such contacts it is natural for individuals to discuss with nurses many personal and family difficulties closely or remotely connected with an immediate health problem. The scope of the workrole of professional nurses includes application of counseling technique in nursing situations.*

Situations in which nurses work offer unusual opportunities to provide counseling as one service among others which nurses make available to people. Under conditions of stress individuals who are in the sickrole are highly motivated to understand what is happening to them as persons. During illness there is often time to reflect upon the meaning of life experiences and to seek help in recognizing and formulating their significance within the situation in which an illness or injury is also given full attention. Nurses are customarily present in such situations. The purview of nurses includes many human events which give rise to troublesome responses in young and old persons alike—the separation

* For a discussion of the entire workrole of nurse see: "Principles of Psychiatric Nursing" in *American Handbook of Psychiatry* (Edited by Sylvano Arieti), Basic Books, N.Y., 1959, Volume II, pp. 1846–1853.

See also: "Therapeutic Concepts," The League Exchange, 26B, National League of Nursing, 10 Columbus Circle, N.Y., 1957, p. 61.

of a sick child from its mother, the reflections of an adolescent boy freshly post-operative following hernia repair, the father of a family undergoing a leg amputation, a young mother who has given birth to a dead baby, a person aware of approaching death due to cancer or old age, and the never anticipated experience of hospitalization for mental illness. Patients in such situations turn to professional nurses as experts who will listen intelligently and who can offer counseling assistance in a way that benefits the patient, as one service among many others which comprise the workrole of nurse practitioner.

THE NEED FOR COUNSELING IS BASED UPON INFERENCE

All of the various other services in the workrole of nurse are at sometime as important as counseling. The nurse is expected, in all situations, to observe and to judge, more or less accurately, by what means favorable improvement can best be facilitated in an immediate situation. Moreover, the nurse must also consider the long-range consequences of the judgments she makes in the present on behalf of the patient. She must determine not only that counseling is needed but that it is *needed more than* rest, sedation, or a particular technical procedure. For example, if a nurse is about to carry out an order to catheterize a patient and observes that the reaction of the patient is not only impeding immediate accomplishment of this task but possibly re-activating older concerns of the patient, the inference that counseling is needed is made. The nurse's recognition of the importance of the physician's order to catheterize the patient, and its significance in relation to study and solution of the medical problem are inherent in preparation for the technical task of carrying out the procedure. However, the nurse also notices that the patient may not comprehend his current show of embarrassment, or understand the basis of his objections to this immediate and necessary task, the technical aspects of which may also not be adequately foreseen. The procedure can be carried out safely, comfortably, and effectively only with the cooperation of patient with nurse; such cooperation may depend upon expression and formulation of immediate reactions to the prospect of catheterization.

RECONSTRUCTING A NURSE–PATIENT RELATIONSHIP TO INCLUDE COUNSELING

The foregoing example indicates that immediate situational counseling is needed and the nurse–patient relationship is re-ordered to

permit attention to needs which take precedence over a technical procedure. The nurse indicates that her role-actions have shifted. Technical apparatus is temporarily put aside. The nurse may pull up a chair
to the bedside, sit down, face the patient, and show by verbal means
or by gesture that counseling is available. She may indicate a time
limit for the emergent task and comment: "You seem to be having a
reaction to being catheterized; let's take twenty minutes to talk about
this before I continue with the procedure." The nurse would then
wait, listen, and discuss with the patient his descriptions of the difficulty
before proceeding with the technical treatment.

TWO TYPES OF COUNSELING IN
NURSING PRACTICE

Immediate situational counseling is the most common and it may be
the only type that can be put to use in short-term nurse–patient relationships. In long-term relationships, development counseling is also made
available by professional nurses.

Immediate situational counseling is offered when there is need for it. Need
is determined by sensitive observation of the demands of a nursing
situation and by inferences drawn by the professional nurse regarding
the significance of a patient's behavior. When the behavior of a patient
—his gestures, words, actions—indicate the presence of feelings or
thoughts which are not fully understood, the ramifications of which
disturb the patient further or complicate and interfere with resolution
of a medical problem, then counseling is indicated. Nursing effort is
directed toward assisting the patient to describe, analyze, and to formulate his immediate responses to the current situation. Time does
not permit penetrating inquiry into details or relations between events
past, present or future although some superficial connections not previously noted by a patient may be recognized in the course of discussing
his experiences with a nurse.

Two major purposes are served by the use of this type of counseling.
The cooperation of the patient is secured through clarification and
understanding of some aspects of immediate response to a facet of the
nursing situation. The patient is also assisted to exercise some skill in
describing and inquiring into his patterns of responding to stressful
situations of minor or major significance to him.

Developmental counseling is used when there is the possibility of a continuing, long-term nurse–patient relationship. It may evolve over a
period of time from repeated use of situational counseling. The practice
of nursing is characterized by sensitive appraisal of developmental needs
as they are expressed through symptomatology and patterns of

participation in the nurse–patient relationship. Such needs are inferred from day-to-day observations of what goes on and from whatever data are made available to nurses in the records and reports of other professional workers. All nurses also use some general organization of useful knowledge about human capacities and developmental tasks, as stated in psychoanalytic, psychiatric, psychological, and nursing literature. Such knowledge provides concepts which the nurse can apply to explain her observations, in part, and which can be used as a suggestive basis for gathering more information relevant to the problem at hand. For example, the definition of the concept of anxiety can be used both for the function of partial interpretation and as structure for securing more data. Likewise, personality theories also provide a frame of reference useful in nursing practice, generally, and particularly in its counseling aspect.

In developmental counseling nursing effort is directed toward gradual recognition of recurring patterns of need and of use of the nursing situation. The aims are to develop and encourage use of latent capacities in the interest of healthier, more productive living outside the nursing situation and as one result of its use. The main purpose is the promotion of self understanding and learning about living through the use of illness as an experience that has meaning.

In long-term relationships continuing and more detailed inquiry are possible. Many connections can be formulated by the patient—between customary social roles and the demands of the sickrole, between illness and preventive health practices, between bodily symptoms and more direct expression of feelings. However, in developmental counseling as in all other intensive therapeutic relationships deeper layers of problems are revealed as surface defenses are recognized and their use attenuated. Therefore, it is used by patient-side nurses who have had preparation adequate for this task. Nevertheless, all nurses make some counseling effort to assist with expressions of developmental problems such as dependence, loneliness, hyperaggressiveness, helplessness, and the like. All nurses have a responsibility to assist patients in moving from dependence, toward independence, then toward interdependence in the nurse–patient relationship and subsequent interpersonal situations. The degree of understanding that develops varies. This type of counseling is most often used by clinical specialists in pediatric and psychiatric nursing.

DEFINITION OF COUNSELING

Counseling is an interpersonal investigative procedure by which a qualified professional person assists a patient or client to describe problematic experiences, and then to examine the data presented in order to gain a clear view of his participation in such experience in light of alternatives open to and chosen by him. Such views, formulated from examination of recurring behavior in past and present experiences, and the connections between them, provide a basis for unique behavior in reaction to similar situations that may arise in the future.

UNIQUE FEATURES OF COUNSELING IN NURSING PRACTICE

Counseling is one aspect of the total workrole of nurses. The need for it, restructuring the nursing situation to include it, and effecting smooth and clearly conceptualized transition from one set of role actions to another are the responsibility of the nurse. The nurse generally comes to the patient to offer help, instead of the client seeking help in the office of a counselor. This involuntary integration is based more often upon the decision of a nurse's registry or a head nurse than upon choice of patient or nurse. It requires particular observance of respect for privacy; counseling is suggested, offered, but the patient can accept and use it or not. The mode of presentation of this service, the patient's interest in it, and the interaction of nurse and patient in initiating a counseling relationship are important elements which determine its use.

FORMAL AND INFORMAL APPROACHES

Some nurses have found it useful to structure a counseling period apart from other activities. In a home situation, a special place and period of time may be designated. A specific term such as "personal discussion" or "homework" may aid in differentiating counseling as serious work, rather than an aspect of social discourse. This differentiation aids in focusing the nature of the work, interest, sustained effort at self-understanding, and in perceiving limits and expectations of the role-actions of expert observer and counselor. This *formal* pattern is established early and often the patient will test the nurse for consistency regarding time and situational arrangements before manifesting sustained voluntary interest. During the counseling period the nurse may indicate disinterest in discussion of current newspaper stories just as during mealtimes she would discourage ventilation of personal problems that could be delayed until the counseling period.

Other nurses have found an *informal* approach more useful, permitting the patient to discuss difficulties at any time. Bathing and feeding are vehicles which facilitate ventilation of feelings and thoughts. Although what is uppermost in the mind of the patient is expressed, attention may be distracted by other activities or the interruption by visitors. However, if the nurse can keep in mind the content verbalized by the patient, significant gestures observed, and the nature of her participation, it can be continued later following a brief summary by the nurse. There is the possibility of premature closure of problems through piecemeal discussion.

PHASES OF COUNSELING

Four phases of the process of counseling are briefly presented below:

Initiation may occur on the invitation of nurse or suggestion of the patient. It may have its beginnings in the period of orientation to the sickrole or occur later following an acute phase of illness. The nurse structures the situation to include counseling, suggests continuation if necessary and feasible, and poses time limits which restrict the extent of discussion. In transitory nurse–patient relationships counseling may not go beyond this phase. When a continuing relationship is possible, this phase includes ventilation of immediate problems, establishing a way of working, the development of rapport, and some inferences are made regarding the extent of need and the possibility of referral through the physician.

Continuation of work includes the purposeful exploration of observed difficulties and patterns of relationship in the nursing situation. Three major problem areas are encountered. Intense anxiety may be experienced, patterns of dependence are revealed, and acting-out of concomitants of unrecognized needs and longings generally connected with dependence occurs. The nurse is obligated to promote her own awareness of what goes on, to keep track of themes, trends, and patterns in the relationship, and to manage her own anxiety constructively throughout. Unless the nurse has these abilities she may find herself caught in the patient's difficulties and extricate herself only to the detriment of the patient.

The main effort in this phase may be the preparation of the patient for more intensive type of psychotherapy. For example, patients who use alcohol often cannot sustain regularized appointments to a physician's office. Moreover, 2–4 hours daily may be given to exploring superficial patterns before reaching a decision that more intensive work is worth the effort. When referral is made the nurse terminates the counseling relation but continues with a wider use of educational and socializing role-actions, to support the patient through initial phases of intensive therapy with another qualified person.

During the phase of continuing work emphasis is on observation, description, analysis, and formulation of feelings and thoughts, noticing connections between patterns used in nurse–patient and other relationships, and validating with the patient regarding the meaning of what is noticed. The nurse does not interpret but assists the patient to render available to both the meaning to him of what goes on.

Termination occurs with referral or at the conclusion of a nurse–patient relationship. Clear statement of time limits at the beginning helps the patient to work in terms of the possible duration. Even so, when the nurse knows that time is short she may have to close off discussion of some problems rather than risk the emergence of irrational expectations, anxiety, and feelings of abandonment without further opportunity for exploration of their significance.

Productive termination includes adequate conceptualization of it in advance, a working summary of the products of the counseling relationship, and an understanding of areas still to be explored and resources available for this work. If the nurse must leave a patient unexpectedly, this fact should be communicated to the next nurse and it can be discussed as an initial problem. Discussion of the patient's future plans and feelings about termination indicate an area of overlap of health teaching and counseling.

The overlapping of socializing and counseling roles tends to put the nurse in the position of being viewed as "friend" or "chum" by the patient. Primary role-actions give rise to the view of nurse as "the unconditional mother" figure. When these views are worked through in the phase of continuation, so that the patient comes to view the nurse as a person whose workrole has many facets determined by situational demand rather than the need of the nurse, then they do not present special problems at the point of termination.

Evaluation of a counseling relationship is an aspect of the three foregoing phases and also a separate phase. A counseling relationship provides opportunity for the patient to learn something new about his experiences in living. It also provides the counselor many opportunities to learn the nature of the problems in living, techniques that work or must be refined in order to maximize constructive intervention in interpersonal difficulties, and it offers a standpoint for self observation. Each session should be scrutinized particularly to clarify, in the view of the counselor, the patterns of participation used by both the counselor and patient. Such patterns should be looked at from the standpoint of their form, intent, and evocative power—that is, the reaction obtained in the other.

Since it is more difficult to make objective appraisals of oneself in, or immediately upon completion of an interview session, evaluation as a fourth phase of counseling should be utilized. Such evaluations when made after some time has elapsed provide some objective detachment

from the immediate involvement in a situation. Fourth phase evaluations are particularly useful when verbatim records or machine recordings have been kept, so that verbal exchanges and nuances of voice
tones can be examined with the benefit of the time distance of a month
or so. The primary question in evaluating counseling data is not "how
well did I help the patient" but "what did I do and on what basis were
what results achieved?"

COUNSELING TECHNIQUE: SETTING TIME LIMITS

Specified time limits permit the patient to determine the extent of
involvement. The nurse indicates when superficial discussion is more
feasible, when continuation of counseling is possible, that extensive help
and referral are needed, or depending on the time limit she may close
off discussion that cannot be handled in the nursing situation. Time
limits are governed by the duration of the medical problem, con-
valescence, and the economic ability of the patient to purchase nursing
services on a luxury basis. The time limits are pointed out repetitively
by the nurse—and the extent of time available, how much of it can be
designated for counseling purposes, and the relationship of time to what
appears to be the extent of the difficulties for which help is needed.

DESIGNATING THE PURPOSE OF COUNSELING

The purposes of counseling can be variously stated: To help the
patient understand himself further in the context of illness, to aid him
to adapt to and learn from the changing patterns of living required by
health practices, and to develop greater skill in responding to stress
situations which affect him. Several other purposes are: securing
collaboration with the workrole of medical personnel, engaging the
latent capacities of the patient and promoting their wider use, and
making the nurse–patient relationship count as a learning experience.

It is the responsibility of the nurse to assist the patient to come to
know the purpose of counseling that is available and to establish the
relationship between it and the process of study and solution of a
medical problem. The nurse can be quite direct about promoting
discussion of thoughts, feelings and difficulties in the nursing situation,
stating in understandable terms why counseling is needed and how it
can be used for the benefit of the patient.

CLARIFYING THE USE OF DATA SECURED
FROM THE PATIENT

Like most people, patients assume that data revealed during counseling will be treated as confidential. However, "nurses notes" represent

the official record of nurse observations and actions and these are available to other personnel. In most instances nurses do not record counseling data due to pressure of other activities. Occasionally it is kept as research data by a nurse. The findings of the nurse are one basis for comparison and for building a comprehensive view of the situation as observed by others, by the nurse, and as described by the patient. However, misuse of data may threaten to dissolve the nurse–patient relationship and so provision to safeguard its integrity must be made. Moreover, the nurse needs to avoid having the patient view her as "informer" and viewing himself as "a thing" whose confidences can be disrespected.

The nurse safeguards the integrity of the relationship by holding in confidence what is revealed personally by the patient. If data relevant to the work of the physician or social worker are developed the nurse points out such relevancies and seeks to secure the cooperation of the patient in open discussion with others for his benefit. In this way the patient is also assisted to conceptualize and experience collaboration among many professional workers.

If the patient states "but I do not want my doctor to know this," then the need for withholding information from an otherwise trusted physician can be explored. It is generally a matter of maintaining prestige and status in the eyes of the physician that impedes frank discussion in the triad nurse–patient–doctor working relationship; the nurse cannot sustain being party to such a need. The fact of a longer period of relationship between nurse and patient makes securing more data inevitable but it does not exclude the physician from knowing more fully the salient points about his patient's patterns of relating to people. It is the nurse–patient relationship that is transitory; the doctor–patient relationship, although based upon contacts of shorter duration, may go on during a lifetime. It is the physician who can make longitudinal studies and get in touch with persons about on-going tendencies and needs; the nurse can only contribute cross-sectional studies of what goes on in the nurse–patient relationship. Nurses assist the physician to share in findings about a patient by securing the voluntary cooperation of the patient but only a nurse can study a nursing situation in which she participates.

SUPPORT AND ENCOURAGEMENT

Many patients require verbal or non-verbal support and encouragement from nurses. Supportive "thereness" is manifested by gestures indicating that the nurse appreciates the pain, discomfort, disdain, embarrassment, which the patient describes. The patient may need the temporary support of physical closenesss, such as having the nurse hold a hand or mop a perspiring brow. The verbal encouragement of "this too shall pass" variety or anticipatory guidance concerning a next step in a new experience, or some indication of "how much longer will it take," all have a place in nursing. Support is communicated through active interest and concern with total welfare. The nurse may intervene when a visitor disparages the efforts or concerns of a patient. She may find it useful to suggest non-medical interests such as hobbies and diversional activities. Some nurses find it useful to use praise when progress is shown; others find it more advantageous to avoid both praise and blame, indicating instead the facts of an accomplishment and utilizing gaps in knowledge inherent in failure as areas requiring health teaching or counseling.

The patient may experience reassurance as one result of these activities. However, the nurse needs to be alert to notice dependence on these techniques to the exclusion of discussion of feelings, thoughts, and actions leading toward self-understanding. Subtle seductive and manipulative maneuvers which the patient unwittingly disguises as bids for support and encouragement need also to be recognized. The most useful reassurance comes with knowing and understanding the significant meaning and full use of one's powers in interpersonal situations.

PASSIVE ASPECTS OF COUNSELING

Non-directive techniques as described by Rogers are used by nurses particularly in initiating a relationship. They permit the direction and content to be determined by the patient. They have a value in alerting the nurse to her own tendencies to become entirely directive and so have a corrective action in relation to other categories of role-actions in which discipline, direction, and advice may be required.

Permissiveness provides opportunity and an atmosphere in which the patient can experience his own use of a situation, the extent and depth of difficulties perceived that he wishes to explore. The patient is left free to ventilate, be selective, withhold, or terminate. However, in other types of counseling the patient can walk out or break appointments; in nursing abrupt dismissal of the nurse or the subject or long silences may be used instead. Sitting out the patient's silences attentively is sometimes more useful than discussion; it may be a new experience that develops rapport.

Rapport is a felt relationship based upon mutual trust, respect and shared satisfaction or interest that partially precedes the development of an active working relationship. It often develops as an outcome of the patient's recognition of the ability and willingness of the nurse to take pains to provide comfort and to meet demands in all aspects of the nursing situation. In the counseling relationship it involves recognition of willingness to struggle toward clarity in regard to a problem and its solution. Struggling with the problem, instead of the patient, requires tolerance of pathology and active inquiry despite slowness and ineptness on the part of the patient. It requires the ability to focus interest and attention on a task at hand and ability to sustain and widen that focus in an evolving way.

A shared feeling of satisfaction between nurse and patient is often communicated by empathy, and is not unlike the satisfaction response that is reciprocally communicated between a loving mother and her comfortable infant. *Emphatic observation* is also a tool the nurse uses to sense disturbances in the patient and in the nurse–patient relationship; these data are then discussed, formulated, and in part validated in the active aspects of counseling.

ACTIVE ASPECTS OF COUNSELING

Listening and *observing* for threads of meaning in what the patient does or describes gives the nurse a basis for framing *direct questions* which aid the patient to notice and to formulate how his situation looks to him. The interview technique described by Sullivan and others suggests the intricacies of the detailed inquiry. In nursing, marginal interviews that are time-limited make use of the same principles with more limited aims. The nurse can take on a more active role once rapport is established. She frames questions to keep anxiety at minimum for the patient and yet to secure what she must know about the nurse–patient relationship in order to improve it in the interest of the patient.

Note taking may be necessary so that the nurse can review her work and grasp the broad outlines of difficulties raised by several patients with whom she works. The use and disposition of notes are clearly outlined to the patient if notes are made during counseling sessions.

SUMMARY

The nurse–patient relationship is initiated, developed, terminated, and governed throughout primarily by the medical problem and its requirements. Counseling role-actions are one category of many that make up the workrole of nurses. The method of counseling involves consideration of movement from one set of role-actions to another, but it is based upon the same general principles as other forms of professional effort which have to do with improvement of interpersonal relations.

Two types of counseling are used: immediate situational counseling is the more commonly used in all types of nursing situations; developmental counseling is used particularly in pediatric and psychiatric nursing. Counseling has many purposes but the most important is helping the patient to use contacts with nurses as experiences in learning something valuable about interpersonal relations.

BIBLIOGRAPHY

BRAYFIELD, ARTHUR H.: 1950. *Readings in Modern Methods of Counseling*. New York: Appleton–Century–Crofts.

GARRETT, ANNETTE M.: 1942. *Interviewing, Its Principles and Methods*. New York: Family Welfare Association of America.

GREGG, DOROTHY E.: 1954. "The Psychiatric Nurse's Role." *American Journal of Nursing*, **54**, 7, pp. 848–51.

JOHNSON, RUTH V.: 1954. "A Counseling Program is More than the Counselor." *American Journal of Nursing*, **54**, 2, pp. 173–4.

PEPLAU, HILDEGARD E.: 1952. *Interpersonal Relations in Nursing*. New York: G. P. Putman's Sons.

ROGERS, CARL R.: 1951. *Client-Centered Therapy*. Boston: Houghton Mifflin Co.

SCHWEBEL, MILTON, and HARRIS, ELLA F.: 1951. *Health Counseling*. New York: Chartwell House, Inc.

STEVENSON, IAN: 1954. "The Nurse and Her Patient in Long-term Cases." *American Journal of Nursing*, **54**, 12, pp. 1462–4.

SULLIVAN, HARRY S.: 1953. *The Interpersonal Theory of Psychiatry*. New York: W. W. Norton & Co., Inc.

———: 1954. *The Psychiatric Interview*. New York: W. W. Norton & Co., Inc.

TUDOR, GWEN E.: 1952. "A Sociopsychiatric Nursing Approach to Intervention in a Problem of Mutual Withdrawal on a Mental Hospital Ward." *Psychiatry*, 15, pp. 193–217.

Counseling Techniques in Psychiatric Social Work

TESSIE D. BERKMAN

Professor, New York University
New York

THE PRACTICE of psychiatric social work has developed within the past half century during periods characterized by social and economic changes unprecedented in our country. In common with all social work, this practice has, therefore, fallen heir to certain problems of communication which are unavoidable during such periods. The marked changes experienced by social work in general and casework in particular have permitted too little opportunity for formalization of the content of its experience. Psychiatric social work has moved forward, as have other social work practices, in advance of clear and tested formalization of methods and techniques utilized. In addition, the enrichment of practice gained through association with psychiatry has not occurred without cost in terms of a clear delineation of each area of practice. The confusions which have resulted make it important to provide a definition of psychiatric social work early in any discussion of it.

Two perspectives on psychiatric social work will be briefly differentiated here. One is based on a social work practice which takes place within a setting wherein responsibility for the diagnosis and treatment of psychiatric patients is assumed by the medical profession. The other is based on qualities deriving from a mastery of psychiatric concepts and an ability to adapt and integrate them into social work practice. The permeation of the qualitative attributes derived from the use of psychiatric concepts into the body of all social work has led to the

inclusion of a wide range of social work practices under the latter definition. A definition based on the ultimate responsibility of psychiatry is,
therefore, the only realistic one in delineating a specific psychiatric
social work area. This chapter will, therefore, be written from the point
of view that psychiatric social work counseling is a practice which takes
place in a setting wherein the responsibility for the diagnosis and
treatment of mentally ill persons is assumed by the profession of
psychiatry.

Psychiatric social work counseling, or counseling in collaboration
with the practice of psychiatry, in its essential attributes does not differ
from other forms of counseling. The basic features of a recognized body
of knowledge, and skill in its application to the counseling situation,
form the fabric of counseling in any field. There are, however, certain
features which emerge with greater emphasis in psychiatric social work
counseling. Such stress or emphasis creates the qualitative aspects of
this field of practice. This chapter is devoted, therefore, to an underscoring of certain factors which assume unusual urgency in the equipment of the counselor working in a psychiatric setting.

The specific features of psychiatric social work counseling may be
considered in terms of (1) areas of special knowledge, (2) the nature
of the collaborative pattern and (3) specific skills and techniques. These
three components in a worker's equipment are, of course, interrelated
and inseparable. They are considered separately in this chapter solely
in the interest of clarity of presentation. Not only does one not exist
without the other, but they exert reciprocal influences creating a
quality which emerges as the equipment of the psychiatric social work
counselor.

AREAS OF SPECIAL KNOWLEDGE

The fact that a counseling which derives its function in terms of the
psychiatric illness of the patient requires a degree of mastery of psychiatric knowledge should require no elaboration. Whether the counselor
works directly with the patient or whether he counsels with a relative in
the interest of the patient's recovery, the service can be offered in a
truly helpful manner only if the patient's illness is understood. The
increase in the range of emotional disorders for which psychiatry has
assumed responsibility, as well as the deepening of the understanding
of each disorder, tends to increase the body of knowledge with which
the psychiatric social work counselor must be familiar. Behavior, which
in earlier periods was considered criminal, anti-social, or just plain
"ornery," has gradually been included within the province of psychiatric disorders, particularly as psychoanalytic thinking has cast new light

on actions which have previously been little understood. In a similar way, new knowledge of the psychodynamics underlying the difficulties of the near-normal, socially conforming person has extended the boundaries of psychoneurotic illness. Increased understanding of psychotic processes, derived from many sources including psychoanalysis, has in the same way increased the available knowledge in this the earliest recognized and still in many ways the most problematic area of psychiatric illness.

This is not to say that the psychiatric social work counselor must be trained as a psychiatrist and also as a counselor. To the contrary, his essential skill is in the area of counseling. But it must be emphasized that a knowledge of the particular psychiatric illness from which the patient suffers is essential. It follows, therefore, that the increasing volume of this knowledge places new and heavy demands on the equipment of the psychiatric social work counselor.

A body of knowledge essential in the equipment of the psychiatric social work counselor which has received less attention than psychiatry concerns the laws and statutes affecting the mentally ill patient. This body of knowledge is, of course, particularly applicable in cases where the patient is, has been, or is being considered for legal commitment. The counselor working in a hospital devoted to treatment of the legally committed patient cannot avoid the necessity for mastery of this body of knowledge which so vitally affects the life of the patient. However, it would appear to be equally important for the counselor working with any patient to have a thorough understanding of such legal provisions. This is essential if for no other reason than that the potentiality for the need for the protection offered by such legal provisions can never be routinely dismissed.

The legal measures providing protection necessary in certain types of psychiatric illness may, however, be considered as but one side of the coin. On the reverse appear the legal responsibility which society has accorded to the profession of medicine for the diagnosis and treatment of psychiatric illness. The responsibility of the psychiatric social work counselor at this point in the development of his practice has no such legal sanction of its own but derives its sanction from association with the profession at whose door society has placed responsibility for the patient.

The equipment of the psychiatric social work counselor should, therefore, include specific knowledge from the disciplines other than his own which have specialized knowledge deriving from medical and legal responsibility for psychiatric illness. Such knowledge forms an essential foundation to the practice of counseling with the psychiatric patient.

THE NATURE OF THE COLLABORATIVE PATTERN

The second feature differentiating psychiatric social work counseling from some other forms of counseling grows out of the collaborative process wherein a counseling service is related to a psychiatric service offered to a patient. Such collaboration may and does assume a wide variety of patterns.* Among the interrelated factors which influence a particular pattern certain major ones may be identified: (1) the nature of the psychiatric setting, whether in-patient or out-patient, and whether tax or privately supported; (2) the person to whom counseling is made available, the patient himself, his relative, or possibly another person closely associated with him; (3) the age of the patient, child, adolescent, or adult; (4) the nature of the illness or illnesses for which treatment is offered; and (5) the philosophy of collaboration evolved between psychiatrist and counselor.

Historically, the contribution of the social worker was first sought by psychiatry in the interest of a return to the community of the patient who had been hospitalized. Historically also, such counseling in the interest of the hospitalized patient was devoted to work with the relative. However, in recent years increased counseling has been made available for the patient himself.† As the hospitalized patient approaches recovery and begins to move into a return to the community, his needs have emerged as those for which counseling has proved to be appropriate and effective.

The collaborative pattern in counseling with the psychiatric patient who is not in need of hospital treatment has no such tradition for its guidance. This patient, who comes from work and home to the out-patient clinic or private psychiatrist's office, is more likely to be suffering from a psychiatric illness other than psychosis, and in these terms his illness represents a more recently recognized responsibility of psychiatry. Conversely, he is a person with whom the social workers have had a long history of experience, particularly in regard to the overt expressions of his problems. For these, and other reasons impossible to summarize within the space available here, a wider range of difference in the philosophy of collaboration has been developed in work with the patient who is not in a hospital as compared with practice within a hospital structure. Such philosophies are naturally reflected in a wide range in the pattern of psychiatrist–social worker collaboration. It is

* KRUGMAN, MORRIS: 1950. "A Study of Current Trends in the Use and Coordination of Services of Psychiatrist, Psychologists and Social Workers," *American Journal of Orthopsychiatry*, XX, No. 1.

† BERKMAN, TESSIE D.: 1953. *Practice of Social Workers in Psychiatric Hospitals and Clinic*, pp. 42–43. American Association of Social Workers, New York.

particularly important, therefore, for psychiatrist and counselor to achieve understanding and clarity in relation to a way of working, particularly on an out-patient basis.

Considerations of age of patient and the matter of whether counseling is offered to a client or his relative offer specific features which affect the nature of counseling in many areas of practice. In work with psychiatric patients such considerations are very closely related to the factor of the specific attributes of the particular illness itself. In working with psychiatric patients of any age, and in working with their relatives, the nature of the illness emerges as a prime consideration. Adaptations of generic counseling principles in relation to various psychiatric illnesses call for a refinement and differentiation of skills and a constant sensitivity to the verbalized and non-verbalized needs of the patient. The number of factors which influence the collaboration between the psychiatrist and counselor place unusual demands on the responsibility of each profession in arriving at an effective delineation of teamwork. The flexibility and experimentation implicit in the variety of patterns which exist would appear to be a reflection of healthy development in this matter. They may be considered as an indication of joint effort in moving toward a pattern in which the skill of one member of this team complements that of the other in the interest of the most effective treatment for the psychiatric patient.

SPECIFIC SKILLS AND TECHNIQUES

Mastery of certain bodies of knowledge and clarity in the way of working in a particular collaborative pattern constitute the foundation and milieu of psychiatric social work but do not of themselves provide any guarantee of skill. The translation of knowledge into skill in any counseling derives from the personality equipment of the counselor. It is assumed, therefore, that any person carrying responsibility for counseling has achieved a professional discipline of his personality in the interest of the person being served. This includes attributes of acceptance and understanding, skill in the use of oneself in the development of a counseling relationship, and ability to select the particular refinement of method appropriate to the need presented at any point in the counseling process.

As has been pointed out, counseling in relation to a psychiatric illness places particular demands on certain areas of skill due to features of the illness itself. Such skills are reflections of many personality attributes, some of which may be considered under the following designations: (1) basic attitudes towards psychiatric illness, (2) understanding of the stigma attached to psychiatric illness, (3) awareness of subtle feelings of personal responsibility for the causation of psychiatric illness, (4) ability to relate to the impact growing out of the expression of psychiatric illness. These four areas are not offered as a comprehensive delineation of the equipment of the psychiatric social work counselor. They are considered to be important because they demonstrate basic personality attributes of the psychiatric social worker which are related to skill in this area of counseling.

BASIC ATTITUDES TOWARD PSYCHIATRIC ILLNESS

Counseling in the interest of any seriously ill person demands a realistic appraisal of his illness and of the means available for facilitating recovery from it. It requires particularly an acceptance of the condition as an illness and an identification with the patient's potentiality for mobilizing himself in the direction of recovery and health. There is, perhaps, no area of illness which places as great a demand on the counselor's fundamental attitude towards the health-illness balance as that of psychiatric illness. The permeation of the various expressions of such illness throughout the structure of the personality of the psychiatric patient in a sense runs counter to any concept of "complete recovery." Although the attitudes of the members of the helping professions are no longer imprisoned within the ideology of a "hopeless illness," this new freedom does not of itself guarantee an appreciation of what may and what may not be expected of the psychiatric patient in his movement in the direction of health.* An extremely slow degree of movement may be the utmost of which a psychiatric patient is capable at a certain time. An attitude reflecting a true appreciation of this matter may require considerable time and experience for its development and integration into personality of the counselor.

An essential for counseling with psychiatric patients is therefore an attitude which recognizes the significance of minute steps in the direction of recovery as well as an appreciation of more rapid ones. Measurement of recovery in terms of greatly improved social functioning, advanced economic and personal achievement, and increased relaxation and happiness in many instances can be made only in terms of what may appear to be infinitesimal change.

The above caution should, of course, not be interpreted in a way that denies nor minimizes rapid movement, dramatic recovery, or new peaks of healthy functioning which the psychiatric patient is frequently able

* The marked shift in attitude toward the possibility of recovery from mental illness is made clear in the report of a relative's conference with a psychiatrist several decades ago. See *Nijinsky* by Romola Nijinsky, New York: Simon and Shuster, 1947, p. 428.

to achieve. Such happy changes in the reorganization of the patient's utilization of his strengths can and do take place. However, the counselor, as a rule, has less difficulty in moving along with such developments. On the other hand, particularly for the counselor new to work with the severely ill patient, there may be a need for self-discipline in achieving a basic acceptance of the small degree of change which, for the psychiatric patient, represents a giant step in the direction of health.

In common with counseling in any area, the ability to adapt to the movement of the client at a particular point in the counseling process emerges almost as a sixth sense in the personality equipment of the counselor. In instances where only a slow movement is possible, a failure to accept this, even in the most subtle way, cuts off the little growth the client is capable of at the time. On the other hand, a constantly alert sensitivity to potentialities for recovery create a strength subtly recognized by the client and unconsciously utilized by him as a major dynamic in the fullest use of the potentialities he possesses.

STIGMA ATTACHED TO PSYCHIATRIC ILLNESS

The growth and dissemination of knowledge in the field of psychiatry has tended to dissipate the feelings of stigma which, until very recently in our culture, have been associated with psychiatric illness. That the counselor's attitude should reflect complete freedom from any remnant of a feeling of stigma or fear in this regard should require no elaboration. It is, furthermore, important that the counselor not assume that his attitude, or that achieved in his social group, is paralleled in the feelings of the person with whom he may be working. The very existence of the illness may operate against the achievement of such freedom. Persons who appear to have achieved a high degree of objectivity in this matter may be prey to an upsurging of archaic emotion, activated by the appearance of psychiatric illness. Thus feelings of intense shame, subterfuges for hiding from others any knowledge of the out-caste behavior, and denial of its existence as a means of hiding it from oneself are common phenomena. Such feelings, only recently subjected to the rays of science, tend to arise under the pressure exerted by the emergence of the illness itself. In any case, it should never be taken for granted that a feeling of stigma does not exist.

It is important for the counselor to be alert to expressions pointing to feelings of stigma early in the counseling process. A realistic coming to terms about even the most simple problem growing out of the illness may be sabotaged by permitting undercurrents of emotion of shame and failure to exist unrecognized and unexpressed. Available psychological energy may be consumed in a wasteful or destructive way by permitting "concealment, like a worm in the bud to feed" on the resources of the person struggling with his adjustment to the illness in himself or in a person with whom he is identified.

FEELINGS OF PERSONAL RESPONSIBILITY FOR CAUSATION OF PSYCHIATRIC ILLNESS

Closely related to the deep-rooted shame and stigma long associated with psychiatric illness is the feeling of the relative that he has been directly responsible for its causation. As new psychological knowledge illuminates personality development, the influence of key persons in the childhood environment is high-lighted. Such emphasis on the responsibility of the adult associated with the small child tends to heighten feelings of guilt in parents. Frequently exaggerated to an irrational degree, these feelings cause acute and disabling pain.

The knowledge of the interplay of parent and child attitudes has made possible the development of modern, enlightened techniques in the fields of child guidance, parent education, and nursery school education. The same knowledge must be scrutinized carefully and utilized with caution in counseling in relation to psychiatric illness lest it serve to intensify an existing irrational sense of responsibility on the part of the relative. Or perhaps it may be better stated that this new knowledge provides an asset in any counselor's equipment only when his attitude reflects an acceptance of the parent (and of his part in the creation of the child's personality) of the same non-judgmental quality which seems more easily to flow in the direction of the child.

Counseling in the interest of psychiatric patients continually provides evidence that the relative's feelings of guilt and personal responsibility emerge with a universality paralleled only by the diversity in the manner of expression. It follows that sensitivity to the pain of a parent, whose feelings in this area are deep rooted, is a *sine qua non* in counseling with them. However, the husband may experience as acute feelings of guilt in relation to a wife's illness, and wife for that of the husband. In like manner, the son or daughter of the parent who is a psychiatric patient does not easily escape the impact of these emotions.

The sense of responsibility for the creation of the illness experienced by the patient himself stems from extremely complicated factors within the illness itself. Traditionally, any consideration of such feelings, particularly those which include a goal of enabling the patient to achieve some insight into them, falls within the responsibility of the psychiatrist. However, irrespective of the nature of the division of labor with the psychiatrist, the counselor must be constantly sensitive to this area of the patient's feelings. In offering counseling to the patient, the worker must be prepared to deal with any reflections of self-blame and guilt which impinge on the counseling activity.

IMPACT OF THE EXPRESSION OF PSYCHIATRIC ILLNESS

The demands which are made on the personality attributes of the psychiatric social work counselor may be observed in dramatic form in terms of the extreme and frequently irrational features which may characterize the expression of the psychiatric patient. The overt and at times highly personalized expressions of hostility of the patient call for a highly sustained quality of acceptance on the part of the counselor. Implicit in such acceptance is the absence of any remnant of fear or discomfort. Any personalized reaction, however subtle or controlled, to the violence or attack which may suddenly emerge in the patient's expression, creates a hazard to the development of the helping relationship which is essential in the counseling process. The relaxation of the attitude of the counselor, reflecting the disappearance of the fear normally arising in response to attack, can be achieved only through continued experience in working with such expressions of feeling.

The acceptance of extreme or irrational behavior should not be confused with a belief that the patient's thinking and feeling represent correct perceptions of himself or others. Such a response carries the danger of the opposite hazard of an over-identification with the patient or with the situation created by his illness. Over-identification prevents the development of a helping relationship and creates an impasse no less serious than that created when remnants of the counselor's "normal" response to personalized hostility are present. As is true of any attitude not helpful to the patient, a tendency towards over-identification requires self-discipline and careful scrutiny. This creates a particular demand on the counselor because there may be an element of seduction which the counselor early in his experience may find it difficult to withstand.

The fine balance between a freedom from discomfort at the personalized hostility of the patient and the development of a disciplined understanding is achieved neither quickly nor easily. Continued experience in working with psychiatric patients can do a great deal in the achievement of such a balance but, of course, can offer no guarantee of it. As is true of any personality attributes essential in any area of counseling, self-scrutiny must be integrated into the experience if old attitudes are to be modified. In these terms the goal of self-awareness on the part of the counselor assumes great importance if effective work is to be done in counseling with psychiatric patients.

CONCLUSION

This chapter is written from the point of view that generic casework principles underlie the practice of counseling in any area. An attempt has been made, therefore, to offer a definition of psychiatric social work and to touch upon certain features which exert influence on the way generic principles are adapted to the counseling practice which takes place in relation to psychiatry.

In addition to the mastery of certain specialized areas of knowledge, the counselor in psychiatric social work must be able to work in collaboration with the practice of psychiatry. This makes necessary a thorough familiarity with the various factors which influence the collaborative process. There is required also an ability to develop a pattern of teamwork with the purpose of offering the most effective psychiatric service to the patient.

Essential skill in counseling in the interest of the psychiatric patient in the last analysis derives from certain personality attributes of the counselor. Specifically, such skill grows out of basic attitudes precluding expression of certain responses usually associated with the manifestations of psychiatric illness. Such responses, if permitted undisciplined expression, hamper and obstruct the fullest use of the counseling relationship. The counselor in psychiatric social work who has achieved a discipline of such attitude becomes free to offer to patient or relative the use of his knowledge and counseling skill in the many and varied ways which grow out of the individualized need of each situation.

Counseling Handicapped Children and Their Parents

IRVING KAYE

Community Counseling Center
Jamaica, New York

THE HANDICAPPED child has recently become a focus of the lay public's attention. But this "sympathy" has not necessarily been translated to its fullest potentials in constructive practice. Needless to say we have gone a long way from some of the practices of Sparta, Greece and ancient Rome. It was not uncommon then to destroy infants who were obviously afflicted with extreme physical and mental handicaps. In Europe, specifically North Germany, the early law recognized the right of parents to kill deformed offspring. The general attitude was to regard deformity as a blight sent by God or as punishment for sin. Ridicule and contempt was the lot for those who deviated in any degree. Towards the latter part of the Middle Ages the handicapped came to be regarded superstitiously. At the birth of a handicapped child, the feeling was that a diabolical mother stole the right child and substituted her own. Both the ignorant and the informed believed that if such children—known as changelings—were maltreated enough the mothers would come again to get them and bring back the rightful child. Also prevalent during this period was the belief that an "evil eye" could be cast on a pregnant woman and thus cause deformity in her child.

The first beginning of hope for the improvement of conditions for the handicapped began to appear in the 18th century. The motivating force seemed to be the removal of the handicapped person from the community, not for his sake, but for the convenience of the members of the community who were outraged by the presence of a handicapped person in their midst. However, because of this, monasteries and other religious facilities were thrown open or converted into institutions for the care of the handicapped. The rise of these shelters gave the handicapped asylum, but did nothing in a constructive way to better their conditions.

With the opening of the 19th century a number of our practices began to change, but unfortunately not our attitudes. The phenomenal advance in medicine and the other physical sciences ushered in an era wherein it was felt that many disabilities could now be cured. When our expectations did not materialize, the demand for the segregation of the handicapped in institutions to remove them from society was reinforced. However, with the advance in knowledge and the increasing attention of the medical profession, the improvement in the lot of many of our handicapped grew rapidly. Attention began to be paid to some of the psychological as well as physical problems of the children and adults who were suffering from disabilities. This trend was accelerated by the insights gained from dynamic psychiatry which brought into sharp focus the observation that reactions to a handicapping condition are not always related to the extent of the injury but are very often colored by the person's feelings and attitudes about his handicap. With the advance in our knowledge, professionals in the field began to be dissatisfied with the one-dimensional, disability-focused approach to the handicapped. They began to realize that the functioning of a person with, and in spite of his disability, is the result of multiple and complex, as well as interrelated factors. The familiar experience of a child with a slight disability becoming immobilized, while another child with a far more extensive disability functioning above and beyond his expected limitations, required a more valid scientific explanation than was possible with the knowledge at hand. Thus was ushered in a period during which we began to look at the handicapped child as a total human being—with feelings and attitudes about his handicap and about the effects of the handicap on himself and on his family. The logical next step of focusing on the social and environmental conditions in which the handicapped child found himself was inevitable. When we began to look more closely at these factors, we began to see more clearly that the feelings of the handicapped child are shaped in the main by the reactions of significant people around him, and especially his parents. Investigators began to report the findings that a child's valuation or devaluation of his own body tends to reflect the value ascribed to it by those who take care of him. The emotional interaction between mother and infant, it was found, proceeds on a nonverbal level mainly—through bodily contact and sounds. Thus, the way the mother nurses, holds, and takes care of his needs conveys to the infant her feelings and attitudes toward him as well as towards his body. As the child grows, the mother's approval or disapproval of his body or any part of it begins to be conveyed verbally as well as nonverbally. The child senses and imitates these parental attitudes. In fact, some workers in the field report that the child perceives and imitates parental defenses against anxiety as well as their attitudes toward his body and its parts.

With this shift from the purely medical and specific-therapy approach to that of looking at the total child and his total life situation, it became obvious that we, somehow, had overlooked another significant part of the problem—the parents of the handicapped child.

In considering the parents of handicapped children, we must first be aware of the basic concepts held by all parents in relation to their children in our American culture. Parents in Twentieth-century American society are expected to make all kinds of sacrifices to give their children more opportunity and more material things than it was possible for them to have when they were children. Our child-centered culture leaves little doubt that we regard parents as less important than their children. When difficulties develop the conviction that they have failed in some way has been fostered by our educative efforts to such an extent that most parents begin to wonder where they have erred. To understand this phenomenon better we need to look more closely at the impact on a family when a handicapped child is brought in. Handicapped children do not, like normal children "just grow" if granted a fairly favorable emotional and physical milieu. Such children, especially if the handicap is extensive, need special medical treatment, perhaps assistance in feeding, dressing and toileting. And then there may be long periods of discouragement and frustration with no tangible rewards for such tremendous investments of time and effort. Is it any wonder that the introduction of the handicapped child produces severe strains on families? Professional workers need to be alert to characteristic trouble spots. For one thing, weaknesses in the relationship between husband and wife need to be strengthened lest hitherto minor differences become magnified. In families where both parents share the responsibility for the care of children, the father may be willing to take on a great deal more responsibility. However, where the father's role has been minimal, the increase in burdens may be on the mother alone. In such situations, we need to be alert to the attempts by the father to withdraw even further and leave the total care of the child to his wife. We need to recognize and accept the fact that neither the father nor mother have to give up his or her life for the handicapped child. With help and sharing of burdens, whether they be psychological or physical, most parents show a remarkable ability to handle responsibilities which at the beginning seem overwhelming. Where burdens are not lightened, the handicapped child's needs can become the center of family life to the exclusion of parental needs and the needs of other children in the family. In such cases the child himself may not be allowed to do what he can. With everything done for him there is limited possibility for trial runs and thus the child loses out in still another way in that he is not given the usual opportunities for normal development and growth toward independence. In addition, double standards of expectations within the family are set up with the handicapped child being excused from normal responsibilities. Siblings, when present, react to this inequality and their resentments add still another burden to the lot of the handicapped child and his parents.

Less frequently we may find parents rejecting or neglecting their handicapped child and making every effort to hide him from the world. Their fears thus override their acceptance of the child and his limitations. Such parents may also withdraw themselves, as well as the child, from all social contacts. This defensive isolation from social contact and group experience limits even further the opportunities for positive experience and adequate satisfaction of the needs of the handicapped child and thus prolongs his feelings of dependency and feelings of being "different." Such parents need encouragement and support of a professional worker to relieve their anxieties and fears. Approval and praise for any positive steps toward resuming social contacts can be extremely helpful. Then there is another way in which parents of handicapped children may handle the strains and added responsibilities. Not too infrequently the professional worker is faced by parents, who, with unrealistic optimism, will deny that the handicap poses any problem for them or their child. Thus, the statement that a severely handicapped child is "doing fine" may be given by the parents to all inquiries. The professional person needs to be alert to this defensive reaction against deep hurt and frustrating reality. Such defenses usually crumble when parents are given half a chance by an interested, sympathetic and helpful worker. Some parents seem to be overwhelmed with a sense of guilt, the source of which is unknown to them. In extreme cases such parents will need intensive psychiatric care. In milder cases, such parents can be helped through group or individual counseling to accept the handicapping condition for what it is rather than as a punishment for some deeply felt strivings which the parents cannot tolerate.

It is not difficult to visualize why the family of the handicapped child is particularly susceptible to disharmony and even disorganization if we examine the dynamics. Just what does it mean to become the parents of a handicapped child? Parents look forward to the birth of their baby. When it is born handicapped, all their plans and dreams seem destroyed. Their conscious and unconscious needs are frustrated. They feel disappointed, shocked, and even guilty. Some of the responsibility for the latter reaction, as we have seen earlier, can be traced to our cultural emphases involving an optimistic faith in ourselves and a taking of responsibility for what we and our children accomplish. With the introduction of a handicapped child, disturbing questions begin to gnaw at parents. "What is wrong with me?" "With my wife?" "What did I do wrong?" "Why did it happen to me?" Unfortunately, too, parents have come to judge themselves in comparative terms with their neighbors in relation to their children. The disability thus becomes an affront to family standing in the community. It is a reminder to the whole world and to the family itself that they have not been able to produce a normal child. Is it surprising then that parent-child relationship becomes strained and distorted?

Where there are siblings, the relationship between the handicapped child and his brothers or sisters becomes more complex and difficult. A number of reactions may occur depending upon such factors as the general atmosphere or tone in the family, the extent and severity of the handicapping condition, the age of the handicapped child, and the age of the other children. Some siblings may become afraid that they, too, will become handicapped (it will rub off on them) and so avoid the whole situation as well as the handicapped child. Others may become protective. Some siblings may react and become resentful because of the overprotection and undue attention that the handicapped child receives. Where the family is able to cope with the "unnatural situation in a natural way," the reactions of siblings may not be too different basically than one observes among children who are not handicapped.

Thus, as we can see any defect or handicap in a child greatly influences the feelings and attitudes of those around him, especially his parents. If the handicap is extensive the parents and other children need as much understanding and emotional support as does the child who is handicapped. Often, the time spent with the frightened and distraught parents, recognizing their plight and giving them some relief from their burdens, will help a great deal to soften the blow and pave the way for a realistic and constructive adjustment to the handicap.

Only in this way can both the handicapped child and his family be better prepared for the problems that lie ahead. Few, if any parents know or are capable to handle the intense feelings of disappointment, frustration, guilt and resentment which overwhelm them when they are faced with a child who is crippled or handicapped. A handicapped child may belong to a family where there are emotionally healthy parents, insecure parents, or neurotic parents. Very often the child has parents who are able to withstand an average amount of stress but who need help if the stress gets too great. Thus, professionals have become increasingly aware of the way parents of handicapped children have been reaching out for knowledge or help to assist them in understanding, as well as coping with, the needs of their handicapped children. The fact that professionals are "tuned in" with greater frequency is attested by the fact that agencies serving handicapped children have increasingly set up programs to help parents. One such type of program focuses on community action to improve services for all children having a specific handicap. The other type of program usually is geared to helping the parents in their daily living with their handicapped children.

Before going any further in our discussion it would seem expedient to define what we mean by "handicapped." At best it is difficult and often confusing, except in extreme situations, to attempt to separate the "normal" and the "handicapped" child. There is probably no child who is up to par in every respect and very few children who are totally disabled. In reality there exists a wide range of capacities and abilities with no exact line separating the normal from the handicapped. Thus, we need to avoid looking at children suffering from physical and/or mental limitation as a group apart, distinct and identifiable as such. We cannot, however, lose sight of the fact that some children have brain pathology, mental defect, or physical limitations which are so extreme as to make personality development of more than a most limited kind impossible. In other children, however, the limitations are so slight or of such a nature that it is not the handicap itself but the reactions of his family, friends, and society in general that is most important. A noticeable defect may impair functioning as well as handicap a child physically and yet not leave him emotionally crippled. Thus, the child suffering from poliomyelitis, although he may be disabled, has more recently been helped with his adjustment problems as a result of a more understanding attitude among parents and the public at large. From the foregoing one can readily see that the prevalence of handicapping conditions among children will depend to a great extent on the criteria used. Accurate data on the number of handicapped children in the United States are not available, although conservative estimates put the total at 5,615,000. Handicapped children fall into many diagnostic categories. They include children with visible physical deformities and those with diseases occurring deep within the body with few if any obvious visible deformities, but with marked effects on the child's ability to adjust to life, physically and emotionally. Among the latter handicapping conditions which chiefly affect function rather than external appearance are epilepsy, congenital heart disease, rheumatic heart disease, hearing impairment, mental retardation, etc. Children with these handicaps are always answering embarrassing questions about the reasons for their inability to do one thing or another. These children do not appear to be particularly different from healthy children. Yet they have handicaps which impose severe limitations on their behavior.

For our purposes, we shall consider a child handicapped if he has some physical, emotional or mental limitation that makes it necessary for him to receive specialized services in order for him to develop adequately. In this sense, we see that the presence of a handicap places intrinsic limitations on a child as he struggles to reach the ordinary life goals of his age group. A child who cannot hear well or see well will rarely reach the educational or social norms which characterize his normally hearing or seeing peers. Adequate human relationships depend on ease of communications and when there is a block to such communication due to such physical factors as deafness or blindness, the attainment of potentials becomes difficult, even under optimum conditions. Simple motor acts such as grasping, manipulating, and coordinating movements are learned with great difficulty by young handicapped children. When we view the task in the context of organizing such acts into patterns of eating, dressing, bathing, writing, or playing a game we can begin to appreciate the difficulties encountered by the handicapped child. Another factor which plays an important part in influencing and determining a child's responses, is his age at the onset of the handicapping condition. If he has known what it means to be "normal," the disease or injury bringing on the handicapping condition may throw him into a state of anxiety and fear. His concept of "self" may be shattered, especially if a readjustment involving a change in patterns and aspirations is involved. Ordinarily a sudden illness or accident is a blow to the sense of trust and security the child has in the outside world. He begins to doubt himself, once the blow has struck, and even begins to doubt the integrity of his body which he has up to then taken for granted. Especially difficult to handle may be the narrowed limits of achievement and expectations. Where a handicapping condition involves restrictive treatments, frustration may result because of interference with normal activity. The wearing of a cast, the complete restrictions imposed during and immediately following the infectious stage of rheumatic fever, are but a few examples in which severe limitations of movement are an integral part of treatment. Where major surgery is required, it is viewed by most children as a physical and psychic threat. Fears of being punished by mutilation, fears of being abandoned and deserted are usually mobilized by surgical procedures and the inevitable hospitalization and separation from home and family. Many handicapping conditions produce varied degrees of physical discomfort, ranging from slight to severe pain. Such conditions produce a preoccupation with self and internal stimuli. Illness and enforced inactivity may interfere with the developing sense of autonomy. Pleasures of exploring and mastering have to be curtailed. Various restrictions which may be painful and which may be too rigidly enforced may lead to a feeling of helplessness and dependency. Handicapping conditions may even interfere with those components of personality which are being established as well as affecting those that have been already achieved. Thus children from three to six years of age are especially prone to feelings of being punished and mutilated by illness or accident. Adolescents may be affected in their sense of identity and their developing relationship to members of the opposite sex. Especially difficult for children six years to twelve are any curbs on their desire to learn and to achieve.

It is obviously impossible to describe here all or even most of the handicapping conditions or to say much about any one of them. Rather, a few of the common handicapping conditions that occur frequently or that have aroused public concern will be discussed. These conditions are presented to illustrate the variation that disabling conditions involve and to point up the fact that handicaps have much in common in their effects on children, parents, and the community at large.

CHILDREN WITH RHEUMATIC FEVER

Rheumatic fever is a children's disease which usually strikes first at the age of seven or eight but sometimes earlier or later. It is very rare under the age of three. The number of children who have rheumatic fever or its aftermath, rheumatic heart disease, is estimated at 675,000. With this disease there is a real possibility of death and although the young child may not have an understanding of the danger he may reflect the fears of his parents. In addition, any involvement of the heart carries with it the dread that its victim may die suddenly. These fears are heightened by the medical procedures necessary which younger children do not, and even cannot understand. Even more difficult for some children is the regimen of rest and dependency which is laid out for them. By the nature of the illness, that it may recur, the child's and parents' anxieties are heightened. At times, a child with rheumatic fever must be removed to a hospital or to a convalescent home with all the traumatic implications that such a step involves. The physical restrictions, the need to isolate a child from his peers on occasion, tend to interfere with his emotional development. It may also cause a break in his schooling and other activities which give him security and support. One can make few generalizations on the effect of the disease on a particular child. The disease varies in severity and intensity. The effects, aside from the disease itself, will also depend on the personality of the child—some children may be threatened by imposed physical dependency; others welcome it. Most children recover to the extent that they can lead a normal life.

Nevertheless, it is important that attention be paid to the emotional problems all along the line. The parents, if they are to be of maximum help, need to know realistically the medical situation and the prognosis. They need the opportunity to discuss their fears and anxieties. Only with adequate professional guidance can they be helped to understand what meaning the illness has for their child and how they can best meet his needs. Tendencies to hinder or restrict children unduly need to be constantly evaluated on the basis of sound medical advice. Separation from the family, especially, needs to be examined closely in the light of emotional as well as physical effects. Much can be done to help parents with their own burdens so that they can minimize the trauma of rheumatic fever on their children. If we are not "tuned in" to lightening the load that the parents carry, the child's disability can well become the pivot around which underlying emotional tensions of parent and child come to the surface. At one extreme we may get the over-solicitous parent who insists on marked curtailment of the child's activities when such curtailment is not warranted by the degree of the child's disability. Such a child will come to believe that he is far more crippled than he really is. At the other extreme is the overindulgent parent who permits activities that are dangerous in view of the child's disability. Obviously, neither the over-solicitous parent nor over-indulgent parent is acting appropriately in such a situation. Both such parents need help in dealing with the unresolved emotional problems in themselves of which they are often unaware.

CHILDREN WITH CEREBRAL PALSY

Injury to the brain, if severe enough, can alter the functioning of the whole organism. It can result in paralysis, mental deficiency, convulsions, blindness, loss of speech and many other defects or it may cause abnormalities in thought, in behavior and in personality. The type of brain damage which goes under the name of cerebral palsy is applied to any paralysis, weakness, lack of coordination or aberration of the motor system resulting from brain pathology. Except in extreme cases, cerebral palsied children can be greatly aided by well-planned training programs. But it must be remembered that even under optimum conditions few of such children can attain normal speech, gait or other skills.

It is variously estimated that there are approximately 285,000 children in the country suffering from cerebral palsy. Much has been discovered on the way to teach such handicapped children to use other parts of the brain and retrain other muscles to replace those over which they have lost control. However, science has as yet found no way to repair or restore damaged brain cells. As a result, for the foreseeable future the cerebral palsied child will need long and extensive help from a variety of the helping professions. Concomitantly, the parents will need infinite understanding and skilled assistance if they are to be of maximum help to their handicapped children.

Contrary to popular belief there is little association between the degree of physical and mental involvement in cerebral palsy. In some children the physical defect looms largest; in others, the mental defect. But since the brain is affected, we find a multiplicity of symptoms. There may be primary emotional problems because of the particular brain injury. Even in those situations where this is not the case, the nature of the handicap and the way the cerebral palsied child is regarded by the community is likely, and often does cause, secondary emotional and behavior problems. Until very recently the cerebral palsied child was socially stigmatized, usually kept hidden away, out of sight of relatives and friends and others. Because it was felt that they were inevitably feeble-minded, training was not considered possible. With the acceptance by the community that this is a handicap about which something can be done, the picture is changing rapidly. With the increased hope, however, comes greater responsibility and burdening of parents of such children. They need expert professional help for a realistic assessment of the child's potential. Is there a possibility of reasonable success in a training program? Is it a hopeless quest? Will the child be helped best away from home? Can a program geared exclusively to his interests in a residential setting counterbalance staying at home and thereby lose day-by-day evidences of being loved by his parents and family? In severely disabled cases the parents are continually faced with heavy physical and emotional burdens and are constantly struggling with the effect of the total situation on their own lives. Even with these difficult reality factors much can be accomplished through skillful guidance.

CHILDREN WITH EPILEPSY

Reference is found to epilepsy throughout ancient literature. It has been observed among all races, in all parts of the earth, and in all stages of history. In fact, epileptic seizures may be older than man himself for they affect other members of the animal kingdom. Yet, there is no unanimity about the concept of epilepsy and the nature of the disorder is obscure. When examined closely, the condition loses its identity as a separate disease entity and it merges into what has been described as convulsive states, including many epilepsies of different origin. The one common feature noted is the direct influence upon the central nervous system which results in recurring seizures.

Although the cause of epilepsy still eludes medical research, it now seems generally accepted in the field that it is not hereditary. Also, mental deficiency or mental deterioration is not a necessary concomitant or consequence of seizures. Due to the social stigma attached to this condition it is almost impossible to determine with any degree of accuracy how many children are afflicted with epilepsy. It is variously estimated that there are 400,000 epileptic children in the country. Of that number fewer than 1500 such children received treatment under the Crippled Children's Program of the Children's Bureau of the United States Department of Health, Education and Welfare in 1958. How many others were treated privately is not known. Unfortunately, the reluctance of parents, because of shame, fear and guilt to seek the very constructive help that is available, either through public or private sources, indicates again the price we all pay for adverse community attitudes. It is such attitudes and feelings which directly interfere with the normal development of children afflicted with epilepsy. These attitudes also prevent the epileptic child from using whatever capacities and potentials he may possess. As long as the community remains skeptical of the effectiveness of therapy, it is doubtful that many facilities for treatment will be established or that much support will be given to research. And yet, the reality is that with present medical knowledge and skills the great majority of epileptic children can be relieved of most of their seizures.

Epilepsy with its attendant, visible and terror-inspiring symptoms are deeply upsetting to many persons. This situation coupled with the mistaken beliefs that epilepsy is evidence of a bad heredity and that it is associated with mental defect and retardation have most telling repercussions in parental attitudes and feelings about their children who are subject to seizures. In view of this, parents of epileptic children urgently need help if the children are to benefit from the scientific advances that have been made. Because they are more prone to shame and guilt feelings than parents of children with other handicapping conditions, the development of group discussions and action is a most hopeful one. It is in such meetings with others who are similarly situated that gives these parents reassurance. The mere knowledge that others have the same problem relieves parents of being terribly alone and different which they inevitably feel when they meet only parents of normal children. The group meeting itself is constructive since normal group solidarity tends to overcome the sense of helplessness which so many of the parents have. Through such groups, too, parents benefit from what others have tried in the care of their children and in meeting adverse community attitudes. But more than anything else parents of epileptic children need to gain a perspective so that they do not become paralyzed into accepting a feeling of helplessness and hopelessness about their epileptic children. Only in this way can they come to grips with the problem and help their children fulfill themselves in spite of their handicaps.

CHILDREN WHO ARE BLIND

Seeing is such a vital function that the average person finds it difficult to grasp or even understand the idea of not being able to see. Aggravating this psychological barrier to understanding, is the fear and terror that the possibility of blindness evokes in the seeing. In addition, cultural patterns tend to stereotype blind persons into a single homogeneous group and thus strengthen popular misconceptions and misunderstandings about those who cannot see. The treatment that the blind have received reflects to a large degree the effect of their disability upon the seeing public. Many workers in the field have long felt that the "differentness" and the inability of the great majority of blind people to make an adjustment within our society can be partially traced to those attitudes of the seeing.

The above should not be construed to minimize the heavy burdens carried by those who cannot see. It cannot be forgotten that the blind operate on different realities, since they depend on other than visual perceptions which the seeing person uses mainly. Also, the blind have to depend to a large degree on the seeing if they are to meet even their barest everyday needs. Of necessity, these constant dependencies can and sometimes do destroy self-confidence to a degree that immobilizes all efforts on the part of a blind person to do anything for himself. Thus, more than anything else persons who cannot see need understanding, encouragement and constructive help if they are to make even a minimum adjustment in the seeing world.

The term blind is usually used to denote visual acuity of 20/200 or less by Snellen charts in the better eye with correcting lenses. Also a person is considered blind if his field of vision is so limited that he can see only a very small area at a time. As can be seen this definition covers a wide range. At one end are those who can see—a person may be able to count fingers of the hand a few feet away, or to recognize by sight a person who stands very close. At the other extreme are those who are totally blind. Also, within the group are those born blind or blinded so early in their life that they either have never known sight or have only a dim memory of what things look like. Others become blind at various ages and stages in their growth and development—when they are in grade school or high school—when they have barely learned daily routines of living or at a time when such routines are well established. Most authorities in the field believe that those children who are blinded after five years of age retain their visual orientation and tend to organize new information around their past visual experiences. The congenitally blind person of necessity must be different from the blinded as well as sighted population in his approach to his environment.

The figures on the number of children who are blind are incomplete. It is estimated that there are approximately 25,000 blind children in the country. Happily, the incidence of blindness due to retrolental fibroplasia is now being reduced by controlling the use of oxygen in cases of prematurely born babies. It has been estimated that this condition alone accounted for 49 per cent of blindness in children under 7 years of age.

As with other handicapping conditions the crucial ingredient for adjustment is the kind of relationship that the child has with its parents and other significant persons around him. Blind children, it has been found by workers in the field, are particularly sensitive to the feeling tones of those around them, even though their behavior often does not seem to show it. Thus, parents need skilled help in understanding the behavior of their blind children. Knowledge about what to expect and what often they can do, can minimize the anxiety and severe distress that the parents feel. With such knowledge and understanding parents can help encourage their blind children to reach out to their environment, which is so vitally important to children who cannot see. Moreover, recognition needs to be given by the community to the heavy demands imposed on parents of blind children to the end that services and facilities are provided to enable such parents to meet their children's needs at successive levels of development. One recent encouraging development has been the acceptance by certain nursery schools of selective blind children into their regular programs. Again the success of such efforts is related to the availability of skilled counseling help to both the parents of the blind children and to the staffs of the schools involved. It is in the development and extension of similar programs and services which we take for granted for the sighted that the blind child can look forward with renewed hope for an opportunity to develop into a human being in his own right.

SUMMARY

As we have already observed it is difficult, except in the more extreme situations, to separate the "normal" and the "handicapped" child. Consequently, it is often not the handicap itself but the reactions of family, friends, and society in general to the child's defect that is determining. While the expressed attitudes of the physically normal majority toward the handicapped are mainly positive, their behavior reflects an essentially negative attitude. This is demonstrated by the readiness of leaders in education, for example, to accept segregated schools and classes for the handicapped whereas they would strongly refect similar segregation on any other basis. Also, the handicapped person in our society still has the status of a minority group, reflecting the negative attitudes of the unhandicapped majority who look upon their less fortunate brethren as "different." As a result the handicapped child is often doubly "punished." Because of his handicap the handicapped child has many special needs. However, the community fails to establish resources to meet those needs because of the very fact that those needs are "different." Thus, facilities for the brain damaged child, the blind child, the mentally retarded child and other children with special needs are few and far between. Also, in his personal life the handicapped child is often pulled and pushed by opposing and opposite reactions, acceptance and rejection, with the result that he is often anxious and tense. Learning to live with their handicapped child, and with their feelings about him and his handicap, imposes tremendous stresses and burdens upon parents of such children. Not only the handicapped child but also his distraught and frightened parents need help.

Faced with these problems what can we in the helping professions do? First in emphasis is to highlight the problems that the handicapped child and his family face so that more lenient, understanding and healthier attitudes are developed by the public at large. But more than that is the need on the part of the helping professions to become attuned to the ways in which families of handicapped children keep asking for help with their very real difficulties and problems. Too often we tend to label as parental rejection, cries for assistance to lighten their burdens. So saturated are many of us with the concept of holding the parents responsible, that we lose the opportunity to help. By giving the parents a breathing spell, a little more security, a chance to be free of guilt and remorse, we can soften the blow and help pave the way for their picking up on their burdens and responsibilities. Unless the parents get the help they request and need, the goal of coming to terms with the disturbing situation that the disability has introduced and of being able to accept the child and his handicap on a realistic basis is seldom achieved. The experience of workers in the field is that acceptance of the full nature of the child's handicap is the basis for the parents maintaining their emotional equilibrium. Only then can they begin to gain some of the satisfactions of normal parenthood regardless of the responsibility, hard work and heartbreak that is so often their lot.

Second, we in the helping professions need to use our advantageous position of seeing the deficiencies in social institutions as they affect individuals, to report on our observations and to join with other groups in the promotion of needed community facilities. If services are inadequate or not available, it is incumbent upon us to help educate the community to the need. But even more important, we have an obligation as the delegated "conscience" of the community to give support to community action programs for the establishment of such services.

Third, we must see that the family has access to existant help. At the present time in most large centers of population, the child with an overt handicap may come in contact with a social worker who is in a position to assist him with his problem. However, even in the large cities handicapped children do not necessarily or even usually come to the attention of a professionally trained social worker. Here, as well as in small communities, where professionally trained staff may not be available, it becomes the responsibility of other professional workers in hospitals to be cognizant of the need and therefore refer the family to whatever community facilities exist. In some instances, it is the teacher or public health nurse who must recognize the need for referral. The family spiritual adviser is also in a good position to focus the family's attention on this need for help where it exists.

In conclusion, we must stress that skillful help and adequate services when given to the families of handicapped children, can sustain such families through the many crises and problems of everyday living that they inevitably face. In salvaging the families we are in effect helping save the children. If we allow the family life of the handicapped child to disintegrate, we also give up on the child.

BIBLIOGRAPHY

1. American Heart Association and the National Heart Institute, USPHS: 1950. "Proceedings First National Conference on Cardiovascular Diseases." New York: International Press.
2. AUERBACH, ALPINE B.: July–August 1961. "Group Education for Parents of the Handicapped." *Children*, pp. 135–140.
3. BENDER, LAURETTA: September 1945. "Infants Reared in Institutions: Permanently Handicapped." Bulletin, Child Welfare League of America, New York.
4. BLANK, ROBERT H.: July 1955. "Psychoanalytic Considerations for Professional Workers in the Prevention of Blindness." *Social Casework*, pp. 319–324.
5. BOWLBY, JOHN: 1951. *Maternal Care and Mental Health.* Geneva: World Health Organization of the United Nations.
6. BRAZELTON, T. BERRY, HOLDEN, RICHMOND, and TALBOT, BEATRICE: September 1953. "Emotional Aspects of Rheumatic Fever in Children." *The Jr. of Pediatrics*, **43**, No. 3.

7. Children's Bureau: 1953. "The Preschool Child who is Blind." Folder 39, U.S. Dept. of Health, Education & Welfare, Children's Bureau.

8. Children's Bureau: 1952. "Emotional Problems Associated with Handicapping Conditions in Children." Publications No. 336.

9. Children's Bureau and Office of Education: 1950. "The Child with Cerebral Palsy." Folder 34, Children's Bureau.

10. COLE, NYLA J. and TABOROFF, LEONARD H.: July 1955. "The Psychological Problems of the Congenitally Blind Child." *Amer. Jr. of Orthopsychiatry*, pp. 627–639.

11. COLEMAN, ROSE W., KRIS, ERNST, and PROVENCE, SALLY: 1953. "The Study of Variations of Early Parental Attitudes: a Preliminary Report." *Psychoanalytic Study of the Child*, **8**, pp. 20–47. New York: Inter. Univ. Press.

12. ENGLISH, O. SPURGEON, and PEARSON, GERALD H. J.: 1945. *Emotional Problems of Living*. New York: W. W. Norton & Co., Inc.

13. FREUD, ANNA: 1952. "The Role of Bodily Illness in the Mental Life of Children." *Psychoanalytic Study of the Child*, **7**, pp. 69–81. New York: Inter. Univ. Press.

14. ILG, FRANCES L., and AMES, LOUISE BATES: 1955. *Child Behavior*. New York: Harper.

15. JAHODA, MARIE: October 1953. "The Meaning of Psychological Health." *Social Casework*, pp. 349–354.

16. JOSSELYN, IRENE M.: January 1949. "Emotional Implications of Rheumatic Heart Disease in Children." *Amer. Jr. of Orthopsychiatry*, pp. 87–100.

17. KAYE, IRVING: 1951. "Evidence of Social and Psychological Maladjustment Revealed in a Study of Seventeen Children who have Idiopathic Petit Mal Epilepsy." *Jr. of Child Psychiatry*, **2**, Sect. 2, pp. 115–160.

18. KERBY, C. EDITH: 1952. "Causes and Prevention of Blindness in Children of School Age." Sight Saving Review 22, Vol. I (Pub. 110, Nat. Society For the Prevention of Blindness, Inc.).

19. KLINE, DRAZA: January 1953. "Should Children be Separated from their Parents?" *The Child*, Washington.

20. KOLODNY, RALPH L.: May–June 1957. "Therapeutic Group Work with Handicapped Children." *Children*, pp. 95–101.

21. LENNOX, WILLIAM G.: 1941. *Science and Seizures: New Light on Epilepsy and Migraine*. New York: Harper.

22. LEWIS, RICHARD S., with STRAUSS, ALFRED A., and LEHTINEN, LAURA E.: 1951. *The Other Child. The Brain-injured Child*. New York: Grune & Stratton.

23. MACGREGOR, FRANCES COOKE, ABEL, THEODORA M., BRYT, ALBERT, LAUER, EDITH, and WEISSMAN, SERENA: 1953. *Facial Deformities and Plastic Surgery: A Psychosocial Study*. Springfield: Charles C. Thomas.

24. MILMAN, DORIS H.: July 1952. "Group Therapy with Parents—An Approach to the Rehabilitation of Physically Disabled Children." *The Jr. of Pediatrics*, **42**, No. 2.

25. MOTTO, R. L.: February 1956: "Emotional Factors in Physically Handicapped Children." *California Medicine*, **84**, No. 2.

26. POWERS, ANN M., GRAYSON, MORRIS, and LEVI, JOSEPH: June 1951. "Mother–Child Relationships in Rehabilitation of the Physically Disabled." *Social Casework*, pp. 261–265.

27. RUSK, HOWARD A. and TAYLOR, EUGENE E.: 1953. *Living with a Disability*. New York: McGraw-Hill.

28. SEARS, MACCOBY and LEVIN: 1957. *Patterns of Child Rearing*. Row, Peterson & Co.

29. SULLIVAN, HARRY: 1953. *The Interpersonal Theory of Psychiatry*. New York: W. W. Norton & Co.

Counseling in Alcoholism

RAYMOND G. McCARTHY

Professor of Education
Executive Director
Summer School of Alcohol Studies
Rutgers Center of Alcohol Studies
New Brunswick, N.J.

COUNSELING with alcoholics in a variety of settings has been attempted for generations. The clinic staff, the probation and parole officer, the clergyman, the employer, the family physician and the family friend—each has employed his training or his intuition in an effort to aid the uncontrolled drinker. Such efforts in the past have been generally unsuccessful and discouraging both for the alcoholic and the counselor.

THEORIES ABOUT ALCOHOLISM

Many factors must enter into any evaluation of the reasons for this failure. The nature of the condition has been oversimplified by some groups. Uncontrolled drinking is sometimes interpreted as a consequence of the ingestion of substantial amounts of alcohol with resulting tissue changes which impose a physical craving. On this assumption, counseling involves interpreting the sequence of events to the drinker, advising him not to drink, and expecting that his intelligence and sense of responsibility will enable him to maintain sobriety.

There has been a tendency to focus attention on the act of drinking and its consequences. The popular exhortation, "Why don't you drink the way I do?" has been followed by the alcoholic with disastrous results to him. This has suggested the possibility of a difference in metabolism, in the way the alcoholic's body disposes of alcohol.

Attempts to alter body chemistry have been made via hormone and vitamin injections with only limited and indecisive results.

The psychiatric literature offers several theories on the etiology of alcoholism. These include oral eroticism, latent homosexuality, inadequacy and inferiority in personal and social relations, generalized feelings of anxiety and guilt, and unresolved aggressive drives. The labels psychoneurotic, latent schizophrenic and psychopath occur frequently. Psychiatrists, although they do not agree on the nature of the condition, generally consider the prognosis in alcoholism poor. A few selected patients are treated privately and with good results. Most psychiatric services prefer to devote their limited staff time to cases which promise to respond to therapy more effectively than does the alcoholic.

The lack of agreement among professional groups on the causes of alcoholism has influenced popular thinking and attitudes. There are approximately 70 million users of alcoholic beverages in this country. Between 6 and 7 per cent are in difficulty with drinking and are labeled alcoholics. There is a ratio of 5.5 males to 1 female. Social drinkers, drawing on their personal experiences, believe the alcoholic could control his drinking if he would use a little will power. Because he does not respond as expected, he is said to be lacking in character and personality strengths.

The alcoholic, in self-defence, must deny that he is either a worthless kind of person or a pathological one. He supports his denial by attempting, unsuccessfully, to drink in a controlled manner. When he resumes drinking after a period of sobriety, his friends and some counselors conclude that he does not wish to recover, that he is egocentric, irresponsible, unsuitable for treatment. Severe pathology in personality is assumed to account for the absence of motivation. The projection of failure in treatment to the alcoholic's lack of motivation or his pathology has obscured the possible inadequacy of the counseling service.

NATURE OF ALCOHOLISM

Alcoholism is a form of personality disorder in which acute episodes of drunkenness are conspicuous. Clinical evidence demonstrates that among many uncontrolled drinkers chronic aspects of the disorder operate during periods of sobriety. Apparently the alcoholic experiences a form of emotional imbalance which has its roots in early life situations and is marked by inadequacies in interpersonal relations. Through the depressant action of alcohol on the nervous system, he achieves a pseudounity of personality. Conflicting drives either disappear or are resolved under alcohol. Drinking becomes an adjustment technique which, in the early stages of the progression of alcoholism, may appear to serve a useful function. In the advanced stages of the disorder, drinking accentuates emotional imbalance and personal and social disorganization.

The alcoholic population embraces a cross section of American society. Segments of this population exhibit severe pathology but there is no typical alcoholic personality. Counseling techniques which are effective with one class of patients will not necessarily work with others. Moreover, outside a specialized alcoholism clinic, few counselors have an opportunity to observe cases representative of the various types within the alcoholic population.

The private physician will treat a type of patient rarely seen in the alcoholic ward of a municipal hospital. Parishioners seeking advice from the minister or priest ordinarily exhibit characteristics somewhat different from those of alcoholics in the county jail or in the case load of a probation or parole officer. Relatively few alcoholics seek assistance at social agencies where a high level of counseling is available, although their families appear frequently at family service or municipal welfare offices.

It is misleading to speak of "the alcoholic," although this practice is resorted to as an economy in language. Alcoholics vary in personality assets and limitations, in accessibility to counseling, and in organic and mental pathology. Every person who would counsel an alcoholic has a responsibility to determine to what degree his professional skills are adequate for the specific situation. Referrals should be made to other agencies when indicated as soon as possible. Only in this way can the effectiveness of counseling be determined.

DISTINGUISHING DIFFERENT GROUPS IN THE ALCOHOLIC POPULATION

It becomes necessary for discussion purposes to distinguish certain poorly defined groups of alcoholics. The groups overlap and the characteristics which they exhibit vary widely in degree. Practically speaking, they represent diverse personality and behavior traits clustering around a central point.

One group consists of men and women in the age range 35–48 years, who have demonstrated competence in a profession or field of work, in family and community relations, and in other areas which ordinarily reflect some degree of social adjustment. They are of at least average intelligence, are sensitive to their responsibilities and have some capacity for developing and maintaining interpersonal relations. Yet they are constantly under stress. Their accomplishments have been achieved only with the expenditure of considerable effort. They are uncomfortable much of the time. Small amounts of alcohol relieve their distress but they appear to be psychologically vulnerable to the effects of alcohol. They resort to excessive drinking repetitively and in time the alcoholic fantasy becomes a goal in itself which supersedes ordinary socially approved goals. For most people, drinking is an adjunct to a social situation and terminates automatically with the termination of the situation. For these alcoholics, the social situation is the justification for drinking which, out of control, continues for hours, days or weeks, ending only with physical or financial exhaustion, or when interrupted at home or in a hospital.

A second group consists of men and women who may appear similar in age range and background to those in group one. They may or may not have demonstrated some degree of social competence. However, it is apparent at first contact that there is severe emotional disturbance at the level of a diagnosable psychoneurosis.

The third group is composed of men whose histories reveal only limited capacities for adjustment. They have never achieved sustained success in a job. Many have never married. They are repeaters in the local courts and jails, and frequent the fringe areas of urban communities. Heavy drinking is the practice in the sub-society in which they move.

A fourth group, probably the smallest, consists of borderline cases of mental illness. Their drinking often obscures the basic condition. They are frequently labeled alcoholics although the primary problem is a form of mental disorder.

THE ALCOHOLIC AT THE INITIAL INTERVIEW

An alcoholic in group one ordinarily appears at a counseling center following a drinking episode. His defences are down, his need for acceptance is such that he responds to pressure from family and friends to seek help. He approaches the first interview with mixed feelings, characterized by conflicting drives. He may assert that he has learned his lesson and is through drinking, yet he is able to rationalize his behavior and project the excesses associated with it to some responsibility other than his.

Most alcoholics in group one are sincere in their statements that they have had enough of drunkenness and sprees. But the idea of permanent total abstinence is frightening for alcoholics; they find it impossible to visualize an acceptable existence without recourse to alcohol. They aspire to become social drinkers, notwithstanding past failures. Attainment of controlled drinking for the alcoholic is impossible at the present stage of scientific knowledge of the condition. The compelling nature of the psychological need to drink like his non-alcoholic friends, a need which his intelligence and experience contradicts, is an indication of the seriousness of the emotional distortion of the individual.

The initial interview provides an opportunity for the alcoholic to test the counselor. Some alcoholics have a need to be punished verbally by an authoritarian figure. Criticism enables them to atone for guilt and provides justification for terminating the counseling relationship. Others have the ability to intellectualize their emotional problems. They have read widely, they have many logical answers to the alcoholism problem, and they assure the counselor that now they understand how to manage their lives. Still others exhibit an air of marked dependence and compliance which overlays a substantial amount of hostility and aggression.

Every person seeking help after years of uncontrolled drinking should receive a careful physical and laboratory check-up. Although the popular concept of extreme physical deterioration associated with alcoholism has been modified by clinical experience, organic disturbances which have been obscured by alcohol often require medical attention. Any person undertaking a program of psychological adjustment should maintain maximum physical efficiency. Moreover, a favorable report on a physical examination is reassuring to the alcoholic, who feels guilty because of the harm he imagines his brain, nervous system and other organs have suffered.

THE COUNSELOR AT THE INITIAL INTERVIEW

Because his defenses are down, an impression of the underlying personality of the drinker can be gained by the counselor during the first interview. Most alcoholics will talk about their drinking and this often provides an area for discussion around which pertinent social background information can be gained.

The drinking pattern is important. Whether counseling is concerned with a daily drinker, an episodic or intermittent drinker, or one exhibiting a regular cycle of sprees, the pattern provides clues to the emotional dynamics underlying the alcoholism. The daily drinker may come to an interview mildly under the influence of alcohol. The periodic and the episodic types, however, will remain sober for days and sometimes for weeks. They present the appearance of successful adjustment and the counselor may be misled into thinking that sobriety, and what appears to be a good relationship, are the results of his personal efforts. It may mean only that the cycle which characterizes the man's drinking is at a low point on the curve when he seeks assistance. The counselor should anticipate rising tension, resistance, broken appointments, and eventually a spree, unless he can marshal techniques to prevent this.

An effective response to counseling is unlikely while drinking continues. Nevertheless, it is naive to assume that a daily drinker who is functioning at a relatively low level of psychological development can give up alcohol for more than brief periods until some emotional growth takes place. On the other hand, the patient who is keeping a schedule of interviews but continuing his drinking without change sooner or later must be faced with alternatives.

At the initial interview there should be recognition, though perhaps unspoken, of the ultimate goal of total sobriety as one aspect of recovery. That this needs to be stated openly, that it should be made a condition of further appointments, that promises or pledges should be either given or accepted, is definitely contraindicated.

An important function of the first interview is to determine the nature of the emergency situation which brought the drinker to the agency. Although recovery implies a significant change in the emotional life of the individual, it is unrealistic to expect the alcoholic to be concerned with the emotional past while the immediate present holds serious threats for him. He should be helped to work out a plan of action to cope with the environmental pressures which surround him. The skill he displays in working through these details may indicate his potential for treatment.

There is growing recognition that the counselor in the first interview or two may need to become more active than has been traditional. This means that he will allow himself to appear to become involved to some degree in the situation. That this can be done without jeopardizing the situation has been demonstrated in the Connecticut Commission on Alcoholism Clinics as reported by Jean Sapir, formerly Psychiatric Social Work Supervisor.

"The diffusion of the difficulty in alcoholics, which involves physical distress, social pressure, and emotional torment (one big headache), is characteristic of the new patient on his first entry into the clinic. The physician–caseworker team, by handling realistically the emergency problems presented, can offer an effective initial response to the addictive drinker's conflicted 'cry of help.' His motivation for crossing our threshold is usually a gun at his back in the form of real disaster—social, physical, or mental. Building up a creative rapport between the clinic and this conflicted, fearful, evasive, and above all, tentative new patient is possible only if there is clear recognition of the real crisis in his affairs which brings him to us. Understanding the deeper aspects of his individual problem will at first be a secondary consideration. Help must be extended toward getting him out of his immediate predicament so that he will be motivated to continue contact. Necessary as it will be eventually to treat him like any other medical-psychiatric patient—with regulation of satisfactions and frustrations in the therapist–patient relationship—this approach must be held in reserve during the initial stages of the contact. Because of the nature and urgency of his specific needs, his needs must be met in some measure in these first contacts.

"When an alcoholic comes to a clinic, it is because he thinks the clinic can do something, usually in regard to the predicament his drinking has created. This urgent need usually takes precedence in his mind over the implicit purpose of his coming—treatment of his addictive drinking. It is important that we help him understand that we are aware of his conflict about giving up alcohol—or even seeing it as a problem—and of his wish to utilize contact with us for secondary gains. Some of these secondary gains we should accept as legitimate needs.

". . . The alcoholic often attempts to use the clinic for no other reason than to impress someone that he is 'doing something' about his drinking. Even when his expressed wish for help is genuine, he will attempt, in his drive to maintain the satisfactions of drinking, to engage his therapist in the intellectual game of searching for 'causes' behind his addiction, using this device to sabotage therapeutic efforts to have him face, and do something about, his current drinking."

The experience of a number of clinics indicates that it is preferable to work directly with the alcoholic for a period of time without involving his spouse or another person. This allows the patient to feel that he is taking some action on his own, that he controls the situation, and that he is doing something about his problem independently of pressure from his wife or friends. When it becomes necessary to include the wife in the program, it should be done only with the consent of the alcoholic, unless there is obvious indication of dishonesty in the relationship or irresponsibility associated, for example, with physical or mental illness.

The counselor should be ready at the first interview to make a referral to another treatment source if the situation appears to be one which he cannot or should not attempt to handle. It is unwise for a clergyman, for example, to continue to counsel a seriously disturbed psychoneurotic or latent schizophrenic. He is not only wasting his own time but he also needs to recognize his ethical responsibility to refer the man or woman to a service equipped to deal with the condition. If a good relationship has been established, and with the full understanding of all parties concerned, the counselor may continue to see the alcoholic under an arrangement with the agency responsible for treatment.

COUNSELING INTERVIEWS

The goal in the treatment of alcoholism is to achieve a realignment of emotional forces within the personality so that the need to use alcohol because of internal and external pressures is reduced. This is a long-term process. For many alcoholics in group one, however, it is an attainable goal.

The chances of effective adjustment are frequently reflected in the life history. Alcoholism is only one aspect of a total life pattern. The evidences of early family adjustment, of success in school, at work, in marital life, are significant. The relationship of drinking to dislocation in these areas needs to be evaluated. Assets which have been obscured or blocked by drinking often begin to function and provide the satisfactions requisite to a stabilized emotional equilibrium.

Some alcoholics in the early stages of recovery become overactive and set themselves goals impossible to achieve. They attempt to make up for lost time by undertaking two jobs. Poor work records may force them into positions below their capacity. They accept this in the beginning, but in time become resentful and project their dissatisfactions on their employer, to fellow workers, and to conditions generally. These responses evidence that the emotional curve is beginning to rise, that tension is building up. This is a critical period for the episodic or periodic drinker, a point at which effective counseling is extremely helpful.

The alcoholic needs to learn from actual experience that periods of stress can be tolerated, can be lived through, and that they are transient. If a drinking episode should occur, the counselor has data upon which he can plot the cycle that dominates the patient's life. With this information he can modify his techniques, anticipate upswings of the curve, and help avert future drinking. This also gives opportunity to demonstrate that the precipitating factor in a drinking spree, i.e., a disappointment at home or on the job, is not the basic cause.

Interviews should be relatively frequent during the first weeks of counseling. When necessary, the patient should be seen briefly two or three times a week rather than once a month for a longer interview. Many alcoholics experience mood swings during which their tenuous motivation toward recovery fluctuates. The support of frequent interviews provides a kind of stabilizing force which promotes a continuation and strengthening of the relationship.

The key to recovery is in experiencing. Because of the development of a popular literature on alcoholism, many alcoholics have an intellectual grasp of their problems. Some have an unusual understanding of their emotional difficulties. Intellectualization, however, does not provide the basis for recovery although it may furnish a valuable contribution. On the other hand, interpretations by the counselor of the patient's motivations, feelings and reactions should be given sparingly and only when the patient is psychologically able to benefit from them. Many alcoholics achieve a level of stability without ever having understood the forces which impelled them to drink. That they feel differently, that they are able to deal with situations more comfortably, is sufficient for them.

Contact with the patient may continue for 12 to 24 months, with timely reduction in the frequency of interviews. This is consistent with the principle of meeting the dependency needs of the alcoholic in the initial phases. When this is done with recognition of the reality of the situation, and when a definite plan is established under which the patient assumes more and more independence, there is movement under guidance.

INTERPRETING THE COUNSELING PROCESS TO THE ALCOHOLIC'S FAMILY

The wife and family of an alcoholic frequently feel relieved when he accepts counseling. They have a naive faith that everything will be all right. It is important to interpret to them at the appropriate time that the path may not be a smooth one.

Many alcoholics have a history of remaining sober weeks or even months. When this happens the first or second time, the wife usually feels that things are now under control. But after several years of such failures, she becomes cynical. Many wives are not impressed by the first weeks of sobriety during counseling. They are likely to say, "We've been through all this before and he always gets drunk." This attitude on the part of the wife, while understandable, is not an asset in the treatment process. In other cases, the over-optimistic wife should be prepared for the possibility of a relapse. She may be told that a relapse can have therapeutic value and that the experience of sobriety under counseling can be quite different qualitatively from self-imposed abstinence in the past.

Living in close association with an alcoholic for years is a traumatic experience. His recovery involves changes in the status of the wife which may be difficult for her. The wife may need counseling in order to understand her own feelings about the situation and for the achievement of an emotional climate in the home which will reinforce the equilibrium toward which the alcoholic is working.

An interpretation of the counseling process and the possible outcomes may be needed also by others in the community, for example, the employer, the creditors, the court and correctional officials.

ALCOHOLISM AND PSYCHONEUROSIS

In addition to a medical check up, a psychiatric evaluation of every alcoholic should be made whenever possible. Where a well-developed neurotic pattern underlies the uncontrolled drinking, psychiatric diagnosis and treatment guidance is imperative. The counselor's role in working with the neurotic who is also an uncontrolled drinker, may consist in evaluating the total social situation, interpreting the meaning of psychiatric help to him and preparing him for referral. In a psychiatric clinic, the role of the counselor will be determined by the philosophy under which the psychiatric team operates.

The relationship between psychoneurosis and alcoholism is not entirely clear. In some cases, the neurotic pattern is the primary cause of the uncontrolled drinking. When the neurosis is relieved, the drinking problem can be controlled. Periods of abstinence sometimes produce somatic symptoms, acute anxiety states, and depression. These cases require careful diagnostic study and highly specialized treatment under psychiatric direction. Unfortunately such treatment at the community level is not available to the majority who need it.

Failure to distinguish between alcoholics in the various groups has contributed to the notion that alcoholics do not wish to recover. Resistance to psychiatry due to misunderstanding about it has also led many alcoholics to avoid treatment and has influenced members of some professions against making referrals to psychiatric resources. Alcoholics have been committed to mental institutions for many years. A combination of fear of mental disease associated with excessive drinking and the relatively unsatisfactory results of custodial care in over-crowded state institutions has obscured the importance of psychiatric help for alcoholics.

THE CHRONIC COURT-CASE ALCOHOLIC

Every municipal court and local jail in the country handles large numbers of men charged with drunkenness and breach of the peace. These men congregate in the sub-marginal areas of the large cities and are regular clients of missions and municipal shelters and lodging houses. They are disreputable in appearance and constitute a nuisance to merchants and citizens. For many people they represent the prototype of the alcoholic. Nevertheless there is serious doubt about the extent of alcoholism in this population. One study of a sample of homeless men on Hart Island under the supervision of the New York City Department of Welfare reported:

"Although the use of alcohol has been general among the Hart Island population, the proportion of alcoholics is probably much lower than is popularly assumed. Drinking on Skid Row is one aspect of social conformity. An interruption of drinking is not likely before a break is achieved with the overall social pattern. The outstanding characteristic of these men may be represented by a high degree of dependence expressed by consistent search for institutional forms which gratify the dependency drives."

The history of frequent institutionalization and other indications of inability to function as independent members of society gives little reason for hope that counseling can be effective with this group. For the majority of these men some form of long-term custodial institution may have to be developed. Half-way houses might serve as a next step on the way to rehabilitation for the more promising cases in this group. At this step, counseling could be an effective adjunct.

ALCOHOLISM WITH OTHER PATHOLOGIES

Individuals exhibiting severe organic or psychiatric pathologies are being referred to alcoholism clinics for treatment. Psychotics, epileptics, patients with neurological impairment, the physically or mentally deteriorated, the borderline moron—these are erroneously labeled alcoholics. Most of them must be referred to other specialized services. A few may be carried on a supportive basis in the expectation that some reduction in the frequency and intensity of their drinking may be achieved, to the benefit of the community.

HOSPITAL AND OUTPATIENT TREATMENT

Many alcoholics require 5 to 8 days of hospital care to recover from the physical effects of acute intoxication. With the exception of the psychiatric wards of municipal institutions, few general hospitals accept alcoholics.

Where brief inpatient care is available, there is opportunity to explain to the patient the nature of his condition and the importance of out-patient treatment. In theory, physicians, nurses and chaplains are in a position to do this. In practice, little effort is made, in part because of the lack of available community resources and also because of the attitude of hopelessness felt by many professional people toward alcoholism. The gap between inpatient care and outpatient treatment and follow-up is a difficult one for both patients and the public to bridge. Skilled counseling and referral can be effective in many cases.

GROUP COUNSELING

Frequent reports appear in the literature concerning group work with alcoholics. Some approaches are didactic; others aim at developing insight and support through group participation and identification. This method offers promise in that it helps to break down the social isolation which is a factor in the progression of alcoholism. Sound evaluation of the techniques employed is needed.

GENERAL IMPRESSIONS ON COUNSELING IN ALCOHOLISM

Reports of counseling in alcoholism have not been illuminating. The techniques employed, the degree of involvement of the patient, the role played by the personality of the counselor, and other variables are not clear.

With the development of government sponsored treatment services in approximately two thirds of the states, experiences are being exchanged and tentative observations presented. Techniques in counseling some types of alcoholics are not basically different from those followed in working with other people in trouble. A positive rapport must be established as soon as possible. This is at times difficult because society has condemned alcoholism as a form of weakness and the counselor represents society in the thinking of the alcoholic.

An intensive, exploratory technique based on analytical concepts is not appropriate for many uncontrolled drinkers. A skillfully applied supportive approach in the early sessions can be effective in developing a relationship which will permit employment of more subtle techniques.

An accepting attitude consistently maintained is a requisite for effective counseling. In his resistance, the alcoholic may employ evasive tactics, untruths and manipulations of various kinds in order to avoid facing the realities of his problem. Sapir has summarized the responsibility of the counselor as follows:

"If we are not able to accept these defensive tactics, recognizing them as natural in a sick person, he will sense our withdrawal of trust and, as a consequence, his own participation in treatment will deteriorate. He will not only feel censured and guilty again, but weak and unloved. His magic has failed its purpose of obtaining love. Obviously, it is necessary to be clear about the 'facts' of a situation; but the emotional 'facts' should be a major concern. The way a patient 'makes magic' can tell us much about his emotional needs and development."

Because alcoholism cuts across so many areas—medicine, religion, family life, occupations, economics—every community resource should be brought to bear on it. As evidence accumulates that the community is ready to accept alcoholism as a form of illness, the alcoholic may be able to acknowledge his own condition for what it really is, a personality disorder requiring treatment. When this is achieved, the task of the counselor will be considerably lightened.

BIBLIOGRAPHY

1. CLINEBELL, HOWARD J.: 1956. *Understanding and Counseling the Alcoholic Through Religion and Psychology.* Nashville, Tennessee: Abingdon Press.
2. JELLINEK, E. M.: 1960. *The Disease Concept of Alcoholism.* New Haven, Connecticut: Hillhouse Press.

3. McCarthy, Raymond G. (Ed.): 1959. *Drinking and Intoxication: Selected Readings in Social Attitudes and Controls.* New York: The Free Press; and New Haven, Connecticut: Publications Division, Yale Center of Alcohol Studies.

4. Sapir, J.: 1953. "Relationship Factors in the Treatment of the Alcoholic." *Social Casework,* **34**, pp. 297–303.

5. Schaefer, E. S.: 1954. "Personality Structure of Alcoholics in Outpatient Psycho-Therapy." *Quarterly Journal of Studies on Alcohol,* **15**, pp. 304–319.

6. Vogel, S.: 1953. "An Interpretation of Medical and Psychiatric Approaches in the Treatment of Alcoholism." *Quarterly Journal of Studies on Alcohol,* **14**, pp. 620–631.

7. "Understanding Alcoholism", January 1958 issue of *The Annals* of the American Academy of Political and Social Science. Volume 315. Especially the articles by John D. Armstrong, Joan K. Jackson, Edith S. Lisansky, Earl Rubington, Jean V. Sapir, and Sidney Vogel.

Legal Counseling

H. FRED GOBER

Attorney, Atlanta
Georgia

THE LAWYER by necessity acquires skill in interviewing since a great part of his day is taken up by conferences with clients. In deciding any legal problem all of the facts having a bearing on the problem must be discovered and considered.

The object of all legal investigation is the discovery of the truth. The investigation of truth, the art of ascertaining that which is unknown from that which is known, has occupied the attention of the reflecting part of mankind in every civilized age and country, but inquiries of this nature are nowhere more essential to society than where they are applied to legal controversies. The general security requires that controversies be decided according to law, that is, by applying constant techniques to past court decisions and legislative enactments. Laws are not self-executing and the administration of law assumes the truth of the facts or situation to which it is applied. Every rational system of law provides that the means of proof must be founded on experience and reason including a thoughtful consideration of human nature and conduct, on a consideration of the value of testimony, documentary proof and the circumstances under which said testimony is given or documentary evidence produced. As a professional man the lawyer owes his first duty to the law and, therefore, is duty bound to discover the truth whether it is for his client or against him. In order to decide controversies satisfactorily the lawyer must seek to find all relevant facts so that the controversy may be decided with the assurance that nothing has been overlooked, nothing misunderstood, and everything given its proper weight.

In seeking the truth the lawyer must bear in mind that if litigated the facts will be considered by a judge, the parties, attorneys, the witnesses and perhaps a jury. For this reason the relevant facts must be determined, put in logical order, the possible legal consequences foreseen and the significant legal questions and crucial points isolated.

With the above factors in mind we come to a consideration of the interviewing methods and techniques used by lawyers. After the social amenities have been observed by introducing yourself to a new client or greeting an old client, it is important to give the impression that the lawyer has plenty of time to discuss the client's problem. The importance of getting all facts connected with a particular problem cannot be over emphasized. In this connection the client should be advised, if he does not already know, that anything he says will be kept strictly confidential as inherent in the attorney–client relationship. For the client who is able to do so, it is perhaps best to let him state his problem in his own way. After this has been done the lawyer can then question the client to bring out any matters or facts or questions which the client's narration did not fully cover. Talkative clients may have to be led back into relevant paths and timid ones may need to be encouraged to reveal all the details of their problem. Certain clients may have a pent-up flood of grievances that must find an outlet, and while economy of time may require the lawyer to stem the torrent of explanation, it is important that it be done in such a way as to leave the client convinced of sincere interest in his plight. It is, of course, elementary that phone calls or any other distractions be eliminated entirely or kept to a minimum while the interview is taking place, and the client should be interviewed in a private office away from other persons to insure privacy and instill confidence. The interview may be brought to a close by telling the client that it appears all the necessary preliminary information has been obtained and he will be contacted when needed and kept advised of developments. In some cases, the lawyer may terminate the interview by saying he underestimated the time needed to get all the facts and has another appointment, but will be glad to see the client again at his convenience.

Since the client will later be subjected to a sifting cross-examination by the attorney for the other side in the event the controversy is litigated, it is necessary that the client be courteously cross-examined during the initial interview. In this connection, leading, rhetorical, repetitive and motivating questions may be used.

The lawyer must refrain from using technical or legal language which may be misunderstood by the client. It is important to advise the client of the various steps the lawyer intends to take and the time and expense and uncertainties involved. Many clients will not understand the time required to study the facts, put them in proper perspective, do the required legal research, file suit, keep up with the court calendar, subpoena witnesses, file supplementary pleadings, take depositions, try the case, prepare possible appeals, and the cost involved in each of the foregoing steps.

Courtesy, accuracy, and tact are necessary when contacting persons against whom the client has a possible claim, or witnesses. Whenever the nature of the case permits, the adverse party or his attorney, if he has one, should be immediately contacted by phone. This saves unnecessary trips for the client and unnecessary interviewing time for the attorney. Moreover, the other side may bring up matters and facts which require immediate explanation by the client. The important factors of accuracy, dispatch, and economy are served by using the telephone whenever possible. There are cases, however, which require investigation before adverse parties are contacted.

Since there may be long delays before the client will be called upon to restate what he now remembers, it is advisable to have the client sign a memorandum or statement as to all matters dependent upon his memory. Some lawyers record the interview but this procedure may have the bad effect of making the client tense and ill at ease. Many lawyers find it helpful to take another statement from the client after witnesses have been interviewed.

It is no secret among lawyers that witnesses are normally favorable to the side whose attorney first contacted them. This is so, not because witnesses tend to lie, but because they normally wish to please rather than displease. Lawyers also know that if a group of witnesses are interviewed in the same room their stories tend to be similar, whereas there will be wide variations if interviewed separately about the same event. Of course, a thorough investigation enables the lawyer to assess fairly correctly the strength or weakness of his case, and contacting the adverse party following the investigation is advisable where the case is complicated or the witnesses several in number. To illustrate: If a person sued by a store on an account maintains she did not buy anything or sign the sales slip, a simple comparison of the client's signature and handwriting with that on the sales slip may save considerable time, and immediate contact with the store's attorney is indicated. However, if there had been no signature to compare, it would not be desirable to have the adverse party see your client to assist his identification of the client in court. Perhaps he should not see her even in court, or see her with several of her friends to make an identification an honest one. Or suppose it had been an automobile collision. In a complicated case of this type, the adverse party would not be contacted until after a thorough investigation has been made. If witnesses are available they should be contacted at once, and their signed statements taken. Often, a negative statement, that the witness was in the vicinity of the collision but did not see it, will prevent that person from later appearing as a witness as he hears about the collision from actual witnesses. An on-the-scene investigation should also be undertaken as soon as possible. Measurements, pictures, diagrams, charts and other devices prove of great value in interviewing witnesses, and are valuable in sifting truth and untruth in court. Of course it is of extreme importance that each statement cover all relevant details about the collision. Where the witness was standing, when he first noticed each of the automobiles, the make and model of the cars, the speed of each, was a horn sounded, brakes applied, any other traffic, the width and condition of the high-way, the distance to the nearest intersection, the weather and time of day, the points of impact, skid marks' direction and length, parts of each car damaged, any traffic signs or markers, occupants of each car and their condition, any other witnesses and how they may be located, any state-ments made by anyone at the scene—the above questions and many others should be asked each witness of an automobile collision.

Of course any information given by the client is confidential and should be divulged to others only with his consent. Whenever the opposing party is represented by counsel all contacts should be with the latter. All communications, whether by telephone, letter, or in person, and whether with the opposing party, his attorney, or witnesses, should be courteous and objective. The attorney is seeking nothing more than justice, and he should never assume that his client has a monopoly on the merits of the case. However, the attorney should not attempt to sit in judgment on the merits of his client's case. If the law presents a remedy, it is the duty of the lawyer to achieve the benefits of that remedy for his client if it is possible to do so. On the other hand, as an officer of the court, the lawyer should not burden the court with false or frivolous claims.

The legal interview is sometimes characterized as a short time con-tact as compared with the sometimes longer contact of social workers, particularly in domestic relations cases. This may be generally true but it is not unusual for legal problems to involve successive interviews over a number of years. It is, of course, important that the lawyer be aware of various other resources available to assist the client. It may very well be that some other agency should be consulted in handling a client's problem. The Legal Aid Society stands ready to give legal service and advice to those unable to pay. Family Service societies and welfare agencies may render valuable assistance in family problems. There are many other social and governmental agencies which perhaps should be contacted to effectively solve a client's problem. Almost every family problem has legal and social aspects and the lawyer on occasion should be willing to recognize that another agency is better equipped to handle a particular problem or series of problems. In answering a client's problem the lawyer is of course limited by the framework of law, whereas the social worker is limited only by the total available resources.

The lawyer uses the interviewing methods and teachings of most persons seeking information, but the nature of law with its emphasis on objective truth requires more emphasis on facts than on the emotional make-up of the client. The lawyer will also rely more on cross-examination to elicit the necessary information, whereas cross-examination is misunderstood and frowned on by some interviewers. It may also be true that the lawyer has an easier task than most interviewers as the client comes to him seeking expert legal advice and is in more of a listening mood than he might be for instance in applying for a job or welfare assistance or asking advice about a family problem.

A legal problem to be effectively handled requires that certain facts be discovered. It is human nature for a client to see his case in a light favorable to him. It is no favor to the client to let him waste time and money for court action which the attorney would have advised against bringing if all the facts had been brought out by tactful cross-examination.

The techniques of interviewing are as broad as human knowledge and human personality. A sincere interest in the interviewee's problem and professional competence will usually lead to a favorable result.

Counseling in Correctional Work

NORMAN FENTON

Formerly Deputy Director
State Department of Corrections
Sacramento, California

THE IMPORTANCE TO SOCIETY OF TREATMENT IN CORRECTIONAL INSTITUTIONS

THIS chapter will be more meaningful and appropriate if the reader keeps in mind the fact that over ninety-five percent of the many thousands of offenders sent to prison and almost all who serve their sentences in jail return to free society. Prisoners now behind walls or fences in the jails or prisons of the world, some guarded there by men with rifles and machine guns, will in time return to the community, possibly even to his own neighborhood. Therefore, if only for selfish reasons, people ought to learn about the quality of the diagnostic study and the treatment these men receive while in correctional institutions. Although we shall have little space for it in this chapter, another matter of serious concern (to the public) is how offenders are supervised after they leave prison on parole.

In evaluating a prison, we may start with the use of two general measures. The first is its general orderliness as a community. The press, the movies and TV have given the general public inaccurate and confused notions about penitentiaries. When a prison riot occurs, the newspapers are quick to dramatize the failure of the prison from this standpoint. Yet, for our purposes, the genuinely treatment-oriented prison, with which we are concerned in this chapter, is only rarely featured in the press or the other media mentioned. Such a place is almost as unlikely to have a large-scale riot as would a well-conducted hospital.

The second test of a correctional institution is how well the prisoners do after they leave. The percentage of parolees who get into trouble after their return to society has seemingly been decreasing gradually as diagnostic studies and treatment in prison and supervision on parole have improved; but it is still much too large. In California, where statistical information about ex-prisoners is quite accurate, it has been reported that between one-third and two-fifths of the men who leave prison will again tangle with the law before the completion of their parole. In explaining the failures, we must assume that either our present methods of diagnosis do not bring the underlying causes of criminality to light for effective treatment, or that our prisons are inadequately constructed, equipped and staffed to do what needs to be done for the social adjustment of the inmates. Thus, men are released from prison who are not ready to go. And the obverse is also true, many men who could be on the outside for their own good and without danger to others remain in prison longer than is necessary.

It is encouraging, however, that when newer methods are used, the proportion of parolees who get along satisfactorily in society seems to increase. A recent initial report of an experimental project in California is a good example. It has been concerned with the treatment, largely by group psychotherapeutic methods, of those very difficult-to-adjust parolees with a known history of the use of narcotics. The author of the report, J. Douglas Grant, stated that, "During the first six months of operation, only five percent of the parolees in this program were arrested, compared to an expected arrest rate of fifty percent" (Grant,[10] p. 5). Many such research projects are needed with different kinds of offenders if correctional treatment is to become more effective. This is necessary before even the more advanced prison will do as well in the second test, how well inmates adjust after they leave prison, as in the first, the orderly conduct of the institution.

RECENT PROGRESS IN THE PRISONS

In the prisons, there have been a number of interesting and heartening accomplishments in recent years. These are not unique for any state but represent trends in the advancement of prison management throughout the world. One of the earliest developments in the area of diagnosis in California was the establishment in makeshift quarters of a Reception-Guidance Center at San Quentin wherein were introduced more adequate diagnostic procedures, coupled with some efforts at counseling and guidance. At present, not quite two decades later, California has three such centers, especially planned and constructed for the purpose.* In these places, newly received prisoners are kept away from the general prison population for about two months. Each is given a comprehensive clinical study, receives group guidance to orient him to being in prison, attends group counseling, and receives any necessary emergency treatment, such as medical or dental care.

Students of counseling will be interested in the contents of the case study compiled by the staff in the reception-guidance center. When completed, this initial study has been called the Admission Summary. It resembles diagnostic studies in other guidance centers. The following areas of investigation are included:

1. *The social history* includes the results of an interview with the inmate by a social worker. This is supplemented by data from questionnaires sent by mail to relatives and others, and from court records and other sources.

2. *The criminal history* is developed from information received from other correctional institutions and agencies. The report from the F.B.I. is especially significant. The man's own story of his present offense and his criminal past also contains material of importance to the clinician.

3. *The physical examination* is conducted by a physician.

4. *The vocational analysis* includes data from several hours of testing† and an interview by a vocational psychologist.‡ These data are supplemented by information from inquiries directed to former employers and to institutions.

5. *The educational history* as reported by the inmate is validated when possible by inquiries to the schools they attended. It is supplemented by achievement tests.†

6. *The psychological study*, a routine with all prisoners, consists of tests† and a personal interview.

---

* Prison architecture has until recently been a serious obstacle to the correctional program. Newer designs in construction are offering a better opportunity for treatment to be administered. Conservative architecture, designed primarily for security, is, however, still a great handicap to the treatment program in most prisons.

† The tests in use are changed from time to time. As of August, 1961, the following were reported by the staff at Chino as in use:

1. Tests for prisoners include: California Reading Test-Intermediate, Composite Opinion & Attitude Survey, Parts I & II (includes MMPI), California Mathematics Test-Intermediate, Differential Aptitude Tests-Mechanical Reasoning, Revised Minnesota Paper Form Board Test, Minnesota Clerical Test, Shipley-Hartford Intelligence Scale, Army General Classification Test-First Civilian Edition, Kuder Preference Record-Vocational, Sentence Completion, W.A.Y., Draw A Person.

2. Tests used with inmates having some difficulty with the English language: California Reading Test-Intermediate, Revised Beta Examination (Intelligence), California Mathematics-Elementary, Revised Minnesota Paper Form Board Test, Sentence Completion, W.A.Y., Draw A Person.

The following individual tests are listed in the order of frequency of use: Bender Gestalt, Rorschach, Thematic Apperception Test, Spiral After-effect Test, Wechsler Bellevue Intelligence Scale for Adults, Stanford-Binet Intelligence Test, Forms L & M, Goldstien–Sheerer.

‡ The current civil service title for this worker. Formerly the title vocational counselor was used.

7. *The psychiatric study* is routinely administered when sufficient staff is available. Otherwise, it is done when evidence from other observers indicates its desirability.

8. *The religious background and attitudes* are reported by a chaplain.

9. *Recreational interests and abilities* may be discussed in interviews with any of several members of the staff. They are summarized by the worker who prepares the social history or by a recreation supervisor.

10. *Initial adjustment to prison* is reported by the correctional officers and others on the staff from observations of the inmate's behavior during the initial weeks in prison.

11. Data about *parole plans and prospects* are contributed by all members of the staff.

12. *A summary of the treatability of the individual.* This is a résumé of the case somewhat like what has been called in the past the summary of assets and liabilities in the case. More recently, it has been fortified by the use of predictive measures, including the use of a table of expectancies* in the reception-guidance centers.

The above outline of the contents of the diagnostic study of prisoners illustrates how the currents of thought in penology are flowing toward the diagnosis and treatment of offenders as total personalities. Moreover, it may be noted that the focus of attention is upon the future well-being and social adjustment of prisoners, especially after their release to society. The Admission Summary prepared in a reception-guidance center may be ten or more single-spaced typewritten pages in length. It begins the cumulative case history of the prisoner which accompanies him from the reception-guidance center to any institutions to which he may subsequently be transferred. When he leaves, a summary is available for use by those supervising him on parole. Each part of the correctional system continues the cumulative case history by adding to it what are called, unfortunately not always justifying the name, "progress reports."

From the standpoint of the social welfare, now threatened by the growing statistics of delinquency and crime, experiences in the prisons seem to emphasize the importance of more and deeper counseling in the elementary and secondary schools than at present, to prevent children and youth from entering the road to infamy. When rapport is good, during the clinician's interviews with prisoners, almost all of them express in confidence a profound distress over their situation and a deep desire to overcome their troubles. They express earnestly the wish to leave prison and thereafter to be on the right side in society. When the defensive coverings of seeming indifference or toughness are drawn aside, most prisoners are found to be confused and unhappy human beings seeking help to overcome their waywardness. Undoubtedly, this desire for assistance in understanding themselves in order to gain better control over their behavior may have been present in their earlier years. If this be so, how tragic it is that these persons who wanted such help

* Grant[9] and Wilkins and Mannheim[16] and others have indicated the possibilities of predicting the effects of differential treatment upon inmates.

when younger received their first real counseling experience, not as children or youths, but later in life as inmates in a prison!

EVIDENCES OF RECENT PROGRESS TOWARD TREATMENT IN THE PRISON

1. Some basic changes in the administration of prisons which make treatment possible are illustrated in the recent history of adult correctional work in California. One of the first of these was the compulsory recruitment of employees through civil service examinations introduced in 1945. In that year, for the first time in the history of the State, the selection of employees for the prisons was based upon adequate qualifications.

2. Associated with better recruitment was the establishment of a program of in-service training to up-grade employees.

3. In order to insure that the recommendations based on the comprehensive study of the newly-committed prisoners would be carried out in their subsequent treatment in the California prisons to which they are transferred from the reception-guidance centers, many specialists were added to the institutional staffs. These included psychiatrists, psychologists, psychiatric social workers, librarians, academic and vocational instructors, chaplains, recreational supervisors, dieticians and others, though persons in some of these job classifications had been employed previously in the California prisons. I should add at once that because of continuous increases in population* many more of these specialists still need to be employed by the California prisons in order adequately to carry out its treatment program.

4. Together with the better selection and the instruction of the staff, more and better facilities for training and treatment were added. These included additional vocational shops, classrooms, chapels, hospitals, gymnasia, playing fields, work projects and industrial operations. Staff and facilities for individual and group psychotherapy were also amplified.

5. To accommodate a greatly increased prison population in California, ten new facilities, some of them administered as satellites of older institutions, and many new honor camps were built. These were carefully planned. They have offered more diversified treatment resources and more opportunity to classify the inmates for purposes of treatment.

* The great tragedy of the California prison system has been the excessive growth in inmate population. The number of prisoners has almost quadrupled in the past seventeen years. Overcrowding has been a great obstacle making more difficult the advancement of the treatment program.

6. To evaluate the outcomes of these correctional efforts, a well-staffed Division of Research was also established.

Just listing all too briefly this selection of major advances in correctional work with adults may give the reader an appreciation of how prisons have changed in recent years. For our purposes in this chapter, these developments are obviously of great importance in implementing the program of counseling. It is also easy to see why the prisons in some places have become more satisfactory and interesting places in which to work. In California, the prisons are now able to compete for personnel with other social agencies and even with the schools and colleges. This is confirmed in part by the fact that in the California prisons over half of those employed at present have had some training on the college level. The ferment of new ideas in diagnosis and treatment, and the other recent developments mentioned above have attracted men and women to the prison service who would never have considered working there a decade or two ago.

COUNSELING AND GUIDANCE IN THE PRISONS

After this general account of the development of diagnosis and treatment in the modern prison, let us now consider a sampling of rather specific aspects of the counseling program therein. Four topics have been chosen which may serve to delineate how counseling methods are used in adult correctional institutions. In some of them, notably the first and second, the reader may recognize how heavily they have drawn upon earlier use of similar methods of group guidance in schools or colleges. On the other hand, perhaps the remaining two may offer suggestions of value to the faculties of educational institutions.

I. *Group Guidance in the Prison*

For our purposes, this topic may be re-stated under two headings. We may first ask how inmates are helped to become acquainted with the opportunities available for them by way of training and treatment in the prison system. And, second, how are they given instruction concerning the rules and regulations of the prisons and of the parole board? As a phase of this second heading, we are interested in how the prison informs its inmates, certified opponents of law and order, at some time in their past, regarding the limits to their behavior in the institutions.

1. The literate prisoner may be oriented initially by a brief bulletin of information about prison life and parole distributed in the county

jail.* This publication deals with practical matters such as mail, visits, clothing and the like. It also contains a general statement by the head of the prison system about the opportunities for treatment in prison. This guidance pamphlet was designed to allay certain fears and to correct common misconceptions found among incoming prisoners, which formerly tended to add to their initial emotional upset at imprisonment and to interfere with a good institutional adjustment. It has also been used to give practical information to relatives† and to try to allay their anxieties, sometimes generated by misleading representations of prison life in TV or the movies.

2. A longer and more detailed publication will soon be made available to the men upon arrival in a reception-guidance center. This will be a printed brochure containing a description of the general program of treatment in the California prisons. It will also portray the special character and purpose of each of the prisons and its satellite units, and of the numerous honor camps. This brochure‡ will also be available for the use of relatives.

3. Group meetings for the inmates are held in the reception-guidance centers and also during the first week or so after transfer to one of the prisons, at which the details of life in the prisons are discussed. They are addressed by the official responsible for the different phases of the conduct of the institutions. The subject-matter includes presentations of the opportunities offered to inmates for education, recreation, religious observance, work, training and other treatment. The nature and granting of parole and other important legal matters are discussed. Sometimes the members of the parole board or the chief state parole officer have addressed these groups. In the group orientation of newly arrived prisoners, an effort is made to give information about the program of the correctional system and to answer the inmates' questions.

An interesting feature of group guidance in the prisons is the presentation by inmate representatives of the activities of inmate organizations. These may include not only athletic teams but also, to mention a few examples, Alcoholics Anonymous, dramatics and musical groups, the debating society and the art guild.

4. An interesting example of group guidance may be found in the methods used to orient the inmates to the laws governing the prison

* Entitled, *Information for Men Sentenced to State Prison and for their Families and Friends*, with a Foreword by Richard A. McGee, Director of Corrections, Sacramento, California, March 1959, 8 pages. Among prisoners who are able to read are usually found some who are generous in conveying the information in these and other publications to others who are not able to read. Or this may be done by staff members.

† Other methods of family counseling will be discussed later in this chapter.

‡ Now in press and to be entitled, *A Look Within*.

society. Shortly after transfer from the reception-guidance center, the inmate is given his own copy of a printed book containing the rules and regulations of the prisons. Group orientation is also used to inform inmates about the laws of the prison society. The head custodial officers present discussions of what is considered to be good citizenship in prison. At these informal sessions, the inmates are free to ask questions and may request explanations of the reasons for the rules. These meetings are permissive in character. They are relaxed and friendly; some gentle banter may be permitted. There are no intrusive authoritarian threats. But the point is pleasantly but firmly made that obedience to the rules has to be enforced if the prison is to be an orderly society for the welfare of all who live and work there.

To supplement these contributions of the staff regarding the prison society, there is a talk by the head of what has been called the inmate advisory council.* In each of the California prisons, the inmate advisory council consists of elected representatives from housing units and shops. The council serves as an agency of communication between prison top management and the inmate body. It meets regularly. The warden is usually present and may bring in matters for consideration. Most of the agenda is concerned with items given to council members by their constituents. The presiding officer is an inmate elected by the council. Minutes are kept by the elected secretary. The results of these meetings are reported to the inmate body through announcements on bulletin boards, in the inmate newspaper or over the institutional radio hook-up. These media are also used to convey to the inmate body any changes in the rules and regulations promulgated by the prison or the parole board. In short, the good prison uses group guidance by staff and inmates to try to develop an informed and well-governed society with as many elements of representative government as are reasonably possible.

The methods of group guidance used to help the inmates understand the rules of the institution are effective. In the California prisons only a small percentage of the inmates violate the regulations. Most of the infractions are of a minor character. Usually, the offenders are merely counseled by a senior correctional officer; others may temporarily lose certain privileges, such as attendance at a recreational motion picture. Serious offenses, fortunately very few in number, have in the past resulted in confinement in a disciplinary unit. More recently the California prisons have developed Adjustment Centers where seriously disturbed inmates are confined after a clinically oriented disciplinary court hearing.† Felonious behavior, such as assault with a weapon or

* See Dickson *et al.*[3] for a longer account of the inmate advisory council.
† See Cook *et al.*[2] for a description of the adjustment center.

possession of narcotics, may be reported to the district attorney of the county in which the prison is located for his decision as to prosecution in court.

This account of how the prisons inform inmates regarding the laws of the prison society and how they set limits to the behavior of inmates, may be relevant to similar efforts to control the behavior of young people in society. Parents, teachers, group workers, the police, are faced with the problem of defining for children and youth what behavior in the school and in the neighborhood is acceptable and what is not. The reader may wonder whether some of these procedures in the prisons developed there as group orientation or guidance may offer useful leads as to what may be transmuted for use in educational institutions or elsewhere in the community.

II. *The Conduct of Vocational Guidance in Prisons*

Vocational guidance is considered separately because of its importance for success on parole. Research has indicated, as one would expect, a positive relationship between satisfactory adjustment on parole and vocational competence.[13] In the prison, vocational guidance begins at admission, as pointed out earlier, by tests and interviews and by individual counseling in the reception-guidance centers. There is group orientation first in the reception-guidance centers and later in the prisons concerning opportunities for work and vocational training in relation to possible placement on parole. The inmates are told that the prisons in California have a staff of certificated vocational instructors, well-equipped shops, defined courses of instruction, ample text and reference material, and a sensible and continuous program of guidance. Vocational guidance and training in the modern prison is carried on very much as similar counseling and instruction would be conducted in a good trade school.

After a man is transferred from the reception-guidance center to an institution, an initial guidance conference is held for each inmate. The staff discusses with him either the vocational training or work program, or both, as recommended in the Admission Summary. The inmate may ask questions or raise objections. Most inmates seem interested in cooperating in the program that is evolved by the group. About six months later a follow-up study is made of each inmate, to consider whether or not changes are necessary in his program. Reports are prepared by vocational instructors, work supervisors and others about the inmate's vocational progress, and these are discussed by the classification committee and with the inmate, if he makes a personal appearance at the session. Because of limitations of time and staff, however, inmates are not brought in to these follow-up conferences in some institutions.

All inmates have recourse to various members of the staff for interviews regarding their work or training programs. Each is assigned to a correctional counselor, whose caseload is about two or three hundred. The latter is available for occasional interviews. He keeps track of the general details of what happens to those on his caseload. While the inmate is in the institution, the correctional counselor reports periodically to the paroling authority on the inmate's progress. When the inmate is about to leave prison, the correctional counselor is responsible for the preparation, with the inmate's collaboration, of the plans for what work the man will do during his initial months on parole. This is then transmitted for approval to the staff of the Division of Paroles in the area where he is to go. The parole agent is responsible for checking at first-hand the adequacy of the man's work program after release. Thus, in the modern prison, from his admission to his parole, the inmate may receive vocational guidance and training.

III. *Counseling the Family in the Prison Program*

The following five items represent a sampling of routine methods of counseling and guidance for the close relatives of inmates which have been introduced into the California prisons:

1. An illustrated lecture is presented to relatives visiting the institution. It describes the life of the man in prison. A question period occurs at the end of the lecture.

2. The family may learn about the prison from an illustrated brochure,* mailed to the homes of inmates. Such accounts of the life of the man in prison have been prepared in the prisons with the collaboration of inmates.

3. Conferences may be arranged for relatives concerned with the inmate's program and progress.

4. Written reports about the man's progress may be sent to families upon their request.

5. A text for relatives, "Treatment in Prison—How the Family Can Help," has been prepared for their use.

In addition to these devices, pilot studies have also shown values for the following procedures in family counseling:

1. Attendance of the families at prison functions, such as a meeting of Alcoholics Anonymous, religious services, art exhibits, musical or dramatic events.

2. An orientation lecture by a staff member, held in the community to which close relatives are invited. This is followed by a period for questions and discussion.

* At one institution, the booklet is entitled, *The Life of the Men in the Correctional Training Facility at Soledad, California.* It was printed in the institutional vocational print shop in 1959. It consists of 20 pages and has many illustrations.

3. Meetings for relatives in the community and in the institution conducted by parole agents before men are released during which the nature and conduct of parole are discussed. The role of the family is also considered.

4. Group psychotherapy for couples conducted at the institutions.

As one would anticipate, these procedures have helped greatly to break down the fears, suspicions and even antipathies of many relatives toward the staff of the prison. These undesirable and harmful feelings are replaced in many cases by the desire to cooperate with the institutional authorities and to encourage the inmates to take greater advantage of their opportunities for advancing themselves while in prison. It would be an interesting study in public relations to compare what the parents of students in some of our high schools and colleges know about the programs and the progress of their sons and daughters in these educational institutions with what the wives and parents of inmates in some modern prisons know as a result of this type of counseling program.

IV. *Group Counseling as Practiced in the Prisons of California*

1. *The origin of the program.* In the reception-guidance center, many members of the staff were from the outset involved in individual counseling as they went about their work of preparing the case history. Social workers not only compiled the social histories of inmates but also, as time permitted, assisted them to understand their life situations somewhat better. Clinical psychologists administered tests, interviewed inmates and counseled them. Psychiatrists carried on the various phases of their work, including in exceptional cases some individual and group psychotherapy. Unfortunately, there was not sufficient staff time available for more than a token amount of psychotherapy by these specialists. In addition to the counseling carried on by these clinical specialists, some occasional counseling was given by teachers, correctional officers, physicians, shop foremen and other members of the staff as opportunity offered.

Shortly after the opening of the reception-guidance center at San Quentin in 1944, certificated teachers were employed to give instruction in social living and other academic subjects. Those selected to teach had had some training in educational counseling. Soon after classes in social living were started, inmates were permitted therein to discuss their personal problems and to release their feelings about many aspects of life in prison and society. With experience, the teachers became quite skilled in getting the men to express their attitudes and feelings. Thus, what began as academic classes gradually changed and became what was later called group counseling. Soon it was noted that the inmates seemed to be relieved of some of the tensions, hatreds and misunderstandings which beset them at admission. The morale of the reception-guidance center seemed to improve. Gradually this program, conducted by other than clinical specialists and soon called group counseling, became the major responsibility of the teachers. The term "group counseling" was used to differentiate what they did from group psychotherapy, which had been in use in the prisons for some time and which was conducted by specialists in psychology, psychiatry and psychiatric social work.

Until 1954, group counseling conducted by laymen was carried on only in the reception-guidance centers. At that time, a pilot study was conducted at Folsom State Prison to ascertain whether group counseling could be carried on advantageously in the ordinary prison by other than clinical specialists. The study at Folsom has been reported in the literature (Fenton,[6] pp. 11–15). It was found that many correctional officers, shop foremen, teachers, and other members of the staff could be given training and later, under supervision, were able to conduct group counseling. The pilot study at Folsom was repeated at the other prisons in California with similar encouraging findings (Fenton,[6] pp. 15 ff).

The most striking feature of the group counseling program in the California prisons has been this participation of laymen as group leaders in the program. Although for a number of years, correctional officers (whom the reader may know under the name of prison guards) had been receiving in-service training which told about their alleged roles in treatment, nevertheless they had remained generally rather aloof from the treatment program. Likewise, teachers, shop foremen, and others were kept on the periphery of the treatment program. Now, for the first time, they were permitted to spend time doing what many of them had longed to do, namely, participate actively in what was being done to help the inmates with their personal problems.

2. *Some questions raised about group counseling as a procedure.* What actually occurs in group counseling varies from didactic group orientation to group interaction of a psychological nature, wherein considerations of feelings and attitudes enter.* Some clinicians, hearing that group counseling is carried on by laymen in the California prisons, have voiced anxieties regarding hurtful or disturbing outcomes of such group work, usually without observing the actual procedure. Somewhat surprisingly, none of these anticipated undesirable outcomes have occurred. There have been no incidents of acting-out behavior in the

---

* The concept of a continuum in treatment from superficial orientation to group psychotherapy has been helpful in describing this range of what occurs in group counseling. See Fenton,[8] pp. 38–40.

groups, though at times feelings have run high. In the few cases where evidence of possible mental disorder in an inmate has been displayed in the group sessions, the group leaders have had ample opportunity for conferences with professional caseworkers. They have referred to psychiatrists or psychologists cases they felt were in need of their special services. These inmates after clinical study have either been recommended to remain in group counseling or, if indicated, to be removed from it and given individual or group psychotherapy.

The program of group counseling has contained other protections from the dangers mentioned. The group leaders, who include about one in five of all employees, are a selected group who showed evidence of interest and competence during a two-months' training program concerned with group counseling, for which they volunteered. Also, they may be advised by correctional caseworkers after being assigned to a group as leader. Ideally, the beginning group leader should have with him an experienced person as co-leader during his first meetings. A text[4] has been prepared for the instruction of group leaders; it also serves to bring about some degree of uniformity in the philosophic premises and the methods employed.

Group counseling in the California prisons is now conducted to a large extent by line officers who comprise about sixty percent of the group leaders. In some prisons, the warden and other top officials conduct groups. Likewise, vocational and academic teachers, shop foremen and other tradesmen, and even interested members of the clerical staff, may participate. Vocational instructors and other employees may for administrative reasons be required to conduct group counseling as part of their work assignments. At present there are over 10,000 inmates and more than 700 employees in the program. There are institutions and honor camps where all inmates agree before transfer there to participate in group counseling. For most of the prisons, however, group counseling is largely voluntary and the range of participation is from fifty to seventy percent of the population.

3. *A brief sketch of the procedure.* As for the program itself, the optimal group is about 10 or 12 inmates; unfortunately, some number more. Meetings are held weekly and are about an hour and a half in length. The group leaders utilize, in so far as they are able, the non-directive procedures observed at eight lengthy demonstrations during their training. The content of the session is developed by the group and usually spontaneously. The sessions are privileged occasions; what is said may not be revealed to others outside the group nor recorded anywhere in the inmate's file. The only official report of the inmate's participation in group counseling is a record of his attendance.

There are limits as to what may be discussed in group sessions.

Politics, religion, or gossip about persons in the prison system are to be avoided as topics for discussion. Of course, group leaders vary in their capacity to sustain these limits. In a well-conducted group, the inmates prefer to discuss matters which affect them personally. They are helpful in keeping out irrelevant materials.

4. *Some considerations in the conduct of group counseling.* Group counseling in prison is so recent a development and so little discussed in the literature that no procedures have as yet been generally accepted among workers in this area. The following are merely a sampling of procedures which occur in the California prisons and are presented here as they might be given in a handbook*:

(a) It is advantageous but not necessary for the leader to meet each prospective member of a counseling group individually in advance of the first meeting. Ideally, he should also plan to read their case records before these interviews and to discuss each inmate's needs with his correctional counselor. In telling those who are to be in his group about the nature of group counseling, the leader should be quite frank in explaining what goes on therein, stressing the importance of the inmate's own activity. The personal interview is also a good time to tell them about the limitations of the procedure. For example, that group counseling is not a cure-all and that some problems may be so serious as to require instead intensive psychotherapy.

(b) The first meeting may be started by a brief explanation of group counseling, pointed up perhaps by the use of selected questions on the blackboard concerning some of its goals.† It is essential at first to avoid feeling any compulsion to get the counselees to react immediately. Ordinarily one need not worry lest the inmates should not participate. If the group leader looks at the individuals in the group and pauses as he does so, someone is likely to respond with a question or comment after the initial introduction. Moreover, the fact that some inmates in a group will have attended groups conducted by the more experienced leaders in the reception-guidance centers has proved helpful in introducing group counseling in the institution. At the present time, practically all inmates have attended group counseling during their first weeks in prison.

(c) In starting later sessions, if the blackboard is not used, one may begin by saying, "What would you like to talk about today? What's happened of interest? Any questions?" *There is no one correct way of starting a session. The same thing is true, indeed, in general about other aspects*

* The reader should consult the employee text[4] for a more detailed account of methods of beginning a group and for its subsequent conduct.

† For an illustration of the use of the blackboard in group counseling with alcoholics in a city jail see Lerner,[12] and Fenton,[4] p. 43.

of conducting group counseling. To a certain extent, each counselor will use an individualized approach on the basis of his own knowledge and experience. In addition to willingness to learn, an important criterion for group leaders is their sincerity* and their capacity to accept the inmates and to have them feel that the leader really wants to help them.

(d) At times there may be a pause without outward reaction. If rapport is good, the leader may wait until someone says something. He need not feel under pressure to do anything to keep up the flow of activity, as might be true in an academic classroom. There may be inward activity in the inmates during these pauses. Sometimes a short pause may even be good for rapport. If strong resistance is evident, indicated by a long pause without action, it may be useful to rephrase or pull together the materials discussed previous to the pause or even to bring up again some item of interest discussed earlier by the group. The group leader can appraise his own security in conducting group counseling by how well and comfortably within himself he can handle these pauses.

(e) The group leader cannot always tell whether or not an inmate is getting anything of value from the sessions. Participation is not necessarily the only evidence of change. Sometimes those who are least vocal come out at the end with the most evidence of growth. The leader should, however, be cautious in using any directive methods that strongly encourage participation.

(f) The effort and initiative must be contributed by the group. The leader needs to resist the normal tendency or temptation to contribute something he feels to be helpful. With experience, he should gain more control of the tendency to be overly directive. As often as possible, he should throw any question addressed to him back to the group by asking, "What do you think about this?" and avoid the natural and normal tendency to be directive, to teach, lecture or just talk.

(g) After four or five meetings, the sessions may occasionally be enriched by inviting resource persons to attend. Parole officers have been found to arouse interest. Likewise, after a number of introductory sessions, other members of the prison staff, with the approval of the inmates, may be invited to attend.

(h) Another resource to enrich the movement of a group is the use of motion pictures. There are many excellent ones which deal with mental health problems. Some are listed in the employee text (Fenton,[4]

---

* Group counseling is not free of exploitation by employees who see in it merely a chance for promotion or overtime pay. Fortunately, their number has seemed to be very small.

pp. 193–5). They have been found to be helpful with counseling groups in prisons and other correctional agencies. For films to be useful, careful preparation must be made.* This includes ordinarily an introductory talk before the showing and some possible lines of discussion thereafter. The leader may raise questions to relate the contents of the film to the personal problems of those in his group. Discussion of the spontaneous reactions of the counseling group to the film is usually given priority over any material prepared by the leader.

(i) After the group has met for about ten meetings and rapport has advanced, it has been worthwhile in some groups occasionally to permit an inmate to act as co-leader.

(j) When one member of the group speaks very feelingly, the leader may ask whether someone else would care to describe his own experiences in the same area. It is always good practice to bring another inmate into the discussion, as opportunity offers, when one of them seems to be reacting very strongly and may be overtaxed by his feelings. An effort should be made, even if it means running a little over the time limit, to see that members of the group do not leave the session in a state of too great emotional excitement.

(k) It is desirable to avoid, if possible, starting discussions which may evoke immediate guilt feelings and accompanying rationalization or even resentment. A good example is the discussion sometimes raised by inmates themselves of the satisfactions a man has in prison. In the institution, the inmate has few responsibilities and most of his thinking is done for him. He has a sort of vacation from real life and its problems of earning a living. He does not have to be concerned about a job or other means of helping himself. Why worry about returning to prison? If such irritating or insulting questions arise, it is well to have the group face them fairly and speak frankly. They will usually protest very strongly and feelingly against the implication that they are voluntarily parasites. Inmates seem to like to annoy each other at times by bringing in the viewpoints of those who dislike offenders. The control of these rather heated and pessimistic sessions requires great patience, objectivity and skill in the group leaders.

(l) Role playing may be employed after the group has been meeting for some time. For example, this may be done by setting up a situation wherein members of the group take the parts of victims, and of offenders. Another possibility is a situation wherein are acted out the parts of a correctional officer and an inmate who has violated a rule. Or a mock parole board hearing may be portrayed. Or the situation to be

* Methods for the use of films are given in the training manual (Fenton.[4] pp. 111–23).

acted out might be what goes on when a parole officer and a parolee meet for the first time after the latter has been released.

Role playing may be further developed later on in the psychodrama, wherein scenes are played by the group depicting some particular inmate's personal problem. The sociodrama is another type of dramatic situation wherein, for example, a member of a minority group applies for a job and the prejudiced attitudes toward his employment are portrayed.

(m) Reading assignments in books on mental health and discussions or reports thereon have been used effectively by some leaders. The inmate text[5] has been used systematically in some groups. Discussions of characters in biographies, short stories or novels may be useful in this connection.

(n) At the close of the session, it has been considered good practice for the leader to indicate that time is about up and then for him to summarize briefly the highlights of the day's discussion. Later, an inmate may be permitted to try to do this. The leader's summary is especially desirable in the early meetings. It may help the inmates to understand the purpose and meaning of group counseling. They may obtain a better understanding of what goes on. The summary of the meeting may leave them with a greater awareness of what has been accomplished.

(o) One of the more difficult questions that may be asked by the beginning counselor is, "How do I know I'm getting anywhere with my group?" In answer to this, it is necessary to point out that growth is not easily recognized. No one may expect miracles. Sometimes inmates feel elated and hopeful after sessions, at other times they may be discouraged. This variation of mood is characteristic of all kinds of treatment, being most poignant perhaps in psychoanalysis. Group counseling, like other types of treatment, is, of course, no permanent solvent for moods.

There are periods when the group is sincerely appreciative of group counseling. At other times they may be severely critical. In general there is a progression of targets of hostility. The first are usually law enforcement and judicial officials. Parole agents especially are recipients of hostility voiced by those in the group who have been returned by them to prison. The second target is the group leader, toward whom the group may express hostilities, usually after the group has met a few times and the inmates feel secure enough to do so. They express their hostility by being critical of his ability to conduct a group or they may be sarcastic about any kind of treatment in prison, especially the value of group counseling itself. After these hostilities have been accepted by the group leader without argument or evidence of resentment, perhaps with an expression of amused tolerance, the group may then turn their attention to a third target, themselves, and their part in causing their present predicament.*

The group leader must try to conduct his group on schedule. He should try to begin promptly. He should try to lead his group as thoughtfully and persistently as he can, avoiding, as far as he himself is concerned, feelings either of elation or depression over the character of the session. Usually, outcomes are satisfactory in a group conducted conscientiously and without too much forceful direction over a period of months. The transfer after a time of positive feeling toward the leader, as the group accepts him as a person of good will, may be one of the most rewarding experiences in human life.

5. *The relationship between individual and group counseling.* A valuable accompaniment of group counseling may be noted in the assistance rendered by the group leader in the form of individual counseling. The inmate may approach the group leader before or after the session and ask for advice or guidance with some personal problem. At such informal individual conferences, group leaders may be helpful to their counselees in many details of prison living. It is an accepted part of the group counseling program that when inmates come to group leaders with practical problems, the leaders may, if their knowledge permits, answer their questions. If unable to do so with confidence, then they should know enough about institutional or agency operations to direct the inmate to the individual on the staff most likely to be helpful and even to try to make an appointment for the counselee to confer with him.

Future studies may indicate, as group counseling enters other correctional fields, that probation officers or parole agents may find group counseling of practical value in the more economical handling of their caseloads. Ordinarily, it would seem advisable that they should serve both as the group leaders and as the individual caseworkers for the clients in their group. With a large caseload, group counseling may possibly be a helpful device for assuring that the parole agent or the probation officer will be in touch with his clients more often than is possible through individual appointments in the office or with less effort than when arrangements have to be made for visits to individual residences.

Ideally, individual and group counseling should be combined, as is done in the private practice of psychotherapy as reported by Bach[1] and others. Material that arises in the inmate's mind, but which he hesitates to bring out in the group, may then be discussed in an

* Our discussion here is necessarily quite sketchy. Reports of actual examples of the progression of targets of hostility in groups are more helpful. Some may be found in Fenton,[8] pp. 36–8.

individual counseling session. In practice, when group counseling is adequately administered, there should be occasional opportunities for individual counseling when the inmate earnestly requests it. Unfortunately this has not ordinarily been possible in the California prisons.

6. *Some outcomes of group counseling.* (a) Group counseling has advanced in prison practice because it has been found to be a useful and economical means of helping inmates. In California, the program began as a recourse, tried after some hesitation, when requests for additional clinical staff had been refused by the state financial authorities. Primarily, the device has proved to be a means of enabling the prison to reach inmates not otherwise afforded psychological treatment. We may also note many other values.*

(b) As a result of group counseling, communication among all the human beings in the prison, staff and inmates alike, has greatly improved. It has brought together the custodial and treatment staffs in the pursuit of common goals for the welfare of inmates, as seemingly nothing ever did before in the history of prisons. Group counseling seems to help to integrate the efforts and thinking of these previously divergent functionaries of the prisons. The values of the contributions of clinical specialists have become better known to the line officer. The nature, importance and difficulties of the custodial staff have been understood better by the clinician. The relationships between inmates and staff have become more wholesome. The improvement in the morale of the prisons, after group counseling has been introduced, has been an encouraging development.

(c) Another important outcome of the group counseling program has been the demonstration of the possibility of helpfulness of inmates for each other. A striking use of the peer group in treating their fellows is found in the Alcoholics Anonymous program. Therein, hitherto untreatable people are helped by laymen who have themselves been alcoholics. But in many prisons, administrative procedures are based upon the hypothesis that the only influence one prisoner may have upon another is bad. Parolees are not permitted to associate with each other in society because of this belief. Group counseling has shown that this hypothesis, in part at least, is fallacious. Groups of inmates and parolees help one another, sometimes seemingly more effectively than staff members could have done. An impressive part of the group guidance program for those about to leave on parole in the California prisons has been the contributions of successful parolees. Some of them are brought back to prison for an evening to participate as instructors in the pre-release program. They answer questions about parole

---

* These are reported in somewhat greater detail in Fenton,[8] pp. 57–9.

raised by inmates, often in the picturesque language of the prison yard. The parolees seem to relieve anxiety and instill hope in those about to leave prison. It is doubtful whether a staff member could do this as well as can men who are succeeding on parole.

(d) A number of other values have been found in group counseling which affect the well being of the inmates themselves. The expressions of feelings of members of the group are influential in enabling other inmates therein to recognize similar feelings in themselves. It seems as though they communicate with each other in expressing their feelings and attitudes not only on a verbal but also on a feeling level. This interplay has, moreover, reduced in some the defenses or resistances to the release of feeling in the group. The expressed hopes and good intentions of other inmates, moreover, have seemed to strengthen the listening group to accept their own inner feelings of wanting to be on the right side in society. The reactions of other inmates, the group leader being silent and non-directive, have also been constructive when members of the group have expressed negative or hostile attitudes. The program has permitted inmates to release feelings (grievances, resentment, frustration and the like) without fear or anxiety in the presence of a permissive, non-punishing group leader, and to enable them to profit from being present while others do so.

(e) Basically, inmates have been helped to recognize the significance of emotional conflicts as being the source of symptoms of criminality such as robbery, burglary, or forgery. An inmate previously unaware of the emotional bases of his symptoms or unwilling to recognize this fact, may be brought gradually by the expressions of others in the group to this insight. The inmate may grow to appreciate the significance of repressed, disturbed feelings toward authority-figures (parents, employers, law enforcement officials) as possibly a partial explanation of why he is in prison. To get along on parole, the inmate has to accept himself as someone with costly disturbances of feeling. To profit from group counseling, he must become at least open-minded about the above belief that the release and examination of his inner feelings in the group is likely to be helpful for his future well-being and happiness in society.

(f) Group counseling has permitted the inmate to see his social personality, how he affects others, as it is presented to the group. He can learn the effect upon others of his personality in a permissive setting wherein he is told frankly about his shortcomings by his fellow inmates, not by authority figures. Both good traits and undesirable ones are reported by the group to the individual. Under good and sympathetic guidance, these experiences may be very helpful for growth of personality in the inmates. These may also be situations requiring individual counseling.

30

(g) As mentioned earlier, group leaders do considerable individual counseling. When an inmate raises a practical question regarding his situation in prison or on parole, the group leader may discuss the matter with him or refer him to the staff member likely to help him or to his correctional counselor. These questions may involve such diversified matters as vocational ambitions, attitudes toward relatives, hobbies, or religious interests. In these and other aspects of their work the group counselors render the same services, usually through reference to others on the staff, as is done by individual counselors. With the personality problems referred to in the previous section, individual counseling is sometimes necessary. The group leader may call upon the clinician for help in some cases.

(h) Inmates have been helped to understand how the world of make-believe, of phantasy, plays a part in social maladjustment. The group helps them to see how a disturbed and unhappy person may find relief in daydreaming. They also may learn that the control of actions arising from daydreaming is a problem which faces the inmate who wants to leave prison and not return.

(i) The discussions in the group have impressive educational outcomes. After a few months in group counseling, there is a notable improvement in many inmates in their ability to speak before others. In some cases this may be of considerable value for personality development. Again, their own discussions of many aspects of life in prison and on the outside leads to the consideration of ethical and social principles. This serves as a good informal way of helping inmates to face their future duties and obligations as members of a democratic society. In the counseling groups, they discuss these aspects of their lives on parole from a standpoint that would be taboo among groups of inmates elsewhere in the prison.

(j) Concern with correctional objectives should not blind us to the recognition of recreational values in group counseling. This is not the primary goal of the program, but, as Samuels[15] noted, group counseling brings gratification and relaxation to the members of the group. These pleasant and wholesome feelings, valuable outcomes of group counseling, may be of considerable value for personality development.

(k) For the most part, the above outcomes are of value to the inmate. Administrators of the prisons for their part may add others; for example, from the standpoint of institutional management there is proportionately less disorderliness and greater courtesy and friendliness among inmates who are participating in group counseling than in others who are not.

(l) As already noted, the conscientious and patient group leader will be rewarded for his efforts by many satisfying experiences as he observes the growth toward maturity of individual inmates and the general improvement in morale of the groups involved.* The program may also have influence for good among other inmates who, although not members of a counseling group, appreciate nevertheless the sincerity of the officials who participate in the group counseling program. The potential values of carry-over to parole are also obvious. These can best be assured when the program on parole also includes group counseling.

7. *Studies concerning group counseling.* At present, research† is being conducted to evaluate the group counseling program. In general, the preliminary findings are favorable as regards the effects upon the conduct of the participants and the morale of the institution. The adjustment of counselees as a group within the institution is better. There are fewer disciplinary problems, and the proportion of escapes is less for inmates in group counseling than that recorded for those not in group counseling. Some of these studies, which are difficult to conduct scientifically because of the many variables involved, have nevertheless had fairly satisfactory control groups. The morale of the staff in an institution with one hundred per cent inmate participation in group counseling was reported as definitely superior to that found in the other facilities in the prison system. Of course, it must be realized that other factors, for example, its smaller size, may also have contributed to this high morale rating. These studies are being repeated with more adequate controls. But even if the above mentioned results were discounted greatly, they would still suggest that group counseling has probably made a valuable contribution to institutional operation.

The initial introduction and subsequent development of group counseling in the prisons, although supported and encouraged by the central administration in the State Capitol, was left for decision to the local institutional leadership. After an experimental trial of the program in each of the institutions, the program was subjected to considerable critical study by the warden and his top staff before increasing the number of groups. Since 1954, when group counseling was first tried in its present form, institutional participation has increased greatly, so that at present about one half of the inmates in the California prison system are enrolled in the program. This expansion of group counseling is impressive. However, it offers in itself no final proof as to the value of group counseling in correctional practice.

---

* Other personal values for employees are given in Fenton,[8] pp. 59–60.

† One of the most extensive studies is a five-year research project begun in 1958 at the University of California at Los Angeles under a subsidy [of about two thousand dollars] from the National Institute for Mental Health of the United States Public Health Service.

The findings for the comparative post-release adjustment of counselees compared with others on parole or discharge are encouraging, though in general not startling. Harrison,[11] p. 61, has noted that "we have clearer evidence of the contributions of group counseling to the safe operation of the prison than we do, as yet, for the long-term rehabilitative benefit." An exception is found in the surprisingly high rate of satisfactory adjustment on parole of men from what are called "long-term, low turnover" groups, conducted with the same inmates for a year or more under the same competent and dedicated leaders. Clearly positive results in the form of unusually good records on parole have been reported in follow-up studies of those who attended such groups while in the institution. These favorable findings are being subjected to rigorous review and additional studies have been planned by the Research Division of the Department of Corrections and by other groups.

A major value reported in various observations and studies has been the improvement in communication between inmates and staff.* The long-established separation of inmates and employees, as though in two different cultures, seems to be much less evident. More good will toward each other is expressed by the human beings in the institution. For example, early returns from a study of youthful offenders in a reformatory-type institution indicate a decrease in hostility and in gang behavior there after group counseling had been introduced. According to comments of the staff, the general emotional climate of the place seemed to have improved.

In an investigation at San Quentin, Roberts,[14] p. 75, reported that "The data suggest a change among group counseling inmates from an attitude indicative of strict compliance with or adherence to the prescriptions of the inmate social system, to one indicating a lesser degree of acceptance of these traditional controls. Also suggested, in the responses of the counselees, was a greater degree of acceptance in their social relationship with other individuals and races."

Another possible contribution of group counseling that has been reported is the growth in the interest of custodial officers in their work, accompanied by greater belief in the desirability of treatment for prisoners.† The reason the program has sometimes been called revolutionary is due to these changes in the attitudes and activities of both inmates and the rank and file of institutional employees. These seem to contradict any dogmatic viewpoint that the prison community is by its very nature irreparably divided into the two irreconcilable

* See the statement by Grant, J. D., "The Research Newsletter," Vacaville, California, 1960, March, pp. 1–2.

† Preliminary findings from the research study directed by J. W. Eaton conducted at the University of California at Los Angeles and mentioned earlier.

cultures, the one of the inmates, and the other of the staff. On the contrary, these preliminary studies suggest that when group counseling is effective, there may be not only better co-existence but the beginning of more genuine communication and cooperation between inmates and staff.

The Future of Counseling in Prison

What has been said in this chapter is intended to indicate the importance of individual and group counseling in the treatment of the personality problems of offenders. In the future, prisons and other correctional agencies must develop more extensive use of individual and group psychotherapy conducted by leaders trained in social work, psychology, and psychiatry. They should also utilize individual and group counseling conducted by laymen under the supervision of these specialists. Evidence now being collected seems to indicate that laymen with preliminary training in group counseling and under professional supervision have a valuable contribution to make to the treatment of inmates.

If the counseling program in prison is to be effective, however, the atmosphere of the institution must be supportive. This criterion applies, of course, to any type of institution, correctional, medical, or educational, in which a program of counseling is introduced. The employment of specialist personnel, psychologists, psychiatrists and others, and the use of accepted professional techniques does not guarantee a good counseling program in prison. Nor is the working out of a neat plan of administration on paper, which some authoritarian penologists seem to depend upon, the guarantee of a good counseling program. Instead, the following three criteria must be met if the potential usefulness of a counseling program in a prison is to be realized:

1. The confident, supporting and even enthusiastic leadership of the head of the prison and others in top management.

2. The understanding acceptance of the counseling program by middle management in custody, education, recreation, the library, the chaplaincy, and the clinical center.

3. The acceptance by the clinical specialists of the rank and file of correctional officers, teachers, work supervisors and the clerical staff as worthy colleagues in the treatment program.

If these three criteria are met, then there is a united front of all the staff in the presentation of the treatment program to the inmate. Also there is an atmosphere of treatment generated by this mutual good will in the staff. These staff relationships are important because the theory underlying the treatment program in the prison is that a major cause of criminality has been the destructive effects of other human beings in the lives of its inmates. These influences, according to this theory, have been responsible for developing in the inmates feelings of inferiority, self-pity, resentment, or hate; sometimes, indeed, these or other feelings have been transmuted by inmates into almost complete despair about themselves and their lives.

In the broader sense, if the prison is ever to become a place for treatment like the good hospital, then surrounding the inmate in the prison there should be none but those who can accept him in their hearts as a troubled fellow human being. In hospitals, patients need to be restricted by regulations; so, likewise, in the prison. But in both places there must be a harmony of constructive purposes among the various kinds of employees who compose the staff. In the treatment prison, all employees must understand the values of humanly sympathetic acceptance and be in accord therewith. Then, no longer will the members of the staff of the prison be classified as either custodial or treatment. Instead, the prisons will develop the one true correctional employee. All on the prison staff who are in personal contact with the inmates will be genuinely therapeutic in this outlook and live these concepts in their behavior on the job.

Treatment of prison inmates may then be recognized as drawing greatly upon the use of methods of guidance and counseling. All employees in the prison must understand their roles in the treatment program. First-hand experience in individual and group counseling should be part of the training of all workers in adult correctional institutions if in the coming years prisons are to become places for treatment.

BIBLIOGRAPHY

1. BACH, R.: 1945. *Intensive Group Psychotherapy*. New York: Ronald Press.
2. COOK, A., HEINZE, R. A., FENTON, N.: 1955. "Methods of Handling the Severely Recalcitrant Inmate." *Proc. Amer. Correc. Assoc.*
3. DICKSON, F. R., FENTON, N., and HOLZSCHUH, A.: 1955. "The Inmate Advisory Council." *Proc. Amer. Correc. Assoc.*, pp. 142–46.
4. FENTON, N.: 1957. "An Introduction to Group Counseling in Correctional Service." New York: *Amer. Correc. Assoc.*
5. ——: 1957. "What Will Be Your Life?" New York: *Amer. Correc. Assoc.*
6. ——: 1957. *A Brief Historical Account of Group Counseling in the Prisons of California*. Sacramento: Department of Corrections.
7. ——: 1959. *The Prisoner's Family*. Palo Alto, Calif., Pacific Books.
8. ——: 1961. *Group Counseling—A Preface to Its Use in Correctional and Welfare Agencies*. Sacramento: Institute for the Study of Crime and Delinquency.
9. GRANT, J. D.: 1960. "What Should Research Be Doing for Parole?" *Proc. Amer. Correc. Assoc.*, pp. 297–304. New York.

10. GRANT, J. D.: "Building Operational Research into a Correctional Administrative Statistical System." Sacramento, Calif., 1950, mimeographed, 14 pp.
11. HARRISON, R. M.: "Mental Health Applications in the California Correctional System." The Chatham Conference, Boston University, 1960, pp. 56–57.
12. LERNER, A.: 1953. "An Exploratory Approach in Group Counseling with Male Alcoholic Inmates in a City Jail." *Quar. J. Stud. on Alcohol*, **14**, pp. 427–67.
13. McENTIRE, D.: "Some Factors Associated with Parole Outcome in California." Department of Corrections, Sacramento, 1950.
14. ROBERTS, E. L. R.: "A Study of the Effects of Group Counseling on Association Choices and Status Ascription among Inmates at the California State Prison at San Quentin," Master's Thesis, San Francisco State College, 1960.
15. SAMUELS, J.: "A Review of Present Problems in the Group Counseling Program, Represa, California," 1956, 8 pp., mimeographed.
16. WILKINS, L. T., and MANNHEIM, H.: 1955. "Prediction Methods in Relation to Borstal Training." London: Her Majesty's Stationery Office.

Probation and Parole Counseling

ALFRED R. LOOS

Commissioner
N.Y. State Board of Parole
New York City

INTRODUCTION

IN THIS chapter, only those aspects of counseling which refer to adults are discussed. While it is acknowledged that there are differences in laws in the several States as to the age at which a juvenile legally becomes an adult, it is deemed expedient to define the adult offender as an individual who has attained the age of sixteen years and has been convicted of a criminal offense.

Authorities in the field generally agree that there are at least four main stages in the correctional process which may be described as follows:

Probation. A division of the field of correctional care which is a legal, social, and personal service, operating within the framework of a judicial setting consisting of Intake, Investigation and Supervision for the purpose of protecting Society, preventing delinquency and crime, and rehabilitating the individual.

Institutionalization. A division of the field of correctional care which receives its intake through judicial commitment for the purpose of providing safe custody and supervision, and of developing a treatment program designed to prepare the offender for his reintegration into the community.

Parole. The conditional release of an inmate, usually by a Board of Parole or a Board of Managers, from a penal or reformative institution, under the supervision of a parole officer or agent.

Post Release. Referred to as the discharge of an inmate from a penal or reformative institution, usually at the expiration of the maximum sentence, or at the expiration of the maximum sentence less time off for good behavior, without the supervision of a duly constituted correctional agency.

Since counseling in correctional institutions is described in another chapter, the principal area of interest here will describe counseling in the other segments of the correctional field—Probation, Parole, and Post Release. For purposes of uniformity, therefore, the Probation Officer, the Parole Officer or Agent, and the representative of the private correctional agency, are included in the use of the term—Correctional Counselor.

DIFFERENTIATING FACTORS IN CORRECTIONAL COUNSELING

While the field of Correction has many similarities to other disciplines in the counseling techniques employed, there are a number of differentiating factors involved in the correctional counseling process that serve to distinguish it. Primarily, Probation and Parole are concerned with the protection of society, and this factor must always receive first priority. Additionally, there is usually a specified period of supervision imposed either by administrative or judicial regulation or by statute. The relationship between the offender and the probation or parole counselor is essentially an imposed one.

Common to both Probation and Parole, however, is supervision in the community with all its implications. Society has assigned to the convicted offender the designation of a restricted supervised status with associated obligations by which he may earn return to normal status in society.

In considering Probation and Parole counseling, it is evident there is little fundamental difference between them in the counseling techniques employed. Primarily, Probation selects those offenders who offer the most promising prospects for supervision in the community without institutionalization. It may be considered a screening process which commits to institutions those offenders whose criminal behavior pattern or crime is such that the best interests of society and the offenders are served if they are removed from the community and placed in an institution which provides not only custody but a constructive treatment program as well.

The problem that confronts the paroling authority is the selection of those inmates of correctional institutions who may benefit from a period of supervision under the control of a parole officer or agent. In some cases, the paroling authority is faced with the perplexing question of deciding whether an inmate should be given an opportunity to demonstrate his ability to adjust under supervision in the community or be held to the expiration of his maximum sentence which may extend over many years. The protection of the community is an all-important factor in reaching this decision. The multiple offender with a sentence of short duration is an example of the type of offender the paroling authority may deem advisable to hold until the maximum expiration of sentence. Most correctional authorities agree that some individuals, in the light of available knowledge, are not able to benefit from a period of supervision.

Apart from these differences, authorities in the correctional field agree that the supervision process in Probation and Parole has considerable similarity. Among these similarities is the length of the period of supervision, which may be prescribed by administrative or judicial regulation or statute. Where the period of supervision is prescribed by statute, the correctional counselor learns that there is another limitation upon the treatment process. An offender may have made a very satisfactory community adjustment and may be emotionally and intellectually ready for release or discharge from supervision, but the law prohibits it. The experienced correctional counselor recognizes this limitation, and interprets its restrictions to the offender with minimal impairment as possible to the counseling relationship. Where a satisfactory relationship exists between the offender and the counselor, the individual usually understands his controlled status and accepts it realistically. It is appropriate to mention that the counselor does have at his disposal in such situations the possibility of the relaxation of control through reduced supervision.

Where the period of supervision is subject to judicial or administrative regulation, the correctional counselor is in a more advantageous position because he is able to terminate the control when the offender has succeeded in his social readjustment in the community.

But whatever procedure is followed in the termination of supervision, it must be acknowledged that it is the correctional counselor and not the offender, who legitimately terminates the relationship. The individual does not have the freedom of choice common to other fields of counseling, in the selection of counseling contacts.

It is the usual practice in Probation and Parole to require that the offender report to the Probation or Parole Officer in person, at regular intervals at a designated place. Although some individuals consider this requirement as an obstacle to treatment because of its "compulsive" nature, experience has demonstrated that the competent correctional counselor can utilize these interviews to further the plan of treatment. The frequency of contact with the individual is a decided advantage the correctional counselor has over counselors in other disciplines.

Distinctive to the correctional field is the use of prescribed rules and conditions of Probation and Parole which follow the same pattern in most agencies. Within reasonable limits, it is the duty of the counselor to require the offender to observe the spirit if not the letter, of these rules and conditions. If the reasons for such rules and conditions are analyzed, it is evident these rules and conditions constitute another manifestation of the authoritarian aspect of the correctional process. Since the probationer or parolee has transgressed the laws of society, and has thereby demonstrated his failure to achieve a normal adjustment in the community, the need is apparent for the development of standards of conduct and behavior which will reflect not only the offender's restricted status but also point out to him the course of conduct and behavior which will enable him to discharge his obligations and responsibilities in a socially acceptable manner.

If there is any area in the field of correctional counseling where the skill of the worker is tested critically, it is in the proper understanding and interpretation of Probation and Parole rules and conditions. Fundamental to this understanding is the recognition that these rules and conditions are not ends in themselves but guides to both the counselor and the offender as to what obligations and responsibilities the offender assumes in his restricted status of probationer or parolee.

To maintain that it is possible to develop a set of rules and conditions in Probation and Parole to apply equally and in the same manner to all offenders, is to negate the theory of individual treatment. There are certain administrative rules and conditions that of necessity must apply to all offenders under Probation or Parole supervision. Regular reporting, avoiding the company of other criminals, prompt replies to official correspondence are examples, but the specific rules and conditions which apply primarily to the regulation of conduct and behavior must be interpreted to the offender in the light of his needs. To take a common rule in Probation and Parole, for example, the abstention from alcoholic beverages. The application of this rule to all offenders in the same manner will serve only to complicate the adjustment of the average probationer or parolee. For the offender whose indulgence in alcoholic beverages has been a precipitating factor in his criminal behavior, total abstention must be enforced rigidly. On the other hand, there are offenders who have indulged in alcoholic beverages in moderation prior to their conviction, and this indulgence has not been a factor in their criminal behavior. To insist that the latter group practice total abstention is to engender disrespect for the rules and conditions themselves. If the counselor interprets properly the rules and conditions prescribed by the correctional agency, applies them intelligently, and succeeds in having the offender not only understand but accept them as well, there then is a mutual understanding of the limitations of the counseling relationship. Within this framework, the counselor can reinterpret the authority of the community to the offender. As he experiences authority that has power to help as well as to limit, he learns to accept other aspects of authority required in the community.

Critics of Probation and Parole maintain frequently that when a probationer or parolee is cited for technical violation of the rules and conditions, this constitutes a failure on the part of the correctional agency. However, authorities in Probation and Parole contend that the citing of offenders for technical violations is a sound case work technique and a part of counseling, provided the worker does it with full attention to the client as an individual whose welfare is his primary interest within the social and legal limitations to which both must adjust.

Unlike other counseling agencies, the correctional agency is part of the system of organized social control. This means that every correctional counselor is responsible for teamwork with personnel in law enforcement and the processes of justice, including police, prosecuting attorneys, judges, and others. The successful counselor accepts and discharges this responsibility and works within its framework.

TYPES OF CORRECTIONAL COUNSELING

In the correctional field, counseling may be divided into two principal categories—individual and group counseling.

Group Counseling

Group counseling seems to have made its greatest stride in the correctional institutions. Many State and Federal institutions now have a group therapy or group counseling program as a positive feature of their treatment program. Group counseling has not yet reached the organized status in other areas of the correctional field as it has in the institutions. However, significant progress is being made on both the juvenile and adult level. The Brooklyn Bureau of Social Service and Children's Aid Society have conducted group counseling on a pioneering basis with groups of mothers and problem girls. It was the feeling of the agency that the case workers who conducted counseling groups gained new experience as well as adding a new technique to their professional equipment and refining their case work skills.[1]

In an effort to determine if juvenile probationers could be reached through the group counseling method, the Los Angeles County Probation Office organized counseling groups among juvenile probationers.

Their experience indicated that, overall, boys in the counseling groups made, statistically, a better than average record on probation.[2]

The Bureau of Juvenile Rehabilitations, Washington State Department of Institutions conducted an experiment in group counseling with juvenile parolees. In this situation, the parole counselor who conducted the group counseling program also supervised the parolees, so he was able to function in both an individual and group counseling role.[3]

A few years ago, the Probation Office of the United States District Court for the District of Columbia experimented with group counseling with probationers and parolees. As a result of their experience, these group counseling programs have become an integral part of the case work program. Probation Officers meet weekly for about 90 minutes with probationers and parolees selected from their own case loads.[4]

In 1955, the adult parole division of the Department of Correction of the state of California began experimenting with group counseling for parolees. Candidates for the group were selected by parole agents from among their own case loads. Experiments were considered successful enough to adopt this approach as a special service within the Adult Parole Division. A report of the Department of Corrections, State of California has this to say about parolee group counseling. "This is a technique used by the parole agent which has proved valuable in the treatment of parolees. In an area of treatment where communication is difficult, as between an offender and/or authority figure such as a parole agent, the mutual exchanges between peers as occurs in a group of parolees has proved effective in helping to resolve personal problems."[5]

The John Howard Society of Quebec recently concluded an experiment in group counseling of convicted offenders. It is now an established feature of the agency program. The experience of this agency again demonstrates the soundness of the theory that the family of a convicted offender in confinement must be prepared emotionally to receive him upon his release.[6]

The BARO (Brooklyn Association for the Rehabilitation of Offenders) Civic Center Clinic, New York City is an agency unique in the history of therapy in America. It is the only full time, duly licensed, privately endowed mental hygiene clinic devoted exclusively to the treatment of adult offenders under psychiatric auspices in the United States. The Clinic has adopted the principle—"in many settings group therapy should be the treatment of choice, the preferred treatment, the treatment that may succeed where the usual face-to-face therapy will fail."[7]

The Kings County, New York, Court Probation Department, largely as a result of the experience of the BARO Clinic, cited above, deemed that sufficient evidence existed concerning probationers who had been treated by group processes to warrant the introduction of a group therapy program in the Kings County Court on an experimental basis.[8]

Broadly speaking, the group counseling process follows fundamentally the same techniques and methods used in other forms of group counseling. In the field of probation and parole, experience to date seems to indicate that this approach has some positive values in treatment. There seems to be common agreement that group counseling facilitates communication between the counselor and offender, both on a verbal and non-verbal level; offenders are more apt to ventilate their feelings in a group setting than in an individual interview; offenders relate more easily to identification with an authority figure in group counseling than in individual counseling; the group experience provides the counselor with an opportunity of observing the offender in his social reactions with others of the group which is not possible in the individual counseling session.

The expanding role of group counseling in the fields of Probation and Parole demonstrates it can be utilized effectively as an adjunct to individual counseling and the environmental case work services of these agencies. It adds another technique to the inventory of skills of the correctional counselor.

Individual Counseling

In the correctional field, individual counseling may be defined as a dynamic and personal face-to-face relationship between two individuals, where one seeks to aid the other to accept and discharge his own responsibility for his own choices and decisions, and their consequences. The counseling relationship should afford the offender the opportunity for clearly meeting and firmly clarifying the available alternatives of action and their possible consequences, if the individual is to be aided in accepting new patterns of behavior.

While counseling was recognized historically as a part of the social case work process, it was not definitely identified as such until recent years. Since the probation and parole areas of the correctional field have been allied with the field of social case work for many decades and the staffs of the probation and parole agencies have a similarity in professional education, training and experience, individual counseling is more apt to be on a skilled, professional level.

The field of social case work has developed an organized and systematized body of knowledge which, together with the accredited Schools of Social Work, has raised the field to the level of a profession. Practically the same techniques apply to individual counseling in the probation and parole areas of the correctional field as have been standard practice for decades in the area of social case work. The progress and growth of group counseling in probation and parole give promise of further refinement of the correctional counselor's technique and skills, but for the present, individual counseling is the standard method practiced in the majority of probation and parole agencies.

OBJECTIVES OF INDIVIDUAL COUNSELING

The ultimate objective of the correctional counselor is to assist the individual to become better adjusted to the demands of social living within the limits of his intelligence, capacity and capabilities. All too frequently the correctional counselor establishes goals and standards for the offender which are far beyond his capabilities.

In such instances, it is not surprising that the offender becomes discouraged, the counselor disappointed, and a potential violation of Probation or Parole is in the initial stages of development.

The initial or diagnostic phase of the treatment process consists of accumulating a body of knowledge regarding the individual offender and his problems, obtained through competent and effective social investigation.

The second, or so-called treatment phase of this process, involves the development of a counseling relationship between the counselor and the offender and the use of that relationship to reach specific objectives. The immediate objective of the process is to obtain, as far as it is possible to do so within the framework of the rules and regulations, and the policies of the agency, maximum participation of the offender in this process. Its ultimate objective is to prepare him for independent action in making his own decisions and fully accepting responsibility for them.

With the development of the group counseling process in probation and parole, the importance of integrating this with the individual counseling approach cannot be overemphasized.

UNDERSTANDING THE ETIOLOGY
OF DEVIANT BEHAVIOR

If the counselor is to treat deviations from acceptable standards of social conduct, he must have specialized knowledge of the nature and the circumstances of these deviations and how they relate to each other. To apply the concept of norms, he must understand the principles of law, social psychology, group dynamics and human relations. This understanding is necessary if he is to evaluate accurately and objectively the degree of deviation from normal behavior which has occurred in the case of the particular offender whom he is trying to assist. For professional competency, the counselor should possess some practical knowledge of such subjects as law, sociology, ethics, mental hygiene, anthropology, to some extent at least, and other specialized professions if he is to effectively consider deviations in relation to normal conduct. By the same token, it follows that the counselor be a mature and stable person and have healthy and acceptable standards of conduct acquired through normal personality development.

It is expected that the counselor will understand the psychological factors which tend to influence his own attitudes towards the persons under his supervision as a result of his own home and family life, education, and conditioning through life experience, and therefore maintain an objective and non-judgmental attitude.

Another principle of correctional counseling may be described as Particularization. In the application of this principle, the counselor analyzes his knowledge of the deviations from normal conduct in the particular case, compares them with normal standards of conduct and through the use of a generalization or a series of generalizations, arrives at tentative conclusions with regard to the causes or factors within the individual himself and his environment which have been responsible for the deviations from normal conduct. The use of particularization applies in a positive as well as in a negative sense because the counselor, while analyzing factors within the individual and his environment responsible for deviant conduct, is also evaluating the individual's constructive life experiences and the resources available within himself and his environment which he may use to make a better adjustment. In many instances, these resources are not readily apparent to the offender himself. It should be evident at this point that the principle of particularization constitutes an effort to arrive at an estimate of causality or etiology. Therefore, it is appropriate to emphasize that while the sequence of causality which the counselor is endeavoring to establish may be either on a sociological or psychological level, more likely it will be a combination of both.

THE CORRECTIONAL COUNSELOR–OFFENDER RELATIONSHIP

The counseling, or case work relationship, is the principal medium through which the counselor can use his knowledge of the individual and his skills as a professional worker to fulfill this function and to attain the objectives of the agency.

Correctional counselors can help individuals to discover and face the alternatives open to them, to make responsible voluntary choices of their own from among these alternatives, and then to accept responsibility for the consequences of their own judgments and decisions. The helping or treatment process, from this viewpoint, loses all semblance of control or manipulation of one person by another. It depends rather upon a relationship between counselor and offender within which the offender may, if he is able and willing, ask, receive, and use help in clarifying his own wants and purposes, in relation to the resources available to him, and in ministering his own powers to achieve his chosen ends.

Analysis of these statements regarding the nature of the counseling relationship establishes that it is based upon an understanding and application of fundamental psychological principles. The counselor must understand that he is dealing with a complex subject, namely the mechanisms which motivate human behavior. He must also remember that in dealing in a practical way with relationships and human behavior, he is concerned with the feelings and attitudes of the offender toward himself, the agency and society, as well as his own feelings and attitudes toward the offender, the agency, and society. He must comprehend the significance of the relationship which involves the understanding and the evaluation of the emotional as well as the intellectual factors which motivate human behavior. The former are more difficult to understand, assess, and evaluate than the latter. Actual practice has demonstrated, however, that the former are the more important.

Experienced counselors have witnessed the futility of demonstrating to the offender or members of his family by logical processes, the accepted norms of human behavior, or the action the offender should take in regard to his previous deviations or possible future deviations, without any recognition on the part of the counselor of the emotional factors involved. Although the understanding of emotional factors are now accepted as fundamental in the counseling field, they are even more important in the application of these principles to the supervision of offenders because one of the objectives is to effect a change in an individual who has passed through the hardening and embittering experience of criminal activity, arrest, conviction, and often incarceration.

It is not intended here to imply that an emotional rather than an intellectual appeal should be made to the offender to change his conduct or to take a specific course of action regarding a particular problem. What is consequential, however, is that unless or until the counselor is able to bring about a change in the attitudes and feelings of the offender which are preventing his use of intellectual concepts regarding behavior and conduct, the time spent in generalizing his problems on an intellectual level is needlessly expended. It should be apparent, therefore, that there must be a recognition on the part of the counselor of the emotional factors affecting the offender's attitude and conduct, and that through the counselor-client relationship, the offender himself must change his attitude before he will be able to accept reasoned intellectual help.

The problem of relationship in the correctional field, therefore, largely is a psychological one, the successful handling of which requires maturity and emotional stability on the part of the counselor, together with some knowledge of the subjects of psychology and psychiatry as they relate to motivations and personality development.

ELEMENTS OF THE CORRECTIONAL COUNSELOR–OFFENDER RELATIONSHIP

Essentially, the correctional counselor–client relationship contains the elements of: 1. attitudes of interest and understanding by the counselor; 2. participation and determination by the offender; and 3. the attainment of specific objectives.

Attitudes of interest and understanding. Primarily, it is a relationship fostered by attitudes of interest and understanding on the part of the counselor. The counselor is interested in the offender as an individual and the purpose or objective of his interest is understanding. The counselor's interest is focused upon the offender's development in its sociological and psychological aspects. Not only the offender's environmental experiences, or reality situations, as they are sometimes referred to, but also and more important, the meaning those situations and experiences have had for him as an individual, concern the counselor. This understanding applies not only to the offender's experiences of the distant past and during the school and youth period of his life, but to all of these experiences up to and including his relationship with the counselor who is responsible for the relationship at any given point in the supervision process.

Participation and self-determination by the offender. The counseling relationship is one in which the offender participates as fully as possible within the limitation of his own intellectual and emotional capacities, and within the limitation of his restricted status as well as the administrative framework and functions of the correctional agency. The extent or degree of participation by the offender in this relationship must of necessity be regulated by the capacities of the individual and the needs of the agency. Obviously, the offender who has the limitation of mental deficiency cannot be self-determining to the same extent as the individual who is of normal intelligence. The degree of his participation will depend upon the extent of his intelligence both as indicated by the process of mental testing and his ability to make a social adjustment. The latter will be based upon the evaluation of the counselor who works with him. On the other hand, the offender of normal intelligence may not be able to accept immediate responsibility for full participation in the counseling relationship because he is inhibited by hostility toward society, the counselor, or the correctional agency.

This hostility, of course, is only one of a great range and variety of emotional factors which may impair the offender's ability to participate fully in the counseling relationship. Notwithstanding, it must be the counselor's objective to evaluate the individual's capacity for relationship as fully as possible after the initial contact and to gradually develop the abilities and capacities of the offender to accept responsibility for his own actions. That is the ultimate aim and objective of the counselor–offender relationship.

In the past there has been a great deal of discussion and controversy, and it might be added, futile controversy, as to whether the principle of self-determination can be applied to counseling in the correctional field. While it is not considered feasible to enter into an extensive discussion of the use of authority in correctional counseling at this point, it is sufficient to state that outstanding authorities in both the field of correction and the field of social case work, now agree that the principle of participation and self-determination are not only possible in the area of correctional counseling, but are desirable and necessary, if the objective of permanent community protection is to be achieved. In applying this principle, however, the counselor may not take risks where a choice must be made between the application of the principle and the safety of the community, regardless of how desirable such action might be for the offender concerned.

Within the limitations permitted by agency function and community protection, however, it is the counselor's objective in applying the principle of participation to first evaluate the offender's abilities and capacities to assume a minimum degree of participation in the relationship, and to gradually increase the offender's responsibilities for meeting his own problems and planning his conduct. Through this method, the individual can obtain permanent advantage from the relationship in the form of maturity, and society will benefit in the form of an improved social attitude on the part of the offender.

The attainment of specific objectives. The third essential element in the counselor–offender relationship is that it is a relationship developed for specific purposes. Its immediate purpose or objective is to assist the offender in understanding and effectively dealing with the problems with which he is immediately faced, including his restricted status.

The ultimate goal or objective of this relationship is the development of the offender's ability to undertake independent action and to make free choices within the framework of acceptable standards of conduct.

METHODS OF DEVELOPING THE CORRECTIONAL COUNSELOR–OFFENDER RELATIONSHIP

Having considered the nature and the essential elements of the counselor–offender relationship, it may be timely to consider the means whereby such a relationship may be effectively developed. If the counselor is to develop this relationship fully and effectively, he must use certain positive attitudes in his relationship with the offender, which are based upon his own sincere belief and convictions.

Mutual respect. Correctional counseling, like other forms of counseling, is based upon a recognition of the value of the individual and respect for his dignity as a unique personality. In its practical application, this principle requires that the offender and the counselor meet as equals and that the counselor give to the offender as far as possible, a sense of his own integrity as an individual person. In a negative sense, it requires that the counselor avoid an attitude of superiority or arrogance.

The proper attitude on the part of the counselor will result in a feeling of mutual respect, the counselor respecting the client's dignity as a human being, and the offender respecting the counselor primarily as another human being and, secondarily, as the representative of a public or private agency. Therefore, the first positive step for the counselor to take in the development of the counseling relationship, is to bring about attitudes of mutual respect. In so doing, it is important that the authority vested in the counselor as a representative of the agency, be used only when necessary and that its use be tempered with discretion and tact. Obviously, authority should not be used in a subjective, threatening, unfair or arbitrary way. To develop and maintain the counseling relationship, it is important that the counselor be gentle, yet firm, in his dealings with the offender, never displaying anger or contempt, yet insisting upon courteous compliance with the conditions imposed by the agency.

The attitude of understanding. The counselor must also make a positive effort to understand the offender both as a person and the problem or problems which he presents. The inexperienced, the untrained, or the unanalytical counselor will be inclined to think of the application of this principle in terms of its face value. The implication to such a person most likely would be that intellectual understanding of the offender and his problems, or understanding based upon the counselor's own life experiences and standards of conduct would be adequate. If this were true, however, the development of the counseling relationship, in fact, the use of the entire counseling process, would be comparatively simple. Since emotional components are a major factor in the consideration of the offender and his problems, as well as the counselor, the use of intellectual understanding alone is not adequate. The counselor must develop an ability to view the problems from the standpoint of the offender. He must be able to share in the offender's difficulties and their solution. This does not mean that the counselor will agree with the individual's interpretation of his problems or place the same values upon them; nor does it mean the counselor must accept the offender's standards of behavior as his own or approve of them. It does require that he must understand the offender's point of view, if he is to make an intelligent effort to assist the individual in changing that point of view. In this process, the counselor must be sensitive to the necessity of striking a balance between understanding the offender and his problems as the offender sees them, and understanding them in terms of acceptable norms of conduct. If the counselor's attitude toward the offender is too detached and objective, or if he fails to participate sufficiently with the subject in finding a solution to the problem, he will fail to assist the offender and may create the impression that his interest is not genuine. On the other hand, if the counselor goes too far in seeing the problem from the offender's point of view, his value in the relationship will be limited because he will not think clearly and objectively about it.

Sincerity. In addition to respect and understanding, there is also the need of sincerity. Without it, no satisfactory relationship can exist anywhere. In Probation and Parole, it is of paramount importance because many offenders have a conviction that persons connected with law enforcement or correctional workers are self-seeking and disinterested in their welfare. For this reason, it is important the counselor zealously maintains the sincerity and integrity of his motives. It is essential that he keep his appointments, fulfill promises made, and always treat the offender in an equitable manner.

Confidence. Whenever and wherever respect, understanding and sincerity enter into any relationship, confidence is bound to follow. Confidence is a necessary requisite to acceptance as a leader or supervisor. Unless the offender has confidence in the counselor, he will not reveal himself fully and the counselor's value in the relationship will be limited accordingly. Gaining the confidence of the offender is, therefore, one of the essential goals toward which the counselor should strive.

A friendly reception of the offender initially and the observation of the usual courtesies of man-to-man relationship, go far to create confidence in the counselor on the part of the offender. Likewise, acceptance of the sincerity of the offender's statements that he will make a successful adjustment regardless of how impossible it may seem on the basis of his criminal behavior pattern, will contribute also to the individual's confidence in the counselor. The counselor must be willing to accept the fact that every individual despite the type of crime he commits or the number of times he has been arrested, may be able to rehabilitate himself with the assistance of the counselor, if the proper combination of factors can be achieved. Experience has demonstrated that many multiple offenders make successful social adjustments, while other individuals with little or no previous criminal record, convicted of minor crimes, become chronic offenders. This situation, therefore, offers a continuous challenge to the counselor.

Sympathetic understanding of the offender's problems based upon a sincere interest, enables the counselor to listen attentively and to comprehend fully the individual's statements regarding them. By this approach, the counselor provides the individual with an emotional release and assists him in finding a solution to the immediate problem as well as affording him the opportunity of thinking and feeling in terms of acceptable standards of conduct. Confidence on the part of the counselor and the belief the offender can make a successful community adjustment, will serve as a needed source of reassurance in addition to increasing his confidence in the counselor.

USE OF THE CORRECTIONAL COUNSELOR–OFFENDER RELATIONSHIP

In considering the principles of correctional counseling thus far, it has been demonstrated that through the application of the principles of deviations, norms, and particularization, used in conjunction with a social investigation, the counselor has been provided with a knowledge of the offender, his problems, and his background in terms of these concepts. He has compared the individual's instability and anti-social conduct with accepted standards of conduct, and has come to some tentative conclusions at least, regarding the factors within the offender himself, and his situation which contributed to his behavior. In the process, he has assessed to some extent, the offender's inner strengths and weaknesses, as well as the favorable and unfavorable factors in the environment. For purposes of exposition, it may be said also the counselor has partially applied the counseling concept termed treatment through the development of a dynamic relationship with the offender which contains the essential elements of mutual respect, understanding, confidence, and sincerity. While all of these are important parts of the counseling process, they must be integrated with the further application of the treatment concept of counseling supplemented by the social case work concept of services to the offender.

All relationship has to have a reason for being. Unless the counselor is prepared to put something into the relationship on behalf of his agency, there is little sense in mere contact. Professional relationships are not merely friendly relationships. Contact is not for the sake of contact. Agencies have programs, resources, and limitations—in short, functions—so that the relationship will be used by both the counselor and the offender to accomplish what the agency is equipped to do. The function of the correctional agency has previously been defined as having the objective of permanent protection of the community through the readjustment of the offender, restoring him to society as a constructive rather than a destructive force.

The function of the correctional agency may be accomplished by the counselor through the medium of a counseling relationship. If the counselor is to work toward the ultimate objective of community protection through providing the offender with the opportunity to alter his attitude toward society, the counseling relationship can be used to meet the individual need apparent to the counselor through the diagnostic phases of the treatment process. In using the relationship in this way, the counselor is endeavoring to reach certain planned treatment objectives.

The counselor can assist the offender to varying degrees in two broad areas, the first of which has the objective of meeting the psychological needs, and the second the objective of supplying services or meeting the sociological needs of the individual. The psychological assistance which the counselor may render may be on an emotional or on an intellectual level, or may be a combination of both. Experience in the correctional field warrants the generalization that, in most instances, the intellectual capacities and abilities of the offender cannot be activated and utilized until some of the emotional problems interfering with sound intellectual judgment are resolved. The offender must be helped in altering unhealthy emotional attitudes which are preventing him from understanding his past conduct in terms of what are objective, legal and normal standards of conduct. Similarly, the offender can make use of the sociological services which the counselor can provide, only after he has resolved his emotional difficulties through help in that area, and has come to some intellectual understanding regarding the nature of the services available to him, and genuinely accepts the need for these services.

It is appropriate therefore, to consider how the counselor can utilize the counseling relationship to meet the psychological needs of the offender, first in the area of the emotions; secondly, in the area of intelligence; and then, how the counselor can use the counseling relationship to meet the sociological needs of the parolee through service.

HOW CORRECTIONAL COUNSELING MEETS EMOTIONAL NEEDS

It cannot be over-emphasized that the counseling relationship, if used constructively, can be helpful for the offender. Its significance as a new experience becomes greater in view of the fact that most offenders have experienced a dearth of satisfactory relationships from normal sources in family life, the home, the school, and the community, and many of them have lost the ability to relate to others in a normal way.

A leading authority in the correctional field points out that both freedom and discipline through the counseling relationship can be helpful in cultivating responsible behavior. What the relationship offers that is new and different and, therefore, positively constructive—is the exercise of authority in a way that is not arbitrary, personal, or capricious, but only reasonable, fair and firm. To find and exercise an authority which does not deny the individual's right to be himself, which encourages and cultivates his own difference, which recognizes even his right to fight against authority if he must, but which in the end holds firm to the fundamental conditions upon which social cooperation and integration must rest—this in itself will be a new experience for many an offender. In the regularity of reports and conferences, in the insistent refusal to allow responsibility to be denied, evaded or shifted, in the consistent use of every moment of contact, however fleeting and trivial, to examine the alternatives that are open and the consequences they entail—in this firm structure of purpose and policy and procedure, coupled with the disciplined use of deep human understanding and genuine respect for the individual personality—is symbolized authority without bigotry or meanness, understanding without prejudice, firmness without rigidity, warmth without sentimentality.[9]

HOW CORRECTIONAL COUNSELING PROVIDES PSYCHOLOGICAL SUPPORT

The techniques involved in providing psychological support vary, and in meeting this need, it is important the counselor keep in mind the circumstances of the individual case. In using this method, the counselor may create too great a degree of dependency of the offender upon him and thus vitiate the ultimate objective of the relationship, which is that of fostering independent action. Furnishing psychological support requires the expression of sympathetic understanding of the offender's feelings and an attitude of acceptance of his behavior. Acceptance of behavior, however, must be within the framework of the functions, rules and regulations of the correctional agency.

A direct indication of the counselor's interest in the offender and his desire to help, his expression of confidence that a way can be found to improve his situation, and confidence in his abilities to solve his various difficulties and to make his own decisions, are also steps which may be taken to provide psychological support. A genuine attitude of approval and the expression of that attitude, recognizing the steps that have been taken by the offender to improve his situation, or those steps which he plans to take after discussions with the counselor, may also be used for this purpose.

Psychological support may also be provided through direct encouragement of attitudes which will be helpful in normal family and community life. In some instances, the offender may be encouraged to satisfy his own desires to a healthy degree within the limitations imposed by society, particularly if he tends to be withdrawn or submissive. Participation in certain approved forms of pleasure and recreational activities is another avenue through which psychological support can be provided. Under some circumstances, psychological support may include the giving of advice on contemplated action, or suggestions of appropriate action by the offender.

Use of the counseling relationship to provide either psychological support or new experience does not have as its objective the development of understanding by the offender, but rather that of providing the opportunity for the relief of emotional tensions, increasing self confidence, and the encouragement of healthy normal social functioning through the use of strengths which the offender as a person may not have used previously. Use of the counseling relationship to provide psychological support, has as its objective, therefore, the affording of satisfactory emotional experiences for the offenders, through either individual or group counseling.

As a word of caution, the technique of furnishing psychological support is confined to the area of consciousness and does not involve delving into unconscious motivations, or attempting to give insight to the offender regarding unconscious psychological mechanisms.

HOW CORRECTIONAL COUNSELING MEETS INTELLECTUAL NEEDS

The counseling relationship may be used to meet the offender's intellectual needs, or in a broad sense, to assist the offender in making an intelligent approach to his problems, his attitude and conduct, in two general ways. Each of these may involve a greater or lesser use of intelligence, depending upon the capacity of the individual. They are the techniques of clarification and interpretation, each of which will be discussed separately. The counselor may use the counseling relationship to meet the emotional and intellectual needs of the offender simultaneously, or there may be some over-lapping in the process. It is also important to keep in mind that to some degree at least, the offender's emotional needs must be met and emotional problems resolved, before the relationship can be used to stimulate his intellectual capacities. In using the techniques of clarification and interpretation, it is therefore assumed that any emotional difficulties which may have prevented the effective use of the offender's intellectual capacities, will have been resolved to a sufficient degree to permit a direct approach by the counselor on an intellectual level.

Clarification. In its practical application, it usually accompanies psychological support. The objective of the process is to assist the offender in understanding himself and his environment. It consists in some instances in giving the offender information about the environment or people with whom he has relationships, which he did not possess and without which he cannot foresee clearly what steps he should take. It may be a matter of helping him think through a particular problem, to consider the various alternatives open to him, and to assist him in arriving at a decision with regard to a particular problem or his general conduct. It may be used to assist him in evaluating the attitudes of other people toward him, to understand the motives which may have influenced their action, and to see the needs of others or the results of his own actions as they affect other people. He may be helped through this process to become aware of his own feelings, desires, and attitudes.

In many instances, the offender merely needs the opportunity to talk out his problems to obtain accurate information which will enable him to see clearly the steps he must take toward a solution.

To illustrate this principle, clarification occurs when the counselor helps an individual consider the advantages and disadvantages involved in a specific kind of employment opportunity, or of a particular neighborhood in which he may wish to live, or of association with certain individuals. In the clarification process, the offender is given the opportunity to discuss the problem or situation in question, to weigh the pertinent factors, and to consider the consequences of his decision. Often it is not a course of action which must be decided upon, but rather an understanding of the individual himself, or some other person which may form the general basis for a whole series of actions.

Interpretation. Interpretation, like clarification, has the objective of developing understanding on the part of the offender. It differs from the clarification process only in that the method used by the counselor is more direct. In using it, the counselor makes direct interpretations regarding the effect or significance of the offender's actions or reactions or those of others with whom he is or has been associated. He may do this through asking questions or making comments regarding the inconsistencies in the offender's thinking, or regarding his inappropriate emotional reactions in particular situations. The efforts of the counselor, however, are directed toward helping the offender to think more clearly in a particular situation. Interpretation may be used in any discussion of personal and family problems in pointing out the various alternatives open to the individual. One of the most important areas in which both interpretation and clarification may be used by the counselor is that of assisting the individual in understanding his status as an offender, the objectives and the purpose of the rules and regulations of the agency, as well as his and the counselor's responsibility to the agency.

HOW CORRECTIONAL COUNSELING MEETS SOCIOLOGICAL NEEDS

The sociological needs of the offender are emphasized because social statistics and social investigation of offenders demonstrate, in general, these offenders are persons who have been subjected to varying degrees and kinds of social deprivation.

One may think in a broad sense of meeting the offender's sociological needs through the rendering of services or manipulation of the environment to assist him. At this point, however, attention is focused primarily upon those sociological needs of the individual which require the direct action of the counselor and which the offender is unable to meet himself. In some instances, offenders are capable of understanding and meeting these needs with a minimum of assistance from the counselor and obviously, should be permitted and encouraged to do so.

In other instances, offenders require some help from the counselor such as that previously outlined, which is available to them through the techniques of clarification and interpretation to assist them in understanding their needs. The offenders in this group usually are capable of undertaking a major role in meeting those needs.

In cases where the counselor must take direct action in meeting the sociological needs of the offender, the action to be taken must be based upon accurate information regarding the need.

Sociological services may comprise a wide range of activities. While no useful purpose would be served by endeavoring to list extensively the various services the counselor may make available to the offender, the following constitutes some typical services:

1. Assistance in obtaining a satisfactory home situation.

2. Assistance in procuring suitable employment.

3. Amelioration of unsatisfactory environmental situations.

4. Obtaining medical, surgical, psychiatric, or psychological services where these services may be necessary in solving a particular problem.

5. Rendering assistance in obtaining suitable educational courses in the areas of general education, adult education, social education, or vocational training.

6. Referral to Alcoholics Anonymous and other specialized organizations.

7. Referral to other community social agencies, equipped to deal with special problems.

8. Encouraging participation in family relationships and activities.

9. Use of community recreational facilities and programs.

10. Assistance in working toward financial security through financial planning, budgeting, systematic savings in financial institutions.

11. Referral to libraries or agencies which provide information with regard to specific subjects.

In meeting sociological needs through services, it is important the counselor know the offender's specific needs and have a knowledge of the services of social agencies and other community resources which he may use to assist the offender. Furthermore, it is assumed that the counselor will have established a relationship with staff members of community agencies so that their cooperation in obtaining necessary services will be assured.

In addition to knowing the needs in an individual case and being able to obtain community services to meet the need, the counselor must use the counseling relationship to clarify and interpret the plan to the offender and obtain his acceptance and participation in using the service for his own permanent benefit.

In general, environmental modification or services are undertaken only when pressures upon the offender are beyond his control but can be modified by the counselor, or when such pressures are more likely to yield to change when handled by the counselor rather than the individual. Whenever the offender is able to make such changes himself, it is preferable that he do so.

THE CORRECTIONAL COUNSELING INTERVIEW

In the correctional field, as in other fields of counseling, interviewing is an essential skill. All of the diagnostic information in the correctional process must be obtained through interviews, conducted first with the offender himself, and secondly, through interviews with the offender's relatives, friends, and the personnel of community agencies. Skill in interviewing, therefore, is a vital element in individual treatment.

Interviewing is a normal medium of social intercourse and the average person has conducted interviews or been interviewed on many occasions. The counselor, in common with the social worker or the reporter, uses the interview to accomplish definite goals. Some principles of interviewing as they apply to correctional counseling are discussed here.

Essential Elements in the Interviewing Process. There are four essential elements in the interviewing process used in correctional counseling. These elements, each of which will be treated separately, are:

1. *Participants.* The interview requires the meeting together of one person (the interviewer) with one or more persons for mutual discussion of a problem or problems, in which both parties have an interest, even though the interest of each may be different.

2. *Objectives.* The nature of the interview presupposes that the interviewer, as an individual, and the agency he represents may be helpful to the person interviewed and that there are specific and general objectives attainable through it.

3. *Dynamic nature of the interview.* Success or failure in attaining the objectives of the interview depends upon the interviewer's ability to establish a satisfactory relationship with the person interviewed.

In this relationship a constant mutual evaluation occurs between the interviewer and the person being interviewed, which brings about an alteration of attitudes on the part of each toward the other as the interview progresses.

4. *Use of the counseling relationship in the interview.* The interviewer uses the counseling relationship, in conjunction with his personal qualifications, and the services of his agency, to attain the specific objectives of the interview. A mutually satisfactory relationship may develop at a fairly rapid tempo, or be retarded by resistance on the part of the person interviewed to any help the interviewer might be able to offer. The degree of either mutual participation in working together, or of resistance to it, depends upon a number of factors, probably the most important of which is the ability and skill of the interviewer to resolve resistance and to obtain the cooperation, participation, and understanding of the person being interviewed.

TYPES OF INTERVIEWS USED IN CORRECTIONAL COUNSELING

There are two general classes of interviews used in correctional counseling. They are:

Diagnostic Interviews. The diagnostic interview is that which is conducted in the process of social investigation for the purpose of obtaining information regarding the offender's background and development. Its objective is that of determining the origin and nature of the personal, social, or family problems which he presents.

Treatment Interviews. This interview has as its objective the adjustment of the subject and is one wherein the interviewer, through the counseling relationship, uses the diagnostic information to help the offender find a solution to his problems and to make an acceptable adjustment to his situation and to society. It is well to point out, however, that in the practical application of sound interviewing principles, these two processes of getting information and of using it are not mutually exclusive, because as the interview progresses the interviewer is constantly developing new information and using it to assist in the adjustment process.

Treatment interviews in probation and parole may be further classified according to the setting and the specific objectives of each, as follows: Initial interview, office interview, office report, other interview, home visit interview, employment visit interview. These interviews may be described as follows:

Initial Interview. The interview conducted by the counselor on the occasion of his first supervision contact with the offender. Although it is usually conducted in the office, it may in some instances, be conducted in the offender's home or elsewhere.

Office Interview. An office interview is any interview conducted with the offender at the agency or at a reporting station, other than a regularly scheduled office report.

Office Report. An office report is the offender's personal appearance in accordance with his reporting schedule at the designated reporting place for interview with the counselor.

Other Interview. Interviews so designated are those conducted by the counselor at the agency office, reporting station, or with community agencies regarding a particular case, but with persons other than the offender.

Home Visit. A home visit is a personal contact made by the counselor with the offender, a member of the family, or some other individual at the offender's home.

Employment Visit. A personal contact made by the counselor with the offender's employer at the place of employment.

APPROACH TO THE INTERVIEW

Preparation for the Interview. In correctional counseling, the interview is based upon a comprehensive knowledge of the person interviewed, obtained from unprejudiced sources. In preparing for the interview, all important sources of information should be used fully by the counselor. These sources may include the presentence report, reports from community agencies, supervision records, institutional data, and parole reports, among others.

Planning the Interview. The sources of information referred to above are used in planning the interview in two general ways. Primarily, they are used as a source of information that will be helpful in establishing a counseling relationship with the offender. Information pertaining to his dominant characteristics, such as his interests—whether they lie in the areas of sports, hobbies or other recreational activities, his likes and dislikes or special aversions, and his social, cultural and financial background, will provide the means of getting on common ground with the offender. It will also assist the counselor in relieving the initial emotional tensions and thus facilitate the opening of the interview.

The secondary, but equally important, use of this information is to provide the counselor with a knowledge of the personal, family, and social problems, the motivations and behavior patterns of the offender upon which the specific objectives of the interview may be formulated.

Specific objectives of the interview. Each interview conducted by the counselor should be planned and should have predetermined objectives. The objectives established in a specific interview depend upon the counselor's knowledge and interpretation of the offender's background and the particular problems or needs presented. Assisting the offender in finding a solution to an environmental or sociological problem through a referral to a prospective employer, providing assistance in budgeting or financial planning, or making a referral to a school for vocational training are examples of such objectives. On the other hand, the objective in a particular interview may be that of using the counseling relationship to assist the offender with the problems of social relationships which are fundamentally psychological in nature.

Flexibility in planning of the interview. Although it is important the counselor establish definite objectives in planning each interview, and each interview be related to the preceding one, he must also be prepared to modify these plans as the need arises. Frequently, information develops as an interview progresses, which places a new or different interpretation on information previously available and, therefore, necessitates a change of planning. In some instances, resistance not previously anticipated may be encountered. Other situations may also arise that require flexibility in carrying out the interview as planned.

Manner and attitude of the interviewer. Both of these factors, as well as the personality makeup of the interviewer, play an important part in effective interviewing. Many persons have natural aptitudes for interviewing while others, because of personal makeup, have more limited ability. Among other attributes, the successful interviewer should have trained and organized common sense, supplemented by both native ability and specialized knowledge.

As previously stated, one of the essential elements in the interview is the mutual evaluation process, and the interviewer must approach it with an understanding of his own emotions and prejudices. The counselor must recognize that, like all others, he has feelings and prejudices that will tend to alter his attitude toward the person being interviewed. While it is not necessary he endeavor to submerge or alter his attitudes, it is necessary he recognize their presence and the effect they may have upon his thinking and his attitude toward the offender.

The counselor's attitude will be reflected in his manner, tone of voice, facial expressions, gestures, interest in and concentration upon the conversation, and particularly his sincerity. All of these factors have an important effect upon the offender being interviewed and the development of a satisfactory counseling relationship.

CASE RECORDING IN CORRECTIONAL COUNSELING

While a full description of the process of case recording is not possible within the limits of this chapter, it is appropriate to discuss the subject briefly.

Although a case history has significance in other counseling fields, it assumes greater importance in the field of Correction because of statutory requirements. A significant difference from other counseling situations exists also in that the diagnostic case history is usually completed and available before the Probation or Parole supervision process occurs. Therefore, the correctional counselor must be able to compile a complete diagnostic case history with the wealth of data concerning the development of the offender and his attitudes, with a comprehensive picture of his social setting and the cultural and familial forces which have influenced him, in order to make possible an intelligent and thorough diagnosis, and for a sympathetic understanding of the offender's significant life forces and patterns.

To intelligently develop and execute a plan of treatment, it is equally essential the correctional counselor record in a professional manner the various stages of the supervision process. Whatever type of recording is followed—chronological, topical, or summary—should reflect the steps taken by the worker to effect the treatment plan, the relationship between the worker and offender, the feelings, attitudes, and personality of the offender, as well as a compliance by the offender with the administrative requirements established for him.

QUALIFICATIONS FOR PROBATION
AND PAROLE COUNSELORS

The title "Correctional Counselor" is in common use in correctional institutions in the larger states throughout the United States, but in the probation and parole areas of the correctional field, it is still the practice to classify the comparable position as probation or parole officer or agent. Regardless of the title, the probation or parole officer functions in a capacity that can be designated as "correctional counselor". Using the term generically, the title "Correctional Counselor" has as much applicability to the areas of probation and parole as it does to correctional institutions.

There now seems to be a general acceptance by leading authorities in the probation and parole areas of the correctional field that these areas are identified with the field of social case work. In the adult institutional area of the correctional field, this identification has not received as much acceptance. In the field of adult probation and parole, where the importance of the authoritarian viewpoint cannot be overlooked, the title "probation officer" or "parole officer" is preferred.[10]

Qualifications for the positions of Probation and Parole Officer are not standardized among the various states and counties. From a national viewpoint, the record can be described only as "spotty". There are counties and states where the qualifications and standards are on a professional level with commensurate salaries. On the other hand there are counties and states where the qualifications for the positions of probation and parole officer are distinctly sub-standard.

Rather than enumerate the varying standards existing among the several states it might be more appropriate to describe what are considered to be the minimum qualifications for probation and parole work as determined by the National Council on Crime and Delinquency, formerly the National Probation and Parole Association.[11]

These minimum qualifications are listed as:

I. MINIMUM QUALIFICATIONS FOR ENTERING PROBATION AND PAROLE WORK

    a. *Personality*

        Emotional maturity, broad common sense, capacity to learn by experience, and a fundamental capacity for and interest in the welfare of human beings are basic and irreplaceable requirements for work in the probation and parole field. It goes without saying that such a person must be of good character and balanced personality with special traits of integrity, ability to work with others, an insight into the causes of human behavior, and a general knowledge of his community.

b. *Education*

A bachelor's degree from a college or university of recognized standing, with courses in the social sciences is minimal.

Professional training for probation and parole work in a graduate school of social work maintaining standards acceptable for accredited schools.

c. *Experience*

One year of paid full time experience under supervision in a social welfare agency or similar agency of high standards or one year of graduate work in a recognized school of social work in lieu thereof.

By a "similar agency" is meant one in which such professional work as the following may be done: teaching, personnel work in industry where the applicant did actual adjustment work with individuals and not merely employment service, or casework in an institution or correctional agency.

d. *Internship Training*

Where an agency wishes to substitute a training program of its own for one year of full time paid experience as indicated above, such training program should be an organized program of training, sustained over a period of at least one year and should be more than the usual in-service training program. It should develop, through teaching and supervision the basic knowledge of the fundamentals of the practice of social work through intensive methods with the trainee.

II. SPECIALIZED KNOWLEDGE

a. Anyone who works in the field of probation and parole must have a knowledge of the principles and skill in the practice of social casework.

He must understand the motivations of human behavior, the influence of physical, mental, and emotional health on conduct and family relationships. He must be informed as to community problems and their effect on individual attitudes and behavior.

b. As an administrative agent of the court or parole authority the counselor must be familiar with the laws within which he operates and the powers and limitations of his position.

This includes a knowledge of specific laws and codes affecting probation and parole and others touching upon this work although not directly related to it.

An understanding of these laws and codes is necessary if

technical errors, which may impose an injustice upon the individual under supervision are to be avoided. Probationers and parolees must always be told their legal rights, and how the law or probation or parole conditions limit their rights and activities. Knowledge of the powers and limitations of his position affords protection to the representative in the exercise of many functions which must be carried out expressly as provided for in the law.

c. The counselor or officer—or whatever other title may be used—must be familiar with the operation of related law enforcement agencies in his jurisdiction.

He must have a working knowledge of and a cooperative relationship with the various departments of government which prepare cases for and cooperate with the court or paroling authority, such as the police, the prosecutor, the sheriff, all courts, the penal or correctional institutions.

While the standards of selection and the minimum qualifications enumerated above may be regarded by some correctional workers as unattainable by the majority of probation and parole agencies, it is interesting to note that the State of New York has in operation an organized program of staff developments designed to increase professional staff competency, in both probation and parole on a state-wide basis.

The Division of Probation of the New York State Department of Correction has a bureau of staff development which, among other duties and responsibilities, conducts training programs for city, county and state probation personnel, prepares and executes programs of information and education to interest persons in the file of probation as a vocation.[12]

Scholarships are also granted for graduate training in the field of probation at graduate schools of social work.[13]

A parallel development occurred in the parole field in the State of New York, at a later date. The New York State Board of Parole developed a long range program for recruitment and retention of professional personnel. The program includes, among others, full and part-time scholarship grants. Parole Officer Trainees are also appointed through Civil Service Career Tests. Candidates for this title are required to have a bachelor's degree with a major in one of the social sciences.[14]

OUTSTANDING NEEDS IN THE CORRECTIONAL FIELD

Outstanding needs in the correctional field are many and reflect the diverse viewpoints of authorities in the probation, parole and institutional areas of the correctional field. To cite a few examples: Opinions

32*

vary as to whether there should be a unified Department of Correction responsible for administration and operation of probation, parole and institutional functions, or a separate and independent agency for each of these functions. The field of Public Relations in Corrections has not received the attention and action warranted in all too many jurisdictions. Citizen participation in Correctional Programs is finally receiving recognition principally as a result of a Ford Foundation grant to the National Council on Crime and Delinquency although several states, and the United States Bureau of Prisons have organized programs.[15] Although group counseling is making an impact upon all areas of the correctional field, further studies are needed to establish the effectiveness of the small group approach.

While it is difficult to isolate a single outstanding need and assign it a high priority, possibly the one problem area on which common agreement can be reached is that of research. When the cost of the annual crime bill is considered, one is appalled by the public apathy towards the expenditure of public monies for correctional research programs. Compared with expenditures for research in the public health and mental health fields, public funds for the support of correctional research programs are practically non-existent. Organized and publicly-supported correctional research programs operate in a few jurisdictions, notably in the State of California. In New York State, the Department of Correction and the Board of Parole have separate research units. The Research Division of the Department of Corrections of the State of California conducts continuous experimentation and research to develop new techniques more positive in helping inmate and parolee. The Department of Corrections looks at its research program in this light: "It is hoped that through research efforts we may learn more about the control and treatment of inmates and, in the long run, establish a more efficient and economical correctional system for the State of California."[16]

In an article in the American Journal of Correction, Dr. Alfred C. Schnur while praising the contributions of correctional research, points out the lack of standards in recording in correctional systems, and the uselessness of the typical record for research purposes. He also comments on the lack of coordination in correctional research and the absence of a convenient place of reference for the findings on particular factors. He emphasizes the need for ongoing research of a character that analyzes all the effects of all the present available treatment techniques for all the men undergoing treatment.[17]

REFERENCES

1. Group Counseling in Combating Delinquency—Hanna Grunwald—December 1958 issue of Federal Probation.
2. Group Counseling in Juvenile Probation—Glenn J. Walker—December 1959 issue of Federal Probation.
3. Page 329—October 1961 issue of Crime & Delinquency—An Experiment in Group Counseling with Juvenile Parolees—Charles W. Taylor.
4. Page 49—September 1961 issue of Federal Probation—Group Counseling in Probation—Herbert Vogt.
5. Page 30—1959–60 Biennial Report of the Department of Corrections—State of California.
6. Page 271—1960 Proceedings of the American Correctional Association.
7. Group Therapy with Adult Offenders on Probation and Parole—March 1959 issue of Group Psychotherapy.
8. Group Therapy with Adult Probationers—Sept. 1960 issue of Federal Probation.
9. "Social Work in A Revolutionary Age"—Kenneth Pray—University of Pennsylvania Press—1949.
10. Standards for Selection of Probation & Parole Personnel—National Council on Crime and Delinquency.
11. Standards for Selection of Probation & Parole Personnel—National Council on Crime and Delinquency.
12. McKinney's Consolidated Laws of New York, Correction Law, Section 14–c.
13. McKinney's Consolidated Laws of New York, Correction Law, Section 14–d.
14. Division of Parole, Executive Department, Thirty-first Annual Report 1960.
15. Correctional Research: United Prison Association of Massachusetts, Bulletin No. 10, August 1960—What's New in Citizen Participation in Correctional Programs.
16. State of California—Biennial Report—1959–1960.
17. Schnur, Dr. Alfred C.—New York, N.Y.—Correctional Research: A Review and Critique—American Journal of Correction—January–February 1962.

BIBLIOGRAPHY

Rogers, Carl R.: 1942. *Counseling and Psychotherapy*. New York: Houghton Mifflin Co.

Pray, Kenneth L. M.: 1949. *Social Work in a Revolutionary Age*. Philadelphia: University of Pennsylvania Press.

Studt, Eliot: "Case Work in the Correctional Field." Washington, D.C.: Federal Probation—September 1954.

Manual for Parole Officers: 1954. New York State Division of Parole, Albany, N.Y.

Manual of Correctional Standards: 1954. New York: The American Prison Association.

Kasius, Cora: 1954. *New Directions in Social Work*. New York: Harper.

Larmour, Victoria A.: 1935. Principles of Social Case Work Treatment as Applied to Problems of Parole Supervision. Pamphlet published by New York State Division of Parole, Albany, N.Y.

Manual for Probation Officers in New York State: 1960. Albany, N.Y.: New York State Department of Correction.

Standard Probation and Parole Act: 1955. New York: National Probation and Parole Association.

LINDNER, ROBERT M. and SELIGER, ROBERT V.: 1947. *Handbook of Correctional Psychology*. New York: Philosophical Library.

GIARDINI, G. I.: 1959. *The Parole Process*. Springfield, Ill.: Charles C. Thomas.

NEWMAN, CHARLES L.: 1958. *Source Book on Probation, Parole and Pardons*. Springfield, Illinois.

KRUEGER, GLADYS M.: 1959. *Survey of Probation Officers*. Washington, D.C.: Superintendent of Documents.

Subject Index